Natural Health Bible for Dogs & Cats

Other Books in THE NATURAL VET™ Series

THE *Natural Vet* SERIES

Natural Health Bible for Dogs & Cats

Your A–Z Guide to Over 200 Conditions, Herbs, Vitamins, and Supplements

Shawn Messonnier, D.V.M.

 THREE RIVERS PRESS • NEW YORK

Published by Three Rivers Press. New York, New York.
Member of the Crown Publishing Group, a division of Random House, Inc.
www.crownpublishing.com

THREE RIVERS PRESS and the Tugboat design are registered trademarks of Random House, Inc.

Originally published by Prima Publishing, Roseville, California, in 2001.

THE NATURAL VET series is a trademark of Random House, Inc.

All products mentioned in this book are trademarks of their respective companies.

DISCLAIMER: While the Publisher and the author have designed this book to provide up-to-date information in regard to the subject matter covered, readers should be aware that medical information is constantly evolving. The information presented herein is of a general nature and is not intended as a substitute for professional medical advice. Readers should consult with a qualified veterinarian for specific instructions on the treatment and care of their pet. The author and Random House, Inc., shall have neither liability nor responsibility to any person or entity with respect to any loss, damage, or injury caused or alleged to be caused directly or indirectly by the information contained in this book.

Printed in the United States of America

Library of Congress Cataloging-in-Publication Data
Messonnier, Shawn.
    Natural health bible for dogs & cats : your A–Z guide to over 200 conditions, herbs, vitamins, and supplements / Shawn Messonnier.
        p.   cm. — (The natural vet series)
    Includes bibliographical references and index.
        1. Dogs—Diseases—Alternative treatment. 2. Cats—Diseases—Alternative treatment.
    3. Alternative veterinary medicine. 4. Herbs—Therapeutic use. I. Title.
    SF991 .M47 2000
    636.7'08955—dc21   00-053731

ISBN 0-7615-2673-0

10 9 8 7 6 5 4 3

First Edition

CONTENTS

PART THREE:
DIET

PART FOUR:
OTHER COMPLEMENTARY THERAPIES

FOREWORD

I was first introduced to Dr. Shawn Messonnier, a holistic veterinarian, at a veterinary conference. I was impressed with this young man's sincerity and passion for his work. When Dr. Messonnier discussed with me the scope and breadth of his work in progress, I smiled to myself because I didn't believe that he could really pull off a project of the magnitude that he had planned. I was wrong. After reviewing Dr. Messonnier's *Natural Health Bible for Dogs & Cats*, I am even more impressed with his work.

Many, if not most, of the currently available texts on Complementary and Alternative Veterinary Medicine (CAVM) have been simply compendiums of information without an overriding attempt to integrate these catalogs of information into a cohesive whole that can be used pragmatically, as a practice companion or by the pet owner. That is where I believe this work of Dr. Messonnier's excels: It offers the veterinarian and the pet owner with an interest in CAVM a guide to the appropriate uses of "natural" therapies. Even with my many years of experience in practicing CAVM, I have learned quite a few new things during my review of Dr. Messonnier's detailed and thoroughly written text.

Each holistic veterinarian has his own interpretation of how to practice CAVM. There are those veterinarians in the holistic field who are very negative about the benefits of most, if not all, conventional medical procedures, including vaccinations and pharmaceuticals. I found it refreshing to view Dr. Messonnier's perspective: that it is important that we not "throw the baby out with the bath water." In other words, we shouldn't reject the valuable and safe aspects of our conventional veterinary medical training, but rather, *integrate* the best of both worlds into a superior form of medical practice.

I have found that the following statements summarize the most important aspects of CAVM:

1) Know what the diagnosis is for the patient you are treating, whether you are using conventional or alternative therapies.

2) Teach, and thus empower, the animal's guardian to care for and "heal" the animal.

3) Be a team. The pet's guardian needs a caring and professional veterinarian who has an interest in complementary and alternative therapies. A veterinarian can best guide and direct the owner in the animal's best interests, and can help design the best herbal, dietary, and nutraceutical program for the pet. (I very much approve of the fact that Dr. Messonnier reminds the reader that it is frequently necessary for one's animal to be seen by a veterinarian.)

I have been practicing CAVM for the past thirteen-plus years of my nineteen-year career as a small-animal veterinarian in private practice. For most of that time, I have been "flying without instruments," which is to say that there has not been much available in the veterinary literature that I could use as a guide for my clinical practice. I had to learn everything the hard way: on my own. With this book in hand, you won't need to learn it the hard way as Dr. Messonnier and I have done. This text will provide you with a ready-to-use clinical tool. Or just simply help you understand more about your pet's health.

ROBERT J. SILVER, D.V.M., M.S.

PREFACE

I am a conventional doctor by training, an Aggie from the Lone Star State. I graduated in 1987 from Texas A&M University with a doctorate of veterinary medicine, and in 1991, opened Paws & Claws Animal Hospital, the first referral hospital for dogs, cats, and exotic pets in Plano, Texas.

After using conventional treatments for several years, I became convinced that many pets that were not improving with lifelong use of conventional medications might improve if some type of alternative was available. This desire to improve the quality of my patients' lives led me to become adept at treating pets with a variety of complementary therapies. Due to the success of this idea, I created the Acupuncture and Holistic Animal Health Care Center, the only hospital in the area to offer both conventional and complementary therapies for dogs and cats.

Now, in addition to practicing medicine, I spread the word of holistic health care for pets as a regular columnist for the *Dallas Morning News* and the *Wylie News*. For two years, I hosted Fox Television's "4 Your Pets" pet care show. I serve on the board of the prestigious international journal, *Veterinary Forum,* and I am also founder and editor-in-chief of *Exotic Pet Practice*, the only monthly international publication devoted to the care of exotic pets. Each month I reach over half a million pet owners as the holistic columnist for both *Dog Fancy* and *Cat Fancy* magazines. I also serve as a consultant to Our Pets, a leading manufacturer of natural pet products, and am the holistic veterinarian for www.planet-pets.com.

This book, the *Natural Health Bible for Dogs & Cats*, is part of a new series of health guides called THE NATURAL VET™. With this exciting project I hope to show you ways to care for your pets using safe, natural, alternative treatments for a variety of medical conditions.

I always enjoy hearing from readers. If you would like to contact me regarding the *Natural Health Bible for Dogs & Cats*, for consulting services, or speaking engagements, you may do so at: 2145 W. Park Blvd., Plano, TX 75075; (972) 867-8800; naturalvet@juno.com.

ACKNOWLEDGMENTS

First, a big thanks to all the folks at Prima who have helped make this project possible.

Second, I would like to express my appreciation to all of my clients and their pets. Thank you for putting your trust in me and for choosing a more natural, holistic approach. Seeing the improvement in your pets has continued to encourage my interest in learning about more natural options to help your pets recover from their diseases and maintain their health.

Third, thanks to all of the veterinarians and medical doctors for their input during the development of the *Natural Health Bible for Dogs & Cats.* Attempting to single out those who have been particularly helpful means that someone will invariably get left out, and for this I apologize. I would like to say a special "Thank You" to the following who have been particularly helpful:

Thanks to Dr. Robert Silver. You are inspirational.

Thanks to Dr. Christina Chambreau for your careful editing of the section on homeopathy.

Thanks to Dr. Marilyn Moore for the information on glycoproteins.

Thanks to Dr. Susan Wynn. As moderator of the AHVMA email list, you keep us all in line. Thanks also for all of the up-to-date medical information and literature you bring to our attention.

Finally, thanks to all of the holistic veterinarians who freely share their ideas on the AHVMA email list. Your help is appreciated by all of the clients whose pets benefit from your "in-the-trenches" experiences.

As always, a special thanks to God for all I have, and to my wife, Sandy, and daughter, Erica, for giving me the time to complete this very important and special project. I love you both!

WHAT MAKES THIS BOOK DIFFERENT?

According to statistics, more than 65 million Americans are using natural therapies. Because approximately 75% of these people own pets, and there are over 110 million dogs and cats in the United States, there is a growing need for accurate information on natural therapies for pets. While we often have to extrapolate data from the medical literature and apply the information to pets, and because pets have their own unique needs and requirements, there is also a big need for information specifically related to treating pets.

Until now, there have been few books on natural therapies for pets. Most of them are not written by veterinarians, and none cover conditions or therapies in an easy-to-follow, A–Z guide. In addition, many of the books currently available are written from a subjective point of view, rather than presenting the information in an objective fashion as is done in the *Natural Health Bible for Dogs & Cats*. Finally, many books currently available present conventional therapies in a negative light. In reality, many holistic veterinarians realize the need for combining conventional and complementary therapies in order to provide the best treatment for pets. THE NATURAL VET series, which includes the *Natural Health Bible for Dogs & Cats*, is designed to provide an objective overview of the commonly used conventional and complementary therapies that may benefit your pet. It is my hope that you will constantly refer to the *Natural Health Bible for Dogs & Cats* to find answers for all of your pet's health questions.

WHY CHOOSE NATURAL TREATMENTS?

Natural therapies are chosen for several reasons. First, in some instances there are no conventional treatments available. For example, milk thistle is a wonderful herb to help heal the liver; there are no conventional medications that can do this. Probiotics and glutamine are wonderful natural therapies to heal a diseased intestinal tract, and there are no conventional medicines that can do what these natural therapies do.

Sometimes a natural therapy is chosen to minimize side effects from conventional therapies. Referring to probiotics again, these supplements can minimize damage to the intestinal tract when antibiotic therapy is needed.

Third, many owners view natural therapies as safer than conventional therapies. While some therapies, especially herbal therapies, can be toxic, most natural therapies are safer than conventional medications. As an example, glucosamine and chondroitin are safer for treating pets with arthritis than corticosteroids or nonsteroidal anti-inflammatory medications. For long-term control of pain and inflammation, their use is preferred over conventional therapies for their wide safety margins.

Finally, many natural therapies cost less over the long-term treatment of your pet than conventional therapies. The supplement choline, contained in a product called Cholodin, costs much less to treat a pet with cognitive disorder than does the conventional therapy Anipryl.

INTRODUCTION

The *Natural Health Bible for Dogs & Cats* is divided into four sections: Conditions, Herbs and Supplements, Diet, and Other Complementary Therapies. Boldfaced words with page numbers following indicate cross-referenced material. For example, under Conditions, the natural medicines mentioned show page numbers where you can go right to a description of that substance and read about its uses, dosages, and so forth.

Part One on Conditions describes more than 40 ailments from Addison's disease to vaccinosis, how they affect dogs and cats, and the most common treatments, both natural and conventional. These are the conditions most commonly seen in general veterinary practice.

There are many different medical disorders that affect dogs and cats. The leading internal medical reference book for veterinarians contains almost 2,000 pages discussing these disorders! In the *Natural Health Bible for Dogs & Cats*, I have attempted to address only those conditions for which holistic-minded pet owners most commonly seek advice and treatment. By necessity, many disorders are not discussed here. Your doctor can advise you on less common conditions not discussed in this edition.

Each medical condition is briefly discussed, followed by a review of currently recommended natural and conventional therapies. A greater discussion of the natural treatments (and the more commonly recommended conventional therapies) can be found by turning to the page numbers that follow the mention of each therapy. Which therapy is best suited for your pet is best determined by consultation with your doctor.

Part Two describes herbs, vitamins, minerals, and other supplements—more than 100 natural substances from alfalfa to shiitake mushroom. These natural treatments and complementary therapies are those that an owner is most likely to encounter, as well as those most commonly recommended by holistic veterinarians; other therapies may exist as well. Your doctor, by virtue of training and experience, may choose a different therapy. For example, let's say that your dog is suffering from osteoarthritis, a common cause of lameness in dogs. A doctor who prefers herbal therapies may choose an herbal therapy for treating this condition, even though that is not listed as the complementary therapy most often recommended by holistic doctors for treating this disorder. This does not mean that your doctor's choice of treatment is incorrect, only that it may not be the one recommended here. I encourage you to bring The *Natural Health Bible for Dogs & Cats* with you during your veterinary visit to discuss the recommended therapies with your veterinarian, so the two of you may work as a team to choose the therapy best suited for your pet.

The scientific proof of many of the therapies that are recommended is lacking with respect to well-designed, double-blind placebo-controlled research studies. Most complementary therapies are recommended based upon years of clinical experience, holistic tradition, and in some cases, extrapolation from human medicine. The references at the end of this book will serve as a guide for owners interested in pursuing the scientific literature discussing the various therapies.

Part Three describes the role of diet in the health of your pet. It shows you in detail the elements of a good diet, how to choose quality food, including how to read pet food labels. It teaches you about additives, chemicals, and other ingredients. Raw food, natural foods, and homemade diets are explained in detail. Many diets are described for pets with specific diseases and for conditions such as aging and obesity. What constitutes good nutrition? This and many other questions about animal diets are answered.

Part Four discusses other kinds of alternative therapies, including magnetic therapy, electromagnetic therapy, aromatherapy, glandular therapy, TTouch, chiropractic, orthomolecular medicine, homeopathy, and flower essences. These practices are described and applied to specific conditions.

Finally, keep in mind that the term "holistic" refers to evaluating the "whole" animal and the "whole" range of options that might be selected for treatment. For many conditions, the most holistic approach will involve a rational selection of recommended complementary and conventional therapies. By definition, a "complementary" therapy is used to "complement" rather than to replace a conventional therapy. Depending upon the condition, the "best" therapy could be a conventional treatment, a natural treatment, or often a combination of both. Your doctor can use the suggested conventional and complementary therapies to choose the most appropriate course of action.

RESOURCES USED

As much as possible, the *Natural Health Bible for Dogs & Cats* is based on science. In some cases, this involves extrapolation from the human medical literature. In other cases, controlled studies in pets are used to present the information. In many cases, the information presented has proven effective based upon tradition and years of experience by veterinarians and herbalists, as in the case of homeopathic and herbal remedies. When no controlled studies have been done to "prove" a particular therapy, every attempt has been made to point this out to the reader.

ABOUT HERBAL TREATMENTS

Herbs that are prescribed for pets may be the whole herb or just the active ingredient in the herb. Products vary on whether or not the whole herb or just a part of the herb is included. By using only the active ingredient, the other parts of the herbs (toxins or other ingredients that may make the active ingredient less effective) are not included.

However, by using only the active ingredient, some of the other ingredients that might act in conjunction with the active ingredient are lost. Which way is better is up to debate, although most herbalists prefer products containing the whole herb to take advantage of all of the ingredients contained within the herb.

There are a number of companies making herbs for the human and pet market, and standard quality controls such as those that exist for human pharmaceuticals are lacking in the supplement market. Studies have shown that some products have more or less (and sometimes even none) of the active ingredient listed on the bottle! For this reason, use only products from high-quality, reputable companies. The least expensive generic herbal supplements are likely to be of lowest quality and questionable value.

Quality control is important when choosing herbs. You should only use herbs from companies with strict quality control procedures. Because the potency of herbs deteriorates with time, it is best if the herbal preparation can be specially made for the pet. Since this is usually not possible, your veterinarian should only keep a small supply of herbs on hand so they do not expire quickly. As a rule, any herbal product over 1 year old should be discarded.

Herbs are usually considered "safe" since they are one form of complementary therapy. While this is generally true, many herbs can be quite toxic if taken incorrectly. All medicines are toxic; only the dosage and the length of treatment determine what is toxic and what is safe. Owners should refrain from self-diagnosing and self-medicating, and instead rely upon advice from a knowledgeable holistic veterinarian. Since herbal remedies can interact (sometimes dangerously) with conventional medications, make sure you tell your veterinarian whatever medications your pet is currently taking.

Herbs are usually supplied in powder or capsule form; tinctures can also be found. Many products made for humans can be used in pets. Unfortunately, the "correct" dosage for the pet has not been determined for many herbs and clinical experience and extrapolation from human data is often used. It is hard to find good controlled studies for using herbs in pets since the funding is lacking when compared to that available to pharmaceutical companies.

Dosage Information for Herbs

The following guidelines serve as a starting point for herbal therapy:

Western Herbs

Capsule Form: 1 500 mg capsule/25-pound dog given 2 to 3 times daily; ¼ to ½ capsule/cat given 2 to 3 times daily

Powder Form: 0.5 to 1.5 teaspoons of powder/2-pound dog given 2 to 3 times daily; 0.5 teaspoon/cat given 2 to 3 times daily

Tincture Form: 5 to 10 drops/10 pounds (dog or cat) given 2 to 3 times daily

Alternatively, some herbalists recommend extrapolation based on weight. Since human doses are based on a 150-pound male, a recommended dose of 3 capsules given 3 times daily for this 150-pound male would extrapolate to 1 capsule given 3 times daily for a 50-pound dog.

You should consult with a holistic doctor to determine the best starting dose prior to treating your pet with herbs.

Chinese Herbs

Concentrated Herbs: 1 gram/20 pounds 2 to 3 times daily of concentrated herbs for dogs and cats

Fresh Herbs: 4 gm of fresh herbs/20 pounds 2 to 3 times daily for dogs and cats

The study of herbal therapy can be divided into two schools: Western Herbal Therapy and Traditional Chinese Medicine (TCM). Similar (and often the same) herbs are used by both schools. The main differences between the Western approach and TCM involve the diagnosis and actual herbs used.

With Western Herbal Therapy, a conventional diagnosis is made (as an example, your veterinarian would diagnose arthritis in your pet). With TCM, a diagnosis typical of the Eastern philosophy might be made (for example, the pet with arthritis might be diagnosed as having a Wandering *Bi* syndrome that might exhibit the need for strengthening of the kidney *yang*). It is not too important which diagnosis is made, as the herbal therapy would be similar. The important point is that the proper diagnosis is made by the doctor before beginning therapy!

Another difference among the two schools is the herbs themselves. With the Western philos-

ophy, herbs such as white willow bark or devil's claw might be recommended. With TCM, a combination of herbs with Chinese names such as *du huo* or *tang kuei* might be prescribed (often the herbs have Western names as well). Once again, what is used is not important as long as the correct herb or herbal combination is chosen.

Four Chinese herbal mixes are described in Part Two: Pinellia Combination, Clematis and Stephania Combination, Coptis and Scute Combination, and Rehmannia Six/Rehmannia Eight Combination.

Scientific Basis for Herbs

Herbs have been used for thousands of years prior to the advent of conventional medicine. Much of our knowledge of herbs comes from these thousands of years of experience rather than from double-blind placebo-controlled scientific studies. There are few studies on the use of herbs for treating pets. Therefore, most of our information is extrapolated from human studies and clinical experience in pets. This does not make herbal medicine any less valid, but in fact gives us many thousands of cases treated successfully with a variety of herbal remedies. As science progresses, we will hopefully learn what are the active ingredients of each herb as well as gain an understanding of how these active ingredients work in pets.

ABOUT VITAMINS

Vitamins are nutrients essential to life. They contribute to overall health by performing a number of functions related to regulating metabolism and functioning in the many biochemical functions that occur throughout the body. While they are required in microscopic amounts (thus they are referred to as micronutrients) when compared to proteins, fats, and carbohydrates, they are no less important. Supplying inadequate amounts of vitamins to dogs and cats causes nutritional deficiencies, while supplying too much of a certain synthetic vitamin can cause toxicity.

Vitamins are divided into water-soluble vitamins or fat-soluble vitamins. Water soluble-vitamins are not stored in the body as they are rapidly eliminated through the urinary tract and must be ingested daily. The B-complex vitamins and vitamin C are water-soluble vitamins.

Fat-soluble vitamins require dietary fat for absorption and are stored in the animal's body in the fat (adipose tissue) and liver. Vitamins A, D, E, and K are fat-soluble vitamins. Both water-soluble and fat-soluble vitamins are needed for maintaining health and protecting against diseases.

Recommended Daily Allowance These numbers can be misleading. Many years ago, the U.S. government set levels called the Recommended Daily Allowance, or RDA for vitamins and minerals for people and pets. These RDAs were determined in an attempt to set recommendations for the general public for providing guidelines to *prevent certain diseases* such as scurvy in people that resulted from deficiencies of vitamins and minerals. However, these guidelines were not developed to *optimize health* or take into account the *needs of individuals*. The same problem exists with guidelines for our pets. While pet food manufacturers strive to make sure their diets contain these minimum recommendations, pets probably require more than the RDA of vitamins and minerals. This is especially true of those pets experiencing illness or undergoing periods of stress.

As a result, many holistic doctors prefer to think in terms of *optimum daily needs* or *amounts* (ODA) rather than the recommended (minimal) daily allowances for their patients. These optimum amounts are not easily determined. However, pets with a variety of illnesses can benefit from the use of additional vitamins and minerals. Additionally, pets fed natural (whole food) sources of vitamins (as a preventive or treatment) will receive extra vitamins and minerals without the possibility for toxicity, as these sources are food sources rather than chemically synthesized vitamins and minerals.

Vitamins and minerals do not occur as isolated chemicals in nature, and with rare exceptions (such as a known illness that would require immediate treatment with a particular vitamin, such as the case with a pet suffering from rat poisoning, who would respond to vitamin K), it doesn't make sense from a holistic perspective to think in terms of supplying certain amounts of individual vitamins. Vitamins and minerals work together, synergistically, to allow maximum functioning of these supplements. An excess of a synthetic vitamin or mineral can cause problems, not just in direct toxic effects but also by upsetting the balance intended by nature. For example, puppies fed high levels of vitamin D or calcium can develop skeletal problems such as osteochondrosis. High doses of an isolated B vitamin can cause deficiency of other B vitamins.

Natural or Synthetic Vitamins?

No one would debate that the best way for us to get all of our nutrition is from eating the correct amounts of a well-balanced diet composed of fresh, naturally raised meats and plants. The same concept is true for our pets. However, it is the rare person or pet who actually eats this ideal diet every day. Even if this were possible, there is no way to compensate for those times of disease or stress where additional vitamins and minerals would be needed. Due to the various pollutions and chemicals our pets encounter each day, providing an optimum allowance of these important micronutrients, rather than a minimum daily amount designed to prevent diseases caused by specific isolated vitamin and mineral deficiencies, makes a lot of sense.

In Part Three, Diet, the emphasis is on how processing food destroys many of the nutrients contained in the original ingredients in the diet, including vitamins and minerals. This is why the manufacturers have to add vitamins and minerals back to the foods. This is also why the best diet for a pet is one made at home. When this is not possible, the next best thing is using the most natural, chemical-free, minimally processed food possible and then supplying additional supplements including vitamins and minerals to provide the optimum allowance of nutrients.

Because pets may not obtain all of the nutrients they need from their diets, holistic doctors often recommend supplementation. In Part Three, Diet, you'll see a recommendation for supplements to use for both processed and homemade diets.

One such supplement is a vitamin/mineral supplement. As a pet owner, you will need to make the decision on your choice of vitamin/mineral supplement. Should you choose a natural supplement, or is a synthetic supplement acceptable?

The following information is taken from a report on this subject written by Judith DeCava (as well as several other resources that are listed in the bibliography at the end of the book). The title of the article, appearing in the May/June 1999 issue of *Nutrition News and Views*, is "Of Foods and Supplements." This discussion will give you an overview of why many holistic doctors recommend natural whole food supplements rather than synthetic chemical vitamin and mineral fractions for basic supplementation.

As Ms. DeCava points out, vitamins and minerals are complex organic substances. Vitamins consist of a group of chemically related compounds working together, synergistically. Separating this complex group of compounds into isolated fractions (for example, removing ascorbic acid from the entire vitamin C complex) converts the vitamin complex into a disabled chemical fraction of minimal or no use to living cells.

While the chemical structure of most vitamin complexes has been determined, little is known about all of the interdependent, interactive components. The true potency of the vitamin or mineral complex is through the combined actions of all of the parts, rather than just isolated segments of the complex. There are many phytochemicals (plant chemicals) that have yet to be discovered. Feeding the natural vitamin complex includes all of the compounds that have yet to be discovered.

Why is this important? Let's take a look at some of the current research and see how using whole food complexes are superior to isolated vitamin and mineral fractions. Note that this research is extrapolated from the human literature; similar conclusions are probably applicable to our pets, although controlled studies are lacking.

Large numbers of people taking synthetic beta-carotene had increased risk of cancer. People eating diets high in beta-carotene had reduced levels of cancer. Whole food complexes, as well as diets high in foods containing beta-carotene, provided the protection not found in synthetic beta-carotene supplements. Why? Because whole foods contain not only beta-carotenes but many other carotenoids and numerous phytochemicals not found in isolated beta-carotene supplements. Supplements containing mixed carotenoids are preferred over pure beta-carotene supplements for this reason.

Vitamin E contains antioxidants necessary for maintaining health. Most synthetic supplements contain only alpha tocopherol, yet this is only one of many tocopherols present in the vitamin E complex. Gamma tocopherol is an even better antioxidant than alpha tocopherol, yet it is not included in most synthetic products (look for natural products containing "mixed tocopherols" to get gamma tocopherol as well as the other tocopherols).

What about natural alpha tocopherol (called d-alpha tocopherol, rather than the synthetic form called dl-alpha tocopherol)? Even this natural form (superior to the synthetic form) does not contain the all of the "mixed tocopherols" or all of the other natural food ingredients (phytonutrients) found in natural foods. Without the rest of the vitamin E complex, alpha tocopherol does not improve the immune system and can cause imbalances in the body.

Any synthetic vitamin or mineral can cause similar problems since they are lacking in all of the many nutrients present in natural raw foods and raw food supplements.

For example, in postmenopausal women taking synthetic vitamin E, their LDL levels increased (meaning their oxidation levels increased). Conversely, in women taking a dietary source of vitamin E, there were significant reductions in oxidation levels (decreased LDL). It was theorized that the synthetic "vitamin E," which was actually alpha tocopherol, possibly displaced the protective gamma tocopherol, which might be the more protective component of the vitamin E complex.

High doses of vitamin A supplements increased birth defects in women, whereas similar amounts of vitamin A present in whole foods did not result in birth defects. It was felt that the vitamin A in foods, which are naturally balanced with synergistic cofactors, minerals, trace elements, phytochemicals, and other vitamin complexes might be protective and nontoxic.

Regarding vitamin C, natural forms of vitamin C are preferred to synthetic ascorbic acid, which is actually only part of the vitamin C complex. One great advantage of getting vitamin C from foods rather than from supplements is that you will get many other healthful nutrients at the same time, such as bioflavonoids and carotenes.

This is not to say that synthetic vitamins and minerals should never be used. Sometimes synthetic vitamins and minerals are needed to provide immediate relief for a pet. For example, a pet having seizures as a result of low blood calcium levels (hypocalcemic tetany) needs synthetic calcium immediately or he will die. A pet poisoned by a vitamin K antagonist rodent poison needs vitamin K. Synthetic vitamins and minerals are quite useful for a number of other disorders such as allergies, epilepsy, and inflammatory bowel disease (see the section on **Orthomolecular Medicine,** page 415).

However, for long-term supplementation, when possible, natural whole food sources of vitamins and minerals provide so much more (many constituents of foods have not yet been identified) than chemically synthesized vitamins and minerals.

Every pet's body is unique, and therefore each pet has unique vitamin and mineral requirements. While guidelines such as the RDA (recommended daily allowance) can be used to suggest minimum amounts of vitamins and minerals that are needed to prevent deficiencies, these values in no way tell us what each individual pet requires. Each pet has unique needs that differ from other pets. For example, the growing pet has different requirements from the healthy adult or geriatric pet. The pet with cancer has different nutritional needs from a healthy pet. It is difficult to feed the pet synthetic chemical vitamin and mineral fractions without having any knowledge of the pet's specific nutrient requirements. By feeding the pet whole food complexes, the pet's body can assimilate what it needs without regard for RDA allowances. This selective absorption allows the body to use what it needs and excrete the rest. Chemically synthesized vitamins and minerals do not allow the body to do this; rather, the body must deal with the chemical vitamin or mineral (rather than the natural food complex) in some manner and possibly suffer consequences of biochemical imbalances or

overdoses. While a food can be chemically isolated into individual parts, the body cannot get along just on these isolated fractions. To isolate a separate vitamin or mineral and call it a "nutrient" is similar to isolating the battery of a watch and calling it a watch; it just isn't the same thing.

Is there any use for synthetic vitamin and mineral fractions in pets? Of course.

As a rule, for disease prevention, using whole food supplements that contain the entire vitamin-mineral complexes as they are found in nature appears to be most beneficial. However, as previously mentioned, isolated fractions of vitamins and minerals do have their place in the treatment of selected diseases of pets. The synthetic fraction of vitamin K can quickly stop internal bleeding. Once controlled, natural vitamin K complexes (which contain the part of vitamin K that was chemically synthesized and given to the pet to stop the bleeding as well as the rest of the entire vitamin K complex) can be used to improve the pet's health.

Likewise, a dog or cat who has recently given birth and is suffering seizures as a result of calcium deficiency needs immediate treatment with an injection of synthetic calcium to immediately stop the seizure. Giving the pet an oral nutritional whole food supplement would never be able to save this pet. However, once the pet is stabilized, improving the diet and supplementing with whole food complexes would be warranted. Maintenance with synthetic vitamins and minerals can never replace the nutritional value of natural vitamin and mineral complexes necessary to maintain health and decrease disease.

Natural nutrients, unlike chemically synthesized pieces of the whole complex, work synergistically. For example, vitamin C complex works synergistically with vitamin A and K complexes. Giving chemical ascorbic acid (which in actuality is only the antioxidant part of the entire vitamin C complex and is not the whole vitamin C complex) will interrupt this complex interaction with the other vitamin complexes. Since nature does not produce fractions of vitamins and minerals but rather creates them in their whole forms, these are the forms the body requires. Chemical vitamin and mineral fractions cannot meet the body's needs. The body treats these chemical fractions as drugs and excretes them quickly rather than assimilating them into the body. This is why holistic doctors recommend using whole raw food complexes as vitamin and mineral supplements rather than the use of chemical fractions of these important nutrients.

While it's important to understand that vitamins and minerals do not occur in nature as isolated entities, it is easiest to discuss these compounds in this way. This is especially true when we wish to review any evidence (or lack of evidence) regarding the use of these products as part of a holistic treatment protocol for pets.

ABOUT MINERALS

As with vitamins, minerals (such as calcium, magnesium, sodium, and phosphorus) are required in the body in minute amounts to maintain health and prevent disease. Minerals can appear in one of four forms: inorganic, organic, colloidal, or crystalloidal.

Organic minerals are present in some chemical combination that is peculiar to the reactions of a living cell. Inorganic minerals are present in soil, water, or air and are assimilated by plants and converted into living organic minerals. Inorganic minerals must be converted by the plant or animal into a living organic mineral in order to be used by the plant or pet.

Which form of mineral is "better" depends upon a number of factors, including nutrient interactions, the presence of non-nutritional factors, and physiologic state of the pet. For some minerals (such as selenium, chromium, and iron) the organic form is preferred; for other minerals such as zinc and copper, the "best" form to use is not so clear.

While inorganic minerals can be used by the body, up to 20 times more are needed to get the same effect as would be seen by ingesting organic minerals. Taking these higher doses may upset the body and result in toxicity.

Colloidal minerals are dispersed in a medium, whereas crystalloid minerals are the pure form of the minerals, and can form mineral crystals. Colloidal minerals in a food can be converted into smaller, usable mineral forms; synthetic colloidal mineral products are quite large and may

not be able to be assimilated into the cells of the body. As with vitamins, minerals are best consumed in their raw organic form, which contains the entire mineral complex and necessary cofactors and enzymes.

Cooked and processed pet foods contain minerals in their inorganic forms and cannot furnish nourishment for the cells as quickly as when in a raw organic form. This is one of the reasons why many holistic doctors prefer raw diets (or at least those containing raw vegetables). Supplementing the pet's diet with whole food supplements can also supply minerals (and many other nutrients) in their most available form.

Part Two, Herbs and Supplements, includes some of the most common minerals that might be prescribed for your pet: boron, calcium, chromium, magnesium, manganese, phosphorus, potassium, selenium, sodium, and zinc.

ABOUT MUSHROOMS

Four of the most commonly used medicinal mushrooms—cordyceps, maitake, reishi, and shitake—and their usage are described in Part Two.

Mushrooms have been used for their purported health benefits for hundreds, if not thousands, of years. Recent evidence reveals that many mushrooms contain polysaccharide compounds that may have antibacterial, antiviral, and anti-tumor properties. Some mushrooms are also recommended for stimulation of the immune system, as well as for pets with diseases of the liver, kidneys, or heart.

While there are more than 30,000 species of mushrooms, approximately 50 or so have been used for medicinal purposes.

Mushroom therapy should be undertaken only under veterinary supervision. Owners should not simply go "mushroom hunting" or pull "toadstools" from their yards and feed them to their pets, as this could result in the accidental feeding of poisonous species of fungi that can result in death.

Dosages of the mushrooms vary with the product preparation. If using fresh mushrooms, a generic dosage of 4 to 6 mushrooms can be added to a homemade diet for nutritional support.

ABOUT SUPPLEMENTS

A number of nutritional supplements may be useful for maintaining health or treating disease. Supplements can be useful by themselves or used in conjunction with conventional therapies, depending upon each pet's individual needs. Many pets may be able to take reduced doses of their medications when taking nutritional supplements, with the ultimate goal being to wean them off of all medications.

Keep in mind that even with the variety of supplements we have at our disposal, *supplements are not cure-alls.* No one supplement is perfect for every pet in every situation. How do you decide which supplement to use? That is not an easy answer. Pet owners should know that there is no one "best" product for helping pets with any specific condition. Doctors often have a favorite supplement, based upon available data anecdotal reports, and personal experience. And, if one product doesn't produce the desired effect, your doctor has a choice of other products she can try. Unless the product contains drugs or chemical fillers, there are usually no side effects when these products are used as directed. However, owners should keep in mind that any product, conventional medication or "natural supplement," can have side effects, including death. It has been said that *all products can show toxicity, the determining factor being the dose.* Owners are encouraged not to use supplements without first learning about them and then discussing them with their doctors. Because there is always the potential for supplements interacting with conventional medications, owners should inform their veterinarians of any and all medications or supplements they are currently administering to their pets.

Because the supplement industry is young and not stringently regulated, owners should only use supplements under veterinary supervision.

A recent study showed that among 13 brands of SAMe supplements (a popular supplement for people), only seven were found to contain the labeled amounts of SAMe (S-adenosyl-methionine)! The laboratory doing the testing also found that the labeled amount of SAMe on such products included the weight of the other non-active components.

A number of products containing perna mussel have shown variable results in people, ranging from no effect to very effective.

Several years ago similar problems were found with supplements containing ephedra (ma huang). Some supplements contained less ephedra than indicated on the label, some contained the labeled amount, and some supplements contained more ephedra than indicated on the label. This variation in ephedra concentration even occurred in different batches of the same supplement made by the same manufacturer in a few cases. This underscores the need for consumers to use only those supplements recommended by their doctors or manufactured by companies with good reputations that practice quality control procedures.

Responses seen in pets being treated with supplements may vary among similar products for many reasons, including these:

- Poor quality control is used (for example, the potency of herbs and several other supplements varies with the method of harvesting, agriculture, and preparation of the product).
- Products may carry the same name but differ in the ingredients in various countries as they may have been manufactured by different companies.
- Different species (of plant or animal) may be used in different products.

Some form of quality control among all manufacturers is clearly needed; currently, as was the case years ago in the infancy of the generic drug industry, no such oversight of quality control occurs.

Due to differences in ingredients and the way the pet's body may react to these ingredients, often several products must be tried before a positive response is obtained.

Commonly, doctors will use several supplements (rather than only one supplement) in their treatment of a disease to get an "additive" effect and see results.

Finally, owners should keep in mind that it may take 2 to 3 months before positive effects are seen from supplements as the body "detoxifies" itself and begins assimilating more nutrients.

In choosing a supplement, an ideal supplement should meet the following criteria:

1. *The supplement should be safe and not harm the pet.*
2. *The supplement should be palatable so that the pet will ingest it.*
3. *The supplement must be cost-effective.* If it costs too much, owners won't buy it. However, owners should keep in mind something that is true of supplements: If the supplement can prevent or cure disease, this saves the owner money in veterinary expenses. Therefore, paying a little more for a higher quality supplement will be cost-effective over the life of the pet.
4. *The supplement should be easy for the owner to administer to the pet.* Many medications prescribed by doctors are never given to the pet since owners experience difficulty giving the dog or cat a pill or liquid. While supplements can come in a pill, a liquid, or a flavored chewable tablet form, powdered supplements that are easily sprinkled onto the pet's food may be the easiest for the owner to give the pet. For supplements that only come in pill or capsule form, your veterinarian may be able to have a compounding pharmacist specially prepare an easier-to-administer liquid version of the supplement.
5. *The supplement should not interfere with other therapies that may be necessary for the pet, nor should it interact with other therapies and cause toxicity to the pet.* This is one important reason why owners should not try most supplements on their own without a proper medical diagnosis and veterinary supervision.
6. *The correct dosage of the supplement should be known.* This one requirement of the ideal nutritional supplement is the hardest to meet. Many supplements are recommended based upon anecdotal evidence, extrapolation from the human medical literature, and clinical experience, without any "hard" scientific studies, such as double-blind placebo-controlled studies (the "gold standard" of scientific studies). This doesn't mean the supplements can't be used effectively. Many of our supplements for which the "best" dosage is not known are used safely and effectively in many of our patients. However, because studies

are often lacking for the use of many of our supplements, owners must work closely with their doctors to review the available supplements and try to find the most appropriate dosage possible. When supplements fail to work, it may be simply because we don't know which dose is most effective.

While there are many great supplements for treating a variety of medical problems in pets, there is no "ideal" supplement. Keep these ideas in mind when you look at the supplements described in this book.

DOSAGE INFORMATION

Dosages are based upon information in the scientific literature, as well as on clinical experience and reports from practitioners. In some cases, as with herbs, exact dosages will vary with the product used and the concentration of the final product. In some cases, as with glandular products, an exact dose may not be important, and the recommended amount of the supplement to use is based upon your pet's response to the therapy. (Unlike the case with most conventional medications, a "correct" dose is not critical or may not be possible to state if the therapy has not been carefully tested and the dose is tailored to each pet's needs.) As much as possible, I have tried to state the correct dose. However, the final decision on what to use and how much of any particular supplement to use should rest with your veterinarian.

TERMS YOU SHOULD KNOW

The following terms are used throughout the book. Here are some definitions to help you understand how we use these terms in the context of pet health.

Anecdotal Studies   These studies are not rigidly controlled but rather are the result of clinical experiences and observations reported by various practitioners. While not often thought of as highly as the double-blind placebo-controlled study, in many cases the only "proof" we have for a therapy may be from these experiences shared by those who use them. Often, anecdotal information eventually leads to more controlled studies.

Double-Blind Placebo-Controlled Studies In what is considered the "gold standard" for scientific "proof," these studies are double-blind (neither the researcher administering the therapy nor the patient knows if the treatment is the actual treatment or a placebo), and a placebo is used to compare results with the therapy tested. A placebo is administered "blindly" to some participants to see if these participants also show improvement. As some improvement can always occur with a placebo, the results between the actual therapy tested and the placebo are compared to see if there is a statistical difference.

Placebo Effect Many skeptics question whether or not a pet improves as a result of the placebo effect when treated with a complementary therapy. Of course, this question should also be asked about conventional therapies as well.

There are actually two placebo effects that may occur when a pet is treated with any type of therapy. The first one is the well-known "placebo effect" so commonly discussed when treating people. In this effect, if a doctor prescribes a medication for someone with a sore shoulder and tells the patient that he will improve in 48 hours, and then the patient improves, was it from the treatment or the power of suggestion?

Because our minds can often convince us that we feel better, and can in fact help the body to heal, it's good to know whether the response to a therapy is from the therapy or the mind healing the body. Of course, there is no way for a pet to tell itself to feel better. If I give a pet a medication to make it stop itching, there is no way for me to tell the pet to stop itching. Either the treatment works or it doesn't. This well-known placebo effect, which commonly occurs in people, cannot occur in pets.

Having said this, people who respond to the power of suggestion (placebo effect) simply prove that the body can heal itself without harmful medications. Holistic medical doctors can use the body's healing ability to assist in wellness

without resorting to powerful and expensive medications, and this is a great thing!

The second type of placebo effect occurs in any person or pet. Simply put, some patients will improve no matter what treatment is chosen unless their condition is severe. Therefore, whenever possible, a placebo-controlled trial is helpful when testing a new therapy to compare how many patients get better with the therapy and how many would have improved on their own anyway. This allows doctors to determine if the therapy really worked or if the patient would have improved without therapy over time.

Health Health is not simply the absence of disease. Many animals may appear healthy (they are not demonstrating signs of illness), but in fact they are ill. As an example, a pet with diabetes may not show any clinical signs until the diabetes has advanced, yet blood and urine tests would show changes in glucose concentrations that would allow a diagnosis of diabetes prior to clinical signs. While this pet appears healthy, in reality he has subclinical (not yet evident) diabetes.

Good health implies the ability to resist disease, to respond well to life, and to resist assaults on the various body systems. In short, a healthy pet is one who has a greater overall ability to stay well, not be ill, and to be able to recover from any illness that might afflict the body more quickly than a pet who lacks this overall quality of health. A healthy pet not only "looks healthy," but is in fact truly healthy.

That's why it's so important for pets to have the opportunity for regular medical care, as least annually, just as it is for humans. Since many diseases, such as kidney failure in dogs, take months or years to occur, proper care and early diagnosis are important. Proper nutrition is important for the life of the pet for the same reason. While many of our pets appear "healthy," we know that this may not be the case. Many of these pets, due to an improper diet and lack of regular medical care, are only marginally surviving. Yet, you'll never know it because your pet "appears healthy." Don't be deceived by appearances. Years of eating an improper diet, over-dependence on vaccinations, lack of preventive care, and use of potentially harmful medications when safer natural supplements could be used in their place, can slowly kill your pet without you even knowing it.

THE LIMITATIONS OF THIS BOOK

Remember that no book can substitute for individualized medical care from a qualified veterinarian. Every animal is different and has specific health needs only a doctor can assess. In many cases, it is possible to use combinations of treatments in sophisticated ways that cannot be described in this book. The information here should be regarded as an introduction and a guide, a place to start. The final treatment decision will best be made after evaluation of your pet and consultation with a veterinarian.

Natural
Health Bible
for Dogs & Cats

PART

ONE

Conditions

ADDISON'S DISEASE

Principal Natural Treatments
Glandular therapy

Other Natural Treatments
Natural diet, antioxidants, borage, dandelion leaf, licorice, nettle, Siberian ginseng, spirulina

Addison's disease, also called hypoadrenocorticism, is an uncommon disease of dogs and occurs very rarely in cats. The cause is unknown in some cases; in others it appears as an immune-mediated disorder in which the pet's body makes antibodies that destroy its own adrenal glands. Chronic use of corticosteroids (such as prednisone) can cause secondary Addison's disease if the corticosteroid administration is suddenly stopped rather than gradually withdrawn from the pet.

Clinical signs occur as a result of decreased output of adrenal gland hormones (glucocorticoids and mineralocorticoids). Clinical signs such as weakness or vomiting can be subtle and intermittent; severe and suddenly occurring signs such as shock may also occur. Because many cases are vague, diagnosis is at times difficult to make. A high index of suspicion is needed in order to diagnose the disease in many pets; blood testing is used to make the definitive diagnosis.

PRINCIPAL NATURAL TREATMENTS

The main natural treatments are designed to strengthen and support the adrenal gland. The most common therapy is **glandular therapy** (page 393), which uses whole animal tissues or extracts of the adrenal gland. Current research supports this concept that the glandular supplements have specific activity and contain active substances that can exert physiologic effects.

While skeptics question the ability of the digestive tract to absorb the large protein macromolecules found in glandular extracts, evidence exists that this is possible. Essentially, these glandular macromolecules can be absorbed from the digestive tract into the circulatory system and may exert their biologic effects on their target tissues.

Several studies show that radioactively tagged cells, when injected into the body, accumulate in their target tissues. The accumulation is more rapid by traumatized body organs or glands than healthy tissues, which may indicate an increased requirement for those ingredients contained in the glandular supplements.

In addition to targeting specific damaged organs and glands, supplementation with glandular supplements may also provide specific nutrients to the pet. For example, glands contain hormones in addition to a number of other chemical constituents. These low doses of crude hormones are suitable for any pet needing hormone replacement, but especially for those pets with mild disease or those who simply need gentle organ support.

Glandular supplements also function as a source of enzymes that may encourage the pet to produce hormones or help the pet maintain health or fight disease.

Finally, glandular supplements are sources of active lipids and steroids that may be of benefit to pets.

The dosage of glandular supplements varies with the product used.

These supplements can be used in conjunction with conventional therapies as they are unlikely to be effective by themselves in most patients. The natural treatments are widely used with variable success but have not all been thoroughly investigated and proven at this time.

OTHER NATURAL TREATMENTS

As with any condition, the most healthful natural **diet** (page 314) will improve the pet's overall health. Treatment for hypoadrenocorticism includes **natural diet** (page 335); **antioxidants** (page 158); and herbal remedies such as **borage** (page 167), **dandelion leaf** (page 193), **licorice** (page 234), **nettle** (page 245), Siberian **ginseng** (page 210), and **spirulina** (page 222) to strengthen the adrenal gland. These can be used in conjunction with conventional therapies as they are unlikely to be effective by themselves in most patients.

CONVENTIONAL THERAPY

Conventional therapy for Addison's disease involves administration via injection or oral medications of supplemental mineralocorticoids and glucocorticoids for the life of the pet. Treatment is rewarding and generally quite safe.

 # ALLERGIC DERMATITIS (Atopy, Atopic Dermatitis)

Principal Natural Treatments
Orthomolecular therapy, topical decontamination with frequent hypoallergenic shampooing and conditioning, omega-3 fatty acids, natural diet

Other Natural Treatments
Digestive enzymes; antioxidants; MSM; proanthocyanidins; herbal therapies including the topically applied herbs aloe, witch hazel, licorice, Oregon grape, peppermint, chamomile, calendula, juniper, lavender, rose bark, uva ursi; and the oral herbs alfalfa, aloe vera, burdock root, dandelion, echinacea, feverfew, garlic, German chamomile, *Ginkgo biloba*, goldenseal, licorice root, nettle, red clover, Oregon grape, yarrow, and yellow dock

Allergic dermatitis is among the most common skin diseases seen in private veterinary practice. The technical term for "allergies" is atopic dermatitis, also called atopy. Atopy is a genetic disease in which the dog or cat becomes sensitized to environmental proteins called allergens. In non-allergic pets, these allergens produce no clinical signs. In allergic or atopic dogs and cats, these allergens produce the clinical signs so commonly seen.

Allergic dogs (and probably cats) develop allergen-specific IgE antibodies (and to some extent IgG antibodies as well). These IgE antibodies are involved in Type I hypersensitivity reactions in the pet's body. While the actual immunologic response can be quite complicated, briefly this is what happens to cause allergies in your pet's body: IgE antibody is formed upon exposure to an environmental allergen such as pollen from grasses, weeds, and trees; mold; human dander; fleas; or house dust mites. The IgE antibody attaches to a tissue cell called a mast cell. The next time the pet encounters the allergen, the allergen attaches to the IgE antibody-mast cell combination. Upon attachment to the IgE-mast cell unit, the mast cell de-granulates (disintegrates, "explodes") releasing the many chemicals contained within the cell and cell membrane. Some of these chemicals include histamine, substance P, bradykinin, and various prostaglandins. It is the presence of these chemicals that causes the clinical signs (inflammation, itching, and such) seen in allergic pets.

ALLERGIC DOG BREEDS

Atopic dermatitis is relatively common in dogs and rare in cats. As previously mentioned, atopic dermatitis is a genetic disease. For this reason dogs (and cats) with atopy should not be bred. Due to the genetic component of the disease, certain breeds of dogs have a high incidence of atopic dermatitis. Breeds with a high incidence of allergies include Cairn Terriers, Shar-peis, West Highland White Terriers, Scottish Terriers, Lhasa Apsos, Shih Tzus, Wirehaired Fox Terriers, Dalmations, Pugs, Irish Setters, Boston Terriers, Golden Retrievers, Boxers, English Setters, Labrador Retrievers, Miniature Schnauzers, and Belgian Tervurens. Despite these breed predispositions, allergic dermatitis can occur in any breed of dog. No specific cat breeds have been shown to be predisposed to atopic dermatitis. Some (but not all) studies of atopic dogs show that females are affected more than males.

According to the literature, allergies usually are seen in pets 1 to 3 years of age. However, this figure is a bit misleading. Allergies usually occur within 1 to 3 years of a pet being exposed to environmental allergens. For example, if you live in an environment where there are few environmental allergens, even if your dog had the genetic ability to develop allergies, he would not do so. If you moved to another area where there were many environmental allergens, your genetically predisposed allergic dog or cat would develop signs of allergies within 1 to 3 years of moving into the new environment. (When owners ask if allergies can be cured, the answer is usually "No," although the rare pet will "outgrow" his allergies. If an owner were to move to another state where there were few allergens that affected the dog or cat, the allergic pet, while still technically "allergic," would not show signs of allergies and would appear "cured.")

Despite this well-reported figure of 1 to 3 years of age (or more correctly 1 to 3 years of antigen exposure), some pets do not show signs of allergies until midlife or later. Still others show signs as early as a few months of age, barely starting their puppyhood or kittenhood.

Many allergic pets have seasonal signs, showing itching only during the season when the specific allergens to which they are allergic are most prominent. For example, pets with allergies to Bermuda grass often begin showing allergic signs in the spring when the grass begins to awaken after the winter. Eventually, over many years, most allergic pets will develop signs that last all year long.

ALLERGIES AND INFECTIONS

The typical allergic pet itches but has normal appearing skin (one exception mentioned in a leading dermatology text states that the English Bulldog may have red skin with minimal itching). This helps differentiate atopy from other diseases that cause itchiness but also cause skin lesions (mange, flea allergies, bacterial infections, yeast infections, skin cancer). The itchiness can be mild, moderate, or severe; but most allergic pets do not start off with severe itching (a pet with severe itching is more likely to have mange, fleas, or the rarely seen food allergies).

With time, skin lesions can develop if secondary infections occur or as a result of chronic self-trauma. Many dogs with chronic allergies develop pink or red skin, bronzing of the skin, and darkening of the skin. The pink color is from chronic inflammation (the pink color can also be seen early in the course of the disease). The bronzing color is from pigment in the dog's saliva that discolors the skin and hair (this bronzing, which can also be seen early in the condition for dogs who excessively lick, is particularly striking in light-haired dogs). Darkening of the skin, called hyperpigmentation, can develop in any chronic skin disorder as the result of repeated trauma and inflammation.

Many dogs (and probably cats) with allergies also have flea allergies and chronic bacterial infections. Chronic skin infections are so common in allergic dogs that every dog with chronic skin infections should be screened for atopy (and also for hormonal diseases such as hypothyroidism, another overlooked underlying disorder). Because allergic skin is not "normal" skin, it is predisposed to secondary infections. Most common, staphylococcal bacteria infect the skin, causing small red bumps called papules or small pimple-like lesions called pustules. Scabs can also form when the papules or pustules rupture.

Secondary yeast infections are becoming increasingly common in atopic dogs. Most of the time the yeast *Malassezia* is the causative agent. Dogs with yeast infections are typically quite itchy, greasy (with greasy yellow scales), red, and quite smelly. Yeast infections are often misdiagnosed but should be considered in any dog with the aforementioned clinical signs.

Diagnosis is based upon clinical signs, ruling out other diseases by various tests (skin scrapings, fungal cultures, skin cytology, and blood testing). When needed, intradermal skin testing (allergy testing) can be done. In vitro testing (blood testing) for allergies is not as accurate as skin testing and should not be relied upon if skin testing is available. (Blood testing is inaccurate for testing for food allergies.)

PRINCIPAL NATURAL TREATMENTS

The main natural treatments are designed to reduce itching and inflammation in pets with allergic dermatitis.

Orthomolecular Therapy

Orthomolecular medicine (often called "megavitamin therapy") seeks to use increased levels of vitamins and minerals (mainly antioxidants) to help treat a variety of medical disorders. While daily amounts of vitamins and minerals have been recommended as an attempt to prevent nutritional deficiencies, orthomolecular medicine uses higher doses as part of the therapy for disease.

The pet food industry relies on recommendations by the National Research Council (NRC) to prevent diseases caused by nutrient deficiencies in the "average" pet; yet, the NRC has not attempted to determine the *optimum* amount of nutrients or their effects in treating medical disorders. While a minimum amount of nutrients may be satisfactory in preventing diseases caused by nutrient deficiencies, it is important to realize that there is no "average" pet, and that every pet has unique nutritional needs.

It is unlikely that our current recommendations are adequate to maintain health in every pet. Each pet has unique requirements for nutrients. Additionally, these needs will vary depending upon the pet's health. For example, in times of stress or disease, additional nutrients above and beyond those needed for health will be required. Orthomolecular medicine evaluates the needs of the pet and uses increased nutrients to fight disease.

Note: Owners should not diagnose and treat their pets without veterinary supervision. Many medical disorders present similar symptoms. Also, megavitamin therapy can be toxic if not used properly.

The orthomolecular approach to treating atopic dermatitis uses a hypoallergenic, healthy diet as the starting point. This diet should be free of chemicals, impurities, and by-products. A blood profile is done to rule out endocrine diseases such as Cushing's disease and hypothyroidism, as antioxidants may create changes in blood values that are normally used to screen for

these common disorders. The treatment uses vitamin A (10,000 IU for small dogs and cats, up to 30,000 IU for large dogs), crystalline ascorbic acid (750 mg for small dogs and cats, up to 3,000 mg for large dogs), and vitamin E (800 IU for small dogs and cats, up to 2,400 IU for large dogs). The antioxidant mineral selenium (20 mcg for small dogs and cats, up to 60 mcg for large dogs) is also added to the regimen. Once asymptomatic, a maintenance protocol using lower dosages of vitamins A and E and the mineral selenium is prescribed to reduce the chance for toxicity. Promising results have been seen in many pets treated with this regimen.

Topical Decontamination

Topical decontamination with frequent hypoallergenic shampooing and conditioning is important in removing foreign proteins from the skin and coat of allergic animals. Additionally, frequent bathing and conditioning can temporarily relieve itching in many pets with atopic dermatitis. Products vary. Those with aloe vera and colloidal oatmeal are usually tried first and work on most pets if frequency of bathing is maintained. (Most allergic pets should be bathed every 24 to 48 hours until itching decreases, then 1 to 3 times weekly as needed to control itching.) If aloe vera and oatmeal products do not help decrease itching, medicated products containing antihistamines or corticosteroids can be tried. Finally, residual "leave-on" conditioners can be used to increase contact time between the allergic pet's skin and the hypoallergenic product.

Omega-3 Fatty Acids

Omega-3 fatty acids—eicosapentaenoic acid (EPA) and docosahexaenoic acid (DHA)—are derived from fish oils of coldwater fish (salmon, trout, or most commonly menhaden fish) and flaxseed. Omega-6 fatty acids—linolenic acid (LA) and gamma-linolenic acid (GLA)—are derived from the oils of seeds such as evening primrose, black currant, and borage. Often, fatty acids are added to the diet with other supplements to attain an additive effect.

Just how do the fatty acids work to help in controlling inflammation in pets? Cell membranes contain phospholipids. When membrane injury occurs, an enzyme acts on the phospholipids in the cell membranes to produce fatty acids, including arachidonic acid (an omega-6 fatty acid) and eicosapentaenoic acid (an omega-3 fatty acid). Further metabolism of the arachidonic acid and eicosapentaenoic acid by additional enzymes (the lipooxygenase and cyclooxygenase pathways) yields the production of chemicals called eicosanoids. The eicosanoids produced by metabolism of arachidonic acid are pro-inflammatory and cause inflammation, suppress the immune system, and cause platelets to aggregate and clot; the eicosanoids produced by metabolism of eicosapentaenoic acid are non-inflammatory, not immunosuppressive, and help inhibit platelets from clotting. (There is some overlap and the actual biochemical pathway is a bit more complicated than I have suggested here. For example, one of the by-products of omega-6 fatty acid metabolism is Prostaglandin E_1, which is anti-inflammatory. This is one reason why some research has shown that using certain omega-6 fatty acids can also act to limit inflammation.)

Supplementation of the diet with omega-3 fatty acids works in this biochemical reaction. By providing extra amounts of these non-inflammatory compounds, we try to overwhelm the body with the production of non-inflammatory eicosanoids. Therefore, since the same enzymes metabolize both omega-3 and omega-6 fatty acids, and since metabolism of the omega-6 fatty acids tends to cause inflammation (with the exception of Prostaglandin E_1 by metabolism of omega-6 as mentioned), by supplying a large amount of omega-3 fatty acids, we favor the production of non-inflammatory chemicals.

Many disorders are due to overproduction of the eicosanoids responsible for producing inflammation, including arthritis and atopic dermatitis. Fatty acid supplementation can be beneficial in inflammatory disorders by regulating the eicosanoid production.

In general, the products of omega-3 (specifically EPA) and one omega-6 fatty acid (DGLA) are less inflammatory than the products of arachidonic acid (another omega-6 fatty acid). By changing dietary fatty acid consumption, we can change eicosanoid production right at the cellular level and try to modify (decrease) inflammation within the body. By providing the proper fatty acids, we can use fatty acids as an anti-inflammatory substance. However, since the products of omega-6 fatty acid metabolism (specifically arachidonic acid) are not the sole cause of the inflammation, fatty acid therapy is rarely effective as the sole therapy but is used as an adjunct therapy to achieve an additive effect.

Note: Flaxseed oil is a popular source of alpha-linoleic acid (ALA), an omega-3 fatty acid that is ultimately converted to EPA and DHA. However, many species of pets (probably including dogs) and some people cannot convert ALA to these other more active non-inflammatory omega-3 fatty acids. In one study in people, flaxseed oil was ineffective in reducing symptoms or raising levels of EPA and DHA. While flaxseed oil has been suggested as a less smelly substitute for fish oil, there is no evidence that it is effective when used for the same therapeutic purposes as fish oil. Therefore, supplementation with EPA and DHA is important, and this is the reason flaxseed oil is not recommended as the sole fatty acid supplement for pets. Flaxseed oil can be used to provide ALA and as a coat conditioner.

Dosages

Because of their anti-inflammatory effects, large doses (2 to 4 times the label dose, as the label dose on most products is suspected to be too low to provide anti-inflammatory effects) of omega-3 fatty acids have been shown beneficial in treating allergic dogs and cats. Inhibition of pro-inflammatory prostaglandins, as well as decreased levels of leukotriene B_4 production from white blood cells (leukotriene B_4 is an important mediator in inflammatory skin disorders) is the explanation for the effectiveness of omega-3 fatty acids in allergic pets. As with the other supplements, they often allow doctors to lower the dosages of drugs such as corticosteroids or non-steroidal medications.

Scientific Evidence

In allergic dogs, fatty acid supplements were effective in 11 to 27% of dogs treated (over 50% of allergic cats responded to fatty acid supplements). How well fatty acids work in an allergic pet depends upon a number of factors, including product used, dosage used, and the presence of other diseases that may contribute to itching. Many atopic pets also have flea allergies, bacterial skin infections, yeast skin infections with *Malassezia* organisms, and food hypersensitivity. Until these other concurrent problems are identified and treated properly, simply administering fatty acid supplements to a pet suspected of just having atopic dermatitis is unlikely to be effective. In general, the literature reports that about 20% of allergic (atopic) dogs and 50% of cats may respond partially or totally to fatty acid supplementation.

The Controversies

While many doctors use fatty acids for a variety of medical problems, there is considerable debate about the use of fatty acids. The debate concerns several areas:

What is the "best" dose to use in the treatment of pets? (Most doctors use anywhere from 2 to 10 times the label dose.) Research in the treatment of allergies indicates that the label dose is ineffective. In people, the dosage that showed effectiveness in many studies were 1.4 to 2.8 grams of GLA per day, or 1.7 grams of EPA and 0.9 grams of DHA per day, which is hard for people to obtain from the supplements currently available. If this were shown to be the correct dosage for pets, a 50-pound dog would need to take 10 or more fatty acids capsules per day to obtain a similar dosage, depending upon which supplement (and there are many choices on the market) was used. Therefore, while the studies with omega-3 fatty acids show many potential health benefits, it is almost impossible to administer the large number of capsules needed to approximate the same dosage used in these studies. The best that owners can hope for at this time is to work with their veterinarians and try to increase, as best as possible, the amount of omega-3 fatty acids in the diet to try to get to what seems to be the "preferred" ratio of 5:1, omega-6:omega-3 fatty acids.

What is the "correct" fatty acid to use? Should we use just omega-3 (EPA and DHA) fatty acids, or combine them with omega-6 (GLA) fatty acids? Is there an "ideal" ratio of omega-6 to omega-3 fatty acids? Through research on pets

with atopic dermatitis, the ideal dietary ratio seems to be 5:1 of omega-6:omega-3 fatty acids, although this is also debated.

Is supplementation with fatty acid capsules or liquids the best approach, or is dietary manipulation (adding the "ideal" ratio of omega-6 and omega-3 fatty acids) preferred for the treatment of inflammatory conditions? There are, in fact, diets constructed with this "ideal" ratio. For owners who do not like giving their pets medication, or for those pets who don't take the fatty acid supplements easily, it might be wise to try some of these medically formulated diets (available from your pet's doctor) that contain the fatty acids. (However, because these medicated diets may not be as natural as possible due to the inclusion of by-products and chemical preservatives, holistic pet owners may need to try other options.)

Fish Oils Since processed foods have increased omega-6 fatty acids and decreased omega-3 fatty acids, supplementing the diets of all pets with omega-3 fatty acids seems warranted and will not harm your pet. As discussed above, omega-3 can be derived from fish oils.

Fish oil supplements are usually in the form of a capsule. Since fish oils can easily oxidize and become rancid, some manufacturers add vitamin E to fish oil capsules and liquid products to keep the oil from spoiling (others remove oxygen from the capsule).

The bottom line is that there are many questions regarding the use of fatty acid therapy. More research is needed to determine the effectiveness of the fatty acids in the treatment of various medical problems, as well as the proper doses needed to achieve clinical results. Until definitive answers are obtained, you will need to work with your doctor (knowing the limitations of our current research) to determine the use of these supplements for your pet.

Flaxseed Oil Flaxseed oil is derived from the seeds of the flax plant and has been proposed as a less smelly alternative to fish oil. Flaxseed oil contains alpha-linolenic acid (ALA), an omega-3 fatty acid that is ultimately converted to EPA and DHA. In fact, flaxseed oil contains higher levels of omega-3 fatty acids (ALA) than fish oil. It also contains omega-6 fatty acids.

As mentioned, many species of pets (probably including dogs and cats) and some people cannot convert ALA to these other more active non-inflammatory omega-3 fatty acids. In one study in people, flaxseed oil was ineffective in reducing symptoms or raising levels of EPA and DHA. While flaxseed oil has been suggested as a substitute for fish oil, there is no evidence that it is effective when used for the same therapeutic purposes as fish oil. Unlike the case for fish oil, there is little evidence that flaxseed oil is effective for any specific therapeutic purpose.

Therefore, supplementation with EPA and DHA is important, and this is the reason flaxseed oil is not recommended as the sole fatty acid supplement for pets. Flaxseed oil can be used to provide ALA and as a coat conditioner.

Flaxseed oil does contain lignans, which are currently being studied for use in preventing cancer in people.

The essential fatty acids in flax can be damaged by exposure to heat, light, and oxygen (essentially, they become rancid). For this reason, you shouldn't cook with flaxseed oil. A good product should be sold in an opaque container, and the manufacturing process should keep the temperature under 100° F (some products are prepared by cold extraction methods). Some producers combine the product with vitamin E because it helps prevent rancidity.

The best use of flaxseed oil is as a general nutritional supplement to provide essential fatty acids.

Flaxseed oil appears to be a safe nutritional supplement when used as recommended.

Safety Issues

Fish oil appears to be safe. The most common side effect seen in people and pets is a fish odor to the breath or the skin.

Because fish oil has a mild "blood-thinning" effect, it should not be combined with powerful blood-thinning medications, such as Coumadin (warfarin) or heparin, except on a veterinarian's advice. Fish oil does not seem to cause bleeding problems when it is taken by itself at commonly recommended dosages. Also, fish oil does not appear to raise blood sugar levels in people or pets with diabetes.

Natural Diet

True food allergies are quite rare in pets. Food intolerances, in which the pet develops an allergic response to a non-nutrient in the food (such as an additive) occur in pets, but the true incidence is hard to gauge. While dietary therapy is not a mainstay in the treatment of itchy pets, feeding the best, most natural and holistic diet possible is recommended for at least three reasons:

1. All pets, regardless of the presence of disease, benefit from eating the best diet.
2. Supplements work best when fed with a good diet. Supplements form the foundation of the treatment of many pets with allergic dermatitis, so feeding the best diet to these pets is indicated.
3. Some pets experience modest to dramatic improvement in their skin disorders (less itching, less flakiness, less redness, less body odor, and so on) when fed a wholesome diet even when the diagnosis of "food allergy" is not technically the correct diagnosis. This may be the result of contamination of the commercially purchased diet with additives, chemical preservatives, pesticides, or hormones. It may also occur as the result of processing the food, which removes nutrients from the diet and alters the nutrients. (For example, heating of the foods to temperatures over 400°F causes an increased level of trans-fatty acids.) Many foods contain increased levels of omega-6 fatty acids relative to omega-3 fatty acids; increased omega-6 fatty acids predispose to inflammation. Because feeding a wholesome diet designed to be hypoallergenic is easily done by most owners, dietary therapy is often recommended for pets with skin disorders.

Diets designed for pets with gastrointestinal disease can be useful for pets with skin disorders with some modification. These modified diets are used to assess and treat food allergies as well as assess any improvement in the pet with any skin disorder, including atopic dermatitis. Keep in mind that even itchy pets without a true food allergy may still show improvement when fed the diet used to test and treat food allergies.

There are several medicated diets containing the "correct" amount of fatty acids that supposedly help the pet with allergic dermatitis. Other medicated diets contain novel or chemically modified protein sources that supposedly reduce the allergic reaction and may help the itchy pet. While these diets can and do help some allergic pets, the holistic pet owner should keep two important considerations in mind before feeding these diets. First, it appears that the "correct" ratio of omega-6 to omega-3 fatty acids is 5:1, although more research is necessary before this becomes accepted as fact. While it is difficult to achieve this ratio simply by adding omega-3 fatty acids to the diet, a large amount of research shows positive benefit in some allergic pets when omega-3 fatty acid supplements are added to the diet, even if the 5:1 ratio is not achieved. Therefore these special supplemented diets are not always needed in pets with allergic dermatitis.

Second, most of these special diets may still use animal by-products and chemical preservatives (it is difficult to say that a commercial diet is free of pesticides and preservatives). This practice defeats the purpose of trying to feed pets a natural, wholesome diet. The best diet is a home-prepared one, ideally made with organically grown vegetables and organically raised animal tissues. If your pet will not eat the homemade diet and does require one of these special diets, be sure to work with your veterinarian to pick the one that is most wholesome.

For pets with allergies, hypoallergenic diets can be tried to see if the level of itching and redness decreases. Hypoallergenic diets are those that contain nutrients to which the pet is unlikely to react with an allergic response. The most common allergic foods are protein sources that the pet has eaten for months or years, rather than a new diet to which the pet has just been introduced. As a result, protein sources that the pet has not eaten before are used (most often rabbit, lamb, or venison). Gluten-free carbohydrate sources are used to prevent gluten allergies.

When indicated by the results of the physical examination and history you provide your veterinarian, a food trial might be indicated. To evaluate the response of a pet with a suspected reaction to food, it is necessary to feed the hypoallergenic diet (and nothing else) for at least 8 weeks. Monthly flavored heartworm preventive should be discontinued and replaced with a non-flavored product. Fresh or distilled water can be used. No treats or table scraps can be given to the pet, or the 8-week dietary trial must begin again. The most common reason for failing to improve is one of two causes: the pet's itching is not related to a food allergy/hypersensitivity, or the owner rushes the dietary trial and does not give the pet at least 8 weeks to see whether the hypoallergenic diet will work.

Vitamins and minerals, which most often contain flavoring, are added after the trial, and the pet is assessed for any reaction to these supplements. Because food allergy trials are difficult, they should be done under veterinary supervision.

Glutamine, recommended for pets with inflammatory bowel disease, has also been suggested as a treatment for food allergies, based on the "leaky gut syndrome." This theory holds that in some pets, whole proteins leak through the wall of the digestive tract and enter the blood, causing allergic reactions. Very preliminary evidence suggests that glutamine supplements might reduce leakage through the intestinal walls. It can be tried for pets with allergic skin disease.

Diets for Adult Dogs with Allergies

Note: Before you start to feed your dog or cat a home-prepared diet, it is strongly recommended that you discuss your decision with your veterinarian or a holistic veterinarian in your area. It is essential that you follow any diet's recommendations closely, including all ingredients and supplements. Failure to do so may result in serious health consequences for your pet.

Diets for dogs with allergies must contain protein sources the dog has not previously eaten. Using the basic dog diet (page 346) we would substitute ½ cup of a meat such as rabbit or venison. Brown rice (2-3 cups) or baked or boiled potato with skin (2-3 cups) serves as the carbohydrate source. Canola oil is added as per the basic diet.

The diet provides approximately 650 kcal with 29 grams of protein and 18 grams of fat.

Fresh, raw or slightly steamed vegetables (carrots, broccoli, etc.) can be used as a top dressing for the diet for extra nutrition and variety (approximately ½–1 cup per recipe.) Most vegetables provide approximately 25 kcal per ½ cup.

Since this diet is not totally balanced, vitamins and minerals are added later (in 4-8 weeks), as the dog improves, to balance the diet. Add four bonemeal tablets (10 grain or equivalent) or 1 teaspoon of bonemeal powder to supply calcium and phosphorus with a multi-vitamin mineral supplement using the label instructions.

Alternatively, a natural product from Standard Process (Calcifood Wafers or Calcium Lactate) can be used (use 1 Calcifood Wafer or 2 Calcium Lactate tablets for each 2 bonemeal tablets.)

When possible, natural vitamins made from raw whole foods, rather than synthetic vitamins (although both can be used in combination) are preferred, as the natural vitamins also supply plant phytochemicals, enzymes, and other nutrients not found in chemically- synthesized vitamins. Catalyn from Standard Process can be used as the natural vitamin in this recipe, at a dose of 1 Catalyn per 25 pounds; Canine Plus (VetriScience) could also be used following label dosages.

Add one new ingredient at a time. If itching does not worsen within 3 to 5 days, add another ingredient if desired.

The nutrient composition of the diet will vary depending upon which ingredients are used. In general, the above recipe supplies the daily nutritional and calorie needs for a 20 pound dog. The actual amount to feed will vary based upon the pet's weight (feed less if weight gain, more if weight loss.)

Added supplements which can be beneficial include omega-3 fatty acids, plant enzymes, and a super green food or health blend formula The health blend formula may contain nutrients that could exacerbate the pet's allergies and should only be added after clinical signs resolve.

Diet for Adult Cats with Allergies

Diets for cats with allergies must contain protein sources the cat has not previously eaten.

Using the basic cat diet (page 348) we would substitute ¾ cup of a meat such as rabbit or venison. Canola oil is added as per the basic diet. Taurine (100 mg) is also added.

Since this diet is not totally balanced, vitamins and minerals are added later (in 4–8 weeks), as the cat improves, to balance the diet. Add two to three bonemeal tablets (10 grain or equivalent) or ¾ teaspoon of bonemeal powder to supply calcium and phosphorus with a multi-vitamin mineral supplement using the label instructions.

Alternatively, a natural product from Standard Process (Calcifood Wafers or Calcium Lactate) can be used (use 1 Calcifood Wafer or 2 Calcium Lactate tablets for each 2 bonemeal tablets.)

When possible, natural vitamins made from raw whole foods, rather than synthetic vitamins (although both can be used in combination) are preferred, as the natural vitamins also supply plant phytochemicals, enzymes, and other nutrients not found in chemically-synthesized vitamins. Catalyn from Standard Process can be used as the natural vitamin in this recipe, at a dose of 1 Catalyn per 10 pounds; NuCat (VetriScience) could also be used following label dosages.

Brown rice (½ cup) or baked or boiled potato with skin (¾ cup) can be added to serve as the carbohydrate source, although cats do not have a true carbohydrate requirement.

This diet will provide about 350 kcal with 31 grams of protein and 25 grams of fat, which would provide the daily amount of nutrients needed for a 10 pound cat.

Fresh, raw or slightly steamed vegetables (carrots, broccoli, etc.) can be used as a top dressing for the diet for extra nutrition and variety (approximately ½–1 cup per recipe), although most cats do not like eating vegetables.

Most vegetables provide approximately 25 kcal per ½ cup. Add one new ingredient at a time. If itching does not worsen within 3 to 5 days, add another ingredient if desired.

The nutrient composition of the diet will vary depending upon which ingredients are used. In general, the above recipe supplies the daily nutritional and calorie needs for a 10 pound cat. The actual amount to feed will vary based upon the pet's weight (feed less if weight gain, more if weight loss.)

Added supplements which can be beneficial include omega-3 fatty acids, plant enzymes, and a super green food or health blend formula. The health blend formula may contain nutrients that could exacerbate the pet's allergies and should only be added after clinical signs resolve.

CONVENTIONAL THERAPY

Conventional therapy for atopic dermatitis relies on corticosteroids and antihistamines. **Corticosteroids** (page 419) can be given by injection, by mouth, or by both routes of administration. The most commonly used corticosteroids are prednisone, prednisolone, dexamethasone, and triamcinolone. Corticosteroid injections can be short-acting or longer-acting (depot) injections.

While very effective when used to control itching and inflammation, corticosteroids have both short-term and long-term side effects. Short-term side effects include increased water intake, increased urination, increased appetite, destruction of joint cartilage, and very rarely, either depression or excitability. Long-term side effects that can occur are numerous; they include suppression of the immune system, infections, diabetes, liver disease, osteoporosis, Cushing's disease, and obesity. Side effects, both short- and long-term, are common in dogs but relatively rare in cats.

When needed, short-term use of fast-acting corticosteroids are preferred. Depot injections, while commonly used in cats, should rarely, if ever, be used in dogs. In cats, an occasional depot injection (1 to 3 times per year) is usually not associated with side effects, but when possible, short-acting injections and oral corticosteroids are preferred.

Antihistamines (page 430) may be effective in selected pets with atopic dermatitis. They can be used as the sole conventional therapy or combined with corticosteroids. Any of several antihistamines can be tried to relieve itching and inflammation in allergic pets. Usually, one antihistamine is given for a period of 7 to 10 days; if no response is seen, another antihistamine can be given. Because histamine is not the only chemical that causes signs in allergic pets, histamines are not effective in every atopic pet. Side effects are rare; mainly, sedation (which may resolve in several days) is seen. The main drawback is that most antihistamines must be given 2 to 3 times daily. When effective, antihistamines cause fewer side effects and offer a safer alternative than corticosteroids.

For a greater discussion about the causes and treatments of allergic dermatitis, see *The Allergy Solution for Dogs* (Prima Publishing, 2000).

ARTHRITIS (Osteoarthritis)

Principal Natural Treatments
   Glucosamine, chondroitin, PSGAGs, shark cartilage, bovine cartilage, perna, sea cucumber, acupuncture

Other Natural Treatments
   Natural diet, MSM, antioxidants including vitamin C, omega-3 fatty acids, magnets, natural diets, SAMe, herbs including alfalfa, boswellia, dandelion root, devil's claw, echinacea (rheumatoid arthritis), feverfew (rheumatoid arthritis), German chamomile, ginger, gotu kola, horsetail, licorice, topical capsaicin (cayenne), turmeric, white willow bark, yarrow, yellow dock (rheumatoid arthritis)

Arthritis, or more correctly, osteoarthritis or degenerative joint disease (DJD), is a common condition in dogs and a rare condition in cats. Arthritis technically means "inflammation of the joint." Inflammation is characterized by swelling, stiffness, and pain; therapy is designed to counteract these effects of inflammation.

When possible, the therapy should also slow down the progression of the arthritis or, if possible, actually help the joint to heal.

A joint is the space between two bones. In dogs, the joints commonly affected with arthritis include the knee, shoulder, ankle, elbow, and most commonly, the hips. The joints between the vertebrae of the backbone also commonly develop arthritis. In cats, the backbone, hips, knees, and joints connecting the smaller bones of the feet are often afflicted with osteoarthritis.

The components of the joint include the bones of the joint, ligaments from surrounding muscles that cross the joint space and attach to the bones, and the joint capsule that encloses the joint. The joint capsule contains a thick protective outer layer and a thin inner layer called the synovial membrane. The synovial membrane contains blood vessels and nerves and makes synovial fluid.

The end of each bone is covered with cartilage called articular cartilage, which acts as a shock absorber to protect the bone. The articular cartilage lacks blood vessels and nerves, and is dependent upon diffusion of nutrients from a special fluid in the joint called synovial fluid. The synovial fluid lines the joint space, nourishing the cartilage and acting as a lubricant and shock absorber.

The lack of nerves in the articular cartilage is an important factor in the progression of arthritis. A great amount of damage can occur to the cartilage before the surrounding joint tissues (joint capsule, bones, and ligaments) become inflamed and cause lameness. Because of this, considerable cartilage damage is often present by the time the animal actually feels any pain and shows signs of lameness.

The joint cartilage (articular cartilage) has a unique structure that allows it to handle the stressful loads placed on it as the animal walks and plays. The articular cartilage is made of cartilage cells (called chondrocytes in medical terminology) and the surrounding tissue called matrix. The major components of this cartilage matrix are collagen (a type of protein), water, and proteoglycans. The proteoglycan molecule is made of a central core of protein with numerous side chains of glycosaminoglycans (GAGs). There are several different proteoglycan molecules in the joint cartilage, including chondroitin sulfate (the predominant GAG in cartilage) and keratin sulfate. Glucosamine, a popular treatment for osteoarthritis, is a precursor chemical necessary for glycosaminoglycan synthesis.

As the animal walks and plays, a large amount of stress is placed on all the components of the joint. Biomechanical and biochemical alterations in the joint occur. With years of wear and tear on the joints, the cartilage breaks down and arthritis can develop. As wear and tear continues, the cartilage is disrupted and joint instability results. Chondrocytes, the cells that make up cartilage, are not able to synthesize enough of the proteoglycans to help the cartilage heal. As the chondrocytes become degraded, inflammatory chemicals are released, causing inflammation and further damaging the cartilage. The inflammatory chemicals also disrupt the proteoglycans. With enough degradation of the cartilage, underlying bone might become damaged, and the animal may refuse to use the affected limb. At this point, owners often seek medical care. Some pets can still be helped with nutritional therapies to heal the joint, whereas others may have arthritis that is too advanced to actually allow for healing. The earlier the pet is diagnosed, the greater the chance for healing to occur using natural treatments.

PRINCIPAL NATURAL TREATMENTS

The main natural treatments are designed to reduce pain and inflammation and nourish and heal the cartilage in pets with osteoarthritis.

Glucosamine

Glucosamine and chondroitin are commonly prescribed chondroprotective nutraceuticals.

When we talk about chondroprotective nutraceuticals (nutritional products), we're talking about "cartilage-protective" compounds. Unlike corticosteroids and other medications, these products actually help the cartilage rebuild and repair itself. In essence, they are "cartilage-friendly" products. These compounds also help relieve pain and inflammation. Interestingly, these improvements seem to last for several weeks after glucosamine supplements are discontinued. Chondroprotective agents can be given orally or by injection; often both forms will be used in the severely arthritic and painful pet.

Optimum functioning of the joints is important for pain-free movements by the pet. While any pet can exhibit lameness or arthritis, it is usually the older pet who is more commonly affected. Articular cartilage, that cartilage which lines the joints, must remain healthy to allow the pet to function to his maximum capability. The articular cartilage acts as a shock absorber for the joint, providing a smooth surface between bones to eliminate bone-on-bone contact. As the cartilage is destroyed, bony surfaces contact and irritate each other, causing pain, inflammation, and reduced activity. While corticosteroids and certain non-steroidal medications certainly relieve the pain and inflammation, they further destroy the articular cartilage, making a bad situation even worse.

Cartilage is made of cells called chondrocytes that make a matrix of molecules which add to the strength of the cartilage. This matrix consists of collagen, a protein that connects tissues, and substances called proteoglycans. These proteoglycans are made of glycosaminoglycans (GAGs) and hyaluronic acid. Surrounding the cartilage, and bathing the joint, is joint (synovial) fluid. Cartilage is a tough material that protects the underlying bones and acts as a shock absorber for the joints during movement. There is a normal amount of wear and tear on the joint cartilage. The various cells and fluids are constantly being broken down and synthesized. It is important that the cartilage receive proper nutrition, especially when it is damaged and inflamed. Chondroprotective agents seek to replenish the raw materials that are essential for the healing and synthesis of cartilage, its matrix, and joint fluid.

Various products, each supplying different nutritional products, are available to assist in relieving inflammation and helping cartilage to heal when it is damaged. The following ingredients may be included in the various nutritional chondroprotective products. Each doctor has a "favorite" product. If one doesn't help your pet, your doctor may suggest trying a different product. Keep in mind that these are true holistic products; there are no harmful side effects such as those often encountered with long-term use of corticosteroids or nonsteroidal medications.

Glucosamine is the most common chondroprotective supplement used for the treatment of osteoarthritis. Chondroitin is the second most commonly used supplement for the treatment of osteoarthritis. Glucosamine is produced naturally in the body, where it is a key building block for making cartilage. (It serves as a building block for the glycosaminoglycans and proteoglycans.) Glucosamine is an aminosugar (made from glutamine and glucose) that is incorporated into articular (joint) cartilage. It is supplied as a supplement in one of three forms: glucosamine sulfate, glucosamine hydrochloride (a salt of D-glucosamine; D-glucosamine is eventually converted by the body into glucosamine sulfate), or N-acetylglucosamine. Glucosamine is not usually obtained directly from food; supplements are derived from chitin, a substance found in the shells of shrimp, lobsters, and crabs.

Scientific Evidence

Studies show that while all three forms of glucosamine are effective, glucosamine hydrochloride (which is a salt of D-glucosamine) and glucosamine sulfate were more effective than N-acetylglucosamine. Results take 4 to 8 weeks to develop. Interestingly, these improvements often last for several weeks after glucosamine supplements are discontinued.

Glucosamine is rapidly taken up by cartilage cells and helps stimulate the synthesis of synovial fluid and cartilage and also helps inhibit the destructive enzymes that can destroy cartilage and proteoglycans. The anti-inflammatory aspect of glucosamine may result from the scavenging of harmful free radicals (similar to antioxidants). Glucosamine is used by the cartilage for the synthesis of glycosaminoglycans.

A number of studies in people and pets show that glucosamine is equally effective for treating osteoarthritis when compared to NSAIDs without the side effects. In fact, glucosamine and chondroitin are among the few supplements for which we actually have good studies in people and pets.

For both people and pets, solid evidence indicates that glucosamine supplements effectively relieve pain and other symptoms of osteoarthritis.

In both people and dogs, patients given glucosamine experienced significantly reduced pain and improved movement, to a greater extent than the improvements seen in the placebo groups.

Other studies showed that non-steroidal medications and glucosamine proved equally effective at reducing symptoms. In people, one group that received combination treatment (the nonsteroidal piroxicam plus glucosamine) didn't show significantly better results than either treatment taken alone.

In this same study, after 90 days into the study, treatment was stopped and the participants were followed for an additional 60 days. The benefits of piroxicam rapidly disappeared, but the benefits of glucosamine lasted for the full 60 days.

While there are a number of glucosamine products from reputable manufacturers, many of the early major studies done in pets have used a proprietary product (Cosequin and Cosequin-DS) containing glucosamine and chondroitin. Clinical evidence indicates other products from well-known manufacturers are also effective.

Dosages

Dosages vary depending upon the product. As a guideline for combination products, a starting dose of 1,000 to 1,500 mg of glucosamine with 800 to 1,200 mg of chondroitin is recommended per day for a 50- to 100-pound dog. This dose is then lowered after 4 to 8 weeks.

While arthritis is rare in cats when compared with dogs, clinical experience suggests that glucosamine and chondroitin products may also be quite helpful for arthritic cats. In general, the recommended dosage for smaller dogs is used.

Glucosamine appears to be extremely safe with no side effects; mild GI upset is rarely observed. No significant side effects have been reported in any of the studies of glucosamine.

Chondroitin

Chondroitin sulfate is the major glycosaminoglycan found in cartilage; it also helps inhibit enzymes that are destructive to the joint. Chondroitin sulfate is a naturally occurring substance in the body. A study in the 1998 journal *Osteoarthritis and Cartilage* reported that chondroitin sulfate is an effective treatment for osteoarthritis. Animal cartilage is the only dietary source of chondroitin.

For years, experts stated that oral chondroitin couldn't work because its molecules are so big that it seemed doubtful that they could be absorbed through the digestive tract. However, in 1995, researchers laid this objection to rest when they found evidence that up to 15% of chondroitin is absorbed intact. Another study found that up to 70% of radiolabeled chondroitin sulfate was well absorbed and showed affinity for articular (joint) cartilage. This evidence for chondroitin absorption holds true for pets as well as for people.

Because chondroitin production by the body decreases with aging, supplementation with this compound may be especially helpful for older pets with arthritis.

The effect of both oral and injected chondroitin was assessed in rabbits with damaged cartilage in the knee. After 84 days of treatment, the rabbits that were given chondroitin had significantly more healthy cartilage remaining in the damaged knee than the untreated animals. Receiving chondroitin by mouth was as effective as taking it through an injection. It appears quite likely that chondroitin can slow the progression of osteoarthritis. However, more studies are needed to confirm this very exciting possibility. It would also be wonderful if chondroitin could repair damaged cartilage and thus reverse arthritis, but none of the research so far shows such an effect. Chondroitin may simply stop further destruction from occurring.

How does chondroitin work for osteoarthritis? Scientists are unsure how chondroitin sulfate works, but one of several theories (or all of them) might explain its mode of action. At its most basic level, chondroitin may help cartilage by providing it with the building blocks it needs to repair itself. It is also believed to block enzymes that break down cartilage in the joints. Another theory holds that chondroitin increases the amount of hyaluronic acid in the joints. Hyaluronic acid is a protective fluid that keeps the joints lubricated. Finally, chondroitin may have a mild anti-inflammatory effect.

Chondroitin is often added to supplements containing glucosamine. While significant studies are lacking, some doctors (but not all) feel that adding chondroitin to glucosamine enhances the ability of both substances to repair cartilage due to a synergistic effect.

Chondroitin sulfate, like glucosamine, has not been associated with any serious side effects. Mild digestive distress appears to be the only real concern in people and possibly pets.

Glycosaminoglycans (GAGs)

Glucosamine and chondroitin constitute the major GAGs in the joint cartilage; glycosaminoglycans serve as major components of articular cartilage.

Glycosaminoglycans function by decreasing the presence of harmful pro-inflammatory prostaglandins and other inflammatory enzymes that degrade the cartilage matrix. This results in reduced pain and inflammation, decreased enzymatic destruction of the cartilage, and stimulation of anabolic (cartilage-building) pathways. The GAGs also appear to increase the synthesis of proteoglycans, hyaluronic acid (which acts as a joint lubricant), and collagen.

One novel product called Adequan contains glycosaminoglycans extracted from bovine cartilage and is available in an injectable form. The recommended regimen is a series of 8 injections, 2 each week for 4 weeks. If the pet has responded favorably during the 4-week trial, the pet is then given an injection as needed (usually 1 injection every 1 to 12 months, varying from pet to pet). This injectable product can be used with oral chondroprotective supplements as well. The injectable product can be used to get a faster response than the oral supplements. Further injections are given as needed, or pets can be maintained on oral supplements according to the response seen and the convenience for the pet owner.

Note: This product has also shown effectiveness when flushed into joints during joint surgery, allowing faster and smoother recovery.

Side effects with GAGs are extremely rare but are reported to include a dose-dependent inhibition of blood clotting. Concerned owners may want to have their pets' doctors regularly monitor blood coagulation parameters and use homeopathic remedies to help increase blood-clotting factors.

The following points concerning chondroprotective therapy are important to maximize success when using these supplements:

Safety. They are extremely safe and equally effective when compared to NSAIDs.

Cost. This may be an issue for some pet owners. The typical daily cost of using a glucosamine-chondroitin supplement is approximately $1.50/day for a 50-pound dog. This cost can decrease as the dosage of the supplement is lowered to allow the owner to use the least amount of supplement to maintain pain relief. The comparable cost of the most popular NSAIDS (Rimadyl and EctoGesic) is approximately $2-3/day for a 50-pound dog, making the supplements less expensive, equally effective, and without potential serious side effects.

Early diagnosis. Since these supplements work by acting on living cartilage cells, they are most effective when used early in the course of the disease. This requires adequate and early diagnosis.

Response time. Because they are not drugs but rather nutritional supplements, response may not be seen for 4 to 8 weeks. During the first 4 to 8 weeks, an increased "induction" dose is used and then the dose is lowered as improvement is seen. Additional short-term therapy (with NSAIDs, acupuncture, or other) can be used during the induction phase.

Effectiveness. The supplements can also be used effectively when no clinical signs are present but yet disease exists. In many practices, a number of dogs are diagnosed via screening radiographs with hip dysplasia and started on the supplements pending a decision on the owner's part for surgical correction or until clinical signs occur.

Product purity. Purity of products is an important factor. There are many generic "knock-off" products that sell for much less than patented products produced by reputable manufacturers. Studies that have been done showing the effectiveness of these compounds have used pure grades of products. Products of lesser purity, while often costing less, may also be less effective. Unlike traditional drugs, these compounds are not regulated and labeling can be inaccurate or misleading; manufacturers are not required to analyze their products regarding purity, uniformity, or content. Purchase only quality products from reputable manufacturers as recommended by your doctor.

Recommended reevaluation. Because the chondroprotective supplements are so effective after 4 to 8 weeks in improving signs seen in arthritic pets, the diagnosis should be reevaluated after this period of time if improvement is not seen.

Shark Cartilage

There is a reported link between blood vessel growth and the development of osteoarthritis as well. The synovial (joint) fluid of arthritic pets includes an increasing amount of a chemical called endothelial cell-stimulating angiogenic factor. This chemical encourages growth of new blood vessels in the arthritic joint. It is theorized that by inhibiting angiogenesis (new blood vessel growth), further degeneration of cartilage might be prevented.

In the laboratory, shark cartilage has been shown to contain chemicals that inhibit blood vessel formation. Because arthritis is an inflammatory condition, and inflammation requires blood vessels, it has been suggested that by inhibiting the formation of new blood vessels, shark cartilage can benefit arthritic pets. And in fact, research has shown this to be the case. In studies in both people and in dogs, significant improvement is seen in patients suffering from arthritis. Arthritic pets and people taking shark cartilage supplements often experience increased mobility and decreased pain. In one study, eight of ten dogs showed improvement (improvement was defined as no continuing lameness, lack of swelling and pain, and improved movement) when treated at a dosage of 750 mg/5 kg of body weight for 3 weeks. When treatment was temporarily discontinued, pain and lameness returned. Administering additional shark cartilage at 50% of the original dose resulted in improvement. The relief from pain and inflammation was theorized to occur as a result of decreased blood vessel formation. Improvement may also result from a relief from pain due to the large amount of mucopolysaccharides (GAGs) contained in the cartilage, which can help nourish and heal the cartilage. As a result of studies such as this one, many veterinarians feel it is prudent to prescribe shark cartilage as it can be beneficial in some pets with arthritis and can substitute for therapy with medications like nonsteroidal drugs that have potential side effects. The main problem with using shark cartilage to treat arthritis is the large dosage required. This suggested dosage would require giving a large number of capsules to the pet each day. And

since shark cartilage is among our more expensive supplements, the dosage of shark cartilage needed for medium- to large-breed arthritic dogs would be unaffordable for most pet owners.

While shark cartilage can be helpful for arthritic pets, the concerns mentioned prompt doctors to recommend glucosamine and chondroitin supplements as their first choices for nutritional supplements.

Shark cartilage should not be used in people who have recently suffered a heart attack, in pregnant women, and those who have are recently recovering from deep surgery; similar precautions probably apply toward pets.

Because of conflicting evidence and the potential for impure product (quality-control issues are important for all nutritional supplements), owners should consult with their doctors before using shark cartilage for any medical needs.

Several products on the market supply a much lower dosage of shark cartilage than that listed in the studies reported to date. This lower dosage has proved beneficial in some arthritic dogs. Because shark cartilage is very expensive to use in larger dogs (approximately $40 to $50 for a 2-week supply), some owners are tempted to give less than the recommended dosage to decrease cost. This can be useful after a 1- to 2-month stabilization period. Work with your doctor to determine the most effective dose for your dog. As is often the case with nutritional supplements, we don't know the best or most effective dose for shark cartilage. Therefore, we must use the products currently available and adapt the dosage to the individual pet's needs.

Bovine Cartilage

Bovine cartilage has proven useful in relieving pain and inflammation in human patients with osteoarthritis and rheumatoid arthritis; increased joint mobility was also noted. In dogs treated with bovine cartilage, good results were seen in the treatment of degenerative disk disease and some spinal disorders. Like shark cartilage, bovine cartilage is high in glycosaminoglycans, which can help the body repair damaged joints. Since shark cartilage was found to be 1,000 times more effective in preventing new blood vessel growth, it has replaced bovine cartilage as a favored cartilage product. (See the discussion of shark cartilage to see why this supplement is not the preferred supplement for arthritic pets.) The recommended dose of bovine cartilage is 200 mg/25 pounds of body weight.

Perna

Perna canaliculus, the green-lipped mussel, is a shellfish that is a natural source of highly concentrated glycosaminoglycans (GAGs), including chondroitin, as well as a number of other nutrients, including complex proteins, amino acids, nucleic acids, naturally chelated minerals, and an inhibitor of prostaglandin synthesis, which makes it effective as an anti-inflammatory supplement.

Several studies in people have confirmed improvement in patients with osteoarthritis and rheumatoid arthritis. Ongoing studies, as well as many years of anecdotal evidence, show the benefit of perna in dogs with osteoarthritis. (As is true with most chondroprotective agents, reports of benefit in cats is scant, as arthritis is quite rare in cats when compared to dogs. However, veterinarians are using many "dog" products safely in cats, and improvement has been noted. If you have an arthritic cat, talk with your veterinarian about using any of these supplements in your cat.)

Stabilized powder (Seatone, MacFarlane Laboratories, Surrey Hills, Victoria, Australia) and the lipid extract (Lyprinol, MacFarlane Laboratories, Surrey Hills, Victoria, Australia) showed similar results in people with rheumatoid and osteoarthritis. The lipid extract is a 20-fold concentrate of the original dried mussel. As is true with the powder form, the lipid extract is believed to be a potent but slow-acting anti-inflammatory agent that inhibits cyclooxygenase and 5-lipooxygenase. This is probably via the omega-3 fatty acid (EPA) content of the mussels. In laboratory experiments in rats, the dosage of Lyprinol was 20 mg/kg. In studies in people, a dosage of 300 mg twice daily for the first 30 days followed by a dosage of 150 mg twice daily showed positive results. No dosages for dogs and cats for these specific products have been reported at this time.

Perna is inexpensive and readily accepted by most dogs; the recommended dosage is 300 mg/15 pounds of body weight. A new product that shows favorable results in many pets, called Glyco-Flex Plus, combines the benefits of perna with glucosamine and methylsulfonylmethane (MSM).

Sea Cucumber

The sea cucumber (*Cucumaria frondosa*), also known by the names "trepang" and "beche de mer" is a marine animal related to urchins. It is believed that these organisms inhibit harmful prostaglandins involved in causing pain and arthritis. They are also rich in nutrients needed by cartilage, including chondroitin and mucopolysaccharides, and several vitamins and minerals. One popular product supplies the sea cucumber in a unique "jerky-type" treat (Sea Jerky-R), which dogs find quite palatable. Other compounds found in this product include sea kelp, natural vitamin E, lecithin, garlic, omega-3 fatty acids, and glucosamine hydrochloride. Each jerky treat provides 1,200 mg of chondroitin.

In research testing by an independent laboratory, the product showed excellent anti-inflammatory activity in rats in which inflammation was induced by injection of adjuvant, and no side effects were seen. The anti-inflammatory response was superior to that of Rimadyl and phenylbutazone. This study also showed that Sea Jerky-R had higher anti-inflammatory activity than a product made from perna mussels and a glucosamine/chondroitin supplement, indicating that this product might be preferred if a dog fails to respond to another supplement. (Since the response to various supplements varies among patients, if one fails to provide relief, another should be tried.) However, to my knowledge Sea Jerky-R has not been evaluated in double-blind placebo-controlled studies in dogs with naturally occuring arthritis. Clinical reports from the veterinary community indicate high acceptance and effectiveness.

The recommended dosage for this unique product is one piece of "jerky" per day for a 60- to 70-pound dog.

While it was assumed that the active ingredient in the product was chondroitin, further research showed that while the sea cucumber contains chondroitin, another substance called InflaStatin (now under research and development) appears to be the active ingredient.

These treats are perfect for the dog who is hard to medicate. While some supplements are flavored pills, there are, of course, those dogs who will not eat anything in a pill form. There are also those dogs whose owners simply can't medicate them. This may be because the dog was never taught to take medications as a puppy and now will not allow the owner to give it a pill. There are also owners who find it a hassle to give their dogs pills each day. However, offering the dog a jerky treat is an easy way to allow the pet to receive the daily recommended dose of medication.

The jerky treats can also be used in conjunction with other similar pill supplements, as it is unlikely to overdose a pet on glucosamine or chondroitin. Many owners will give their dogs their recommended amounts of daily pills and also reward the dog with a jerky treat. For those pets with arthritis, most owners and doctors like the idea of giving them a daily treat that is good for them, as is the case with this jerky product.

Acupuncture

Acupuncture is without a doubt one of the most field-tested techniques available in complementary medicine. While it is hard to pinpoint exactly how long acupuncture has been around, evidence indicates that it is easily more than 4,000 years old, having been used in Asian and Indian cultures for many centuries. For skeptics who question the effectiveness of this popular complementary therapy, a large amount of empirical as well as experimental information and studies show the effectiveness of acupuncture. Certainly a therapy that is a mainstay of Traditional Chinese Medicine could not have survived if it were not effective. The theory of Traditional Chinese Medicine has, in fact, served as the basis of acupuncture instruction for over 4,000 years. While there is certainly no substitute for well-documented research using controlled clinical studies, we cannot ignore thousands of years of clinical experience.

One stumbling block to the Western-trained mind trying to understand acupuncture is the lack of scientific explanation as to exactly how acupuncture works. The explanations offered by Traditional Chinese Medicine suffice for practitioners of this ancient art, but confuse the traditional Western mind. However, while a number of physiological theories have been proposed to explain how acupuncture works (see below), we must remain open-minded to the effectiveness of this therapy (and, of course, to all complementary therapies).

The wise reader will remember that while we may not know exactly how acupuncture (or other complementary therapies) actually work, we also do not know exactly how certain modern Western medical treatments work. (For example, even Pfizer's own literature states that exactly how their bestselling nonsteroidal drug Rimadyl works is not known.) If we can use traditional drug therapies without formal proof of how they work, we can also use therapies such as acupuncture without formal proof of how they work.

We do know that acupuncture points lie over free nerve endings wrapped in connective tissue or within the walls of blood vessels; this anatomy may help explain why stimulation of acupuncture points elicits therapeutic effects. Additionally, there is a high concentration of tissue-secretory mast cells in and around acupuncture points. The release of histamine (and probably other chemicals) may explain an important part of acupuncture by causing dilation of surrounding blood vessels and stimulating adjacent nerve terminals.

What Exactly Is Acupuncture?

In its purest sense, acupuncture involves the placement of tiny needles into various parts (acupuncture points) of a pet's body. These needles stimulate the acupuncture points, which can effect a resolution of the clinical signs.

In traditional acupuncture, the acupuncturist places tiny needles at various points on the pet's body. These points are chosen based on diagnostic tests and/or traditional "recipes" or formulas that are known to help pets with specific problems. As mentioned, these acupuncture points correspond to areas of the body that contain nerves and blood vessels. By stimulating these points, acupuncture causes a combination of pain relief, stimulation of the immune system, and alterations in blood vessels, causing a decrease in clinical signs.

While traditional acupuncture uses tiny acupuncture needles to stimulate the specific acupuncture points chosen, other forms of acupuncture also exist. These other forms of acupuncture are often chosen to provide the pet more prolonged stimulation of acupuncture points, as they produce a higher and more continuous level of stimulation.

They include:

- **Laser therapy.** Acupuncture points may be stimulated by low intensity or cold lasers to promote positive physiologic effects associated with healing and decreased pain and inflammation.
- **Aquapuncture.** Aquapuncture utilizes the injection of tiny amounts of fluid (often vitamins, but also sterile water, antibiotics, herbal extracts, analgesics, local anesthetics, corticosteroids, nonsteroidal medications, or electrolyte solutions) at the acupuncture site for a more prolonged effect.
- **Implantation.** To achieve a more prolonged and intense stimulation of acupuncture points, various objects (usually beads made of gold, silver, or stainless steel) are surgically implanted at acupuncture sites.
- **Electroacupuncture.** This form of acupuncture therapy uses a small amount of non-painful electricity to stimulate the acupuncture site for a more intense effect.
- **Moxibustion.** Moxibustion is the burning of an herb (typically *Artesmisia vulgaris*) on or above acupuncture points. The heat from the burning herb gives additional stimulation to the acupuncture points. Care must be taken to avoid burning the patient!
- **Acupressure.** Acupressure involves applying pressure with the fingers to specific acupuncture points. Owners can be taught to apply acupressure at home to the acupuncture points that have been used during veterinary treatments to augment the acupuncture treatments to give further relief from pain and inflammation.

Most holistic doctors usually combine acupuncture with other treatments to achieve a truly "holistic" therapy. For example, for pets with osteoarthritis, nutritional supplements that are designed to heal the damaged cartilage are often added to acupuncture treatment, as acupuncture by itself will not heal damaged cartilage. Once the pet has improved by experiencing decreased pain and inflammation and showing greater mobility, doctors will use acupuncture on an "as-needed" basis when the pet shows increased stiffness.

Safety Issues

As a rule, acupuncture compares quite favorably with traditional therapies (see the discussion below). In some cases, acupuncture may be preferred when conventional therapy is ineffective or potentially harmful (such as long-term therapy for pain relief with medication like corticosteroids or nonsteroidal anti-inflammatory medications). At other times, acupuncture may be used when an owner cannot afford traditional therapy (such as back surgery for intervertebral disk disease or hip replacement surgery for the pet with severe hip dysplasia). It is ideal if doctors discuss both acupuncture and conventional therapies to allow the owner to make the best decision for his pet.

Side effects from acupuncture are rare. Accidental puncture of an underlying vital organ can occur; this usually happens if the incorrect needles (the needles come in various sizes and the correct length of needle must be chosen that corresponds to the size of the pet and the area to be treated) are placed in an area in which there is minimal soft tissue that covers the underlying organs (such as the abdomen). Infection can occur at the site of needle insertion; needles should not be placed in areas in which the skin is infected or inflamed. In rare instances, the needle can break (due to patient movement and incorrect needle placement and removal) and surgery may be needed to remove it.

Some pets require sedation in order to allow insertion of the acupuncture needles. In some animals, clinical signs may worsen for a few days before they improve. (This is not unusual in pets treated with complementary therapies and is explained by the body going through the healing process; additionally, some animals treated with conventional medications also get worse before the medication "kicks in" and the pet begins to show signs of improvement.)

Many owners worry that acupuncture is painful and that their pets will suffer. Usually acupuncture is not painful. Occasionally, the animal will experience some sensation as the needle passes through the skin. Once in place, most animals will relax, and some may become sleepy. Fractious animals (especially cats and nervous dogs) may require mild sedation for treatment. Alternatively, a complementary therapy to calm the pet (such as an herbal remedy or the flower essence called **Rescue Remedy,** page 391) can be used prior to and during acupuncture treatment.

Treatments

The number of acupuncture treatments that a pet will require varies from pet to pet. Usually, owners are asked to commit to 8 treatments (2 to 3/week) to assess whether acupuncture will work. On average, treatments last about 15 to 30 minutes for needle acupuncture, and 5 to 10 minutes for aquapuncture or electroacupuncture. If the pet improves, acupuncture is done "as needed" to control the pet's signs. As previously mentioned, other therapies may be used to decrease the number of visits to the doctor's office for acupuncture.

While acupuncture can be useful for a variety of disorders, most clients seek acupuncture therapy for pets with musculoskeletal or neurological disorders.

Scientific Evidence

Numerous reports in the human medical literature attest to the benefits of acupuncture. One study showed 65% of people treated with chronic neck and shoulder pain achieved long-term improvement after acupuncture, and another study of 22 patients with chronic low back pain showed a 79.1% success rate. Acupuncture was twice as effective as the nonsteroidal anti-inflammatory medication piroxicam.

In pets, one study found that 70% of dogs with chronic degenerative joint disease (osteoarthritis) showed greater than 50% improvement in mobility after treatment with acupuncture.

In pets with osteoarthritis, acupuncture has been theorized to work by relieving muscle spasms around the effective joint, by producing analgesia (pain relief) by stimulating central endorphin-releasing systems, by improving blood circulation to spastic muscles surrounding affected joints, by direct anti-inflammatory effects, and by releasing local trigger points and relieving stiffness.

Traditional Chinese medical theory holds that acupuncture works by unblocking *Qi* and blood in the body's meridians and treating the *Bi* syndrome (osteoarthritis is a *Bi* condition in Chinese medicine).

If acupuncture is used to treat osteoarthritis, it is imperative that a proper diagnosis be made prior to starting therapy. Many pets have been prescribed anti-inflammatory medications (corticosteroids or nonsteroidal anti-inflammatory medications) without a proper diagnosis (orthopedic and neurological examinations plus radiographic evaluation of the injured part). Acupuncture cannot be effective for the treatment of osteoarthritis if the pet does not have osteoarthritis!

Many dogs treated incorrectly for osteoarthritis in fact have neurological disease (most commonly **degenerative myelopathy,** page 60). These dogs require different therapy for their problem than do pets with osteoarthritis and will not usually respond to anti-inflammatory therapy for osteoarthritis. Make sure a proper diagnosis is obtained so that the correct treatment can be administered before signs become so severe that no therapy will be successful!

Conventional therapies may occasionally be needed and used with the natural therapies on "bad days."

OTHER NATURAL TREATMENTS

Additional recommended complementary therapies for pets with osteoarthritis include natural **diet** (page 314), **MSM** (page 242), **antioxidants** including **vitamin C** (page 158), **omega-3 fatty acids** (page 246), **magnets** (page 412), **natural diets** (page 335), and **SAMe** (page 265). Herbs used to treat osteoarthritis include **alfalfa** (page 156), **boswellia** (page 168), **dandelion root** (page 193), **devil's claw** (page 194), **echinacea** (page 195, used for rheumatoid arthritis), **fever-**

few (page 202, used for rheumatoid arthritis), **German chamomile** (page 206), **ginger** (page 207), **gotu kola** (page 221), **horsetail** (page 225), **licorice** (page 234), topical **capsaicin** (page 174), **turmeric** (page 280), **white willow bark** (page 307), **yarrow** (page 308), and **yellow dock** (page 309, used for rheumatoid arthritis).

Many of these natural treatments are widely used with variable success but have not all been thoroughly investigated and proven at this time.

As with any condition, the most healthful natural diet will improve the pet's overall health.

CONVENTIONAL THERAPY

Conventional therapies for osteoarthritis in dogs and cats include the use of corticosteroids or nonsteroidal anti-inflammatory medications (NSAIDs).

Corticosteroids (page 419) can be given by injection, by mouth, or by both routes of administration. The most commonly used corticosteroids are prednisone, prednisolone, dexamethasone, and triamcinolone. Corticosteroid injections can be short-acting or longer-acting (depot) injections.

While very effective when used to relieve pain and inflammation, corticosteroids have both short-term as well as long-term side effects. Short-term side effects include increased water intake, increased urination, increased appetite, destruc-

tion of joint cartilage, and very rarely, either depression or excitability. Long-term side effects that can occur are numerous and include suppression of the immune system, infections, diabetes, liver disease, osteoporosis, Cushing's disease, and obesity. Side effects, both short- and long-term, are common in dogs but relatively rare in cats.

When needed, short-term use of fast-acting corticosteroids is preferred. Depot injections, while commonly used in cats, should rarely, if ever, be used in dogs. In cats, an occasional depot injection (1 to 3 times per year) is usually not associated with side effects, but when possible, short-acting injections and oral corticosteroids are preferred.

Few NSAIDs (pages 421) are approved for dogs; none are approved for cats, and most cannot be safely used in cats. Side effects of NSAID usage include liver disease, kidney disease, ulceration of the stomach and intestinal tract, and possibly further destruction of the joint cartilage.

The safest use of NSAID therapy is to combine NSAIDs with natural treatments designed to restore joint cartilage, as well as relieve pain and inflammation. Once clinical signs improve, NSAIDs are safely used on an "as-needed" basis when the pet experiences a particularly painful day.

For a greater discussion about the causes and treatments of osteoarthritis, see *The Arthritis Solution for Dogs* (Prima Publishing, 2000).

 # ASTHMA

Principal Natural Treatments
   Omega-3 fatty acids, orthomolecular therapy

Other Natural Treatments
   Natural diet, antioxidants, herbs: boswellia, cat's claw, coltsfoot, ephedra, feverfew, garlic, German chamomile, *Ginkgo biloba*, licorice, lobelia, turmeric

Asthma (feline bronchial disease) is an inflammatory disease affecting the smooth muscle of the bronchi of cats (and rarely dogs). The inflammation causes reversible airflow obstruction through smooth muscle constriction, bronchial

wall fluid buildup (edema), and thickening of the mucous glands of the airways. This inflammation, occurring as a result of a reaction (allergy) to environmental allergens (foreign proteins), causes coughing and/or wheezing. Secondary infection (pneumonia) is reported to occur in 24 to 42% of cats with asthma. Because feline heartworm disease can cause signs that mimic asthma, all cats with respiratory signs should be screened for feline heartworm disease. As much as possible, owners should try to minimize environmental factors (such as cigarette smoke, dust, hair spray, and perfume) that can trigger an asthmatic attack.

PRINCIPAL NATURAL TREATMENTS

The main natural treatments are designed to reduce wheezing and inflammation in pets with asthma.

Omega-3 Fatty Acids

Omega-3 fatty acids—eicosapentaenoic acid (EPA) and docosahexaenoic acid (DHA)—are derived from fish oils of coldwater fish (salmon, trout, or most commonly menhaden fish) and flaxseed. Omega-6 fatty acids—linoleic acid (LA) and gamma-linolenic acid (GLA)—are derived from the oils of seeds such as evening primrose, black currant, and borage. Often, fatty acids are added to the diet with other supplements to attain an additive effect.

Just how do the fatty acids work to help in controlling inflammation in pets? Cell membranes contain phospholipids. When membrane injury occurs, an enzyme acts on the phospholipids in the cell membranes to produce fatty acids, including arachidonic acid (an omega-6 fatty acid) and eicosapentaenoic acid (an omega-3 fatty acid). Further metabolism of the arachidonic acid and eicosapentaenoic acid by additional enzymes (the lipooxygenase and cyclooxygenase pathways) yields the production of chemicals called eicosanoids. The eicosanoids produced by metabolism of arachidonic acid are pro-inflammatory and cause inflammation, suppress the immune system, and cause platelets to aggregate and clot; the eicosanoids produced by metabolism of eicosapentaenoic acid are non-inflammatory, not immunosuppressive, and help inhibit platelets from clotting. (There is some overlap and the actual biochemical pathway is a bit more complicated than I have suggested here. For example, one of the by-products of omega-6 fatty acid metabolism is Prostaglandin E_1, which is anti-inflammatory.

(This is one reason why some research has shown that using certain omega-6 fatty acids can also act to limit inflammation.)

Supplementation of the diet with omega-3 fatty acids works in this biochemical reaction. By providing extra amounts of these non-inflammatory compounds, we try to overwhelm the body with the production of non-inflammatory eicosanoids. Therefore, since the same enzymes metabolize both omega-3 and omega-6 fatty acids, and since metabolism of the omega-6 fatty acids tends to cause inflammation (with the exception of Prostaglandin E_1 by metabolism of omega-6 as mentioned), by supplying a large amount of omega-3 fatty acids we favor the production of non-inflammatory chemicals.

Many disorders, including asthma, are due to overproduction of the eicosanoids responsible for producing inflammation. Fatty acid supplementation can be beneficial in inflammatory disorders by regulating the eicosanoid production.

In general, the products of omega-3 (specifically EPA) and one omega-6 fatty acid (DGLA) are less inflammatory than the products of arachidonic acid (another omega-6 fatty acid). By changing dietary fatty acid consumption, we can change eicosanoid production right at the cellular level and try to modify (decrease) inflammation within the body. By providing the proper fatty acids, we can use fatty acids as an anti-inflammatory substance. However, since the products of omega-6 fatty acid metabolism (specifically arachidonic acid) are not the sole cause of the inflammation, fatty acid therapy is rarely effective as the sole therapy but is used as an adjunct therapy to achieve an additive effect.

Note: Flaxseed oil is a popular source of alpha-linoleic acid (ALA), an omega-3 fatty acid that is ultimately converted to EPA and DHA. However, many species of pets (probably including dogs) and some people cannot convert ALA to these other more active non-inflammatory omega-3 fatty acids. In one study in people, flaxseed oil was ineffective in reducing symptoms or raising levels of EPA and DHA. While flaxseed oil has been suggested as a less smelly substitute for fish oil, there is no evidence that it is effective when used for the same therapeutic purposes as fish oil. Therefore, supplementation with EPA and

DHA is important, and this is the reason flaxseed oil is not recommended as the sole fatty acid supplement for pets. Flaxseed oil can be used to provide ALA and as a coat conditioner.

Omega-3 fatty acids have been recommended for the treatment of asthma in pets as this is often a result of inflammation in the airways. While controlled studies are lacking, many doctors feel there is some benefit to their use.

While many doctors use fatty acids for a variety of medical problems, there is considerable debate about the use of fatty acids. The debate concerns several areas:

Dosage

What is the "best" dose to use in the treatment of pets? Most doctors use anywhere from 2 to 10 times the label dose. Research in the treatment of allergies indicates that the label dose is ineffective; the same theory probably holds true for treating asthma, but the research is lacking. In people, the dosage that showed effectiveness in many studies was 1.4 to 2.8 gm of GLA per day, or 1.7 gm of EPA and 0.9 gm of DHA per day, which is hard for people to obtain from the supplements currently available. If this were shown to be the correct dosage for pets, a 50-pound dog would need to take 10 or more fatty acid capsules per day to obtain a similar dosage, depending upon which supplement (and there are many choices on the market) was used. Therefore, while the studies with omega-3 fatty acids show many potential health benefits, it is almost impossible to administer the large number of capsules needed to approximate the same dosage used in these studies. The best that owners can hope for at this time is to work with their veterinarians and try to increase, as best as possible, the amount of omega-3 fatty acids in the diet.

Which Fatty Acid?

What is the "correct" fatty acid to use? Should we use just omega-3 (EPA and DHA) fatty acids, or combine them with omega-6 (GLA) fatty acids? Is there an "ideal" ratio of omega-6 to omega-3 fatty acids? (Through research on pets with atopic dermatitis, the ideal dietary ratio seems to be 5:1 of omega-6:omega-3 fatty acids, although this is also debated. Whether or not this "ideal" dietary ratio is ideal for the treatment of asthma and other inflammatory conditions remains to be seen.

Fatty Acid Supplementation

Is supplementation with fatty acid capsules or liquids the best approach, or is dietary manipulation preferred for the treatment of inflammatory conditions? There are, in fact, diets constructed with this "ideal" ratio (of omega-6 to omega-3 fatty acids). For owners who do not like giving their pets medication, or for those pets who don't take the fatty acid supplements easily, it might be wise to try some of these medically formulated diets (available from your pet's doctor) that contain the fatty acids. (However, because these medicated diets may not be as natural as possible due to the inclusion of by-products and chemical preservatives, holistic pet owners may need to try other options.) These diets, often prescribed as anti-inflammatory diets for pets with allergies, may be useful as a part of the therapy of asthmatic pets.

Fish Oils   Since fish oils can easily oxidize and become rancid, some manufacturers add vitamin E to fish oil capsules and liquid products to keep the oil from spoiling (others remove oxygen from the capsule).

Since processed foods have increased omega-6 fatty acids and decreased omega-3 fatty acids, supplementing the diets of all pets with omega-3 fatty acids seems warranted and will not harm your pet.

The bottom line is that there are many questions regarding the use of fatty acid therapy. More research is needed to determine the effectiveness of the fatty acids in the treatment of various medical problems, as well as the proper doses needed to achieve clinical results. Until definitive answers are obtained, you will need to work with your doctors (knowing the limitations of current research) to determine the use of these supplements for your pet.

Fish oil appears to be safe. The most common side effect seen in people and pets is a fish odor to the breath or the skin.

Because fish oil has a mild "blood-thinning" effect, it should not be combined with powerful blood-thinning medications, such as Coumadin (warfarin) or heparin, except on a veterinarian's advice. Fish oil does not seem to cause bleeding problems when it is taken by itself at commonly recommended dosages. Also, fish oil does not appear to raise blood sugar levels in people or pets with diabetes.

Flaxseed Oil   Flaxseed oil is derived from the seeds of the flax plant and has been proposed as a less smelly alternative to fish oil. Flaxseed oil contains alpha-linolenic acid (ALA), an omega-3 fatty acid that is ultimately converted to EPA and DHA. In fact, flaxseed oil contains higher levels of omega-3 fatty acids (ALA) than fish oil. It also contains omega-6 fatty acids.

As mentioned, many species of pets (probably including dogs and cats) and some people cannot convert ALA to these other more active non-inflammatory omega-3 fatty acids. In one study in people, flaxseed oil was ineffective in reducing symptoms or raising levels of EPA and DHA. While flaxseed oil has been suggested as a substitute for fish oil, there is no evidence that it is effective when used for the same therapeutic purposes as fish oil. Unlike the case for fish oil, there is little evidence that flaxseed oil is effective for any specific therapeutic purpose.

Therefore, supplementation with EPA and DHA is important, and this is the reason flaxseed oil is not recommended as the sole fatty acid supplement for pets. Flaxseed oil can be used to provide ALA and as a coat conditioner.

Flaxseed oil also does contain lignans, which are currently being studied for use in preventing cancer in people.

The essential fatty acids in flax can be damaged by exposure to heat, light, and oxygen (essentially, they become rancid). For this reason, you shouldn't cook with flaxseed oil. A good product should be sold in an opaque container, and the manufacturing process should keep the temperature under 100° F (some products are prepared by cold extraction methods). Some manufacturers combine the product with vitamin E because it helps prevent rancidity.

The best use of flaxseed oil is as a general nutritional supplement to provide essential fatty acids.

Flaxseed oil appears to be a safe nutritional supplement when used as recommended.

Orthomolecular Therapy

Orthomolecular medicine (often called "megavitamin therapy") seeks to use increased levels of vitamins and minerals (mainly antioxidants) to help treat a variety of medical disorders. While daily amounts of vitamins and minerals have been recommended as an attempt to prevent nutritional deficiencies, orthomolecular medicine uses higher doses as part of the therapy for disease.

The pet food industry relies on recommendations by the National Research Council (NRC) to prevent diseases caused by nutrient deficiencies in the "average" pet, yet the NRC has not attempted to determine the *optimum* amount of nutrients or their effects in treating medical disorders. While a minimum amount of nutrients may be satisfactory in preventing diseases caused by nutrient deficiencies, it is important to realize that there is no "average" pet, and that every pet has unique nutritional needs.

It is unlikely that our current recommendations are adequate to maintain health in every pet. Each pet has unique requirements for nutrients. Additionally, these needs will vary depending upon the pet's health. For example, in times of stress or disease, additional nutrients above and beyond those needed for health will be required. Orthomolecular medicine evaluates the needs of the pet and uses increased nutrients to fight disease.

Note: Owners should not diagnose and treat their pets without veterinary supervision. Many medical disorders present similar symptoms. Also, megavitamin therapy can be toxic if not used properly.

The orthomolecular approach to treating asthma uses a hypoallergenic, healthful diet as the starting point. This diet should be free of chemicals, impurities, and by-products. A blood profile is done to rule out endocrine diseases such as Cushing's disease and hypothyroidism, as antioxidants may create changes in blood values that are normally used to screen for these common disorders.

Treatment requires borrowing from treatments recommended for other allergic or inflammatory conditions and uses vitamin A (10,000 IU for small dogs and cats, up to 30,000 IU for large dogs), crystalline ascorbic acid (750 mg for small dogs and cats, up to 3,000 mg for large dogs), and vitamin E (800 IU for small dogs and cats, up to 2,400 IU for large dogs). The antioxidant mineral selenium (20 mcg for small dogs and cats, up to 60 mcg for large dogs) is also added to the regimen. Once asymptomatic, a maintenance protocol using lower dosages of vitamins A and E and the mineral selenium is prescribed to reduce the chance for toxicity.

OTHER NATURAL TREATMENTS

Other complementary therapies for pets with asthma include natural **diet** (page 314) and the following herbs: **boswellia** (page 168), **cat's claw** (page 177), **coltsfoot** (page 189), **ephedra** (page 200), **feverfew** (page 202), **garlic** (page 204), **German chamomile** (page 206), *Ginkgo biloba* (page 208), **licorice** (page 234), **lobelia** (page 236), and **turmeric** (page 280).

Often asthmatic pets still require conventional medications. The supplements can be used in conjunction with conventional therapies as they are often ineffective by themselves in most patients with severe asthma. The natural treatments are widely used with variable success but have not all been thoroughly investigated and proven at this time.

As with any condition, the most healthful **natural diet** (page 335) will improve the pet's overall health.

CONVENTIONAL THERAPY

Conventional therapy for dogs and cats with asthma includes the use of corticosteroids and bronchodilators.

Corticosteroids can be given by injection, by mouth, or by both routes of administration. The most commonly used corticosteroids are prednisone, prednisolone, dexamethasone, and triamcinolone. Corticosteroid injections can be short-acting or longer-acting (depot) injections.

While very effective when used to control inflammation and decrease airway sensitivity, corticosteroids have both short-term as well as long-term side effects. Short-term side effects include increased water intake, increased urination, increased appetite, destruction of joint cartilage, and very rarely, either depression or excitability. Long-term side effects that can occur are numerous and include suppression of the immune system, infections, diabetes, liver disease, osteoporosis, Cushing's disease, and obesity. Side effects, both short- and long-term, are common in dogs but relatively rare in cats.

When needed, short-term use of fast-acting corticosteroids are preferred. Depot injections, while commonly used in cats, should rarely, if ever, be used in dogs. In cats, an occasional depot injection (1 to 3 times per year) is usually not associated with side effects, but when possible, short-acting injections and oral corticosteroids are preferred.

Bronchodilators commonly used to treat arthritis in pets include aminophylline and theophylline. These medications are methylxanthine derivatives that act as respiratory smooth muscle relaxing agents. Biochemically, they work by competing with the enzyme phosphodiesterase, which increases the levels of cyclic AMP, resulting in the release of epinephrine. Increased levels of cyclic AMP may also inhibit two chemicals produced in the body, which contribute to signs seen in asthmatic patients: histamine, and the slow-reacting substance of anaphylaxis (SRS-A). In addition to relaxing respiratory smooth muscles, they also relax the smooth muscles of the blood vessels of the respiratory tract and remove excess fluid from the body via their diuretic actions.

Aminophylline and theophylline should be used cautiously in pets with heart disease, stomach ulcers, hyperthyroidism, kidney disease, liver disease, and high blood pressure. Older pets may be more sensitive to side effects. Preexisting heart arrhythmias may worsen in pets receiving aminophylline or theophylline. Additional side effects include central nervous system stimulation and gastrointestinal stimulation. These medications have a narrow therapeutic index, which means there is a very small difference between the effective dose and the toxic dose.

AUTOIMMUNE DISEASES

Principal Natural Treatments
    Antioxidants, omega-3 fatty acids

Other Natural Treatments
    Natural diet, alfalfa, yellow dock, cordyceps mushrooms

Autoimmune diseases, which occur more commonly in dogs than in cats, are those diseases in which the pet's body forms antibodies attacking its own tissues. The exact cause of autoimmune diseases is not known. However, many doctors feel that the immune system may malfunction as a result of infections or chronic exposure to toxins. The fact that an increased number of cases are seen shortly following repeated immunization prompts many holistic doctors to surmise that vaccinations may be responsible for the formation of autoimmune diseases in some pets.

Commonly diagnosed autoimmune diseases include:

Autoimmune Hemolytic Anemia (AIHA).   In this disorder, the pet forms antibodies against its own red blood cells, causing anemia.

Hypothyroidism.   Discussed in detail later in this section (page 103), the pet forms antibodies against its thyroid gland.

Immune-Mediated Thrombocytopenia (ITP). In this disorder, the pet forms antibodies against its own platelets, causing reduced blood-clotting ability.

Keratoconjunctivitis Sicca (KCS).   Also called "dry eye," dogs with this disorder form antibodies against their tear glands, causing chronic eye disease.

Pemphigus.   A number of disorders make up the pemphigus complex of diseases. In these disorders, the pet forms antibodies against its skin.

Rheumatoid Arthritis (RA).   In this disorder, the pet forms antibodies against its own joint tissues, causing lameness and arthritis.

Systemic Lupus Erythematosus (SLE). Also simply called lupus, in this disorder, the pet forms antibodies against a number of its tissues, including blood cells, skin, and the kidneys.

PRINCIPAL NATURAL TREATMENTS

Antioxidants

Certain vitamins and minerals function in the body to reduce oxidation. Oxidation is a chemical process that occurs within the body's cells. After oxidation occurs, certain by-products such as peroxides and "free radicals" accumulate. These cellular by-products are toxic to the cells and surrounding tissue. The body removes these by-products by producing additional chemicals called antioxidants that combat these oxidizing chemicals.

In disease, excess oxidation can occur and the body's normal antioxidant abilities are overwhelmed. This is where supplying antioxidants can help. By giving your pet's body extra antioxidants, it may be possible to neutralize the harmful by-products of cellular oxidation.

Several antioxidants can be used to supplement pets. Most commonly, the antioxidant **vitamins A** (page 284), **C** (page 297), and **E** (page 302), and the minerals **selenium** (page 268), **manganese** (page 239), and **zinc** (page 310), are prescribed. Other antioxidants, including **N-acetylcysteine** (page 243), **Coenzyme Q$_{10}$** (page 185), *Ginkgo biloba* (page 208), **bilberry** (page 164), **grape seed extract** (page 159), and **pycnogenol** (page 159) may also be helpful for a number of disorders.

There is no "correct" antioxidant to use. Dosage varies with the specific antioxidant chosen.

Following is a brief discussion of a commonly used group of antioxidants called bioflavonoids/proanthocyanidins.

Proanthocyanidins

Proanthocyanidins (also called pycnogenols or bioflavonoids, a class of water-soluble plant-coloring agents; while they don't seem to be essential to life, it's likely that people and pets need them for optimal health) are naturally occurring polyphenolic compounds found in plants. Most often, products containing proanthocyanidins are made from grape seeds or pine bark. These compounds are used for their antioxidant effects against lipid (fat) peroxidation. Proanthocyanidins also inhibit the enzyme cyclooxygenase (the same enzyme inhibited by aspirin and other nonsteroidal medications); cyclooxygenase converts arachidonic acid into chemicals (leukotrienes and prostaglandins), which contribute to inflammation and allergic reactions. Proanthocyanidins also decrease histamine release from cells by inhibiting several enzymes.

Some research suggests that pycnogenol seems to work by enhancing the effects of another antioxidant, vitamin C. Other research suggests that the bioflavonoids can work independently of other antioxidants; as is the case with many supplements, there probably is an additive effect when multiple antioxidants are combined. People taking pycnogenol often report feeling better and having more energy; this "side effect" may possibly occur in our pets as well.

Quercetin is a natural antioxidant bioflavonoid found in red wine, grapefruit, onions, apples, black tea, and, in lesser amounts, in leafy green vegetables and beans. Quercetin protects cells in the body from damage by free radicals and stabilizes collagen in blood vessels.

Quercetin supplements are available in pill and tablet form. One problem with them, however, is that they don't seem to be well absorbed by the body. A special form called quercetin chalcone appears to be better absorbed.

Quercetin appears to be quite safe. Maximum safe dosages for young children, women who are pregnant or nursing, or those with serious liver or kidney disease have not been established; similar precautions are probably warranted in pets.

In people, a typical dosage of proanthocyanidins is 200 to 400 mg 3 times daily. Quercetin may be better absorbed if taken on an empty stomach. The suggested dosage of proanthocyanidin complex in pets is 10 to 200 mg given daily (divided into 2 to 3 doses). The suggested dosage of bioflavonoid complex in pets is 200 to 1,500 mg per day (divided into 2 to 3 doses). The actual dosage of each product will vary with the product and the pet's weight and disease condition.

While there is no specific research showing benefit in specific autoimmune disorders, the use of antioxidants is widely recommended by holistic veterinarians to reduce oxidative damage to tissues that may occur in various autoimmune disorders. More research on antioxidants and other complementary therapies in the treatment of autoimmune disorders is needed.

Omega-3 Fatty Acids

Omega-3 fatty acids—eicosapentaenoic acid (EPA) and docosahexaenoic acid (DHA)—are derived from fish oils of coldwater fish (salmon, trout, or most commonly menhaden fish) and flaxseed. Omega-6 fatty acids—linoleic acid (LA) and gamma-linolenic acid (GLA)—are derived from the oils of seeds such as evening primrose, black currant, and borage. Often, fatty acids are added to the diet with other supplements to attain an additive effect.

Just how do the fatty acids work to help in controlling inflammation in pets? Cell membranes contain phospholipids. When membrane injury occurs, an enzyme acts on the phospholipids in the cell membranes to produce fatty acids including arachidonic acid (an omega-6 fatty acid) and eicosapentaenoic acid (an omega-3 fatty acid). Further metabolism of the arachidonic acid and eicosapentaenoic acid by additional enzymes (the lipooxygenase and cyclooxygenase pathways) yields the production of chemicals called eicosanoids. The eicosanoids produced by metabolism of arachidonic acid are pro-inflammatory and cause inflammation, suppress the immune system, and cause platelets to aggregate and clot; the eicosanoids produced by metabolism of eicosapentaenoic acid are non-inflammatory, not immunosuppressive, and help inhibit platelets from clotting. (There is some overlap and the actual biochemical pathway is a bit more complicated than I have suggested here. For example, one of the by-products of omega-6 fatty acid metabolism is Prostaglandin E_1, which is anti-inflammatory. This is one reason why some research has shown that using certain omega-6 fatty acids can also act to limit inflammation.)

Supplementation of the diet with omega-3 fatty acids works in this biochemical reaction. By providing extra amounts of these non-inflammatory compounds, we try to overwhelm the body with the production of non-inflammatory eicosanoids. Therefore, since the same enzymes metabolize both omega-3 and omega-6 fatty acids, and since metabolism of the omega-6 fatty acids tends to cause inflammation (with the exception of Prostaglandin E_1 by metabolism of omega-6 as mentioned), by supplying a large amount of omega-3 fatty acids we favor the production of non-inflammatory chemicals.

Many disorders are due to overproduction of the eicosanoids responsible for producing inflammation. Fatty acid supplementation can be beneficial in inflammatory disorders by regulating the eicosanoid production. While not proven, many holistic veterinarians recommend anti-inflammatory agents such as omega-3 fatty acids in an attempt to regulate the immune response in pets with autoimmune disorders. While controlled studies are lacking, many doctors feel there is some benefit to their use.

In general, the products of omega-3 (specifically EPA) and one omega-6 fatty acid (DGLA) are less inflammatory than the products of arachidonic acid (another omega-6 fatty acid). By changing dietary fatty acid consumption, we can change eicosanoid production right at the cellular level and try to modify (decrease) inflammation within the body. By providing the proper (anti-inflammatory) fatty acids, we can use fatty acids as an anti-inflammatory substance. However, since the products of omega-6 fatty acid metabolism (specifically arachidonic acid) are not the sole cause of the inflammation, fatty acid therapy is rarely effective as the sole therapy but is used as an adjunct therapy to achieve an additive effect.

Note: Flaxseed oil is a popular source of alpha-linoleic acid (ALA), an omega-3 fatty acid that is ultimately converted to EPA and DHA. However, many species of pets (probably including dogs) and some people cannot convert ALA to these other more active non-inflammatory omega-3 fatty acids. In one study in people, flaxseed oil was ineffective in reducing symptoms or raising levels of EPA and DHA. While flaxseed oil has been suggested as a less smelly substitute for fish oil, there is no evidence that it is effective when used for the same therapeutic purposes as fish oil. Therefore, supplementation with EPA and DHA is important, and this is the reason flaxseed oil is not recommended as the sole fatty acid supplement for pets. Flaxseed oil can be used to provide ALA and as a coat conditioner.

While many doctors use fatty acids for a variety of medical problems, there is considerable debate about the use of fatty acids. The debate concerns several areas:

Dosages

What is the "best" dose to use in the treatment of pets? Most doctors use anywhere from 2 to 10 times the label dose. Research in the treatment of allergies indicates that the label dose is ineffective; the same theory probably holds true for treating autoimmune disorders, but the research is lacking. In people, the dosage that showed effectiveness in many studies was 1.4 to 2.8 gm of GLA per day, or 1.7 gm of EPA and 0.9 gm of DHA per day, which is hard for people to obtain from the supplements currently available. If this were shown to be the correct dosage for pets, a 50-pound dog would need to take 10 or more fatty acids capsules per day to obtain a similar dosage, depending upon which supplement (and there are many choices on the market) was used. Therefore, while the studies with omega-3 fatty acids show many potential health benefits, it is almost impossible to administer the large number of capsules needed to approximate the same dosage used in these studies. The best that owners can hope for at this time is to work with their veterinarians and try to increase, as best as possible, the amount of omega-3 fatty acids in the diet.

Which Fatty Acid?

What is the "correct" fatty acid to use? Should we use just omega-3 (EPA and DHA) fatty acids, or combine them with omega-6 (GLA) fatty acids? Is there an "ideal" ratio of omega-6 to omega-3 fatty acids? (Through research on pets with atopic dermatitis, the ideal dietary ratio seems to be 5:1 of omega-6:omega-3 fatty acids, although this is also debated. Whether or not this "ideal" dietary ratio is ideal for the treatment of autoimmune disorders and other inflammatory conditions remains to be seen.)

Fatty Acid Supplementation

Is supplementation with fatty acid capsules or liquids the best approach, or is dietary manipulation preferred for the treatment of inflammatory conditions? There are, in fact, diets constructed with this "ideal" ratio (of omega-6 to omega-3 fatty acids). For owners who do not like giving their pets medication, or for those pets who don't take the fatty acid supplements easily, it might be wise to try some of these medically formulated diets (available from your pet's doctor) that contain the fatty acids. (However, because these medicated diets may not be as natural as possible due to the inclusion of by-products and chemical preservatives, holistic pet owners may need to try other options.) These diets, often prescribed as anti-inflammatory diets for pets with allergies, may be useful as a part of the therapy of autoimmune disorders in pets.

Fish Oils   Since fish oils can easily oxidize and become rancid, some manufacturers add vitamin E to fish oil capsules and liquid products to keep the oil from spoiling (others remove oxygen from the capsule).

Since processed foods have increased omega-6 fatty acids and decreased omega-3 fatty acids, supplementing the diets of all pets with omega-3 fatty acids seems warranted and will not harm your pet.

The bottom line is that there are many questions regarding the use of fatty acid therapy. More research is needed to determine the effectiveness of the fatty acids in the treatment of various medical problems, as well as the proper doses needed to achieve clinical results. Until definitive answers are obtained, you will need to work with your doctor (knowing the limitations of current research) to determine the use of these supplements for your pet.

Fish oil appears to be safe. The most common side effect seen in people and pets is a fish odor to the breath or the skin.

Because fish oil has a mild "blood-thinning" effect, it should not be combined with powerful blood-thinning medications, such as Coumadin (warfarin) or heparin, except on a veterinarian's advice. Fish oil does not seem to cause bleeding problems when it is taken by itself at commonly recommended dosages. Also, fish oil does not appear to raise blood sugar levels in people or pets with diabetes.

Flaxseed Oil   Flaxseed oil is derived from the seeds of the flax plant and has been proposed as a less smelly alternative to fish oil. Flaxseed oil contains alpha-linolenic acid (ALA), an omega-3 fatty acid that is ultimately converted to EPA and DHA. In fact, flaxseed oil contains higher levels of omega-3 fatty acids (ALA) than fish oil. It also contains omega-6 fatty acids.

As mentioned, many species of pets (probably including dogs and cats) and some people cannot convert ALA to these other more active non-inflammatory omega-3 fatty acids. In one study in people, flaxseed oil was ineffective in reducing symptoms or raising levels of EPA and DHA. While flaxseed oil has been suggested as a substitute for fish oil, there is no evidence that it is effective when used for the same therapeutic purposes as fish oil. Unlike the case for fish oil, there is little evidence that flaxseed oil is effective for any specific therapeutic purpose.

Therefore, supplementation with EPA and DHA is important, and this is the reason flaxseed oil is not recommended as the sole fatty acid supplement for pets. Flaxseed oil can be used to provide ALA and as a coat conditioner.

Flaxseed oil also does contain lignans, which are currently being studied for use in preventing cancer in people.

The essential fatty acids in flax can be damaged by exposure to heat, light, and oxygen (essentially, they become rancid). For this reason, you shouldn't cook with flaxseed oil. A good product should be sold in an opaque container, and the manufacturing process should keep the temperature under 100° F (some products are prepared by cold extraction methods). Some manufacturers combine the product with vitamin E because it helps prevent rancidity.

The best use of flaxseed oil is as a general nutritional supplement to provide essential fatty acids.

Flaxseed oil appears to be a safe nutritional supplement when used as recommended.

These supplements can be used in conjunction with conventional therapies as they are unlikely to be effective by themselves in most patients. The natural treatments are widely used with variable success but have not all been thoroughly investigated and proven at this time.

As with any condition, the most healthful natural diet will improve the pet's overall health.

OTHER NATURAL TREATMENTS

Other therapies that can be tried include the herbs **alfalfa** (page 156), **yellow dock** (page 309), and **cordyceps mushrooms** (page 191).

CONVENTIONAL THERAPY

Specific therapies vary with the disease. In general, conventional therapies rely on immunosuppressive medications such as corticosteroids or stronger chemotherapeutic drugs to decrease the overactive immune system.

 # BLADDER CANCER

Principal Natural Treatments
  Natural diet, antioxidants, omega-3 fatty acids

Other Natural Treatments
  DMG, Coenzyme Q$_{10}$, glycoproteins, proanthocyanidins, soy isoflavones, immunostimulant herbs: alfalfa, aloe vera (Acemannan), astragalus, burdock, dandelion leaf, dandelion root, echinacea, garlic, ginseng, goldenseal, hawthorn, licorice, marshmallow, milk thistle, nettle, red clover, St. John's wort, turmeric, yellow dock; immunostimulant mushrooms: maitake, reishi

Bladder cancer most commonly occurs in older dogs and rarely in older cats. The tumor most commonly affecting the bladder is transitional cell carcinoma. Clinical signs of bladder cancer include increased frequency of urination, painful urination or a burning sensation during urination, excessive licking at the genitals, and occasionally blood in the urine. Increased thirst, increased volume of urine, and urinary incontinence are rarely associated with bladder cancer and are more typical of kidney disease and diabetes. However, some dogs with bladder cancer can exhibit urinary incontinence. A new test using a urine sample is available to screen dogs for bladder cancer.

PRINCIPAL NATURAL TREATMENTS

The following therapies are designed to boost the immune system and slow the spread of cancer. These therapies can be used in conjunction with conventional therapies as they are unlikely to be effective by themselves in most patients. The natural treatments are widely used with variable success but have not all been thoroughly investigated and proven at this time.

Natural Diet

While there are no controlled studies showing the value of diet in supporting the pet with bladder cancer, there are studies showing the benefits of dietary therapy when combined with conventional therapies in dogs with lymphoma. Since this diet is designed to reduce the growth and spread of cancer, it is often recommended for dogs and cats with any type of cancerous disease.

Studies demonstrate that both people and pets with inadequate nutrition cannot metabolize chemotherapy drugs adequately, which predisposes them to toxicity and poor therapeutic response. This makes proper diet and nutritional supplementation an important part of cancer therapy.

Several metabolic derangements are common in the cancer patient. First, cancer patients often have hyperlactatemia (increased lactic acid in the blood). In addition, since metabolism of simple carbohydrates produces lactate, a diet with a minimum of these carbohydrates might be preferred.

Research has shown a pronounced decrease in certain amino acids, such as arginine, in the plasma of cancer patients. If left uncorrected, these amino acid deficiencies could result in serious health risks to the patient. Supplementation with the deficient amino acids might improve immune function and positively affect treatment and survival rates.

Weight loss often occurs in cancer patients as a result of cachexia (wasting). Most of the weight loss seen in cancer patients experiencing cancer cachexia occurs as a result of depleted body fat stores. Tumor cells, unlike normal healthy cells, have difficulty utilizing lipids for energy. Dogs with lymphoma fed diets high in fat had longer remission periods than dogs fed high carbohydrate diets.

While there are often many treatment options for the various malignancies experienced by our patients, we often overlook the simple aspect of nutrition. In the next decade, prevention and treatment will most likely include a focus on nutrition in veterinary medicine, just as our counterparts are now doing in the human medical field. The research is out there: There is no doubt that cancer patients have deranged nutrient metabolism that can negatively affect the outcome of conventional therapies. Additions of omega-3 fatty acids and antioxidant vitamins and minerals to the diet of cancer patients may help improve survival and possibly decrease the chances of pets contracting cancer in those who are currently cancer-free.

The n/d Diet

Recently, Hill's Pet Food Company introduced the first cancer diet for dogs called n/d. The diet contains increased protein and fat, decreased carbohydrates, increased omega-3 fatty acids, and increased arginine (the reasons for this formulation are discussed on page 32). The composition

of the diet is: protein, 37%; fat, 32%; carbohydrates, 21%; arginine, 3.1% (647 mg/100 kcal); and omega-3 fatty acids from fish oil, 7.3% (1,518 mg/100 kcal). In controlled studies, dogs with lymphoma (lymphosarcoma) who were being treated with chemotherapy and being fed n/d had increased survival times when compared with dogs being treated with the same chemotherapy medications and eating a controlled diet. Similar findings were found for dogs with nasal and oral cancer who were treated with radiation therapy and eating n/d. The conclusions from this study showed that survival time increased 56%; quality of life improved due to decreased pain in dogs treated with radiation; remission periods were longer; and metabolic changes seen in pets with cancer were reversed.

While these findings are quite impressive, there is no evidence that this diet helps dogs or cats with other forms of cancer. Despite this need for additional research, it is likely that any pet with any type of cancer could benefit from this or similar diets (see below for further discussion).

There are three potential problems with diet n/d:

1. It is an expensive diet, especially for owners of large-breed dogs.
2. It is only available in a canned variety, most likely due to the high fat content.
3. The protein source is an animal by-product, beef lung. (Owners who desire the most holistic and natural diet possible might object to this protein source.)

A homemade diet that approximates n/d can be attempted. However, due to the high level of omega-3 fatty acids in the food, it is difficult (if not impossible) and expensive to prepare a similar diet at home.

Tofu (**soy** protein, page 274) protects the intestinal tract from damage that could occur with certain chemotherapy drugs and result in diarrhea. While not proven, tofu diets might be preferred for pets with cancer, especially those whose treatment regimen includes chemotherapy.

The homemade anticancer diet for dogs should have the following nutrient levels: protein, 35 to 40%; fat, 30%; and carbohydrates, 20%.

Cats can have higher protein and fat levels and minimal or no carbohydrates (cats do not have a strict dietary carbohydrate requirement).

Antioxidants can be added to the diet. However, high doses of antioxidants might interfere with any chemotherapy medications such as doxorubicin (Adriamycin) that work to kill cancer cells by oxidation. Several studies indicate that high levels of antioxidants may help cancer cells grow and spread. For example, a recent study showed that cancer cells contain high levels of vitamin C, probably serving as an antioxidant to protect the cancer cell from oxidation. Because of the possibility of high levels of antioxidants interfering with treatment or cure, you should discuss this topic with your pet's oncologist (cancer specialist) prior to using increased levels of antioxidants.

Arginine decreases tumor growth and spread (metastasis); therefore, supplemental arginine is useful for pets with cancer. **Glutamine** may retard the cachexia (wasting) seen in many pets with cancer and may help protect against intestinal injury. However, some experimental studies have shown no benefit and occasionally show increased vomiting or diarrhea in pets supplemented with glutamine. At this time, there is no clear-cut evidence for or against glutamine supplementation. The need for glutamine will vary from case to case.

Other recommendations include adding 60 to 100 mg of Coenzyme Q_{10} (an antioxidant) and 500 mg of vitamin E/450 kcals of food. The precaution mentioned above concerning antioxidants should be heeded: They may interfere with chemotherapy medications.

Finally, many holistic veterinarians will add fresh vegetables (especially those high in indoles and antioxidants), such as broccoli, kale, cabbage, and fresh garlic. Other supplements (see page 33) can be used as needed. Your veterinarian can decide which additional supplements might be helpful after consultation with you and a thorough examination of your pet.

Diet for Dogs with Bladder Cancer

Note: Before you start to feed your dog or cat a home-prepared diet, it is strongly recommended that you discuss your decision with your veterinarian or a holistic veterinarian in your area. It is essential that you follow any diet's recommendations closely, including all ingredients and supplements. Failure to do so may result in serious health consequences for your pet.

½ cup tofu, raw, firm
1 cup boiled lentils
2 cups of potatoes boiled with skin
2 teaspoons chicken fat or canola oil
¹⁄₁₀ teaspoon salt
Multivitamin/mineral supplement

This diet provides 775 kcal and supports the daily needs of a 25-pound dog. It also provides 43.9 gm of protein and 22 gm of fat. Adding 2 tablespoons canned sardines increases the protein content by 6.2 gm and the fat content by 4.6 gm.

Variations

1. Add arginine at 647 mg/100 kcal of food.
2. Add omega-3 fatty acids (fish oil) at 1,518 mg/100 kcal. This is very difficult to do, as the average omega-3 fatty acid capsule contains 180 mg. Work with your doctor to increase the fatty acid content as much as possible (adding fish such as salmon to the diet can help achieve this goal).
3. Occasionally substitute ⅓ pound of cooked chicken, turkey, or lowfat beef for the tofu (in which case the lentils can be eliminated).
4. Occasionally substitute 2 cups of rice or macaroni for the potatoes.
5. Add fresh, raw or steamed vegetables to increase the level of natural vitamins and minerals, as well as add flavor. Most vegetables provide approximately 25 kcal per ½ cup.
6. Add 4 bonemeal tablets (10-grain or equivalent) or 1 teaspoon of bonemeal powder to supply calcium and phosphorus with a multivitamin/mineral supplement. Follow the label instructions. Alternatively, use a natural product from Standard Process (1 Calcifood Wafer or 2 Calcium Lactate tablets) for each 2 bonemeal tablets.
7. When possible, use natural vitamins made from raw whole foods, rather than synthetic vitamins (although both can be used in combination), as the natural vitamins also supply plant

phytochemicals, enzymes, and other nutrients not found in chemically synthesized vitamins. Use either Catalyn from Standard Process (at a dose of 1 Catalyn per 25 pounds) or Canine Plus from VetriScience (following label dosages) as the natural vitamin in this recipe.

Diets for Cats with Bladder Cancer

½ pound chicken
½ large hard-boiled egg
½ ounce clams, chopped in juice
4 teaspoon chicken fat or canola oil
⅛ teaspoon potassium chloride
100 mg taurine
Multivitamin/mineral supplement

This diet provides 471 kcal, 53.1 gm of protein, and 27.4 gm of fat, and provides the daily needs for a 15-pound cat.

Variations

1. Add arginine at 647 mg/100 kcal of food. This is a recommendation for dogs and has not been proven in cats.
2. Add omega-3 fatty acids (fish oil) at 1,518 mg/ 100 kcal. This is very difficult to do, as the average omega-3 fatty acid capsule contains 180 mg. Work with your doctor to increase the fatty acid content as much as possible (adding fish such as salmon to the diet can help achieve this goal). This is a recommendation for dogs and has not been proven in cats.
3. Occasionally add ⅓ cup of rice, macaroni, or potatoes. However, cats do not have a proven need for dietary carbohydrates, and adding additional carbohydrates supplies substrate (food) for cancer cells.
4. Add fresh raw or steamed vegetables to increase the level of natural vitamins and minerals, as well as add flavor. Most vegetables provide approximately 25 kcal per ½ cup. Many cats, however, will not eat vegetables.
5. Add 3 bonemeal tablets (10-grain or equivalent) or ¾ teaspoon of bonemeal powder to supply calcium and phosphorus with a multivitamin/mineral supplement, following the label instructions. Alternatively, use a natural product from Standard Process (1 Calcifood Wafer or 2 Calcium Lactate tablets for each 2 bonemeal tablets) as the natural vitamin in this recipe.
6. When possible, use natural vitamins made from raw whole foods, rather than synthetic vitamins (although both can be used in combination), as the natural vitamins also supply plant phytochemicals, enzymes, and other nutrients not found in chemically synthesized vitamins. Use either Catalyn from Standard Process (at a dose of 1 Catalyn per 10 pounds) or NuCat from VetriScience (following label dosages) as the natural vitamin in this recipe.

Antioxidants

Certain vitamins and minerals function in the body to reduce oxidation. Oxidation is a chemical process that occurs within the body's cells. After oxidation occurs, certain by-products such as peroxides and "free radicals" accumulate. These cellular by-products are toxic to the cells and surrounding tissue. The body removes these by-products by producing additional chemicals called antioxidants that combat these oxidizing chemicals.

In disease, excess oxidation can occur and the body's normal antioxidant abilities are overwhelmed. This is where supplying antioxidants can help. By giving your pet's body extra antioxidants, you may find it possible to neutralize the harmful by-products of cellular oxidation.

Several antioxidants can be used to supplement pets. Most commonly, the antioxidant **vitamins A** (page 284), **C** (page 297), and **E** (page 302), and the minerals **selenium** (page 268), **manganese** (page 239), and **zinc** (page 310) are prescribed. Other antioxidants, including **N-acetylcysteine** (page 243), **Coenzyme Q₁₀** (page 185), *Ginkgo biloba* (page 208), **bilberry** (page 164), **grape seed extract** (page 159), and **pycnogenol** (page 159) may also be helpful for a number of disorders.

There is no "correct" antioxidant to use. Dosage varies with the specific antioxidant chosen.

Following is a brief discussion of a commonly used group of antioxidants called bioflavonoids/ proanthocyanidins.

Proanthocyanidins

Proanthocyanidins are naturally occurring polyphenolic compounds found in plants; most often products containing proanthocyanidins are made from grape seed or pine bark. Proanthocyanidins are also called pycnogenols or bioflavonoids, a class of water-soluble plant coloring agents. While they don't seem to be essential to life, it's likely that people and pets need them for optimal health. These compounds are used for their antioxidant effects against lipid (fat) peroxidation. Proanthocyanidins also inhibit the enzyme cyclo-oxygenase (the same enzyme inhibited by aspirin and other nonsteroidal medications); cyclo-oxygenase converts arachidonic acid into chemicals (leukotrienes and prostaglandins), which contribute to inflammation and allergic reactions. Proanthocyanidins also decrease histamine release from cells by inhibiting several enzymes.

Proanthocyanidins, by potentiating the immune system (via enhancement of T-lymphocyte activity and modulation of neutrophil and macrophage responses), are often recommended for use in the treatment of pets with cancer.

Some research suggests that pycnogenol seems to work by enhancing the effects of another antioxidant, vitamin C. Other research suggests that the bioflavonoids can work independently of other antioxidants; as is the case with many supplements, there probably is an additive effect when multiple antioxidants are combined. People taking pycnogenol often report feeling better and having more energy; this "side effect" may possibly occur in our pets as well.

Quercetin is a natural antioxidant bioflavonoid found in red wine, grapefruit, onions, apples, black tea, and, in lesser amounts, in leafy green vegetables and beans. Quercetin protects cells in the body from damage by free radicals and stabilizes collagen in blood vessels. Test-tube and animal research also suggests that quercetin might be able to help prevent tumors in hamsters or enhance the effects of cancer-fighting drugs.

Quercetin supplements are available in pill and tablet form. One problem with them, however, is that they don't seem to be well absorbed by the body. A special form called quercetin chalcone appears to be better absorbed.

Quercetin appears to be quite safe. Maximum safe dosages for young children, women who are pregnant or nursing, or those with serious liver or kidney disease have not been established; similar precautions are probably warranted in pets.

In people, a typical dosage of proanthocyanidins is 200 to 400 mg 3 times daily. Quercetin may be better absorbed if taken on an empty stomach. The suggested dosage of proanthocyanidin complex in pets is 10 to 200 mg given daily (divided into 2 to 3 doses.) The suggested dosage of bioflavonoid complex in pets is 200 to 1,500 mg per day (divided into 2 to 3 doses). The actual dosage of each product will vary with the product and the pet's weight and disease condition.

Because some types of chemotherapy and radiation therapy may rely on cellular oxidation for their effects, antioxidants should not be used without veterinary supervision in pets with cancer undergoing chemotherapy or radiation therapy.

Omega-3 Fatty Acids

Omega-3 fatty acids (eicosapentaenoic acid (EPA) and docosahexaenoic acid (DHA) are derived from fish oils of coldwater fish (salmon, trout, or most commonly menhaden fish) and flaxseed, whereas omega-6 fatty acids (linoleic acid (LA) and gamma-linolenic acid (GLA) are derived from the oils of seeds such as evening primrose, black currant, and borage. Often, fatty acids are added to the diet with other supplements to attain an additive effect.

In transplanted tumor models, omega-3 fatty acids reduced tumor development while omega-6 fatty acids stimulated tumor development. Omega-3 fatty acids have been shown to inhibit tumor growth as well as the spread of cancer (metastasis). Reduced radiation damage in the skin was also seen following supplementation with omega-3 fatty acids.

The use of omega-3 fatty acids can promote weight gain and may have anticancer effects, and so warrants special mention. In people, the use of omega-3 fatty acids, such as those found in fish oils, improves the immune status, metabolic status, and clinical outcomes of cancer patients. These supplements also decrease the duration of hospitalization and complication rates in people with gastrointestinal cancer. In animal models, the omega-3 fatty acids inhibit the formation of tumors and metastasis (spread of the cancer). Fi-

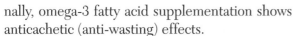
nally, omega-3 fatty acid supplementation shows anticachetic (anti-wasting) effects.

Note: Flaxseed oil is a popular source of alpha-linoleic acid (ALA), an omega-3 fatty acid that is ultimately converted to EPA and DHA. However, many species of pets (probably including dogs) and some people cannot convert ALA to these other more active non-inflammatory omega-3 fatty acids. Also, flaxseed oil contains omega-6 fatty acids which are not recommended in pets with cancer. In one study in people, flaxseed oil was ineffective in reducing symptoms or raising levels of EPA and DHA. While flaxseed oil has been suggested as a less smelly substitute for fish oil, there is no evidence that it is effective when used for the same therapeutic purposes as fish oil. Therefore, supplementation with EPA and DHA is important, and this is the reason flaxseed oil is not recommended as the sole fatty acid supplement for pets. Flaxseed oil can be used to provide ALA and as a coat conditioner.

While many doctors use fatty acids for a variety of medical problems, there is considerable debate about the use of fatty acids. The debate concerns several areas:

Dosages

What is the "best" dose to use in the treatment of pets? (Most doctors use anywhere from 2 to 10 times the label dose.) The recommended dosage for pets with cancer is approximately 1,500 mg/100 kilocalories of food (the amount added to Prescription Diet n/d, discussed below). In order to get this dose, depending upon the product selected, you would need to feed your dog about 5 capsules per 100 kcal of diet. This is a lot of fatty acid capsules!

Which Fatty Acid?

Is supplementation with fatty acid capsules or liquids the best approach, or is dietary manipulation preferred for the treatment of cancer? There is one diet, Prescription Diet n/d, made for dogs with cancer. This diet contains the "proper" amount of omega-3 fatty acids, and it is impossible to add enough fatty acids in the form of supplements to equal the amount found in n/d. However, the protein source for the diet,

beef lung, is not the most wholesome protein source, which is a concern for holistic pet owners. Many owners use some of the n/d with a homemade diet plus additional fatty acids to achieve a compromise.

Studies done in dogs with lymphoma and nasal tumors have shown that dogs eating the n/d showed increased disease-free intervals and survival times when compared with similarly treated dogs not eating this diet. While research has not been reported in dogs with other cancers or in cats with cancers, it is recommended to use fatty acid supplementation in pets with any kind of cancer due to the potential benefit. More research will be needed to give us good information in this area.

Fish Oils   Since fish oils can easily oxidize and become rancid, some manufacturers add vitamin E to fish oil capsules and liquid products to keep the oil from spoiling (others remove oxygen from the capsule).

The bottom line is that there are many questions regarding the use of fatty acid therapy. More research is needed to determine the effectiveness of the fatty acids in the treatment of various cancers, as well as the proper doses needed to achieve clinical results. Until definitive answers are obtained, you will need to work with your doctors (knowing the limitations of current research) to determine the use of these supplements for your pet.

Fish oil appears to be safe. The most common side effect seen in people and pets is a fish odor to the breath or the skin.

Because fish oil has a mild "blood-thinning" effect, it should not be combined with powerful blood-thinning medications, such as Coumadin (warfarin) or heparin, except on a veterinarian's advice. Fish oil does not seem to cause bleeding problems when it is taken by itself at commonly recommended dosages. Also, fish oil does not appear to raise blood sugar levels in people or pets with diabetes.

Flaxseed Oil   Flaxseed oil is derived from the seeds of the flax plant and has been proposed as a less smelly alternative to fish oil. Flaxseed oil contains alpha-linolenic acid (ALA), an omega-3 fatty acid that is ultimately converted to EPA and DHA. In fact, flaxseed oil contains higher levels of omega-3 fatty acids (ALA) than fish oil. It also contains omega-6 fatty acids.

As mentioned, many species of pets (probably including dogs and cats) and some people cannot convert ALA to these other more active non-inflammatory omega-3 fatty acids. In one study in people, flaxseed oil was ineffective in reducing symptoms or raising levels of EPA and DHA. While flaxseed oil has been suggested as a substitute for fish oil, there is no evidence that it is effective when used for the same therapeutic purposes as fish oil. Unlike the case for fish oil, there is little evidence that flaxseed oil is effective for any specific therapeutic purpose.

Therefore, supplementation with EPA and DHA is important, and this is the reason flaxseed oil is not recommended as the sole fatty acid supplement for pets. Flaxseed oil can be used to provide ALA and as a coat conditioner.

Flaxseed oil also contains lignans, which are currently being studied for use in preventing cancer in people. To date, we have no information to recommend their use in pets with cancer.

The essential fatty acids in flax can be damaged by exposure to heat, light, and oxygen (essentially, they become rancid). For this reason, you shouldn't cook with flaxseed oil. A good product should be sold in an opaque container, and the manufacturing process should keep the temperature under 100° F (some products are prepared by cold extraction methods.) Some manufacturers combine the product with vitamin E because it helps prevent rancidity.

The best use of flaxseed oil is as a general nutritional supplement to provide essential fatty acids. It appears to be a safe nutritional supplement when used as recommended.

OTHER NATURAL TREATMENTS

There are no "cures" for bladder cancer. Any of the other therapies recommended for general support of the cancer patient may be useful, including: **DMG** (page 194), **Coenzyme Q10** (page 185), **glycoproteins** (page 214), **proanthocyanidins** (page 27), immunostimulant herbs: **alfalfa** (page 156), **aloe vera** (Acemannan, page 156), **astragalus** (page 160), **burdock** (page 170), **dandelion leaf** (page 193), **dandelion root** (page 193), **echinacea** (page 195), **garlic** (page 204), **ginseng** (page 210), **goldenseal** (page 220), **hawthorn** (page 223), **licorice** (page 234), **marshmallow** (page 240), **milk thistle** (page 241), **nettle** (page 245), **red clover** (page 262), **St. John's wort** (page 276), **turmeric** (page 280), **yellow dock** (page 309); immunostimulant mushrooms: **maitake** (page 238), **reishi** (page 264), and **shiitake** (page 272).

CONVENTIONAL THERAPY

Conventional therapies for pets with bladder cancer include surgical removal when possible (usually the cancer is too advanced when discovered for surgery to help). Radiation therapy offers only local control and is seldom used due to the good effects gained with chemotherapy. Chemotherapy, mitoxantrone, often combined with the drug, piroxicam, has shown a 75% subjective improvement with a 36% tumor response rate.

BLADDER INFECTIONS

Principal Natural Treatments
  Natural diet, cranberry extract

Other Natural Treatments
  Coenzyme Q10, omega-3 fatty acids, vitamin E, antioxidants, herbs: alfalfa, dandelion leaf, echinacea, goldenseal, horsetail, marshmallow, plantain, Oregon grape, uva ursei, yarrow; and maitake mushrooms

Bladder infections usually occur as bacteria normally living in and around the lower urinary tract ascend (go up) the urinary tract through the urethra and infect the normally sterile bladder. Clinical signs of either bladder infections or bladder stones are similar and include increased frequency of urination, painful urination or a burning sensation during urination, excessive licking at the genitals, and occasionally blood in the urine. Increased thirst, increased volume of urine, and urinary incontinence are rarely associated with bladder disease and are more typical of kidney disease and diabetes.

PRINCIPAL NATURAL TREATMENTS

Natural Diet

The same diet recommended for controlling struvite bladder stones is recommended for dogs and cats with chronic bladder infections. If processed foods must be fed, most holistic veterinarians prefer canned diets (which contain large amounts of water) rather than dry foods.

Dietary therapy is a useful adjunct (and possible preventive measure) for pets with bladder infections. Since most infections commonly form in alkaline urine (urine with a high pH), diets should help maintain an acidic urine (low pH) as much as possible. Diets with animal-based protein sources are most important in maintaining an acidic pH (vegetarian or cereal-based diets are more likely to cause an alkaline urine).

While urinary acidifiers can be useful, some doctors discourage their use as the exact dosage that is safe and effective is often not known. If urinary acidifiers are used for short-term acidification, a natural therapy such as **cranberry** extract (see page 38) might be preferred to conventional medications (such as methionine).

Diet for Dogs with Bladder Infections

Note: Before you start to feed your dog or cat a home-prepared diet, it is strongly recommended that you discuss your decision with your veterinarian or a holistic veterinarian in your area. It is essential that you follow any diet's recommendations closely, including all ingredients and supplements. Failure to do so may result in serious health consequences for your pet.

⅔ cup lowfat cottage cheese
1 large hard-boiled egg
2 cups long grain, cooked brown rice
2 teaspoons chicken fat or canola oil
½ ounce brewer's yeast
¼ teaspoon potassium chloride (salt substitute)

This diet provides 780 kcal (enough to fulfill the daily amount required for a 25-pound dog), 42.9 gm protein, 22 gm fat, 92 mg sodium/100 kcal (a high-sodium diet).

Variations

1. Substitute 4 ounces of tuna (in water without sodium) or ¼ pound of lean ground beef (or ground chicken or lamb) for the sardines.
2. Substitute 2 to 3 cups of potato, cooked with the skin, or 2 cups of cooked macaroni for the rice.
3. Supply vitamins and minerals as follows: 4 bonemeal tablets (10-grain or equivalent) or 1 teaspoon of bonemeal powder to supply calcium and phosphorus with a multivitamin/mineral supplement using the label instructions. Alternatively, use a natural product from Standard Process (1 Calcifood Wafer or 2 Calcium Lactate tablets for each 2 bonemeal tablets).
4. When possible, use natural vitamins made from raw whole foods, rather than synthetic vitamins (although both can be used in combination), as the natural vitamins also supply plant phytochemicals, enzymes, and other nutrients not found in chemically synthesized vitamins. Use either Catalyn from Standard Process (at a dose of 1 Catalyn per 25 pounds) or Canine Plus from VetriScience (following label dosages) for the natural vitamins in this recipe.
4. For extra nutrition and variety, use fresh, raw, or slightly steamed vegetables, such as carrots or broccoli (approximately ½ to 1 cup per recipe) as a top dressing for the diet. Most vegetables provide approximately 25 kcal per ½ cup.
5. Add supplements that can be beneficial, such as omega-3 fatty acids, plant enzymes, and a super green food or health blend formula.

Note: If adding vegetables or other supplements, monitor urine pH when feeding the diet with these supplements and without the supplements to be sure the pH does not change from acid to alkaline. Some dogs have a difficult time producing acid urine even when fed the above diet or when administered urinary acidifiers.

Diet for Cats with Bladder Infections

3½ ounces firm raw tofu
2¼ ounces sardines, canned in tomato sauce
½ ounce clams, chopped in juice
½ yolk of large hard-boiled egg
⅓ cup long grain, cooked brown rice
2 teaspoons chicken fat or canola oil
½ ounce brewer's yeast
100 mg taurine

This diet provides 501 kcal (enough to fulfill the daily amount required for a 16-pound cat), 37.4 gm protein, 29.6 gm fat, 62.2 mg sodium/100 kcal (a high-sodium diet).

Variations

1. Substitute 2 ounces of tuna (in water without sodium), 2 ounces of canned salmon (with bones), 2⅔ ounces of chicken breast, 4 ounces of lean ground beef, or 4 ounces of lean ground lamb for the sardines.
2. Substitute ⅓ cup of potato, cooked with the skin, or ⅓ cup of cooked macaroni for the rice.
3. Supply vitamins and minerals as follows: 1 bonemeal tablet (10-grain or equivalent) or ¼ teaspoon of bonemeal powder to supply calcium and phosphorus with a multivitamin/mineral supplement using the label instructions. Alternatively, use a natural product from Standard Process (1 Calcifood Wafer or 2 Calcium Lactate tablets for each 2 bonemeal tablets).
4. When possible, use natural vitamins made from raw whole foods, rather than synthetic vitamins (although both can be used in combination), as the natural vitamins also supply plant phytochemicals, enzymes, and other nutrients not found in chemically synthesized vitamins. Use either Catalyn from Standard Process (at a dose of 1 Catalyn per 10 pounds) or NuCat from VetriScience (following label dosages) as the natural vitamin in this recipe.
4. For nutrition and variety, use fresh, raw or slightly steamed vegetables, such as carrots or broccoli (approximately ½ to 1 cup per recipe), as a top dressing for the diet. (Many cats, however, will not eat vegetables.) Most vegetables provide approximately 25 kcal per ½ cup.
5. Add supplements that can be beneficial, such as omega-3 fatty acids, plant enzymes, and a super green food or health blend formula.

Note: If adding vegetables or other supplements, monitor urine pH when feeding the diet with these supplements and without the supplements to be sure the pH does not change from acid to alkaline.

Diets for cats with struvite stones should contain 20 to 40 mg/100 kcal of magnesium and 125 to 250 mg/100 kcal of phosphorus. These levels are higher than those recommended by the NRC for adult cats. Eliminating the oil and rice from this diet will further increase the magnesium and phosphorus.

Cranberry

The cranberry plant, a relative of the common blueberry plant, has been used as food and as a treatment of bladder diseases.

Research has shown that drinking cranberry juice makes the urine more acidic. Since common urinary tract infections in pets (especially dogs) are caused by bacteria such as E. coli, which function best in alkaline urine, many holistic doctors promote cranberry juice extracts for treating bladder infections. In addition, since the most common bladder stones in dogs and cats, and the sand-like gravel and microscopic crystals that are often encountered in cats with feline lower urinary tract disease (FLUTD, formerly called FUS) form in alkaline urine, acidifying the urine with supplements such as cranberry extracts may prove helpful.

However, contrary to early reseach in people, it now appears that acidification of the urine is not so important as cranberry's ability to block bacteria from adhering to the bladder wall. Preventing bacterial adhesion to the bladder wall prevents infection and allows the bacteria to be washed out with the urine.

Cranberry juice is believed to be most effective as a form of prevention. When taken regularly, it appears to reduce the frequency of recurrent bladder infections in women prone to develop them. Cranberry may also be helpful during a bladder infection but not as reliably. Similar findings are lacking in pets but may be applicable.

In people, the recommended dosage of dry cranberry juice extract is 300 to 400 mg twice daily, or 8 to 16 ounces of juice daily. Pure cranberry juice (not sugary cranberry juice cocktail with its low percentage of cranberry) should be used for best effect.

For pets, the recommended dosage varies with the product. One recommended product used in cats suggests a daily dose of 250 mg of cranberry extract. Cranberry juice is not recommended, as it is all but impossible to get most pets to drink enough of the juice to be effective.

There are no known risks of this food for adults, children, or pregnant or nursing women, nor are there any known risks in pets. However, cranberry juice may allow the kidneys to excrete certain drugs more rapidly, thereby reducing their effectiveness. All weakly alkaline drugs may be affected, including many antidepressants and prescription painkillers.

In dogs and cats, the push to acidify the urine through prescription-type diets has led to a slight increase in oxalate stones in the bladder, which are more common in acid urine. Pets taking cranberry extract would be more prone to develop crystals and stones such as oxalate stones, which are more common in acid urine. However, since the crystals and stones that form in alkaline urine are much more commonly diagnosed, pets with chronic stones (and cats with chronic

FLUTD) would probably benefit from acidification of the urine even with the slight risk of stones forming in acid urine. Discuss this with your veterinarian.

OTHER NATURAL TREATMENTS

Other therapies to consider for the pet with bladder disease include **Coenzyme Q10** (page 185), **omega-3 fatty acids** (page 246), **vitamin E** (page 302), **antioxidants** (page 158), as well as the herbs **alfalfa** to alkalinize the urine (page 156), **dandelion leaf** (page 193), **echinacea** (page 195), **goldenseal** (page 220), **horsetail** (page 225), **marshmallow** (page 240), **plantain** (page 256), **Oregon grape** (page 251), **uva ursi** (page 281), **yarrow** (page 308), and **maitake mushrooms** (page 238).

These therapies can be used in conjunction with conventional therapies as needed. The natural treatments are widely used with variable success but have not all been thoroughly investigated and proven at this time.

CONVENTIONAL THERAPY

Conventional therapies for pets with bladder infections require the use of antibiotics for 2 to 3 weeks, or longer for chronic infections. Recurring bladder infections often indicate an underlying problem, such as bladder stones or bladder cancer. In the absence of these other problems, pets with chronic bladder infections may require lifelong treatment with antibiotics and special diets to acidify the urine. Alternatively, urinary acidifiers can also be used for the treatment of chronic bladder infections. There is an increased incidence of oxalate stones in patients who maintain an acid urine as the result of using acidifiers (oxalate stones form in acid urine, whereas the more common struvite stones prefer alkaline urine).

BLADDER STONES

Principal Natural Treatments
Natural diet, no dry food (preferably no processed foods), cranberry extract

Other Natural Treatments
Coenzyme Q$_{10}$, omega-3 fatty acids, vitamin E, antioxidants, herbs: alfalfa to alkalinize the urine, dandelion leaf, echinacea, goldenseal, horsetail, marshmallow, plantain, Oregon grape, uva ursi, yarrow; maitake mushrooms

Bladder stones form as microscopic crystals precipitate in the bladder, in the form of one or more stones. Clinical signs of bladder stones are similar to those seen in dogs and cats with other disorders of the bladder and include increased frequency of urination, painful urination or a burning sensation during urination, excessive licking at the genitals, and occasionally blood in the urine. Increased thirst, increased volume of urine, and urinary incontinence are rarely associated with bladder stones and are more typical of kidney disease and diabetes. In dogs, stones are usually associated with infections, as the infection provides a locus for stone formation; in cats, stones are rarely seen with infections.

PRINCIPAL NATURAL TREATMENTS

Homemade diets are preferred for pets with chronic bladder disorders such as bladder stones. If processed foods must be fed, most holistic veterinarians prefer canned diets (which contain large amounts of water) rather than dry foods.

Several different types of stones can occur in the bladder and urinary system of cats and dogs. Generally, struvite stones (composed of the minerals magnesium, ammonium, and phosphate) are most commonly diagnosed. Clinical signs of bladder stones in cats and dogs include frequent urination (pollakiruia), straining to urinate (dysuria), and blood in the urine (hematuria). Radiographs (x rays) of the entire urinary system are taken to determine if stones are present in the kidneys, ureters, bladder (the most common location for urinary stones), or urethra. Not every type of stone is easily visualized on radiographs (struvite stones are easily visualized though), and often another test such as an abdominal ultrasound is needed to allow for a definitive diagnosis.

Dietary therapy is a useful adjunct (and possible preventive measure) for pets with struvite stones. Since the struvite stones most commonly form in alkaline urine (urine with a high pH) when the urine is saturated with magnesium, ammonium, or phosphate, diets should help maintain an acidic urine (low pH) as much as possible. Diets with animal-based protein sources are most important in maintaining an acidic pH (vegetarian or cereal-based diets are more likely to cause an alkaline urine).

In cats, struvite stones most commonly form in the absence of a bladder infection (unlike the situation in dogs, in which a bladder infection is usually the initiating factor in causing the formation of stones). Unless a secondary infection is present, large amounts of urinary bleeding is encountered, or surgery is performed for stone removal, antibiotic therapy is usually not needed in cats with struvite bladder stones.

In cats, crystals, stones, and the condition called feline lower urinary tract disease (FLUTD) most commonly form in cats (which are true carnivores adapted to eating meat-based diets) fed dry commercial foods (which are usually high in vegetable materials and grains). Most holistic veterinarians see a lower incidence of these urinary disorders in cats fed meat-based homemade diets.

Diets designed for cats with struvite bladder stones are designed to produce an acid urine (pH lasting 4 to 6 hours after feeding of 6.2 to 6.6 in cats fed free-choice), which allows for crystals and stones to be dissolved. While some commercial foods have decreased levels of magnesium and phosphorus, it has recently been shown that these minerals only contribute to stone formation if the urine is alkaline. If the urine can be maintained with an acidic pH, the dietary concentration of magnesium and phosphorus do not need to be lowered below recommended daily amounts. In fact, reducing the magnesium levels in cat food can cause increased excretion of calcium from the kidneys, leading to the formation of calcium oxalate stones in the bladder. In fact, the increased incidence of calcium oxalate stones in cats and dogs has coincided with an increased use of commercial "stone" diets containing reduced magnesium and phosphorus (often labeled under the term "ash"). Feeding recommended levels of phosphate to normal cats does not promote stone formation. Phosphate is needed to allow the urine to maintain an acid pH, which helps discourage crystal and stone formation. To increase urination (which reduces the amount of time crystals can form and remain in the bladder), extra salt (sodium chloride) can be added to the diet.

In dogs, struvite stones most commonly form as a result of a urinary tract infection. The infection serves as a nidus for stone formation in alkaline urine saturated with magnesium, ammonium, and phosphorus. The infection must be treated (usually with an extended course of antibiotics for at least 2 to 3 weeks) in order for crystals and stones to dissolve. Diets for dogs with struvite stones contain reduced amounts of high-quality proteins (to reduce urea in urine), and reduced levels of phosphorus and magnesium to reduce the concentration of these minerals in alkaline urine. Diets designed for dogs with struvite bladder stones contain near normal levels of minerals such as magnesium; reduced magnesium levels may increase the risk of formation of calcium oxalate stones. To increase urination (which reduces the amount of time crystals can form and remain in the bladder), extra salt (sodium chloride) can be added to the diet.

While urinary acidifiers can be useful, some doctors discourage their use, as the exact dosage that is safe and effective is often not known. If urinary acidifiers are used for short-term acidification, a natural therapy such as **cranberry** extract (page 38) might be preferred to conventional medications (such as methionine).

Diet for Dogs with Bladder Stones

Note: Before you start to feed your dog or cat a home-prepared diet, it is strongly recommended that you discuss your decision with your veterinarian or a holistic veterinarian in your area. It is essential that you follow any diet's recommendations closely, including all ingredients and supplements. Failure to do so may result in serious health consequences for your pet.

> ⅔ cup lowfat cottage cheese
> 1 large hard-boiled egg
> 2 cups long grain, cooked brown rice
> 2 teaspoons chicken fat or canola oil
> ½ ounce brewer's yeast
> ¼ teaspoon potassium chloride (salt substitute)

This diet provides 780 kcal (enough to fulfill the daily amount required for a 25-pound dog), 42.9 gm protein, 22 gm fat, 92 mg sodium/100 kcal (a high-sodium diet).

Variations

1. Substitute 4 ounces of tuna (in water without sodium) or ¼ pound of lean ground beef (or ground chicken or lamb) for cottage cheese.
2. Substitute 2 to 3 cups of potato, cooked with the skin, or 2 cups of cooked macaroni for the rice.
3. Supply vitamins and minerals as follows: 4 bonemeal tablets (10-grain or equivalent) or 1 teaspoon of bonemeal powder to supply calcium and phosphorus with a multivitamin/mineral supplement using the label instructions. Alternatively, use a natural product from Standard Process (1 Calcifood Wafer or 2 Calcium Lactate tablets for each 2 bonemeal tablets).

   When possible, use natural vitamins made from raw whole foods, rather than synthetic vitamins (although both can be used in combination), as the natural vitamins also supply plant phytochemicals, enzymes, and other nutrients not found in chemically synthesized vitamins. Use either Catalyn from Standard Process (at a dose of 1 Catalyn per 25 pounds) or Canine Plus from VetriScience (following label dosages) as the natural vitamin in this recipe.
4. For extra nutrition and variety, use fresh, raw or slightly steamed vegetables, such as carrots or broccoli (approximately ½ to 1 cup per recipe), as a top dressing for the diet. Most vegetables provide approximately 25 kcal per ½ cup.

5. Add supplements that can be beneficial, such as omega-3 fatty acids, plant enzymes, and a super green food or health blend formula.

Note: If adding vegetables or other supplements, monitor urine pH when feeding the diet with these supplements and without the supplements to be sure the pH does not change from acid to alkaline. Some dogs have a difficult time producing acid urine even when fed the previous diet or when administered urinary acidifiers.

Diet for Cats with Bladder Stones

> *3½ ounces firm raw tofu*
> *2¼ ounces sardines, canned in tomato sauce*
> *½ ounce clams, chopped in juice*
> *½ yolk of large hard-boiled egg*
> *⅓ cup long grain, cooked brown rice*
> *2 teaspoons chicken fat or canola oil*
> *½ ounce brewer's yeast*

This diet provides 501 kcal (enough to fulfill the daily amount required for a 16-pound cat), 37.4 gm protein, 29.6 gm fat, 62.2 mg sodium/100 kcal (a high-sodium diet).

Variations

1. Substitute 2 ounces of tuna (in water without sodium), 2 ounces of canned salmon (with bones), 2⅔ ounces of chicken breast, 4 ounces of lean ground beef, or 4 ounces of lean ground lamb for the sardines.
2. Substitute ⅓ cup of potato, cooked with the skin, or ⅓ cup of cooked macaroni for the rice.
3. Supply vitamins and minerals as follows: 1 bonemeal tablet (10-grain or equivalent) or ¼ teaspoon of bonemeal powder to supply calcium and phosphorus with a multivitamin/mineral supplement according to the label instructions. Alternatively, use a natural product from Standard Process (either 1 Calcifood Wafer or 2 Calcium Lactate tablets for each 2 bonemeal tablets).

When possible, use natural vitamins made from raw whole foods, rather than synthetic vitamins (although both can be used in combination), as the natural vitamins also supply plant phytochemicals, enzymes, and other nutrients not found in chemically synthesized vitamins. Use either Catalyn from Standard Process (at a dose of 1 Catalyn per 10 pounds) or NuCat from VetriScience (following label dosages) as the natural vitamin in this recipe.

4. For extra nutrition and variety, use fresh, raw or slightly steamed vegetables, such as carrots or broccoli (approximately ½ to 1 cup per recipe) as a top dressing for the diet. Many cats, however, will not eat vegetables. Most vegetables provide approximately 25 kcal per ½ cup.
5. Add supplements that can be beneficial, such as omega-3 fatty acids, plant enzymes, and a super green food or health blend formula.

Note: If adding vegetables or other supplements, monitor urine pH when feeding the diet with these supplements and without the supplements to be sure the pH does not change from acid to alkaline.

Diets for cats with struvite stones should contain 20 to 40 mg/100 kcal of magnesium and 125 to 250 mg/100 kcal of phosphorus. These levels are higher than those recommended by the NRC for adult cats. Eliminating the oil and rice from this diet will further increase the magnesium and phosphorus.

Cranberry

The cranberry plant, a relative of the common blueberry plant, has been used as food and as a treatment of bladder diseases.

Research has shown that drinking cranberry juice makes the urine more acidic. Since common urinary tract infections in pets (especially dogs) are caused by bacteria such as E. coli, which function best in alkaline urine, many holistic doctors promote cranberry juice extracts for treating bladder infections. Additionally, since the most common bladder stones in dogs and cats, and the sand-like gravel and microscopic crystals that are often encountered in cats with feline lower urinary tract disease (FLUTD, formerly called FUS) form in alkaline urine, acidifying the urine with supplements such as cranberry extracts may prove helpful.

However, contrary to early reseach in people, it now appears that acidification of the urine is not so important as cranberry's ability to block bacteria from adhering to the bladder wall. Preventing bacterial adhesion to the bladder wall prevents infection and allows the bacteria to be washed out with the urine.

Cranberry juice is believed to be most effective as a form of prevention. When taken regularly, it appears to reduce the frequency of recurrent bladder infections in women prone to develop them. Cranberry may also be helpful during a bladder infection but not as reliably. Similar findings are lacking in pets but may be applicable.

In people, the recommended dosage of dry cranberry juice extract is 300 to 400 mg twice daily, or 8 to 16 ounces of juice daily. Pure cranberry juice (not sugary cranberry juice cocktail with its low percentage of cranberry) should be used for best effect.

For pets, the recommended dosage varies with the product. One recommended product used in cats suggests a daily dose of 250 mg of cranberry extract. Cranberry juice is not recommended, as it is all but impossible to get most pets to drink enough of the juice to be effective.

There are no known risks of this food for adults, children, or pregnant or nursing women, nor are there any known risks in pets. However, cranberry juice may allow the kidneys to excrete certain drugs more rapidly, thereby reducing their effectiveness. All weakly alkaline drugs may be affected, including many antidepressants and prescription painkillers.

In dogs and cats, the push to acidify the urine through prescription-type diets has led to a slight increase in oxalate stones in the bladder, which are more common in acid urine. Pets taking cranberry extract would be more prone to develop crystals and stones such as oxalate stones which are more common in acid urine. However, since the crystals and stones that form in alkaline urine are much more commonly diagnosed, pets with chronic stones (and cats with chronic FLUTD) would probably benefit from acidification of the urine even with the slight risk of stones forming in acid urine. Discuss this with your veterinarian.

OTHER NATURAL TREATMENTS

Other therapies to consider for the pet with bladder stones include **Coenzyme Q10** (page 185), **omega-3 fatty acids** (page 246), **vitamin E** (page 302), **antioxidants** (page 158), as well as the herbs **alfalfa** to alkalinize the urine (page 156), **dandelion leaf** (page 193), **echinacea** (page 195), **goldenseal** (page 220), **horsetail** (page 225), **marshmallow** (page 240), **plantain** (page 256), **Oregon grape** (page 251), **uva ursi** (page 281), **yarrow** (page 308), and **maitake** mushrooms (page 238).

These therapies can be used in conjunction with conventional therapies as needed. The natural treatments are widely used with variable success but have not all been thoroughly investigated and proven at this time.

CONVENTIONAL THERAPY

Conventional therapies for pets with bladder stones requires the use of antibiotics to eliminate any underlying infections (see page 105). Surgery is usually necessary and recommended for removal of bladder stones. Alternatively, several diets are available through veterinarians marketed as "stone-dissolving" diets. These diets typically contain reduced ash (mineral) content and high amounts of urinary acidifiers. They are only effective against struvite (magnesium ammonium phosphate) stones, which are the most common stone seen in pets with bladder stones. Their advantage is that if the pet has struvite stones and if the diet works, surgery is avoided. The diets typically take 4 to 6 months to dissolve the stones.

The disadvantages to "stone-dissolving" diets include:

- *Cost.* Due to repeated veterinary visits and radiographic procedures, using diet is usually no less expensive than surgical removal of the stones.
- *Limited efficacy.* The diets only dissolve struvite stones, and there is no way to definitively diagnose the type of stone without removing it then performing a crystal analysis on the stone. If the diets do not dissolve the stone, surgery is still indicated.
- *Less than natural ingredients.* These processed diets may contain chemicals, by-products, and fillers.

Cancer

Urinary acidifiers can also be used for the prevention of some types of stones. Long-term control with urinary acidifiers is often recommended, although no long-term, controlled studies have been done that support decreased infections and stones from this approach. While probably not harmful (especially if natural acidifiers such as cranberry extract are used), there is an increased incidence of oxalate stones in patients who maintain an acid urine as the result of using acidifiers (oxalate stones form in acid urine, whereas the more common struvite stones prefer alkaline urine).

 CANCER

Principal Natural Treatments
Natural diet, omega-3 fatty acids, glycoproteins, antioxidants

Other Natural Treatments
Coenzyme Q_{10}, proanthocyanidins, DMG, soy isoflavones, larch, immunostimulant herbs: alfalfa, aloe vera (Acemannan), astragalus, burdock, dandelion leaf, dandelion root, echinacea, garlic, ginseng, goldenseal, hawthorn, licorice, marshmallow, milk thistle, nettle, red clover, St. John's wort, turmeric, yellow dock; immunostimulant mushrooms: maitake, reishi, cordyceps

Cancer is among the most feared diseases by pet owners. For many owners, the diagnosis brings grief, uncertainty, fear, and a general feeling of hopelessness.

While it is true that cancers can result in the untimely death of our pets, not all cancers carry a poor prognosis. For example, many solid tumors, if diagnosed early, respond quite well to surgical removal before they have spread. In these instances, early surgery is curative.

Other cancers may not be diagnosed until they have already spread. In these instances, treatment may not cure the pet but instead will provide a comfortable, extended life for the pet. In this latter case, the goal is to prolong life, but also ensure the pet is comfortable and has a good quality of life in whatever time remains. For most pets, the diagnosis of cancer is not an immediate death sentence, but rather the chance to begin therapy. Few cancers truly spread quickly. By keeping up with regular veterinary examinations and laboratory tests, early diagnosis of cancer is possible in most dogs and cats.

What Causes Cancer?

A common question among pet owners is "What causes cancer?" There are actually several recognized causes of cancers in pets.

Viruses. In cats, the feline leukemia virus, feline sarcoma virus, and feline immunodeficiency virus directly or indirectly (through suppression of the immune system) cause cancer.

Toxins. In dogs, exposure to certain chemicals including 2,4-D can cause cancer. Various food additives have also demonstrated carcinogenic activity in laboratory animals, prompting many owners to prepare food at home or select diets that do not contain these synthetic additives and preservatives.

Vaccinations. Doctors are now beginning to realize that in a very small percentage of cats, frequent immunizations may cause certain solid tumors to develop. This is a very controversial topic, and the exact reason why a very rare number of cats who receive vaccinations (or other injectable medications) develop cancer is not known. Current evidence suggests that in genetically susceptible pets, some component of the vaccine (or of any injection) may cause a local reaction that becomes cancer. See the section on **Vaccinosis** (page 147) for more information on what is now called "injection site sarcoma."

Genetics. Some pets are genetically prone to cancers. For example, among dogs, the Boxer is well-known to develop cancers at a much higher rate than many other breeds. Large breed dogs such as Retrievers have a higher incidence of malignant tumors of the spleen and liver. These examples may be a result of the inheritability of certain types of cancers, similar to the situation that occurs with some types of cancers in people (retinoblastoma) that occur as a result of genetic defects.

Aging. Most cancers occur in older pets. The exact reason is not known, but it seems that these older pets may have decreased functioning of the immune system.

Normally, as cells divide, mutations arise. In most pets, these abnormal, mutated cells are killed by their immune systems. Cancers arise when the immune system fails to kill these mutated cells. This seems to occur at a higher frequency in older pets.

On a cellular level, here is how cancer forms and spreads:

It is known that malignant cellular transformation is associated with a series of genetic changes occurring within the cell. Cells contain proto-oncogenes, normal sequences of DNA which regulate cellular responses to external signals that stimulate cell growth and reproduction. Proto-oncogenes are called simply oncogenes if their level of expression is altered so that the cell gains the potential for malignant transformation. Oncogenes may be activated in an aberrant manner in several ways, including:

- Point mutations can occur as a result of cell damage, altering the behavior of normal genes.
- Amplification of oncogenes can occur, altering the processing of cellular signals.
- Tumor suppressor genes, normally acting to restrict cell proliferation, can be diminished, allowing the formation and spread of cancer.

Once these cellular defects occur, mutated (cancerous) cells can reproduce and spread, causing what is called "cancer."

PRINCIPAL NATURAL TREATMENTS

The main natural treatments are designed to boost the immune system and reduce the spread of cancer.

These can be used in conjunction with conventional therapies as they are unlikely to be effective by themselves in most patients. The natural treatments are widely used with variable success but have not been thoroughly investigated and proven at this time.

Natural Diet

While there are no controlled studies showing the value of diet in supporting the pet with every type of cancer, there are studies showing the benefits of dietary therapy when combined with conventional therapies in dogs with lymphoma and nasal tumors. Since this diet is designed to reduce the growth and spread of cancer, it is often recommended for dogs and cats with any type of cancerous disease.

Studies demonstrate that both people and pets with inadequate nutrition cannot metabolize chemotherapy drugs adequately, which predisposes them to toxicity and poor therapeutic response. This makes proper diet and nutritional supplementation an important part of cancer therapy.

There are several metabolic derangements common in the cancer patient. First, cancer patients often have hyperlactatemia (increased lactic acid in the blood). Additionally, since metabolism of simple carbohydrates produces lactate, a diet with a minimum of these carbohydrates might be preferred.

Research has shown a pronounced decrease in certain amino acids such as arginine in the plasma of cancer patients. If left uncorrected, these amino acid deficiencies could result in serious health risks to the patient. Supplementation with the deficient amino acids might improve immune function and positively affect treatment and survival rates.

Weight loss often occurs in cancer patients as a result of cachexia (wasting). Most of the weight loss seen in cancer patients experiencing cancer cachexia occurs as a result of depleted body fat stores. Tumor cells, unlike normal healthy cells, have difficulty utilizing lipids for energy. Dogs with lymphoma fed diets high in fat had longer remission periods than dogs fed high carbohydrate diets.

While there are often many treatment options for the various malignancies experienced by our patients, we often overlook the simple aspect of nutrition. In the next decade, prevention and treatment will most likely include a focus on nutrition in veterinary medicine, just as our counterparts are now doing in the human medical field. The research is out there: There is no doubt that cancer patients have deranged nutrient metabolism that can negatively affect the outcome of conventional therapies. Additions of omega-3 fatty acids and antioxidant vitamins and minerals to the diet of cancer patients may help improve survival and possibly decrease the chances of pets contracting cancer in those who are currently cancer-free.

The n/d Diet

Recently, Hill's Pet Food Company introduced the first cancer diet for dogs called n/d. The diet contains increased protein and fat, decreased carbohydrates, increased omega-3 fatty acids, and increased arginine (the reasons for this formulation are discussed later). The composition of the diet is: protein, 37%; fat, 32%; carbohydrates, 21%; arginine, 3.1% (647 mg/100 kcal); omega-3 fatty acids from fish oil, 7.3% (1,518 mg/100 kcal). In controlled studies dogs with lymphoma (lymphosarcoma) that were being treated with chemotherapy and being fed n/d had increased survival times when compared with dogs being treated with the same chemotherapy medications and eating a controlled diet. Similar findings were found for dogs with nasal and oral cancer that were treated with radiation therapy and eating n/d. The conclusions from this study showed that: survival time increased 56%; quality of life improved due to decreased pain from dogs treated with radiation; remission periods were longer; and metabolic changes seen in pets with cancer were reversed.

While these findings are quite impressive, there is no evidence that this diet helps dogs or cats with other forms of cancer. Despite this need for additional research, it is likely that any pet with any type of cancer could benefit from this or similar diets (see below for further discussion.)

There are three potential problems with diet n/d:

1. It is an expensive diet, especially for owners of large breed dogs.

2. It is only available in a canned variety, most likely due to the high fat content.
3. The protein source is an animal by-product, beef lung. (Owners who desire the most holistic and natural diet possible might object to this protein source.)

A homemade diet that approximates n/d can be attempted. However, due to the high level of omega-3 fatty acids in the food it is difficult (if not impossible) and expensive to prepare a similar diet at home.

Tofu (soy protein) protects the intestinal tract from damage that could occur with certain chemotherapy drugs and result in diarrhea. While not proven, tofu diets might be preferred for pets with cancer, especially those whose treatment regimen includes chemotherapy.

The homemade anticancer diet for dogs should have the following nutrient levels: protein, 35 to 40%; fat, 30%; carbohydrates, 20%. Cats can have higher protein and fat levels and minimal or no carbohydrates (cats do not have a strict dietary carbohydrate requirement).

Antioxidants can be added to the diet. However, high doses of antioxidants might interfere with any chemotherapy medications, such as doxorubicin (Adriamycin), that work to kill cancer cells by oxidation. Several studies indicate that high levels of antioxidants may help cancer cells grow and spread. For example, a recent study showed that cancer cells contain high levels of vitamin C, probably serving as an antioxidant to protect the cancer cell from oxidation. Because of the possibility of high levels of antioxidants interfering with treatment or cure, you should discuss this topic with your pet's oncologist (cancer specialist) prior to using increased levels of antioxidants.

Arginine decreases tumor growth and spread (metastasis); supplemental arginine is useful for pets with cancer. Glutamine may retard the cachexia (wasting) seen in many pets with cancer and may help protect against intestinal injury. However, some experimental studies have shown no benefit and occasionally increased vomiting or diarrhea in pets supplemented with glutamine. At this time, there is no clear-cut evidence for or against glutamine supplementation. The need for glutamine will vary from case to case.

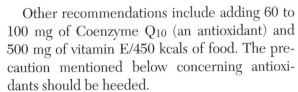

Other recommendations include adding 60 to 100 mg of Coenzyme Q$_{10}$ (an antioxidant) and 500 mg of vitamin E/450 kcals of food. The precaution mentioned below concerning antioxidants should be heeded.

Finally, many holistic veterinarians will add fresh vegetables (especially those high in indoles and antioxidants), such as broccoli, kale, cabbage, and fresh garlic. Other supplements (see below) can be used as needed. Your veterinarian can decide which additional supplements might be helpful after consultation with you and a thorough examination of your pet.

Diet for Dogs with Cancer

Note: Before you start to feed your dog or cat a home-prepared diet, it is strongly recommended that you discuss your decision with your veterinarian or a holistic veterinarian in your area. It is essential that you follow any diet's recommendations closely, including all ingredients and supplements. Failure to do so may result in serious health consequences for your pet.

> ½ cup raw tofu
> 1 cup boiled lentils
> 2 cups of potatoes boiled with skin
> 2 teaspoons chicken fat or canola oil
> ¹⁄₁₀ teaspoon salt
> Multivitamin/mineral supplement

This diet provides 775 kcal and supports the daily needs of a 25-pound dog. It also provides 43.9 gm of protein and 22 gm of fat. Adding 2 tablespoons canned sardines increases the protein content by 6.2 gm and the fat content by 4.6 gm.

Variations

1. Add arginine at 647 mg/100 kcal of food.
2. Add omega-3 fatty acids (fish oil) at 1,518 mg/100 kcal. This is very difficult to do, as the average omega-3 fatty acid capsule contains 180 mg. Work with your doctor to increase the fatty acid content as much as possible (adding fish such as salmon to the diet can help achieve this goal.)
3. Occasionally substitute ⅓ pound of cooked chicken, turkey, or lowfat beef for the tofu (in which case the lentils can be eliminated).

4. Occasionally substitute 2 cups of rice or macaroni for the potatoes.
5. Add fresh, raw or steamed vegetables to increase the level of natural vitamins and minerals, as well as add flavor. Most vegetables provide approximately 25 kcal per ½ cup.
6. Add 4 bonemeal tablets (10-grain or equivalent) or 1 teaspoon of bonemeal powder to supply calcium and phosphorus with a multivitamin/mineral supplement. Follow the label instructions. Alternatively, use a natural product from Standard Process (1 Calcifood Wafer or 2 Calcium Lactate tablets) for each 2 bonemeal tablets.
7. When possible, use natural vitamins made from raw whole foods, rather than synthetic vitamins (although both can be used in combination), as the natural vitamins also supply plant phytochemicals, enzymes, and other nutrients not found in chemically synthesized vitamins. Use either Catalyn from Standard Process (at a dose of 1 Catalyn per 25 pounds) or Canine Plus from VetriScience (following label dosages) as the natural vitamin in this recipe.

Diet for Cats with Cancer

> ½ pound chicken
> ½ large hard-boiled egg
> ½ ounce clams, chopped in juice
> 4 teaspoon chicken fat or canola oil
> ⅛ teaspoon potassium chloride
> 100 mg taurine
> Multivitamin/mineral supplement

This diet provides 471 kcal, 53.1 gm of protein, and 27.4 gm of fat and provides the daily needs for a 15-pound cat.

Variations

1. Add arginine at 647 mg/100 kcal of food. This is a recommendation for dogs and has not been proven in cats.
2. Add omega-3 fatty acids (fish oil) at 1,518 mg/100 kcal. This is very difficult to do, as the average omega-3 fatty acid capsule contains 180 mg. Work with your doctor to increase the fatty acid content as much as possible (adding fish such as salmon to the diet can help achieve this goal). This is a recommendation for dogs and has not been proven in cats.

3. Occasionally add ⅓ cup of rice, macaroni, or potatoes. However, cats do not have a proven need for dietary carbohydrates, and adding additional carbohydrates supplies substrate (food) for cancer cells.

4. Add fresh, raw or steamed vegetables to increase the level of natural vitamins and minerals, as well as add flavor. Most vegetables provide approximately 25 kcal per ½ cup. Many cats, however, will not eat vegetables.

5. Add 3 bonemeal tablets (10-grain or equivalent) or ¾ teaspoon of bonemeal powder to supply calcium and phosphorus with a multivitamin/mineral supplement, following the label instructions. Alternatively, use a natural product from Standard Process (1 Calcifood Wafer or 2 Calcium Lactate tablets for each 2 bonemeal tablets) as the natural vitamin in this recipe.

6. When possible, use natural vitamins made from raw whole foods, rather than synthetic vitamins (although both can be used in combination), as the natural vitamins also supply plant phytochemicals, enzymes, and other nutrients not found in chemically synthesized vitamins. Use either Catalyn from Standard Process (at a dose of 1 Catalyn per 10 pounds) or NuCat from VetriScience (following label dosages) as the natural vitamin in this recipe.

Omega-3 Fatty Acids

Omega-3 fatty acids—eicosapentaenoic acid (EPA) and docosahexaenoic acid (DHA)—are derived from fish oils of coldwater fish (salmon, trout, or most commonly menhaden fish) and flaxseed. Omega-6 fatty acids—linoleic acid (LA) and gamma-linolenic acid (GLA)—are derived from the oils of seeds such as evening primrose, black currant, and borage. Often, fatty acids are added to the diet with other supplements to attain an additive effect.

In transplanted tumor models, omega-3 fatty acids reduced tumor development while omega-6 fatty acids stimulated tumor development. Omega-3 fatty acids have been shown to inhibit tumor growth as well as the spread of cancer (metastasis.) Reduced radiation damage in the skin was also seen following supplementation with omega-3 fatty acids.

The use of omega-3 fatty acids can promote weight gain and may have anticancer effects, and so warrants special mention. In people, the use of omega-3 fatty acids, such as those found in fish oils, improves the immune status, metabolic status, and clinical outcomes of cancer patients. These supplements also decrease the duration of hospitalization and complication rates in people with gastrointestinal cancer. In animal models, the omega-3 fatty acids inhibit the formation of tumors and metastasis (spread of the cancer). Finally, omega-3 fatty acid supplementation shows anticachetic (anti-wasting) effects.

Note: Flaxseed oil is a popular source of alpha-linoleic acid (ALA), an omega-3 fatty acid that is ultimately converted to EPA and DHA. However, many species of pets (probably including dogs) and some people cannot convert ALA to these other more active non-inflammatory omega-3 fatty acids. Also, flaxseed oil contains omega-6 fatty acids which are not recommended in pets with cancer. In one study in people, flaxseed oil was ineffective in reducing symptoms or raising levels of EPA and DHA. While flaxseed oil has been suggested as a less smelly substitute for fish oil, there is no evidence that it is effective when used for the same therapeutic purposes as fish oil. Therefore, supplementation with EPA and DHA is important, and this is the reason flaxseed oil is not recommended as the sole fatty acid supplement for pets. Flaxseed oil can be used to provide ALA and as a coat conditioner.

While many doctors use fatty acids for a variety of medical problems, there is considerable debate about the use of fatty acids. The debate concerns several areas:

Dosage

What is the "best" dose to use in the treatment of pets? Most doctors use anywhere from 2 to 10 times the label dose. The recommended dosage for pets with cancer is approximately 1,500 mg/100 kilocalories of food (the amount added to Prescription Diet n/d, discussed on page 49). In order to get this dose, depending upon the product selected, you would need to feed your dog about 5 capsules per 100 kcal of diet. This is a lot of fatty acid capsules!

Is supplementation with fatty acid capsules or liquids the best approach, or is dietary manipulation preferred for the treatment of cancer? There is one diet, Prescription Diet n/d, made for dogs with cancer. This diet contains the "proper" amount of omega-3 fatty acids, and it is impossible to add enough fatty acids in the form of supplements to equal the amount found in n/d. However, the protein source for the diet, beef lung, is not the most wholesome protein source, which is a concern for holistic pet owners. Many owners use some of the n/d with a homemade diet plus additional fatty acids to achieve a compromise.

Studies done in dogs with lymphoma and nasal tumors have shown that dogs eating the n/d showed increased disease-free intervals and survival times when compared with similarly treated dogs not eating this diet. While research has not been reported in dogs with other cancers or in cats with cancers, it is recommended to use fatty acid supplementation in pets with any kind of cancer due to the potential benefit. More research will be needed to give us good information in this area.

Fish Oils   Since fish oils can easily oxidize and become rancid, some manufacturers add vitamin E to fish oil capsules and liquid products to keep the oil from spoiling (others remove oxygen from the capsule).

The bottom line is that there are many questions regarding the use of fatty acid therapy. More research is needed to determine the effectiveness of the fatty acids in the treatment of various cancers, as well as the proper doses needed to achieve clinical results. Until definitive answers are obtained, you will need to work with your doctors (knowing the limitations of our current research) to determine the use of these supplements for your pet.

Fish oil appears to be safe. The most common side effect seen in people and pets is a fish odor to the breath or the skin.

Because fish oil has a mild "blood-thinning" effect, it should not be combined with powerful blood-thinning medications, such as Coumadin (warfarin) or heparin, except on a veterinarian's advice. Fish oil does not seem to cause bleeding problems when it is taken by itself at commonly recommended dosages. Also, fish oil does not appear to raise blood sugar levels in people or pets with diabetes.

Flaxseed Oil   Flaxseed oil is derived from the seeds of the flax plant and has been proposed as a less smelly alternative to fish oil. Flaxseed oil contains alpha-linolenic acid (ALA), an omega-3 fatty acid that is ultimately converted to EPA and DHA. In fact, flaxseed oil contains higher levels of omega-3 fatty acids (ALA) than fish oil. It also contains omega-6 fatty acids.

As mentioned, many species of pets (probably including dogs and cats) and some people cannot convert ALA to these other more active non-inflammatory omega-3 fatty acids. In one study in people, flaxseed oil was ineffective in reducing symptoms or raising levels of EPA and DHA. While flaxseed oil has been suggested as a substitute for fish oil, there is no evidence that it is effective when used for the same therapeutic purposes as fish oil. Unlike the case for fish oil, there is little evidence that flaxseed oil is effective for any specific therapeutic purpose.

Therefore, supplementation with EPA and DHA is important, and this is the reason flaxseed oil is not recommended as the sole fatty acid supplement for pets. Flaxseed oil can be used to provide ALA and as a coat conditioner.

Flaxseed oil also contains lignans, which are currently being studied for use in preventing cancer in people. To date, we have no information to recommend their use in pets with cancer.

The essential fatty acids in flax can be damaged by exposure to heat, light, and oxygen (essentially, they become rancid). For this reason, you shouldn't cook with flaxseed oil. A good product should be sold in an opaque container, and the manufacturing process should keep the temperature under 100° F (some products are prepared by cold extraction methods.) Some manufacturers combine the product with vitamin E because it helps prevent rancidity.

The best use of flaxseed oil is as a general nutritional supplement to provide essential fatty acids.

Flaxseed oil appears to be a safe nutritional supplement when used as recommended.

Glycoproteins

Glycoproteins are protein molecules bound to carbohydrate molecules. Glycoprotein molecules coat the surface of every cell with a nucleus in the human body. The body uses the glycoproteins on cell surface glycoconjugates as communication or recognition molecules. These communications may then result in other cellular events, including secretion of bioactive substances (interferon, interleukin-1, complement), ingestion of bacteria and cell debris, inhibition of adherence necessary for bacterial infection, and the spread of cancer cell metastasis.

Scientists have identified eight sugars, glycoforms, found on human cell surfaces that are involved in cellular recognition processes. Of the 200 such sugars occurring naturally in plants, to date only these eight have been identified as components of cellular glycoproteins. These eight sugars that are essential for glycoconjugate synthesis (mannose, galactose, fucose, xylose, glucose, sialic acid, N-acetylglucosamine, N-acetylgalactosamine) can be readily absorbed and directly incorporated into glycoproteins and glycolipids.

Recent research has found specific cell surface glycoforms to be characteristic of many disease conditions. In some people with rheumatoid arthritis, some of these patients' defense cells (IgG antibody) bear malformed glycoproteins. These cells are missing required galactose molecules; the extent to which the galactose molecules are missing correlates with disease severity and reverses in disease remission. In people with cancer, more than 20 different malignancies are known to be associated with characteristic glycoproteins.

Glyconutritional supplements are designed to provide substrates for the body to use in building part of the glycoconjugates on cell surfaces. These supplements, most commonly acemannan and mannose, are designed to make the necessary sugars available to the cells quicker and in greater quantity.

Acemannan is a glycoprotein (a long chain of mannan polymers with random o-acetyl groups) derived from the aloe vera plant that has been shown to increase the body's production of immune-modulating chemicals, including interleukins 1 and 6, interferon-gamma, and Prostaglandin E_2 and tumor necrosis factor alpha by macrophages. Acemannan also enhances macrophage phagocytosis and nonspecific cytotoxicity, which increases the ability of white blood cells (macrophages) to destroy infectious organisms. Glycoproteins such as acemannan also offer antiviral activity as well as bone marrow stimulating activity.

Scientific Evidence

Acemannan has been approved as an adjunct therapy for solid tumors called fibrosarcomas. Intralesional injection into the tumor (2 mg weekly for up to 6 weeks), combined with intraperitoneal injections (1 mg/kg of body weight given weekly for 6 weeks, followed by monthly injections for one year), has been shown to be effective in shrinking tumors (via necrosis and inflammation).

All eight of the glycoconjugate sugars are readily absorbed from the intestines when taken orally. Studies have shown intact mannose molecules are rapidly absorbed from the intestine of rats into the blood, elevate the blood mannose levels by 3- to 10-fold, and is cleared from the blood within hours. The conclusion reached was that mannose was absorbed from the intestinal tract into the blood and from the blood into the cells. These studies suggest that dietary mannose may make a significant contribution to glycoform synthesis in mammals.

Other human and animal ingestion studies show that mannose is readily absorbed, and is cleared from the blood over several hours; some of the mannose was incorporated into glycoproteins. After absorption into the blood, glycoconjugate sugars generally become distributed (usually as glycoproteins and glycolipids) into body fluids, organs, and various body tissues.

In one study, healthy humans were given radiolabeled galactose, mannose, or glucose. This study showed that galactose and mannose were directly incorporated into human glycoproteins without first being broken down into glucose. The conclusion was that specific dietary sugars could represent a new class of nutrients and that the use of these nutrients could have important consequences. Therapy with mannose offers a treatment that is easy to administer and is nontoxic.

Most of the essential glycoconjugate sugars have demonstrated an ability to inhibit cancer growth and the spread of tumor cells both in vitro and in vivo (in experiments in pets and people). The ability of the glycoproteins to inhibit tumor growth may be related to their ability to alter the activities of the immune system. Glycoconjugate sugars stimulate white blood cells (macrophages), which secrete interferons. The interferons activate natural killer cells that help eliminate cancer cells. The glycoproteins may inhibit the spread of tumor cells by preventing them from adhering to each other as a result of competitive inhibition of glycoconjugate receptor binding.

Adverse effects caused by glycoconjugate sugars are rare and usually occur when they are injected or when doses greatly exceed levels that would be expected in normal diets. For pets being treated with the most commonly used glycoproteins (acemannan and mannose), side effects would not be expected. (Popular glycoprotein supplements used in pets are manufactured by Carrington Laboratories and Mannatech Laboratories.)

Antioxidants

Certain vitamins and minerals function in the body to reduce oxidation. Oxidation is a chemical process that occurs within the body's cells. After oxidation occurs, certain by-products such as peroxides and "free radicals" accumulate. These cellular by-products are toxic to the cells and surrounding tissue. The body removes these by-products by producing additional chemicals called antioxidants that combat these oxidizing chemicals.

In disease, excess oxidation can occur and the body's normal antioxidant abilities are overwhelmed. This is where supplying antioxidants can help. By giving your pet's body extra antioxidants, you may find it possible to neutralize the harmful by-products of cellular oxidation.

Several antioxidants can be used to supplement pets. Most commonly, the antioxidant **vitamins A** (page 284), **C** (page 297), and **E** (page 302), and the minerals **selenium** (page 268), **manganese** (page 239), and **zinc** (page 310) are prescribed. Other antioxidants, including **N-acetylcysteine** (page 243), **Coenzyme Q10**

(page 185), *Ginkgo biloba* (page 208), **bilberry** (page 164), **grape seed extract** (page 159), and **pycnogenol** (page 159) may also be helpful for a number of disorders. There is no "correct" antioxidant to use. Dosage varies with the specific antioxidant chosen.

Following is a brief discussion of a commonly used group of antioxidants called bioflavonoids/proanthocyanidins.

Proanthocyanidins are naturally occurring polyphenolic compounds found in plants; most often products containing proanthocyanidins are made from grape seed or pine bark. Proanthocyanidins are also called pycnogenols or bioflavonoids, a class of water-soluble plant coloring agents. While they don't seem to be essential to life, it's likely that people and pets need them for optimal health. These compounds are used for their antioxidant effects against lipid (fat) peroxidation. Proanthocyanidins also inhibit the enzyme cyclooxygenase (the same enzyme inhibited by aspirin and other nonsteroidal medications); cyclooxygenase converts arachidonic acid into chemicals (leukotrienes and prostaglandins), which contribute to inflammation and allergic reactions. Proanthocyanidins also decrease histamine release from cells by inhibiting several enzymes.

Proanthocyanidins, by potentiating the immune system (via enhancement of T-lymphocyte activity and modulation of neutrophil and macrophage responses), are often recommended for use in the treatment of pets with cancer.

Some research suggests that pycnogenol seems to work by enhancing the effects of another antioxidant, vitamin C. Other research suggests that the bioflavonoids can work independently of other antioxidants; as is the case with many supplements, there probably is an additive effect when multiple antioxidants are combined. People taking pycnogenol often report feeling better and having more energy; this "side effect" may possibly occur in our pets as well.

Quercetin is a natural antioxidant bioflavonoid found in red wine, grapefruit, onions, apples, black tea, and, in lesser amounts, in leafy green vegetables and beans. Quercetin protects cells in the body from damage by free radicals and stabilizes collagen in blood vessels. Test-tube and animal research also suggests that quercetin might be able to help prevent tumors in hamsters or enhance the effects of cancer-fighting drugs.

Quercetin supplements are available in pill and tablet form. One problem with them, however, is that they don't seem to be well absorbed by the body. A special form called quercetin chalcone appears to be better absorbed.

Quercetin appears to be quite safe. Maximum safe dosages for young children, women who are pregnant or nursing, or those with serious liver or kidney disease have not been established; similar precautions are probably warranted in pets.

In people, a typical dosage of proanthocyanidins is 200 to 400 mg 3 times daily. Quercetin may be better absorbed if taken on an empty stomach. The suggested dosage of proanthocyanidin complex in pets is 10 to 200 mg given daily (divided into 2 to 3 doses.) The suggested dosage of bioflavonoid complex in pets is 200 to 1,500 mg per day (divided into 2 to 3 doses). The actual dosage of each product will vary with the product and the pet's weight and disease condition.

Because some types of chemotherapy and radiation therapy may rely on cellular oxidation for their effects, antioxidants should not be used without veterinary supervision in pets with cancer undergoing chemotherapy or radiation therapy.

OTHER NATURAL TREATMENTS

Other therapies to consider include **DMG** (page 194), **Coenzyme Q$_{10}$** (page 185), **proanthocyanidins** (page 27), **larch** (page 231); immunostimulant herbs **alfalfa** (page 156), **aloe vera** (Acemannan, page 156), **astragalus** (page 160), **burdock** (page 170), **dandelion leaf** (page 193), **dandelion root** (page 193), **echinacea** (page 195), **garlic** (page 204), **ginseng** (page 210), **goldenseal** (page 220), **hawthorn** (page 223), **licorice** (page 234), **marshmallow** (page 240), **milk thistle** (page 241), **nettle** (page 245), **red clover** (page 262), **St. John's wort** (page 276), **turmeric** (page 280), **yellow dock** (page 309); immunostimulant mushrooms: **maitake** (page 238), **reishi** (page 264), **shiitake** (page 272), and **cordyceps** (page 191).

These therapies can be used in conjunction with conventional therapies as they are unlikely to be effective by themselves in most patients. The natural treatments are widely used with variable success but have not all been thoroughly investigated and proven at this time.

CONVENTIONAL THERAPY

Conventional therapies for pets with cancer make use of a combination of surgery, chemotherapy, and radiation therapy.

Surgery

Surgery is the treatment of choice for solid tumors. Surgery can be curative if the entire solid tumor can be removed before it has metastasized (spread throughout the body by way of blood or lymphatic vessels). In the case of most small skin tumors, surgery is curative. When the entire tumor cannot be removed, surgery can be used to "debulk" the tumor (debulking removes as much of the tumor as possible). After debulking, additional therapy (chemotherapy or radiation) is used in an attempt to kill any remaining cells, as well as any cells that may have already spread from the original cancer site.

But does every tumor need to be removed? Of course not! Many of the pets seen for cancer consultations have benign fatty tumors, cysts, or warts that usually do not require surgical removal. With rare exception (an obvious wart), the only way to determine whether the lump is a benign lesion or a malignant cancer is through a biopsy.

Fortunately, most lumps are easily biopsied in the office with a small needle, in a procedure called aspiration cytology. In this procedure, a small needle, typically a 23- to 25-gauge needle, is gently inserted into the lump. The doctor aspirates a few cells or small amount of fluid, which are placed on a microscope slide, stained, and examined in the office.

Within minutes the doctor can usually tell whether the lump is benign or malignant. Most benign lumps grow slowly if at all and don't usually need removal. Malignant masses should be removed as soon as feasible after additional testing (x rays, blood tests) has been done to determine if the cancer has spread.

It is vital that all lumps be biopsied! Some doctors diagnose tumors as "cysts" or "fatty tumors" by only looking or feeling the lumps; some of these "cysts" or "fatty tumors" in fact turn out to be malignant tumors when biopsied. The only mass that can be correctly diagnosed by visual inspection is the common papilloma or wart. All other masses, both benign lumps and cancerous tumors, look and feel the same. If your doctor says the lump doesn't need to be biopsied, *get a second opinion!*

Some tumors are so large by the time of diagnosis, or are in a location making surgery difficult if not impossible, that surgery is not an option. In these cases, some other form of treatment must be performed. To make the surgery as safe as possible, a thorough diagnostic workup including blood tests must be done prior to anesthesia.

Radiation

Radiation involves the use of radioactive materials, usually some type of x ray, to kill the tumor cells. It can be used alone or in combination with surgery or chemotherapy. Radiation is not effective against every type of cancer, so it's necessary to work closely with a radiation specialist to determine which tumors are radiosensitive and are most likely to respond to this form of therapy.

Most pets tolerate radiation therapy quite well, but treatments usually require full anesthesia to administer the radiation. Common side effects of treating tumors with radiation include hair loss, burning of the skin, and discoloration of the skin. A new form of therapy for dogs with lymphosarcoma is whole body irradiation. In this procedure, the dog is anesthetized and half of the body is irradiated. Several weeks later, the procedure is repeated and the other half of the body is irradiated. The procedure has been reported to give dogs with lymphosarcoma a longer life expectancy (2 to 3 years) than with conventional chemotherapy (12 to 18 months). The most common side effects, which last 1 to 2 weeks, are nausea, vomiting, diarrhea, and lethargy. Nutritional support and herbal therapies can be useful to minimize side effects of whole body irradiation, as well as any other radiation therapies for the pet with radiosensitive cancers.

Chemotherapy

Chemotherapy is effective against many but not all tumors. As is the case with radiation therapy, some cancers are sensitive to chemotherapy whereas others are not. Usually the goal of chemotherapy is not to cure but rather to prolong life before the cancer returns. Unlike the case with people, side effects of chemotherapy, such as vomiting and hair loss, are rare. However, pets must be monitored closely for other, more serious side effects. These side effects vary with the actual drug used, but include kidney disease, heart disease, and bone marrow suppression. Working with a knowledgeable cancer specialist is critical. Most pets do quite well with chemotherapy and suffer few side effects. Nutritional support and herbal therapies can be useful to minimize side effects of chemotherapy.

 # CATARACTS

Principal Natural Treatments
  Antioxidants, bilberry, topical succus cineraria

Other Natural Treatments
  None

Cataracts are a common eye disorder of older dogs and, very rarely, older cats. While they can occur secondarily to diabetes, or can occur in young pets as a congenital problem, they are most often an aging change in the lens of the eye. Cataracts are technically an opacification and calcification of the lens in the eye. They can be a mild problem (immature cataracts) that minimally affects vision, or they can be a severe problem (mature to hypermature cataracts) that cause blindness. A common eye disorder of older pets that does not interfere with vision but is often confused by owners with cataracts is a condition called nuclear sclerosis. In this condition, the lens of the eye becomes slightly cloudy, but unlike a cataract it does not interfere with vision.

PRINCIPAL NATURAL TREATMENTS

As with any disorder, a natural diet goes a long way in maintaining the health of the pet. Supplementation with antioxidants and the herb bilberry may be helpful.

Topically applied succus cineraria has also helped in anecdotal reports among holistic veterinarians.

Antioxidants

Certain vitamins and minerals function in the body to reduce oxidation. Oxidation is a chemical process that occurs within the body's cells. After oxidation occurs, certain by-products such as peroxides and "free radicals" accumulate. These cellular by-products are toxic to the cells and surrounding tissue. The body removes these by-products by producing additional chemicals called antioxidants that combat these oxidizing chemicals.

In disease, excess oxidation can occur and the body's normal antioxidant abilities are overwhelmed. This is where supplying antioxidants can help. By giving your pet's body extra antioxidants, it may be possible to neutralize the harmful by-products of cellular oxidation. While not proven in pets, there is some evidence in pets that antioxidants (especially mixed carotenoids and **vitamins C,** page 297, and **E,** page 302) may prevent or slow the progression of cataracts.

Several antioxidants can be used to supplement pets. Most commonly, the antioxidant **vitamins A** (page 284), **C** (page 297), and **E** (page 302), and the minerals **selenium** (page 268), **manganese** (page 239), and **zinc** (page 310) are prescribed. Other antioxidants, including **N-acetylcysteine** (page 243), **Coenzyme Q10** (page 185), *Ginkgo biloba* (page 208), **bilberry** (page 164), **grape seed extract** (page 159), and

pycnogenol (page 159) may also be helpful for a number of disorders.

There is no "correct" antioxidant to use. Dosage varies with the specific antioxidant chosen.

Following is a brief discussion of a commonly used group of antioxidants called bioflavonoids/proanthocyanidins.

Proanthocyanidins are naturally occurring polyphenolic compounds found in plants; most often products containing proanthocyanidins are made from grape seed or pine bark. Proanthocyanidins are also called pycnogenols or bioflavonoids, a class of water-soluble plant coloring agents. While they don't seem to be essential to life, it's likely that people and pets need them for optimal health. These compounds are used for their antioxidant effects against lipid (fat) peroxidation. Proanthocyanidins also inhibit the enzyme cyclooxygenase (the same enzyme inhibited by aspirin and other nonsteroidal medications); cyclooxygenase converts arachidonic acid into chemicals (leukotrienes and prostaglandins), which contribute to inflammation and allergic reactions. Proanthocyanidins also decrease histamine release from cells by inhibiting several enzymes.

Some research suggests that pycnogenol seems to work by enhancing the effects of another antioxidant, vitamin C. Other research suggests that the bioflavonoids can work independently of other antioxidants; as is the case with many supplements, there probably is an additive effective when multiple antioxidants are combined. People taking pycnogenol often report feeling better and having more energy; this "side effect" may possibly occur in our pets as well.

Quercetin is a natural antioxidant bioflavonoid found in red wine, grapefruit, onions, apples, black tea, and, in lesser amounts, in leafy green vegetables and beans. Quercetin protects cells in the body from damage by free radicals and stabilizes collagen in blood vessels.

Quercetin supplements are available in pill and tablet form. One problem with them, however, is that they don't seem to be well absorbed by the body. A special form called quercetin chalcone appears to be better absorbed.

Quercetin appears to be quite safe. Maximum safe dosages for young children, women who are

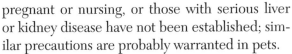

pregnant or nursing, or those with serious liver or kidney disease have not been established; similar precautions are probably warranted in pets.

In people, a typical dosage of proanthocyanidins is 200 to 400 mg 3 times daily. Quercetin may be better absorbed if taken on an empty stomach. The suggested dosage of proanthocyanidin complex in pets is 10 to 200 mg given daily (divided into 2 to 3 doses.) The suggested dosage of bioflavonoid complex in pets is 200 to 1,500 mg per day (divided into 2 to 3 doses). The actual dosage of each product will vary with the product and the pet's weight and disease condition.

While there is no specific research in pets showing benefit in preventing and treating cataracts, the use of antioxidants is widely recommended by holistic veterinarians to reduce oxidative damage to tissues that may occur in the lenses of the eyes.

Bilberry

Bilberry, related to blueberry, is most commonly taken internally by people to help with disorders of the eyes, including macular degeneration and cataract formation, due to its antioxidant effects. Its flavonoid compounds (anthocyanosides) are the most pharmacologically active. These flavonoids have several effects, including improved capillary strength (once again due to vitamin C), decreased platelet clumping, lowering of blood sugar (making it potentially useful for diabetic pets), and protective effects against gastric ulcers (due to increased mucus production). Bilberry's anthocyanosides have a special attraction to the retina, which may explain this herb's apparent usefulness in eye diseases.

Bilberry is used throughout Europe today for the treatment of poor night vision and day blindness in people. Regular use of bilberry is also thought to help prevent or treat other eye diseases such as macular degeneration, diabetic retinopathy, and cataracts.

In pets, bilberry can be tried in pets with cataracts (combining it with other antioxidants including vitamin E). Results have been variable.

Bilberry is a food and as such is quite safe. Do not use in pets on hypoglycemic therapy without veterinary supervision. In people, rare side effects such as mild digestive distress, skin rashes, and drowsiness can be seen. Safety in patients with severe liver or kidney disease is not known. There are no known drug interactions. Bilberry does not appear to interfere with blood clotting.

Cineraria

Cineraria is an herbal remedy recommended for dogs and cats with cataracts. The juice is diluted at least 50:50 with artificial tears. Anecdotal reports indicate that pets with cataracts appear to have improved vision, although the opacity of the lens may not decrease. If cineraria will work, it will usually occur with the first bottle.

The main natural treatments are designed to reduce cloudiness of the lens in the eyes.

For pets with mild, early cataracts, these therapies may be effective by themselves. For pets with more severe cataracts, conventional therapies may be indicated. The natural treatments are widely used with variable success but have not all been thoroughly investigated and proven at this time.

As with any condition, the most healthful natural diet will improve the pet's overall health.

CONVENTIONAL THERAPY

Mild cataracts that do not interfere with vision require no treatment. Cataracts that interfere with vision may need to be surgically removed; an artificial intraocular lens replacement may be recommended. Prior to surgery, pets are screened for other eye disorders (such as retinal degeneration) that may occur with cataracts and also cause blindness.

COGNITIVE DISORDER (Senility)

Principal Natural Treatments
Choline/lecithin

Other Natural Treatments
Natural diet, antioxidants: vitamin E, SAMe, omega-3 fatty acids; herbs: alfalfa, astragalus, *Ginkgo biloba,* ginseng, gotu kola, horsetail; glandulars, DMG, Coenzyme Q$_{10}$, plant enzymes

Canine cognitive disorder (canine cognitive dysfunction) is a medical condition associated with age-related deterioration of a dog's cognitive functioning. The condition most commonly affects dogs 11 years of age and older. The results of several recent studies showed that 48% of dogs 8 years of age and older, 62% of dogs 11 to 16 years of age, and 100% of dogs 16 years of age and older exhibited at least one of the changes that occurs in dogs with cognitive disorder. The changes occur as a result of physical and chemical changes within the cerebrum of the dog, including deposition of beta amyloid protein (similar to Alzheimer's patients), atrophy from nerve cell death, myelin degeneration, intraneuronal lipofuscin accumulation, decreased neurotransmitter activity, or increased activity of monoamine oxidase-B (MAO-B, an enzyme that breaks down the neurotransmitter dopamine).

Clinical signs include those changes owners often refer to as "senility" (which does not occur in pets), such as disorientation, "acting old," increased sleep (especially during the day), altered interactions with family members, loss of housetraining, decreased ability to recognize familiar people and surroundings, decreased hearing, restlessness, decreased desire to perform favorite tasks (such as walking), standing in the corner, and barking at inanimate objects.

There is no diagnostic test for cognitive disorder. The diagnosis is made after ruling out other diseases that can also alter mental state (internal disorders such as liver or kidney diseases, cardiac diseases, and especially hypothyroidism) via laboratory testing (usually blood and urine testing).

The condition appears to occur in cats as well, but is not as well defined or researched. Additionally, there is no approved conventional treatment for feline cognitive disorder.

Note: Many older dogs and cats that act "old" in fact have suffered for years from other chronic problems such as osteoarthritis or periodontal disease. Following proper diagnosis and treatment, these pets misdiagnosed as acting "old" will act "young" again as a result of decreased pain and infection.

PRINCIPAL NATURAL TREATMENTS

Choline/Lecithin

Lecithin contains a substance called phosphatidylcholine (PC) that is presumed to be responsible for its medicinal effects. Phosphatidylcholine is a major part of the membranes surrounding our cells. However, when phosphatidylcholine is consumed, it is broken down into choline rather than being carried directly to cell membranes. Choline acts like folic acid, TMG (trimethylglycine), and SAMe (S-adenosylmethionine) to promote methylation. It is also used to make acetylcholine, a nerve chemical essential for proper brain function.

Choline and phosphatidylcholine are effective for treating human neurological disorders with presumed choline deficiencies including tardive dyskinesia, Huntington's chorea, and Friedreich's ataxia.

For use as a supplement or a food additive, lecithin is often manufactured from soy.

One choline-containing product that has been used successfully in pets is Cholodin. Cholodin contains choline (40 mg per pill), phosphatidylcholine (as lecithin, 40 mg per pill), DL-methionine, and vitamins and minerals. Choline provides methyl groups used by the body in a number of biological reactions and acts as a precursor of acetylcholine. Phosphatidylcholine (lecithin) in part of the plasma membrane of mammalian cells also provides additional choline for acetylcholine synthesis. Methinonine and inositol also are involved in neurotransmitter metabolism.

Studies have shown effectiveness in improving neurological function in pets with cognitive disorder (often referred to incorrectly as "senility" in older pets). For those pets who respond favorably, Cholodin, given at 1 to 2 pills daily for a small dog or cat, and 2 to 4 pills given daily for a large dog, can be used in place of the drug Anipryl (selegiline) which has recently been approved for use in canine cognitive disorder.

Lecithin is believed to be generally safe. However, some people taking high dosages (several grams daily) experience minor but annoying side effects, such as abdominal discomfort, diarrhea, and nausea. Maximum safe dosages for young children, pregnant or nursing women, or those with severe liver or kidney disease have not been determined; the same precautions are probably warranted in pets.

OTHER NATURAL TREATMENTS

Additional complementary therapies for pets with cognitive disorder include **natural diet** (page 335), **antioxidants** (specifically **vitamin E,** page 302), **SAMe** (page 265), **omega-3 fatty acids** (page 246), the herbs **alfalfa** (page 156), **astragalus** (page 160), *Ginkgo biloba* (page 208), **ginseng** (page 210), **gotu kola** (page 221),

horsetail (page 225), **glandulars** (page 393), **DMG** (page 194), **Coenzyme Q10** (page 185), and plant **enzymes** (page 197).

These therapies can be used in conjunction with conventional therapies as needed. The natural treatments are widely used with variable success but have not all been thoroughly investigated and proven at this time.

As with any condition, the most healthful natural diet will improve the pet's overall health.

CONVENTIONAL THERAPY

The conventional therapy for cognitive disorder is a medication called Anipryl (selegiline, also called l-deprenyl), which has a complex set of mechanisms of action. It appears to work by increasing dopamine neurotransmitter levels in the brain via its inhibition of the enzyme monoamine oxidase-B (MAO-B). It should not be used in pets receiving opioid medications, amitraz (Mitaban, a commonly used dip for pets with mange), other antidepressants (tricyclics such as amitriptyline and SSRI's such as fluoxetine (Prozac), and ephedrine. Side effects include vomiting, diarrhea, lack of appetite, restlessness, lethargy, salivation, and trembling. Owners must use the product for at least 30 to 60 days to assess the effectiveness of Anipryl in treating dogs with cognitive disorder. The drug is not approved for use in cats at this time. For dogs with hypothyroidism as the cause of their cognitive disorder, thyroid supplementation is prescribed.

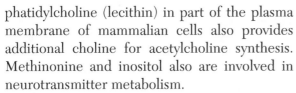 **CONSTIPATION** (Obstipation, Megacolon)

Principal Natural Treatments
  Natural diets

Other Natural Treatments
  Chickweed, dandelion root, Oregon grape, slippery elm, yellow dock

Constipation, often suspected by pet owners but in fact rarely diagnosed, occurs when the pet is unable to properly evacuate his bowels. As a result, the feces remain in the colon where

water from the fecal material continues to be absorbed by the colon. The fecal matter dries out and forms a hard mass. While constipation can occur in dogs (usually as a result of eating large amounts of foreign material), true constipation usually occurs in cats.

Cats can develop an unusual form of constipation or obstipation (severe constipation) called megacolon. In this disorder of unknown cause, the colon loses its ability to effectively contract and cause voiding of feces.

PRINCIPAL NATURAL TREATMENTS

The main natural treatments are designed to induce normal bowel movements.

These can be used in conjunction with conventional therapies when they are not effective by themselves in most patients. The natural treatments are widely used with variable success but have not been thoroughly investigated and proven at this time.

Natural diets recommended for pets with obesity, especially those with natural laxatives such as fibrous vegetables like pumpkin and squashes, are recommended for cats with constipation (see below).

Diet for Cats with Constipation

Note: Before you start to feed your dog or cat a home-prepared diet, it is strongly recommended that you discuss your decision with your veterinarian or a holistic veterinarian in your area. It is essential that you follow any diet's recommendations closely, including all ingredients and supplements. Failure to do so may result in serious health consequences for your pet.

> *5 ounces salmon, canned with bone (low-salt)*
> *⅓ cup long grain, cooked rice*
> *¼ teaspoon salt or salt substitute*
> *100 mg taurine*

This diet provides 284 kcal, 30.2 gm of protein, and 10.4 gm of fat. Feed this recipe to a cat who weighs 11 pounds.

Variations

1. Substitute 4 to 8 ounces of tuna or ½ pound of chicken, beef, or lamb for the salmon.
2. Rice is optional, as cats do not have a strict dietary carbohydrate requirement.
3. For extra nutrition and fiber and variety, add fresh, raw or slightly steamed vegetables, such as carrots or broccoli (approximately ½ to 1 cup per recipe, ½ cup of vegetables add about 30 kilocalories to the diet) as a top dressing for the diet. Pumpkin or squash can be fed to add extra fiber as well. Most cats will not eat vegetables, however.
4. Feed this diet in divided amounts at least twice daily and preferably 4 to 6 times daily. Frequent small meals will allow more frequent movements of the digestive tract and can encourage frequent eliminations.

OTHER NATURAL TREATMENTS

Other therapies that may be helpful include herbs such as **chickweed** (page 179), **dandelion root** (page 193), **Oregon grape** (page 251), **slippery elm** (page 273), and **yellow dock** (page 309). These therapies can be used in conjunction with conventional therapies, as they are unlikely to be effective by themselves in most patients with severe disease. The natural treatments are widely used with variable success but have not all been thoroughly investigated and proven at this time.

CONVENTIONAL THERAPY

Usually an enema is needed (often administered under sedation or light anesthesia) to evacuate the colon. Drug therapy or surgery is required for cats with megacolon due to the chronic and lifelong nature of this disorder.

CUSHING'S DISEASE

Principal Natural Treatments
Glandular therapy

Other Natural Treatments
Natural diet, antioxidants, herbs: astragalus, burdock, dandelion root, nettle, Siberian ginseng

Cushing's disease, hyperadrenocorticism, results in overproduction of adrenal gland hormones, most commonly glucocorticoids. The disorder is relatively common in middle-aged to older dogs and rare in cats. Cushing's disease usually occurs as a result of a benign (non-cancerous) tumor of the pituitary gland. Rarely, a tumor (benign or cancerous) of the adrenal gland(s) may occur. Long-term administration of corticosteroids causes a steroid-induced Cushing's syndrome that usually resolves whenever the pet is weaned off the steroids.

Clinical signs resemble those seen in older pets with other diseases such as kidney disease or diabetes mellitus. Pets with Cushing's disease often have increased water intake, increased urine output, increased appetite, and weight gain. Secondary infections of the skin and bladder are common in pets with Cushing's disease.

PRINCIPAL NATURAL TREATMENTS

Glandular Therapy

The most common therapy is glandular therapy, which uses whole animal tissues or extracts of the adrenal gland. Current research supports this concept that the glandular supplements have specific activity and contain active substances that can exert physiologic effects.

While skeptics question the ability of the digestive tract to absorb the large protein macromolecules found in glandular extracts, evidence exists that this is possible. Therefore, these glandular macromolecules can be absorbed from the digestive tract into the circulatory system and may exert their biologic effects on their target tissues.

Several studies show that radiolabeled cells, when injected into the body, accumulate in their target tissues. The accumulation is more rapid by traumatized body organs or glands than healthy tissues, which may indicate an increased requirement for those ingredients contained in the glandular supplements.

In addition to targeting specific damaged organs and glands, supplementation with glandular supplements may also provide specific nutrients to the pet. For example, glands contain hormones in addition to a number of other chemical constituents. These low doses of crude hormones are suitable for any pet needing hormone replacement, but especially for those pets with mild disease or those who simply need gentle organ support.

Glandular supplements also function as a source of enzymes that may encourage the pet to produce hormones or help the pet maintain health or fight disease.

Finally, glandular supplements are sources of active lipids and steroids that may be of benefit to pets.

The dosage of glandular supplements varies with the product used.

OTHER NATURAL TREATMENTS

Useful treatments can include natural **diet** (page 314); **antioxidants** (page 158); and herbal therapies: **astragalus** (page 160), **burdock** (page 170), **dandelion root** (page 193), **nettle** (page 245), and Siberian **ginseng** (page 210). These therapies are not curative but are used to support and nourish the adrenal gland.

As with any condition, the most healthful natural diet will improve the pet's overall health.

These can be used in conjunction with conventional therapies as they are unlikely to be effective by themselves in most patients. The natural treatments are widely used with variable success but have not all been thoroughly investigated and proven at this time.

CONVENTIONAL THERAPY

Lysodren, a drug related to DDT, is the preferred conventional therapy. The new medication Anipryl can be used, but response is variable. Other medications such as ketoconazole may also be effective in some pets. Treatment is life long, and pets must be regularly monitored for side effects.

 # DEGENERATIVE MYELOPATHY

Principal Natural Treatments
    Antioxidants (especially vitamin E and B vitamins), spinal cord glandulars and myelin specific protein, N-acetylcysteine, aminocaproic acid

Other Natural Treatments
    Natural diet, L-carnitine

Degenerative myelopathy is a common cause of neurological dysfunction of the rear limbs (posterior paralysis) of dogs. Other causes include intervertebral disk disease, spinal tumors, hypothyroidism, and cauda equina syndrome. Most commonly, middle-aged to older larger breed dogs, especially German Shepherds, are affected (in the past, the condition was called German Shepherd myelopathy). The disorder is slowly progressive and often confused with hip dysplasia; many pets mistakenly diagnosed with hip dysplasia in fact have degenerative myelopathy. (To complicate things, some dogs have both hip dysplasia and degenerative myelopathy at the same time!) Changes in the spinal cord causing the neurological signs include demyelination (destruction of the myelin sheath surrounding the spinal cord) and degeneration of axons (nerve tracts).

The exact cause of degenerative myelopathy is unknown. However, many doctors feel that this is an autoimmune disorder in which antibodies are formed by the dog against spinal cord protein. Holistic veterinarians propose that since vaccinated dogs have higher levels of auto-antibodies, there may be an association with overvaccination. Definitive proof of this theory is lacking, although the suggestion is plausible. The disease mimics multiple sclerosis in people.

Diagnosis is made by ruling out other causes of similar clinical signs, including intervertebral disk disease, spinal cord tumors, hip dysplasia, cauda equina syndrome, and hypothyroidism.

PRINCIPAL NATURAL TREATMENTS

The main natural treatments are designed to reduce inflammation in the spinal cord. The natural treatments are widely used with variable success but have not all been thoroughly investigated and proven at this time. As with any condition, the most healthful natural diet will improve the pet's overall health.

Definitive proof of the effectiveness of any therapy for degenerative myelopathy is lacking. However, the following therapies have been recommended and anecdotally used with variable success in some dogs with degenerative myelopathy:

Antioxidants

Spinal cord glandulars and myelin specific protein, N-acetylcysteine, and aminocaproic acid are used. Two particularly useful products are called Antiox-Q and Antiox-QCB. Antiox-Q is a mixture of the vitamin regimen recommended for dogs with degenerative myelopathy. This is a convenient form of medication, because it enables the dog to get all the correct amounts of the vitamins in a single dose instead of many doses of each individual vitamin.

Antiox-Q is given 5 ml twice a day if your dog weighs more than 50 pounds, or 2.5 ml twice a day if less than 50 pounds. Each 5 ml dose of Antiox-Q contains all the following vitamins at their recommended dosages:

Vitamin	Recommended Dosage
Bovine cartilage/gelatin	750 mg
Coenzyme Q$_{10}$	50 mg
Vitamin E	1,000 IU
Gamma-linolenic acid	100 mg
Omega-3 fatty acid (flaxseed oil)	500 mg
Selenium	100 mcg
Gingko extract	100 mg
Beta-carotene	12,500 IU
Olive oil	2.5 ml
Pantothenic acid/calcium pantothenate	50 mg
Vitamin B$_{12}$	50 mg
Thiamine	50 mg
Riboflavin (vitamin B$_2$)	50 mg
Niacin	50 mg
Pyridoxine	50 mg
Folic acid	400 mcg

Antiox-QCB contains all of the previously mentioned vitamins in addition to curcumin (500 mg) and bromelain (200 mg supplying 2,400 GDU per gram), which are natural anti-inflammatory agents. Taken together, these two herbs assist in the absorption of each other from the gastrointestinal tract, which increases their effects. It should be administered on an empty stomach or the curcumin and bromelain will not have their natural anti-inflammatory effects. These products have been formulated in consultation with Dr. Roger Clemmons, one of the leading researchers on degenerative myelopathy, by Westlab Pharmacy (352) 373-8111, toll free at (800) 4WESTLA, e-mail at info@westlabpharmacy.com.

OTHER NATURAL TREATMENTS

Other natural treatments include natural **diet** and **L-carnitine** (page 175).

CONVENTIONAL THERAPY

There are no approved conventional therapies for the treatment of degenerative myelopathy. Many pets, incorrectly diagnosed as having hip dysplasia, are treated with corticosteroids or NSAIDs, which will not correct degenerative myelopathy (although rare patients will show minor improvement with corticosteroid therapy).

 # DENTAL DISEASE (Periodontal Disease, Gingivitis, Stomatitis)

Principal Natural Treatments
Coenzyme Q$_{10}$, antioxidants, orthomolecular therapy

Other Natural Treatments
Natural diet, neem (antibacterial), colloidal silver, olive leaf extract, bioflavonoids, lactoferrin, N-acetylcysteine, GAGs, DMG, reishi mushrooms, L-glutamine, antibacterial herbs: aloe vera, astragalus, boswellia, echinacea, garlic, German chamomile (topical), ginger, goldenseal (topical), gotu kola, horsetail (urinary system), licorice, marshmallow, Oregon grape, sage, St. John's wort, turmeric, uva ursi; topical lemon juice

Periodontal disease is the most common infectious (caused by bacteria) disease in dogs and cats. It is estimated that 80% or more of dogs and cats between the ages of 1 and 3 years

have some evidence of periodontal disease that requires treatment.

Normal teeth should be white. Gums should be light pink, except in those breeds with pigmented

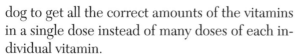

gums (such as Chows). While all pets have some amount of noticeable breath odor, pets with periodontal disease have noticeably disagreeable odors, from months to years of decay. While bad breath per se is no big deal, what causes bad breath is a big deal—and a very serious problem that ultimately will shorten a pet's life. The bad breath is just one sign of periodontal disease and is caused by bacteria and their toxins destroying the teeth and gums. Left untreated, the bacteria and their toxins can cause serious health problems for the pet.

Periodontal disease in pets, as in people, is caused by bacteria and plaque. With time, plaque hardens and becomes the yellow-brown tartar commonly seen on the teeth. As bacteria and plaque accumulate, toxins are produced. Over time, these toxins destroy the teeth and gums. Excess tartar, foul breath, loose teeth, bleeding teeth and gums, inflamed and reddened gums, and actual pus coming from the tooth sockets are seen as a result of severe destruction of the oral tissues of the jaw. Gingivitis-stomatitis is a painful inflammatory condition of the gums and other tissues of the mouth.

Periodontal disease is not just confined to the mouth. Its effects are felt throughout the body, and this disease is the main source of infection and inflammation elsewhere in the body. The foundation of any holistic health-care program involves treating disease; and pets with dirty, infected teeth must be treated to eliminate chronic sources of infection and inflammation that can cause harm within the body. Many older dogs and cats that act "old" in fact have suffered for years from periodontal disease. Upon a proper dental scaling under anesthesia, most of these pets will act "young" again as a result of decreased pain and infection.

The term "dental disease" can refer to any problem with a pet's teeth and gums, such as a tumor, a broken tooth, improper dentition that might require orthodontics, or more commonly an infection of the teeth and gums.

As mentioned, periodontal disease, caused by bacteria and their toxins destroying the teeth and gums, can cause other health problems for pets. Every time the dog or cat inhales, it is inhaling bacteria and toxins into its lungs. Whenever the pet swallows, it is swallowing bacteria and bacterial toxins into its stomach and intestines. Whenever it eats, bacteria and their toxins enter the bloodstream. Over several months or years, these bacteria and toxins can cause heart, liver, kidney, lung, and gastrointestinal disease or organ failure. These problems become more severe as the pet ages due to chronic infection, chronic stimulation of the immune system, and chronic wear and tear on aging organs that may not be able to handle this constant load of bacteria and bacterial toxins. To help prevent early death from these devastating diseases, and to relieve the pain associated with dental infections, early treatment of oral infections (periodontal disease) is essential.

The treatment depends upon the severity of the disease. Most pets who have early periodontal disease can be treated by their veterinarians with an ultrasonic scaling and antibiotics if needed. More severe disease often requires advanced dental procedures such as root canals, extractions, and gum surgery best performed by referral to a specialist. Often oral radiographs (x rays) will detect disease under the gums that would normally go undetected in the more severe cases.

For most pets, an annual dental cleaning will suffice. Some pets may need treatment more frequently. Smaller breeds of dogs often require a cleaning twice each year. Pets with diseases such as heart disease, diabetes, liver or kidney disease, or any problems with their immune systems should have their periodontal infections treated as often as needed to prevent serious complications. For example, recent studies showed that bacteria were often found on abnormal heart valves in pets with heart disease. These bacteria were identical to the ones cultured from the infected teeth and gums. It is no coincidence that many pets with heart disease also have periodontal disease. If left untreated, periodontal disease can cause a heart infection called bacterial endocarditis. This condition is life-threatening and very difficult and expensive to treat. One of the most important things to do with pets with heart disease (as well as any chronic disease) is to make sure they have their teeth cleaned at least annually if not more often.

Any pet with heart disease needs to have any type of infection prevented at all costs.

While many pet owners (especially those with older pets) worry about anesthesia, modern anesthesia is very safe in our older pets. Every pet should have a thorough examination and some sort of laboratory testing, usually blood or urine testing, prior to the anesthetic procedure. There is no reason to deprive an older pet of a necessary procedure just because anesthesia might be needed. As long as the pet is treated holistically and the anesthesia is safely administered, older pets can have dental cleanings done safely as needed.

Anything the owner can do to decrease infection, such as regular brushing using a product prescribed by the veterinarian, can decrease the number of treatments needed each year. At-home care by owners can go a long way in controlling periodontal infections. Regular brushing with a veterinary dental product, such as a chlorhexidine solution, will significantly slow down the return of periodontal disease. Most pets can easily be trained to accept daily brushing.

PRINCIPAL NATURAL TREATMENTS

Coenzyme Q$_{10}$

Coenzyme Q$_{10}$ (ubiquinone) is a powerful fat-soluble antioxidant that is found in every cell in the body. It plays a fundamental role in the mitochondria, the parts of the cell that produce energy from food. Coenzyme Q$_{10}$ appears to control the flow of oxygen within the cells as well as functioning as an antioxidant to reduce damage to cells by harmful free radicals. Every cell in the body needs CoQ$_{10}$, but there is no U.S. Recommended Dietary Allowance since the body can manufacture CoQ$_{10}$ from scratch.

Because CoQ$_{10}$ is found in all animal and plant cells, we obtain small amounts of this nutrient from our diet. However, it would be hard to get a therapeutic dosage from food.

While CoQ$_{10}$ is most commonly recommended for pets with heart disease, anecdotal studies suggest that by acting as an antioxidant it may also help pets with gingivitis.

CoQ$_{10}$ may also help periodontal (gum) disease (by reducing the size and improving the health of periodontal pockets, as well as decreasing inflammation, redness, bleeding, and pain) and diabetes in people and pets.

In people, the typical recommended dosage of CoQ$_{10}$ is 30 to 300 mg daily, often divided into 2 or 3 doses. CoQ$_{10}$ is fat-soluble and is better absorbed when taken in an oil-based soft gel form rather than in a dry form such as tablets and capsules. In pets, the typical dosage is 30 mg every 24 to 48 hours, although your veterinarian may alter this dosage depending upon your pet's size and individual needs. (Some doctors feel that increasing the dosage is necessary for larger pets; for example, 80 mg every 24 to 48 hours might be recommended daily for a 100-pound dog.)

CoQ$_{10}$ appears to be extremely safe. No significant side effects have been found; however, pets with severe heart disease should not take CoQ$_{10}$ (or any other supplement) except under a veterinarian's supervision.

The maximum safe dosages of CoQ$_{10}$ for young children, pregnant or nursing women, or those with severe liver or kidney disease has not been determined; the same is true for pets of similar circumstances.

Antioxidants

Certain vitamins and minerals function in the body to reduce oxidation. Oxidation is a chemical process that occurs within the body's cells. After oxidation occurs, certain by-products such as peroxides and "free radicals" accumulate. These cellular by-products are toxic to the cells and surrounding tissue. The body removes these by-products by producing additional chemicals called antioxidants that combat these oxidizing chemicals.

In disease, excess oxidation can occur and the body's normal antioxidant abilities are overwhelmed. This is where supplying antioxidants can help. By giving your pet's body extra antioxidants, it may be possible to neutralize the harmful by-products of cellular oxidation. Since oxidative damage may contribute to periodontal disease and severe gingivitis, many holistic veterinarians recommend antioxidants to decrease inflammation in the mouth (although clinical studies are lacking at this time).

Several antioxidants can be used to supplement pets. Most commonly, the antioxidant **vitamins A** (page 284), **C** (page 297), and **E** (page 302) and the minerals **selenium** (page 268), **manganese** (page 239), and **zinc** (page 310) are prescribed. Other antioxidants, including **N-acetylcysteine** (page 243), **Coenzyme Q10** (page 185), *Ginkgo biloba* (page 208), **bilberry** (page 164), **grape seed extract** (page 159), and **pycnogenol** (page 159) may also be helpful for a number of disorders.

There is no "correct" antioxidant to use. Dosage varies with the specific antioxidant chosen.

Following is a brief discussion of a commonly used group of antioxidants called bioflavonoids/proanthocyanidins.

Proanthocyanidins

Proanthocyanidins are naturally occurring polyphenolic compounds found in plants; most often products containing proanthocyanidins are made from grape seed or pine bark. Proanthocyanidins are also called pycnogenols or bioflavonoids, a class of water-soluble plant coloring agents. While they don't seem to be essential to life, it's likely that people and pets need them for optimal health. These compounds are used for their antioxidant effects against lipid (fat) peroxidation. Proanthocyanidins also inhibit the enzyme cyclooxygenase (the same enzyme inhibited by aspirin and other nonsteroidal medications); cyclooxygenase converts arachidonic acid into chemicals (leukotrienes and prostaglandins), which contribute to inflammation and allergic reactions. Proanthocyanidins also decrease histamine release from cells by inhibiting several enzymes.

Some research suggests that pycnogenol seems to work by enhancing the effects of another antioxidant, vitamin C. Other research suggests that the bioflavonoids can work independently of other antioxidants; as is the case with many supplements, there probably is an additive effect when multiple antioxidants are combined. People taking pycnogenol often report feeling better and having more energy; this "side effect" may possibly occur in our pets as well.

Quercetin is a natural antioxidant bioflavonoid found in red wine, grapefruit, onions, apples, black tea, and, in lesser amounts, in leafy green vegetables and beans. Quercetin protects cells in the body from damage by free radicals and stabilizes collagen in blood vessels.

Quercetin supplements are available in pill and tablet form. One problem with them, however, is that they don't seem to be well absorbed by the body. A special form called quercetin chalcone appears to be better absorbed.

Quercetin appears to be quite safe. Maximum safe dosages for young children, women who are pregnant or nursing, or those with serious liver or kidney disease have not been established; similar precautions are probably warranted in pets.

In people, a typical dosage of proanthocyanidins is 200 to 400 mg 3 times daily. Quercetin may be better absorbed if taken on an empty stomach. The suggested dosage of proanthocyanidin complex in pets is 10 to 200 mg given daily (divided into 2 to 3 doses.) The suggested dosage of bioflavonoid complex in pets is 200 to 1,500 mg per day (divided into 2 to 3 doses). The actual dosage of each product will vary with the product and the pet's weight and disease condition.

Orthomolecular Therapy

Orthomolecular medicine (often called "megavitamin therapy") seeks to use increased levels of vitamins and minerals (mainly antioxidants) to help treat a variety of medical disorders. While daily amounts of vitamins and minerals have been recommended as an attempt to prevent nutritional deficiencies, orthomolecular medicine uses higher doses as part of the therapy for disease.

The pet food industry relies on recommendations by the National Research Council (NRC) to prevent diseases caused by nutrient deficiencies in the "average" pet; yet, the NRC has not attempted to determine the *optimum* amount of nutrients or their effects in treating medical disorders. While a minimum amount of nutrients may be satisfactory in preventing diseases caused by nutrient deficiencies, it is important to realize that there is no "average" pet, and that every pet has unique nutritional needs.

It is unlikely that our current recommendations are adequate to maintain health in every pet. Each pet has unique requirements for nutrients. Additionally, these needs will vary depending upon the pet's health. For example, in times of stress or disease additional nutrients above and beyond those needed for health will be required. Orthomolecular medicine evaluates the needs of the pet and uses increased nutrients to fight disease.

Note: Owners should not diagnose and treat their pets without veterinary supervision. Many medical disorders present similar symptoms. Also, megavitamin therapy can be toxic if not used properly.

Cats, and rarely dogs, develop severe inflammation and/or infection of the gums and surrounding oral tissues called gingivitis-stomatitis. The cause of this painful condition is unknown but appears to be a severe immune response to oral antigens. Because cats with feline leukemia virus or feline immunodeficiency virus may present with chronic dental disease or gingivitis, cats with recurring gingivitis, stomatitis, or dental disease should be tested for these immunosuppressive viral infections.

Traditionally, many cats can be treated conventionally with frequent dental cleanings, oral antibiotics, and corticosteroids. In severe cases, cats need all teeth extracted to cure the condition.

Orthomolecular therapy for cats or dogs with severe gingivitis involves administration of high doses of vitamins A, C, and E and selenium to improve cell-mediated immunity and decrease local oxidation that may contribute to destruction of the oral tissues. The antioxidants are administered locally and may also be rubbed onto the gums. Dental cleanings (as needed) and administration of antibiotics and/or corticosteroids are administered as needed at the start of therapy and during any flareups. A small number of cases have shown significant improvement when other (conventional) therapies have failed.

Treatment uses vitamin A (10,000 IU for small dogs and cats, up to 30,000 IU for large dogs), crystalline ascorbic acid (750 mg for small dogs and cats, up to 3,000 mg for large dogs), and vitamin E (800 IU for small dogs and cats, up to 2,400 IU for large dogs). The antioxidant mineral selenium (20 mcg for small dogs and cats, up to 60 mcg for large dogs) is also added to the regimen. Once asymptomatic, a maintenance protocol using gradually lower dosages of vitamins A and E and the mineral selenium are prescribed to reduce the chance for toxicity. Promising results have been seen in many pets treated with this regimen.

OTHER NATURAL TREATMENTS

In addition to dental cleanings as needed, the following therapies may be of benefit: natural **diet** (page 335), **neem** (see antibacterial, page 244), **colloidal silver** (page 186), **olive leaf extract** (page 246), **bioflavonoids** (page 27), **lactoferrin** (page 230), **N-acetylcysteine** (page 243), **GAGs** (page 218), **DMG** (page 194), **reishi mushrooms** (page 264), **L-glutamine** (page 213); antibacterial herbs: **aloe vera** (page 156), **astragalus** (page 160), **boswellia** (page 168), **echinacea** (page 195), **garlic** (page 204), **German chamomile** (topical, page 206), **ginger** (page 207), **goldenseal** (topical, page 220), **gotu kola** (page 221), **horsetail** (urinary system, page 225), **licorice** (page 234), **marshmallow** (page 240), **Oregon grape** (page 251), **sage** (page 264), **St. John's wort** (page 276), **turmeric** (page 280), **uva ursi** (page 281), and topical lemon juice.

Severe cases of stomatitis in older pets that have decreased salivary production may improve by administering a drop of lemon juice 1 to 3 times daily in their mouths to stimulate intense saliva production and wash the debris field away. This clears the mouth of potentially troublesome bacteria that lead to stomatitis since they would accumulate in normal animals in the cheek area.

These can be used in conjunction with conventional therapies when needed. The natural treatments are widely used with variable success but have not all been thoroughly investigated and proven at this time.

As with any condition, the most healthful natural diet will improve the pet's overall health.

CONVENTIONAL THERAPY

Conventional therapy for dental disease involves regular dental cleanings. This means ultrasonic cleanings done under anesthesia, usually one to two times per year for most pets (more often for pets with chronic diseases such as heart disease, diabetes, or Cushing's disease), corticosteroids (to relieve the severe inflammation that may occur in cats, and rarely dogs) with gingivitis-stomatitis (a painful inflammatory condition of the gums and other tissues of the mouth), and antibiotics (to decrease bacterial infections that make up the tartar and destroy the periodontal tissues). Maintenance with dog and cat toothpastes or solutions containing chlorhexidine can decrease the frequency of dental cleanings that are required.

DIABETES

Principal Natural Treatments
  Natural diet, glandular therapy, chromium, vanadium

Other Natural Treatments
  Omega-3 fatty acids, vitamin B$_6$, alanine, glutamine, DMG, glycoproteins, N-acetylcysteine, proanthocyanidins, bilberry, burdock root, calendula, dandelion leaf, dandelion root, garlic, gymnema, marshmallow, panax ginseng, yucca

Diabetes mellitus is a common endocrine pancreatic disorder of cats and dogs. The incidence of diabetes in cats and dogs is reported to be anywhere from 1 in 100 to 1 in 500 pets.

Diabetes is classified as type I or type II. Type I diabetes is also called insulin-dependent diabetes. In this disorder, there is destruction of the beta cells (insulin-producing cells) of the pancreas. Treatment involves replacing insulin through insulin injections given 1 to 2 times per day.

Type II diabetes is also called non-insulin-dependent diabetes, as insulin is usually not required for treating pets with this disorder. Insulin resistance and dysfunctional beta cells, rather than permanent destruction of beta cells, are seen in pets with type II diabetes.

Type I diabetes is the most common type. Most (if not all) dogs with diabetes have type I diabetes; approximately 50 to 70% of cats have type I diabetes, with the remainder having type II diabetes.

Causes of type 1 diabetes include immune-mediated destruction of the beta cells of the pancreas in dogs and amyloidosis (deposition of amyloid protein in the pancreas) in cats. Other causes of diabetes in dogs and cats include obesity (probably the most common cause of type II diabetes in cats), genetics, infection, pancreatitis, and administration of certain medications (corticosteroids, progesterone compounds).

PRINCIPAL NATURAL TREATMENTS

Treatments for pets with diabetes include: natural diet/high-fiber diet/ high-protein/low carb (the so-called **"meat and vegetables" diet**, page 358), exercise, glandular therapy, chromium, and vanadium.

Natural Diet

Dietary therapy is useful in both dogs and cats with diabetes. Most diabetic dogs require insulin as they have type I diabetes (insulin-dependent diabetes). Many cats may not require insulin, as they have type II diabetes (non-insulin-dependent diabetes). These cats are most likely to respond to therapies that may include dietary therapy, nutritional supplementation, and exercise.

While not proven, some holistic veterinarians believe that years of feeding corn-based foods to cats (which amounts to feeding a high-carbohydrate food to a true carnivore, which is not natural) may be contributing to the high incidence of diabetes in cats.

The homemade diet recommended for dogs with diabetes is composed of 50 to 55% high-quality complex carbohydrates (oats, vegetables, potato) with no simple sugars (such as sucrose, which may be included in commercial processed diets, especially soft-moist foods). Fat is restricted (no more than 20%), and moderate amounts of protein (15 to 30%) are included.

Diets high in complex carbohydrates (fibers) allow slower digestion and absorption of carbohydrates, which helps prevent wide fluctuations in blood glucose levels by minimizing postprandial glucose concentrations (postprandial refers to the period after a meal is eaten when blood glucose is most likely to spike to a high level, usually within 1 to 4 hours after eating). High complex carbohydrate diets also appear to increase the sensitivity of the cells of the body to insulin, which can improve blood sugar regulation. Carbohydrates such as vegetables, oats, and potatoes are more slowly digested and absorbed than rice and are preferred sources of carbohydrates for inclusion in the diets of diabetic dogs.

Soluble and insoluble fibers are carbohydrates commonly included in diets for dogs with diabetes. Soluble fibers (such as guar gum, which can be sprinkled on food at 8 gm/400 kcal of food) reduce blood sugar levels by absorbing water and forming gels that slow movement of food from the stomach, reduce absorption of glucose, and increase the passage of food throughout the intestinal tract (which serves to slow glucose absorption). Insoluble fibers (such as wheat bran added to the diet at 8 gm/400 kcal of food) have similar effects. Pumpkin, squashes, and similar vegetables can be used to add fiber to pet diets. Products such as sugar-free Metamucil can also be added to the pet's diet to provide additional fiber.

Dogs and cats with diabetes who are thin should not be fed high-fiber diets initially as they may continue to lose weight. These pets should be fed wholesome maintenance diets with small amounts of fiber added slowly once normalization of weight is achieved.

Diet for Dogs with Diabetes

Note: Before you start to feed your dog or cat a home-prepared diet, it is strongly recommended that you discuss your decision with your veterinarian or a holistic veterinarian in your area. It is essential that you follow any diet's recommendations closely, including all ingredients and supplements. Failure to do so may result in serious health consequences for your pet.

1¼ cups oatmeal or rolled oats, cooked
3½ ounces (¼ cup) kidney beans
1 large hard-boiled egg
1 cup mixed vegetables, cooked and drained

This diet provides 452 kcal, 24.5 gm protein, 8.9 gm fat, and supports the daily caloric needs of a 12- to 13-pound dog.

Variations

1. Substitute ⅓ pound chicken or turkey breast and 2 cups of potato cooked with the skin on for the rolled oats and the kidney beans. If this substitution is made, also add 30 gm (1 ounce) of wheat bran to the diet.
2. Add 1½ to 2 bonemeal tablets (10-grain or equivalent) or ½ teaspoon of bonemeal powder to supply calcium and phosphorus with a multivitamin/mineral supplement, using the label instructions. Alternatively, use a natural product from Standard Process (1 Calcifood Wafer or 2 Calcium Lactate tablets for each 2 bonemeal tablets).
3. When possible, use natural vitamins made from raw whole foods, rather than synthetic vitamins (although both can be used in combination), as the natural vitamins also supply plant phytochemicals, enzymes, and other nutrients not found in chemically-synthesized vitamins.
4. Use either Catalyn from Standard Process (at a dose of 1 Catalyn per 25 pounds) or Canine Plus from VetriScience (following label dosages) as the natural vitamin in this recipe.

Diet for Cats with Diabetes

Most doctors also recommend similar diets for diabetic cats. However, cats are true carnivores and require meat in their diets. Therefore, the diet that may prove most helpful for diabetic cats uses the maintenance diet with added fiber. However, keep in mind that cats will usually not accept diets high in fiber.

⅓ to ½ pound of ground meat (turkey, chicken, lamb, beef)
½ to 1 large hard-boiled egg
½ ounce of clams chopped in juice
4 teaspoons chicken fat or canola oil
⅛ teaspoon potassium chloride (salt substitute)
100 mg taurine

If using ½ pound of chicken and ½ egg, the diet will provide 471 kcal, 53.1 gm of protein, and 27.4 gm of fat. An adult indoor 10-pound cat requires approximately 300 kcal of energy per day, an adult outdoor 10-pound cat requires approximately 360 kcal of energy per day, and a 5-pound kitten requires approximately 300 kcal of energy per day. See table 3.2 on page 346 for more information and feeding guidelines.

Variations

1. Substitute tuna (4 ounces in water without salt), sardines (4 to 6 ounces in tomato sauce), or other fish (such as 5 ounces of salmon) for the meat protein. For occasional variety, substitute ½ to ⅔ cup of tofu. Since cats are true carnivores, most doctors prefer to recommend tofu on only an occasional basis.

2. Add ⅓ cup of potato (cooked with the skin), rice, or macaroni, although cats do not have a defined dietary requirement for carbohydrates.

3. Supply vitamins and minerals as follows: 3 to 4 bonemeal tablets (10-grain or equivalent) or ¾ to 1 teaspoon of bonemeal powder to supply calcium and phosphorus with a multivitamin/mineral supplement, using the label instructions. Alternatively, use a natural product from Standard Process (1 Calcifood Wafer or 2 Calcium Lactate tablets for each 2 bonemeal tablets).

4. When possible, add natural vitamins made from raw whole foods, rather than synthetic vitamins (although both can be used in combination), as the natural vitamins also supply plant phytochemicals, enzymes, and other nutrients not found in chemically synthesized vitamins. Use either Catalyn from Standard Process (at a dose of 1 Catalyn per 10 pounds) or NuCat from VetriScience (following label dosages) as the natural vitamin in this recipe.

5. For extra nutrition and variety, use fresh, raw or slightly steamed vegetables, such as carrots or broccoli (approximately ½ to 1 cup per recipe) as a top dressing for the diet. (Many cats, however, will not eat vegetables.) Most vegetables provide approximately 25 kcal per ½ cup.

6. The nutrient composition of the diet will vary depending upon which ingredients are used. See the table on page 284 to determine how much to feed your kitten or adult cat. The actual amount to feed will vary based upon the pet's weight (feed less if weight gain, more if weight loss).

7. Extra fiber can be added by supplementing with kidney beans (⅛ cup), oatmeal (¼ cup), wheat bran (¼ ounce), pumpkin or squashes, and sugar-free fiber products such as Metamucil.

Chromium

Chromium is a trace mineral in the body. Chromium's role in maintaining good health was discovered in 1957, when scientists extracted a substance known as glucose tolerance factor (GTF) from pork kidney. GTF, which helps the body maintain normal blood sugar levels, contains chromium as the active component. GTF binds to and potentiates the activity of insulin.

Chromium is necessary for pancreatic beta cell sensitivity (beta cells make insulin), insulin binding, insulin receptor enzymes, and insulin receptor sites. Supplemental chromium tends to balance glucose metabolism, benefiting both hypoglycemic (low blood sugar) and diabetic patients. One explanation for this is that chromium may improve C-peptide levels, leading to enhanced pancreatic beta cell function.

Supplementing with chromium can lower blood lipids, which may make it beneficial in people and pets with elevated blood cholesterol levels.

Chromium's most important function is to help regulate the amount of glucose in the blood. Insulin regulates the movement of glucose out of the blood and into cells. It appears that insulin uses chromium as a cofactor to allow glucose to pass through the cell membrane and enter the cell.

Based on chromium's close relationship with insulin, this trace mineral has been studied as a treatment for diabetes. The results have been positive: Chromium supplements appear to improve blood sugar control in people with diabetes.

Chromium has principally been studied for its possible benefits in improving blood sugar control in people with diabetes. Reasonably good evidence suggests that people with adult-onset (type II) diabetes may show some improvement when given appropriate dosages of chromium. Individuals with childhood-onset (type I) diabetes may respond as well. Finally, chromium also appears to help treat problems with blood sugar control that are too mild to deserve the name "diabetes." Putting all the results together, it does appear that chromium supplementation can be helpful in treating diabetes, both type I and type II. However, more work needs to be done to determine the optimum dosage.

Tissue levels of chromium in people and pets is often low due to limited uptake of chromium by plants as well as limited absorption by people and pets.

As mentioned, it has been theorized that many Americans may be chromium-deficient.

Preliminary research done by the U.S. Department of Agriculture (USDA) in 1985 found low chromium intakes in a small group of people studied. Although large-scale studies are needed to show whether Americans as a whole are chromium-deficient, we do know that many traditional sources of chromium, such as wheat, are depleted of this important mineral during processing. Some researchers believe that inadequate intake of chromium may be one of the causes for the rising rates of adult-onset diabetes. However, the matter is greatly complicated by the fact that we lack a good test to determine chromium deficiency.

While chromium is found in drinking water, especially hard water, concentrations vary so widely throughout the world that drinking water is not a reliable source. The most concentrated sources of chromium are brewer's yeast (not nutritional or torula yeast) and calf liver. Two ounces of brewer's yeast or 4 ounces of calf liver supply between 50 and 60 mcg of chromium. Other good sources of chromium are whole-wheat bread, wheat bran, and rye bread. Potatoes, wheat germ, green pepper, and apples offer modest amounts of chromium.

Calcium carbonate interferes with the absorption of chromium.

People may have a difficult time absorbing and synthesizing chromium if it is not attached to a substrate such as picolonic acid (chromium picolinate) or nicotinic acid (chromium nicotinate). In people, concerns have been raised over the use of the picolinate form of chromium in individuals suffering from affective or psychotic dis-orders, because picolinic acids can change levels of neurotransmitters.

Safety Issues

Recently, there has been the suggestion that chromium picolinate may cause damage to DNA, especially when combined with ascorbic acid. Alternative forms of chromium, such as that in the GTF form that can be extracted from foods such as yeast, contain no picolinic acid and may be safer. Additionally, while there are many forms of chromium available for supplementation, supplementation with an organic form (such as GTF) is recommended as this organically bound form of chromium is absorbed better and is more available to the pet than inorganic forms of chromium. More research is needed on this topic, although the use of the GTF form may be preferred until results are in.

Chromium appears to be safe in people when taken at a dosage of 50 to 200 mcg daily. However, concern has been expressed since chromium is a heavy metal and might conceivably build up and cause problems if taken to excess. Recently, there have been a few reports of kidney damage in people who took a relatively high dosage of chromium: 1,200 mcg or more daily for several months. For this reason, the dosage found most effective for individuals with type II diabetes—1,000 mcg daily—might present some health risks. Similar concerns are probably applicable for pets.

For pets with diabetes that may respond to chromium supplementation, a decreased dosage of insulin may be needed; medical supervision is essential before decreasing insulin.

The recommended dosages for the use of chromium in pets with diabetes is 50 to 300 mcg per day. Typically, a dosage of 200 mcg/cat of chromium picolinate is recommended. However, since picolinate may cause damage to DNA, more research is needed in this area. Using the chromium GTF natural supplement would be a safer alternative, although research using this form to determine the proper dosage has not been done. Work with your veterinarian to determine whether chromium supplementation can be used in your pet.

Calcium carbonate supplements may interfere with the absorption of chromium.

The maximum safe dosages of chromium for young children, women who are pregnant or nursing, or those with severe liver or kidney disease have not been established; similar concerns are probably warranted in pets.

Vanadium

Vanadium is a mineral, and evidence from animal studies suggests it may be an essential micronutrient.

In people as well as pets, there are no well-documented uses for vanadium, and *there are serious safety concerns regarding its use.* However, vanadium has been proposed to be of benefit to patients with diabetes as vanadium has insulin-like properties and may inhibit protein tyrosine phosphatase (PTP).

Studies in rats with and without diabetes suggest that vanadium may have an insulin-like effect, reducing blood sugar levels. Based on these findings, preliminary studies involving human subjects have been conducted, with promising results.

Based on promising animal studies, high doses of vanadium, like chromium, have been tested as an aid to controlling blood sugar levels in people with diabetes. However, animal studies suggest that taking high doses of vanadium can be harmful.

In various studies in people, vanadium has been used at doses thousands of times higher than is present in the diet, as high as 125 mg per day. However, there are serious safety concerns about taking vanadium at such high doses. Many doctors do not recommend that people exceed the nutritional dose of 10 to 30 mcg daily (some people with diabetes are prescribed 50 to 100 mcg/day).

To date, most doctors feel that studies using vanadium were all too small to be taken as definitive proof. More research is needed to definitely establish whether vanadium is effective (not to mention safe) for the treatment of diabetes.

New organic forms of vanadium have been synthesized—vanadyl acetylacetonate, vanadyl 3-ethylacetylacetonate, and bis (maltolato) oxovanadium. These forms appear to be safer than vanadyl sulfate and are well tolerated in diabetic cats.

In small studies in cats, the use of vanadium did improve clinical signs and reduce blood glucose levels with minimal signs of toxicity.

In pets with diabetes, dosages of 0.2 mg/kg daily for vanadium and 1 mg/kg daily for vanadyl sulfate seem safe. Some holistic veterinarians adapt the recommended human dose of vanadium to pets, using 50 mcg/day for small dogs and cats, 75 mcg per day for medium-sized dogs, and 100 mcg per day for larger dogs. The dosage of ½ of a capsule of Super Vanadyl Fuel (Twin Laboratories, Hauppauge, New York) given once daily on the food of diabetic cats appears safe. However, you should not administer vanadium (or chromium) to your pets unless under veterinary supervision.

With insulin-resistant type II diabetics, vanadium may help balance glucose levels by increasing glycogen synthesis (glycogen is a storage form of glucose). Because vanadium mimics many of the effects of insulin, it may improve blood sugar balance. In some studies, vanadium supplements have been shown to lower plasma glucose levels, improve insulin sensitivity, increase glucose uptake, and decrease blood fat levels in type I and type II diabetes.

Studies of diabetic rats suggest that, at high dosages, vanadium can accumulate in the body until it reaches toxic levels. Based on these results, high dosages of vanadium can't be considered safe for human use; similar concerns are probably reasonably applied to dogs and cats.

Glandular Therapy

Glandular therapy is also used in the treatment of diabetes.

This therapy uses whole animal tissues or extracts of the pancreas. Current research supports this concept that the glandular supplements have specific activity and contain active substances that can exert physiologic effects.

While skeptics question the ability of the digestive tract to absorb the large protein macromolecules found in glandular extracts, evidence exists that this is possible. Therefore, these glandular macromolecules can be absorbed from the digestive tract into the circulatory system and may exert their biologic effects on their target tissues.

Several studies show that radiolabeled cells, when injected into the body, accumulate in their target tissues. The accumulation is more rapid by traumatized body organs or glands than healthy tissues, which may indicate an increased requirement for those ingredients contained in the glandular supplements.

In addition to targeting specific damaged organs and glands, supplementation with glandular supplements may also provide specific nutrients to the pet. For example, glands contain hormones in addition to a number of other chemical constituents. These low doses of crude hormones are suitable for any pet needing hormone replacement, but especially for those pets with mild disease or those that simply need gentle organ support.

Glandular supplements also function as a source of enzymes that may encourage the pet to produce hormones or help the pet maintain health or fight disease.

Finally, glandular supplements are sources of active lipids and steroids that may be of benefit to pets.

The dosage of glandular supplements varies with the product used.

OTHER NATURAL TREATMENTS

Other therapies include exercise, **omega-3 fatty acids** (page 246), **vitamin B₆** (page 294), alanine, **glutamine** (page 213), **DMG** (page 194), **glycoproteins** (page 214), **N-acetylcysteine** (200 to 1,500 mg/day, page 243), **proanthocyanidins** (page 27); herbs: **bilberry** (page 164), **burdock root** (page 170), **calendula** (page 173), **dandelion leaf** (page 193), **dandelion root** (page 193), **garlic** (page 204), **gymnema** (page 223), **marshmallow** (page 240), ***Panax ginseng*** (page 210), and **yucca** (page 309).

These can be used in conjunction with conventional therapies, as they are unlikely to be effective by themselves in most patients with severe diabetes. The natural treatments are widely used with variable success but have not all been thoroughly investigated and proven at this time.

As with any condition, the most healthful natural diet will improve the pet's overall health.

CONVENTIONAL THERAPY

Conventional therapy for pets with type I diabetes is with the injectable drug insulin, which works to lower blood sugar. Oral hypoglycemic agents (which lower blood sugar) can be used but are not routinely prescribed for most diabetic pets. In cats with non-insulin-dependent diabetes (and possibly in any pet with type I or type II diabetes), dietary therapy (usually a higher fiber diet containing increased amounts of soluble and insoluble fiber designed to reduce obesity and minimize fluctuations in blood glucose) and exercise (when possible) may be effective in lowering blood sugar and controlling clinical signs.

 # DIARRHEA (See Inflammatory Bowel Disease)

 # DISTEMPER

Common Natural Treatments
  Homeopathic nosode

Other Natural Treatments
  None. No cure, but nutritional support: natural diet, antioxidants, homeopathic nosodes, supplements for infectious diseases

Canine distemper is a viral disease affecting dogs of all ages, but mainly unvaccinated or partially vaccinated puppies. The severity of the disease and the tissues infected vary with the particular strain of the virus infecting the pet and the pet's immune system; pets with antibody titers

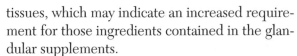

over 1:100 typically do not develop the disease. Typical clinical signs resemble those of kennel cough in the early stages of the disease, namely runny eyes and a runny nose. As the disease progresses, the pet develops a thicker purulent (pus) discharge of the eyes and nose, and develops a cough due to pneumonia. Lack of appetite, fever, and general lethargy also occur. Occasionally secondary skin infections arise and resemble pimples on the abdominal skin. The pads of the feet may thicken and become hard (distemper is often referred to as "hardpad" disease). Neurological complications, usually chomping of the jaw or seizures, develop later in the disease and are often the reason most pets with distemper are euthanized.

PRINCIPAL NATURAL TREATMENTS

Homeopathic Nosodes

Nosodes, a special type of homeopathic remedy, are prepared from infectious organisms, such as distemper virus and staphylococcus bacteria. Remember that no matter what the source of the remedy, the actual ingredients are diluted in preparing the remedy. No measurable amount of the original source for the remedy remains, only the vital energy or life force, which imparts healing properties to the remedy. No harm will come to your pet regardless of the toxicity of the original compound used in the preparation of the remedy.

But do nosodes work? Some doctors seem to prefer nosodes manufactured by specific homeopathic pharmacies, as they feel there is a definite difference in the ability of nosodes to stimulate the immune system. In their opinions, the manufacturer of the nosode is important and some vaccination nosodes work better than others.

To prevent disease, nosodes are supposed to work in the same manner as conventional vaccines, namely by stimulating antibodies to fight off infections. Nosodes have been reported to control outbreaks of infectious disease in animals in a kennel situation. While good controlled studies are lacking, homeopathic veterinarians have reported success in some patients when treating infectious disease with the homeopathic nosode.

OTHER NATURAL TREATMENTS

There is no cure for distemper, although many holistic doctors report anecdotal cases of cure using nutritional support such as a natural **diet** (page 314) and **antioxidants** (page 158), in addition to the homeopathic nosode. Supplements listed under the heading of **Infectious Diseases** (page 105) may also be used.

The natural treatments are widely used with variable success but have not all been thoroughly investigated and proven at this time.

As with any condition, the most healthful natural diet will improve the pet's overall health.

CONVENTIONAL THERAPY

There is no treatment for distemper, and most pets are euthanized once seizures develop. Supportive care includes antibiotics, force-feeding, and fluid therapy.

 # EAR INFECTIONS

Principal Natural Treatments
Herbal drops with aloe vera and calendula

Other Natural Treatments
None

Ear infections in dogs and cats are caused by bacteria, yeasts, or **ear mites** (page 132).

Chronic ear infections occur in certain breeds such as Retrievers and Spaniels due to anatomic abnormalities or lifestyle (frequent swimming). Chronic ear infections may also be caused by underlying abnormalities such as **food allergies** (page 3), **atopy** (page 3), or **hypothyroidism** (page 103). Accurate diagnosis requires examination of the ear discharge under a microscope (ear cytology). A medicated ear flushing (sedation is often required) will clean the ear and allow the owners to apply treatment more easily.

PRINCIPAL NATURAL TREATMENTS

The treatment utilizes herbal ear drops containing herbs such as **aloe vera** (page 156) and **calendula** (page 173). Aloe is often used topically as a soothing rinse or topical preparation. Aloe contains a number of beneficial chemicals. The prostaglandins in aloe have beneficial effects on inflammation, allergy, and wound healing. While many would profess to appreciate the healing effect of aloe on wounds and burns, no properly designed scientific studies have been completed that could tell us just how effective aloe really is for these conditions. Topical aloe gel may improve the rate of healing of minor cuts and scrapes, although one report suggests that aloe can actually impair healing in severe wounds.

Aloe has antibacterial and antifungal effects; the antibacterial effects have been compared to silver sulfadiazine.

Calendula, also called the pot marigold, is an herb related to the sunflower. It is useful as an anti-inflammatory herb and for its antibacterial and antifungal properties. The various oils in the flowers (such as essential oils and flavonoids) assist in cell healing and decrease bacteria and fungi in the wounded part. Diluted calendula is often recommended for ear infections, eye infections, and topical treatment of minor wounds. It may also be helpful topically for pets with ringworm. Internally, calendula can treat inflammation and infection of the digestive and urinary systems.

Calendula may induce abortions and should be avoided in pregnant animals. Calendula contains a small amount of salicylate in the leaves and stems. While unlikely to be harmful due to the small amount of salicylate, to be safe for long-term use, it should only be used internally under veterinary supervision in cats.

As with any condition, the most healthful natural diet will improve the pet's overall health.

CONVENTIONAL THERAPY

Conventional therapy utilizes antibiotic or antifungal ear drops (combined with corticosteroids in the drops to relieve inflammation). Therapy, following a medicated ear flush in the doctor's office, must be given for 2 to 3 weeks in most cases.

EPILEPSY

Principal Natural Treatments
  Natural diet, choline/lecithin, orthomolecular therapy

Other Natural Treatments
  Bach flower essences, DMG, taurine, thyroid supplement/glandulars, herbs: *Ginkgo biloba,* gotu kola, kava kava, skullcap, valerian; B vitamins, magnesium, tyrosine in combination with taurine; bugelweed, dandelion leaf, burdock, red clover

Epilepsy is the name given to seizural disorders in dogs and cats for which there is no identifiable cause. Primary epilepsy is the result of functional cerebral disturbances without obvious cause other than a possible hereditary predisposition.

For a diagnosis of epilepsy to be made, other causes of seizures (including poisoning, infection, tumors, and cranial trauma) must be ruled out through diagnostic testing. While true epilepsy can occur in pets of any age, most commonly

Epilepsy

dogs and cats with epilepsy begin demonstrating seizures between 6 months and 5 years of age.

Seizures occur in epileptic pets as hyperexcitable neurons within the brain that show activity. As the development of progressive and refractory seizures correlates with the number of seizures, early diagnosis and treatment are important in preventing a worsening of future seizures. Generally, conventional anti-epileptic medicine is not prescribed unless the pet has at least one seizure per month, as the goal of treatment is to reduce, rather than to eliminate, seizure frequency, severity, and length.

PRINCIPAL NATURAL TREATMENTS

Natural Diet

A number of pets with epilepsy have been reported (through anecdotal reports) to show improvement upon dietary manipulation. Suggested dietary changes (which may decrease a food hypersensitivity that causes the pet to seizure) include: diets free of red meat, homemade diets free of common dietary allergens (beef, chicken, corn), diets free of preservatives, and diets using minimally processed foods. Some pets may also be sensitive to the flavoring in monthly or daily heartworm preventative medications; therefore, using a non-flavored product may also be helpful when dietary manipulation alone is not successful. Since seizures are a medical problem, owners should not try dietary manipulation without a proper diagnosis and veterinary supervision.

Choline/Lecithin

Lecithin contains a substance called phosphatidylcholine (PC) that is presumed to be responsible for its medicinal effects. Phosphatidylcholine is a major part of the membranes surrounding our cells. However, when phosphatidylcholine is consumed, it is broken down into choline rather than being carried directly to cell membranes. Choline acts like folic acid, TMG (trimethylglycine), and SAMe (S-adenosylmethionine) to promote methylation. It is also used to make acetylcholine, a nerve chemical essential for proper brain function.

Choline and phosphatidylcholine are effective for treating human neurological disorders with presumed choline deficiencies including tardive dyskinesia, Huntington's chorea, and Friedreich's ataxia.

For use as a supplement or a food additive, lecithin is often manufactured from soy.

One choline-containing product that has been used successfully in pets is Cholodin. Cholodin contains choline, phosphatidylcholine, DL-methionine, and vitamins and minerals. Choline provides methyl groups used by the body in a number of biological reactions and acts as a precursor of acetylcholine. Phosphatidylcholine (lecithin) is part of the plasma membrane of mammalian cells and also provides additional choline for acetylcholine synthesis. Methionine and inositol also are involved in neurotransmitter metabolism.

Due to its ability to interact with cells of the nervous system, Cholodin is also recommended for pets with epilepsy. Studies have shown decreased seizure frequency in pets supplemented with products containing increased levels of choline and phosphatidylcholine. Cholodin, given at 1 to 2 pills daily for a small dog or cat, and 2 to 4 pills daily for a large dog, and other choline-containing products can be tried to determine effectiveness under your veterinarian's supervision. Do not stop anti-epileptic drugs without your veterinarian's permission.

Lecithin is believed to be generally safe. However, some people taking high dosages (several grams daily) experience minor but annoying side effects, such as abdominal discomfort, diarrhea, and nausea. Maximum safe dosages for young children, pregnant or nursing women, or those with severe liver or kidney disease have not been determined; the same precautions are probably warranted in pets.

Orthomolecular Therapy

Orthomolecular medicine (often called "megavitamin therapy") seeks to use increased levels of vitamins and minerals (mainly antioxidants) to help treat a variety of medical disorders. While daily amounts of vitamins and minerals have been recommended as an attempt to prevent nutritional deficiencies, orthomolecular medicine uses higher doses as part of the therapy for disease.

The pet food industry relies on recommendations by the National Research Council (NRC) to prevent diseases caused by nutrient deficiencies in the "average" pet, yet the NRC has not attempted to determine the *optimum* amount of nutrients or their effects in treating medical disorders. While a minimum amount of nutrients may be satisfactory in preventing diseases caused by nutrient deficiencies, it is important to realize that there is no "average" pet, and that every pet has unique nutritional needs.

It is unlikely that our current recommendations are adequate to maintain health in every pet. Each pet has unique requirements for nutrients. Additionally, these needs will vary depending upon the pet's health. For example, in times of stress or disease additional nutrients above and beyond those needed for health will be required. Orthomolecular medicine evaluates the needs of the pet and uses increased nutrients to fight disease.

Note: Owners should not diagnose and treat their pets without veterinary supervision. Many medical disorders present similar symptoms. Also, megavitamin therapy can be toxic if not used properly.

As mentioned under **Natural Diets** (page 335), correcting the diet is important as there is anecdotal evidence that food hypersensitivity may be the cause of seizures in some pets. A small number of cases treated concurrently with anticonvulsant medicines plus antioxidants have shown promise and allowed a reduction or elimination of seizures. While more cases must be treated before any conclusions can be reached, using antioxidant vitamins and minerals may be helpful in selected patients with epilepsy.

Treatment uses **vitamin A** (10,000 IU for small dogs and cats, up to 30,000 IU for large dogs), crystalline ascorbic acid (750 mg for small dogs and cats, up to 3,000 mg for large dogs), and vitamin E (800 IU for small dogs and cats, up to 2,400 IU for large dogs). The antioxidant mineral **selenium** (20 mcg for small dogs and cats, up to 60 mcg for large dogs) is also added to the regimen. Once asymptomatic, a maintenance protocol using gradually lower dosages of vitamins A and E and the mineral selenium are prescribed to reduce the chance for toxicity. Promis-

ing results have been seen in many pets treated with this regimen.

OTHER NATURAL TREATMENTS

Bach flower essences (page 388), **DMG** (page 194), **taurine** (page 278), thyroid supplement/**glandulars** (page 393); herbs: *Ginkgo biloba* (page 208), **gotu kola** (page 221), **kava kava** (page 229), **skullcap** (page 273), **valerian** (page 282), **B vitamins** (page 288), and **magnesium** (page 237).

Note: Some doctors have reported success with tyrosine, given in combination with taurine at 5 to 10 mg per pound (of each supplement) of body weight 1 to 2 times daily, which may also reduce seizures by increasing the seizure threshold.

These therapies can be used in conjunction with conventional therapies as they are unlikely to be effective by themselves in most patients with severe disease. The natural treatments are widely used with variable success but have not been thoroughly investigated and proven at this time.

As with any condition, the most healthful natural diet will improve the pet's overall health.

CONVENTIONAL THERAPY

Conventional therapy involves various anticonvulsant medications, including phenobarbital, potassium bromide, or valium.

Phenobarbital is commonly used to control seizures in dogs and cats with epilepsy. Side effects include increased thirst, urination, and appetite; occasionally, excessive sedation and a wobbly gait are seen, especially as the dosage increases. Increased liver enzymes, which may or may not be associated with liver damage, can be seen, as can anemia. Dogs and cats taking phenobarbital should be reevaluated periodically and have regular blood profiles to monitor side effects and therapeutic blood levels (generally every 3 to 6 months).

Potassium bromide is not approved for use in dogs and cats but has become a popular medication for the control of seizures in dogs. It appears to be a safer medication than phenobarbital (fewer side effects), although phenobarbital rarely produces any significant side effects in dogs. Potassium bromide can be used in dogs as the sole therapeutic agent, in combination with phenobarbital (if needed), or in place of phenobarbital for those dogs whose seizures are not adequately controlled with phenobarbital or who suffer from secondary liver disease as a result of phenobarbital therapy. Many doctors are now using potassium bromide as the initial (and often only) medical therapy for dogs with epilepsy.

Side effects of potassium bromide may include tremors, stupor, wobbly gait, lack of appetite, vomiting, and constipation. Potassium bromide may rarely cause pancreatitis when it is used in combination with phenobarbital or primidone (another anticonvulsant that is rarely used in dogs). Dogs placed on low-salt diets may have increased bromide toxicity as a result of decreased chloride ion levels. Extra salt in the diet, as well as use of diuretics, may decrease the blood levels of bromide and increase the frequency of seizures. Dogs taking potassium bromide should be reevaluated periodically and have regular blood profiles to monitor side effects and therapeutic blood levels (generally every 3 to 6 months).

Valium is most commonly used as an injection for pets in status epilepticus, which is a state of active, ongoing seizures. Valium is not usually used as a sole medication for treating dogs with epilepsy, although it may be used as the sole agent in treating epileptic cats. Oral administration of diazepam has been rarely associated with severe liver disease in cats. Cats taking diazepam on a regular basis should be frequently tested for liver disease.

FELINE IMMUNODEFICIENCY VIRUS INFECTION (FIV)

Principal Natural Treatments
Glycoproteins such as acemannan, orthomolecular therapy

Other Natural Treatments
Natural diet, antioxidants, DMG, alfalfa, aloe vera, astragalus, boswellia, burdock, dandelion leaf, dandelion root, echinacea, garlic, German chamomile, ginger, ginseng, goldenseal, gotu kola, hawthorn, horsetail, licorice, marshmallow, milk thistle, nettle, Oregon grape, red clover, sage, St. John's wort, turmeric, yarrow, yellow dock; mushrooms: reishi, shiitake, cordyceps, maitake; homeopathic nosodes

---

Feline immunodeficiency virus (FIV) affects mainly cats with exposure to the outdoor environment; most commonly, intact males are infected. The virus is spread by biting. Once infected, most cats do not develop the disease for many years (the median age of healthy infected cats is 3 years of age, whereas the median age of clinically ill cats is 10 years of age, indicating a latent period of an average of 7 years).

Primary FIV infections present with fever and lymph node enlargement. The most typical signs seen in infected FIV-positive cats are chronic diseases, such as diarrhea, skin infections, and dental disease. However, any clinical signs (such as seizures) can occur as the signs that are seen depend upon the specific body tissue infected by the virus. Cats who persistently test positive on the blood tests for the virus will usually be infected for life.

PRINCIPAL NATURAL TREATMENTS

Glycoproteins such as acemannan (see **aloe vera,** page 156) may be helpful, or orthomolecular therapy.

Glycoproteins

Glycoproteins are protein molecules bound to carbohydrate molecules. Glycoprotein molecules coat the surface of every cell with a nucleus in the human body. The body uses the glycoproteins on cell surface glycoconjugates as communication or recognition molecules. These communications may then result in other cellular events, including secretion of bioactive substances (interferon, interleukin-1, complement), ingestion of bacteria and cell debris, inhibition of adherence necessary for bacterial infection, and the spread of cancer cell metastasis.

Scientists have identified eight sugars, glycoforms, found on human cell surfaces glycoforms that are involved in cellular recognition processes. Of the 200 such sugars occurring naturally in plants, to date only these eight have been identified as components of cellular glycoproteins. These eight sugars that are essential for glycoconjugate synthesis (mannose, galactose, fucose, xylose, glucose, sialic acid, N-acetylglucosamine, N-acetylgalactosamine) can be readily absorbed and directly incorporated into glycoproteins and glycolipids.

Recent research has found specific cell surface glycoforms to be characteristic of many disease conditions. In some patients with rheumatoid arthritis, some defense cells (IgG antibody) bear malformed glycoproteins. These cells are missing required galactose molecules; the extent to which the galactose molecules are missing correlates with disease severity and reverses in disease remission. In people with cancer, more than 20 different malignancies are known to be associated with characteristic glycoproteins.

Glyconutritional supplements are designed to provide substrates for the body to use in building part of the glycoconjugates on cell surfaces. These supplements, most commonly acemannan and mannose, are designed to make the necessary sugars available to the cells quicker and in greater quantity.

Acemannan is a glycoprotein (a long chain of mannan polymers with random o-acetyl groups) derived from the aloe vera plant that has been shown to increase the body's production of immune-modulating chemicals, including interleukins 1 and 6, interferon-gamma, and Prostaglandin E_2 and tumor necrosis factor alpha by macrophages. Acemannan also enhances macrophage phagocytosis and nonspecific cytotoxicity, which increases the ability of white blood cells (macrophages) to destroy infectious organisms. Glycoproteins such as acemannan also offer antiviral activity as well as bone marrow stimulating activity.

Scientific Evidence

Acemannan has been proposed as an adjunctive therapy for cats with feline immunodeficiency virus. In one study of feline immunodeficiency virus (FIV) infections, a 75% survival rate was obtained for cats in Stage 3, 4, or 5 (seriously ill cats for which life expectancy is up to one year for Stage 4 cats and 1 to 6 months for stage 5 cats). Cats showed increased body weight, decreased lymph node size, and a reduction in sepsis (infections that are commonly seen in end stage FIV cats). Neutrophil counts improved, as well as lymphocyte counts, indicating an improvement in the immune status of the infected cats. Cats responded regardless of route of administration of acemannan (weekly IV injection or weekly subcutaneous injection, of 2 mg/kg acemannan, or daily oral administration of 100 mg/cat acemannan). No signs of toxicity were noted in any cats, although four cats given the IV injections showed an immediate allergic reaction, which commonly occurs in cats given IV push injections of very large molecular weight compounds such as acemannan).

In these studies, all cats remained virus positive but experienced a noticeable improvement in the quality of life. While acemannan (and other glycoproteins) may be helpful for cats with immunodeficiency viral infections, more studies are needed to determine what if any true long-term benefit infected cats might experience. At the current time, acemannan and other glycoproteins such as mannose, one of eight glycoproteins found in the oral supplement, Ambrotose, probably serve as a useful treatment option for this chronic feline viral disease for which conventional therapies really do not exist (conventional therapies are of no particular benefit and serve mainly to support the sick cat).

All eight of the glycoconjugate sugars are readily absorbed from the intestines when taken orally. Studies have shown intact mannose molecules are rapidly absorbed from the intestine of rats into the blood, elevating the blood mannose levels by 3- to 10-fold, and mannose is cleared from the blood within hours. The conclusion reached was that mannose was absorbed from the intestinal tract into the blood and from the blood into the cells. These studies suggest that dietary mannose may make a significant contribution to glycoform synthesis in mammals.

Other human and animal ingestion studies show that mannose is readily absorbed, and is cleared from the blood over several hours; some of the mannose was incorporated into glycoproteins. After absorption into the blood, glycoconjugate sugars generally become distributed (usually as glycoproteins and glycolipids) into body fluids, organs, and various body tissues.

In one study, healthy humans were given radiolabeled galactose, mannose or glucose. This study showed that galactose and mannose were directly incorporated into human glycoproteins without first being broken down into glucose. The conclusion was that specific dietary sugars could represent a new class of nutrients and that the use of these nutrients could have important consequences. Therapy with mannose offers a treatment that is easy to administer and is nontoxic.

Glycoconjugate sugars have been shown to kill bacteria and viruses and prevent infection caused by them. For example, mannose acts to prevent bacterial infection by binding to the sites on the bacteria and preventing attachment of the bacteria to sites on the cells of the host. Glycoconjugate sugars display anti-viral activity as a result of their ability to stimulate macrophages to release interferon. They also interfere with normal virus function.

Adverse effects caused by glycoconjugate sugars are rare and usually occur when they are injected or when doses greatly exceed levels that would be expected in normal diets. For pets being treated with the most commonly used glycoproteins (acemannan and mannose), side effects would not be expected.

(Popular glycoprotein supplements used in pets are manufactured by Carrington Laboratories and Mannatech Laboratories.)

Orthomolecular Therapy

Orthomolecular medicine (often called "megavitamin therapy") seeks to use increased levels of vitamins and minerals (mainly antioxidants) to help treat a variety of medical disorders. While daily amounts of vitamins and minerals have been recommended as an attempt to prevent nutritional deficiencies, orthomolecular medicine uses higher doses as part of the therapy for disease.

The pet food industry relies on recommendations by the National Research Council (NRC) to prevent diseases caused by nutrient deficiencies in the "average" pet; yet, the NRC has not attempted to determine the *optimum* amount of nutrients or their effects in treating medical disorders. While a minimum amount of nutrients may be satisfactory in preventing diseases caused by nutrient deficiencies, it is important to realize that there is no "average" pet, and that every pet has unique nutritional needs.

It is unlikely that our current recommendations are adequate to maintain health in every pet. Each pet has unique requirements for nutrients. Additionally, these needs will vary depending upon the pet's health. For example, in times of stress or disease additional nutrients above and beyond those needed for health will be required. Orthomolecular medicine evaluates the needs of the pet and uses increased nutrients to fight disease.

While orthomolecular therapy of FIV infection has not been reported, it might be worth a try as it has shown helpful in some cats with feline leukemia virus infection. Orthomolecular therapy of feline leukemia utilizes 750 mg of sodium ascorbate, 750 IU of vitamin A, and 75 IU of vitamin E. A number of cats on this protocol tested negative for leukemia virus within 2 years of initial diagnosis on both ELISA and IFA tests. Also, many cats displaying signs of chronic illness became devoid of symptoms. Since false negative test results are possible, all cats testing negative on blood ELISA testing treated with orthomolecular therapy should have follow-up IFA testing done.

OTHER NATURAL TREATMENTS

Other therapies such as **natural diet** (page 314), **antioxidants** (page 158), and **DMG** (page 194) may be useful. The immune-boosting herbs include: **alfalfa** (page 156), **aloe vera** (page 156), **astragalus** (page 160), **burdock** (page 170), **dandelion leaf** (page 193), **dandelion root** (page 193), **echinacea** (page 195), **garlic** (page 204), **ginseng** (page 210), **goldenseal** (page 220), **hawthorn** (page 223), **licorice** (page 234), **marshmallow** (page 240), **milk thistle** (page

241), **nettle** (page 245), **red clover** (page 262), **St. John's wort** (page 276), **turmeric** (page 280), and **yellow dock** (page 309). The herbs for infections include **aloe vera** (page 156), **astragalus** (page 160), **boswellia** (page 168), **echinacea** (page 195), **garlic** (page 204), **German chamomile** (topical, page 206), **ginger** (page 210), **goldenseal** (topical, page 220), **gotu kola** (page 221), **horsetail** (urinary system, page 225), **licorice** (page 234), **marshmallow** (page 240), **Oregon grape** (page 251), **sage** (page 264), **St. John's wort** (page 276), **turmeric** (page 280), and **yarrow** (page 308). Mushrooms such as **reishi** (page 264), **shiitake** (page 272), **cordyceps** (page 191), and **maitake** (page 238) are also recommended. **Homeopathic** nosodes may be helpful.

The natural treatments are widely used with variable success but have not been thoroughly investigated and proven at this time.

CONVENTIONAL THERAPY

There is no cure for FIV infection. Clinical signs are treated as needed; chronic infections are treated with antibiotics. Supportive care for cats with fever and lack of appetite (such as fluid therapy and force-feeding) are used as needed; human alpha-interferon may be helpful.

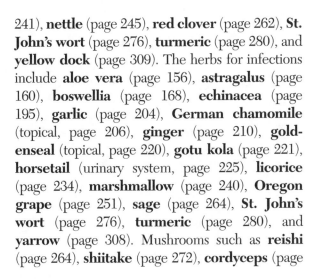

FELINE INFECTIOUS PERITONITIS (FIP)

Principal Natural Treatments
Glycoproteins such as acemannan, orthomolecular therapy

Other Natural Treatments
Natural diet, antioxidants, DMG, alfalfa, aloe vera, astragalus, boswellia, burdock, dandelion leaf, dandelion root, echinacea, garlic, German chamomile, ginger, ginseng, goldenseal, gotu kola, hawthorn, horsetail, licorice, marshmallow, milk thistle, nettle, Oregon grape, red clover, St. John's wort, turmeric, yarrow, yellow dock; mushrooms: reishi, cordyceps, and maitake; homeopathic nosodes

Feline infectious peritonitis is a disease caused by systemic infection with a feline corona virus. FIP can occur in any cat; most are less than one year of age. Two forms of the disease occur, the dry form and the wet form. The dry form causes the formation of pyogranulomas (abscesses) in various organs of the body. Clinical signs depend upon the organ affected (seizures if the brain is infected, paralysis if the spinal cord is affected, blindness if the eyes are affected, kidney failure if the kidneys are affected, and so forth). The wet form, which is the form usually seen in younger patients, causes fluid to leak from the blood vessels and accumulate in the chest (causing difficulty breathing) and/or abdomen (creating a pot-bellied appearance). Once infected, most cats with the wet form die or are euthanized. Cats with the dry form can potentially live a normal life depending upon the organ involved.

PRINCIPAL NATURAL TREATMENTS

There is no cure for FIP. Similar immune-supporting remedies that are recommended for cats with FeLV or FIV may be helpful, but most cases of the wet form are ultimately fatal. Supportive therapies include glycoproteins such as acemannan and orthomolecular therapy.

Glycoproteins

Glycoproteins are protein molecules bound to carbohydrate molecules. Glycoprotein molecules coat the surface of every cell with a nucleus in the human body. The body uses the glycoproteins on cell surface glycoconjugates as communication or recognition molecules. These communications may then result in other cellular events, including secretion of bioactive substances (interferon, interleukin-1, complement), ingestion of bacteria and cell debris, inhibition of adherence necessary for bacterial infection, and the spread of cancer cell metastasis.

Scientists have identified eight sugars, glycoforms, found on human cell surfaces that are involved in cellular recognition processes. Of the 200 such sugars occurring naturally in plants, to date only these eight have been identified as components of cellular glycoproteins. These eight sugars that are essential for glycoconjugate synthesis (mannose, galactose, fucose, xylose, glucose, sialic acid, N-acetylglucosamine, N-acetylgalactosamine) can be readily absorbed and directly incorporated into glycoproteins and glycolipids.

Recent research has found specific cell surface glycoforms to be characteristic of many disease conditions. In some patients with rheumatoid arthritis, some defense cells (IgG antibody) bear malformed glycoproteins. These cells are missing required galactose molecules; the extent to which the galactose molecules are missing correlates with disease severity and reverses in disease remission. In people with cancer, more than 20 different malignancies are known to be associated with characteristic glycoproteins.

Glyconutritional supplements are designed to provide substrates for the body to use in building part of the glycoconjugates on cell surfaces. These supplements, most commonly acemannan and mannose, are designed to make the necessary sugars available to the cells quicker and in greater quantity.

Acemannan is a glycoprotein (a long chain of mannan polymers with random o-acetyl groups) derived from the aloe vera plant that has been shown to increase the body's production of immune-modulating chemicals including interleukins 1 and 6, interferon-gamma, and Prostaglandin E_2 and tumor necrosis factor alpha by macrophages. Acemannan also enhances macrophage phagocytosis and nonspecific cytotoxicity, which increases the ability of white blood cells (macrophages) to destroy infectious organisms. Glycoproteins such as acemannan also offer antiviral activity as well as bone marrow stimulating activity.

Scientific Evidence

While acemannan has been proposed as an adjunctive therapy for cats with feline leukemia virus infection and feline immunodeficiency virus, there are no definitive studies showing its use in the treatment of FIP. However, since the therapy is safe and there are no conventional therapies, using acemannan may be of help to the cat infected with FIP.

All eight of the glycoconjugate sugars are readily absorbed from the intestines when taken orally. Studies have shown intact mannose molecules are rapidly absorbed from the intestine of rats into the blood, elevating the blood mannose levels by 3- to 10-fold, and mannose is cleared from the blood within hours. The conclusion reached was that mannose was absorbed from the intestinal tract into the blood and from the blood into the cells. These studies suggest that dietary mannose may make a significant contribution to glycoform synthesis in mammals.

Other human and animal ingestion studies show that mannose is readily absorbed, and is cleared from the blood over several hours; some of the mannose was incorporated into glycoproteins. After absorption into the blood, glycoconjugate sugars generally become distributed (usually as glycoproteins and glycolipids) into body fluids, organs, and various body tissues.

In one study, healthy humans were given radiolabeled galactose, mannose, or glucose. This study showed that galactose and mannose were directly incorporated into human glycoproteins without first being broken down into glucose. The conclusion was that specific dietary sugars could represent a new class of nutrients and that the use of these nutrients could have important consequences. Therapy with mannose offers a treatment that is easy to administer and is nontoxic.

Glycoconjugate sugars have been shown to kill bacteria and viruses and prevent infection by them. For example, mannose acts to prevent bacterial infection by binding to the sites on the bacteria and preventing attachment of the bacteria to sites on the cells of the host. Glycoconjugate sugars display anti-viral activity as a result of their ability to stimulate macrophages to release interferon. They also interfere with normal virus function.

Adverse effects caused by glycoconjugate sugars are rare and usually occur when they are injected or when doses greatly exceed levels that would be expected in normal diets. For pets

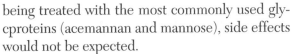

being treated with the most commonly used gly-cproteins (acemannan and mannose), side effects would not be expected.

(Popular glycoprotein supplements used in pets are manufactured by Carrington Laboratories and Mannatech Laboratories.)

Orthomolecular Therapy

Orthomolecular medicine (often called "megavitamin therapy") seeks to use increased levels of vitamins and minerals (mainly antioxidants) to help treat a variety of medical disorders. While daily amounts of vitamins and minerals have been recommended as an attempt to prevent nutritional deficiencies, orthomolecular medicine uses higher doses as part of the therapy for disease.

The pet food industry relies on recommendations by the National Research Council (NRC) to prevent diseases caused by nutrient deficiencies in the "average" pet, yet the NRC has not attempted to determine the *optimum* amount of nutrients or their effects in treating medical disorders. While a minimum amount of nutrients may be satisfactory in preventing diseases caused by nutrient deficiencies, it is important to realize that there is no "average" pet, and that every pet has unique nutritional needs.

It is unlikely that our current recommendations are adequate to maintain health in every pet. Each pet has unique requirements for nutrients. Additionally, these needs will vary depending upon the pet's health. For example, in times of stress or disease additional nutrients above and beyond those needed for health will be required. Orthomolecular medicine evaluates the needs of the pet and uses increased nutrients to fight disease.

While no studies show effectiveness in cats with FIP, orthomolecular therapy of cats with leukemia infection has shown promise in some cats and might be worth trying in cats infected with FIP. Orthomolecular therapy of feline leukemia utilizes 750 mg of sodium ascorbate, 750 IU of vitamin A, and 75 IU of vitamin E. A number of cats on this protocol tested negative for leukemia virus within 2 years of initial diagnosis on both ELISA and IFA tests. Also, many cats displaying signs of chronic illness became devoid of symptoms. Since false negative test re-sults are possible, all cats testing negative on blood ELISA testing treated with orthomolecular therapy should have follow-up IFA testing done.

OTHER NATURAL TREATMENTS

Other therapies such as **natural diet** (page 335), **antioxidants** (page 158), **DMG** (page 194); immune-boosting herbs **alfalfa** (page 156), **aloe vera** (page 156), **astragalus** (page 160), **burdock** (page 170), **dandelion leaf** (page 193), **dandelion root** (page 193), **echinacea** (page 195), **garlic** (page 204), **ginseng** (page 210), **goldenseal** (page 220), **hawthorn** (page 223), **licorice** (page 234), **marshmallow** (page 240), **milk thistle** (page 241), **nettle** (page 245), **red clover** (page 262), **St. John's wort** (page 276), **turmeric** (page 280), **yellow dock** (page 309). Herbs for infections include **aloe vera** (page 156), **astragalus** (page 160), **boswellia** (page 168), **echinacea** (page 195), **garlic** (page 204), **German chamomile** (topical, page 206), **ginger** (page 207), **goldenseal** (topical, page 220), **gotu kola** (page 221), **horsetail** (urinary system, page 225), **licorice** (page 234), **marshmallow** (page 240), **Oregon grape** (page 251), **sage** (page 264), **St. John's wort** (page 276), **turmeric** (page 280), **yarrow** (page 308). Mushrooms such as **reishi** (page 264), **shiitake** (page 272), **cordyceps** (page 191), and **maitake** (page 238) are also recommended. **Homeopathic** nosodes may be helpful.

There is no cure for FIP. Similar immune-supporting remedies that are recommended for cats with FeLV or FIV may be helpful, but most cases of the wet form are ultimately fatal. The natural treatments are widely used with variable success but have not been thoroughly investigated and proven at this time.

CONVENTIONAL THERAPY

There is no cure for FIP. Cats with the wet form may respond temporarily to antibiotics, corticosteroids, or other chemotherapeutic drugs, and to human alpha-interferon. Cats with the dry form often live a normal life depending upon the organ affected. Otherwise, no specific treatment is available.

FELINE LEUKEMIA VIRUS INFECTION (FeLV)

Principal Natural Treatments

Glycoproteins such as acemannan, orthomolecular therapy

Other Natural Treatments

Natural diet, antioxidants, DMG, alfalfa, aloe vera, astragalus, burdock, dandelion leaf, dandelion root, echinacea, garlic, ginseng, goldenseal, hawthorn, licorice, marshmallow, milk thistle, nettle, red clover, St. John's wort, turmeric, yellow dock, boswellia, ginger, gotu kola, horsetail, Oregon grape, sage, yarrow; mushrooms such as reishi, cordyceps, and maitake; homeopathic nosodes

Feline leukemia virus infection is a viral infection that is spread between cats by prolonged contact with saliva or nasal secretions. Infection most commonly occurs in outdoor male cats between 1 to 6 years of age. Approximately 30% of exposed cats are persistently viremic (and remain infected), 30% are transiently viremic (infected with the virus and then cure themselves of the infection), and the remaining 40% of cats are latently infected and test negative on blood testing (the infection resides somewhere in the body such as the spleen, lymph nodes, or bone marrow but not in the blood).

Similar to infection with the FIV virus, the most typical signs seen in infected FeLV positive cats is chronic disease, such as diarrhea, skin infections, and dental disease. Cancerous tumors may also occur. Any clinical signs (such as seizures) can occur as the signs that are seen depend upon the specific body tissue infected by the virus. Cats who persistently test positive on the blood tests for the virus will usually be infected for life.

PRINCIPAL NATURAL TREATMENTS

Glycoproteins

Glycoproteins are protein molecules bound to carbohydrate molecules. Glycoprotein molecules coat the surface of every cell with a nucleus in the human body. The body uses the glycoproteins on cell surface glycoconjugates as communication or recognition molecules. These communications may then result in other cellular events, including secretion of bioactive substances (interferon, interleukin-1, complement), ingestion of bacteria and cell debris, inhibition of adherence necessary for bacterial infection, and the spread of cancer cell metastasis.

Scientists have identified eight sugars, glycoforms, found on human cell surfaces that are involved in cellular recognition processes. Of the 200 such sugars occurring naturally in plants, to date only these eight have been identified as components of cellular glycoproteins. These eight sugars that are essential for glycoconjugate synthesis (mannose, galactose, fucose, xylose, glucose, sialic acid, N-acetylglucosamine, N-acetylgalactosamine) can be readily absorbed and directly incorporated into glycoproteins and glycolipids.

Recent research has found specific cell surface glycoforms to be characteristic of many disease conditions. In some patients with rheumatoid arthritis, some defense cells (IgG antibody) bear malformed glycoproteins. These cells are missing required galactose molecules; the extent to which the galactose molecules are missing correlates with disease severity and reverses in disease remission. In people with cancer, more than 20 different malignancies are known to be associated with characteristic glycoproteins.

Glyconutritional supplements are designed to provide substrates for the body to use in building part of the glycoconjugates on cell surfaces. These supplements, most commonly acemannan and mannose, are designed to make the necessary sugars available to the cells quicker and in greater quantity.

Acemannan is a glycoprotein (a long chain of mannan polymers with random o-acetyl groups) derived from the aloe vera plant that has been shown to increase the body's production of immune-modulating chemicals including interleukins-1 and 6, interferon-gamma, and Prostaglandin E_2 and tumor necrosis factor alpha by macrophages. Acemannan also enhances macrophage phagocytosis and non-specific cytotoxicity, which increases the ability of white blood cells (macrophages) to destroy infectious organisms. Glycoproteins such as acemannan also offer antiviral activity as well as bone marrow stimulating activity.

Scientific Evidence

Acemannan has been proposed as an adjunctive therapy for cats with feline leukemia virus infection. No definitive studies of large numbers of cats have shown the cats to revert to a negative viral status, although the administration of acemannan did appear to prolong the life of the cats. In sick cats with leukemia virus infection, 29 out of 41 cats survived a 12-week study period using intraperitoneal acemannan (2 mg/kg weekly for the first 6 weeks of the study). Two months following the 12-week study, 21 cats were still alive (1 had died, 5 cats could not be followed up as their owners had moved). In a similar study of sick cats that were leukemia positive and not treated with acemannan, 40 out of 46 cats died or were euthanized within 5 days of diagnosis.

In these studies, all cats remained virus positive but experienced a noticeable improvement in the quality of life. While acemannan (and other glycoproteins) may be helpful for cats with leukemia viral infections, more studies are needed to determine what if any true long-term benefit infected cats might experience. At the current time, acemannan and other glycoproteins such as mannose (Ambrotose) probably serve as a useful treatment option for this chronic feline viral disease for which conventional therapies really do not exist (conventional therapies are of no particular benefit and serve mainly to support the sick cat).

All eight of the glycoconjugate sugars are readily absorbed from the intestines when taken orally. Studies have shown intact mannose molecules are rapidly absorbed from the intestine of rats into the blood, elevating the blood mannose levels by 3- to 10-fold, and mannose is cleared from the blood within hours. The conclusion reached was that mannose was absorbed from the intestinal tract into the blood and from the blood into the cells. These studies suggest that dietary mannose may make a significant contribution to glycoform synthesis in mammals.

Other human and animal ingestion studies show that mannose is readily absorbed, and is cleared from the blood over several hours; some of the mannose was incorporated into glycoproteins. After absorption into the blood, glycoconjugate sugars generally become distributed (usually as glycoproteins and glycolipids) into body fluids, organs, and various body tissues.

In one study, healthy humans were given radiolabeled galactose, mannose, or glucose. This study showed that galactose and mannose were directly incorporated into human glycoproteins without first being broken down into glucose. The conclusion was that specific dietary sugars could represent a new class of nutrients and that the use of these nutrients could have important consequences. Therapy with mannose offers a treatment that is easy to administer and is nontoxic.

Adverse effects caused by glycoconjugate sugars are rare and usually occur when they are injected or when doses greatly exceed levels that would be expected in normal diets. For pets being treated with the most commonly used glycoproteins (acemannan and mannose), side effects would not be expected.

(Popular glycoprotein supplements used in pets are manufactured by Carrington Laboratories and Mannatech Laboratories.)

Orthomolecular Therapy

Orthomolecular medicine (often called "megavitamin therapy") seeks to use increased levels of vitamins and minerals (mainly antioxidants) to help treat a variety of medical disorders. While daily amounts of vitamins and minerals have been recommended as an attempt to prevent nutritional deficiencies, orthomolecular medicine uses higher doses as part of the therapy for disease.

The pet food industry relies on recommendations by the National Research Council (NRC) to prevent diseases caused by nutrient deficiencies in the "average" pet; yet, the NRC has not attempted to determine the *optimum* amount of nutrients or their effects in treating medical disorders. While a minimum amount of nutrients may be satisfactory in preventing diseases caused by nutrient deficiencies, it is important to realize that there is no "average" pet, and that every pet has unique nutritional needs.

It is unlikely that our current recommendations are adequate to maintain health in every pet since each pet has unique requirements for nutrients. Additionally, these needs will vary depending upon the pet's health. For example, in times of stress or disease additional nutrients above and beyond those needed for health will be required. Orthomolecular medicine evaluates the needs of the pet and uses increased nutrients to fight disease.

Orthomolecular therapy of feline leukemia utilizes 750 mg of sodium ascorbate, 750 IU of **vitamin A** (page 284), and 75 IU of **vitamin E** (page 302). A number of cats on this protocol tested negative for leukemia virus within 2 years of initial diagnosis on both ELISA and IFA tests. Also, many cats displaying signs of chronic illness became devoid of symptoms. Since false negative test results are possible, all cats testing negative on blood ELISA testing treated with orthomolecular therapy should have follow-up IFA testing done.

OTHER NATURAL TREATMENTS

Other therapies are recommended, such as **natural diet** (page 335), **antioxidants** (page 158), **DMG** (page 194); immune-boosting herbs including **alfalfa** (page 156), **aloe vera** (page 156), **astragalus** (page 160), **burdock** (page 170), **dandelion leaf** (page 193), **dandelion root** (page 193), **echinacea** (page 195), **garlic** (page 204), **ginseng** (page 210), **goldenseal** (page 220), **hawthorn** (page 223), **licorice** (page 234), **marshmallow** (page 240), **milk thistle** (page 241), **nettle** (page 245), **red clover** (page 262), **St. John's wort** (page 276), **turmeric** (page 280), and **yellow dock** (page 309). Herbs for infections include **aloe vera** (page 156), **astragalus** (page 160), **boswellia** (page 103), **echinacea** (page 195), **garlic** (page 204), **German chamomile** (topical, page 206), **ginger** (page 207), **goldenseal** (topical, page 220), **gotu kola** (page 221), **horsetail** (urinary system, page 225), **licorice** (page 234), **marshmallow** (page 240), **Oregon grape** (page 251), **sage** (page 264), **St. John's wort** (page 276), **turmeric** (page 280), **yarrow** (page 308). Mushrooms such as **reishi** (page 264), **shiitake** (page 272), **cordyceps** (page 191), and **maitake** (page 238) are also recommended. **Homeopathic nosodes** (page 411) may be helpful.

CONVENTIONAL THERAPY

As with FIV infection, there is no cure for FeLV infection. Clinical signs are treated as needed; chronic infections are treated with antibiotics. Supportive care for cats with fever and lack of appetite (such as fluid therapy and force-feeding) are used as needed; human alpha-interferon may be helpful.

 # FELINE LOWER URINARY TRACT DISEASE (FLUTD)

Principal Natural Treatments
  Natural diet, cranberry extract

Other Natural Treatments
  Coenzyme Q$_{10}$, omega-3 fatty acids, vitamin E, antioxidants, Bach flower essences (emotional component), herbs: alfalfa (to alkalinize the urine), dandelion leaf, echinacea, goldenseal, horsetail, marshmallow, plantain, Oregon grape, uva ursi, yarrow

Feline lower urinary tract disease (FLUTD, formerly called FUS, feline urological syndrome) is the most commonly diagnosed disorder of the bladder in cats.

Clinical signs of FLUTD include increased frequency of urination, painful urination or a burning sensation during urination, excessive licking at the genitals, and occasionally blood in the urine.

Owners commonly and mistakenly assume that cats with FLUTD are constipated, as affected cats spend a lot of time in the litter box attempting to eliminate. Increased thirst, increased volume of urine, and urinary incontinence are rarely associated with bladder disease and are more typical of kidney disease and diabetes.

FLUTD is a common problem in cats of any age, usually resulting from struvite crystals forming in urine with an alkaline, or (high) pH, which irritate the bladder (and may form struvite stones). Some cats have FLUTD without the presence of crystals, and in whom the urine is an acid (low) pH. About 25% of cats with FLUTD have an anatomic abnormality called a vesicourachal diverticulum. This pouch on the end of the bladder predisposes the animal to bladder disease. Most cases occur in cats (male or females) between 2 and 6 years of age, although struvite stones are most commonly seen in female cats that are between 1 and 2 years of age. Male cats are more likely to develop obstruction of the urethra (the tube leading from the bladder to the urethral opening) due to their anatomy (a long, narrow urethra, compared with the female cat's short, wide urethra). Cats with FLUTD may show any of the following signs: increased frequency of urination, painful urination or a burning sensation during urination, excessive licking at the genitals, and occasionally blood in the urine. Urethral obstruction is caused by mucus and/or crystals which "clog up" the urethra. Cats with urethral obstruction often spend a large amount of time in the litter box, causing many owners to mistakenly believe that the cats are constipated, but, in fact, true constipation is rare in dogs and cats.

The cause of FLUTD is unknown, although many doctors believe that cats eating dry foods (which in general contain more minerals such as magnesium per kcal of food than wet foods) predispose cats to this problem. Many holistic doctors claim that cats eating any processed foods are more likely to present with FLUTD, whereas switching to a homemade natural diet is preventative/curative. While some cats (2% or so) may have urinary tract infections, most cats have idiopathic disease (meaning the cause is unknown). Decreased water intake and therefore decreased urination may predispose cats to FLUTD.

While mineral (specifically magnesium) content of food has been blamed on causing FLUTD, it appears that the pH of the urine has more influence on the development of the crystals which are often seen in cats with FLUTD. Cats fed processed food tend to have a higher pH (which favors struvite crystal formation) than cats fed meals at specific times.

PRINCIPAL NATURAL TREATMENTS

A natural diet with no dry food (and preferably no processed foods) and cranberry extract are the main natural treatments.

Natural Diet

The same diet recommended for controlling struvite bladder stones is recommended for cats with FLUTD. If processed foods must be fed, most holistic veterinarians prefer canned diets (which contain large amounts of water) rather than dry foods.

Dietary therapy is a useful adjunct (and possible preventive measure) for cats with struvite crystals and stones. Since the struvite stones most commonly form in alkaline urine (urine with a high pH) when the urine is saturated with magnesium, ammonium, or phosphate, diets should help maintain an acidic urine (low pH) as much as possible. Diets with animal-based protein sources are most important in maintaining an acidic pH (vegetarian or cereal-based diets are more likely to cause an alkaline urine).

In cats, struvite crystals and stones most commonly form in the absence of a bladder infection (unlike the situation in dogs, in which a bladder infection is usually the initiating factor in causing the formation of stones). Unless a secondary infection is present, large amounts of urinary bleeding are encountered, or surgery is performed for stone removal; antibiotic therapy is usually not needed in cats with struvite bladder stones.

Crystals, stones, and the condition called feline lower urinary tract disease (FLUTD), most commonly form in cats (which are true carnivores adapted to eating meat-based diets) fed dry commercial foods (which are usually high in vegetable materials and grains). Most holistic veterinarians see a lower incidence of these urinary disorders in cats fed meat-based homemade diets.

Diets designed for cats with struvite crystals or bladder stones are designed to produce an acid urine (pH lasting 4 to 6 hours after feeding, which allows for crystals and stones to be dissolved. While some commercial foods have decreased levels of magnesium and phosphorus, it has recently been shown that these minerals only contribute to stone formation if the urine is alkaline. If the urine can be maintained with an acidic pH, the dietary concentrations of magnesium and phosphorus do not need to be lowered below recommended daily amounts. In fact, reducing the magnesium levels in cat food can cause increased excretion of calcium from the kidneys, leading to the formation of calcium oxalate stones in the bladder. In fact, the increased incidence of calcium oxalate stones in cats and dogs has coincided with an increased use of commercial "stone" diets containing reduced magnesium and phosphorus (often labeled under the term "ash"). Feeding recommended levels of phosphate to normal cats does not promote stone formation. Phosphate is needed to allow the urine to maintain an acid pH, which helps discourage crystal and stone formation. To increase urination (which reduces the amount of time crystals can form and remain in the bladder), extra salt (sodium chloride) can be added to the diet.

While urinary acidifiers can be useful, some doctors discourage their use as the exact dosage that is safe and effective is often not known. If urinary acidifiers are used for short-term acidification, a natural therapy such as cranberry extract might be preferred to conventional medications (such as methionine).

Diet for Cats with FLUTD

Note: Before you start to feed your dog or cat a home-prepared diet, it is strongly recommended that you discuss your decision with your veterinarian or a holistic veterinarian in your area. It is essential that you follow any diet's recommendations closely, including all ingredients and supplements. Failure to do so may result in serious health consequences for your pet.

3½ ounces firm raw tofu
2¼ ounces sardines, canned in tomato sauce
½ ounce clams, chopped in juice
½ yolk of large hard-boiled egg

⅓ cup long grain, cooked brown rice
2 teaspoons chicken fat or canola oil
½ ounce brewer's yeast
100 mg taurine

This diet provides 501 kcal (enough to fulfill the daily amount required for a 16-pound cat), 37.4 gm protein, 29.6 gm fat, 62.2 mg sodium/100 kcal (a high-sodium diet).

Variations

1. Substitute 2 ounces of tuna (in water without sodium), 2 ounces of canned salmon (with bones), 2⅔ ounces of chicken breast, 4 ounces of lean ground beef, or 4 ounces of lean ground lamb for the sardines.
2. Substitute ⅓ cup of potato, cooked with the skin, or ⅓ cup of cooked macaroni for the rice.
3. Supply vitamins and minerals as follows: 1 bonemeal tablet (10-grain or equivalent) or ¼ teaspoon of bonemeal powder to supply calcium and phosphorus with a multivitamin/mineral supplement, using the label instructions. Alternatively, use a natural product from Standard Process (1 Calcifood Wafer or 2 Calcium Lactate tablets for each 2 bonemeal tablets).
4. When possible, use natural vitamins made from raw whole foods, rather than synthetic vitamins (although both can be used in combination), as the natural vitamins also supply plant phytochemicals, enzymes, and other nutrients not found in chemically synthesized vitamins. Use either Catalyn from Standard Process (at a dose of 1 Catalyn per 10 pounds) or NuCat from VetriScience (following label dosages) as the natural vitamin for this recipe.
5. For extra nutrition and variety, use fresh, raw or slightly steamed vegetables, such as carrots or broccoli (approximately ½ to 1 cup per recipe) as a top dressing for the diet. (Many cats, however, will not eat vegetables.) Most vegetables provide approximately 25 kcal per ½ cup.
6. Add supplements that can be beneficial, such as omega-3 fatty acids, plant enzymes, and a super green food or health blend formula.

Note: If adding vegetables or other supplements, urine pH should be monitored when feeding the diet with these supplements and without the supplements to be sure the pH does not change from acid to alkaline.

Diets for cats with struvite stones should contain 20 to 40 mg/100 kcal of magnesium and 125 to 250 mg/100 kcal of phosphorus. These levels are higher than those recommended by the NRC for adult cats. Eliminating the oil and rice from this diet will further increase the magnesium and phosphorus.

Cranberry

The cranberry plant, a relative of the common blueberry plant, has been used as food and as treatment of bladder diseases.

Research has shown that drinking cranberry juice makes the urine more acidic. Since common urinary tract infections in pets (especially dogs) are caused by bacteria such as E. coli, which function best in alkaline urine, many holistic doctors promote cranberry juice extracts for treating bladder infections. In addition, since the most common bladder stones in dogs and cats, and the sand-like gravel and microscopic crystals that are often encountered in cats with feline lower urinary tract disease (FLUTD, formerly called FUS) form in alkaline urine, acidifying the urine with supplements such as cranberry extracts may prove helpful.

However, contrary to early reseach in people, it now appears that acidification of the urine is not so important as cranberry's ability to block bacteria from adhering to the bladder wall. Preventing bacterial adhesion to the bladder wall prevents infection and allows the bacteria to be washed out with the urine.

Cranberry juice is believed to be most effective as a form of prevention. When taken regularly, it appears to reduce the frequency of recurrent bladder infections in women prone to developing them. Cranberry may also be helpful during a bladder infection but not as reliably. Similar findings are lacking in pets but may be applicable.

In people, the recommended dosage of dry cranberry juice extract is 300 to 400 mg twice daily, or 8 to 16 ounces of juice daily. Pure cranberry juice (not sugary cranberry juice cocktail with its low percentage of cranberry) should be used for best effect.

For pets, the recommended dosage varies with the product. One recommended product used in cats recommends a daily dose of 250 mg of cranberry extract. Cranberry juice is not recommended, as it is all but impossible to get most pets to drink enough of the juice to be effective.

There are no known risks of this food for adults, children, or pregnant or nursing women, nor are there any known risks in pets. However, cranberry juice may allow the kidneys to excrete certain drugs more rapidly, thereby reducing their effectiveness. All weakly alkaline drugs may be affected, including many antidepressants and prescription painkillers.

In dogs and cats, the push to acidify the urine through prescription-type diets has led to a slight increase in oxalate stones in the bladder, which are more common in acid urine. Pets taking cranberry extract would be more prone to develop crystals and stones such as oxalate stones which are more common in acid urine. However, since the crystals and stones that form in alkaline urine are much more commonly diagnosed, pets with chronic stones (and cats with chronic FLUTD) would probably benefit from acidification of the urine even with the slight risk of stones forming in acid urine. Discuss this with your veterinarian.

OTHER NATURAL TREATMENTS

Coenzyme Q10 (page 185), **omega-3 fatty acids** (page 246), **vitamin E** (page 302), **antioxidants** (page 158), **Bach flower essences** for the emotional component (page 388). Use the following herbs: **alfalfa** to alkalinize the urine (page 156), **dandelion leaf** (page 193), **echinacea** (page 195), **goldenseal** (page 220), **horsetail** (page 225), **marshmallow** (page 240), **plantain** (page 256), **Oregon grape** (page 251), **uva ursi** (page 281), and **yarrow** (page 308).

These natural treatments are widely used with variable success but have not all been thoroughly investigated and proven at this time.

CONVENTIONAL THERAPIES

The treatment of FLUTD is controversial because the exact cause is unknown. Cats with an anatomic problems (such as bladder stones or vesicourachal diverticulum) should have these problems corrected through surgery (although some stone-dissolving diets might help correct certain types of bladder stones in cats). Cats with FLUTD have improved with no treatment, with antibiotic treatment (even though less than 10% of cats with FLUTD have bladder infections), and with anti-anxiety medications (such as amitriptyline). Cats with urethral obstruction must be anesthetized and have a urethral catheter placed through the urethra and into the bladder in order to allow urination.

There are several prescription-type diets available through veterinarians that may decrease the formation of crystals. These diets typically contain reduced ash (mineral) content and high amounts of urinary acidifiers. Urinary acidifiers can also be used for the prevention of FLUTD. There is an increased incidence of oxalate stones in cats who maintain an acid urine as the result of using acidifiers (oxalate stones form in acid urine, whereas the more common struvite stones prefer alkaline urine).

FELINE UPPER RESPIRATORY TRACT INFECTIONS

Principal Natural Treatments
Homeopathic nosodes

Other Natural Treatments
Natural diet, antioxidants, herbs: alfalfa, aloe vera, astragalus, burdock, dandelion leaf, dandelion root, echinacea, garlic, ginseng, goldenseal, hawthorn, licorice, marshmallow, milk thistle, nettle, red clover, St. John's wort, turmeric, yellow dock, boswellia, German chamomile, ginger, gotu kola, horsetail, Oregon grape, sage, yarrow; mushrooms: reishi, shiitake, cordyceps, maitake

Upper respiratory infections are common in kittens and rare in most adult cats. Common infectious organisms include the *Bordetella* bacterium, feline herpes virus (viral rhinotracheitis), feline calicivirus, *Mycoplasma*, and *Chlamydia psittaci*. Infection occurs as a result of contact with the organism, which is present in nasal, eye, and salivary secretions from infected or diseased cats. Common clinical signs include discharge from the eyes and nose. The discharge is usually initially clear and then becomes thicker and yellow or green as secondary infections occur. Most kittens and cats recover from their infections. Kittens infected with herpes virus become chronically infected and may continue to spread the virus throughout life. These kittens may become cats who are chronically diseased and suffer from respiratory infections, because the infection cannot be cured.

PRINCIPAL NATURAL TREATMENTS

Homeopathic Nosodes

Nosodes, a special type of homeopathic remedy, are prepared from infectious organisms such as distemper virus and staphylococcus bacteria. Remember that no matter what the source of the remedy, the actual ingredients are diluted in preparing the remedy. No measurable amount of the original source for the remedy remains, only the vital energy or life force, which imparts healing properties to the remedy. No harm will come to your pet regardless of the toxicity of the original compound used in the preparation of the remedy.

But do nosodes work? Some doctors seem to prefer nosodes manufactured by specific homeopathic pharmacies, as they feel there is a definite difference in the ability of nosodes to stimulate the immune system. In their opinions, the manufacturer of the nosode is important and some vaccination nosodes work better than others.

To prevent disease, nosodes are supposed to work in the same manner as conventional vaccines, namely by stimulating antibodies to fight off infections. Nosodes have been reported to control outbreaks of infectious disease in animals in a kennel situation. While good controlled studies are lacking, homeopathic veterinarians have reported success in some patients when treating infectious disease with the homeopathic nosode.

OTHER NATURAL TREATMENTS

Complementary therapies are used to boost the immune system and keep the eyes clear of discharge. They include **natural diet** (page 335), **antioxidants** (page 158); immune-boosting herbs: **alfalfa** (page 156), **aloe vera** (page 156), **astragalus** (page 160), **burdock** (page 170), **dandelion leaf** (page 193), **dandelion root** (page 193), **echinacea** (page 195), **garlic** (page 204), **ginseng** (page 210), **goldenseal** (page 220), **hawthorn** (page 223), **licorice** (page 234), **marshmallow** (page 240), **milk thistle** (page 241), **nettle** (page 245), **red clover** (page 262), **St. John's wort** (page 276), **turmeric** (page 280), **yellow dock** (page 309), herbs for infections: **aloe vera** (page 156), **astragalus** (page 160), **boswellia** (page 168), **echinacea** (page 195), **garlic** (page 204), **German chamomile** (topical, page 206), **ginger** (page 207), **goldenseal** (topical, page 220), **gotu kola** (page 221), **horsetail** (urinary system, page 225), **licorice** (page 234), **marshmallow** (page 240), **Oregon grape** (page 251), **sage** (page 264), **St. John's wort** (page 276), **turmeric** (page 280), **yarrow** (page 309); and mushrooms: **reishi** (page 264), **shiitake** (page 272), **cordyceps** (page 191), and **maitake** (238).

These can be used in conjunction with conventional therapies as needed. The natural treatments are widely used with variable success but have not all been thoroughly investigated and proven at this time.

As with any condition, the most healthful natural diet will improve the pet's overall health.

CONVENTIONAL THERAPY

Antiviral medications may be prescribed in severe cases. Usually, oral antibiotics are used (to treat secondary infections or primary *Bordetella*, *Mycoplasma*, or *Chlamydia* infections) as well as medicated eye drops. Most kittens recover within 1 to 2 weeks.

FLEAS (And Ticks)

Principal Natural Treatments
　　None

Other Natural Treatments
　　Neem, citronella, diatomaceous earth, sodium polysorbate, beneficial nematodes, garlic (oral), burdock root (oral), dandelion (oral), red clover (oral), feverfew (topical), pyrethrum (topical), mullein (Rotenone, oral), Canadian fleabane (oral), and pennyroyal oil (oral, potential toxicity!)

Fleas are the most common external pest causing irritation and discomfort to dogs and cats. Flea infestations are not usually fatal; however, puppies, kittens, and debilitated pets can become quite ill and even die due to blood loss from heavy flea infestation (fleas suck blood from their hosts). Fleas most commonly cause irritation to infested pets. Dogs and cats with flea allergies can experience intense itching and secondary skin infections. *Only one flea bite is necessary to cause severe signs in flea-allergic pets; in many flea-allergic pets, no fleas are ever found.*

Finally, fleas are also the intermediate host for the common dog and cat tapeworm. Finding tapeworms in the pet's feces, or finding flea fecal material ("flea dirt," small black flecks of blood located on the pet that turn red when mixed with water) is evidence of flea infestation even if no adult fleas are seen.

Treating fleas either with natural or conventional therapies (or both) require treating the pet, indoor environment, and outdoor environment. Owners should keep in mind that there are four stages of the flea life cycle: adult (the only stage that occurs on the pet and makes up 5 to 10% of the entire flea population), egg, larvae, and cocoon. *Since 90 to 95% of the flea population (the eggs, larvae, and cocoons) occur in the environment (house and yard) rather than on the pet, flea-control programs must concentrate their efforts there, or the programs will fail.*

OTHER NATURAL TREATMENTS

While generally considered to be less toxic than even the newer, safer chemicals recommended for flea control, the main drawback to using natural treatments for flea control on the pet is the need for frequent application. Natural products are quite useful in the environment and usually do not require frequent applications.

Treatments for flea control on the pet and in the environment include **neem** (page 244), citronella, diatomaceous earth, sodium polysorbate, and beneficial homeopathic nematodes. Herbs to be given orally include **garlic** (page 204), **burdock root** (page 170), **dandelion** (page 193), and **red clover** (page 262). Herbs to be given topically include **feverfew** (page 202), **pyrethrum** (page 261), mullein, **Canadian fleabane** (page 203), and **pennyroyal oil** (page 252), which has potential toxicity. (See **pennyroyal oil** in Part Two, Herbs and Supplements.)

The natural treatments are widely used with variable success but have not all been thoroughly investigated and proven at this time.

As with any condition, the most healthful natural diet will improve the pet's overall health.

CONVENTIONAL THERAPY

Conventional therapies involve the use of various chemicals such as carbamates, organophosphates, synthetic pyrethrins, and insect growth regulators such as methoprene, to kill fleas. There are no conventional treatments to eliminate the cocoon stage of the flea life cycle.

The newer conventional therapies for flea (and tick) control appear to be safer and work better than products available years ago. Ideally, problems are best prevented rather than treated. Since the advent of products such as Program, Advantage, and Frontline, owners can now have year-round or season-round prevention for their pets rather than wait until severe flea infestation occurs. Preventing problems allows owners to use fewer chemicals in their approach than waiting to treat problems that require more chemicals used for greater lengths of time.

The newer chemicals work much better than past treatments of toxic dips, powders, sprays, and collars. By their modes of action and application, they are safer for pets, owners, and the environment. Still, these products are chemicals; when possible, more natural preventive measures are recommended. In addition, when possible, these (and other unnecessary) chemicals should be avoided in pets with chronic diseases, including allergies, cancer, epilepsy, feline leukemia virus infection, feline immunodeficiency infection, autoimmune diseases, and any other conditions where extraneous application or ingestion of chemicals is best avoided.

Toxicity that occurs with conventional flea treatments mainly involves the central nervous system, usually by inhibiting acetylcholinesterase, the enzyme that degrades the major nerve transmitter acetylcholine. Using the products only on an as-needed basis, following label directions, and working with your veterinarian to use the least toxic products (for example, a pyrethrin outdoor spray or methoprene indoors rather than an organophosphate) will allow most products to be used safely when indicated.

GASTROINTESTINAL DISEASE
(See Inflammatory Bowel Disease)

 # HEART DISEASE (Cardiomyopathy, Valvular Heart Disease, Congestive Heart Failure)

Principal Natural Treatments
Taurine, carnitine, hawthorn, natural diet, Coenzyme Q$_{10}$

Other Natural Treatments
Omega-3 fatty acids, antioxidants, glandulars, DMG, bugleweed, burdock, coptis, dandelion leaf, devil's claw (possible anti-arrhythmic), garlic, ginger, *Ginkgo biloba,* goldenseal, gotu kola, hawthorn, goldenseal, Oregon grape, red clover, and maitake mushrooms

In dogs and cats, the most common types of heart disease include cardiomyopathy and valvular heart disease. Congestive heart failure occurs late in the course of any type of heart disease as the heart muscle fails to adequately pump blood throughout the body.

Valvular heart disease is the most common heart disease in dogs, occurring most commonly in older small breed dogs (the prevalence is estimated at 75% of dogs over 16 years of age). This condition occurs as the heart valves (most commonly the mitral valves that separate the left atrium from the left ventricle) degenerate as a result of acquired chronic structural changes in the valves. Small nodules of myxomatous degeneration occur in the valves, causing them to thicken, become irregular, and retract from each other. This retraction allows blood to flow in a "backward" direction as well as a forward direction. This abnormal blood flow causes "regurgitation" of blood, which is heard through the stethoscope as a result of turbulence caused by the regurgitation. With time, coughing and exercise intolerance may occur as regurgitation worsens and the heart can no longer adapt, leading to early congestive heart failure.

Dogs may also be afflicted with cardiomyopathy, where the heart muscle itself is actually diseased. Larger breeds of dogs (especially Boxers and Doberman Pinschers) may be afflicted with dilated cardiomyopathy, although increasing incidence is reported in Cocker Spaniels. The average age of affected dogs is 4 to 8 years. The cause is unknown, although the higher incidence in purebred dogs when compared to mixed breed dogs suggests a genetic cause. Additionally, L-carnitine or taurine deficiency has been shown in some dogs.

In dilated cardiomyopathy, the heart enlarges as the heart muscle progressively becomes thinner. The thinner muscle does not pump blood adequately, and with time congestive heart failure occurs.

Cats with heart disease are most commonly affected with hypertrophic cardiomyopathy. In the past, dilated cardiomyopathy was also common. Recent evidence that taurine deficiency contributed to most cases of feline dilated cardiomyopathy has resulted in manufacturers increasing the amounts of taurine in commercial cat foods. As a result, dilated cardiomyopathy is rare in cats today (unless owners prepare food at home and do not adequately supplement with taurine. This is especially problematic if owners insist on feeding cats vegetarian diets, as vegetables do not contain taurine.

Hypertrophic cardiomyopathy appears to be genetic in origin in cats. Hypertrophic cardiomyopathy most commonly occurs in younger (4- to 8-year-old) male cats. In this condition, the heart muscle thickens, often to the point where the chambers of the heart diminish in size to the point where little blood is able to be pumped around the body. This lack of forward movement of blood results in heart failure in severe, chronic cases of hypertrophic cardiomyopathy. In some cases of cardiomyopathy in cats, emboli (a collection of clotted platelets) forms in the heart and travels to another area of the body, most commonly the lower aorta. This embolus then causes lack of blood to the body part served by the blocked aorta, usually one or both hind limbs, causing paralysis. Often this secondary effect of cardiomyopathy prompts the client to bring in the cat for a veterinary visit, allowing the diagnosis of the underlying heart disease.

PRINCIPAL NATURAL TREATMENTS

Taurine

Supplementation with taurine may be beneficial in both cats and dogs with heart disease. In cats with taurine deficiency that results in dilated cardiomyopathy, clinical improvement is usually seen within 2 to 3 weeks following supplementation; 250 to 500 mg of taurine daily is suggested. Improvements in the EKG and radiographs will often take 3 to 6 weeks. The goal of taurine supplementation is to achieve plasma taurine levels of at least 60 nmol/mL (normal cats usually have levels >40 nmol/mL). Not all cats with dilated cardiomyopathy have taurine deficiency as the cause of the cardiomyopathy; those cats with normal taurine levels would not be expected to respond to supplementation with taurine (although since taurine supplementation is safe, any cat with heart disease could probably receive a diet containing additional taurine).

In dogs, dilated cardiomyopathy can also occur, leading to congestive heart failure. Preliminary work shows that supplementation with taurine may be beneficial in American Cocker Spaniels and Golden Retrievers with dilated cardiomyopathy. Supplementation with taurine (500 mg twice daily) and L-carnitine (1,000 mg twice daily) in a small number of dogs with low plasma taurine levels resulted in improvement in a few of the patients. Since American Cocker Spaniels are predisposed to dilated cardiomyopathy with concurrent taurine (and possibly) carnitine deficien-

cies, supplementation with these two compounds is suggested for Cocker Spaniels with dilated cardiomyopathy (although not all researchers agree on this recommendation, supplementation is safe even in those cases where it is difficult to determine if it is truly needed).

Dogs with chronic valvular disease (leaky heart valves), the most common heart disease reported in dogs, usually have normal plasma taurine levels, making routine supplementation unlikely to be of benefit.

Taurine deficiency can be diagnosed based upon testing levels in the blood. Plasma levels are more indicative of recent taurine intake; whole blood levels are more suggestive of chronic taurine intake. However, even with normal blood levels, it is possible that levels of taurine in the heart muscle cells might not be adequate. Even for those pets without low blood taurine levels, supplementation can be tried without side effects.

Carnitine

Decreased carnitine levels may also be related to dilated cardiomyopathy in dogs, especially in Boxers, Doberman Pinschers, and American Cocker Spaniels. Carnitine deficiency is difficult to diagnose and usually requires a heart biopsy for a definitive diagnosis. Carnitine supplementation of 2 gm (2,000 mg) given 3 times daily is often recommended for dogs with cardiomyopathy.

Carnitine can also be used for pets with any type of heart disease (and is included in some heart supplements), but definitive proof for its use in heart diseases other than cardiomyopathy caused by carnitine deficiency is lacking. However, as with taurine, since carnitine supplementation is safe, supplementation will not hurt and other nutrients in the supplements (such as antioxidants and herbs) may be useful.

Carnitine is abundant in red meat (higher in beef than in chicken or turkey) and dairy products, which form the basis of the diets listed on page 95. Diets high in cereal grains and plants (which account for many commercial diets) may not support adequate carnitine levels in the heart.

Supplemental carnitine may improve the ability of certain tissues to produce energy. This effect has led to the use of carnitine in various muscle diseases as well as heart conditions, as carnitine accumulates in both skeletal and cardiac muscle. There is no dietary requirement for carnitine. However, a few individuals have a genetic defect that hinders the body's ability to make carnitine. In dogs, a subset of pets with dilated cardiomyopathy that show variable response to carnitine supplementation has been identified (this was first shown in Boxers).

In addition, diseases of the liver, kidneys, or brain may inhibit carnitine production. Heart muscle tissue, because of its high energy requirements, is particularly vulnerable to carnitine deficiency.

The principal dietary sources of carnitine are meat and dairy products, but to obtain therapeutic dosages a supplement is necessary.

In people, carnitine is taken in three forms: L-carnitine (for heart and other conditions), L-propionyl-carnitine (for heart conditions), and acetyl-L-carnitine (for Alzheimer's disease). The dosage is the same for all three forms.

Carnitine is primarily used for heart-related conditions. Without adequate carnitine to transport fatty acids into heart muscle cells, reduced levels of energy are available to the heart.

In people, fairly good evidence suggests that it can be used along with conventional treatment for angina or chest pain, to improve symptoms and reduce medication needs. When combined with conventional therapy, it may also reduce mortality after a heart attack. A few studies suggest that carnitine may be useful for cardiomyopathy.

Several small studies have found that carnitine, often in the form of L-propionyl-carnitine, can improve symptoms of congestive heart failure. There is better evidence for Coenzyme Q10 for this condition, and in fact, some veterinarians may prescribe both supplements.

In people, carnitine may help reduce death rate after a heart attack. In a 12-month, placebo-controlled study, 160 individuals who had experienced a heart attack received 4 g of L-carnitine or placebo daily, in addition to other conventional medication. The mortality rate in the treated group was significantly lower than in the placebo group, 1.2% versus 12.5% respectively. There were also improvements in heart rate, blood pressure, angina (chest pain), and blood lipids. A larger double-blind study of 472 people found that carnitine may improve the chances of survival if given within 24 hours after a heart attack. As a rule, pets do not experience "heart attacks" as people do. Pets can experience sudden onset of congestive heart failure due to valvular disease or cardiomyopathy. Whether or not administering carnitine following an acute episode improves survival is unknown.

Weak evidence in people suggests that carnitine may be able to improve cholesterol and triglyceride levels. In carnitine deficiency, increased blood trigylceride levels can occur.

In pets, heart levels (myocardial levels) of carnitine have been found to be low in up to 40% of dogs suffering with dilated cardiomyopathy. Diagnosing carnitine deficiency is difficult, as blood levels do not correlate with levels in heart muscle cells (although low plasma carnitine levels appear to be predictive of low mycardial carnitine concentration). Researchers must do heart muscle biopsies in order to determine myocardial carnitine deficiency. If the heart is unable to concentrate carnitine, levels can fall quite low despite normal blood levels. Studies show that only 20% of dogs with dilated cardiomyopathy with myocardial deficiency also had low blood levels of carnitine. Most dogs with myocardial carnitine deficiency and dilated cardiomyopathy suffer from a membrane transport defect that prevents adequate levels of carnitine moving from the blood into the heart muscle cells (in these pets, blood levels of carnitine are usually normal or higher than normal).

The dosage of carnitine recommended for dogs with carnitine deficiency cardiomyopathy is 50 mg/kg 3 times daily, or alternatively 2,000 mg per pet 3 times daily. Rare side effects include diarrhea and flatulence (intestinal gas). Improved heart function, appetite, and exercise tolerance are often noted within 2 months following supplementation in some dogs.

Note: Carnitine supplementation has also been suggested for pets with other heart diseases, including endocardiosis (valvular heart disease), ischemic heart disease, and congestive heart failure. Definitive proof is lacking, although carnitine supplementation is safe and can be tried for pets with these other cardiac disorders under veterinary supervision.

To sum up, current benefits and recommendations regarding carnitine supplementation for dogs with heart disease include:

1. Since true carnitine deficiency may exist in a small number of dogs such as Boxers with dilated cardiomyopathy, supplementation with L-carnitine may be of benefit in these pets.
2. In some dogs with dilated cardiomypathy (approximately the 40% that have myocardial carnitine deficiency), supplementation may improve clinical signs and cause some improvement in the echocardiograms of these patients.
3. Supplementation with L-carnitine may improve survival in some dogs with dilated cardiomyopathy, especially those who have myocardial carnitine deficiency.

The main disadvantage of carnitine supplementation is the cost, approximately $75 per month. While carnitine deficiency is not the cause of dilated cardiomyopathy in most dogs, supplementation is safe and can be used as an adjunct to other therapies.

L-carnitine in its three forms appears to be safe, even when taken with medications. People are advised not to use forms of carnitine known as "D-carnitine" or "DL-carnitine," as these can cause angina, muscle pain, and loss of muscle function (probably by interfering with L-carnitine). The maximum safe dosages for young children, pregnant or nursing women, or those with severe liver or kidney disease have not been established; similar precautions are probably warranted in pets.

Natural Diet

Dietary therapy is designed to regulate sodium levels. In heart failure, sodium is retained rather than being excreted by the kidneys. Sodium retains fluid in the body, which causes fluid to leak from the blood vessels into the lungs, liver, and other organs causing the signs (coughing, abdominal fluid, and such) seen in pets with congestive heart failure.

To reduce sodium retention, salt is reduced in diets designed for pets with heart disease. Since commercial pet foods have excessive amounts of sodium to increase palatability and act as a preservative, these diets are not recommended for pets with heart disease. There are several medicated diets prepared for pets with heart disease. However, they may contain by-products and chemical preservatives that are not always consistent with a holistic nutritional program, although they may have a place in the management of heart disease if the owner cannot prepare a homemade diet or if the pet will not eat the homemade diet. Homemade diets can fit the need for holistic, low-sodium diets.

Pets with heart failure may have low potassium levels resulting from decreased food intake (common in pets with heart failure) and the use of diuretics such as furosemide (Lasix). Even with normal blood levels, cellular levels of potassium may be decreased. Extra potassium can be supplied using supplements or potassium chloride (salt substitute). Discuss this with your veterinarian before beginning potassium supplementation.

Magnesium may also be decreased in pets with heart failure, once again due to reduced food intake and use of diuretics. Magnesium depletion is difficult to prove based on blood levels as, similar to potassium, blood levels do not coincide with cellular levels. Magnesium supplementation under veterinary supervision may be warranted.

Supplementation with Coenzyme Q_{10}, taurine, and carnitine may be helpful in pets with heart disease and heart failure. Taurine deficiency can cause dilated cardiomyopathy in cats. This disease is quite rare today as pet food manufacturers have increased the levels of taurine in commercial pet foods. Cats are true carnivores. Unlike dogs, they cannot make enough taurine to meet their daily needs and must receive taurine from their diets. Homemade diets for cats containing animal proteins such as meat or fish contain adequate taurine levels. However, processing results in loss of taurine if the meat juices are removed. Pouring the juices over the diet, or feeding raw meats if the owner is comfortable with this—see the discussion in Part Three, page 336, on feeding raw diets—can replace this taurine. Eggs and cottage cheese contain little or no taurine and must be supplemented with taurine. Vegetarian diets (including tofu-based diets) do not supply taurine as plants do not make taurine; these diets must also be supplemented with taurine to meet the cat's needs.

Diet for Adult Dogs with Heart Disease

Diets for dogs with heart disease are usually lower in sodium and higher in potassium.

Extra fat can be added to maintain weight if weight loss due to heart failure occurs. The basic dog diet (page 346) can be used, but do not add extra salt. In the place of eggs, ⅓ pound lean ground beef or chicken or other meat can be used. Canola oil is added as per the basic diet.

The diet provides approximately 900 kcal with 45 grams of protein and 37 grams of fat.

Fresh, raw or slightly steamed vegetables (carrots, broccoli, etc.) can be used as a top dressing for the diet for extra nutrition and variety (approximately ½–1 cup per recipe.)

Most vegetables provide approximately 25 kcal per ½ cup.

Five bonemeal tablets (10 grain or equivalent) or 1–1¼ teaspoon of bonemeal powder to supply calcium and phosphorus with a multi-vitamin mineral supplement using the label instructions is added. Alternatively, a natural product from Standard Process (Calcifood Wafers or Calcium Lactate) can be used (use 1 Calcifood Wafer or 2 Calcium Lactate tablets for each 2 bonemeal tablets.)

When possible, natural vitamins made from raw whole foods, rather than synthetic vitamins (although both can be used in combination) are preferred, as the natural vitamins also supply plant phytochemicals, enzymes, and other nutrients not found in chemically-synthesized vitamins. Catalyn from Standard Process can be used as the natural vitamin in this recipe, at a dose of 1 Catalyn per 25 pounds; Canine Plus (VetriScience) could also be used following label dosages.

The nutrient composition of the diet will vary depending upon which ingredients are used. In general, the above recipe supplies the daily nutritional and calorie needs for a 30 pound dog.

The actual amount to feed will vary based upon the pet's weight (feed less if weight gain, more if weight loss.)

Added supplements which can be beneficial include omega-3 fatty acids, plant enzymes, and a super green food or health blend formula The health blend formula may contain excess sodium that could be harmful (check with the manufacturer.)

Diet for Adult Cat with Heart Disease

Diets for cats with heart disease are usually lower in sodium and higher in potassium.

Extra fat can be added to maintain weight if weight loss due to heart disease occurs. The basic cat diet (page 348) can be used, but do not add extra salt. Low sodium tuna or salmon (5-6 ounces) could be substituted for the meat for variation. Brown or white rice (½ cup) can be added if desired.

Taurine (100-500 mg) should also be added.

The diet provides approximately 550 kcal with 55 grams of protein and 30 grams of fat.

Fresh, raw or slightly steamed vegetables (carrots, broccoli, etc.) can be used as a top dressing for the diet for extra nutrition and variety (approximately ½ -1 cup per recipe), but most cats do not like eating vegetables.

Two bonemeal tablets (10 grain or equivalent) or ¼ - ½ teaspoon of bonemeal powder to supply calcium and phosphorus with a multi-vitamin mineral supplement using the label instructions is added. Alternatively, a natural product from Standard Process (Calcifood Wafers or Calcium Lactate) can be used (use 1 Calcifood Wafer or 2 Calcium Lactate tablets for each 2 bonemeal tablets.)

When possible, natural vitamins made from raw whole foods, rather than synthetic vitamins (although both can be used in combination) are preferred, as the natural vitamins also supply plant phytochemicals, enzymes, and other nutrients not found in chemically- synthesized vitamins. Catalyn from Standard Process can be used as the natural vitamin in this recipe, at a dose of 1 Catalyn per 10 pounds; NuCat (VetriScience) could also be used following label dosages.

The nutrient composition of the diet will vary depending upon which ingredients are used. In general, the above recipe supplies the daily nutritional and calorie needs for a 10-11 pound cat. The actual amount to feed will vary based upon the pet's weight (feed less if weight gain, more if weight loss.)

Added supplements which can be beneficial include omega-3 fatty acids, plant enzymes, and a super green food or health blend formula The health blend formula may contain excess sodium that could be harmful (check with the manufacturer.)

Hawthorn

Hawthorn is a well-known heart and vascular tonic, often being prescribed for pets with early congestive heart failure. It may be a possible alternative to digitalis. Hawthorn also possesses antioxidant properties. Although not as potent as foxglove, hawthorn is much safer. The active ingredients in foxglove are the drugs digoxin and digitoxin. However, hawthorn does not appear to have any single active ingredient, although the flavonoids and proanthocyanidins have been suggested as the active components. This has prevented it from being turned into a drug.

Like foxglove and the drugs made from it, hawthorn appears to improve the heart's pumping ability. But it offers one very important advantage. Digitalis and some other medications that increase the power of the heart also make it more irritable and liable to dangerous irregularities of rhythm. In contrast, hawthorn has the unique property of both strengthening the heart and stabilizing it against arrhythmias by lengthening what is called the refractory period, the short period following a heartbeat during which the heart cannot beat again. Many irregularities of heart rhythm begin with an early beat. Digitalis shortens the refractory period, making such a premature beat more likely, while hawthorn protects against such potentially dangerous breaks in the heart's even rhythm. Also, with digitalis, the difference between the proper dosage and the toxic dosage is very small. Hawthorn has an enormous range of safe dosing.

In people, several double-blind studies strongly suggest that hawthorn is an effective treatment for congestive heart failure. Comparative studies suggest that hawthorn is about as effective as a low dose of the conventional drug captopril (a relative of enalapril, used in pets with heart failure), although whether it produces the same long-term benefits as captopril is unknown.

Due to the flavonoid content, hawthorn is often recommended for pets with heart disease, heartworm disease, and kidney disease. The flavonoids appear to decrease "leakiness" of the capillaries, improve cardiac blood flow by dilating coronary arteries, and improve the contractility of the heart. Hawthorn may also be useful in controlling mild heart arrhythmias. It may act by inhibiting the enzyme phosphodiesterase or as an ACE inhibitor, making it a possible substitute for drugs such as enalapril (Enacard). Doctors may prescribe hawthorn for pets undergoing chemotherapy, especially when the drug chosen for chemotherapy may produce cardiac side effects.

In people, the standard dosage of hawthorn is 100 to 300 mg 3 times daily of an extract standardized to contain about 2 to 3% flavonoids or 18 to 20% procyanidins. Full effects appear to take several weeks or months to develop.

In pets, a recommended dosage of 100 mg/25 to 50 pounds of body weight twice daily has been used with positive results.

Hawthorn is safe to feed to animals; older animals that may be prone to heart or kidney disease can be given hawthorn on a daily basis. Caution is warranted in pets with low blood pressure and hypertrophic cardiomyopathy. In people, side effects are rare, mostly consisting of mild stomach upset and occasional allergic reactions (skin rash).

Safety in young children, pregnant or nursing women, or those with severe liver, heart or kidney disease has not been established. Similar concerns in pets are probably warranted.

Coenzyme Q10

Coenzyme Q10 (ubiquinone) is a powerful fat-soluble antioxidant that is found in every cell in the body. It plays a fundamental role in the mitochondria, the parts of the cell that produce energy from food. Coenzyme Q_{10} appears to control the flow of oxygen within the cells as well as functioning as an antioxidant to reduce damage to cells by harmful free radicals. Every cell in the body needs CoQ_{10}, but there is no U.S. Recommended Dietary Allowance since the body can manufacture CoQ_{10} from scratch.

Because CoQ_{10} is found in all animal and plant cells, we obtain small amounts of this nutrient from our diet. However, it would be hard to get a therapeutic dosage from food.

CoQ_{10} appears to assist the heart muscle during times of stress, perhaps by helping it use energy more efficiently. While CoQ_{10}'s best-established use is for congestive heart failure, ongoing research suggests that it may also be useful for other types of heart problems and for a wide variety of additional illnesses. Preliminary research has shown reduced levels of CoQ_{10} in the hearts of people and pets with heart disease.

In people, the typical recommended dosage of CoQ_{10} is 30 to 300 mg daily, often divided into 2 or 3 doses. CoQ_{10} is fat-soluble and is better absorbed when taken in an oil-based soft gel form rather than in a dry form such as tablets and capsules. In pets, the typical dosage is 30 mg every 24 to 48 hours, although your veterinarian may alter this dosage depending upon your pet's size and individual needs. (Some doctors feel that increasing the dosage is necessary for larger pets; for example, 80 mg every 24 to 48 hours might be recommended for a 100-pound dog.)

In people, the best-documented use of CoQ_{10} is for treating congestive heart failure and when taken along with conventional medications, not instead of them. People with congestive heart failure have significantly lower levels of CoQ_{10} in their heart muscle cells than healthy people. While this does not prove that CoQ_{10} supplements will help people with heart failure, it has prompted researchers to try using CoQ_{10} as a treatment for heart failure. In people, at least nine double-blind studies have found that CoQ_{10} supplements can markedly improve symptoms and objective measurements of heart function when they are taken along with conventional medication.

Weaker evidence suggests that it may be useful for cardiomyopathy (several small studies suggest that CoQ_{10} supplements are helpful for some forms of cardiomyopathy) and other forms of heart disease. It has also been suggested as a treatment for high blood pressure (although the scientific evidence for this use is weak) and to prevent heart damage caused by certain types of cancer chemotherapy (such as adriamycin). Since CoQ_{10} might conceivably interfere with the action of other chemotherapy drugs due to its antioxidant activity (although there is no good evidence that it does so), check with your veterinarian before using CoQ_{10} if your pet has cancer that requires chemotherapy.

CoQ_{10} may also help periodontal (gum) disease (by reducing the size and improving the health of periodontal pockets, as well as decreasing inflammation, redness, bleeding, and pain) and diabetes in people and pets. Since most pets with heart disease also have periodontal disease, an extra benefit might be achieved in pets with heart disease taking CoQ_{10}.

In experiments in dogs, Coenzyme Q_{10} was found to exert a protective effect against oxidative injury to the heart. Stabilization of body weight, improved clinical status, and a slowing of the progression of signs has been seen in dogs with heart disease treated with Coenzyme Q_{10}.

CoQ_{10} appears to be extremely safe. No significant side effects have been found; however, pets with severe heart disease should not take CoQ_{10} (or any other supplement) except under a veterinarian's supervision.

The maximum safe dosages of CoQ_{10} for young children, pregnant or nursing women, or those with severe liver or kidney disease have not been determined; the same is true for pets of similar circumstances.

OTHER NATURAL TREATMENTS

Treatments for pets with cancer include **omega-3 fatty acids** (page 246), **antioxidants** (page 158), **glandulars** (page 393), **DMG** (page 194), and the herbs **bugleweed** (page 170), **burdock** (page 170), **coptis** (page 190), **dandelion leaves** (page 193), **devil's claw** (possible anti-arrhythmic, page 194), **garlic** (page 204), **ginger** (page 207), *Ginkgo biloba* (page 208), **goldenseal** (page 220), **gotu kola** (page 221), **Oregon grape** (page 251), **red clover** (page 262), and **maitake** mushrooms (page 238).

These can be used in conjunction with conventional therapies as they are unlikely to be effective by themselves in most patients with severe heart disease. The natural treatments are widely used with variable success but have not all been thoroughly investigated and proven at this time.

As with any condition, the most healthful natural diet will improve the pet's overall health.

CONVENTIONAL THERAPY

Conventional therapy for heart disease includes medications such as diuretics and various cardiac drugs (digitalis, calcium-channel blockers, ACE inhibitors).

The most commonly used and safest diuretic is furosemide (Lasix). This loop diuretic is structurally related to the sulfonamide antibiotics. Furosemide works to increase excretion of fluid and electrolytes from the body. The medication should be decreased in pets with kidney failure and should be used with caution where there are preexisting electrolyte imbalances, diabetes mellitus, and liver disease. Pets should be monitored for electrolyte imbalances, especially potassium deficiency. The risk of side effects (including kidney failure) increases when furosemide is used concurrently with other medications, including aminoglycoside antibiotics, enalapril, NSAIDs, and corticosteroids. Furosemide may alter in-

sulin requirements in diabetic pets, and the effects of theophylline may increase in pets taking furosemide.

Calcium-channel blockers commonly used include diltiazem or verapamil. By blocking the calcium channels in the cells of heart muscles and the smooth muscles of blood vessels, these medications dilate arteries and slow heart rate. Overdosage may cause excessive slowing of the heart, low blood pressure, and heart failure.

Digitalis is a synthetic medication that is a purified form of the active ingredient in the purple foxglove plant. Digoxin and digitoxin are the two most commonly prescribed digitalis medications. These drugs work to slow heart rate and strengthen the contractile force of the heart. Side effects include various heart arrhythmias, vomiting, diarrhea, and lack of appetite. These medications have a narrow therapeutic index, which means there is a very small difference between the effective dose and the toxic dose.

A newer class of medications commonly used in the treatment of various cardiac disorders in dogs and cats are angiotensin-converting enzyme inhibitors (ACE inhibitors). Enalapril is the most commonly prescribed ACE inhibitor (captopril is another popular ACE inhibitor). Enalapril, after biochemical conversion in the liver to the more active form, enalaprilat, prevents the formation of angiotensin II by inhibiting the angiotensin-converting enzyme. Side effects include loss of appetite, vomiting, and diarrhea. Low blood pressure and kidney failure can occur when ACE inhibitors are combined with diuretics, including furosemide. NSAIDs may reduce the effectiveness of ACE inhibitors, especially when the ACE inhibitors are used to control high blood pressure.

 # HEARTWORM DISEASE

Principal Natural Treatments
None

Other Natural Treatments
Black walnut, wormwood, homeopathic nosodes

Heartworms are caused by the parasite *Dirofilaria immitis* and are transmitted by the bite of the mosquito. When a dog or cat is bitten by a mosquito infected with heartworms, the immature larvae carried by the mosquito enter through the mosquito bite in the skin. From the site of the mosquito bite, the larvae continue to molt and travel through the pet's body. Approximately 6 months after infection, the mature larvae enter the pet's heart and pulmonary vessels in the lungs and finish their maturation into adult heartworms. In dogs, most of the worms reside in the pulmonary vessels in the lungs (except in heavy infections, where the worms can live in pulmonary vessels, the heart, and the vena cava); in cats, due to a lower number of worms, the heartworms are most likely to reside in the heart.

It is important to differentiate between heartworm infection and heartworm disease. A pet whose body contains heartworms in said to be infected with heartworms. Heartworm disease occurs when an infected pet shows clinical signs of infection, including difficulty breathing, fluid in the lungs or abdomen, vomiting, diarrhea, weight loss, or sudden collapse and death. In cats, chronic vomiting or asthmatic-like signs are often the only signs seen in cats with heartworm infection and heartworm disease. Most dogs infected with heartworms are not suffering from heartworm disease at the time of diagnosis.

Diagnosis of heartworm infection in dogs is by finding microfilaria (baby heartworms) on a concentration or filter test, or by finding antigen (foreign protein) from adult female worms on an occult test. Many dogs (40% or more) will not have microfilaria and will have an occult (adult-only) infection. Additionally, the microfilaria of a benign subcutaneous worm *Dipetalonema reconditum*, can be confused with the microfilaria of *Dirofilaria immitis*. For these reasons, it is imperative that dogs screened for heartworms have an occult test or both an occult test and a microfilaria test, especially before heartworm treatment is instituted.

Diagnosis of heartworm infection in cats is more difficult, as cats usually do not harbor microfilaria and have fewer worms in their bodies than dogs (see the next discussion). In cats, diagnosis can be made through a combination of tests, including occult testing for antibody and antigen detection, chest radiographs (x rays), CBC, blood chemistry profile, and cardiac ultrasound.

HEARTWORM INFECTION/ DISEASE IN CATS VERSUS DOGS

Here are some key differences in heartworm infection/disease of dogs and cats.

Heartworm in Dogs

- Heartworms live an average of 3 to 5 years before dying naturally.
- A minimal number to many microfilaria are seen.
- The average number of adult heartworms is 15, and more are possible.
- Clinical signs of heartworm disease are rare when few worms are present.
- The incidence of infection/disease is high in endemic areas if preventative medicine is not used.

Heartworm in Cats

- Heartworms live approximately 2 years.
- Microfilaria are very rarely seen.
- The average number of adult heartworms is 1 to 3.
- Clinical signs of heartworm disease can occur even when 1 to 3 worms are present.
- The incidence of infection/disease in endemic areas is lower than in dogs (25%).

OTHER NATURAL TREATMENTS

There are several protocols listed in the holistic literature for the treatment of canine heartworm infection/disease. Unfortunately, no controlled studies showing their effectiveness have been completed, although the veterinarians who use these protocols have reported success in some cases. Many of these cases have not been followed long term, and many holistic practitioners do not recommend them due to their questionable effectiveness. In some protocols, the dogs were also placed on monthly heartworm preventative medication (Heartgard), which has been shown to actually kill adult worms after continuous usage, making interpretation of results from alternative treatments difficult. Some protocols also make use of more toxic herbs such as wormwood and black walnut.

For owners who wish to try one of these protocols, they must be administered under strict veterinary supervision to minimize toxicity. Pets should receive regular follow-up testing (occult heartworm tests) to determine effectiveness (or lack of effectiveness) if an alternative protocol is used. For owners who wish to use the conventional medical therapy combined with some type of complementary therapy, patient support (of the heart and liver) can be accomplished by various nutritional supplements and herbal preparations. Support of the heart and liver with herbs and glandulars can be beneficial in supporting the patient during conventional treatment.

Diatomaceous earth, while reportedly effective for helping control some intestinal parasites, is not effective in preventing or treating heartworm infection/disease.

These protocols can be used in conjunction with conventional therapies as they are unlikely to be effective by themselves in most patients. The natural treatments are widely used with variable success but have not all been thoroughly investigated and proven at this time.

As with any condition, the most healthful natural diet will improve the pet's overall health.

CONVENTIONAL THERAPY

In the past, an arsenical (arsenic-containing) medication called Caparsolate was the only medication available for treating heartworm infection in dogs. While it is effective, there is very little difference in the treatment dose and the toxic dose, making it imperative that the medication be carefully administered. Additionally, the compound was very caustic and had to be given intravenously. If any of the four required doses of Caparsolate leaked out of the vein, severe damage to the surrounding tissue was possible.

While there are still some veterinarians who use Caparsolate, a newer product called Immiticide is currently considered the treatment of choice. The medication is safer than Caparsolate, requires only two injections, and the medication is designed to be given intramuscularly rather than intravenously.

Heartworm treatment is safer in dogs who are infected but not suffering from heartworm disease. Pre-treatment diagnostic tests (chest radiographs, urinalysis, and blood profiles) are necessary prior to treating dogs infected with heartworms or showing signs of heartworm disease to minimize side effects from therapy.

When administered properly to dogs with heartworm infection, treatment is generally safe and without side effects (especially when Immiticide is used). Treatment is generally recommended due to the overall safety of treatment (when properly administered in selected patients) and the long life cycle of the parasite.

Treatment of cats with heartworm infection or disease presents some difficulty. Neither Caparsolate nor Immiticide is approved for use in cats. Additionally, cats with heartworm disease are likely to suffer potentially fatal pulmonary embolisms after treatment with Caparsolate (estimates are that 30 to 50% of cats treated for heartworm infection/disease are likely to experience a life-threatening crisis within 3 weeks of treatment). Many doctors choose supportive care (usually corticosteroids) for the vomiting or asthmatic-like signs seen in cats with heartworm disease rather than treat the cat with Caparsolate or Immiticide, due to the shortened life expectancy of heartworms in cats as compared to dogs and the potential for adverse reactions when using the conventional medications in cats.

Prevention of heartworms can be accomplished with daily (dog) or monthly (dog and cat) administration of heartworm preventative medications. Dogs showing evidence of microfilaria in their blood may react (severely) with the diethylcarbamazine in the daily preventative medication. Additionally, if an owner misses more than 24 to 48 hours (a short window when heartworm infection can occur) between dosing, the dog can become infected. Therefore, most, if not all, pets would have greater heartworm protection with minimal side effects using the monthly preventatives. The monthly preventatives contain extremely low doses of medications. These medications, while only given monthly, do not actually last in the body for an entire month but just for a few days. Therefore, the holistic pet owner can feel comfortable using them. Most holistic veterinarians would recommend that pet owners not use the combination products that contain both heartworm preventative medication and flea preventative medication (Sentinel). As a rule, if the pet doesn't need additional chemicals (as in the case of flea preventative medication), it shouldn't be used.

Homeopathic heartworm nosodes have been suggested as an alternative to conventional medications to prevent heartworm disease. No studies are available suggesting their effectiveness. For owners who choose to use the nosodes, semiannual heartworm testing should be done to allow early detection of infection if it should occur.

HYPERTHYROIDISM

Principal Natural Treatments
　Glandular therapy, astragalus (cats only), bugleweed (cats only), lemon balm (cats only)

Other Natural Treatments
　Homeopathic thyroidium, whole food supplements: raw broccoli or Phytolin

In cats, hyperthyroidism results from functional thyroid adenomatous hyperplasia (growth of the glandular cells) or adenoma (a benign tumor). Rarely, a cancerous tumor (adenocarcinoma) causes feline hyperthyroidism. One or both lobes of the thyroid gland are involved (70% of cases involve both thyroid glands).

Most cats with hyperthyroidism are older pets (10 years of age and older).

The most common clinical signs include hyperactivity, weight loss, increased appetite, vomiting, or diarrhea. In some cases (apathetic hyperthyroidism, which occurs in approximately 5% of cases), the cat does not experience these classic signs. Instead, the cat may act more lethargic, eat less, and generally act depressed or weak.

Diagnosis is made by finding elevated thyroid hormone levels on a blood profile. Other common geriatric diseases whose clinical signs mimic hyerthyroidism, such as kidney disease and diabetes, should be screened for as well. Secondary problems such as mild liver or heart disease usually resolve when the underlying hyperthyroidism is treated. Because older cats can also have kidney disease that may worsen if the hyperthyroidism is treated, cats with hyperthyroidism must be carefully screened for kidney disease prior to treatment of hyperthyroidism.

PRINCIPAL NATURAL TREATMENTS

Treatments include glandular therapy and the herbs **astragalus** (page 160), **bugleweed** (page 170), and **lemon balm** (page 234).

Glandular Therapy

Glandular therapy is recommended for cats with hyperthyroidism.

Glandular therapy uses whole animal tissues or extracts of the thyroid gland. Current research supports this concept that the glandular supplements have specific activity and contain active substances that can exert physiologic effects.

While skeptics question the ability of the digestive tract to absorb the large protein macromolecules found in glandular extracts, evidence exists that this is possible. Therefore, these glandular macromolecules can be absorbed from the digestive tract into the circulatory system and may exert their biologic effects on their target tissues.

Several studies show that radiolabeled cells, when injected into the body, accumulate in their target tissues. The accumulation is more rapid by traumatized body organs or glands than healthy tissues, which may indicate an increased requirement for those ingredients contained in the glandular supplements.

In addition to targeting specific damaged organs and glands, supplementation with glandular supplements may also provide specific nutrients to the pet. For example, glands contain hormones in addition to a number of other chemical constituents. These low doses of crude hormones are suitable for any pet needing hormone replacement, but especially for those pets with mild disease or those who simply need gentle organ support.

Glandular supplements also function as a source of enzymes that may encourage the pet to produce hormones or help the pet maintain health or fight disease.

Finally, glandular supplements are sources of active lipids and steroids that may be of benefit to pets.

The dosage of glandular supplements varies with the product used.

Astragalus

Astragalus is used to strengthen the immune system and acts as an antibacterial and anti-inflammatory herb. As a result, many doctors prescribe this herb for pets with various infections and for those with chronic illnesses, including cancer.

In cats, astragalus is often recommended for the treatment of hyperthyroidism. It can also be used to help the body recover from long-term steroid therapy and for pets with kidney disease, as this herb improves kidney circulation.

Astragalus membranaceous is safe, but other species of astragalus can be toxic. Do not use in pets with diseases resulting from an overactive immune system (autoimmune diseases).

Bugleweed

Bugleweed may be useful for cats with mild hyperthyroidism. Frequent doses of the herbal extract must be given for several days before any result may be detected.

Like digitalis, bugleweed can be helpful in heart conditions in which the heart's contractions should be strengthened and the rate (pulse) decreased.

Bugleweed can also act as a diuretic and remove excess fluid from the lungs, as might occur in congestive heart failure.

Bugleweed can be useful for pain relief; it does not contain salicylic acid so it can be used safely in cats.

Do not use in pregnant animals.

Lemon Balm

Lemon balm may be useful in cats with hyperthyroidism to decrease thyroid output and possibly decrease blood pressure.

As with the other herbs mentioned, controlled studies are hard to find, and herbs may not be helpful in cats with severe disease. The dosage of herbs varies with the product used. Guidelines are given in the Introduction to the book under the section *About Herbal Treatments*.

OTHER NATURAL TREATMENTS

Other therapies include homeopathics (Homeopathic thyroidium), and whole food supplements. Use raw broccoli mixed in a homemade diet, as much possible; or if the cat does not eat raw broccoli, use a whole food broccoli supplement such as Phytolin from Standard Process.

These can be used in conjunction with conventional therapies as they are unlikely to be effective by themselves in most patients. The natural treatments are widely used with variable success but have not all been thoroughly investigated and proven at this time.

As with any condition, the most healthful natural diet will improve the pet's overall health.

SAFETY ISSUES

Because vegetables such as broccoli and cabbage can depress thyroid hormone if eaten in large amounts, they should not be fed (or only fed in small amounts) to dogs with hypothyroidism. The herbs mentioned above, in the section Other Natural Treatments, while useful in treating cats with hyperthyroidism, *should be avoided in dogs* to prevent a worsening of clinical signs. Treatments to avoid in dogs include astragalus, bugleweed, and lemon balm.

CONVENTIONAL THERAPY

Three conventional therapies are recommended for cats with hyperthyroidism. Surgical removal of the thyroid gland can be performed. However, anesthesia is needed for this procedure; and while geriatric cats can be safely anesthetized, the other options for treatment usually do not require anesthesia and are usually preferred. Second, surgery, especially in severely hyperthyroid cats, is associated with significant morbidity (illness and trauma) and mortality, as well as the chance for postoperative calcium imbalances due to damage or inadvertent removal of the associated parathyroid glands.

Medical therapy, most commonly with methimazole (Tapazole), is another conventional option for treating hyperthyroidism. The medicine is given for the life of the cat and is very successful in lowering levels of thyroid hormones. Rare side effects include lack of appetite, vomiting, lethargy, facial dermatitis, and low red cell, platelet, and white blood cell counts. Liver disease is also a possible side effect. Cats experiencing abnormal blood or liver profiles or facial dermatitis are at risk of future serious side effects and must have their medication stopped and another form of treatment instituted.

The third and most commonly used treatment for cats with hyperthyroidism is radioactive iodine[131]. While this sounds quite drastic, it may be the safest conventional treatment for hyper-

thyroid cats. Side effects are extremely rare, and most cats are completely cured after one treatment. Hypothyroidism, or low thyroid output, is a rare side effect of treatment that can easily be treated with thyroid replacement hormone if needed. Because radioactive iodine cures the hyperthyroid conditions, and because cats with underlying kidney disease could develop kidney failure when cured of their hyperthyroid conditions, it is essential that cats be screened for kidney disease prior to radioactive iodine treatment. The major concern among owners is that cats treated with radioactive iodine must be hospitalized for one week or more until they are no longer excreting radioactive iodine in their urine or feces.

A fourth, newer proposed treatment for feline hyperthyroidism is injection of ethanol directly into the affected thyroid gland using ultrasound to guide the procedure (the procedure is called percutaneous ethanol ablation). Early studies appear positive, although some cases involved laryngeal paralysis secondary to leakage of ethanol from the thyroid gland and inflammation of the recurrent laryngeal nerve. More research is needed to determine whether percutaneous ethanol ablation will become a safe and effective therapy for treating feline hyperthyroidism.

 # HYPOTHYROIDISM

Principal Natural Treatments
Glandular thyroid supplement

Other Natural Treatments
None

Hypothyroidism is the most common endocrine (hormonal) disease of dogs and is most commonly seen in middle-aged to older dogs. The average age of dogs with hypothyroidism is 7 years of age. While any breed can be affected, increased incidence of hypothyroidism is seen in Labrador and Golden Retrievers, Shetland Sheepdogs, Great Danes, Irish

Setters, Doberman Pinschers, and Old English Sheepdogs.

The cause of hypothyroidism is believed to be immune-mediated thyroiditis, caused by the dog's body forming antibodies against its own thyroid gland. Idiopathic follicular atrophy, a condition of unknown cause where the thyroid gland follicles are lost and replaced by fat or connective tissue, is also seen in dogs with hypothyroidism. Rarely, thyroid cancer can also cause hypothyroidism.

Clinical signs classically seen in dogs with hypothyroidism include lethargy, weight gain, hair loss, seborrhea, and chronic skin infections (any dog with chronic skin infections or other skin disorders should be tested for hypothyroidism). Less commonly seen clinical signs in dogs with thyroid disease include neurological disorders (any kind of neurological disorder can be caused by hypothyroidism), infertility, behavioral disorders, heart disorders, and gastrointestinal disorders. Because hypothyroidism is so common in dogs and can cause any clinical signs, thyroid testing should be a part of the normal clinical workup for any sick dog.

PRINCIPAL NATURAL TREATMENTS

Treatment for dogs with hypothyroidism involves the use of glandular thyroid supplement, with or without the use of synthetic medication.

Glandular Therapy

Glandular therapy uses whole animal tissues or extracts of the thyroid gland. Current research supports this concept that the glandular supplements have specific activity and contain active substances that can exert physiologic effects.

While skeptics question the ability of the digestive tract to absorb the large protein macromolecules found in glandular extracts, evidence exists that this is possible. Therefore, these glandular macromolecules can be absorbed from the digestive tract into the circulatory system and may exert their biologic effects on their target tissues.

Several studies show that radiolabeled cells, when injected into the body, accumulate in their target tissues. The accumulation is more rapid by traumatized body organs or glands than healthy tissues, which may indicate an increased requirement for those ingredients contained in the glandular supplements.

In addition to targeting specific damaged organs and glands, supplementation with glandular supplements may also provide specific nutrients to the pet. For example, glands contain hormones in addition to a number of other chemical constituents. These low doses of crude hormones are suitable for any pet needing hormone replacement, but especially for those pets with mild disease or those who simply need gentle organ support.

Glandular supplements also function as a source of enzymes that may encourage the pet to produce hormones or help the pet maintain health or fight disease.

Finally, glandular supplements are sources of active lipids and steroids that may be of benefit to pets.

The dosage of glandular supplements varies with the product used.

SAFETY ISSUES

Because vegetables such as broccoli and cabbage can depress thyroid hormone if eaten in large amounts, they should not be fed (or only fed in small amounts) to dogs with hypothyroidism.

CONVENTIONAL THERAPY

Supplementation with synthetic thyroid medication is the treatment (usually given for the life of the dog) for canine hypothyroidism. Blood testing done twice yearly should be done to monitor the dog's thyroid levels, allowing the dosage of medication to be adjusted as needed.

INFECTIONS (Viral/Bacterial/Fungal)

Principal Natural Treatments
None

Other Natural Treatments
Natural diet, antioxidants, orthomolecular therapy, colloidal silver, neem, olive leaf extract, aloe vera, astragalus, boswellia (ulcerative colitis), echinacea, garlic, German chamomile (topical), ginger, goldenseal (topical), gotu kola, horsetail (urinary system), licorice, marshmallow, Oregon grape, sage, St. John's wort, turmeric, uva ursi (urinary infections, alkaline urine), yarrow, reishi and maitake mushrooms, and homeopathic nosodes

There are a number of infectious diseases in dogs and cats. Most commonly encountered are bacterial infections, although viral and fungal infections are also seen. Specific diseases that commonly occur in dogs and cats are discussed throughout this section.

OTHER NATURAL TREATMENTS

Complementary therapies for pets with various infections include **natural diet** (page 335), **antioxidants** (page 158), **orthomolecular therapy** (page 415), **colloidal silver** (page 186), **neem** (page 244), **olive leaf extract** (page 246), the herbs **aloe vera** (page 156), **astragalus** (page 160), **boswellia** (for ulcerative colitis, page 168), **echinacea** (page 195), **garlic** (page 204), **German chamomile** applied topically (page 206), **ginger** (page 207), **goldenseal** applied topically (page 220), **gotu kola** (page 221), **horsetail** for infections of the urinary system (page 225), **licorice** (page 234), **marshmallow** (page 240), **Oregon grape** (page 251), **sage** (page 264), **St. John's wort** (page 276), **turmeric** (page 280), **uva ursi** for infections of the urinary system with alkaline urine (page 281), **yarrow** (page 308), **reishi** (page 264) and **maitake** mushrooms (page 238). **Homeopathic nosodes** (page 411) may be helpful.

These can be used in conjunction with conventional therapies, as they are unlikely to be effective by themselves in most patients with severe infections. The natural treatments are widely used with variable success but have not all been thoroughly investigated and proven at this time.

As with any condition, the most healthful natural diet will improve the pet's overall health.

CONVENTIONAL THERAPY

Conventional therapies for infectious diseases involve the use of antibiotics (for bacterial infections), antifungal medications (for fungal infections such as ringworm), and antiviral medications (for viral infections). A greater discussion of **antibiotic therapy,** the most common antimicrobial therapy in veterinary medicine, can be found on page 427.

 # INFLAMMATORY BOWEL DISEASE (Diarrhea)

Principal Natural Treatments
Glutamine, natural diet, orthomolecular therapy, antioxidants, enzymes, prebiotics/probiotics

Other Natural Treatments
MSM, omega-3 fatty acids, glucosamine, DMG, aloe vera, boswellia (ulcerative colitis), calendula, chamomile, marshmallow, raspberry leaf, and slippery elm

Inflammatory bowel disease is the name given to a group of conditions that are characterized by pathologic evidence of inflammation of the intestinal tract which is associated with (usually chronic and persistent) gastrointestinal signs.

The clinical signs most commonly seen in pets with inflammatory bowel disease often reflect the location of the intestinal lesions (inflammation). Vomiting, diarrhea, and/or weight loss are usually observed. Lesions affecting the upper GI (gastrointestinal) tract (stomach and upper small intestine) are more likely to cause vomiting, whereas lesions of the lower small intestinal tract and colon are more likely to cause diarrhea.

Causes of inflammatory bowel disease are numerous and include parasites (whipworms, giardia), fungi (histoplasmosis, prototheccosis), bacteria (*Salmonella, Campylobacter,* pathogenic *E. coli),* food allergy/hypersensitivity, cancer (lymphosarcoma, adenocarcinoma), and idiopathic (unknown cause named by the type of pathogenic white blood cells seen in biopsy specimens such as eosinophilic, lymphocytic-plasmacytic, or granulomatous). Most commonly, the idiopathic classification of inflammatory bowel disease is seen in dogs and cats. While there is no known cause of idiopathic inflammatory bowel disease, most doctors suspect some type of allergy as this is an immune disease. The allergy or sensitivity might be due to the diet (many mild cases can respond to dietary manipulation), bacterial antigens, or self-antigens (an autoimmune disorder). Allergies to food components usually involve cereal grains (wheat, barley, and oats, all of which contain gluten, a common dietary protein in many cereal grains), meats, and rarely eggs.

Leaky Gut Syndrome, Intestinal Dysbiosis, Intestinal Hyperpermeability

The human and veterinary literature discuss a condition called the "leaky gut syndrome." This theory holds that in some people and pets, whole proteins leak through the wall of the digestive tract due to a hyperpermeable condition, and enter the blood, causing allergic reactions. These reactions may include food allergies, arthritis, autoimmune diseases, impaired nutrient absorption, and chemical sensitivities. It is theorized that many chronic diseases, often treated for years with various conventional medications, may in fact result from leaky gut syndrome.

One organism that has been postulated to be responsible for some of the signs seen in people and pets with leaky gut syndrome is the common yeast *Candida albicans.* This yeast has been observed to enter the bloodstream from the intestinal tract, and may cause chronic allergies. Overgrowth of this yeast and other organisms may occur in pets with chronic intestinal disease and in pets undergoing chronic antibiotic or NSAID therapy. The organisms can produce toxins that cause leaky gut syndrome. The increased intestinal permeability may allow greater absorption of the microorganisms and their toxins, causing further harm.

While controlled studies are lacking, holistic doctors often attempt gastrointestinal detoxification (using enzymes, prebiotics, probiotics, glutamine, and so forth) for pets with many diseases in an attempt to heal a leaky gut that may be contributing to clinical signs or disease.

PRINCIPAL NATURAL TREATMENTS

Glutamine

Glutamine, or L-glutamine, is an amino acid derived from another amino acid, glutamic acid. There is no daily requirement for glutamine as the body can make its own. High-protein foods such as meat, fish, beans, and dairy products are excellent sources of glutamine. Severe stresses may result in a temporary glutamine deficiency.

Glutamine plays a role in the health of the immune system, digestive tract, and muscle cells, as well as other bodily functions. It appears to serve as a fuel for the cells that line the intestines (it serves as a primary energy source for the mucosal cells that line the intestinal tract). Because stress on the intestinal cells that can occur in chronic inflammatory bowel disease can increase the need for glutamine as the body replaces the cells lining the intestinal tract, glutamine is often recommended for pets with chronic bowel disorders (including inflammatory bowel disease).

It has also been suggested as a treatment for food allergies, based on the "leaky gut syndrome." This theory holds that in some pets, whole proteins leak through the wall of the digestive tract and enter the blood, causing allergic reactions. Preliminary evidence suggests that glutamine supplements might reduce leakage through the intestinal walls. However, there is little real evidence that it works as a treatment for true food allergies, although it is highly recommended for pets with various bowel disorders.

Glutamine, being one of the body's amino acids, is thought to be a safe supplement when taken at recommended dosages. Because many anti-epilepsy drugs work by blocking glutamate stimulation in the brain, high dosages of glutamine may overwhelm these drugs and pose a risk to pets with epilepsy. If your pet is taking anti-seizure medications, glutamine should only be used under veterinary supervision.

Maximum safe dosages for young children, pregnant or nursing women, or those with severe liver or kidney disease have not been determined; similar precautions are probably warranted in pets. Recommended dosages in pets are 250 to 3,000 mg daily.

Natural Diet

Dietary therapy is an important part of any treatment plan for pets with inflammatory bowel disease in addition to other conventional or complementary therapies. Avoiding foods which exacerbate the bowel inflammation is important.

Severe inflammation of the intestinal tract can cause increased absorption of large food particles (molecules) that normally do not cross the intestinal barrier, possibly causing the formation of auto-antibodies, which may lead to autoimmune diseases (and further intestinal damage). Bacteria and yeasts (such as *Candida albicans*) may overgrow in the intestines of pets with chronic gastrointestinal disease and treated for extended periods of time with antibiotics, and may contribute through toxin formation to leaky gut syndrome and food allergies or hypersensitivities. Many of these pets may require chronic therapy with medications (such as corticosteroids and antibiotics) and/or natural supplements (probiotics, glutamine and so on). Dietary therapy is quite helpful in these pets and, when combined with appropriate supplements in pets with mild disease, may be the only therapy needed.

The diet for pets with gastrointestinal disease should contain highly digestible nutrients. The typical diet is low in fat, contains hypoallergenic and easily digestible carbohydrate and protein sources. Diets requiring minimal digestion reduce digestive enzyme production protecting the intestinal tract. Excess fat aggravates diarrhea; excess dietary sugars and glutens are not easily digested in pets with gastrointestinal disease. Fiber may be added during the recovery stage if needed to allow continued healing or to prevent diarrhea in pets with chronic gastroenteritis; potatoes and vegetables serve as healthful, natural sources of fiber.

Boiled white rice, which is highly digestible, is the recommended carbohydrate source. Alternatively, tapioca or potatoes can be used if pets cannot tolerate rice (which is very rare) or if they will not eat rice-based diets. Gluten-based grains (wheat, barley, rye, oats) can cause persistent diarrhea due to gluten sensitivity and are not recommended.

Proteins that are highly digestible and have a high biological value, such as cottage cheese or tofu, are recommended. Cottage cheese is easily digested and most pets do not have milk protein allergies. Meat can also be tried, although some pets may lose tolerance to meat (and develop a temporary sensitivity to meat during injury to the intestinal tract caused by vomiting or diarrhea). Additionally, meat stimulates more acid to be secreted in the stomach than tofu. If meat is to be fed, lowfat beef or preferably chicken or turkey can be tried.

Diet for Dogs with Inflammatory Bowel Disease

Dogs with gastrointestinal disease need diets with highly digestible protein that are also low in fat. Low-fat cottage cheese (½-⅔ cup) is used to provide protein (tofu with ⅛ teaspoon of added salt can be used if the dog refuses cottage cheese.)

Brown or white rice (2 cups) is an easily digestible carbohydrate source (boiled or baked potato can be tried if the dog refuses rice.) Potassium can be added using supplements such as Tumil-K (available through veterinarians) or by adding ¼-½ teaspoon of salt supplement (potassium chloride.)

This diet would provide approximately 500 kcal with 27 grams of protein and 2 grams of fat.

Two to three bonemeal tablets (10 grain or equivalent) or ¾ teaspoon of bonemeal powder to supply calcium and phosphorus with a multi-vitamin mineral supplement using the label instructions is added as the pet improves.

Alternatively, a natural product from Standard Process (Calcifood Wafers or Calcium Lactate) can be used (use 1 Calcifood Wafer or 2 Calcium Lactate tablets for each 2 bonemeal tablets.)

When possible, natural vitamins made from raw whole foods, rather than synthetic vitamins (although both can be used in combination) are preferred, as the natural vitamins also supply plant phytochemicals, enzymes, and other nutrients not found in chemically-synthesized vitamins. Catalyn from Standard Process can be used as the natural vitamin in this recipe, at a dose of 1 Catalyn per 25 pounds; Canine Plus (VetriScience) could also be used following label dosages.

Fresh, raw or slightly steamed vegetables (carrots, broccoli, etc.) can be used as a top dressing for the diet for extra nutrition and variety as the pet improves.

Most vegetables provide approximately 25 kcal per ½ cup.

In general, the above recipe supplies the daily nutritional and calorie needs for a 12-13 pound dog. The actual amount to feed will vary based upon the pet's weight (feed less if weight gain, more if weight loss.)

Diet for Cats with
Inflammatory Bowel Disease

Note: Before you start to feed your dog or cat a home-prepared diet, it is strongly recommended that you discuss your decision with your veterinarian or a holistic veterinarian in your area. It is essential that you follow any diet's recommendations closely, including all ingredients and supplements. Failure to do so

may result in serious health consequences for your pet.

Cats with gastrointestinal disease can do well with a slight variation of the basic cat diet (page 348.) The canola oil and clams should be eliminated. Cats can be fed simply the protein source (such as chicken or turkey, with or without the egg) or a small amount of brown or white rice (¼-½ cup) can be added if desired.

Potassium can be added using supplements such as Tumil-K (available through veterinarians) or by adding ¼-½ teaspoon of salt supplement (potassium chloride.)

Add 100 mg of taurine.

This diet would provide approximately 275 kcal with 30 grams of protein and 16 grams of fat.

One to two bonemeal tablets (10 grain or equivalent) or ¼-½ teaspoon of bonemeal powder to supply calcium and phosphorus with a multi-vitamin mineral supplement using the label instructions is added as the pet improves. Alternatively, a natural product from Standard Process (Calcifood Wafers or Calcium Lactate) can be used (use 1 Calcifood Wafer or 2 Calcium Lactate tablets for each 2 bonemeal tablets.)

When possible, natural vitamins made from raw whole foods, rather than synthetic vitamins (although both can be used in combination) are preferred, as the natural vitamins also supply plant phytochemicals, enzymes, and other nutrients not found in chemically-synthesized vitamins.

Catalyn from Standard Process can be used as the natural vitamin in this recipe, at a dose of 1 Catalyn per 10 pounds; NuCat (VetriScience) could also be used following label dosages.

Fresh, raw or slightly steamed vegetables (carrots, broccoli, etc.) can be used as a top dressing for the diet for extra nutrition and variety as the pet improves.

Most vegetables provide approximately 25 kcal per ½ cup, although most cats will not eat vegetables.

In general, the above recipe supplies the daily nutritional and calorie needs for a 9-10 pound cat. The actual amount to feed will vary based upon the pet's weight (feed less if weight gain, more if weight loss.)

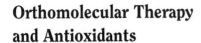
Orthomolecular Therapy and Antioxidants

Orthomolecular medicine (often called "megavitamin therapy") seeks to use increased levels of vitamins and minerals (mainly antioxidants) to help treat a variety of medical disorders. While daily amounts of vitamins and minerals have been recommended as an attempt to prevent nutritional deficiencies, orthomolecular medicine uses higher doses as part of the therapy for disease.

The pet food industry relies on recommendations by the National Research Council (NRC) to prevent diseases caused by nutrient deficiencies in the "average" pet, yet the NRC has not attempted to determine the *optimum* amount of nutrients or their effects in treating medical disorders. While a minimum amount of nutrients may be satisfactory in preventing diseases caused by nutrient deficiencies, it is important to realize that there is no "average" pet, and that every pet has unique nutritional needs.

It is unlikely that our current recommendations are adequate to maintain health in every pet. Each pet has unique requirements for nutrients. Additionally, these needs will vary depending upon the pet's health. For example, in times of stress or disease additional nutrients above and beyond those needed for health will be required. Orthomolecular medicine evaluates the needs of the pet and uses increased nutrients to fight disease.

The principles of **orthomolecular medicine** are summarized in Part Four, Other Complementary Therapies.

Note: Owners should not diagnose and treat their pets without veterinary supervision. Many medical disorders present similar symptoms. Also, megavitamin therapy can be toxic if not used properly.

As with other conditions, the initial approach to orthomolecular therapies involves a hypoallergenic diet free of by-products, chemical preservatives, fillers, and artificial colorings and flavorings to decrease potential hypersensitivity within the gastrointestinal tract.

Treatment uses **vitamin A** (10,000 IU for small dogs and cats, up to 30,000 IU for large dogs) and **vitamin E** (800 IU for small dogs and cats, up to 2,400 IU for large dogs). The antioxidant mineral **selenium** (20 mcg for small dogs and cats, up to 60 mcg for large dogs) is also added to the regimen. Once asymptomatic, a maintenance protocol using gradually lower dosages of vitamins A and E and the mineral selenium are prescribed to reduce the chance for toxicity.

Ascorbic acid is not used due to its cholinergic effect on the intestinal tract which can worsen diarrhea.

Plant Enzymes

Enzymes are used for a variety of functions in the pet's body. Cellular processes, digestion, and absorption of dietary nutrients are dependent upon the proper enzymes. Most commonly owners often think of enzymes as necessary for digestion of food. In fact, enzymes produced by the pancreas are essential for digestion of nutrients in the diet. Once properly digested by pancreatic enzymes, the dietary nutrients can be absorbed by the pet.

The pancreas produces amylase, lipase, and various proteases. Amylase is used for digesting carbohydrates, lipase is used for digesting fats, and proteases are used by the body to digest proteins.

While it is true that the pancreas produces enzymes to aid in food digestion, additional enzymes found in the diet contribute to digestion and absorption as well and may enhance feed efficiency (maximizing the utilization of nutrients in the diet). Natural raw diets contain a number of chemicals, including enzymes not found in processed diets. Processing often alters the nutrients found in a pet's food, depleting it of important nutrients and enzymes (enzymes are broken down in the presence of temperatures in the range of 120 to 160° F. and in the presences of freezing temperatures). Supplying additional enzymes through the use of supplementation can replenish enzymes absent in processed foods. Even pets on natural raw diets can often benefit from additional enzymes, which is why they are often recommended as a supplement.

In addition, various stressors such as illness, stress, allergies, food intolerance, age (older pets may have reduced digestive enzyme capability), and various orally administered medications (antibiotics) can decrease gastrointestinal function. This results in poor digestion and absorption of the nutrients in the diet. Supplying digestive enzymes at these times can improve digestion and absorption.

How Do Enzymes Work?

There is nothing magical about the enzymes themselves. They only work by liberating essential nutrients from the pet's diet. While we don't know all the wonderful things that enzymes do, it is known that certain enzyme supplements can increase the absorption of essential vitamins, minerals, and certain fatty acids from the diet. Increased absorption of zinc, selenium, vitamin B_6, and linoleic acid have been detected following plant enzyme supplementation (specifically in a small study using a plant enzyme product called Prozyme).

Doctors can prescribe pancreatic enzymes, microbial enzymes, or plant (vegetable) enzymes. Pancreatic enzymes are adequate for pets with pancreatic disease where enzyme production and function is inadequate.

Enzymes have been recommended for treating pets with various disorders, including inflammatory bowel disease. The plant enzymes are active over a much wider pH range (pH 3 to 9) than pancreatic enzymes and are the preferred enzymes for most patients. Plants contain the enzyme cellulase. Dogs and cats do not normally have cellulase in their bodies, and that's why they can only digest some of the plant material in their diets.

Supplementation with enzyme products that contain cellulase in addition to the normal lipase, amylase, and proteases found in many supplements seems to be more advantageous to pets with medical problems as these products liberate chemicals such as zinc, selenium, and linoleic acid that might be bound by fiber.

In one study, supplementing the diet with additional zinc did not confer the same benefits (improved growth rate and efficiency) as supplementing with plant enzymes. Apparently the plant enzymes liberate other nutrients in the diet in addition to zinc resulting in positive benefits that did not occur simply by increasing the nutrient zinc.

Since response is variable regarding the product used, if one supplement does not help another might.

Since enzymes are inactivated by heat, they cannot be added to warm food or mixed with warm water. Rather, they are simply sprinkled onto the food (at room temperature) at the time of feeding.

Enzyme supplementation is inexpensive, safe, and easy to administer in pill or powder form. Your doctor can help you decide which product is best for your pet's condition.

The dosage of plant enzymes varies with the product used.

Probiotics/Prebiotics

Probiotics are defined as normal viable bacteria residing in the intestinal tract that promote normal bowel health. Probiotics are given orally and are usually indicated for use in intestinal disorders in which specific factors can disrupt the normal bacterial population, making the pet more susceptible to disease. Specific factors that can disrupt the normal flora of the bowel include surgery, medications (including steroids and nonsteroidal anti-inflammatory drugs), antibiotics (especially when used long-term), shipping, birthing, weaning, illness such as parvovirus infection, and dietary factors (poor-quality diet, oxidative damage, stress). Improving the nutritional status of the intestinal tract may reduce bacterial movement across the bowel mucosa (lining), intestinal permeability, and systemic endotoxemia. In addition, probiotics may supply nutrients to the pet, help in digestion, and allow for better conversion of food into nutrients.

Prebiotics are food supplements that are not digested and absorbed by the host but improve health by stimulating the growth and activity of selected intestinal bacteria. Currently, there are no well-conducted studies on prebiotics.

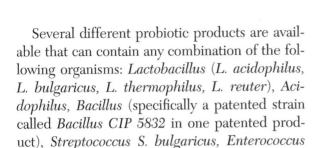

Several different probiotic products are available that can contain any combination of the following organisms: *Lactobacillus* (*L. acidophilus, L. bulgaricus, L. thermophilus, L. reuter*), *Acidophilus, Bacillus* (specifically a patented strain called *Bacillus CIP 5832* in one patented product), *Streptococcus S. bulgaricus, Enterococcus* (*E. faecium*) *Bifidobacterium, B. bifidus,* and *Saccharomyces* (*S. boulardii,* which is actually a beneficial yeast rather than a bacterium).

The intestinal tract, especially the large intestine (colon) is home to millions of bacteria, most of which are harmless, and in fact are beneficial to the pet. The intestinal bacteria are essential to digestion and the synthesis of vitamin K and many of the B vitamins.

Your pet's intestinal tract has billions of bacteria and yeasts, and some of these internal inhabitants are more helpful than others. *Acidophilus* and related probiotic bacteria not only help the digestive tract function, but also reduce the presence of less healthful organisms by competing with them for the limited space available.

There are several proposed mechanisms by which probiotics can protect your pet from harmful bowel bacteria: Probiotics produce inhibitory chemicals that reduce the numbers of harmful bacteria and possibly toxin production by these harmful bacteria; probiotics may block the adhesion of harmful bacteria to intestinal cells; probiotics may compete for nutrients needed for growth and reproduction by harmful bacteria; or probiotics may degrade toxin receptors located on intestinal cells, preventing toxin absorption and damage by toxins produced by harmful intestinal bacteria. Supplementing with probiotics may also stimulate immune function of the intestinal tract.

Antibiotics can disturb the balance of the intestinal tract by killing friendly bacteria. When this happens, harmful bacteria and yeasts can move in, reproduce, and take over. This is especially true in pets on long-term (several months) antibiotic therapy, and for pets with chronic diarrhea.

Conversely, it appears that the regular use of probiotics can generally improve the health of the gastrointestinal system.

The use of probiotics for treating diarrhea as well as maintaining health is quite controversial, with no clear scientific evidence (for health maintenance). Although many holistic doctors believe that they are helpful and perhaps even necessary for health, there is no daily requirement for probiotic bacteria. Probiotics are living creatures, not chemicals, so they can sustain themselves in the body unless something comes along to damage them, such as antibiotics.

Cultured dairy products such as yogurt and kefir are good sources of acidophilus and other probiotic bacteria. However, many yogurt products do not contain any living organisms or only contain small numbers of organisms.

Some pets will eat these foods, and others won't. Also, if the pet has any lactose intolerance, he may not tolerate yogurt well and may experience diarrhea (although this is rare). Most doctors recommend supplements to provide the highest doses of probiotics and avoid any lactose intolerance.

Various probiotics, while usually producing the same beneficial effects, may function differently within the intestinal tract. For example, *Lactobacillus acidophilus* produces lactic acid to lower the pH of the intestines and acts as an intestinal bacterial colonizer, *L. casei* lowers oxidation processes, and *L. lactis* acts on hydrogen peroxide as well as amylase and proteases.

Dosages of Probiotics

Dosages of acidophilus and other probiotics are expressed not in grams or milligrams, but in billions of organisms. A typical daily dose in people should supply about 3 to 5 billion live organisms. One popular pet supplement provides 500 million viable cells to be given per 50 pounds of body weight. The suggested dosage range of probiotics for pets is approximately 20 to 500 million microorganisms.

Some doctors recommend that when administering antibiotics, the probiotic should be given at least 2 hours later, several times per day, and when the antibiotic treatment has been completed, owners should double or triple the probiotic dose for 7 to 10 days.

Another recommendation is that if taking several species of probiotics, *Acidophilus* is reported to flourish best if taken in the morning, and the *Bifidus* when taken at night. It is suspected that this may follow the diurnal acid/alkaline tide that the body utilizes as part of the detoxification process. However, this is not proven. The most important thing is that, regardless of when they are taken, probiotics should be taken when using (extended) antibiotic therapy and other conditions for which these supplements are indicated (such as bowel disorders).

Because probiotics are not drugs but living organisms, the precise dosage is not so important. They should be taken regularly to reinforce the beneficial bacterial colonies in the intestinal tract, which may gradually push out harmful bacteria and yeasts growing there.

The downside of using a living organism is that probiotics may die on the shelf. The container label should guarantee living *Acidophilus* (or *Bulgaricus*, and so on) at the time of purchase, not just at the time of manufacture.

Scientific Evidence

There is fairly good evidence that many probiotics can help with various types and causes of diarrhea. *Saccharomyces boulardii, Enterococcus faecium,* and *Lactobacillus spp.* have been shown to help prevent antibiotic-induced diarrhea. *Saccharomyces* has demonstrated the most promise for use in diarrhea caused by the intestinal bacterium *Clostridium difficile,* a common cause of bacterial overgrowth in pets and people (*Lactobacillus spp.* are also helpful in bacterial overgrowth). Some evidence suggests that a particular type of probiotic, *L. reuteri,* can help treat diarrhea caused by viral infections in children. According to several studies conducted on the subject, it appears that regular use of acidophilus can help prevent "traveler's diarrhea" (an illness caused by eating contaminated food).

There are no known safety problems with the use of *Acidophilus* or other probiotics. Occasionally, some people notice a temporary increase in digestive gas (the same could occur in pets).

If your pet is taking antibiotics, it may be beneficial to supplement with probiotics at the same time, and to continue them for a couple of weeks after the course of drug treatment has stopped.

This will help restore the balance of natural bacteria in the digestive tract.

Fructo-oligosaccharides

In people, it is often suggested that in addition to taking probiotics, patients take fructo-oligosaccharides, supplements that can promote thriving colonies of helpful bacteria in the digestive tract. Fructo-oligosaccharides (FOS) are naturally occurring sugars found in many fruits, vegetables and grains. (Fructo means "fruit," and an oligosaccharide is a type of carbohydrate.) These non-digestible complex carbohydrates resist digestion by salivary and intestinal digestive enzymes and enter the colon where they are fermented by bacteria such as *Bifidobacterium* and *Bacteroides spp.*

The most beneficial effect of fructo-oligosaccharides is the selective stimulation of the growth of *Bifidobacterium,* thus significantly enhancing the composition of the colonic microflora and reducing the number of potential pathogenic bacteria. *Lactobacillus,* another beneficial bacteria, was also seen to proliferate with addition of FOS supplements. Because FOS increases the colonization of healthy bacteria in the gut, they are considered to be a prebiotic rather than a probiotic.

Taking FOS supplements is thought to foster a healthy environment for the beneficial bacteria living in the intestinal tract. Studies using FOS at a dosage of 0.75% to 1.0% (dry matter basis) showed decreased *E. coli* and increased lactobacilli intestinal bacteria in cats and dogs. The typical daily dose of fructo-oligosaccharides for people is between 2 and 8 g. The correct dose for pets has not been determined. One supplement contains 50 mg per dose for a 50-pound dog; research on FOS showed positive benefits when the dosage was 0.75% to 1.0% of the food when fed on a dry matter basis.

OTHER NATURAL TREATMENTS

These treatments include **MSM** (page 242), **omega-3 fatty acids** (page 158), **glucosamine** (page 212), **DMG** (page 194), **aloe vera** (page 156), **boswellia** for ulcerative colitis (page 168),

calendula (page 173), **chamomile** (page 178), **marshmallow** (page 240), **raspberry leaf** (page 261), and **slippery elm** (page 273).

These can be used in conjunction with conventional therapies as needed. The natural treatments are widely used with variable success but have not all been thoroughly investigated and proven at this time.

CONVENTIONAL THERAPY

Most pets with inflammatory bowel disease are treated with various anti-inflammatory medications, including corticosteroids, sulfasalazine, or in serious cases the chemotherapy agent azathio-

prine. These therapies are often combined with antimicrobial medications (tylosin, metronidazole). Usually the pet is treated with a high (immunosuppressive) dose of anti-inflammatory medication and is slowly, over several months, weaned off the medicine or weaned to the lowest dose that controls the clinical signs. There is potential danger in using high doses of corticosteroids, including side effects such as pancreatitis, increased susceptibility to infection, and gastrointestinal ulceration or perforation. Using gastrointestinal protectant medications such as sucralfate, misoprostol, or omeprazole may decrease some of these side effects.

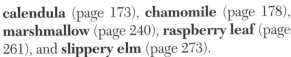

INTERVERTEBRAL DISK DISEASE

Principal Natural Treatments
  Acupuncture

Other Natural Treatments
  Homeopathics, antioxidants

Intervertebral disk disease is a common cause of neck or back pain and/or paralysis in small breeds of dogs. Large breeds of dogs and cats are less commonly affected by intervertebral disk disease. While any breed of dog (or cat) can be affected, the dog breeds most commonly affected include Dachshunds, Shih Tzus, Lhasa Apsos, and similar breeds.

The disorder occurs as a result of degeneration of the shock-absorbing disks located in between the bones (vertebrae) of the back (spinal column). In Type I disk disease (the type most commonly seen in small breeds, although at least one author reports an increased incidence in Doberman Pinschers), the outer part of the disk (the annulus fibrosis) degenerates and ruptures, allowing the inner part of the disk (the nucleus pulposus) to extrude into the spinal canal. The extruding nucleus puts pressure on the spinal cord. The amount of pressure determines the signs seen. Minor pressure usually causes pain

and possibly mild proprioceptive defects (causing a wobbly gait). More severe pressure can cause sudden and severe paralysis.

Diagnosis is made by clinical signs, radiography (x rays), and specialized radiographic procedures (myelogram, MRI). Conventional therapy can involve medical therapy or surgical therapy. Medical therapy, consisting of strict confinement (cage rest) with corticosteroids and/or muscle relaxants, is indicated for pets with mild clinical signs. However, the incidence of recurrence of disk disease is greater in pets treated medically rather than surgically. Estimates are that 30 to 40% of dogs treated medically have a recurrence at some time.

Acute paralysis, or chronic recurrence of mild signs, indicates the need for surgical removal of the disk. Pets with acute paralysis present a true emergency. In the presence of paralysis with the retention of deep pain on neurological examination, surgery should be performed within 12 to 24 hours. In the presence of paralysis but the absence of deep pain on neurological examination, surgery is less successful and the prognosis is poor.

PRINCIPAL NATURAL TREATMENTS

The most common natural treatment therapy for pets with disk disease is **acupuncture**.

Acupuncture

Acupuncture is without a doubt one of the most field-tested techniques available in complementary medicine. While it is hard to pinpoint exactly how long acupuncture has been around, evidence indicates that it is easily more than 4,000 years old, having been used in Asian and Indian cultures for many centuries. For skeptics who question the effectiveness of this popular complementary therapy, a large amount of empirical as well as experimental information and studies show the effectiveness of acupuncture. Certainly a therapy that is a mainstay of Traditional Chinese Medicine (TCM) could not have survived if it were not effective. The theory of Traditional Chinese Medicine has in fact served as the basis of acupuncture instruction for over 4,000 years. While there is certainly no substitute for well-documented research using controlled clinical studies, we cannot ignore thousands of years of clinical experience.

One stumbling block to the Western-trained mind trying to understand acupuncture is the lack of scientific explanation as to exactly how acupuncture works. The explanations offered by Traditional Chinese Medicine suffice for practitioners of this ancient art, but confuse the traditional Western mind. However, while a number of physiological theories have been proposed to explain how acupuncture works (to follow), we must remain open-minded to the effectiveness of this therapy (and, of course, to all complementary therapies).

The wise reader will remember that while we may not know exactly how acupuncture (or other complementary therapies) actually work, we also do not know exactly how certain modern Western medical treatments work. (For example, even Pfizer's own literature states that exactly how their bestselling nonsteroidal drug Rimadyl works is not known.) If we can use traditional drug ther-

apies without formal proof of how they work, we can also use therapies such as acupuncture without formal proof of how they work.

We do know that acupuncture points lie over free nerve endings wrapped in connective tissue or within the walls of blood vessels; this anatomy may help explain why stimulation of acupuncture points elicits therapeutic effects. Additionally, there is a high concentration of tissue-secretory mast cells in and around acupuncture points. The release of histamine (and probably other chemicals) may explain an important part of acupuncture by causing dilation of surrounding blood vessels and stimulating adjacent nerve terminals.

How Does Acupuncture Work?

Exactly how does acupuncture work? There are in fact several proposed theories that attempt to explain how acupuncture exerts its effects. No one theory fully explains how acupuncture works; the actual mechanisms are complex and likely interrelated.

The theories that explain the workings of acupuncture include:

Gate Theory. Inhibitory neurons close a "gate" to ascending pain fibers and thus prevent pain from reaching the higher brain centers that allow conscious recognition of pain. There is a large amount of evidence that acupuncture can induce local pain relief; acupuncture points with the highest proportion of type A nerve fibers relative to type C nerve fibers provide the best regional pain relief. However, while probably accounting for some of the action of acupuncture, the gate theory does not explain the delayed onset of some of the effects seen with acupuncture therapy.

Humoral Theory. Local anesthesia results from some combination of endogenous chemicals including opioids, serotonin, and cholinergic and adrenergic compounds. These compounds are increased as a result of acupuncture. Additionally, humoral immunity is enhanced during acupuncture treatment.

Autonomic Nervous System. Stimulation of acupuncture points can cause autonomic nervous system dilation of blood vessels (the so-called "somatovisceral reflex"). This helps explain why stimulating points on the skin can exert strong influences on internal organs. Acupuncture may produce these effects by stimulating cyclic AMP (cAMP) which causes release of catecholamine hormones from the adrenal gland; the catecholamines then affect cellular functions such as dilation of blood vessels.

Local Effects. Acupuncture produces local effects including increased local tissue immune function, increased blood supply, and muscle and tissue relaxation as well as local pain relief.

Bioelectrical Theory. Acupuncture channels (called "meridians") allow transmission of nervous impulses because of their low electrical impedance (electrical impedances can be measured at acupuncture points). Acupuncture points boost the DC signals carried by the meridian, which short-circuits the current and blocks the pain impulse.

What Exactly Is Acupuncture?

In its purest sense, acupuncture involves the placement of tiny needles into various parts (acupuncture points) of a pet's body. These needles stimulate the acupuncture points, which can effect a resolution of the clinical signs.

In traditional acupuncture, the acupuncturist places tiny needles at various points on the pet's body. These points are chosen based on diagnostic tests and/or traditional "recipes" or formulas that are known to help pets with specific problems. As mentioned, these acupuncture points correspond to areas of the body which contain nerves and blood vessels. By stimulating these points, acupuncture causes a combination of pain relief, stimulation of the immune system, and alterations in blood vessels, causing a decrease in clinical signs.

While traditional acupuncture uses tiny acupuncture needles to stimulate the specific acupuncture points chosen, other forms of acupuncture also exist. These other forms of acupuncture are often chosen to provide the pet more prolonged stimulation of acupuncture points, as they produce a higher and more continuous level of stimulation. They include:

Laser therapy. Acupuncture points may be stimulated by low intensity or cold lasers to promote positive physiologic effects associated with healing and decreased pain and inflammation.

Aquapuncture. Aquapuncture utilizes the injection of tiny amounts of fluid (often vitamins, but also sterile water, antibiotics, herbal extracts, analgesics, local anesthetics, corticosteroids, nonsteroidal medications, or electrolyte solutions) at the acupuncture site for a more prolonged effect.

Implantation. To achieve a more prolonged and intense stimulation of acupuncture points, various objects (usually beads made of gold, silver, or stainless steel) are surgically implanted at acupuncture sites.

Electroacupuncture. This form of acupuncture therapy uses a small amount of non-painful electricity to stimulate the acupuncture site for a more intense effect.

Moxibustion. Moxibustion is the burning of an herb (typically Artesmisia vulgaris) on or above acupuncture points. The heat from the burning herb gives additional stimulation to the acupuncture points. **Care must be taken to avoid burning the patient!**

Acupressure. Acupressure involves applying pressure with the fingers to specific acupuncture points. Owners can be taught to apply acupressure at home to the acupuncture points that have been used during veterinary treatments to augment the acupuncture treatments to give further relief from pain and inflammation.

SAFETY ISSUES

As a rule, acupuncture compares quite favorably with traditional therapies. In some cases, acupuncture may be preferred when conventional therapy is ineffective or potentially harmful. At other times, acupuncture may be used when an owner cannot afford traditional therapy.

Side effects from acupuncture are rare. Accidental puncture of an underlying vital organ can occur. When this happens, it is usually because the incorrect needles (the needles come in various sizes and the correct length of needle must be chosen that corresponds to the size of the pet and the area to be treated) are placed in an area in which there is minimal soft tissue that covers the underlying organs (such as the abdomen). Infection can occur at the site of needle insertion; needles should not be placed in areas in which the skin is infected or inflamed. In rare instances, the needle can break (due to patient movement and incorrect needle placement and removal), and surgery may be needed to remove it.

Some pets require sedation in order to allow insertion of the acupuncture needles. In some animals, clinical signs may worsen for a few days before they improve. (This is not unusual in pets treated with complementary therapies and is explained by the body going through the healing process. In addition, some animals treated with conventional medications also get worse before the medication "kicks in" and the pet begins to show signs of improvement.)

Many owners worry that acupuncture is painful and that their pets will suffer. Usually acupuncture is not painful. Occasionally, the animal will experience some sensation as the needle passes through the skin. Once in place, most animals will relax and some may become sleepy. Fractious animals (especially cats and nervous dogs) may require mild sedation for treatment. Alternatively, a complementary therapy to calm the pet (such as an herbal remedy or the flower essence called **Rescue Remedy,** page 391) can be used prior to and during acupuncture treatment.

In addition to acupuncture, cage rest is critical to prevent additional stress to the spinal cord, which could increase clinical signs of symptoms. When acupuncture therapy is chosen, the use of corticosteroids should be avoided whenever possible as corticosteroid administration decreases the effectiveness of acupuncture. However, if corticosteroids are needed to provide immediate relief (decreased pain and inflammation), they should be used. In this case, additional acupuncture treatments may be needed.

Treatments

The number of acupuncture treatments that a pet will require varies from pet to pet. Usually, owners are asked to commit to 8 treatments (2 to 3/week) to assess if acupuncture will work. On average, treatments last about 15 to 30 minutes for needle acupuncture, and 5 to 10 minutes for aquapuncture or electroacupuncture. If the pet improves, acupuncture is done "as needed" to control the pet's signs. As previously mentioned, other therapies may be used to decrease the number of visits to the doctor's office for acupuncture.

Results

Acupuncture can be effective for pets with neurological disorders such as intervertebral disk disease. While the effectiveness of acupuncture treatment compares favorably with corticosteroids and surgical therapy, for pets in whom surgery is indicated, acupuncture should not replace therapy unless the patient is a poor surgical candidate or the owner is unable to afford surgery. Simply put, *pets that require surgery to treat or cure a problem should have surgery and not a complementary therapy unless there are valid reasons that surgery should not or cannot be performed.*

Intervertebral disk disease commonly affects the middle to lower back (thoracolumbar area) or the neck (cervical area).

Back Disk Disease

Pets with intervertebral disk disease of the thoracolumbar area (thoracolumbar disk disease) are graded based upon clinical signs; the grading allows a more accurate prognosis to be given. The four grades of thoracolumbar disk disease are:

- *Grade I:* Pets have back pain as their only clinical sign.
- *Grade II:* Pets have back pain plus rear leg paresis (partial paralysis) and ataxia (wobbly gait).
- *Grade III:* Pets have back pain and rear leg paralysis (total paralysis), and some dogs and cats may not have control over bladder and colon function.
- *Grade IV:* Pets have paralysis and no conscious pain perception in the rear legs.

Neck Disk Disease

Pets with intervertebral disk disease of the neck area (cervical disk disease) are also graded based upon clinical signs; the grading allows a more accurate prognosis to be given. The three grades of cervical disk disease are:

- *Grade I:* Pets have only neck pain present.
- *Grade II:* Pets have neck pain plus show proprioceptive deficits (ataxia, or a wobbly gait), of the front or rear legs.
- *Grade III:* Pets have neck pain and paralysis of the front and rear legs, and some dogs and cats may not have control over bladder and colon function.

The mechanism of how acupuncture works for pets with intervertebral disk disease of the neck or back are not yet fully understood. Acupuncture may eliminate trigger points (local points of tenderness and muscle spasms and tightness) and abolish muscle pain and stiffness. Acupuncture may also augment endogenous release of corticosteroids to relieve pain and inflammation, but this is disputed by some holistic veterinarians.

Scientific Evidence

How does disk disease respond to treatment with acupuncture?

Grade I back disk disease: For pets with thoracolumbar intervertebral disk disease, 90% recover after 2 to 3 acupuncture treatments over a 1- to 2-week treatment period.

Grade II back disk disease: For pets with grade II disk disease, approximately 90% of treated pets receiving 3 to 4 treatments over 3 weeks of treatment recovered.

These results indicate that for pets with grade I or II thoracolumbar intervertebral disk disease, the results of treatment with acupuncture are comparable to therapy with conventional medications (corticosteroids) or surgical disk decompression. However, while acupuncture can effectively relieve the clinical signs (pain, wobbly gait, and so forth) seen in pets with disk disease, surgery may be preferred for pets with recurring clinical signs as only surgery can prevent recurrence of the problem by removing the damaged disks. (Of patients treated with acupuncture, 10 to 25% may have recurrences of their clinical signs and require surgery.)

Grade III back disk disease: For pets with grade III thoracolumbar intervertebral disk disease, 80% recover after 5 to 6 acupuncture treatments over a 6-week treatment period.

Grade IV back disk disease: For pets with grade IV thoracolumbar intervertebral disk disease, less than 25% of patients recover after 10 or more treatments over 3 to 6 months of treatment.

Acupuncture is only half as effective as immediate decompressive surgery for pets with grade IV intervertebral disk disease. Since few dogs with Grade IV thoracolumbar intervertebral disk disease recover from their clinical signs (paralysis, lack of deep pain) regardless of treatment, the prognosis for these dogs is quite grave. However, even for those pets with this grave prognosis, acupuncture is recommended if the owner chooses not to have surgery done in the possible (although slight) chance that the pet might recover.

Grade I neck disk disease: For pets with grade I cervical intervertebral disk disease, approximately 80% recover after 3 to 4 treatments over 1 to 2 weeks.

Grade II neck disk disease: For pets with grade II disk disease, 67% recover after 5 to 6 treatments over 3 to 4 weeks of therapy.

Grade III neck disk disease: As of this writing, too few grade III cervical intervertebral disk disease patients have been described to evaluate results properly.

Approximately 33% of pets with cervical intervertebral disk disease relapse within 3 years, requiring additional treatment. For pets with chronic disk disease, surgery may be indicated to prevent future recurrences. (Surgical removal of damaged disks prevents recurrences of these disks from causing future disease; however, other disks could conceivably develop disease at a future time for which additional treatment would be needed.)

To summarize, in general, the results of treating pets with intervertebral disk disease with acupuncture approximate those of surgery. However, surgical removal of the damaged disks prevents the possibility of future episodes of disk disease and the chance of relapse (for those damaged disks) is gone. Surgery is recommended for pets with grade IV disk disease (any pet with paralysis and absence of deep pain) within 24 hours to maximize the chance of cure. However, the prognosis for recovery for these pets is poor even with surgery.

Acupuncture should only be performed on these pets if presented after more than 24 hours or if owner is unable to afford surgery. The chance for recovery following surgery in these pets is very low once 24 hours has elapsed due to the high possibility of permanent neurological damage. If the pet is not in severe pain, acupuncture should be attempted as there is unlikely to be any harm to the pet from acupuncture therapy and a few pets may recover.

OTHER NATURAL TREATMENTS

Homeopathics and **antioxidants** can be used in conjunction with conventional therapies as needed. The natural treatments are widely used with variable success, but, with the exception of acupuncture, have not all been thoroughly investigated and proven at this time. Pets with total paralysis are often better treated with surgery depending upon the results of the neurological examination performed at the initial presentation.

As with any condition, the most healthful natural diet will improve the pet's overall health.

CONVENTIONAL THERAPY

Conventional therapies rely on corticosteroids, muscle relaxants, and surgery when indicated.

 # INTESTINAL PARASITES

Principal Natural Treatments
   Garlic

Other Natural Treatments
   Black walnut (potential toxicity), German chamomile, goldenseal, licorice, Oregon grape, wormwood (potential toxicity), yarrow, yucca, pumpkin seeds, digestive enzymes, reishi mushrooms, homeopathics: *filix mas, nat phos, chenopodium*

Intestinal parasites are commonly seen in puppies and kittens, and less commonly in adult dogs and cats. The following parasites occur most commonly in pets: roundworms, hookworms, whipworms, tapeworms, coccidia, and a protozoal organism called *Giardia*. In the majority of the cases, puppies and kittens contract roundworms and tapeworms from their mother around the time of birth. With the exception of tapeworms and coccidia, the other parasites have zoonotic potential, meaning they are transmissible to people through fecal ingestion.

These parasites are easily transmitted between pets via infected feces, with the exception of tapeworms, which are spread by the ingestion of infected fleas.

The most common clinical signs of intestinal parasites include diarrhea, weight loss, general unthriftiness, and occasionally vomiting. Puppies and kittens with roundworms may have a "pot-bellied" appearance. Signs are more common in puppies and kittens and those pets that are generally "unhealthy." Hookworms can cause anemia, which can be fatal in puppies and kittens and "unhealthy" pets. Whipworms and *Giardia*, which are very difficult to detect on routine fecal examinations (unlike the other parasites), can be the cause of unexplained chronic weight loss and diarrhea.

Because the parasites can be present without clinical signs, and because the parasites can be transmitted to other pets and people, regular fecal examinations (at least twice yearly) are recommended by most veterinarians and the Centers for Disease Control (CDC). Additionally, most veterinarians and the CDC recommend regular deworming of puppies and kittens (up to approximately 3 to 4 months of age) as most, if not all, puppies and kittens have been exposed to roundworms and hookworms.

PRINCIPAL NATURAL TREATMENT

Garlic

Garlic contains a number of nutrients and a number of sulfur compounds that have been shown to have medical qualities, especially allicin and alliin.

Raw garlic can kill a wide variety of microorganisms by direct contact, including fungi, bacteria, viruses, and protozoa.

Garlic is recommended for pets with tapeworms; it has shown effectiveness in treating people with roundworms and hookworms and is often recommended for dogs and cats with these or other parasites.

When used for infections and possibly parasite control, the "allicin potential" of the garlic compound used is important. Since allicin is an unstable compound that is easily destroyed, fresh garlic or products with an identified allicin potential should be used when garlic is chosen for treating infections. (Because it is hard to know if a prepared formula has the guaranteed amount of allicin listed on the label unless the product comes from a reputable manufacturer, many herbalists recommend using fresh garlic cloves when the allicin content is important.)

For prepared products, the product should provide a daily dose of at least 10 mg of alliin or a total allicin potential of 4,000 micrograms (4 to 5 mg), which approximates 1 clove (4 grams) of garlic. (In people, a typical dosage of garlic is 900 mg daily of a garlic powder extract standardized to contain 1.3% alliin, providing about 12,000 mcg of alliin daily. This recommendation needs to be extrapolated for use in pets.) Many manufacturers claim an allicin potential "at the time of manufacture." This is not helpful as it does not reveal the allicin potential of the finished product and whether or not the product is stable. Read the label carefully.

However, there is a great deal of controversy over the proper dosage and form of garlic. In people, most everyone agrees that one or two raw garlic cloves a day are adequate for most purposes, but virtual trade wars have taken place over the potency and effectiveness of various dried, aged, or deodorized garlic preparations. The problem has to do with the way garlic is naturally constructed.

A relatively odorless substance, alliin, is one of the most important compounds in garlic. When garlic is crushed or cut, an enzyme called allinase is brought in contact with alliin, turning it into allicin. The allicin itself then rapidly breaks down into entirely different compounds. Allicin is most responsible for garlic's strong odor. It can also blister the skin and kill bacteria, viruses, and fungi. Presumably the garlic plant uses allicin as a form of protection from pests and parasites. It also may provide much of the medicinal benefits of garlic.

When powdered garlic is put in a capsule, it acts like cutting the bulb. The chain reaction starts once the garlic is powdered: Alliin contacts allinase, yielding allicin, which then breaks down. Unless something is done to prevent this process, garlic powder won't have any alliin or allicin left by the time you buy it.

Some garlic producers declare that alliin and allicin have nothing to do with garlic's effectiveness and simply sell products without it. This is particularly true of aged powdered garlic and garlic oil. But others feel certain that allicin is absolutely essential. However, in order to make garlic relatively odorless, they must prevent the alliin from turning into allicin until the product is consumed. To accomplish this feat, they engage in marvelously complex manufacturing processes, each unique and proprietary. How well each of these methods works is a matter of finger-pointing controversy.

When possible, raw garlic cloves are probably preferred.

SAFETY ISSUES

Too much garlic can be toxic to pets, causing Heinz body anemia. As a rule, follow label directions for commercially prepared products (such as those recommended for flea control) and for feeding fresh garlic: 1 clove per 10 to 30 pounds of body weight per day. There do not appear to be any animal toxicity studies on the most commonly used form of garlic: powdered garlic standardized to alliin content.

Garlic should not be used in pets with anemia. Do not use in pets scheduled for surgery due to the possibility of increased bleeding times (refrain from use at least 1 week before and 1 week after surgery).

Garlic may cause excess intestinal gas (reduce the dosage if this occurs).

Taking garlic at the same time as taking ginkgo or high-dose vitamin E might conceivably cause a risk of bleeding problems.

OTHER NATURAL TREATMENTS

Treatments for deworming pets include the herbs **black walnut** (potential toxicity, page 167), **garlic** (page 204), **German chamomile** (page 206), **goldenseal** (page 220), **licorice** (page 234), **Oregon grape** (page 251), **wormwood** (potential toxicity, page 308), **yarrow** (page 308), **yucca** (page 309), pumpkin seeds (a 50% kill of tapeworms), digestive **enzymes** (page 197), **reishi**

mushrooms (page 264), and the homeopathics, filix mas, nat phos, and chenopodium.

These can be used in conjunction with conventional therapies as needed. The natural treatments are widely used with variable success but have not been thoroughly investigated and proven at this time.

As with any condition, the most healthful natural diet will improve the pet's overall health.

CONVENTIONAL THERAPY

Conventional therapies for intestinal parasites involve the use of any of several medications, including pyrantel pamoate, febendazole, metronidazole, and praziquantel.

In the past, deworming medications were quite toxic and often caused severe clinical signs such as vomiting and diarrhea in pets treated with these medications. The currently used deworming medications are quite safe and usually 100% effective when used correctly, by following the correct deworming protocol. As a result, many holistic doctors use them for treating pets with intestinal parasites as they are effective and often safer than other deworming options, such as some of the commonly recommended herbal deworming products wormwood and black walnut.

 # KENNEL COUGH

Principal Natural Treatments
   Homeopathic nosodes

Other Natural Treatments
   Natural diet, antioxidants, orthomolecular therapy, colloidal silver, neem, olive leaf extract, aloe vera, astragalus, echinacea, garlic, ginger, gotu kola, licorice, marshmallow, Oregon grape, sage, St. John's wort, turmeric, yarrow, reishi and maitake mushrooms

Kennel cough (infectious tracheobronchitis) is a common disease of dogs and rarely of cats. It is most commonly caused by the *Bordetella* bacterium (dogs and cats) or the adenovirus (dogs) or parainfluenza virus (dogs). Usually, kennel cough occurs as a result of exposure to in-

fected pets (through boarding), although this is not necessary for a pet to develop kennel cough.

Clinical signs include coughing, gagging, and retching; many owners mistakenly believe their pets are choking on something. Vaccination is available to decrease the incidence of disease.

PRINCIPAL NATURAL TREATMENT

Homeopathic Nosodes

Nosodes, a special type of **homeopathic** remedy, are prepared from infectious organisms such as distemper virus and *Staphylococcus* bacteria. Remember that no matter what the source of the remedy, the actual ingredients are diluted in preparing the remedy. No measurable amount of the original source for the remedy remains, only the vital energy or life force, which imparts healing properties to the remedy. No harm will come to your pet regardless of the toxicity of the original compound used in the preparation of the remedy.

But do nosodes work? Some doctors seem to prefer nosodes manufactured by specific homeopathic pharmacies, as they feel there is a definite difference in the ability of nosodes to stimulate the immune system. In their opinions, the manufacturer of the nosode is important and some vaccination nosodes work better than others.

To prevent disease, nosodes are supposed to work in the same manner as conventional vaccines, namely by stimulating antibodies to fight off infections. Nosodes have been reported to control outbreaks of infectious disease in animals in a kennel situation. While good controlled studies are lacking, homeopathic veterinarians have reported success in some patients when treating infectious disease with the homeopathic nosodes.

OTHER NATURAL TREATMENTS

The same general recommendations made for pets with any infectious disease can be tried, including **natural diet** (page 335), **antioxidants** (page 158), **orthomolecular therapy** (page 415), **colloidal silver** (page 186), **neem** (page 244), **olive leaf extract** (page 246), herbs: **aloe vera** (page 156), **astragalus** (page 160), **echinacea** (page 195), **garlic** (page 204), **ginger** (page 271), **gotu kola** (page 221), **licorice** (page 234), **marshmallow** (page 240), **Oregon grape** (page 251), **sage** (page 264), **St. John's wort** (page 276), **turmeric** (page 280), **yarrow** (page 308), **reishi** (page 264) and **maitake** mushrooms (page 238).

These can be used in conjunction with conventional therapies as needed. The natural treatments are widely used with variable success but have not all been thoroughly investigated and proven at this time.

As with any condition, the most healthful natural diet will improve the pet's overall health.

CONVENTIONAL THERAPY

Treatment with antibiotics, corticosteroids, and antitussives (cough suppressants) are the mainstay of therapy for pets with kennel cough.

KIDNEY DISEASE

Principal Natural Treatments
  Natural diet, omega-3 fatty acids

Other Natural Treatments
  Astragalus, burdock, dandelion leaf, echinacea, garlic, *Ginkgo biloba,* gotu kola, hawthorn, marshmallow, B vitamins, glandular supplements

Kidney disease involves any insult to the kidneys. If the insult continues, the kidneys can experience failure. Kidney failure can be divided into either acute kidney failure or chronic kidney failure.

Acute kidney failure can occur in dogs and cats of any age, although most commonly younger pets are affected. Acute kidney failure can occur from a number of causes. Prerenal causes (not directly involving damage to the kidney) of acute kidney failure include low blood pressure, low blood volume, heart failure, and certain medications such as nonsteroidal anti-inflammatory medications and ACE inhibitors such as enalapril, a drug marketed as Enacard used for pets with heart disease. Renal causes (involving direct damage to the kidneys) of acute kidney failure include intrinsic kidney diseases, toxins that directly attack the kidneys (such as antifreeze poisoning or aminoglycoside antibiotics), cancer of the kidney, kidney trauma (kidney stones, direct trauma), congenital disorders (polycystic kidney disease, renal cortical hypoplasia), and infections (leptospirosis in dogs, feline infectious peritonitis in cats). Postrenal causes (involving a blockage of urine outflow from the kidneys or bladder) of acute kidney failure include bladder stones, urethral stones, bladder cancer, and feline lower urinary tract disease (including urinary tract obstruction that is most commonly seen in male cats).

Treatment of acute kidney failure involves intravenous fluid therapy (or periotoneal dialysis) to decrease the uremic toxins that accumulate in the blood, antibiotics if needed for infectious causes, antidotes for poisoning, and removal of any blockages or obstructions that may be causing the kidney failure. Many pets with acute kidney failure die despite intensive therapy. Those who recover are considered cured.

Chronic kidney failure is the most common form of kidney failure in dogs and cats, and is one of the major causes of illness and death in older dogs and cats. Several studies have shown that the mean ages of dogs and cats with kidney failure were 7.0 years for dogs and 7.5 years for cats. Most pets with chronic kidney failure are older than 10 years old, and the incidence increases with age.

The pathologic (microscopic) diagnosis of kidney failure in dogs and cats includes disorders such as glomerulonephritis, amyloidosis, tubulointerstitial nephritis, and occasionally, lymphoma cancer. Regardless of the actual microscopic diagnosis, the actual cause of chronic kidney failure in most pets is unknown. Initiating factors causing chronic kidney failure remain unclear in most cases, and much controversy has

been raised in speculating exactly what causes older pets to develop kidney failure. According to one author, Dr. Donald Strombeck, in *Home-Prepared Dog & Cat Diets* (ISUP, 1999), the increased incidence of kidney disease may be related to feeding processed pet foods, as the incidence has increased since the increase in the popularity of these diets. Dr. Strombeck theorizes that increased levels of vitamins and minerals (especially vitamin D, calcium, and phosphorus) added to processed foods may, over time, damage the kidneys ultimately leading to kidney failure. However, while kidney failure is common in older pets, not every older pet eating processed food develops kidney failure. Other contributing factors seem to be involved as well. Feeding properly balanced homemade diets, and avoiding unnecessary use of chemicals, vaccinations, and infections are potential solutions to decrease the possibility of kidney failure. Dental infections, the most common infectious disorder in dogs and cats, is easily treated by regular dental cleanings, removing oral bacteria before it can travel throughout the body causing liver, heart, or kidney infections.

PRINCIPAL NATURAL TREATMENTS

Natural Diets

There are several dietary nutrients to consider altering in pets with kidney disease and kidney failure, including protein, phosphorus, sodium, potassium, and fatty acids.

Protein Protein restriction is often recommended for pets with kidney disease and kidney failure. Dietary protein is broken down to acid products that are normally excreted by the kidneys. Diseased kidneys cannot excrete these acid products and other toxins as efficiently as normal kidneys. As these products accumulate in the blood, signs of uremia and kidney failure (excess thirst, excess urination, decreased appetite, foul breath, lethargy) occur. Amino acids containing sulfur, as well as extra phosphorus in the diet, contribute to the formation of these acid products and toxins. Excess phosphorus in the body, as occurs in pets with kidney failure, can combine with calcium-forming crystals. These crystals can precipitate into the kidneys and other organs, further contributing to terminal kidney and multiorgan failure. By reducing ingredients in the diet that contain sulfurous amino acids and phosphorus, we can promote kidney health and reduce kidney damage.

Animal sources of protein (meat) are high in sulfur-containing amino acids and phosphorus. Plant protein sources contain less sulfurous amino acids and phosphorus and also minerals such as potassium and magnesium that contribute to an alakaline urine, promoting kidney health. Proteins of high biological value that contain little phosphorus are preferred for pets with kidney disease and kidney failure.

Eggs contain the protein of the highest biological value and are often recommended for pets with kidney disease or kidney failure. However, eggs also contain sulfurous amino acids, which could contribute to acidosis. Egg protein can be safely fed to most pets with kidney disease without contributing to acidosis—except in terminal kidney failure or if blood testing reveals acidosis.

While plant proteins do contain less sulfurous amino acids, the biological value of their proteins is less than egg protein so more protein would need to be fed if plant proteins were selected as the protein source for the diet. This extra protein would require more waste products to be excreted by already damaged kidneys, which is why egg protein is usually recommended for kidney diets. Tofu can be used as a compromise if the pet cannot tolerate egg protein.

Phosphorus By decreasing meat in the diet, we also reduce phosphorus levels (which are often severely elevated in pets with kidney failure). Phosphorus may be more toxic than protein in pets with kidney failure. Whenever we decrease protein, we also decrease phosphorus. Phosphorus-binding agents, given orally, can be useful in pets with elevated blood phosphorus levels if the following diet, which is low in phosphorus, cannot maintain acceptable phosphorus levels.

Sodium While high blood pressure (hypertension) is rare in pets, it can occur as a result of

kidney failure in dogs and cats (and in cats with hyperthyroidism, which can occur concurrently with kidney failure). Most commercial diets have excessive levels of sodium to improve palatability and act as a preservative. Sodium restriction in the diets listed here can be a first line defense against hypertension.

Potassium Kidney failure usually results in potassium loss through the failing kidneys, even if the blood potassium level is normal (blood levels of potassium do not reflect cellular levels). Unless increased potassium blood levels are detected (which can occur in some pets with kidney failure), extra potassium supplementation can be of benefit. Potassium chloride, a salt substitute, is recommended in the diets; other sources of potassium supplementation can be obtained through your veterinarian.

The following diets are starting points for feeding pets with kidney disease and kidney failure. Check with your veterinarian to determine the exact needs for your pet.

Diet for Dogs with Kidney Disease

Dogs with kidney disease may do well on the basic dog diet (page 346.) If kidney failure is present, the diet is adapted to offer lower protein and phosphorus with increased potassium. High quality protein (1-2 hardboiled eggs) is used as the protein source; brown (or white) rice, or baked (or boiled) potato with skin (3 cups of either carbohydrate source) is added to the egg(s.) Canola oil is added as per the basic diet. The diet provides approximately 600 kcal with 15-20 grams of protein and 18 grams of fat.

This diet provides approximately 300% potassium, 50% phosphorus, and 115% of the daily requirements for sodium. Extra potassium (potassium chloride or potassium supplement) can be used if needed; check with your veterinarian.

Fresh, raw or slightly steamed vegetables (carrots, broccoli, etc.) can be used as a top dressing for the diet for extra nutrition and variety and to help bind intestinal phosphorus (approximately ½ to 1 cup per recipe.) Most vegetables provide approximately 25 kcal per ½ cup.

Calcium carbonate or calcium lactate (which may bind phosphorus) is used rather than bonemeal to decrease the phosphorus levels;1 ½-2 pills of either calcium source are added to the diet. If reduced phosphorus is not needed, 3 bonemeal tablets (10 grain or equivalent) or ¾ teaspoon of bonemeal powder to supply calcium and phosphorus with a multi-vitamin mineral supplement using the label instructions is added. Alternatively, a natural product from Standard Process (Calcifood Wafers or Calcium Lactate) can be used (use 1 Calcifood Wafer or 2 Calcium Lactate tablets for each 2 bonemeal tablets.)

When possible, natural vitamins made from raw whole foods, rather than synthetic vitamins (although both can be used in combination) are preferred, as the natural vitamins also supply plant phytochemicals, enzymes, and other nutrients not found in chemically-synthesized vitamins. Catalyn from Standard Process can be used as the natural vitamin in this recipe, at a dose of 1 Catalyn per 25 pounds; Canine Plus (VetriScience) could also be used following label dosages.

The nutrient composition of the diet will vary depending upon which ingredients are used. In general, the above recipe supplies the daily nutritional and calorie needs for a 20 pound dog. The actual amount to feed will vary based upon the pet's weight (feed less if weight gain, more if weight loss.)

Added supplements which can be beneficial include omega-3 fatty acids (page 246) which may be helpful for pets with kidney disease. Check with your veterinarian for guidelines.

Diet for Cats with Kidney Disease

Cats with kidney disease may do well on the basic cat diet (page 348.) If kidney failure is present, the diet is adapted to offer lower protein and phosphorus with increased potassium. High quality protein (1-2 hardboiled eggs) is used as the protein source (2-3 ounces of salmon or tuna, or 3-4 ounces of poultry or beef can be substituted.) Since cats do not require carbohydrates, none need be added, although adding ½ cup brown or white rice, or baked or boiled potato with skin is acceptable. Canola oil is added as per the basic diet. Taurine (100 mg) is also added. The diet provides approximately 300 kcal with 15 grams of protein and 14 grams of fat. This diet provides approximately 200% potassium, 45%

phosphorus, and 160% of the daily requirements for sodium. Extra potassium (potassium chloride or potassium supplement) can be used if needed; check with your veterinarian.

Calcium carbonate or calcium lactate (which may bind phosphorus) is used rather than bonemeal to decrease the phosphorus levels;1 ½ pills of either calcium source are added to the diet. If reduced phosphorus is not needed, 2-3 bonemeal tablets (10 grain or equivalent) or ¾ teaspoon of bonemeal powder to supply calcium and phosphorus with a multi-vitamin mineral supplement using the label instructions is added. Alternatively, a natural product from Standard Process (Calcifood Wafers or Calcium Lactate) can be used (use 1 Calcifood Wafer or 2 Calcium Lactate tablets for each 2 bonemeal tablets.)

When possible, natural vitamins made from raw whole foods, rather than synthetic vitamins (although both can be used in combination) are preferred, as the natural vitamins also supply plant phytochemicals, enzymes, and other nutrients not found in chemically-synthesized vitamins. Catalyn from Standard Process can be used as the natural vitamin in this recipe, at a dose of 1 Catalyn per 10 pounds; NuCat Plus (VetriScience) could also be used following label dosages.

The nutrient composition of the diet will vary depending upon which ingredients are used. In general, the above recipe supplies the daily nutritional and calorie needs for a 10 pound cat. The actual amount to feed will vary based upon the pet's weight (feed less if weight gain, more if weight loss.)

Added supplements which can be beneficial include omega-3 fatty acids (pg xx,) which may be helpful for pets with kidney disease. Check with your veterinarian for guidelines.

Omega-3 Fatty Acids

Omega-3 fatty acids can increase beneficial (anti-inflammatory) prostaglandins; these prostaglandins can reduce inflammation in the kidney and improve blood flow to the kidneys (a vasodilatory effect.) Since omega-3 fatty acids can also lower blood cholesterol and triglycerides, this effect can also benefit pets with kidney disease as dogs and cats with induced kidney disease have elevated levels of blood cholesterol and trigly-

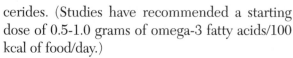

cerides. (Studies have recommended a starting dose of 0.5-1.0 grams of omega-3 fatty acids/100 kcal of food/day.)

Omega-3 fatty acids—eicosapentaenoic acid (EPA) and docosahexaenoic acid (DHA)—are derived from fish oils of coldwater fish (salmon, trout, or most commonly menhaden fish) and flaxseed. Omega-6 fatty acids—linoleic acid (LA) and gamma-linolenic acid (GLA)—are derived from the oils of seeds such as evening primrose, black currant, and borage. Often, fatty acids are added to the diet with other supplements to attain an additive effect.

Just how do the fatty acids work to help in controlling inflammation in pets? Cell membranes contain phospholipids. When membrane injury occurs, an enzyme acts on the phospholipids in the cell membranes to produce fatty acids, including arachidonic acid (an omega-6 fatty acid) and eicosapentaenoic acid (an omega-3 fatty acid). Further metabolism of the arachidonic acid and eicosapentaenoic acid by additional enzymes (the lipooxygenase and cyclooxygenase pathways) yields the production of chemicals called eicosanoids. The eicosanoids produced by metabolism of arachidonic acid are pro-inflammatory and cause inflammation, suppress the immune system, and cause platelets to aggregate and clot; the eicosanoids produced by metabolism of eicosapentaenoic acid are non-inflammatory, not immunosuppressive, and help inhibit platelets from clotting. (There is some overlap and the actual biochemical pathway is a bit more complicated than I have suggested here. For example, one of the by-products of omega-6 fatty acid metabolism is Prostaglandin E_1, which is anti-inflammatory. This is one reason why some research has shown that using certain omega-6 fatty acids can also act to limit inflammation.)

Supplementation of the diet with omega-3 fatty acids works in this biochemical reaction. By providing extra amounts of these non-inflammatory compounds, we try to overwhelm the body with the production of non-inflammatory eicosanoids. Therefore, since the same enzymes metabolize both omega-3 and omega-6 fatty acids, and since metabolism of the omega-6 fatty acids tend to cause inflammation (with the exception of Prostaglandin E_1 by metabolism of omega-6 as men-

tioned above) by supplying a large amount of omega-3 fatty acids, we favor the production of non-inflammatory chemicals.

Many disorders are due to overproduction of the eicosanoids responsible for producing inflammation, including kidney disease. While more research is needed, preliminary studies show that fatty acid supplementation may be beneficial in pets with kidney disease by regulating the eicosanoid production. Ongoing studies seem to support the belief that supplementation with omega-3 fatty acids may benefit pets with kidney disease or kidney failure.

In general, the products of omega-3 (specifically EPA) and one omega-6 fatty acid (DGLA) are less inflammatory than the products of arachidonic acid (another omega-6 fatty acid.) By providing the proper (anti-inflammatory) fatty acids, we can use fatty acids as an anti-inflammatory substance. However, since the products of omega-6 fatty acid metabolism (specifically arachidonic acid) are not the sole cause of the inflammation, fatty acid therapy is rarely effective as the sole therapy but is used as an adjunct therapy to achieve an additive effect.

Note: Flaxseed oil is a popular source of alpha-linoleic acid (ALA), an omega-3 fatty acid that is ultimately converted to EPA and DHA. However, many species of pets (probably including dogs) and some people cannot convert ALA to these other more active non-inflammatory omega-3 fatty acids. In one study in people, flaxseed oil was ineffective in reducing symptoms or raising levels of EPA and DHA. While flaxseed oil has been suggested as a less smelly substitute for fish oil, there is no evidence that it is effective when used for the same therapeutic purposes as fish oil. Therefore, supplementation with EPA and DHA is important, and this is the reason flaxseed oil is not recommended as the sole fatty acid supplement for pets. Flaxseed oil can be used to provide ALA and as a coat conditioner.

The Controversies

While many doctors use fatty acids for a variety of medical problems, there is considerable debate about the use of fatty acids. The debate concerns several areas:

What is the "best" dose to use in the treatment of pets? Most doctors use anywhere from 2 to 10 times the label dose. Research in the treatment of kidney disease indicates that the label dose is ineffective.

While current research shows that a starting dose of 0.5 to 1.0 grams of omega-3 fatty acids/100 kcal of food/day seems to work, more research may fine-tune this dose.

While the studies with omega-3 fatty acids show many potential health benefits, it is almost impossible to administer the large number of capsules needed to approximate the same dosage used in these studies. The best that owners can hope for at this time is to work with their veterinarians and try to increase, as best as possible, the amount of omega-3 fatty acids in the diet to try to get the recommended amount.

Is supplementation with fatty acid capsules or liquids the best approach, or is dietary manipulation preferred for the treatment of kidney disease? There are in fact, diets constructed with extra omega-3 fatty acids. For owners who do not like giving their pets medication, or for those pets who don't take the fatty acid supplements easily, it might be wise to try some of these medically formulated diets (available from your pet's doctor) that contain the fatty acids. However, because these medicated diets may not be as natural as possible due to the inclusion of by-products and chemical preservatives, holistic pet owners may need to try other options. These diets, often prescribed as anti-inflammatory diets for pets with allergies, may be useful as a part of the therapy of kidney disease in pets.

Fish Oils   Since fish oils can easily oxidize and become rancid, some manufacturers add vitamin E to fish oil capsules and liquid products to keep the oil from spoiling (others remove oxygen from the capsule).

The bottom line is that there are many questions regarding the use of fatty acid therapy. More research is needed to determine the effectiveness of the fatty acids in the treatment of various medical problems, as well as the proper doses needed to achieve clinical results. Until definitive answers are obtained, you will need to work with your doctors (knowing the limitations of our current research) to determine the use of these supplements for your pet.

Fish oil appears to be safe. The most common side effect seen in people and pets is a fish odor to the breath or the skin.

Because fish oil has a mild "blood-thinning" effect, it should not be combined with powerful blood-thinning medications, such as Coumadin (warfarin) or heparin, except on a veterinarian's advice. Fish oil does not seem to cause bleeding problems when it is taken by itself at commonly recommended dosages. Also, fish oil does not appear to raise blood sugar levels in people or pets with diabetes.

Flaxseed Oil   Flaxseed oil is derived from the seeds of the flax plant and has been proposed as a less smelly alternative to fish oil. Flaxseed oil contains alpha-linolenic acid (ALA), an omega-3 fatty acid that is ultimately converted to EPA and DHA. In fact, flaxseed oil contains higher levels of omega-3 fatty acids (ALA) than fish oil. It also contains omega-6 fatty acids.

As mentioned, many species of pets (probably including dogs and cats) and some people cannot convert ALA to these other more active non-inflammatory omega-3 fatty acids. In one study in people, flaxseed oil was ineffective in reducing symptoms or raising levels of EPA and DHA. While flaxseed oil has been suggested as a substitute for fish oil, there is no evidence that it is effective when used for the same therapeutic purposes as fish oil. Unlike the case for fish oil, there is little evidence that flaxseed oil is effective for any specific therapeutic purpose.

Therefore, supplementation with EPA and DHA is important, and this is the reason flaxseed oil is not recommended as the sole fatty acid supplement for pets. Flaxseed oil can be used to provide ALA and as a coat conditioner.

Flaxseed oil also does contain lignans, which are currently being studied for use in preventing cancer in people.

The essential fatty acids in flax can be damaged by exposure to heat, light, and oxygen (essentially, they become rancid). For this reason, you shouldn't cook with flaxseed oil. A good product should be sold in an opaque container, and the manufacturing process should keep the temperature under 100° F (some products are prepared by cold extraction methods). Some manufacturers combine the product with vitamin E because it helps prevent rancidity.

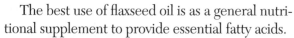
The best use of flaxseed oil is as a general nutritional supplement to provide essential fatty acids.

Flaxseed oil appears to be a safe nutritional supplement when used as recommended.

OTHER NATURAL TREATMENTS

The herbs **astragalus** (page 160), **burdock** (page 170), **dandelion leaf** (page 193), **echinacea** (page 195), **garlic** (page 204), *Ginkgo biloba* (page 208), **gotu kola** (page 221), **hawthorn** (page 223), **marshmallow** (page 240), and supplements of **B vitamins** (page 288), and **glandular therapy** (page 393) may be useful.

These can be used in conjunction with fluid therapy as they are unlikely to be effective by themselves in most patients. The natural treatments are widely used with variable success but have not all been thoroughly investigated and proven at this time.

As with any condition, the most healthful natural diet will improve the pet's overall health.

CONVENTIONAL THERAPY

Conventional therapies are supportive and include:

- *Fluid therapy:* Given intravenously in critical cases (Subcutaneous fluids can be administered by owners at home following stabilization and for maintaining adequate hydration of the pet.)
- *Antibiotics:* Given when needed

- *Medications to decrease vomiting:* Given when vomiting results from uremic toxins
- *Medications to stimulate red blood cell production:* Given in cases of secondary anemia, which is seen in many pets with chronic kidney failure

Some cats with kidney failure are candidates for kidney transplantation; this is not routinely done in dogs. Continuous ambulatory peritoneal dialysis is another option for treating either acute or chronic kidney failure. However, due to potential complications, this technique is rarely used. Special diets low in protein, phosphorus, and sodium, with increased B vitamins and omega-3 fatty acids, are often recommended for dogs and cats with kidney failure. The use of these diets in older pets without kidney failure, but who simply show mildly elevated kidney enzymes on blood testing, is controversial and not now recommended by most veterinarians. Reducing protein concentration in geriatric pets is not recommended or needed and does not prevent kidney failure. Geriatric pets can benefit from reduced sodium and phosphorus levels but do not need protein restriction; many geriatric diets actually have increased levels of highly digestible, high-quality protein. (See pages 123–124 for a greater discussion of dietary therapy of pets with kidney disease.) Unlike acute kidney failure, chronic kidney failure cannot be cured as it results from chronic and permanent changes to aging kidneys.

LIVER DISEASE

Principal Natural Treatments
Natural diet, milk thistle

Other Natural Treatments
Choline, carnitine, arginine, boswellia, burdock, chaparral, dandelion root, licorice, nettle, Oregon grape, red clover, turmeric, yellow dock, maitake mushrooms

Liver disease is the catch-all term that is applied to any medical disorder affecting the liver and usually causing elevated blood levels of liver enzymes.

As with kidney disease, liver disease can be divided into both acute and chronic liver disease. Causes of acute liver disease include toxins (a number of drugs have been implicated in causing acute liver disease, including Tylenol, Rimadyl, Valium, tetracycline, sulfa drugs, and *Amanita* (mushroom poisoning); hepatic lipidosis (fatty liver disease), trauma, heatstroke, and infections (canine infectious hepatitis). Causes of chronic liver disease include genetics, infections (canine infectious hepatitis, leptospirosis), toxins (anticonvulsants, Rimadyl), and idiopathic hepatitis.

Feline cholangiohepatitis is a common inflammatory liver disease in cats that may be associated with infection of bacteria from the intestines that ascend the biliary tract (bile ducts).

Certain breeds of dogs are prone to chronic hepatitis and cirrhosis (an end stage of liver disease in which liver tissue is replaced with fibrous tissue). Doberman Pinschers (especially females), American and English Cocker Spaniels, Bedlington Terriers, and West Highland White Terriers are the breeds associated with chronic liver disease and cirrhosis.

Clinical signs of liver disease include lack of appetite, vomiting, diarrhea, increased thirst, increased urination, lethargy, jaundice, and seizures.

Liver disease is diagnosed by blood and urine tests, abdominal radiographs (x rays), and abdominal ultrasound. Liver biopsy is needed to determine the cause of liver disease.

A common (probably the most common) liver disease in cats is hepatic lipidosis (fatty liver disease). This occurs in cats (and sometimes dogs) as a result of starvation and weight loss (hepatic lipidosis can occur in cats who do not eat for as little as 72 hours). Depletion of certain nutrients (choline, carnitine, arginine) impairs metabolism of fat, resulting in fat deposition (rather than removal) from the liver.

PRINCIPAL NATURAL TREATMENTS

Natural Diet

Dietary therapy is a mainstay of treating the pet with liver disease, as there are few conventional medications that actually treat liver disease.

High quality and highly digestible carbohydrates are recommended to supply energy for the pet. Inferior types of carbohydrates that are undigested are fermented by intestinal bacteria, which increases the bacteria in the colon. These bacteria then break down dietary proteins and produce extra ammonia, which is absorbed into the body and contributes to toxicity in pets with liver disease. Frequent feedings of high-quality, simple carbohydrates such as white rice and potatoes are recommended. Vegetables act as a source of complex carbohydrates and provide fiber; the fiber helps bind intestinal toxins and promotes bowel movements to remove these toxins (by-products of protein digestion and bacterial fermentation of undigested foods) from the body.

Proteins provided by the diet must be of high biological value to reduce the production of ammonia, a by-product of protein digestion. Most commercial foods contain proteins that are not of high biological value. (Many commercial foods may also contain excess vitamin A, copper, and bacterial endotoxins, all of which contribute to the clinical signs in pets with liver disease.) Unless your doctor recommends protein restriction (usually only needed by pets with encephalopathy, a condition producing neurological signs in pets with severe liver disease), normal amounts of protein should be fed as protein is needed by the liver during repair.

Studies show that dogs with liver disease fed diets containing meat-based proteins have shorter survival times and more severe clinical signs than dogs with liver disease fed milk-based or soy-based protein diets. Cats require higher protein diets than dogs. While it may be more beneficial to cats to also feed them diets based on milk-based or soy-based proteins, most cats prefer meat-based diets. Cats fed milk-based or soy-based proteins must have supplemental taurine (100 to 200 mg/day), as milk has minimal taurine and soy (tofu) has no taurine.

In cats, hepatic lipidosis (fatty liver disease) is the most common liver disease and is secondary to starvation (often seen in overweight cats who go without eating for as little as 3 to 5 days). Hepatic lipidosis is a secondary complication of anorexia and obesity rather than a true primary liver disease. Force-feeding cats to help heal the liver and correct the underlying problem is the treatment for hepatic lipidosis. This often requires tube feeding of special diets. When feasible, high-fat (approximately 30%) enteral diets

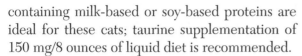

containing milk-based or soy-based proteins are ideal for these cats; taurine supplementation of 150 mg/8 ounces of liquid diet is recommended.

Adding the amino acids arginine or citrulline to the diet may be indicated, as these amino acids accelerate conversion of highly toxic ammonia to urea, reversing the clinical signs of toxicity that may occur in pets with liver disease. Glycine may decrease the toxicity that affects the kidneys when the chemotherapy drug cisplatin is administered.

Fat is used in the diet for energy. Even pets with fatty liver disease (hepatic lipidosis) do well on diets containing 20 to 25% fat. Free fatty acids contribute to increased blood ammonia by interfering with ammonia metabolism. Dietary fats do not contribute to increased blood levels of free fatty acids; fasting or starvation will contribute to increased levels of free fatty acids. Therefore, pets with liver disease should have diets containing adequate amounts of fats and should receive frequent small feedings. Additionally, small frequent feedings reduce protein breakdown by the body (which can worsen clinical signs), improve glucose metabolism (preventing hypoglycemia), and decrease intestinal ammonia concentrations.

Increasing levels of **vitamin A** (page 284) and copper can contribute to liver damage; excess supplementation should be avoided. **Zinc** (page 310) supplementation may be of benefit as many pets with liver disease are deficient in zinc, and zinc can reduce copper absorption. Adding **vitamins C** (page 297), **E** (page 302), and **K** (page 305) may be warranted for pets with liver disease. Vitamin E protects against metabolism of lipids in cell membranes. Vitamin K is needed for proper blood clotting, which can be a problem in pets with severe liver disease. While dogs and cats, unlike people, can make vitamin C in the liver and do not normally require this vitamin, liver disease may decrease the amount of vitamin C. Supplementation with these vitamins under veterinary supervision may be helpful.

Diet for Dogs with Liver Disease

Dogs with liver disease need different protein sources than those to fed to normal pets.

The basic dog diet (page 346) is adapted by using cottage cheese (½ cup) and soy protein (typically tofu, ⅔ cup) as the primary protein sources (yogurt can be tried if cottage cheese is refused by the dog.) While not all dogs like cottage cheese or soy protein, try to avoid egg and meat protein whenever possible. Adding 1½ to 2 cups of brown or white rice plus the canola oil and potassium chloride as in the basic dog diet completes the diet (adding a few ounces of raw or undercooked potato can increase bowel movements which may decrease bowel toxins.) This diet would provide approximately 650 kcal with 36 grams of protein and 20 grams of fat.

Fresh, raw or slightly steamed vegetables (carrots, broccoli, etc.) can be used as a top dressing for the diet for extra nutrition and variety and to help bind intestinal phosphorus approximately ½ to 1 cup per recipe.) Most vegetables provide approximately 25 kcal per ½ cup.

Three to four bonemeal tablets (10 grain or equivalent) or ¾-1 teaspoon of bonemeal powder to supply calcium and phosphorus with a multi-vitamin mineral supplement using the label instructions is added. Alternatively, a natural product from Standard Process (Calcifood Wafers or Calcium Lactate) can be used (use 1 Calcifood Wafer or 2 Calcium Lactate tablets for each 2 bonemeal tablets.)

When possible, natural vitamins made from raw whole foods, rather than synthetic vitamins (although both can be used in combination) are preferred, as the natural vitamins also supply plant phytochemicals, enzymes, and other nutrients not found in chemically-synthesized vitamins. Catalyn from Standard Process can be used as the natural vitamin in this recipe, at a dose of 1 Catalyn per 25 pounds; Canine Plus (VetriScience) could also be used following label dosages.

The nutrient composition of the diet will vary depending upon which ingredients are used. In general, the above recipe supplies the daily nutritional and calorie needs for a 20 pound dog. The actual amount to feed will vary based upon the pet's weight (feed less if weight gain, more if weight loss.)

Supplementation may be necessary for pets with liver disease. The following recommendations are made, but check with your pet's veterinarian to determine the individual needs of your pet.

Vitamin C or ascorbic acid: 25 mg/kg/day (Ascorbic acid, but not natural vitamin C, can cause release of copper from the liver which can worsen clinical signs; add small amounts daily and work up to the recommended dosage if clinical signs do not worsen, or preferably use natural vitamin C.)

Vitamin E: 500 mg/day

Zinc: 3 mg/kg/day of zinc gluconate, 2 mg/kg/day of zinc sulfate, or 2 mg/kg/day of zinc acetate (Divide these doses into 3 daily doses; zinc acetate may cause less intestinal irritation.)

Vitamin B: Additional supplementation with B vitamins are important.

Diet for Cats with Liver Disease

Cats with liver disease need different protein sources than normal pets.

The basic cat diet (page 348) is adapted by using cottage cheese (½ cup) and soy protein (typically tofu, ⅔ cup) as the primary protein sources (yogurt can be tried if cottage cheese is refused by the dog.) While not all cats like cottage cheese or soy protein, try to avoid egg and meat protein whenever possible. If this is not possible, try using ⅓ pound of turkey instead of the cottage cheese and tofu. Adding ⅓ cup of brown or white rice plus the canola oil and potassium chloride as in the basic cat diet completes the diet (adding a few ounces of raw or undercooked potato can increase bowel movements which may decrease bowel toxins.) Add 100 mg of taurine. This diet would provide approximately 450 kcal with 40 grams of protein and 22 grams of fat to meet the daily caloric needs of a 15 pound cat.

Fresh, raw or slightly steamed vegetables (carrots, broccoli, etc.) can be used as a top dressing for the diet for extra nutrition and variety and to help bind intestinal phosphorus (approximately ½-1 cup per recipe.) Most vegetables provide approximately 25 kcal per ½ cup. Most cats do not like vegetables.

Two to three bonemeal tablets (10 grain or equivalent) or ¾-1 teaspoon of bonemeal powder to supply calcium and phosphorus with a multi-vitamin mineral supplement using the label instructions is added. Alternatively, a natural product from Standard Process (Calcifood Wafers or Calcium Lactate) can be used (use 1 Calcifood Wafer or 2 Calcium Lactate tablets for each 2 bonemeal tablets.)

When possible, natural vitamins made from raw whole foods, rather than synthetic vitamins (although both can be used in combination) are preferred, as the natural vitamins also supply plant phytochemicals, enzymes, and other nutrients not found in chemically-synthesized vitamins. Catalyn from Standard Process can be used as the natural vitamin in this recipe, at a dose of 1 Catalyn per 10 pounds; NuCat (VetriScience) could also be used following label dosages.

The nutrient composition of the diet will vary depending upon which ingredients are used. In general, the above recipe supplies the daily nutritional and calorie needs for a 15 pound cat. The actual amount to feed will vary based upon the pet's weight (feed less if weight gain, more if weight loss.)

Supply vitamins and minerals as follows:

Bonemeal: 2 to 3 bonemeal tablets (10-grain or equivalent) or ¾ to 1 teaspoon of bonemeal powder to supply calcium and phosphorus with a multivitamin/mineral supplement using the label instructions. Alternatively, use a natural product from Standard Process (1 Calcifood Wafer or 2 Calcium Lactate tablets for each 2 bonemeal tablets).

Vitamin C or ascorbic acid: 25 mg/day (Ascorbic acid, but not natural vitamin C, can cause release of copper from the liver which can worsen clinical signs; add small amounts daily and work up to the recommeded dosage if clinical signs do not worsen, or preferably use natural vitamin C.)

Vitamin E: 100 mg/day

Zinc: 3 mg/kg/day of zinc gluconate, 2 mg/kg/day of zinc sulfate, or 2 mg/kg/day of zinc acetate (Divide these doses into 3 daily doses; zinc acetate may cause less intestinal irritation.)

B vitamins: Additional supplementation is warranted, especially thiamine as cats can easily develop thiamine deficiency with decreased food intake, are important.

Taurine: 50 to 100 mg per cat per day, or add ½ to 1 ounce chopped clams to the diet. (These recommendations are extrapolated from recommendations for dogs as the exact requirements are not known for cats.)

Milk Thistle

Milk thistle is well known for use in liver disease. Its silymarin content has been shown effective in treating liver disease. Milk thistle compounds are usually standardized to 70 to 80% silymarin. Milk thistle is one of the few herbs that has no real equivalent in the world of conventional medicine.

The active ingredients in milk thistle appear to be four substances known collectively as silymarin, of which the most potent is named silibinin. When injected intravenously, silibinin is one of the few known antidotes to poisoning by the deathcap mushroom, *Amanita phalloides*. Animal studies suggest that milk thistle extracts can also protect against many other poisonous substances, from toluene to the drug acetaminophen.

Silymarin appears to function by displacing toxins trying to bind to the liver as well as by causing the liver to regenerate more quickly. It may also scavenge free radicals and stabilize liver cell membranes. However, milk thistle is not effective in treating advanced liver cirrhosis, and only the intravenous form can counter mushroom poisoning.

Silymarin protects the liver as an antioxidant (it is more potent than vitamin E), by increasing glutathione levels, and by inhibiting the formation of damaging leukotrienes. Silymarin also stimulates the production of new liver cells, replacing the damaged cells.

Due to its liver support, milk thistle is often used anytime the pet becomes ill to support the liver. It can also be used anytime drugs are given to the pet that could be toxic to the liver, especially chemotherapy medicines for treating cancer, heartworm treatment medications, and long-term use of other medications (such as antibiotics and corticosteroids).

In people, treatment produces a modest improvement in symptoms of chronic liver disease, such as nausea, weakness, loss of appetite, fatigue, and pain. Liver enzymes as measured by blood tests frequently improve, and if a liver biopsy is performed, there may be improvements on the cellular level. Some studies have shown a reduction in death rate among those with serious liver disease.

A new form of silymarin, in which the compound is bound to phosphatidylcholine, has been shown to have greater bioavailability than unbound silymarin.

It is best not to use milk thistle as a daily preventive supplement but rather reserve its use for conditions where the liver is under stress.

The standard dosage of milk thistle is 100 mg per 25 lb of weight, 2 to 3 times a day. In people, the best results are seen at higher doses (140 to 200 mg 3 times daily of an extract standardized to contain 70% silymarin); the bound form is dosed at 100 to 200 mg twice daily.

SAFETY ISSUES

Do not use milk thistle in pregnant animals. Long-term use may alter blood liver enzymes. High doses may cause diarrhea.

On the basis of its extensive use as a food, milk thistle is believed to be safe for pregnant or nursing women, and researchers have enrolled pregnant women in studies. However, safety in young children, pregnant or nursing women, and individuals with severe renal disease has not been formally established. Similar precautions in pets are probably warranted.

OTHER NATURAL TREATMENTS

These treatments include the nutrients **choline** (page 180), **carnitine** (page 175), and **arginine** (page 160), and the herbs **boswellia** (page 168), **burdock** (page 170), **chaparral** (page 178), **dandelion root** (page 193), **licorice** (page 234), **nettle** (page 245), **Oregon grape** (page 251), **red clover** (page 262), **turmeric** (page 280), **yellow dock** (page 309), and **maitake mushrooms** (page 238).

CONVENTIONAL THERAPY

There is no specific treatment for liver disease in dogs and cats, unless a specific toxin is identified.

Supportive care includes intravenous fluids and force-feeding. Force-feeding is the treatment of choice for cats with hepatic lipidosis; feeding usually requires feeding through a gastrotomy (stomach) tube for 2 to 3 months. Antibiotics and/or corticosteroids may be indicated, for example, for feline cholangiohepatitis.

MANGE

Principal Natural Treatments
None

Other Natural Treatments
Natural diet, homeopathic sulfur, garlic, echinacea, mullein flower oil (ear mites), yellow dock oil (ear mites), reishi mushrooms (ear mites)

Mange is caused by microscopic insects called mites. The most common types of mange are demodectic mange (common in puppies; rare in adult dogs, kittens, and cats), sarcoptic mange (scabies in puppies and dogs), notoedric mange (scabies in kittens and cats), and otodectic mange (ear mites in puppies, dogs, kittens, and cats). Demodectic mange is a genetic disease and is not transmissible between pets. The other types of mange are transmissible between pets and can in fact be transmitted between pets and their owners. Mange is a common cause of skin disease in pets and may be difficult to diagnose in some pets.

OTHER NATURAL TREATMENTS

Variable success with mange can be achieved with a natural **diet** (page 314); **homeopathic sulfur** (page 403), and the herbs **garlic** (page 204) and **echinacea** (page 195). For ear mites, **mullein flower oil** (page 388) or **yellow dock** (page 309), and **reishi mushrooms** (page 264) can be tried.

These can be used in conjunction with conventional therapies as they are unlikely to be effective by themselves in most patients with severe disease. The natural treatments are widely used with variable success but have not been thoroughly investigated and proven at this time.

As with any condition, the most healthful natural diet will improve the pet's overall health.

CONVENTIONAL THERAPY

Most conventional therapies for demodectic, sarcoptic, and notoedric mange require medicated dips or shampoos. Despite the potential toxicity and side effects that can occur with some dips, most are administered safely to the majority of pets with mange. The drug ivermectin can be used for most types of mange, but it is toxic at the dose required to treat mange in Collie-type dogs. Ear mites can be treated with oral or injectable ivermectin or topical drops (which must be administered for 4 weeks along with some type of body treatment, usually a flea spray, to effectively break the mite life cycle and kill the mites).

OBESITY

Principal Natural Treatments
Natural Diet

Other Natural Treatments
Chromium, carnitine, boron, cayenne, ginger, mustard, hydroxycitric acid, chitosan, Coenzyme Q_{10}

Obesity, defined as an increase in body weight of at least 15% above what would be normal for the size of the pet, is the most common nutritional disease in pets. As with people, obesity results from an excess caloric intake relative to the expenditure of energy.

Many owners question a link between spaying or neutering the pet and obesity. Reduction of the male and female hormones (as a result of neutering or spaying, respectively), does not cause obesity per se. However, if the metabolic rate decreases as a result of neutering or spaying, and if the intake of calories is not adjusted, obesity can result.

Because diseases such as hypothyroidism and diabetes mellitus can be associated with obesity, obese pets should be screened for these disorders prior to treatment.

PRINCIPAL NATURAL TREATMENTS

Natural Diet

Obesity is a severe and debilitating illness. It is the most common nutritional disease in pets and people; estimates suggest that up to 45% of dogs and up to 13% of cats are obese. Many doctors think these estimates are quite low judging by the number of obese pets they see every day in practice. With rare exception (the presence of a disease like thyroid disease), obese pets are made that way, not born that way. In the wild, few, if any, animals are obese. They eat to meet their calorie needs, and are always moving, playing, fighting, mating, and hunting for food (exercising).

How can you decide if your pet fits the definition of "obese?" Current medical opinion states that a pet is obese if it weighs 15% or more over its ideal weight. Pets that weigh 1 to 14% over

their ideal weight are considered "overweight" but not yet "obese."

While pet owners often use the pet's actual weight to gauge obesity, it is probably more accurate to use a body composition score. Body composition, measured by looking at the pet from the top and sides and feeling the areas over the ribs and spine more accurately reflects obesity than a certain magical number. It also gives us something more concrete to shoot for. For example, while most people who diet strive to achieve a certain numerical weight, a more accurate assessment would be to strive for a certain look. While losing 10 pounds might be an admirable goal, being able to lose a few inches around the waist or fit into a smaller pair of pants is really the ultimate goal. This is not to suggest that you can't have a target weight when designing a weight-control program for your pet, only that this magic number is only a rough guideline of what your pet's "best" weight might be to treat obesity. Many doctors prefer to use the weight as a guideline but ultimately use the look and feel (measured by the body composition score) of the pet to know when we have reached our ultimate goal.

Can pet owners prevent obesity? Keep in mind that most obese pets are made that way, not born that way. Many owners give their pets treats and snacks and feed them whenever the pet begs for food. In essence, these owners are setting their pets up for all of the medical problems that can occur with obesity. While many people who constantly reward these begging behaviors believe that they are being kind and loving owners, they are actually killing their pets with kindness.

Problems that are associated with obesity in pets and people are numerous and include orthopedic problems (including **arthritis,** page 11), ruptured ligaments, **intervertebral disk disease** (page 113), difficulty breathing, reduced capacity for exercise (and in severe cases any movement at all), heat intolerance, increased chance for complications due to drug therapy (it is more difficult to accurately dose medications in obese pets), cardiac problems, hypertension, and **cancer** (page 44). When you keep in mind that the excess body fat occurs in the body cavities of the chest and abdomen (often being deposited there first) as well as under the skin (what we see as "fat"), it is not surprising that so many medical problems can be associated with obesity.

The treatment of obesity requires a controlled low-calorie, lowfat diet with a sensible exercise program. Other natural treatments include nutritional supplements (to follow), which might help reduce weight in selected patients.

Prior to starting a weight-reduction diet and exercise regimen, it is important that your pet receive a blood profile to rule out diseases previously discussed, such as **diabetes** (page 66) or **hypothyroidism** (page 103), that may cause or contribute to obesity. Presence of these diseases would require treatment in addition to dietary therapy.

If your dog or cat needs to lose weight, he should be on a weight-reduction diet (ideally a natural, wholesome, homemade diet) recommended by your veterinarian. Store-bought "Lite" foods are not designed for weight loss, but rather weight maintenance once weight loss has been achieved. Therefore, they are not usually recommended for pets requiring weight loss. Additionally, since most of these diets do not contain natural healthful ingredients, it is unlikely they would be recommended as part of a weight-loss program unless other diets could not be used.

There are several commercial weight-loss or obesity-reduction diets. While they are effective in reducing weight in many pets, they may also contain artificial ingredients and by-products. If these diets are used, it would be wise to switch to a homemade diet or a more wholesome (natural) processed "Lite" or maintenance diet *once weight reduction has been achieved.*

Any food (including carbohydrates and proteins) can be converted to and stored as fat if not needed by the body for another metabolic process. Feeding fat is more likely to contribute to fat deposition in fat cells than feeding protein or carbohydrates. Therefore, lower fat diets are preferred for weight loss in pets.

Foods that increase metabolism, such as vegetables that are high in fiber, are included in weight-loss diets. Fiber, contained in vegetables, decreases fat and glucose absorption; fluctuating glucose levels cause greater insulin release. Since insulin is needed for fat storage, decreased or stable levels are preferred. Fiber also binds to fat in the intestinal tract and increases movement of the food in the intestines, which is of benefit to the obese pet.

Weight-Control Diet for Dogs

Note: Before you start to feed your dog or cat a home-prepared diet, it is strongly recommended that you discuss your decision with your veterinarian or a holistic veterinarian in your area. It is essential that you follow any diet's recommendations closely, including all ingredients and supplements. Failure to do so may result in serious health consequences for your pet.

½ pound of cooked chicken
2 cups of cooked long grain rice
¼ teaspoon salt or salt substitute

This diet provides approximately 624 kcal, 49.4 gm of protein, and 4.7 gm of fat. It supplies the daily caloric needs for weight loss in a 45- to 50-pound dog.

This diet supplies the calories required for weight reduction in a dog who normally weighs 47 to 48 pounds (non-obese weight). In other words, it should be fed to a dog who weighs more than 47 to 48 pounds but whose ideal weight would be approximately 47 to 48 pounds.

Variations

1. Substitute 4 egg whites (cooked) or ½ cup cottage cheese (1% fat) for the chicken. Usually beef and lamb are too high in fat for canine weight reduction diets.
2. Substitute 3 cups of cooked potatoes (with skins) for the rice.

3. For extra nutrition and fiber and variety, use fresh, raw or slightly steamed vegetables, such as carrots or broccoli as a top dressing for the diet. Use approximately ½ to 1 cup per recipe (½ cup of vegetables add about 30 kilocalories to the diet).

4. If the weight-reduction diet is prescribed for a dog with osteoarthritis, omega-3 fatty acids may be prescribed to help relieve the inflammation and pain seen in pets with osteoarthritis. Including omega-3 fatty acids adds few calories to the diet (approximately 10 kilocalories, depending upon the brand). Because omega-3 fatty acids can be helpful for arthritic pets, and because they also increase the metabolic rate (which burns calories), they may be useful in the diets of obese, arthritic pets.

5. Feed this diet in divided amounts at least twice daily and preferably 4 to 6 times daily. Frequent small meals will allow the pet to feel full all of the time (feeling full reduces appetite and the need to beg, although many dogs who beg have been unintentionally rewarded by their owners for this behavior). Feeding frequent small meals also results in additional weight loss as some of the food consumed is immediately burned into heat (thermogenesis). Frequent feeding results in more burning of calories.

6. Supply vitamins and minerals as follows: 4 bonemeal tablets (10-grain or equivalent) or ¾ to 1 teaspoon of bonemeal powder to supply calcium and phosphorus with a multivitamin/mineral supplement, using the label instructions. Alternatively, use a natural product from Standard Process (1 Calcifood Wafer or 2 Calcium Lactate tablets) for each 2 bonemeal tablets. When possible, use natural vitamins made from raw whole foods, rather than synthetic vitamins (although both can be used in combination), as the natural vitamins also supply plant phytochemicals, enzymes, and other nutrients not found in chemically synthesized vitamins. Use either Catalyn from Standard Process (at a dose of 1 Catalyn per 25 pounds) or Canine Plus from VetriScience (following label dosages) as the natural vitamin in this recipe.

7. Add supplements that can be beneficial, such as plant enzymes, and a super green food or health blend formula.

Weight Control Diet for Cats

5 ounces salmon, canned with bone (low-salt)
⅓ cup long grain rice, cooked
¼ teaspoon salt or salt substitute
100 mg taurine

This diet provides 284 kcal, 30.2 gm of protein, and 10.4 gm of fat. Feed 75% of this recipe to a cat who would normally weigh 11 pounds, 67% to a cat who would normally weigh 10 pounds, and 60% to a cat who would normally weigh 9 pounds.

Variations

1. Substitute 4 to 8 ounces of tuna or ½ pound of chicken for the salmon. Beef, lamb, and sardines usually have too much fat to be used in feline weight-reduction diets.

2. Rice is optional, as cats do not have a strict dietary carbohydrate requirement.

3. Salmon contains omega-3 fatty acids. Omega-3 fatty acids are often prescribed for pets with osteoarthritis to relieve pain and inflammation; additional supplementation with omega-3 fatty acids may or may not be needed. Each extra-strength omega-3 fatty acid capsule contains approximately 10 calories. Omega-3 fatty acids increase metabolic rate so more energy is burned, which can aid weight loss.

4. For extra nutrition, fiber, and variety, use fresh, raw or slightly steamed vegetables, such as carrots or broccoli as a top dressing for the diet. Add approximately ½ to 1 cup per recipe (½ cup of vegetables add about 30 kilocalories to the diet). Most cats will not eat vegetables, however.

5. Feed this diet in divided amounts at least twice daily and preferably 4 to 6 times daily. Frequent small meals will allow the pet to feel full all of the time. (Feeling full reduces appetite and the need to beg, although many cats that beg have been unintentionally rewarded by their owners for this behavior.) Feeding frequent small meals also results in additional weight loss, as some of the food

consumed is immediately burned into heat (thermogenesis). Frequent feeding results in more burning of calories.

OTHER NATURAL TREATMENTS

While not meant to replace diet and exercise, the following supplements may be beneficial as part of a weight-loss program: **chromium** (page 182), **carnitine** (page 175), **boron** (page 168), the herbs **cayenne** (page 174), **ginger** (page 207), and mustard, **hydroxycitric acid** (page 226), **chitosan** (page 179), and **Coenzyme Q10** (page 185).

The natural treatments are widely used with variable success but have not been thoroughly investigated and proven at this time.

A regular program of supervised exercise is also important for pets on a weight-reduction program.

CONVENTIONAL THERAPY

The treatment of obesity involves restricting calories and increasing the metabolic rate via a controlled exercise program. Using store-bought "Lite" diets is not usually adequate, as these diets are not designed for weight loss but rather weight maintenance. Additionally, since many store-bought diets may contain chemicals, by-products, and fillers, they would not be a part of a holistic pet program. Homemade restricted calorie diets would be the first choice for dietary therapy for obese pets; processed "obesity-management" diets available through veterinarians would be the second-best choice as some of these diets may also contain chemicals, by-products, and fillers. These "obesity-management" diets are used until the target weight is obtained, then replaced with a homemade maintenance diet if possible.

 # PARVOVIRUS

Principal Natural Treatments
    Homeopathic nosodes, glutamine, probiotics

Other Natural Treatments
    Aloe vera juice, boswellia, calendula, chamomile, German chamomile, marshmallow, raspberry leaf, slippery elm

Parvoviral infection, caused by canine parvovirus 2 (CPV-2) commonly affects young puppies. Kittens and cats have their own parvovirus that causes panleukopenia. However, vaccination is so effective that this disease is very rarely seen. Clinical signs are usually seen 5 to 12 days after the puppy is exposed to infected feces. The signs seen depend on the virulence of the virus, the amount of virus ingested, and the breed of puppy infected. Certain breeds such as Doberman Pinschers, Rottweilers, Pit Bulls, and Labrador Retrievers may be more severely infected than others. Signs seen include depression, lack of appetite, and vomiting, followed in 24 to 48 hours by diarrhea (often bloody). Diagnosis is made on clinical signs and testing of the feces for the virus.

PRINCIPAL NATURAL TREATMENTS

Homeopathic Nosodes

Nosodes, a special type of homeopathic remedy, are prepared from infectious organisms, such as distemper virus and staphylococcus bacteria. Remember that no matter what the source of the remedy, the actual ingredients are diluted in preparing the remedy. No measurable amount of the original source for the remedy remains, only the vital energy or life force, which imparts healing properties to the remedy. No harm will come to your pet regardless of the toxicity of the original compound used in the preparation of the remedy.

But do nosodes work? Some doctors seem to prefer nosodes manufactured by specific homeopathic pharmacies, as they feel there is a definite difference in the ability of nosodes to stimulate the immune system. In their opinions, the manufacturer of the nosode is important and some vaccination nosodes work better than others.

To prevent disease, nosodes are supposed to work in the same manner as conventional vaccines, namely by stimulating antibodies to fight off infections. To treat disease, nosodes have been reported to control outbreaks of infectious disease in animals in a kennel situation. While good controlled studies are lacking, homeopathic veterinarians have reported success in some patients when treating infectious disease with the homeopathic nosode.

Glutamine

Glutamine, or L-glutamine, is an amino acid derived from another amino acid, glutamic acid.

There is no daily requirement for glutamine, as the body can make its own. High-protein foods such as meat, fish, beans, and dairy products are excellent sources of glutamine. Severe stresses may result in a temporary glutamine deficiency.

Glutamine plays a role in the health of the immune system, digestive tract, and muscle cells, as well as other bodily functions. It appears to serve as a fuel for the cells that line the intestines (it serves as a primary energy source for the mucosal cells that line the intestinal tract). Because stress on the intestinal cells that can occur in parvovirus infection can increase the need for glutamine as the body replaces the cells lining the intestinal tract, glutamine is often recommended for pets with parvovirus.

It has also been suggested as a treatment for food allergies, based on the "leaky gut syndrome." This theory holds that in some pets, whole proteins leak through the wall of the digestive tract and enter the blood, causing allergic reactions. Preliminary evidence suggests that glutamine supplements might reduce leakage through the intestinal walls.

However, there is little real evidence that it works as a treatment for true food allergies, although it is highly recommended for pets with various bowel disorders.

Glutamine, being one of the body's amino acids, is thought to be a safe supplement when taken at recommended dosages. Because many anti-epilepsy drugs work by blocking glutamate stimulation in the brain, high dosages of glutamine may overwhelm these drugs and pose a risk to pets with epilepsy. If your pet is taking anti-seizure medications, glutamine should only be used under veterinary supervision.

Maximum safe dosages for young children, pregnant or nursing women, or those with severe liver or kidney disease have not been determined; similar precautions are probably warranted in pets. Recommended dosages in pets are 250 to 3,000 mg daily.

Probiotics/Prebiotics

Probiotics are defined as normal viable bacteria residing in the intestinal tract that promote normal bowel health. Probiotics are given orally and are usually indicated for use in intestinal disorders in which specific factors can disrupt the normal bacterial population, making the pet more susceptible to disease. Specific factors which can disrupt the normal flora of the bowel include surgery, medications (including steroids and nonsteroidal anti-inflammatory drugs), antibiotics (especially when used long-term), shipping, birthing, weaning, illness such as parvovirus infection, and dietary factors (poor quality diet, oxidative damage, stress). Improving the nutritional status of the intestinal tract may reduce bacterial movement across the bowel mucosa (lining), intestinal permeability, and systemic endotoxemia. Additionally, probiotics may supply nutrients to the pet, help in digestion, and allow for better conversion of food into nutrients.

Prebiotics are food supplements that are not digested and absorbed by the host but improve health by stimulating the growth and activity of selected intestinal bacteria. Currently, there are no well-conducted studies on prebiotics.

There are several different probiotic products available which can contain any combination of the following organisms: *Lactobacillus* (*L. acidophilus, L. bulgaricus, L. thermophilus, L. reuteri*), *Acidophilus, Bacillus* (specifically a patented strain called *Bacillus CIP 5832* in one patented product), *Streptococcus S. bulgaricus,*

Enterococcus (E. faecium), Bifidobacterium, B. bifidus, and *Saccharomyces (S. boulardii,* which is actually a benficial yeast not a bacterium).

The intestinal tract, especially the large intestine (colon) is home to millions of bacteria, most of which are harmless and in fact beneficial to the pet. The intestinal bacteria are essential to digestion and the synthesis of vitamin K and many of the B vitamins.

As mentioned, your pet's intestinal tract contains billions of bacteria and yeasts. Some of these internal inhabitants are more helpful than others. *Acidophilus* and related probiotic bacteria not only help the digestive tract function, they also reduce the presence of less healthful organisms by competing with them for the limited space available.

How Probiotics Work

There are several proposed explanations about the mechanisms by which probiotics can protect your pet from harmful bowel bacteria:

- produce inhibitory chemicals that reduce the numbers of harmful bacteria and possibly toxin production by these harmful bacteria
- may block the adhesion of harmful bacteria to intestinal cells
- may compete for nutrients needed for growth and reproduction by harmful bacteria
- may degrade toxin receptors located on intestinal cells, preventing toxin absorption and damage by toxins produced by harmful intestinal bacteria
- may also stimulate immune function of the intestinal tract

Antibiotics can disturb the balance of the intestinal tract by killing friendly bacteria. When this happens, harmful bacteria and yeasts can move in, reproduce, and take over. This is especially true in pets on long-term (several months) antibiotic therapy, and for pets with chronic diarrhea.

Conversely, it appears that the regular use of probiotics can generally improve the health of the gastrointestinal system.

The use of probiotics for treating diarrhea as well as maintaining health is quite controversial,

with no clear scientific evidence (for health maintenance). Although many holistic doctors believe that they are helpful and perhaps even necessary for health, there is no daily requirement for probiotic bacteria. Probiotics are living creatures, not chemicals, so they can sustain themselves in the body unless something comes along to damage them, such as antibiotics.

Cultured dairy products such as yogurt and kefir are good sources of acidophilus and other probiotic bacteria. However, many yogurt products do not contain any living organisms or only contain small numbers of organisms.

Some pets will eat these foods, and others won't. Also, if the pet has any lactose intolerance, he may not tolerate yogurt well and may experience diarrhea (although this is rare). Most doctors recommend supplements to provide the highest doses of probiotics and avoid any lactose intolerance.

Various probiotics, while usually producing the same beneficial effects, may function differently within the intestinal tract. For example, *Lactobacillus acidophilus* produces lactic acid to lower the pH of the intestines and acts as an intestinal bacterial colonizer, *L. casei* lowers oxidation processes, and *L. lactis* acts on hydrogen peroxide as well as amylase and proteases.

Dosages

Dosages of acidophilus and other probiotics are expressed not in grams or milligrams, but in billions of organisms. A typical daily dose in people should supply about 3 to 5 billion live organisms. One popular pet supplement provides 500 million viable cells to be given per 50 pounds of body weight. The suggested dosage range of probiotics for pets is approximately 20 to 500 million microorganisms.

Some doctors recommend that when administering antibiotics, the probiotic should be given at least 2 hours later, several times per day, and when the antibiotic treatment has been completed, owners should double or triple the probiotic dose for 7 to 10 days.

Another recommendation is that if taking several species of probiotics, *Acidophilus* is reported to flourish best if taken in the morning, and the

Bifidus when taken at night. It is suspected that this may follow the diurnal acid/alkaline tide that the body utilizes as part of the detoxification process. However, this is not proven. The most important thing is that, regardless of when they are taken, probiotics should be taken when using (extended) antibiotic therapy and other conditions for which these supplements are indicated (as treatment for bowel disorders, for example).

Because probiotics are not drugs but living organisms, the precise dosage is not so important. They should be taken regularly to reinforce the beneficial bacterial colonies in the intestinal tract, which may gradually push out harmful bacteria and yeasts growing there.

The downside of using a living organism is that probiotics may die on the shelf. The container label should guarantee living *Acidophilus* (or *Bulgaricus*, and so on) at the time of purchase, not just at the time of manufacture.

There is fairly good evidence that many probiotics can help with various types and causes of diarrhea. *Saccharomyces boulardii*, *Enterococcus faecium*, and *Lactobacillus spp.* have been shown to help prevent antibiotic-induced diarrhea. *Saccharomyces* has demonstrated the most promise for use in diarrhea caused by the intestinal bacterium *Clostridium difficile*, a common cause of bacterial overgrowth in pets and people (*Lactobacillus spp.* are also helpful in bacterial overgrowth). Some evidence suggests that a particular type of probiotic, *L. reuteri*, can help treat diarrhea caused by viral infections in children. According to several studies conducted on the subject, it appears that regular use of acidophilus can help prevent "traveler's diarrhea" (an illness caused by eating contaminated food.

There are no known safety problems with the use of *Acidophilus* or other probiotics. Occasionally, some people notice a temporary increase in digestive gas (the same could occur in pets.)

If your pet is taking antibiotics, it may be beneficial to supplement with probiotics at the same time, and to continue them for a couple of weeks after the course of drug treatment has stopped. This will help restore the balance of natural bacteria in the digestive tract.

Fructo-oligosaccharides

In people, it is often suggested that in addition to taking probiotics, patients take fructo-oligosaccharides, supplements that can promote thriving colonies of helpful bacteria in the digestive tract. Fructo-oligosaccharides (FOS) are naturally occurring sugars found in many fruits, vegetables and grains. (Fructo means "fruit," and an oligosaccharide is a type of carbohydrate.) These non-digestible complex carbohydrates resist digestion by salivary and intestinal digestive enzymes and enter the colon where they are fermented by bacteria such as *Bifidobacterium* and *Bacteroides spp.*

The most beneficial effect of fructo-oligosaccharides is the selective stimulation of the growth of *Bifidobacterium*, thus significantly enhancing the composition of the colonic microflora and reducing the number of potential pathogenic bacteria. *Lactobacillus*, another beneficial bacteria, was also seen to proliferate with addition of FOS supplements. Because FOS increases the colonization of healthy bacteria in the gut, they are considered to be a prebiotic rather than a probiotic.

Taking FOS supplements are thought to foster a healthy environment for the beneficial bacteria living in the intestinal tract. Studies using FOS at a dosage of 0.75% to 1.0% (dry matter basis) showed decreased E. coli and increased lactobacilli intestinal bacteria in cats and dogs. The typical daily dose of fructo-oligosaccharides for people is between 2 and 8 g. The correct dose for pets has not been determined. One supplement contains 50 mg per dose for a 50-pound dog; research on FOS showed positive benefits when the dosage was 0.75% to 1.0% of the food when fed on a dry matter basis.

OTHER NATURAL TREATMENTS

Other natural treatments include **aloe vera** juice (page 156), **boswellia** (page 168), **calendula** (page 173), **chamomile** (page 178), **German chamomile** (page 206), **marshmallow** (page 240), **raspberry leaf** (page 261), and **slippery elm** (page 273). These can be used in conjunction with conventional therapies, as they are unlikely to be effective by themselves in most patients. The natural treatments are widely used with variable success but have not all been thoroughly investigated and proven at this time.

As with any condition, the most healthful natural diet will improve the pet's overall health.

CONVENTIONAL THERAPY

Supportive care includes: antibiotics (to control secondary infections), intravenous fluid therapy, force-feeding, replacement of serum protein when needed, and medications such as corticosteroids or nonsteroidal anti-inflammatory medications to control inflammation in the intestines.

PERIODONTAL DISEASE (See Dental Disease)

RICKETTSIAL DISEASES

Principal Natural Treatments
Omega-3 fatty acids, antioxidants

Other Natural Treatments
Alfalfa, aloe vera, astragalus, burdock, dandelion leaf, dandelion root, echinacea, garlic, ginseng, goldenseal, hawthorn, licorice, marshmallow, milk thistle, nettle, red clover, St. John's wort, turmeric, yellow dock, homeopathic nosodes

Rickettsial diseases are those caused by rickettsia, microscopic organisms that are not quite bacteria and not quite viruses. In dogs, the most common rickettsial diseases are ehrlichiosis, Lyme disease, and Rocky Mountain spotted fever. The rickettsial organisms that cause each of these diseases are carried by ticks and transmitted to the pet within 24 hours after the tick bites and attaches to the pet. Tick control is useful to decrease the spread of these diseases. Rickettsial diseases are zoonotic, meaning they can be transmitted to people. However, an infected pet can only transmit the disease to a person through a tick bite and not by directly infecting the person itself. Tick control is therefore important to decrease the chance of spreading the disease to the pet owner as well.

Clinical signs vary with the specific disease. Listed below are common types and symptoms.

Ehrlichiosis. Clinical signs are varied and may include fever, lack of appetite, anemia (pale gums), decreased platelet count, weight loss, abdominal pain, enlarged lymph nodes, enlarged

spleen, difficulty breathing, swollen joints, eye abnormalities (blindness, redness, cloudiness of the cornea), discharge from the eyes, and diarrhea.

Lyme Disease. Clinical signs can include swollen and painful joints, enlarged lymph nodes, fever, change in personality, and seizures.

Rocky Mountain Spotted Fever. Clinical signs are varied and are almost identical to those seen in dogs with ehrlichiosis. The signs may include fever, lack of appetite, anemia (pale gums), decreased platelet count, weight loss, abdominal pain, enlarged lymph nodes, enlarged spleen, difficulty breathing, swollen joints, eye abnormalities (blindness, redness, cloudiness of the cornea), discharge from the eyes, and diarrhea.

PRINCIPAL NATURAL TREATMENTS
Omega-3 Fatty Acids

Omega-3 fatty acids—eicosapentaenoic acid (EPA) and docosahexaenoic acid (DHA)—are derived from fish oils of coldwater fish (salmon, trout, or most commonly menhaden fish) and flaxseed. Omega-6 fatty acids—linoleic acid (LA) and gamma-linolenic acid (GLA)—are derived from the oils of seeds such as evening primrose, black currant, and borage. Often, fatty acids are added to the diet with other supplements to attain an additive effect.

Just how do the fatty acids work to help in controlling inflammation in pets? Cell membranes contain phospholipids. When membrane injury occurs, an enzyme acts on the phospholipids in the cell membranes to produce fatty acids including arachidonic acid (an omega-6 fatty acid) and eicosapentaenoic acid (an omega-3 fatty acid). Further metabolism of the arachidonic acid and eicosapentaenoic acid by additional enzymes (the lipooxygenase and cyclooxygenase pathways) yields the production of chemicals called eicosanoids. The eicosanoids produced by metabolism of arachidonic acid are pro-inflammatory and cause inflammation, suppress the immune system, and cause platelets to aggregate and clot; the eicosanoids produced by metabolism of eicosapentaenoic acid are non-inflammatory, not immunosuppressive, and help inhibit platelets from clotting. There is some overlap and the actual biochemical pathway is a bit more complicated than I have suggested here. For example, one of the by-products of omega-6 fatty acid metabolism is Prostaglandin E_1, which is anti-inflammatory. This is one reason why some research has shown that using certain omega-6 fatty acids can also act to limit inflammation.)

Supplementation of the diet with omega-3 fatty acids works in this biochemical reaction. By providing extra amounts of these non-inflammatory compounds, we try to overwhelm the body with the production of non-inflammatory eicosanoids. Therefore, since the same enzymes metabolize both omega-3 and omega-6 fatty acids, and since metabolism of the omega-6 fatty acids tend to cause inflammation (with the exception of Prostaglandin E_1 by metabolism of omega-6 as mentioned above), by supplying a large amount of omega-3 fatty acids we favor the production of non-inflammatory chemicals.

Many disorders are due to overproduction of the eicosanoids responsible for producing in-flammation. Fatty acid supplementation may be beneficial in inflammatory disorders by regulating the eicosanoid production, although controlled studies are lacking.

In general, the products of omega-3 (specifically EPA) and one omega-6 fatty acid (DGLA) are less inflammatory than the products of arachidonic acid (another omega-6 fatty acid). By changing dietary fatty acid consumption, we can change eicosanoid production right at the cellular level and try to modify (decrease) inflammation within the body. By providing the proper (anti-inflammatory) fatty acids, we can use fatty acids as an anti-inflammatory substance. However, since the products of omega-6 fatty acid metabolism (specifically arachidonic acid) are not the sole cause of the inflammation, fatty acid therapy is rarely effective as the sole therapy but is used as an adjunct therapy to achieve an additive effect.

Note: Flaxseed oil is a popular source of alpha-linoleic acid (ALA), an omega-3 fatty acid that is ultimately converted to EPA and DHA. However, many species of pets (probably including dogs) and some people cannot convert ALA to these other more active non-inflammatory omega-3 fatty acids. In one study in people, flaxseed oil was ineffective in reducing symptoms or raising levels of EPA and DHA. While flaxseed oil has been suggested as a less smelly substitute for fish oil, there is no evidence that it is effective when used for the same therapeutic purposes as fish oil. Therefore, supplementation with EPA and DHA is important, and this is the reason flaxseed oil is not recommended as the sole fatty acid supplement for pets. Flaxseed oil can be used to provide ALA and as a coat conditioner.

Dosages

What is the "best" dose to use in the treatment of pets? Most doctors use anywhere from 2 to 10 times the label dose. Research in the treatment of allergies indicates that the label dose is ineffective; higher doses may also be indicated in pets with ricketssial diseases. In people, the dosage that showed effectiveness in many studies were 1.4 to 2.8 gm of GLA per day, or 1.7 gm of EPA and 0.9 gm of DHA per day, which is hard for people to obtain from the supplements currently available. If this were shown to be the correct dosage for pets, a 50-pound dog would need to take 10 or more fatty acid capsules per day to obtain a similar dosage, depending upon which supplement (and there are many choices on the market) was used. Therefore, while the studies with omega-3 fatty acids show many potential health benefits, it is almost impossible to administer the large number of capsules needed to approximate the same dosage used in these studies. The best that owners can hope for at this time is to work with their veterinarians and try to increase, as best as possible, the amount of omega-3 fatty acids in the diet to try to get to what seems to be the "preferred" ratio of 5:1, omega-6:omega-3 fatty acids.

What is the "correct" fatty acid to use? Should we use just omega-3 (EPA and DHA) fatty acids, or combine them with omega-6 (GLA) fatty acids? Is there an "ideal" ratio of omega-6 to omega-3 fatty acids? (Research on pets with atopic dermatitis suggests that the ideal dietary ratio seems to be 5:1 of omega-6:omega-3 fatty acids, although this is also debated.)

Is supplementation with fatty acid capsules or liquids the best approach, or is dietary manipulation (adding the "ideal" ratio of omega-6 and omega-3 fatty acids) preferred for the treatment of inflammatory conditions? There are in fact, diets constructed with this "ideal" ratio. For owners who do not like giving their pets medication, or for those pets who don't take the fatty acid supplements easily, it might be wise to try some of these medically formulated diets (available from your pet's doctor) that contain the fatty acids. However, because these medicated diets may not be as natural as possible due to the inclusion of by-products and chemical preservatives, holistic pet owners may need to try other options.

Fish Oils   Since fish oils can easily oxidize and become rancid, some manufacturers add vitamin E to fish oil capsules and liquid products to keep the oil from spoiling (others remove oxygen from the capsule.)

Since processed foods have increased omega-6 fatty acids and decreased omega-3 fatty acids, supplementing the diets of all pets with omega-3 fatty acids seems warranted and will not harm your pet.

The bottom line is that there are many questions regarding the use of fatty acid therapy. More research is needed to determine the effectiveness of the fatty acids in the treatment of various medical problems, as well as the proper doses needed to achieve clinical results. Until definitive answers are obtained, you will need to work with your doctors (knowing the limitations of our current research) to determine the use of these supplements for your pet.

Fish oil appears to be safe. The most common side effect seen in people and pets is a fish odor to the breath or the skin.

Because fish oil has a mild "blood-thinning" effect, it should not be combined with powerful blood-thinning medications, such as Coumadin (warfarin) or heparin, except on a veterinarian's advice. Fish oil does not seem to cause bleeding problems when it is taken by itself at commonly recommended dosages. Also, fish oil does not appear to raise blood sugar levels in people or pets with diabetes.

Flaxseed Oil   Flaxseed oil is derived from the seeds of the flax plant and has been proposed as a less smelly alternative to fish oil. Flaxseed oil contains alpha-linolenic acid (ALA), an omega-3 fatty acid that is ultimately converted to EPA and DHA. In fact, flaxseed oil contains higher levels of omega-3 fatty acids (ALA) than fish oil. It also contains omega-6 fatty acids.

As mentioned, many species of pets (probably including dogs and cats) and some people cannot convert ALA to these other more active non-inflammatory omega-3 fatty acids. In one study in people, flaxseed oil was ineffective in reducing symptoms or raising levels of EPA and DHA. While flaxseed oil has been suggested as a substitute for fish oil, there is no evidence that it is effective when used for the same therapeutic purposes as fish oil. Unlike the case for fish oil, there is little evidence that flaxseed oil is effective for any specific therapeutic purpose.

Therefore, supplementation with EPA and DHA is important, and this is the reason flaxseed oil is not recommended as the sole fatty acid supplement for pets. Flaxseed oil can be used to provide ALA and as a coat conditioner.

Flaxseed oil also does contain lignans, which are currently being studied for use in preventing cancer in people.

The essential fatty acids in flax can be damaged by exposure to heat, light, and oxygen (essentially, they become rancid). For this reason, you shouldn't cook with flaxseed oil. A good product should be sold in an opaque container, and the manufacturing process should keep the temperature under 100° F (some products are prepared by cold extraction methods). Some manufacturers combine the product with vitamin E because it helps prevent rancidity.

The best use of flaxseed oil is as a general nutritional supplement to provide essential fatty acids.

Flaxseed oil appears to be a safe nutritional supplement when used as recommended.

Antioxidants

Certain vitamins and minerals function in the body to reduce oxidation. Oxidation is a chemical process that occurs within the body's cells. After oxidation occurs, certain by-products such as peroxides and "free radicals" accumulate. These cellular by-products are toxic to the cells and surrounding tissue. The body removes these by-products by producing additional chemicals called antioxidants that combat these oxidizing chemicals.

In disease, excess oxidation can occur and the body's normal antioxidant abilities are overwhelmed. This is where supplying antioxidants can help. By giving your pet's body extra antioxidants, it may be possible to neutralize the harmful by-products of cellular oxidation.

Several antioxidants can be used to supplement pets. Most commonly, the antioxidant **vitamins A** (page 284), **C** (page 297), and **E** (page 302) and the minerals **selenium** (page 268), **manganese** (page 239), and **zinc** (page 310) are prescribed. Other antioxidants, including **N-acetylcysteine** (page 243), **Coenzyme Q10** (page 185), *Ginkgo biloba* (page 208), **bilberry** (page 164), **grape seed extract** (page 159), and **pycnogenol** (page 159) may also be helpful for a number of disorders.

There is no "correct" antioxidant to use. Dosage varies with the specific antioxidant chosen.

Following is a brief discussion of a commonly used group of antioxidants called bioflavonoids/proanthocyanidins; see the specific pages listed previously for information on other antioxidants.

Proanthocyanidins

Proanthocyanidins (also called pycnogenols or bioflavonoids; while they don't seem to be essential to life, it's likely that people and pets need them for optimal health) are naturally occuring polyphenolic compounds found in plants. Most often products containing proanthocyanidins are made from grape seed or pine bark. These compounds are used for their antioxidant effects against lipid (fat) peroxidation. Proanthocyanidins also inhibit the enzyme cyclooxygenase (the same enzyme inhibited by aspirin and other nonsteroidal medications); cyclooxygenase converts arachidonic acid into chemicals (leukotrienes and prostaglandins) which contribute to inflammation and allergic reactions. Proanthocyanidins also decrease histamine release from cells by inhibiting several enzymes.

Some research suggests that pycnogenol seems to work by enhancing the effects of another antioxidant, vitamin C. Other research suggests that the bioflavonoids can work independently of other antioxidants; as is the case with many supplements, there probably is an additive effect when multiple antioxidants are combined. People taking pycnogenol often report feeling better and having more energy; this "side effect" may possibly occur in our pets as well.

Quercetin is a natural antioxidant bioflavonoid found in red wine, grapefruit, onions, apples, black tea, and, in lesser amounts, in leafy green vegetables and beans. Quercetin protects cells in the body from damage by free radicals and stabilizes collagen in blood vessels.

Quercetin supplements are available in pill and tablet form. One problem with them, however, is that they don't seem to be well absorbed by the body. A special form called quercetin chalcone appears to be better absorbed.

Quercetin appears to be quite safe. Maximum safe dosages for young children, women who are pregnant or nursing, or those with serious liver or kidney disease have not been established; similar precautions are probably warranted in pets.

In people, a typical dosage of proanthocyanidins is 200 to 400 mg 3 times daily. Quercetin may be better absorbed if taken on an empty stomach. The suggested dosage of proanthocyanidin complex in pets is 10 to 200 mg given daily (divided into 2 to 3 doses). The suggested dosage of bioflavonoid complex in pets is 200 to 1,500 mg per day (divided into 2 to 3 doses). The actual dosage of each product will vary with the product and the pet's weight and disease condition.

While there is no specific research showing benefit in specific rickettsial diseases, the use of antioxidants is widely recommended by holistic veterinarians to reduce oxidative damage to tissues that may occur. More research on antioxidants and other complementary therapies in the treatment of rickettsial diseases is needed.

OTHER NATURAL TREATMENTS

The herbs **alfalfa** (page 156), **aloe vera** (page 156), **astragalus** (page 160), **burdock** (page 170), **dandelion leaf** (page 193), **dandelion root** (page 193), **echinacea** (page 195), **garlic** (page 204), **ginseng** (page 210), **goldenseal** (page 220), **hawthorn** (page 223), **licorice** (page 234), **marshmallow** (page 240), **milk thistle** (page 241), **nettle** (page 245), **red clover** (page 262), **St. John's wort** (page 276), **turmeric** (page 280), **yellow dock** (page 309); the **glycoprotein acemannan** (page 156), and **homeopathic nosodes** (page 411) may each be helpful.

These can be used in conjunction with conventional therapies, as they are unlikely to be effective by themselves in most patients. The natural treatments are widely used with variable success but have not all been thoroughly investigated and proven at this time.

As with any condition, the most healthful natural diet will improve the pet's overall health.

CONVENTIONAL THERAPY

Tetracyclines such as doxycycline are the treatment of choice and generally will cure most cases. For pets that are critically ill, hospitalization with intravenous fluid therapy, transfusions, and force feeding are necessary.

RINGWORM

Principal Natural Treatments
  None

Other Natural Treatments
  Topical herbal shampoos with calendula and goldenseal, natural diet, the herbs astragalus, dandelion leaf, echinacea, garlic, German chamomile, gotu kola, Oregon grape, sage, turmeric, yellow dock, homeopathic sulfur

Ringworm is a common fungal infection mainly affecting puppies and kittens. The disease is highly contagious between pets and may be easily transmitted between infected pets and their owners. Owners should note that most cases of ringworm in people are *not* caused by exposure to pets, however. Clinical signs include hair loss, usually in a circular or "ring-shaped" pattern. However, ringworm can look like any skin disease. In kittens, tiny scabs (miliary lesions) may also occur in infected pets.

OTHER NATURAL TREATMENTS

Topical therapy with herbal shampoos containing **calendula** (page 173) and **goldenseal** (page 220) may be helpful. In addition, a natural **diet** (page 314) is indicated. Herbs to boost the immune system and help with infections are **astragalus** (page 160), **dandelion leaf** (page 193), **echinacea** (page 195), **garlic** (page 204), and **German chamomile** (topically, page 206), **gotu kola** (page 221), **Oregon grape** (page 251),

sage (page 264), **turmeric** (page 280), and **yellow dock** (page 309).

These natural treatments are designed to reduce growth of the fungus and inflammation in pets with allergic dermatitis.

They can be used in conjunction with conventional therapies as they are unlikely to be effective by themselves in most patients with severe ringworm infections. The natural treatments are widely used with variable success but have not been thoroughly investigated and proven at this time.

As with any condition, the most healthful natural diet will improve the pet's overall health.

CONVENTIONAL THERAPY

Conventional therapy utilizes medicated shampoos, and, in serious infections, oral antifungal medications, usually griseofulvin.

 # URINARY INCONTINENCE

Principal Natural Treatments
   Rehmannia Six or Eight formulas, soy protein/isoflavones

Other Natural Treatments
   Gingko biloba, mullein, shiitake mushrooms, glandular therapy

Urinary incontinence means that the pet cannot totally control his ability to urinate. Typically, urinary incontinence causes a "leaky bladder." Clinical signs often seen include finding "wet spots" under the pet where he sleeps, and seeing dribbling urine as the pet moves about.

Urinary incontinence can be seen in young pets, including puppies and kittens, but is usually seen in middle-aged to older pets. The exact cause is unknown, although since incontinence often responds to estrogen or testosterone supplementation following spaying and neutering, hormonal factors obviously play a factor in maintaining the tone of the urethra and preventing leakage of urine. Other hormonal imbalances such as hypothyroidism, and rarely bladder tumors, also can lead to urinary incontinence. Bladder tumors usually also cause increased frequency of urination, painful urination, or a burning sensation during urination, excessive licking at the genitals, and occasionally blood in the urine.

PRINCIPAL NATURAL TREATMENTS

Rehmannia Six or Rehmannia Eight

This well-known Chinese herbal formula is used as a kidney yin and blood tonic for pets with kidney disease (excess water) or urinary incontinence. Ingredients include rehmannia, cornus, dioscorea, moutan, hoelen, alisma (**Rehmannia Six,** page 262), and cinnamon bark and aconite (**Rehmannia Eight**, page 262). The herbs regulate water balance in the body.

Soy Protein/Isoflavones

The soybean has been prized for centuries in Asia as a nutritious, high-protein food with many potential uses. For example, in pets with severe liver disease, diets using soy protein are preferred to decrease formation of chemicals that may be toxic to the pet. Today soy protein is popular for people as a cholesterol-free meat and dairy substitute (soy burgers, soy yogurt, tofu hot dogs, and tofu cheese can be found in a growing number of grocery stores alongside the traditional white blocks of tofu).

In addition to protein, soybeans contain chemicals that are similar to estrogen. These may be the active ingredients in soy protein formulations, although this is not known for sure.

Due to the estrogenic effects, soy protein also seems to reduce the common menopausal symptom known as "hot flashes" in women. Unlike estrogen, soy appears to reduce the risk of uterine cancer. While its effect on breast cancer is not as well established, there are reasons to believe that soy can help reduce breast cancer risk as well due to the isoflavone content.

In pets, soy isoflavones have been proposed as a natural therapy for canine urinary incontinence at a starting dose of 2 mg per pound twice daily. The dosage can be increased if there is no response in 7 to 10 days. However, the pet should be examined regularly and have laboratory tests to check for signs of hyperestrogenism, which is a potential side effect. The correct dosage has not been determined, nor has it been determined if there is any long-term harm with this therapy. If signs of estrogenism do not occur, the regimen is likely to be safe for pets.

As a food that has been eaten for centuries, soy protein is believed to be quite safe. However, the isoflavones in soy could conceivably have some potentially harmful hormonal effects in certain specific situations. In particular, we don't know if high doses of soy are safe for women who have already had breast cancer (for more information, see the chapter on **isoflavones,** page 274). They may also interact with hormone medications.

For people taking zinc, iron, or calcium supplements, it has been suggested that it may be best to eat soy at a different time of day to avoid absorption problems. Patients taking the medications estrogen, tamoxifen, or raloxifene might experience interactions if eating large amounts of soy as it is possible that soy might interfere with their effects. The same precautions may also be warranted in pets.

Isoflavones are water-soluble chemicals found in many plants; soy protein contains a fair amount of isoflavones. One group of isoflavones is known as phytoestrogens (plant estrogens), so named because they cause effects in the body somewhat similar to those of estrogen. The most investigated natural isoflavones, genistein and daidzen, are found in soy products and the herb red clover. Another isoflavone, ipriflavone, is an intentionally modified form of daidzen used as a seminatural drug. Ipriflavone is a synthesized type of phytoestrogen that possesses the bone-stimulating effects of estrogen without any estrogen-like activity elsewhere in the body. After 7 successful years of experiments with animals, human research was started in 1981. Today, ipriflavone is available in over 22 countries and in most drugstores in the United States as a nonprescription dietary supplement. It is an accepted treatment for osteoporosis in people in Italy, Turkey, and Japan.

Like estrogen, ipriflavone appears to slow bone breakdown. Since it does not appear to have any estrogenic effects anywhere else in the body, it shouldn't increase the risk of breast or uterine cancer.

Isoflavones appear to work by latching on to the same places (receptor sites) on cells and not allowing actual estrogen to attach. In this way, when there is not enough estrogen in the body, isoflavones can partially make up for it; but when there is plenty of estrogen, they can partially block its influence. In people, the net effect of this interaction may be to reduce some of the risks of excess estrogen (breast and uterine cancer), while still providing some of estrogen's benefits (preventing osteoporosis).

Roasted soybeans have the highest isoflavone content, about 167 mg for a 3.5-ounce serving. Tempeh is next, with 60 mg; followed by soy flour, with 44 mg. Processed soy products such as soy protein and soymilk contain about 20 mg per serving. Similar isoflavones are also found in the herb red clover. The synthetic isoflavone ipriflavone is not found in foods and must be obtained as a supplement.

Dosages

The proper dosage of the synthetic isoflavone ipriflavone has been well established through human studies: 200 mg 3 times daily, or 300 mg twice daily.

The optimum dosage of natural isoflavones obtained from food is not known. We know that Japanese women eat up to 200 mg of isoflavones daily, but we don't really know what amount of natural isoflavones is ideal. Most experts recommend 25 to 60 mg daily for people.

In pets, a dosage for soy isoflavones of 2 mg per pound of body weight twice daily has been suggested as an alternative therapy for dogs with urinary incontinence (as mentioned above). Long-term side effects are unknown, and pets taking soy isoflavones should be monitored for side effects associated with estrogen, including bone marrow suppression.

Safety Issues

Natural soy isoflavones have not been subjected to rigorous safety studies. However, because they are consumed in very high quantities among those who eat traditional Asian diets, they are thought to be safe when used at the recommended dosages. However, because isoflavones work somewhat like estrogen, there are at least theoretical concerns that they may not be safe for women who have already had breast cancer.

Nearly 3,000 people have used the seminatural isoflavone ipriflavone in clinical studies, with no more side effects than those taking placebo. However, because ipriflavone is metabolized by the kidneys, individuals with severe kidney disease should have their ipriflavone dosage monitored by a physician. Similar precautions are warranted in pets until we have more information on the usage and safety of soy isoflavones. Feeding pets soy-based diets (tofu) are not likely to be of any harm.

OTHER NATURAL TREATMENTS

The natural treatments of **Gingko biloba** (page 208), **mullein** (page 243), **shiitake mushrooms** (page 272), and **glandular therapy** (page 393) are widely used with variable success, but have not all been thoroughly investigated and proven at this time.

As with any condition, the most healthful natural diet will improve the pet's overall health.

CONVENTIONAL THERAPY

Conventional therapies for pets with urinary incontinence uses estrogen or testosterone. Due to the chance of severe side effects, including genital cancers and bone marrow suppression, treatment with these hormones is not usually the first choice. Dogs with hypothyroidism can improve with thyroid supplementation.

Using certain medications such as phenylpropanolamine is a safer first-choice alternative and can be used for long-term control, usually without any side effects.

VACCINOSIS

Principal Natural Treatments
  Thuja, lyssin, homeopathic nosodes

Other Natural Treatments
  None

Vaccinosis is the term given to the chronic reaction of the body against repeated immunization. Many holistic veterinarians and owners are concerned about the frequent (and most likely unnecessary) immunization of pets for just about every disease imaginable.

Minor side effects often seen following immunization include fever, stiffness, joint soreness, lethary, and decreased appetite.

A number of more serious conditions have been proven or proposed to be the result of excessive immunization, and animals run the risk of adverse reactions as increasing amounts of foreign antigens are injected into them. Since vaccination involves altering the immune system, it is not surprising that occasionally adverse effects involving the immune system as a result of immunization also occur. These include:

- Injection-site sarcomas (an aggressive cancer of cats that may occur in 1:1000 to 1:10,000 cats following any injection; vaccines are implicated more than other injectable medications)
- Collapse with autoimmune hemolytic anemia (decreased red blood cell count) or thrombocytopenia (decreased platelet count)
- Liver failure
- Kidney failure
- Bone marrow suppression
- Immune suppression
- Systemic lupus erythematosus
- Rheumatoid arthritis
- Food allergy
- Atopic dermatitis (allergic disease as a result of immunization is suspected to occur as a result of an augmented immune response to the vaccine and/or other allergens/immugens, the so-called "allergic breakthrough" phenomenon
- Glomerulonephritis/renal amyloidosis (different types of immune kidney diseases)
- Seizures
- Bloating
- Hypothyroidism
- Hyperthyroidism

The administration of vaccines may also interfere with the interpretation of various test results. For instance, dogs vaccinated for Lyme disease will be positive on the screening test for this disorder, necessitating a follow-up test to differentiate between the vaccine and the actual presence of the disease. Cats vaccinated against any disease may show a positive titer on the standard corona virus test, called the FIP test.

Both killed vaccines (containing adjuvant to stimulate a greater immune response) and modified live vaccines have been implicated in vaccine reactions. Many vaccine reactions seem to occur following booster immunization with vaccines containing a number of antigens (such as 5-way or 7-way vaccines).

Injection-Site Sarcomas

A recent phenomenon diagnosed in cats is a condition called injection-site sarcoma. This aggressive cancer is estimated to occur in 1:1,000 to 1:10,000 cats. The tumors usually occur between 3.5 months and 3.5 years following injection. Any

vaccine (or injectable substance) can be associated with sarcomas; recently, the injectable flea-control product Program has been reported to possibly be associated with injection-site sarcomas in three cats.

Following injection, inflammation results—usually as a result of the adjuvant in the medication or vaccine (the adjuvant is a chemical added to increase local inflammation and a more intense immune reaction). The amount of chronic inflammation occurring at the site of the injection is related to the cat's risk of developing injection-site sarcoma (the more inflammation the greater the risk). Since vaccines are often given annually in the same site on the cat's body, it is no surprise that risk increases with the number of vaccines given on one site.

Not all cats will develop injection-site sarcoma as a result of an injection. Most cats do not develop injection-site sarcomas despite inflammation at the injection site. Apparently, there is some interaction between intense inflammation and tumor oncogenes, which ultimately results in tumor formation following injections. In fact, preliminary research has shown that sarcomas associated with vaccines had overexpression of the c-jun gene (a gene that is related to cancer development in animals species, an oncogene) when compared to sarcomas not related to vaccine injection. The working hypothesis as to why some rare cats develop injection-site sarcomas (and most cats do not) is that something in the injections (probably adjuvant) causes persistent inflammation at the injection site, which in some way stimulates the cat's oncogenes to overreact and develop tumors. In other words, it appears that some cats may be genetically predisposed to developing injection-site sarcomas, and the inflammation following immunization is the trigger to set this reaction in motion.

Sarcomas in many cats may also appear unrelated to injections of medications or vaccinations. When compared to sarcomas that are not related to injections, injection-site sarcomas are typically more aggressive and are characterized by rapid growth and ulceration, are usually not encapsulated, and infiltrate and extend along fascial (surrounding connective tissue) planes. Complete removal is difficult, and local recurrence is common. As a result, an aggressive first surgery to remove as much of the tumor as possible is recommended. Cats with tumors located on the leg had a better prognosis than cats with tumors on the body (probably as a result of amputation of the affected limb as the surgical treatment). Median survival is approximately 576 days (most of these cats had additional therapy, such as radiation therapy, in addition to surgical removal of the tumor). Cats with injection-site sarcomas should never be revaccinated.

Currently, vaccine protocols are under review as manufacturers attempt to determine the maximum (and not just the currently published minimum) levels of duration. Additionally, while not proven, removing adjuvant from vaccines and using vaccines made from recombinant DNA technology (rather than from whole killed, or modified live, viral and bacterial organisms) may reduce vaccine-site sarcomas. However, early data from recombinant vaccines against human and mouse viruses has shown potentially dangerous side effects such as damage to T lymphocytes.

Current recommendations are for most immunizations to be given at least annually. This recommendation came about as a result of several findings. First, in the late 1950s, it was shown that ⅓ of puppies immunized against distemper did not maintain protective titers at one year following immunization. Second, as vaccination became widespread and infectious diseases decreased, it was believed that there would be a lack of natural exposure needed to maintain a regular boosting of the immune system required to give long-term population immunity. Third, annual vaccination was shown to reduce the incidence of infectious diseases such as distemper.

Rabies is usually a 3-year vaccine, meaning that immunity lasts at least 3 years. Some state laws require annual immunization, even though the 3-year vaccine is used. Canine bordetella intranasal vaccine is usually administered every 6 months.

There are ongoing research projects where the goal is to attempt to determine the maximum duration of immunity of vaccines in pets. This presents quite a challenge, as there are a number of vaccine manufacturers whose vaccines must be tested. The results of these tests will most likely need to be repeated to verify their accuracy. Results of the tests (and retesting) will probably take at least 5 to 10 years or more. Not until then can current vaccination protocols be changed with confidence.

The Titers Tests

An alternative to routine vaccination of every pet is the use of vaccine (antibody) titers. These simple blood tests can give us information about an individual pet's antibody status in relation to specific diseases.

In simple terms, antibodies are proteins made by the pet's white blood cells (specifically B lymphocytes). These antibodies are made whenever a pet contacts an infectious organism (virus or bacteria, as a result of a natural infection) or is vaccinated (the vaccine uses low doses of infectious organisms, tricking the immune system to form protective antibodies without causing disease as might occur in a natural infection). Using a titer test reveals each pet's antibody status. These results are then interpreted in an attempt to determine whether the pet is currently protected against a specific infectious disease or if the pet may require immunization.

There are both pros and cons to the use of vaccine (antibody) titers to determine the need to immunize pets.

Pros in Using the Titers Tests

- Easy to perform
- Inexpensive (usually less than $50)
- Gives specific information about each individual patient, allowing the doctor and owner to make a rational and informed decision
- Replaces the current recommendation for annual vaccination for every pet regardless of actual need

Cons to Using the Titers Tests

1. While inexpensive, the extra cost may prohibit some owners from taking advantage of the testing.
2. Some diseases will not be titered; rather, automatic immunization will still be given. This is the case for the rabies vaccine. The 3-year rabies vaccine (used by most if not all practitioners) only needs to be given every 3 years. Some

states require more frequent immunization regardless of the 3-year duration of immunity. These states may not accept titer information and would still require immunization, regardless of titer status.

3. Not all diseases produce a measurable titer. For example, antibody levels have been shown to correlate with protection against canine distemper virus, canine parvovirus, canine adenovirus, feline panleukopenia virus, and Lyme disease. Serum titers do not correlate with protection for the following diseases: kennel cough (*Bordetella bronchiseptica* and parainfluenza), canine coronavirus, feline enteric coronavirus, and feline chlamydial infection. Cellular immunity (rather than antibodies) provide protection against feline rhinotracheitis virus and feline infectious peritonitis virus, making titers inaccurate in interpreting protection for these diseases. Antibody levels (IgG titers) do provide information about protection against canine leptospirosis, although immunity against this disease following vaccination with inactivated leptospirosis organisms is generally believed to be short-lived (6 to 12 months). There is still adequate protection due to the cellular immunity the vaccines for these diseases produce.

4. Titers, like vaccines, are not perfect. There is no guarantee that a pet with an adequate titer (or an annual vaccination) will not become infected or become ill with a disease. The titer only tells us that the pet should have adequate antibodies to fight off the infectious organism and that the pet possesses the ability to mount a secondary antibody response (and fight off the disease).

5. There is no agreed-upon correct titer level for determining protective titers. Currently, doctors must use all of the conflicting information available and make an educated decision regarding what constitutes an "adequate, protective" titer.

What Constitutes the "Correct" Titer?

Unfortunately, we do not have an adequate answer to this important question. The significance of titers depends on the disease, the state of vaccination, the time of exposure, and the immune system. The presence of titers does not guarantee protection, and likewise the absence of titers does not guarantee that a pet will become ill if exposed to an infectious organism. One study showed that transplanting memory cells (lymphocytic white blood cells) to native mice from exposed mice allowed the naive (unexposed) mice to adopt these memory cells, making the animal fully immune.

Titers are currently used by vaccine manufacturers as one way of proving that puppies and kittens immunized with their vaccines are protected against infection. After much research, companies have determined what constitutes a protective titer (for their vaccine) when the puppy or kitten is adequately immunized. Puppies and kittens properly immunized and exhibiting a protective titer would not be expected to develop a disease if they come into contact with an infectious organism.

The value of protective titers vary with individual vaccines. Additionally, these titers are adequate to ensure protection for vaccinated puppies and kittens. Are these same values appropriate for adult dogs and cats who have received numerous vaccinations over many years? Would lower values also be appropriate for these pets? The biggest question is whether animals with low or no titers and the possibility of memory cells, which might be able to develop antibodies upon disease exposure, should be vaccinated. Since we have no good, inexpensive test for the memory cells (and also the cellular immunity, which is also important to protect pets against infectious diseases), the use of titers, while helpful, is not perfect.

To date, the answers to these questions is unknown, and this complicates our use of vaccine titers until more information becomes available.

Common recommendations for protective titers vary with the study. For example, protective titers have been reported as follows:

Protective Titers

Canine Distemper:	>1:5; >1:20, >1:96
Canine Parvovirus:	>1:5, >1:80
Feline Calicivirus:	>1:16, >1:24, >1.32
Feline Panleukopenia:	>1.40
Feline Herpes Virus	>1:16

Currently, the use of titers is not perfect but gives us some information about each individual pet. Most holistic doctors will consider immunization if the pet fails to detect a titer of 1:5 or greater, although some will use the upper end of the titers as mentioned above. The presence of any titer for those diseases in which titer information correlates with disease protection indicates the ability of the pet to respond to immunization and possibly infection. More research is needed to determine which vaccines induce the longest lasting protection, and how titer levels correlate with these specific vaccines.

The best recommendations at this point are as follows:

- While not perfect, titers are the only inexpensive way to assess each pet's unique vaccine needs.
- Standardized testing should be adopted, along with an agreed-upon "correct" level to constitute a protective titer. This may be difficult, as each vaccine manufacturer would need to determine the "correct" level for each vaccine produced.
- Any titer indicates the ability of the pet to respond to immunization. The higher the titer, the greater the antibody level at the time of the testing. As long as the pet has protective immunity, however, vaccines are not needed as they do not "boost" the immune system.
- Until we have more information, we probably need to use published studies by vaccine manufacturers showing the levels of titers that afforded vaccinated puppies and kittens protection from disease challenge. On average, this is a titer somewhere around 1:64.
- At this time, most holistic veterinarians use a combination of blood titers plus their knowledge of the pet's lifestyle to determine whether or not to vaccinate. For example, an outdoor cat is at higher risk of coming in contact with cats who may transmit infectious diseases. The need for this cat to be adequately immunized is greater than the cat who never leaves the house except to go for a veterinary visit 1 to 2 times each year and has little chance of ever contracting an infectious disease. A veterinary practice located in an area with a large concentration of parvo virus cases will probably stress current immunization in an attempt to protect any pets who may not be currently immunized. Because of the pet's need to withstand infection and disease, a strong immune system maintained by a healthful diet supplemented with quality nutritional supplements is of paramount importance.

Homeopathic vaccine nosodes (see page 411 for additional discussion on homeopathy and nosodes) can be used in place of immunizations, and homeopathic remedies such as Thuja can be given at the time of whatever immunization is needed in an attempt to minimize any "vaccine reaction." While many doctors who practice homeopathy feel that nosodes are helpful in this regard, controlled studies showing their effectiveness in preventing disease is lacking. Drs. Christopher Day, John Saxton, and Richard Pitcairn have all reported positive effects when using nosodes in place of conventional vaccines. However, a recently conducted preliminary controlled trial failed to show effectiveness of parvo nosode protecting against a street virus challenge. For this reason, the routine recommendation of replacing vaccines with nosodes is controversial and not recommended by all holistic veterinarians. Owners who use nosodes as a replacement for conventional vaccinations may be required to sign a legal release indicating they understand the questionable effectiveness of nosodes as a replacement for vaccination.

Pets with chronic immune disorders (such as cancer, allergies, epilepsy, kidney disease, heart disease, liver disease, thyroid disease) may be at increased risk for further immune damage from the unecessary use of chemicals such as flea products, preservatives in most commercial pet foods, and vaccines. While controversial, most holistic doctors do not recommend ever administering vaccines to pets with any chronic, serious disorder, especially those involving the immune system. Pets with mild problems (such as well-controlled allergies) can probably be vaccinated safely. This is an individual decision, as many disorders seem to appear shortly after immunization, and chronic disorders may be exacerbated (such as more itching in allergic pets, more seizures in an epileptic pet) following immunization. While rare, pets in remission following a diagnosis of cancer have been known to relapse following immunization; as a rule, most doctors do not recommend ever revaccinating pets with cancer. Pets undergoing stress (illness) should not be immunized. Dogs and cats who have experienced vaccine reactions, as well as those whose closely related family members have a documented clinical illness following immunization should probably not be overvaccinated, and possibly not vaccinated at all. Pets undergoing anesthetic procedures should probably not be immunized in most cases.

The following recommendations seem prudent for pets who must receive vaccinations. This list is extrapolated from an article by P. Rivera in *Journal AHVMA*, titled, "Vaccinations and Vaccinosis."

Recommendations for Vaccination

- Only immunize healthy pets.
- Don't expose vaccinated pets to sick pets or unvaccinated pets for at least 2 to 3 weeks following immunization. (Shedding of viral particles can occur in the feces of pets vaccinated with modified-live viruses.)
- Consider the animal's lifestyle when deciding when to immunize and which vaccines to administer. (What diseases is the pet most likely to encounter considering its lifestyle?)
- Don't let vaccines substitute for proper medical care: good diet, supplements, prevention of disease via regular dental cleanings, and necessary laboratory testing.
- Don't vaccinate pregnant animals.
- Don't vaccinate animals during their estrus (heat) cycles.

PRINCIPAL NATURAL TREATMENTS

Treatment and/or prevention of vaccine reactions utilizing the homeopathic remedy **Thuja** or **lyssin** (see **Homeopathy**, page 394) may help counteract any potential negative effects of immunization that might be contributing to the pet's current disease. In place of conventional vaccines, homeopathic nosodes may provide protection (see warning). Pets at risk of vaccine reactions should have blood titers checked or possibly not be immunized.

Nosodes

For example, the distemper nosode is made from the distemper virus or secretions from a dog infected with distemper. A variety of nosodes are available, both for the treatment of infectious diseases and for vaccination against some of these diseases.

Other nosodes that have been used with success include bowel nosodes (useful in disorders that disturb the normal gastrointestinal bacterial flora), Morgan-Bach nosode (useful for disorders of the digestive and respiratory systems and in some skin disorders), Proteus-Bach nosode (for nervous system disorders), and the Gaertner-Bach nosode (useful in malnourished pets with gastrointestinal disorders and worms).

Many homeopathic physicians prefer to use nosodes in place of conventional vaccines as part of the annual immunization regimen. Vaccinations are somewhat homeopathic in the sense that they are made from altered infectious organisms, and are administered in a diluted form. By administering these infectious organisms, we attempt to stimulate the dog's immune system to prevent against infectious diseases.

There are several concerns with conventional vaccines. First, it appears that many dogs may not need vaccinations each year against every infectious organism. Some dogs may have immunity that lasts longer than one year after vaccination with some of our current vaccines. These dogs would not really benefit from an additional immunization until their immunity had waned.

Second, we know that conventional vaccinations do cause both short-term and long-term side effects. Some of these are relatively benign, such as mild swelling or pain after the vaccination. Other reactions can be more severe or even fatal, including inducing immune-mediated diseases, such as anemia and low platelet counts. In cats, we are now seeing vaccine-induced cancers. While these have not been reported in dogs yet, we are still right to be concerned about this side effect developing in vaccinated dogs in the future (for more about vaccinations, see the guide *Vaccination: What You Must Know Before You Vaccinate Your Dog*).

Homeopathic doctors therefore usually recommend the administration of homeopathic nosodes in place of conventional vaccines. Since the nosodes do not contain measurable amounts of infectious product, they are without any side effects.

Nosodes Versus Vaccines

But do nosodes work? Some doctors seem to prefer nosodes manufactured by specific homeopathic pharmacies, as they feel there is a definite difference in the ability of nosodes to stimulate the immune system. In their opinions, the manufacturer of the nosode is important and some vaccination nosodes work better than others.

Nosodes are supposed to work in the same manner as conventional vaccines, namely by stimulating antibodies to fight off infections. While not opposed to using vaccine nosodes, I do question how effective they might be when compared to conventional vaccination protocols.

One way to test whether they work is to subject them to the same testing vaccine companies use. After vaccinating a number of dogs with nosodes, these dogs should then be exposed to the infectious organisms to see if they become infected or remain protected. While this technique may be acceptable in the laboratory, owners would not want to subject their dogs to potentially fatal doses of infectious organisms just to see whether nosodes work.

There is another way to evaluate the ability of nosodes to work. First, run antibody titers to see whether the pet's immune system needs stimulation. If the titers are low, administer the nosode. After administering them to the dog, run antibody titers to see whether the nosodes have effectively stimulated the immune system. If the antibody titer is high, then the nosode has been effective. Otherwise, the nosode has failed to work properly.

In addition to or in place of homeopathic nosodes are topical vaccines. These vaccines may be administered orally or topically. In dogs, the kennel cough vaccine is a topical vaccine given intranasally. The benefit of this topical vaccine is that we stimulate the immune system topically, causing the formation of large amounts of local antibodies. Since the organisms causing kennel cough (parainfluenza virus and *Bordetella bronchiseptica* bacterium) enter via the nasal cavity, local immunity is probably preferred to systemic immunity that may occur with the injectable subcutaneous kennel cough vaccine. Another important benefit of topical vaccines is the reduced risk of side effects. While short-term sneezing may occur after intranasal administration, concerns over chronic systemic immune system stimulation are not usually warranted with intranasal vaccination. Additionally, the risk of accine-induced tumors (fibrosarcoma tumors, which may occur very rarely in cats and may become a problem in dogs in the future, but to date have not been reported in dogs) does not occur with topical vaccination.

This approach to running antibody titers is what I suggest as a new approach to our traditional practice of vaccinating dogs. Instead of routinely administering vaccines to dogs who may not need them and may suffer from their overuse, run antibody titers to see whether vaccinations are indicated.

I have not seen any conclusive studies showing that this approach of running titers, administering nosodes, and then doing follow-up titers to see if the nosodes were effective in stimulating the dog's antibodies really works. Therefore, it is hard for me to give an unconditional recommendation to using nosodes in place of conventional vaccines. Still, some doctors do believe nosodes can be effective in protecting the pet against infectious diseases. It may be that the nosodes, like conventional vaccines, also stimulate the cell-mediated part of the immune system. This part of the immune system is also important in protecting dogs against infectious diseases like parvovirus and distemper. It is very difficult to easily and inexpensively measure this part of the immune system. Still, if nosodes work by stimulating the cell-mediated immunity, they could still offer protection despite the fact that measurable antibody titers are not detected.

Owners must discuss this matter with their doctors. I feel uncomfortable with using nosodes in place of vaccines if no measurable titer is detected, although I have no problem using them annually when antibody titers are detected, as an extra measure of protection (without the side effects of vaccinations). For owners who are totally opposed to annual vaccinations, nosodes should be administered. Titers can be run following nosode administration to evaluate whether the nosode was effective in stimulating this part of the immune system.

CONVENTIONAL THERAPY

There is no conventional therapy for vaccinosis. For pets with acute (allergic) vaccine reactions, treatment with corticosteroids, antihistamines, and/or epinephrine is curative in most cases. Pets with vaccine reactions should ideally not be revaccinated in the future (especially those with severe allergic reactions). If for some reason the pet must be revaccinated, vaccines should be split (one shot now, one 3 weeks later), and pretreatment with low-dose corticosteroid and/or antihistamine should be used, along with the homeopathic remedy Thuja.

Herbs and Supplements

ALFALFA *(Medicago sativa)*

Common Uses

Allergies, arthritis, cognitive disorder, cancer, urinary disorders (acidic urine)

Alfalfa contains many nutrients (protein, vitamins, and minerals) and chlorophyll (which serves as an antioxidant).

THERAPEUTIC USES

Alfalfa is purported to be one of the best herbal therapies for arthritis.

Alfalfa possesses cancer-preventing properties by inactivating chemicals that can cause cancer.

The vitamin K content of alfalfa makes it valuable in pets with bleeding disorders. Conversely, excess doses might interfere with blood clotting due to the coumarin (an anticoagulant) content in alfalfa.

Alfalfa is often fed to animals who need to gain weight.

Alfalfa can make urine alkaline and is useful in those **bladder** conditions (page 36) where a more alkaline urine is needed (likewise, it should not be used in pets whose medical conditions require an acid urine).

Due to the large content of nutrients, many doctors recommend it for pets who require increased mental nutrition (older pets, especially those with cognitive disorder).

SAFETY ISSUES

Alfalfa is generally regarded safe. The seeds can cause blood disorders due to L-canavanine and should be avoided. Animals sensitive to pollen may be sensitive to fresh alfalfa.

ALOE VERA (Acemannan)

Common Uses

Allergies (topical and herbal rinse), diarrhea (juice), cancer, infections

Aloe is often used topically as a soothing rinse or topical preparation. Aloe contains a number of beneficial chemicals. The prostaglandins in aloe have beneficial effects on inflammation, allergy, and wound healing. While many would profess to appreciate the healing effect of aloe on wounds and burns, there have never been any properly designed scientific studies that can tell us just how effective aloe really is for these conditions.

Topical aloe gel may improve the rate of healing of minor cuts and scrapes, although one report suggests that aloe can actually impair healing in severe wounds.

THERAPEUTIC USES

Acemannan, a polysaccharide immune stimulant found in aloe vera, may be helpful for pets with **allergies** (page 3), skin infections, and other diseases (**feline leukemia** (page 82), **feline immunodeficiency virus infection** (page 76) that suppress the immune system.

Acemannan is approved for use as part of the therapy for treating fibrosarcoma tumors in pets. A further discussion of acemannan and other glycoproteins can be found under **Glycoproteins** (page 214).

Aloe has antibacterial and antifungal effects; the antibacterial effects have been compared to silver sulfadiazine.

In people, aloe has been used internally as a laxative or tonic (lower doses) for the gastrointestinal system.

Oral aloe vera is also sometimes recommended to treat AIDS, diabetes, asthma, stomach ulcers, and general immune weakness. While the evidence for benefit in these conditions is slight to nonexistent, one of the constituents of aloe, acemannan, does seem to possess numerous interesting effects. Test-tube and animal studies suggest that it may stimulate immunity and inhibit the growth of viruses. Aloe vera is definitely not a proven treatment for any of these conditions.

DOSAGES

Aloe is best used externally. Aloe extracts such as acemannan can be used as injectable medicines or externally.

SAFETY ISSUES

If used internally, aloe possesses strong purgative properties that can result in severe diarrhea due to the anthroquinones located in the latex skin. The juice, while bitter, can be used in small doses and is safer.

In pets, aloe should only be used externally without direct veterinary supervision; internal application can result in strong laxative effects due to its anthroquinone (aloin) content. Acemannan can be used safely internally.

Do not use in pregnant or lactating animals. In people, oral aloe is not recommended for those with severe liver or kidney disease; the same warning is probably justified in pets.

AMINOCAPROIC ACID (ACA)

Common Uses
Degenerative myelopathy

Like NAC, ACA is a medication that is often recommended by holistic veterinarians for dogs suffering from degenerative myelopathy.

THERAPEUTIC USES

Aminocaproic acid (page 60) works by inhibiting the process of fibrinolysis (the breakdown of fibrin, a protein needed for proper blood clotting) and can reverse states that are associated with excessive fibrinolysis. Degenerative myelopathy is theorized (but not proven) to be caused by an autoimmune response (possibly from overvaccinating dogs) attacking the nervous system of dogs, which leads to progressive neural tissue damage. Since this is an autoimmune response, immune complexes circulate in the blood, leading to endothelial cell damage in the blood vessels of the central nervous system. This causes fibrin to be deposited around blood vessels. When the fibrin degrades, inflammatory cells are stimulated to migrate into the lesions, which leads to tissue damage. While not proven, it is possible that aminocaproic acid may limit or stop this process.

DOSAGES

Aminocaproic acid is made in a 250mg/ml oral solution. This can be mixed with chicken broth, using 2 ml of the drug and 1 ml of chicken broth. The recommended dosage is 500 mg (3 ml of the above combination) given 3 times a day with or without food. Aminocaproic acid can be stored at room temperature with the lid tightly closed.

ANTINEOPLASTONS

Possible Use
  Tumors

These products are fractions of peptides derived from blood and urine. Early studies show some benefit in people with a variety of tumors. However, this is very preliminary research and more research is needed before any meaningful conclusions can be made.

ANTIOXIDANTS

Common Uses
  Anti-inflammatory, arthritis, allergies, asthma, cancer

Certain vitamins and minerals function in the body to reduce oxidation. Oxidation is a chemical process that occurs within the body's cells. After oxidation occurs, certain by-products such as peroxides and "free radicals" accumulate. These cellular by-products are toxic to the cells and surrounding tissue. The body removes these by-products by producing additional chemicals called antioxidants that combat these oxidizing chemicals.

THERAPEUTIC USES

In disease, excess oxidation can occur and the body's normal antioxidant abilities are overwhelmed. This is where supplying antioxidants can help. By giving your pet's body extra antioxidants, it may be possible to neutralize the harmful by-products of cellular oxidation.

SOURCES

There are several antioxidants that can be used to supplement pets. Most commonly, the antioxidant vitamins A, C, and E, and the minerals selenium, manganese, and zinc are prescribed. These are all found in Part Two, under their own individual listings. Other antioxidants, including superoxide dismutase, glutathione, cysteine,

Coenzyme Q_{10}, *Ginkgo biloba*, bilberry, grape seed extract, and pycnogenol may also be helpful for a number of disorders.

Proanthocyanidins

Also called pycnogenols or bioflavonoids, this class of water-soluble plant-coloring agents, which contain naturally occurring polyphenolic compounds, are found in plants (most often products containing proanthocyanidins are made from grape seed or pine bark). While they don't seem to be essential to life, it's likely that people and pets need them for optimal health. These compounds are used for their antioxidant effects against lipid (fat) peroxidation. Proanthocyanidins also inhibit the enzyme cyclooxygenase (the same enzyme inhibited by aspirin and other nonsteroidal medications); cyclooxygenase converts arachidonic acid into chemicals (leukotrienes and prostaglandins), which contribute to inflammation and allergic reactions. Proanthocyanidins also decrease histamine release from cells by inhibiting several enzymes.

The actions of the proanthocyanidins make them useful in treating pets with various inflammatory disorders including allergies, asthma, and arthritis.

Inhibiting enzymes involved in the destruction of collagen (callagenase, elastase, hyaluronidase) is a proposed mechanism of proanthocyanidins in the treatment of arthritis, in addition to the anti-inflammatory actions.

Proanthocyanidins, by augmenting the immune system (via enhancement of T-lymphocyte activity and modulation of neutrophil and macrophage responses), are often recommended for use in the treatment of pets with cancer.

Pycnogenol

This antioxidant is promoted as an anti-arthritis agent in people. Pycnogenol is a group of chemicals from the bark of pine trees native to southern France and is a mixture of bioflavonoids, which inhibit the prostaglandins that cause inflammation. (Bioflavonoids isolated from grape seed are also recommended for arthritic disorders for their anti-inflammatory effect.) In addition to its use in people to help control arthritis, it is also suggested for use in patients suffering from adult attention deficit disorder.

Some research suggests that pycnogenol seems to work by enhancing the effects of another antioxidant, vitamin C. Other research suggests that the bioflavonoids can work independently of other antioxidants; as is the case with many supplements, there probably is an additive effective when multiple antioxidants are combined. People taking pycnogenol often report feeling better and having more energy; this "side effect" may possibly occur in our pets as well.

Quercetin

Quercetin is a natural antioxidant bioflavonoid found in red wine, grapefruit, onions, apples, black tea, and, in lesser amounts, in leafy green vegetables and beans. Quercetin protects cells in the body from damage by free radicals and stabilizes collagen in blood vessels.

Another intriguing finding is that quercetin may help prevent immune cells from releasing histamine, the chemical that initiates the itching, sneezing, and swelling of an allergic reaction. Based on this very preliminary research, quercetin is often recommended as a treatment for allergies and asthma. This recommendation is based on test-tube research showing that quercetin prevents histamine release from mast cells (allergy cells). It also may block other substances involved with allergies, although there is no evidence so far

that taking quercetin supplements will reduce your pet's symptoms.

In people, quercetin may help protect against heart attacks and strokes.

Quercetin supplements are available in pill and tablet form. One problem with them, however, is that they don't seem to be well absorbed by the body. A special form called quercetin chalcone appears to be better absorbed. Test-tube and animal research also suggests that quercetin might be able to help prevent tumors in hamsters or enhance the effects of cancer-fighting drugs. An animal study found that quercetin might protect rodents with diabetes from forming cataracts. Another intriguing finding of test-tube research is that quercetin seems to prevent a wide range of viruses from infecting cells and reproducing once they are inside cells. One study found that quercetin produced this effect against herpes simplex, polio virus, flu virus, and respiratory viruses. However, none of this research tells us whether humans or pets taking quercetin supplements can hope for the same benefits. Much more research needs to be done on the use of quercetin for these conditions.

DOSAGES

In people, a typical dosage of proanthocyanidins is 200 to 400 mg 3 times daily. Quercetin may be better absorbed if taken on an empty stomach. The suggested dosage of proanthocyanidin complex in pets is 10 to 200 mg given daily (divided into 2 to 3 doses). The suggested dosage of bioflavonoid complex in pets is 200 to 1,500 mg per day (divided into 2 to 3 doses.) The actual dosage of each product will vary with the product and the pet's weight and disease condition.

SAFETY ISSUES

In general, antioxidants can be useful for a variety of conditions. Because some types of chemotherapy and radiation therapy may rely on cellular oxidation for their effects, antioxidants should not be used without veterinary supervision in pets with cancer undergoing chemotherapy or radiation therapy. For a greater discussion on the use of high doses of antioxidants in the therapy of various diseases in pets, called ortho-molecular medicine, see Part Four, Other Complementary Therapies.

Quercetin appears to be quite safe. Maximum safe dosages for young children, women who are pregnant or nursing, or those with serious liver or kidney disease have not been established; similar precautions are probably warranted in pets.

ARGININE

Common Uses
   Liver disease, heart disease, cancer

Arginine is an essential amino acid found in many foods. It plays a role in several biochemical processes in the body, including cell division, wound healing, immune functions, hormone secretion, and the removal of ammonia from the body. Arginine is also involved in the formation of nitric oxide which relaxes blood vessels.

THERAPEUTIC USES

Doses of of 500 to 3,000 mg per day are recommended.

SAFETY ISSUES

Since arginine is an amino acid, supplementation is believed to be safe. Maximum safe doses have not, however, been established.

ASTRAGALUS *(Astragalus membranaceus)*

Common Uses
   Cancer, infections, kidney disease, hyperthyroidism in cats

Astragalus is used to strengthen the immune system and acts as an anti-inflammatory.

THERAPEUTIC USES

Many doctors prescribe astragalus for pets with various infections and chronic illnesses, including **cancer** (page 44). In cats, it is often recommended for the treatment of hyperthyroidism.

Astragalus can be used to help the body recover from long-term steroid therapy and for pets with **kidney disease** (page 121), as this herb improves kidney circulation.

SAFETY ISSUES

The medicinal herb *Astragalus membranaceous* is safe; many other species are toxic. For hyper-immune disorders (autoimmune diseases, diabetes) and disorders with diminished immune systems with low white blood cell counts (feline leukemia and immunodeficiency diseases), it may be wise to avoid this herb, as astragalus is used for immune stimulation. It is best used early in the course of the disease to stimulate the immune system. Do not use to treat hypothyroidism.

BETA-CAROTENE

Common Uses
Nutritional supplement

Beta-carotene belongs to a family of natural chemicals known as carotenes or carotenoids. Scientists have identified nearly 600 different carotenes, including lycopene and lutein. Widely found in plants, carotenes (along with another group of chemicals, the bioflavonoids) give color to fruits, vegetables, and other plants.

Beta-carotene and vitamin A are sometimes described as if they were the same thing. This is because the dog's body converts beta-carotene into vitamin A. However, there are significant differences between the two.

THERAPEUTIC USES

Beta-carotene is a particularly important carotene from a nutritional standpoint, because the dog's body easily transforms it to vitamin A (cats lack the enzymes to do this and must be supplied with pre-formed vitamin A). While vitamin A supplements themselves can be toxic when taken to excess, if you give your dog beta-carotene, his body will make only as much vitamin A as needed.

Beta-carotene is also often recommended because it is an antioxidant like vitamins C and E. However, although there is a great deal of evidence in people that the carotenes (all of them, not just beta-carotene) found in food can provide a variety of health benefits (from reducing the risk of cancer to preventing heart disease), there is little to no evidence that high doses of purified beta-carotene supplements are good for you or your dog.

In people, beta-carotene has been suggested for the treatment of a number of disorders, including cancer prevention and treatment, heart disease prevention, and cataract prevention, but there is little to no evidence that it works. Other proposed uses include osteoarthritis, rheumatoid arthritis, asthma, depression, epilepsy, high blood pressure, and immunodeficiency conditions (AIDS in people).

SOURCES

For those owners who feed their pets homemade diets, or who supplement their pets' diets with raw or lightly steamed vegetables, dark green and orange-yellow vegetables are good sources of beta-carotene. These include carrots, sweet potatoes, squash, spinach, romaine lettuce, broccoli, apricots, and green peppers.

Note: All the significant positive evidence for beta-carotene applies to food sources, not supplements.

DOSAGES

While controversial, it is unknown at the present time whether it is advisable to take dosages of beta-carotene much higher than the recommended allowance for nutritional purposes. It is probably much better to feed dogs increased amounts of fresh vegetables and use whole food supplements (see Part Three, Diet, for a greater discussion of this controversy).

It is difficult to recommend beta-carotene supplements for any use other than to supply nutritional levels of vitamin A in dogs; many synthetic vitamins use beta-carotene rather than vitamin A to do this.

Evidence in people suggests that *mixed* carotenes found in food can protect against cancer and heart disease. However, supplements that contain only purified beta-carotene may actually be harmful (while whole food supplements that contain mixed carotenoids would not be harmful and can be helpful). It is unknown if this same evidence applies to pets.

Similarly, although mixed carotenes found in food seem to slow the progression of **cataracts** (page 53), pure beta-carotene alone does not seem to work. Dietary beta-carotene may also slow down the progression of **osteoarthritis** (page 11), but it is not known whether beta-carotene supplements work for this purpose.

SCIENTIFIC EVIDENCE

In people, the story of beta-carotene and cancer is full of contradictions. It starts in the early 1980s, when the cumulative results of many studies suggested that people who eat a lot of fruits and vegetables are significantly less likely to get cancer. A close look at the data pointed to carotenes as the active ingredients in fruits and vegetables. It appeared that a high intake of dietary carotene could dramatically reduce the risk of lung cancer, bladder cancer, breast cancer, esophageal cancer, and stomach cancer.

The next step was to give carotenes to people and see whether it made a difference. Researchers used purified beta-carotene instead of mixed carotenes, because it is much more readily available. They studied people in high-risk groups, such as smokers, because it is easier to see results when you look at people who are more likely to develop cancer to begin with. However, the results were surprisingly unfavorable.

The anticancer bubble burst for beta-carotene in 1994 when the results of the Alpha-Tocopherol, Beta-Carotene (ATBC) study came in. These results showed that beta-carotene supplements did not prevent lung cancer, but actually increased the risk of getting it by 18%. This trial had followed 29,133 male smokers in Finland who took supplements of 50 IU of vitamin E (alpha-tocopherol, which is actually only one of the tocopherols found in vitamin E but which is erroneously used synonymously with "vitamin E"), 20 mg of beta-carotene, both, or placebo daily for 5 to 8 years. (In contrast, vitamin E was found to reduce the risk of cancer, especially prostate cancer.)

In January 1996, researchers monitoring the Beta-Carotene and Retinol Efficacy Trial (CARET) confirmed the prior bad news with more of their own: The beta-carotene group had 46% more cases of lung cancer deaths. This study involved smokers, former smokers, and workers exposed to asbestos. Alarmed, the National Cancer Institute ended the $42 million CARET trial 21 months before it was planned to end.

At about the same time, the 12-year Physicians' Health Study of 22,000 male physicians was finding that 50 mg of beta-carotene taken every other day had no effect, good or bad, on the risk of cancer or heart disease. In this study, 11% of the participants were smokers and 39% were ex-smokers. Interestingly, higher levels of carotene intake *from the diet* were associated with lower levels of cancer.

What is the explanation for this apparent discrepancy? It could be that beta-carotene alone is not effective. The other carotenes found in fruits and vegetables may be more important for preventing cancer than beta-carotene. One researcher has suggested that taking beta-carotene supplements actually depletes the body of other beneficial carotenes.

The situation with beta-carotene and heart disease is rather similar to that of beta-carotene and cancer. Numerous studies suggest that carotenes as a whole can reduce the risk of heart disease. However, isolated beta-carotene may not help prevent heart disease and could actually increase the risk in people (and possibly pets, although the type of heart disease in people, coronary artery disease, is quite different from the various heart disorders, including valvular disease and cardiomyopathy, seen in pets).

The bottom line: As with cancer, the mixed carotenoids *found in foods* seem to be helpful for people with heart disease, but beta-carotene supplements do not.

A high dietary intake of beta-carotene appears to slow the progression of osteoarthritis by as much as 70%, according to a study in which researchers followed 640 individuals over a period of 8 to 10 years. However, again we don't know whether purified beta-carotene supplements work the same way as beta-carotene from food sources.

SAFETY ISSUES

At recommended dosages, beta-carotene is very safe in people and pets. The only side effects reported from beta-carotene overdose are diarrhea and a yellowish tinge to the skin and mucous membranes, which disappear once beta-carotene supplements are decreased or stopped.

This research on beta-carotene has not been reported in pets, since no studies have been done. While extrapolation from the human literature to the veterinary literature is not perfect and is not always applicable, until (and if) we ever have studies involving beta-carotene in dogs, it would be prudent to consider the research presented in people.

In light of this evidence, high-dose beta-carotene may slightly increase the risk of heart disease and cancer in people and possibly dogs (keep in mind that dogs do not routinely acquire the same type of heart disease reported in people). The solution: Feed your dogs fresh vegetables (as a top dressing to the regular diet) or use whole food supplements to obtain beta-carotene and other carotenoids found in food and the vitamin A complex.

The drug methotrexate (used in treating some cancers) and colchicine can impair beta-carotene absorption.

 # BETAINE HYDROCHLORIDE

Common Possible Uses
Anemia, asthma, diarrhea, allergies, heartburn

Betaine hydrochloride is a source of hydrochloric acid, a naturally occurring chemical in the stomach that helps digest food by breaking up fats and proteins. Stomach acid also aids in the absorption of nutrients through the walls of the intestines into the blood and protects the gastrointestinal tract from harmful bacteria. Betaine hydrochloride is not an essential nutrient, and no food sources exist.

A major branch of alternative medicine known as naturopathy has long held that low stomach acid is a widespread problem that interferes with digestion and the absorption of nutrients. Betaine hydrochloride is one of the most common recommendations for this condition (along with the more folksy apple cider vinegar).

Betaine is also sold by itself, without the hydrochloride molecule attached. In this form, it is called TMG (trimethylglycine). TMG is not acidic, but recent evidence in people suggests that it may provide certain health benefits of its own.

THERAPEUTIC USES

Based on theories about the importance of stomach acid, betaine has been recommended for a wide variety of problems, including anemia, asthma, diarrhea, excess intestinal yeast, food allergies, allergies, rheumatoid arthritis, and thyroid conditions. In people, other suggested uses include atherosclerosis, excess candida (yeast), gallstones, inner ear infections, gastrointestinal ulcers, and heartburn. Unfortunately, there is as yet no real scientific research on its effectiveness for any of these conditions.

SAFETY ISSUES

Betaine hydrochloride should not be given to pets with ulcers. Betaine seldom causes any obvious side effects, but it has not been put through rigorous safety studies. In particular, safety for young children, pregnant or nursing women, or those with severe liver or kidney disease has not been established; similar precautions are probably warranted in pets.

BILBERRY *(Vaccinium myrtillus)*

Common Uses
Diabetes, eye diseases

Bilberry, related to the blueberry, came to popularity during World War II, when British Royal Air Force pilots reported that eating bilberry jam improved their night vision.

THERAPEUTIC USES

Bilberry is most commonly taken internally in people to help with disorders of the eyes, including macular degeneration and cataract formation due to its antioxidant effects. Its flavonoid compounds (anthocyanosides) are the most pharmacologically active. These flavonoids have several effects, including collagen stabilization (due to their vitamin C content), which may make them useful for pets with arthritis. Other effects include improved capillary strength (once again due to vitamin C), decreased platelet clumping, lowering of blood sugar (making it potentially useful for diabetic pets), and protective effects against gastric ulcers (due to increased mucus production). Bilberry's anthocyanosides have a special attraction to the retina, which may explain this herb's apparent usefulness in eye diseases.

Bilberry is used throughout Europe today for the treatment of poor night vision and day blindness in people. Regular use of bilberry is also thought to help prevent or treat other eye diseases such as macular regeneration, diabetic retinopathy, and cataracts.

European physicians additionally believe that bilberry's blood vessel stabilizing properties also make it useful as a treatment before surgery to reduce bleeding complications, as well as for other blood vessel problems such as easy bruising, but the evidence as yet is only suggestive. On the basis of very limited evidence, bilberry has also been suggested as a treatment for improving blood sugar control in people with diabetes, as well as for reducing the risk of atherosclerosis.

Bilberry can be tried in pets with **cataracts** (page 53) (combining it with other antioxidants including vitamin E), **arthritis** (page 21), ulcers, and **diabetes** (page 66) (if not yet on hypoglycemic therapy).

SAFETY ISSUES

Bilberry is a food and as such is quite safe. Do not use in pets on hypoglycemic therapy without veterinary supervision. In people, rare side effects such as mild digestive distress, skin rashes, and drowsiness can be seen. Safety in patients with severe liver or kidney disease is not known. There are no known drug interactions.

Bilberry does not appear to interfere with blood clotting.

BIOTIN (Biocytin, brewer's yeast)

Common Uses
Healthy skin and hair coat

Possible Use
Diabetes

Biotin is a water-soluble B vitamin that plays an important role in metabolizing energy. Biotin also acts by assisting four essential enzymes that metabolize down fats, carbohydrates, and proteins.

Biotin aids in cell growth, fatty acid production, and in the utilization of other B vitamins and proteins. Biotin is needed for healthy skin and hair, and helps relieve muscle pain. Raw egg whites contain avidin, a protein that binds to biotin in the intestines and causes biotin deficiency. This can be avoided by not feeding raw egg whites to pets in large quantities for extended periods of time. Cooked egg whites are safe as the cooking inactivates the avidin.

THERAPEUTIC USES

Extra biotin (as well as the other B vitamins) may be needed in pets on chronic antibiotic therapy.

Preliminary evidence suggests that supplemental biotin can help reduce blood sugar levels in people with either type I (childhood-onset) or type II (adult-onset) diabetes. Biotin may also reduce the symptoms of diabetic neuropathy.

Weak evidence suggests that biotin supplements can promote healthy nails and eliminate cradle cap in infants.

Although biotin is a necessary nutrient, pets usually get about one-half of their daily requirement from bacteria living in the digestive tract. Actual biotin deficiency is uncommon, except in the case of ingestions of large quantities of raw egg white.

SOURCES

Good dietary sources of biotin include brewer's yeast, nutritional (torula) yeast, whole grains, nuts, egg yolks, meat, milk, poultry, soybeans, sardines, saltwater fish, legumes, liver, cauliflower, bananas, and mushrooms.

SAFETY ISSUES

Biotin appears to be quite safe.

 # BLACK AND GREEN TEA *(Camellia sinensis)*

Common Uses
Cancer prevention

Both black and green tea are made from the same plant. The highest quality teas are derived from the young shoots comprising the first two or three leaves plus the growing bud; poorer quality teas are made from leaves located farther down the stems. Green tea is preferred as more of the active substances (catechins) remain in the less-processed green form. Green tea contains high levels of substances called polyphenols (catechins) known to possess strong antioxidant, anticarcinogenic, and even antibiotic properties. The four major green tea catechins are epicatechin, epigallocatechin, epicatechin gallate, and epigallocatechin gallate (EGCg), the most potent and physiologically active antioxidant of the four catechins. A typical cup of green tea contains between 300 and 400 mg of polyphenols, of which 10 to 30 mg is EGCg.

THERAPEUTIC USES

Black tea contains theoflavins and theorubigins, which also inhibit cancer-promoting agents, and protect against oxidative damage.

A growing body of evidence in both human and animal studies suggests that regular consumption of green tea can reduce the incidence of a variety of cancers, including colon, pancreatic, and stomach cancers. Cancer inhibition seems to be related to anti-tumor activity by inhibiting urokinase (uPA, an enzyme used by human cancers to invade cells and spread), inhibiting angiogenesis (the formation of new blood vessels used by cancers to grow and spread), and possibly by inhibiting vascular endothelial growth factor, inhibition of an NADH oxidase known as quinol oxidase or NOX (NOX activity is needed for growth of normal cells, and an overactive form of NOX called tNOX allows tumor cells to grow; EGCc inhibits tNOX but not NOX).

Also, giving green tea with the chemotherapy drug doxorubicin decreased heart toxicity often seen with doxorubicin administration (by decreasing doxorubicin concentration in the heart cells) and increased doxorubicin concentration in cancer cells.

Green tea has also been shown to maintain white blood cell counts in human patients undergoing radiation or chemotherapy.

Other proposed benefits of green tea include: reduced cholesterol and triglycerides, arterial relaxation (via an increase in nitric oxide and intracellular calcium), inhibition of platelet clumping (via the amino acid theanne in the tea, which inhibits thromboxane), immune enhancement (by increased production of B-cells), treating infections (by inhibiting bacterial enzymes and inhibiting viral absorption onto cell membranes), possible lower blood sugar in diabetic pets (although one study has made the assertion that regular consumption of tea by children increases their development of diabetes), antioxidant activity (increased levels of seroxide dismutase in the blood and increased activity of glutathione S-transferase and catalase in the liver), liver protection, and kidney protection.

SCIENTIFIC EVIDENCE

While the observational preclinical studies used to draw these conclusions (both experimental laboratory testing in lab animals and in vitro studies) support the health benefits of tea (especially green tea), studies in people have been misleading and do not always show consistent results. Epidemiological studies have turned up both positive and negative results on the health benefits of green tea; not everyone who examines the data concludes that green tea has been proven effective. However, most doctors feel that there are health benefits to the use of green tea despite the inconclusive clinical studies.

Studies suggest that people drinking 3 cups of green tea daily have increased protection against cancer. The typical consumption of green tea in the average Japanese tea drinker is 10 cups per day (1,000 mg of EGCg/day). However, because not everyone wants to take the time to drink green tea, manufacturers have offered extracts that can be taken in pill form. A typical dosage is 100 to 150 mg 3 times daily of a green tea extract standardized to contain 80% total polyphenols and 50% epigallocatechin gallate. Whether these extracts work as well as the real thing remains unknown, although some studies have shown effectiveness. Since pets will not drink this much tea each day, and it is unknown whether the extracts are effective, the use of green tea in pets to prevent cancer is speculative at best and remains to be seen. Black tea applied topically appears to soothe discomfort in the mouth that is associated with radiation-induced damage (radiation mucositis). Applying black or green tea to pets with gingivitis or oral ulcerations may be soothing. Because the results of most tests appear encouraging, many veterinarians are supportive of the use of green tea for pets with a variety of medical disorders, especially cancers.

SAFETY ISSUES

Black and green tea are generally regarded as safe. Green tea does contain caffeine, although at a lower level than black tea or coffee, and can therefore cause insomnia, nervousness, and the other well-known symptoms of excess caffeine intake. Due to the potential for platelet inhibition and increased bleeding, pets taking anticoagulant medications such as aspirin must be monitored carefully for bleeding. EGCg has provoked asthmatic attacks in a small number of asthmatic patients working in a tea factory. Tea has a low sodium but high potassium content; pets with elevated potassium levels (end-stage kidney failure) should not take green tea. Green tea should not be given to infants and young children as it may cause iron metabolism problems and microcytic anemia; similar precautions probably apply in pets.

For pets taking MAO inhibitors, the caffeine in green tea could cause serious problems.

BLACK WALNUT (*Juglans nigra*)

Common Uses
Intestinal parasites (potential toxicity)

The hulls of black walnut are recommended for use as a deworming agent in pets. The active ingredients are purported to be tannins and alkaloids.

THERAPEUTIC USES

Black walnut has been used to treat dogs and cats with tapeworms.

There have been anecdotal reports of black walnut being effective against heartworms. However, there is no proof of this nor any controlled studies backing up this claim. Some experienced holistic veterinarians use black walnut to first "weaken" the heartworms to make conventional therapy more effective, but once again controlled studies are lacking to support this claim. Heartworm prevention is preferred to treatment.

If your doctor is skilled at using black walnut, it can be used in an attempt to rid the pet of heartworms; however, in most if not all cases conventional therapy (perhaps also using herbs such as milk thistle to support the liver and other supplements to strengthen the heart) will need to be administered.

SAFETY ISSUES

Black walnut is usually considered to be too toxic to use without veterinary supervision. There are reports of toxicity due to fungal contamination. The tannins and alkaloids may lead to vomiting and diarrhea. Most conventional dewormers (and other herbal deworming preparations) are much safer

 # BORAGE (*Borago offinalis*)

Common Uses
Adrenal, Addison's disease, Cushing's disease

Borage is a plant with vivid, star-shaped flowers that are usually bright blue.

THERAPEUTIC USES

Borage oil (from the seeds), leaves, and flowers may be used as herbal supplements. Borage is often recommended as an adrenal gland stimulant. While not as powerful as licorice, it is often tried in cases of mild adrenal gland dysfunction (both in **Addison's disease** (page 2) and in cases of extended corticosteroid usage where there is temporary adrenal gland exhaustion). Borage may also be useful as an expectorant in patients with productive bronchitis, and as a mild diuretic. Applied topically, borage can act as an astringent and anti-inflammatory agent. The fatty acid content may help decrease blood cholesterol, blood pressure, and aid in the treatment of cardiovascular disorders. However, GLA, an omega-6 fatty acid, is found in high amounts in borage. Since omega-6 fatty acids are pro-inflammatory compounds, supplementation with omega-3 fatty acids such as those found in fish oil may be preferred for the treatment of medical disorders (see **Oral Fatty Acids,** page 246).

SAFETY ISSUES

Borage leaves contain small amounts of compounds (alkaloids) that can be toxic to the liver; therefore, borage should not be used in pets with liver disease or in pregnant animals. Use of large amounts of borage, or prolonged ingestion of large amounts should be avoided.

BORON

Common Uses
   Arthritis

Boron seems to assist in the proper absorption of calcium, magnesium, and phosphorus from foods, and slows the loss of these minerals through urination.

THERAPEUTIC USES

In people, boron is recommended for the therapy of osteoarthritis, osteoporosis, and rheumatoid arthritis, although the evidence is weak for its effectiveness. Boron may speed up the burning of calories in people.

In pets, supplements for **osteoarthritis** (page 11) and **obesity** (page 133) may contain boron, although as with people good studies are lacking showing its effectiveness.

SOURCES

Good sources of include leafy vegetables, raisins, prunes, nuts, non-citrus fruits, and grains.

SAFETY ISSUES

Boron is considered to be fairly safe unless used at extremely high doses.

BOSWELLIA *(Boswellia serrata)*

Common Uses
   Arthritis, asthma, infections (ulcerative colitis), liver disease

Investigations of boswellia have shown that the herb contains certain substances known as boswellic acids, which appear to possess anti-inflammatory properties. Studies have shown the anti-inflammatory effects are comparable to phenylbutazone and other nonsteroidal medications. The anti-inflammatory action may be due to inhibition of leukotrienes, potent products similar to prostaglandins.

THERAPEUTIC USES

In addition to its use for its anti-inflammatory properties, other preliminary research suggests that boswellia may improve the biochemical structure of cartilage by prolonging the half-life of glycosaminoglycans in the cartilage.

The resin was found to be effective in people with ulcerative colitis (mimicking the action of sulfasalazine, an antibiotic often prescribed to treat this disorder).

In pets, boswellia is often recommended for rheumatoid arthritis, **osteoarthritis** (page 11), **liver disease** (page 127), **asthma** (page 21), and **diarrhea** (page 71).

SCIENTIFIC EVIDENCE

In two studies in people with rheumatoid arthritis, one study found benefit in those taking boswellia and another study found no benefit.

The conclusion was that while boswellia might be helpful, more research is needed. There has not been any formal study of boswellia's effectiveness in osteoarthritis.

SAFETY ISSUES

Boswellia can cause diarrhea, skin inflammation, and nausea in people (and possibly in pets). Boswellia should not be used in conjunction with nonsteroidal medications, in pregnant animals, or those with severe liver or kidney disease.

 # BOVINE CARTILAGE (See Also Glycosaminoglycans)

Common Uses
  Arthritis

Bovine cartilage, derived from the trachea (windpipe) of cattle, is often recommended for the treatment of arthritis in pets.

THERAPEUTIC USES

Bovine cartilage has proved useful in relieving pain and inflammation in human patients with osteoarthritis and rheumatoid arthritis; increased joint mobility was also noted. In dogs treated with bovine cartilage, good results were seen in the treatment of degenerative disk disease and some spinal disorders. Like shark cartilage, bo-

vine cartilage is high in glycosaminoglycans, which can help the body repair damaged joints. Since shark cartilage was found to be 1,000 times more effective in preventing new blood vessel growth, it has replaced bovine cartilage as a favored cartilage product (see the discussion under **Shark Cartilage,** page 271).

DOSAGES

The recommended dose of bovine cartilage is 200 mg/25 pounds of body weight.

 # BROMELAIN (See Enzymes)

Bromelain

BUGLEWEED *(Lycopus virginicus)*

Common Uses
Diuretic, heart conditions, hyperthyroidism in cats

Bugleweed is native to North America and is from the mint family. It is closely related to gypsyweed (*L. europaeus*).

THERAPEUTIC USES

Bugleweed may be useful for cats with mild **hyperthyroidism** (page 101). Frequent doses of the herbal extract must be given for several days before any result may be detected.

Like digitalis, bugleweed can be helpful in heart conditions in which the heart's contractions should be strengthened and the rate (pulse) de-creased. Bugleweed can also act as a diuretic and remove excess fluid from the lungs, as might occur in congestive heart failure.

Bugleweed can be useful for pain relief; it does not contain salicylic acid so it can be used safely in cats.

SAFETY ISSUES

Bugleweed is considered safe but should not be used in pregnant or nursing animals as it can constrict blood vessels and may have hormonal properties. Do not use in pets with hypothyroidism.

BURDOCK ROOT *(Arctium lappa, Arctim minor)*

Common Uses
Allergies, diabetes, diuretic, fleas (oral), cancer, kidney disease, liver disease

Burdock is an herb well-known for its cleansing properties as well as diuretic effects.

THERAPEUTIC USES

Burdock is also a good herb for use as a liver tonic. It is also known for its effects in any skin condition with oiliness, flakiness, and inflammation. Its diuretic action removes toxins and wastes from the body. This herb is useful in any situation in which toxins have built up and need to be eliminated from the body, including pets eating low-quality processed foods.

Burdock has been shown to contain chemicals that remove environmental toxins from the body, acting as an antioxidant to remove harmful free radicals from the body. This action has also led burdock to be used in the treatment of cancer. Burdock was also a primary ingredient in the fa-mous (or infamous) **Hoxsey cancer treatment** (page 226).

Harry Hoxsey was a former coal miner who parlayed a traditional family remedy for cancer into the largest privately owned cancer treatment center in the world, with branches in 17 states. It was shut down in the 1950s by the FDA. Harry Hoxsey himself subsequently died of cancer. Other herbs in his formula included red clover, poke, prickly ash, bloodroot, and barberry. Burdock is also found in the famous herbal cancer remedy Essiac. Despite this historical enthusiasm, there is no significant evidence that burdock is an effective treatment for cancer or any other illness.

While burdock has been recommended for these various conditions, unfortunately there is as yet no real scientific evidence for any of these uses.

SAFETY ISSUES

As a food commonly eaten in Japan (it is often found in sukiyaki), burdock root is believed to be safe. However, in 1978, the *Journal of the American Medical Association* caused a brief scare by publishing a report of burdock poisoning. Subsequent investigation showed that the herbal product involved was actually contaminated with the poisonous chemical atropine from an unknown source.

Burdock is extremely safe and can be fed to most pets on a long-term basis. Safety in young children, pregnant or nursing women, or those with severe liver or kidney disease is not established; similar precautions are warranted in pets.

If your pet is taking insulin, it is possible that burdock will increase its effect.

CALCIUM

Common Uses
Nutritional supplement with drug therapy or homemade diets

Calcium is the most abundant mineral in the body, making up nearly 2% of the pet's total body weight. More than 99% of the calcium in the body is found in bones. Calcium is primarily used as a structural component of bones and teeth and also as a messenger that enables cells to respond to hormones and nerve transmitting chemicals. Many enzymes depend on calcium in order to work properly, as do the nerves, heart, and blood-clotting mechanisms. Calcium is absorbed from the diet in the intestinal tract under vitamin D regulation.

In people, supplemental calcium is most commonly prescribed for the treatment of osteoporosis and premenstrual syndrome (PMS). Other uses include colon polyps and cancer prevention, hypertension (high blood pressure), high cholesterol, preeclampsia, attention deficit disorder, migraine headaches, and periodontal disease. Calcium seems to work best when combined with vitamin D.

Supplemental calcium is available in a number of forms, including calcium carbonate, dolomite, oyster shell calcium, bonemeal, calcium citrate, calcium citrate malate, tricalcium phosphate, calcium lactate, calcium gluconate, calcium aspartate, calcium orotate, and calcium chelate. Calcium bicarbonate is the only form of calcium that can be ionized in the blood, but calcium bicarbonate is not stable when synthetically produced.

Calcium lactate is most easily converted in the body to calcium bicarbonate, and as a result it is the form preferred by many doctors. Recent studies have shown that calcium citrate is better absorbed than calcium carbonate and some other forms of calcium.

SOURCES

Milk (or soy milk fortified with calcium), cheese, and other dairy products are excellent sources of calcium. Other sources of calcium include orange juice, fish canned with its bones (for example, sardines), dark green vegetables, nuts and seeds, and calcium-processed tofu.

Most pets get their calcium from bones in the diet or supplements added to the diet.

If calcium supplements are prescribed (as they are with the homemade diets listed in Part Three, which one is "best"? There is no real good answer to that.

Natural forms of supplements often come from bones, shells, or the earth (bonemeal, oyster shell, and dolomite). Bonemeal is often heated. See Part Three on Diet.

However, there are concerns that the natural forms of calcium supplements may contain significant amounts of lead. The lead concentration should always be less than 2 parts per million, although this is not often listed on the label.

Calcium carbonate is one of the least expensive forms of calcium, but it can cause constipation and bloating. Feeding it to the pet with meals improves absorption, because stomach acid is released to digest the food. Studies indicate calcium carbonate is not as well absorbed as calcium citrate.

Chelated calcium is calcium bound to an organic acid (citrate, citrate malate, lactate, gluconate, aspartate, or orotate). The chelated forms of calcium offer some significant advantages and disadvantages compared with calcium carbonate.

One advantage is that chelated forms are well absorbed regardless of stomach acid. A disadvantage is that chelated calcium is often more expensive than calcium carbonate.

Furthermore, calcium may interfere with the absorption of chromium, iron, manganese, and magnesium. If these supplements are prescribed, it is best to administer them to the pet at a different time from when you administer the calcium supplement.

THERAPEUTIC USES

Low blood calcium (hypocalcemia) can occur in pets eating an all-meat diet (meat is low in calcium; meat diets should be supplemented with bones or calcium supplements). The disease seen with low blood calcium as a result of improper diet is called nutritional secondary hyperparathyroidism. The condition is very rare in dogs and cats (except in those eating all meat, non-supplemented diets) and quite common in pet reptiles and birds (who are often fed the incorrect diet.) Correcting the diet cures the disorder.

Dogs and cats with kidney failure can also develop a form of hypocalcemia called renal secondary hyperparathyroidism; calcium supplementation and/or efforts to lower blood phosphorus levels are indicated, as kidney failure cannot be cured.

Hypocalcemia also may occur in pets (predominantly small breed dogs) immediately before or shortly after giving birth (postpartum hypocalcemia). Intravenous calcium supplementation corrects the seizures seen in pets suffering from this disorder.

Pets suffering from pancreatitis may also show low blood calcium.

High blood calcium (hypercalcemia) most commonly is seen in dogs and cats suffering from poisoning with vitamin D rodenticides (rodent poisons) or with cancers, especially lymphosarcoma and anal sac adenocarcinoma. High blood calcium levels in an otherwise normal pet should prompt the doctor to look for undiscovered cancers).

DOSAGES

The Association of American Feed Control Officials (AAFCO) recommendation is 320 mg/kg of body weight per day (puppies), 119 mg/kg of body weight per day (dogs), 400 mg/kg of body weight per day (kittens), and 128 mg/kg of body weight per day (cats).

SAFETY ISSUES

In general, mild calcium supplementation is safe but is not necessary for most pets unless there are medical reasons to recommend supplementation (or unless the owner prepares the pet's diet at home).

However, excess supplementation with calcium has been linked to skeletal problems (osteochondrosis) in large breed growing puppies.

Pets with cancer or parathyroid gland problems (hyperparathyroidism) should not receive calcium supplementation without veterinary supervision.

Extra calcium supplementation should also generally be avoided in pets with kidney or bladder stones composed of calcium oxalate crystals.

People taking corticosteroids, colchicine, isoniazid (INH), long-term sulfa antibiotics, heparin, aluminum hydroxide, digoxin, methotrexate, dilantin (phenytoin), or phenobarbital may need more calcium. This may also apply to pets, although additional calcium supplementation is usually not prescribed.

Pets taking antibiotics in the tetracycline or quinolone (such as enrofloxacin, brand name Baytril) family should take prescribed calcium at a different time of day because calcium interferes with the medications' absorption.

Pets taking thiazide diuretics, calcium-channel blockers, or atenolol should not receive extra calcium except under veterinary supervision.

Pets taking antacids (such as Zantac, active ingredient ranitidine, or Prilosec, active ingredient omeprazole) may not be able to absorb calcium carbonate well and should receive a different type of calcium supplement.

 # CALENDULA *(Calendula officinalis)*

Common Uses
Allergies (herbal rinse) diarrhea, diabetes

Calendula, also called the pot marigold, is an herb related to the sunflower.

THERAPEUTIC USES

It is useful as an anti-inflammatory herb and for its antibacterial and antifungal properties. The various oils in the flowers (including essential oils and flavonoids) assist in cell healing and decrease bacteria and fungi in the wounded part. Diluted calendula is often recommended for **ear infections** (page 72), eye infections, and topical treatment of minor wounds. It may also be helpful topically for pets with **ringworm** (page 144). Internally, calendula can treat inflammation and infection of the digestive and urinary systems.

SAFETY ISSUES

Calendula may induce abortions and should be avoided in pregnant animals. Calendula contains a small amount of salicylate in the leaves and stems. While unlikely to be harmful due to the small amount of salicylate, to be safe for long-term use, it should only be used internally under veterinary supervision in cats.

 # CANADIAN FLEABANE

Common Uses
Fleas (topical)

The fleabane plant has been used as an insecticide. It contains limonene, a compound that has shown effectivess in killing fleas.

SAFETY ISSUES

While limonene (d-limonene) is usually safe in pets, little information is available about the safety of fleabane. It is highly allergenic and may cause upper respiratory irritation.

CAPSAICIN (Cayenne, Capsicum)

Common Uses
  Arthritis (topical)

Capsaicin is the chemical that produces the hot sensation in peppers.

THERAPEUTIC USES

Capsaicin is incorporated into topical creams that are quite popular with people. It has shown effectiveness when rubbed onto sore joints of people with osteoarthritis or rheumatoid arthritis. Capsaicin first stimulates but then blocks small pain fibers by depleting them of the nerve transmitter called substance P. In people, the only side effect from topical application is the warm sensation felt when the cream is applied.

While they might be effective, capsaicin creams are unlikely to be of much use in pets due to the amount of hair covering the skin. Additionally, it is possible that the cream used for people might be too uncomfortable for pets. And finally, unless bandaged, it is unlikely that the cream would have much contact with the pet's skin as pets are likely to lick off the cream, especially if there is any discomfort (burning sensation) associated with the cream.

Cayenne contains carotenes which act as antioxidants when given orally. Since capsaicin can open blocked blood vessels, its use can be considered (although not yet reported) as part of the therapy of cats with embolization secondary to cardiomyopathy. It may be included in herbal therapies for pets with **heart disease** (page 91), as it has been reported to strengthen the heart and blood vessels and reduces platelet clumping (blood clotting).

In people, cayenne pepper taken internally has recently been widely touted as a treatment for heart disease by those who have found it useful for themselves or others, but there is no scientific evidence that it is effective. However, a small amount of evidence suggests that oral use of cayenne can protect your stomach against damage caused by anti-inflammatory drugs; similar benefit may or may not occur in pets.

Capsaicin powder (or cayenne) can be applied to minor wounds (including nails trimmed too close) to stop bleeding.

SAFETY ISSUES

Cayenne can be irritating to mucous membranes; avoid use in animals with sensitive skin. Animals with sensitive digestive or urinary system disorders, as well as pregnant animals, should not be given cayenne orally.

Contrary to some reports, cayenne does not appear to aggravate stomach ulcers and may in fact offer protection against ulcers caused by corticosteroids and nonsteroidal anti-inflammatory medications.

In people taking the asthma drug theophylline, cayenne might increase the amount absorbed, possibly leading to toxic levels. Oral cayenne may increase the effect of sedative drugs. These same warnings may also apply to pets.

CARNITINE (L-carnitine, L-acetyl-carnitine, L-propionyl-carnitine)

Common Uses
Nutritional supplement

Carnitine is an amino acid the body uses to turn fat into energy. Specifically, carnitine is required for transporting long-chain, fatty acids into the cells, which is essential to the conversion of fatty acids into energy for the cells, especially heart muscle cells. It is not normally considered an essential nutrient because the body can manufacture all it needs in the liver from lysine, methionine, and vitamins C, B$_1$, and B$_6$. However, supplemental carnitine may improve the ability of certain tissues to produce energy. This effect has led to the use of carnitine in various muscle diseases as well as heart conditions, as carnitine accumulates in both skeletal and cardiac muscle. There is no dietary requirement for carnitine. However, a few individuals have a genetic defect that hinders the body's ability to make carnitine. In dogs, a subset of pets with dilated cardiomyopathy that show variable response to carnitine supplementation has been identified (this was first shown in Boxers).

In addition, diseases of the liver, kidneys, or brain may inhibit carnitine production. Heart muscle tissue, because of its high energy requirements, is particularly vulnerable to carnitine deficiency.

SOURCES

The principal dietary sources of carnitine are meat and dairy products, but to obtain therapeutic dosages a supplement is necessary. The main disadvantage of carnitine supplementation is the cost, approximately $75 per month.

THERAPEUTIC USES

Carnitine is primarily used for heart-related conditions. Without adequate carnitine to transport fatty acids into heart muscle cells, reduced levels of energy are available to the heart.

Carnitine supplementation has also been suggested for pets with other heart diseases, including endocardiosis (**valvular heart disease** (page 91)), ischemic heart disease, and **congestive heart failure** (page 91). Definitive proof is lacking, although carnitine supplementation is safe and can be tried for pets with these other cardiac disorders under veterinary supervision. In addition to helping the heart muscle, supplementing with carnitine may improve appetite and overall performance.

Current benefits and recommendations regarding carnitine supplementation for dogs with heart disease include:

- Since true carnitine deficiency may exist in a small number of dogs such as Boxers with dilated cardiomyopathy, supplementation with L-carnitine may be of benefit in these pets.
- In some dogs with dilated cardiomyopathy (approximately the 40% who have myocardial carnitine deficiency), supplementation may improve clinical signs and cause some improvement in the echocardiograms of these patients.
- Supplementation with L-carnitine may improve survival in some dogs with dilated cardiomyopathy, especially those that have myocardial carnitine deficiency.

SCIENTIFIC EVIDENCE

In people, fairly good evidence suggests that it can be used along with conventional treatment for angina or chest pain, to improve symptoms and reduce medication needs. When combined with conventional therapy, it may also reduce mortality after a heart attack. A few studies suggest that carnitine may be useful for cardiomyopathy.

Several small studies in people have found that carnitine, often in the form of L-propionyl-carnitine, can improve symptoms of congestive heart failure. There is better evidence for Coenzyme Q_{10} for this condition (in fact some veterinarians may prescribe both supplements for pets with various heart conditions, including heart failure).

In people, carnitine may help reduce the chance of death after a heart attack. In a 12-month, placebo-controlled study, 160 individuals who had experienced a heart attack received 4 g of L-carnitine daily, or placebo, in addition to other conventional medication. The mortality rate in the treated group was significantly lower than in the placebo group: 1.2% versus 12.5% respectively. There were also improvements in heart rate, blood pressure, angina (chest pain), and blood lipids. A larger double-blind study of 472 people found that carnitine may improve the chances of survival if given within 24 hours after a heart attack. As a rule, pets do not experience "heart attacks" as people do. Pets can experience sudden onset of congestive heart failure due to valvular disease or cardiomyopathy. Whether or not administering carnitine following an acute episode improves survival is unknown.

Evidence also suggests that one particular form of carnitine, L-acetyl-carnitine, may be helpful in Alzheimer's disease, although a more recent larger study found no benefit. Dogs and cats do not get true Alzheimer's disease, but instead suffer from cognitive disorder (what many owners mistakenly refer to as "senility"). Whether or not L-acetyl-carnitine may be helpful for pets with cognitive disorder is unknown at this point.

Weak evidence in people suggests that carnitine may be able to improve cholesterol and triglyceride levels. In people, carnitine is recommended at 500 mg per day to reduce fat deposits. Research is needed to determine whether this recommendation would be of benefit to overweight pets.

In carnitine deficiency, increased blood trigylceride levels can occur.

In pets, heart levels (myocardial levels) of carnitine have been found to be low in up to 40% of dogs suffering with dilated cardiomyopathy. Diagnosing carnitine deficiency is difficult, as blood levels do not correlate with levels in heart muscle cells (although low plasma carnitine levels appear to be predictive of low mycardial carnitine concentration). Researchers must do heart muscle biopsies in order to determine myocardial carnitine deficiency. If the heart is unable to concentrate carnitine, levels can fall quite low despite normal blood levels. Studies show that only 20% of dogs with dilated cardiomyopathy and myocardial deficiency also had low blood levels of carnitine. Most dogs with myocardial carnitine deficiency and dilated cardiomyopathy suffer from a membrane transport defect that prevents adequate levels of carnitine moving from the blood into the heart muscle cells (in these pets, blood levels of carnitine are usually normal or higher than normal).

DOSAGES

The dosage recommended for dogs with myocardial carnitine deficiency and dilated cardiomyopathy is 50 mg/kg 3 times daily, or alternatively 2,000 mg per pet 3 times daily. Rare side effects include diarrhea and flatulence (intestinal gas). Improved heart function, appetite, and exercise tolerance are often noted within 2 months following supplementation in some dogs.

SAFETY ISSUES

While carnitine deficiency is not the cause of dilated cardiomyopathy in most dogs, supplementation is safe and can be used as an adjunct to other therapies.

While cats do not typically have carnitine deficiencies as a cause of their cardiomyopathies, carnitine can be used in cats with heart disorders although it is not known if supplementation would be of benefit. Carnitine may also be helpful for cats (and dogs) with hepatic lipidosis (fatty liver disease) at 25 to 50 mg/kg 3 times daily.

L-carnitine in its three forms appears to be safe, even when taken with medications. People are advised not to use forms of carnitine known as "D-carnitine" or "DL-carnitine," as these can cause angina, muscle pain, and loss of muscle function (probably by interfering with L-carnitine). The maximum safe dosages for young children, pregnant or nursing women, or those with severe liver or kidney disease have not been established; similar precautions are probably warranted in pets.

Pets that are taking antiseizure medications, particularly phenytoin (Dilantin) or phenobarbital, may need extra carnitine, especially those with heart disease.

 # CAT'S CLAW *(Uncaria tomentosa)*

Common Uses
Asthma

In people, cat's claw is a popular herb used to treat cancer, diabetes, ulcers, arthritis, and infections, as well as to assist in recovery from childbirth. It is also used as a contraceptive.

THERAPEUTIC USES

In pets, cat's claw is used for the treatment of abscesses, **arthritis** (page 11), dermatitis, **cancer** (page 44), urinary infections, and for boosting the immune system. It appears to have immune stimulating and anti-inflammatory activity. It may be useful for **feline leukemia virus** (page 82) and **feline immunodeficiency infections** (page 76) in cats.

Cat's claw is considered a promising treatment for viral diseases such as herpes, shingles, and AIDS. Its possible use for treating allergies, stomach ulcers, osteoarthritis, and rheumatoid arthritis is also being studied. However, the best description of the present state of affairs is that we don't yet know whether cat's claw really works. It certainly is not a proven treatment for cancer.

SCIENTIFIC EVIDENCE

Scientific studies of cat's claw conducted in Peru, Italy, Austria, and Germany have yielded numerous intriguing findings, but as yet no conclusive proof of any healing benefit.

SAFETY ISSUES

Cat's claw appears to be safe in pets. However, European physicians believe that it should not be taken in conjunction with hormone treatments, insulin, or vaccines. Safety in young children, pregnant or nursing women, or those with severe liver or kidney disease is not established; similar precautions may be warranted in pets.

 # CETYL MYRISTOLEATE

Common Uses
Arthritis

Cetyl myristoleate (CM) is a fatty acid ester of a common fatty acid (myristoleic acid) commonly found in fish oils, dairy butter, and animal fat. The mechanism of action of CM is unknown but it may act similarly to omega-3 fatty acids (its effects are often seen more quickly and last longer than when fatty acids supplements are used by themselves, however). Some doctors have proposed that CM can reprogram certain types of white blood cells (memory T-cells); others suggest that hyper-immune responses by the body are normalized and that CM may function as a joint

Cetyl Myristoleate

lubricant as well as an anti-inflammatory. See more discussion under Glycosaminoglycans.

THERAPEUTIC USES

Veterinarians using a product called Myristin in combination with another product called Myrist-Aid (which contains glucosamine, MSM, and other herbs and antioxidants) have reported success in dogs with **osteoarthritis** (page 11).

It appears that CM may be quite successful for treating many pets with arthritis without side effects; more studies are recommended.

SCIENTIFIC EVIDENCE

A major multi-center study involving people with rheumatoid arthritis showed significant improvement in 63.3% of patients using CM alone, with 87% improvement in patients using CM and glucosamine. No adverse reactions were seen except for mild gastrointestinal (GI) symptoms in five patients (the same signs were seen in three patients receiving a placebo).

DOSAGES

Doctors using CM products have recommended a dosage of 385 mg twice daily for small dogs and cats, 770 mg twice daily for medium dogs, and 1,155 mg twice daily for large dogs, all dosages given with digestive enzymes for maximum absorption.

 # CHAMOMILE (See German Chamomile)

Common Uses
  Allergies (herbal rinse), diarrhea

 # CHAPARRAL *(Larrea tridentata)*

Common Uses
  Antibacterial (topical), antifungal (topical)

Chaparral is an herb that has been recommended for a number of conditions. It has been used to treat tumors, liver disease, and as a sunscreen. Most herbalists use chaparral for its antibacterial and antifungal properties.

THERAPEUTIC USES

Chaparrall is typically used to treat infections caused by bacteria, fungi, or amoebas. The lignan nordihydroguaiarectic acid (NDGA) is believed to be the active ingredient. Chaparrall's toxicity limits its internal use, and most doctors recommend it for topical control of infections.

SAFETY ISSUES

Ingestion can cause severe liver damage. It is important that pet's be prevented from licking chaparral off when applied topically. If this is not possible, chaparall should not be used.

CHICKWEED

Common Uses
Constipation

Chickweed is a safe herb useful for its soothing properties. The entire plant, fresh juice, or salves and ointments containing chickweed can be used.

THERAPEUTIC USES

Chickweed is useful for its soothing and lubricating properties. While recommended to assist in the treatment of **constipation** (page 57), it may also be useful to control hairballs. Irritations of the oral cavity or esophagus may also be relieved by the administration of chickweed. Topically, chickweed poultices may cool and soothe minor burns and skin irritations, and can be helpful for pets with localized dry, itchy spots.

SAFETY ISSUES

Chickweed is generally considered safe, but the rare pet may be allergic; large quantities may have a laxative effect. To check for allergies, a small amount should be applied to the skin first to check for inflammation, hives, or other signs of sensitivity. If no reaction occurs, feed a small amount and watch for vomiting, diarrhea, or hives.

If no reaction occurs, use as directed by your veterinarian.

CHITOSAN

Common Uses
Obesity

Chitosan is a dietary supplement made from the outer skeletons of shellfish. The product is purported to bind to fat in the intestines, which prevents the absorption of fat. Studies are inconclusive regarding how well the product works in people or pets. One veterinary company is purported to be developing a product containing chitosan at this time. Time will tell if it will be of value in any diet programs for pets.

CHOLINE (Egg lecithin, soy lecithin, phosphatidylcholine in lecithin) (See also Lecithin)

Common Uses
Cognitive disorder

Choline, unlike other B vitamins which are synthesized by intestinal bacteria, is synthesized in the liver.

Choline is needed for the proper transmission of nerve impulses and is a constituent of acetylcholine, the major neurotransmitter. Choline is a structural element of cell membranes (as the chemical phosphatidylcholine) that promotes lipid transport and acts as a source of methyl groups (after it is transformed into betaine) for various chemical reactions in the body. Choline acts like folic acid, TMG (trimethylglycine), and SAMe (S-adenosylmethionine) to promote methylation.

It appears that phosphatidylcholine is presumed to be responsible for the medicinal effects of choline supplementation.

Choline is also useful for proper functioning and regulation of the liver and gallbladder. This vitamin aids in hormone production and minimizes fat accumulation in the liver by regulating fat and cholesterol metabolism.

In people, choline (or lecithin) supplementation has been recommended for the treatment of a variety of disorders, including elevated blood cholesterol, liver disease, and psychological and neurological disorders (such as Tourette's syndrome, Alzheimer's disease, and bipolar disorder). The evidence supporting the treatment of these disorders with choline is slim; since supplementation is safe and some studies have shown benefit, the use of choline is often recommended.

THERAPEUTIC USES

In pets, choline is used as a natural therapy for seizures and **cognitive disorder** (page 56). There is good evidence for its use in dogs with seizures and cognitive disorder; anecdotal evidence suggests effectiveness in cats with these medical problems as well.

Choline is also recommended for pets with **liver** (page 127) and gallbladder diseases, especially those resulting from fat accumulation in the liver (fatty liver disease called hepatic lipidosis). Pets with high levels of blood cholesterol (as seen in dogs with hypothyroidism and in the genetic disorder hyperlipidemia in Miniature Schnauzers) may also respond to choline supplementation, although controlled studies are lacking. However, choline and methionine should not be used if hepatic encephalopathy (acidosis and brain depression) are present.

Since choline is present in myelin sheaths (the sheath surrounding nerves) as sphingomyelin, supplementation of pets with demyelinating disorders (such as canine degenerative myelopathy) may be indicated, although once again controlled studies are lacking.

Choline is present in the diet as lecithin, choline, or sphingomyelin.

SOURCES

Choline can be found in egg yolks, lecithin, meat, milk, whole grains, soybeans, soy, and natural fats.

DOSAGES

The AAFCO recommendation for choline is 1,200 ppm for dogs and 2,400 ppm for cats.

SAFETY ISSUES

Choline supplementation is believed to be generally safe. While rarely reported, side effects such as anemia may be seen in dogs receiving three or more times the apparent choline requirement (anemia has been reported in dogs receiving 150 mg of choline). However, many holistic veterinarians use high levels of choline in pets with cognitive disorder without apparent ill effects. Monitoring pets receiving high levels of choline for anemia seems warranted.

CHONDROITIN

Common Uses
Osteoarthritis

Chondroitin sulfate is the major glycosaminoglycan found in cartilage; it also helps inhibit enzymes that are destructive to the joints. Chondroitin sulfate is a naturally occurring substance in the body.

THERAPEUTIC USES

A study in the 1998 journal, *Osteoarthritis and Cartilage*, reported that chondroitin sulfate is an effective treatment for **osteoarthritis** (page 11).

Because chondroitin production by the body decreases with aging, supplementation with this compound may be especially helpful for older pets with arthritis.

SOURCE

Animal cartilage is the only dietary source of chondroitin.

SCIENTIFIC EVIDENCE

For years, experts stated that oral chondroitin couldn't work because its molecules are so big that it seemed doubtful that they could be absorbed through the digestive tract. However, in 1995, researchers laid this objection to rest when they found evidence that up to 15% of chondroitin is absorbed intact. Another study found that up to 70% of radiolabeled chondroitin sulfate was well absorbed and showed affinity for articular (joint) cartilage. This evidence for chondroitin absorption holds true for pets as well as people.

The effect of both oral and injected chondroitin was assessed in rabbits with damaged cartilage in the knee. After 84 days of treatment, the rabbits that were given chondroitin had significantly more healthy cartilage remaining in the damaged knee than the untreated animals. Receiving chondroitin by mouth was as effective as taking it through an injection. It appears quite likely that chondroitin can slow the progression of osteoarthritis. However, more studies are needed to confirm this very exciting possibility. It would also be wonderful if chondroitin could repair damaged cartilage and thus reverse arthritis, but none of the research so far shows such an effect. Chondroitin may simply stop further destruction from occurring.

How does chondroitin work for osteoarthritis? Scientists are unsure how chondroitin sulfate works, but one of several theories (or all of them) might explain its mode of action. At its most basic level, chondroitin may help cartilage by providing it with the building blocks it needs to repair itself. It is also believed to block enzymes that break down cartilage in the joints. Another theory holds that chondroitin increases the amount of hyaluronic acid in the joints. Hyaluronic acid is a protective fluid that keeps the joints lubricated. Finally, chondroitin may have a mild anti-inflammatory effect.

Chondroitin is often added to supplements containing glucosamine. While significant studies are lacking, some doctors (but not all) feel that adding chondroitin to glucosamine enhances the ability of both substances to repair cartilage due to a synergistic effect.

SAFETY ISSUES

Chondroitin sulfate, like glucosamine, has not been associated with any serious side effects. Mild digestive distress appears to be the only real concern in people and possibly pets.

CHROMIUM (chromium picolinate, chromium polynicotinate, chromium chloride, high-chromium brewer's yeast)

Common Uses
Diabetes

Chromium is a trace mineral in the body. Chromium's role in maintaining good health was discovered in 1957, when scientists extracted a substance known as glucose tolerance factor (GTF) from pork kidney. GTF, which helps the body maintain normal blood sugar levels, contains chromium as the active component. GTF binds to and potentiates the activity of insulin.

Chromium is necessary for pancreatic beta cell sensitivity (beta cells make insulin), insulin binding, insulin receptor enzymes, and insulin receptor sites. Supplemental chromium tends to balance glucose metabolism, benefiting both hypoglycemic (low blood sugar) and diabetic patients. One explanation for this is that chromium may improve C-peptide levels, leading to enhanced pancreatic beta cell function.

THERAPEUTIC USES

Supplementing with chromium can lower blood lipids, which may make it beneficial in people and pets with elevated blood cholesterol levels.

Chromium's most important function is to help regulate the amount of glucose in the blood. Insulin regulates the movement of glucose out of the blood and into cells. It appears that insulin uses chromium as a cofactor to allow glucose to pass through the cell membrane and enter the cell.

Based on chromium's close relationship with insulin, this trace mineral has been studied as a treatment for **diabetes** (page 66). The results have been positive: Chromium supplements appear to improve blood sugar control in people with diabetes.

Tissue levels of chromium in people and pets is often low due to limited uptake of chromium by plants as well as limited absorption by people and pets.

SCIENTIFIC EVIDENCE

Recent evidence also suggests that chromium supplements might help dieters lose fat and gain lean muscle tissue, probably through its effects on insulin (by increasing the body's sensitivity to insulin). Since decreased sensitivity to insulin can contribute to weight gain (as often happens in diabetic patients), supplying additional chromium (usually at a dose of 200 to 400 mcg/day) is recommended for weight control in people. Research is needed to determine whether chromium would be of benefit to overweight pets.

As mentioned, it has been theorized that many Americans may be chromium-deficient. Preliminary research done by the U.S. Department of Agriculture (USDA) in 1985 found low chromium intakes in a small group of people studied. Although large-scale studies are needed to show whether Americans as a whole are chromium-deficient, we do know that many traditional sources of chromium, such as wheat, are depleted of this important mineral during processing. Some researchers believe that inadequate intake of chromium may be one of the causes for the rising rates of adult-onset diabetes. However, the matter is greatly complicated by the fact that we lack a good test to determine chromium deficiency.

SOURCES

While chromium is found in drinking water, especially hard water, concentrations vary so widely throughout the world that drinking water is not a reliable source. The most concentrated sources of chromium are brewer's yeast (not nutritional or torula yeast) and calf liver. Two ounces of brewer's yeast or 4 ounces of calf liver supply between 50 and 60 mcg of chromium.

Other good sources of chromium are whole-wheat bread, wheat bran, and rye bread. Potatoes, wheat germ, green pepper, and apples offer modest amounts of chromium.

DOSAGES

The recommended dosages for the use of chromium in pets with diabetes is 50 to 300 mcg per day. Typically, a dosage of 200 mcg/cat of chromium picolinate is recommended. However, since picolinate may cause damage to DNA, more research is needed in this area. Using the chromium GTF natural supplement would be a safer alternative, although research using this form to determine the proper dosage has not been done. Work with your veterinarian to determine if chromium supplementation can be used in your pet.

SAFETY ISSUES

Calcium carbonate supplements may interfere with the absorption of chromium.

People may have a difficult time absorbing and synthesizing chromium if it is not attached to a substrate such as picolonic acid (chromium picolinate) or nicotinic acid (chromium nicotinate). In people, concerns have been raised over the use of the picolinate form of chromium in individuals suffering from affective or psychotic disorders, because picolinic acids can change levels of neurotransmitters.

Recently, there has been the suggestion that chromium picolinate may cause damage to DNA, especially when combined with ascorbic acid. Alternative forms of chromium, such as that in the GTF form that can be extracted from foods such as yeast, contain no picolinic acid and may be safer. Additionally, while many forms of chromium are available, supplementation with an organic form (such as GTF) is recommended as this organically bound form of chromium is absorbed better and is more available to the pet than inorganic forms of chromium. More research is needed on this topic, although the use of the GTF form may be preferred until results are in.

Chromium appears to be safe in people when taken at a dosage of 50 to 200 mcg daily. However, concern has been expressed since chromium is a heavy metal and might conceivably build up and cause problems if taken to excess. Recently, there have been a few reports of kidney damage in people who took a relatively high dosage of chromium: 1,200 mcg or more daily for several months. For this reason, the dosage found most effective for individuals with type II diabetes, 1,000 mcg daily, might present some health risks. Similar concerns are probably applicable for pets.

For pets with diabetes who may respond to chromium supplementation, a decreased dosage of insulin may be needed; medical supervision is essential before decreasing insulin.

The maximum safe dosages of chromium for young children, women who are pregnant or nursing, or those with severe liver or kidney disease has not been established; similar concerns are probably warranted in pets.

CINERARIA *(Cineraria maritima)*

Common Uses
  Cataracts

Cineraria is an herbal remedy recommended for dogs and cats with **cataracts** (page 53). The juice is diluted at least 50:50 with artificial tears. Anecdotal reports indicate that pets with cataracts appear to have improved vision, although the opacity of the lens may not decrease. If cineraria will work, it will usually occur with the first bottle.

CLEMATIS AND STEPHANIA COMBINATION

Common Uses
  Weak hind limbs, hip dysplasia, lumbosacral pain

This herbal formula contains a variety of herbs including gentiana, achyranthis, ginger, angelica, siler, notopterygium, hoelen, stephania, atractylodes, peony, persica, rehmannia, tang kuei, and ligusticum.

CHINESE HERBS

This is one of a variety of Chinese herbal formulas for treating pets. Because of the Chinese diagnosis and classification of diseases, the ingredients in each formula may vary. Individual Chinese pharmacists include herbs in their tented formulas based upon their experiences. However, they can compound formulas to the needs of an individual pet.

For example, a Western diagnosis of allergies allows a selection of treatment based upon this diagnosis. In Traditional Chinese Medicine (TCM), diagnosis and treatment are based upon the need to rebalance the patient so that the individual, not the disease, is treated. As an example, with TCM we might be concerned about selecting herbs to circulate Qi, nurture Yin, or invigorate Yang. This system has been used for thousands of years, even prior to the advent of Western medicine, and the herbal treatments have been passed down through time.

This doesn't mean that Chinese herbal formulas cannot be used based upon a Western diagnosis, only that if the herbal formula doesn't work, it might indicate the need for another formula or a correct TCM diagnosis so that the correct remedy can be selected.

THERAPEUTIC USES

Clematis and Stephania Combination is a Chinese herbal formula used for pets with weak hind limbs, stiffness, hip dysplasia, or lumbosacral pain.

DOSAGES

Use 1 gm/20 pounds, 2 to 3 times daily of concentrated herbs for dogs and cats; 4 gm of fresh herbs/20 pounds, 2 to 3 times daily for dogs and cats; tinctures 5 to 10 drops/20 pounds, 2 to 3 times daily for dogs and cats.

Alternatively, some herbalists recommend extrapolation based on weight. Since human doses are based on a 150-pound male, a recommended dose of 3 capsules given 3 times daily for this 150-pound male would extrapolate to 1 capsule given 3 times daily for a 50-pound dog. There are some suggestions that dogs and cats require more herb per pound of body weight than humans. This would suggest that a 10-pound cat should receive 20% of the recommended human dosage, whereas a 25-pound dog should receive 25% of the human dosage.

You should consult with a holistic doctor to determine the best starting dose prior to treating your pet with herbs.

Herbs are usually supplied in powder or capsule form; tinctures can also be found. Many products made for humans can be used in pets. Unfortunately, the "correct" dosage for the pet has not been determined for many herbs, and clinical experience and extrapolation from human data is often used. The lower dosage is usually used and the dosage increased if needed. Compared to traditional drug therapy, herbal treatments usually take longer (several weeks or longer) before an effect is seen. As with Western herbal therapy, quality control in the manufacturing of the product used is important, and only herbs from reliable companies should be used.

SAFETY ISSUES

While many herbs are used safely in pets, remember that many potent drugs (such as digitalis, vincristine, and aspirin) were first described in plants and herbs and have actually been extracted from plants and herbs. This means that working with your holistic veterinarian before using herbal remedies in your pet is essential. For example, a recent report of a Chinese herbal cream used in people for skin disorders showed a high level of the steroid dexamethasone in the product, with the highest levels in the products recommended for children. Other reports of the product ma huang, which contains the potent drug ephedra, revealed varying levels of ephedra in a number of products tested. Stories such as these reinforce the need for proper medical care and advice when using herbs.

 # COENZYME Q$_{10}$

Common Uses
Heart disease, obesity

Coenzyme Q$_{10}$ (ubiquinone) is a powerful fat-soluble antioxidant that is found in every cell in the body. It plays a fundamental role in the mitochondria, the parts of the cell that produce energy from food. Coenzyme Q$_{10}$ (CoQ$_{10}$) appears to control the flow of oxygen within the cells as well as functioning as an antioxidant to reduce damage to cells by harmful free radicals. Every cell in the body needs CoQ$_{10}$, but there is no U.S. Recommended Dietary Allowance since the body can manufacture CoQ$_{10}$ from scratch. Because CoQ$_{10}$ is found in all animal and plant cells, we obtain small amounts of this nutrient from our diet. However, it would be hard to get a therapeutic dosage from food.

THERAPEUTIC USES

In dogs and cats, CoQ$_{10}$ has been recommended for the treatment of **heart disease** (page 91), **periodontal disease** (page 140), **diabetes** (page 66), immune problems, and decreased physical performance. Since Coenzyme Q$_{10}$ levels decrease in people and pets as they age, supplementation of older pets may be warranted, especially to correct the decline in immune system functioning as happens in older pets.

CoQ$_{10}$ appears to assist the heart during times of stress on the heart muscle, perhaps by helping it use energy more efficiently. While CoQ$_{10}$'s best-established use is for congestive heart failure, ongoing research suggests that it may also be useful for other types of heart problems and for a wide variety of additional illnesses. Preliminary research has shown reduced levels of CoQ$_{10}$ in the hearts of people and pets with heart disease.

DOSAGES

In people, the typical recommended dosage of CoQ$_{10}$ is 30 to 300 mg daily, often divided into 2 or 3 doses. CoQ$_{10}$ is fat soluble and is better absorbed when taken in an oil-based soft gel form rather than in a dry form, such as tablets and capsules. In pets, the typical dosage is 30 mg every 24 to 48 hours, although your veterinarian may alter this dosage depending upon your pet's size and individual needs. (Some doctors feel that increasing the dosage is necessary for larger pets; for example, 80 mg every 24 to 48 hours might be recommended daily for a 100-pound dog).

SCIENTIFIC EVIDENCE

In people, the best-documented use of CoQ$_{10}$ is for treating congestive heart failure when taken along with conventional medications, not instead of them. People with congestive heart failure have significantly lower levels of CoQ$_{10}$ in their heart muscle cells than healthy people. While this does not prove that CoQ$_{10}$ supplements will help people with heart failure, it has prompted researchers to try using CoQ10 as a treatment for heart failure. In people, at least nine double-blind studies have found that CoQ10 supplements can markedly improve symptoms and objective measurements of heart function when they are taken along with conventional medication.

Weaker evidence suggests that it may be useful for cardiomyopathy (several small studies suggest that CoQ10 supplements are helpful for some forms of cardiomyopathy) and other forms of heart disease. It has also been suggested as a treatment for high blood pressure (although the scientific evidence for this use is weak) and to prevent heart damage caused by certain types of cancer chemotherapy (such as adriamycin). Since CoQ10 might conceivably interfere with the action of other chemotherapy drugs due to its antioxidant activity (although there is no good evidence that it does so), check with your veterinarian before using CoQ10 if your pet has cancer that requires chemotherapy.

CoQ10 may also help periodontal (gum) disease (by reducing the size and improving the health of periodontal pockets, as well as decreasing inflammation, redness, bleeding, and pain) and diabetes in people and pets.

Coenzyme Q10 is used to transport and break down fat into energy. In people, Coenzyme Q10 levels were found to be low in approximately 50% of obese individuals. Supplementation with Coenzyme Q10 resulted in accelerated weight loss in overweight people. It may be of benefit in overweight pets and at the recommended dosage no side effects have been seen. Consult with your doctor about using Coenzyme Q10 to help in a weight-reduction program for your pet.

In experiments in dogs, Coenzyme Q10 was found to exert a protective effect against oxidative injury to the heart. Stabilization of body weight, improved clinical status, and a slowing of the progression of heart disease has been seen in dogs with heart disease treated with Coenzyme Q10.

SAFETY ISSUES

There may be depletion of CoQ10 associated with certain medications: cholesterol-lowering drugs in the statin family, such as lovastatin (Mevacor), simvastatin (Zocor), and pravastatin (Pravachol); oral diabetes drugs (especially glyburide, phenformin, and tolazamide); beta-blockers (specifically propranolol, metoprolol, and alprenolol); antipsychotic drugs in the phenothiazine family, tricyclic antidepressants, diazoxide, methyldopa, hydrochlorothiazide, clonidine, and hydralazine. Supplementation with CoQ10 might prove useful.

CoQ10 appears to be extremely safe. No significant side effects have been found; however, pets with severe heart disease should not take CoQ10 (or any other supplement) except under a veterinarian's supervision.

The maximum safe dosages of CoQ10 for young children, pregnant or nursing women, or those with severe liver or kidney disease has not been determined; the same is true for pets of similar circumstances.

COLLOIDAL SILVER

Common Uses
Infections

Colloidal silver has been recommended for treating several internal and external problems in pets. Some doctors and pet owners have reported good results when other treatments have failed.

Depending upon the manufacturer of colloidal silver (which is not the same thing as silver sulfadiazine), the actual quantity of silver in the bottles is not always guaranteed. Some doctors have reported that bottles of the product had bacteria or fungus growing in the bottles, which makes one wonder about the potential antimicrobial action of some products.

Colloidal silver is produced by the electrocolloidal method, which extracts microscopic particles from silver. These microscopic particles pass out of the body into the urine and feces. Because the colloidal silver maintains a positive electrical charge, it should only be contained in dark glass bottles (plastic maintains a negative electrical charge and neutralizes the colloidal silver).

THERAPEUTIC USES

Silver, in the form of silver sulfadiazine (Silvadene), is quite useful for treating topical **bacterial infections** (page 105), especially severe infections caused by gram negative bacterial species (*Pseudomonas spp.* and *Aeromonas spp.*).

Both human and veterinary medical doctors have reported success when the product is used orally or topically in a variety of infectious disorders.

SCIENTIFIC EVIDENCE

University studies show effective and quick antimicrobial kill of *Staphylococcus epidermidis*, *Staphylococcus aureus*, *Enterococcus faecalis*, *Salmonella typhimurium*, *Pseudomonas aeruginosa*, and *Candida albicans* using colloidal silver (the product tested was manufactured by SilverKare) when incubated at the recommended 30 ppm.

DOSAGES

One use of colloidal silver that anecdotally has shown some success is the treatment of cats with either acute or chronic sinus infections. A drop of colloidal silver is placed in each eye and in the nostrils; it can also be added to the drinking water or given orally.

SAFETY ISSUES

While quality varies among manufacturers, properly produced colloidal silver appears safe and effective in many conditions. To date, no infectious organisms appear to have developed resistance to colloidal silver.

In 1997, the FDA issued an opinion on silver products (silver salts, which are not the same as colloidal silver). These products are not approved in any animal species, and the FDA is not aware of any substantial scientific evidence that supports the safe and effective use of silver salts for any animal disease condition.

In the Federal Register (October 15, 1996), the FDA proposed to establish that all over-the-counter human drug products containing colloidal silver ingredients or silver salts for internal or external use are not generally recognized as safe and effective and are misbranded. This proposal has now been withdrawn.

While short-term use of some products has not resulted in any reported side effects, there is always the potential for argyria (silver poisoning) in improperly made products and those containing silver salts. According to several scientific publications mentioned in the Federal Register proposal (October 15, 1996), the human consumption of silver may result in argyria, a permanent ashen-gray or blue discoloration of the skin, conjunctiva, and internal organs. However, this has not been seen in people or pets using properly manufactured colloidal silver.

While more reports and controlled studies are needed, preliminary anecdotal reports appear encouraging. Because of the potential benefits of colloidal silver, owners should discuss this therapy with their veterinarians for possible use in the treatment of infectious disorders.

Colloidal Silver

COLOSTRUM/LACTOFERRIN

Common Uses
Arthritis

Colostrum is the antibody-rich fluid produced from the mother during the first day or two after birth. However, most commercial colostrum preparations come from cows. Whether cow antibodies are good for humans or pets is unclear, although many holistic veterinarians anecdotally report positive results with both colostrum and the more concentrated form called lactoferrin. Lactoferrin is a component of colostrum. By concentrating the intended nutrient (lactoferrin), instead of having a tiny amount of it as found in colostrum, the effect may be maximized in the body.

Ideally, colostrum should come from a dairy that does not use hormones, pesticides, or medications in the cows, which could concentrate in the colostrum.

Purine and pyrimidine complexes are the active fractions found in colostrum, the first milk produced by mammals. Purine nucleotides are involved in virtually all cellular processes and play a major role in structural, metabolic, energetic and regulatory functions. Like arabinogalactans, they have been shown to stimulate the activity of natural killer white blood cells. Colostrum contains cytokines and other protein compounds that can act as biological response modifiers.

THERAPEUTIC USES

In pets, colostrum has been recommended and anecdotally found useful for the treatment of wounds (promotes healing of insect bites, abscesses, ruptured cysts, warts, and surgical incisions when applied topically to the wound), gingivitis, as an aid to proper functioning and motility of the intestinal tract, **diarrhea** (page 71), colitis, **inflammatory bowel disease** (page 105), **constipation** (page 57), food **allergies** (page 3), and **arthritis** (page 11). Very often colostrum is used with other treatments; these other treatments might be reduced or eliminated after the pet has been taking colostrum.

Research supports its use in the treatment of rheumatoid arthritis and osteoarthritis as well as other autoimmune conditions. Nucleotides also may play an important role in essential fatty acid metabolism, and may have a positive effect on the functions of the gastrointestinal tract and the liver.

Colostrum is often sold as an "immune stimulant." However, if it works it all, it would most likely function by directly fighting parasites, bacteria, and viruses. There is no particular reason to believe it does strengthen the immune system, although it has been purported to establish homeostasis in the thymus gland, which functions in regulating the immune system. More research is needed to determine whether colostrum works in this manner.

DOSAGES

The usual recommended dosage of colostrum is 10 g daily in people; in pets, the recommendation is to feed it free-choice in powder form at least 30 minutes or longer before feeding, usually once daily in the morning.

The recommended dosage for cats with gingivitis is 40 mg/kg applied topically to the gums.

SCIENTIFIC EVIDENCE

There is some evidence that colostrum can help prevent certain infectious diseases, but other studies have found it ineffective.

A specialized form of colostrum was tested for its ability to prevent infection in people with the common parasite cryptosporidium. One group of healthy volunteers was given colostrum before receiving an infectious dose of cryptosporidium, while the other group was given placebo. Those who took colostrum experienced less diarrhea and appeared to experience a lower-grade infection.

Several other studies indicate that colostrum may relieve diarrhea and other symptoms associated with cryptosporidium in people with AIDS.

Another study suggests that colostrum might prevent mild infections with the Shigella parasite from becoming severe. However, a different study looking at Bangladeshi children infected with *Helicobacter pylori* (the organism that causes digestive ulcers) found no benefits. Also, no benefit was seen in a study on rotavirus (another parasite that causes diarrhea in children).

There is evidence that lactoferrin works in cats with stomatitis secondary to FIV (feline immunodeficiency virus) infection (the study showed no evidence for colostrum). It is theorized that lacto-ferrin may have two functions. Lactoferrin may bind iron that is essential for bacterial growth, and it may stimulate local (IgA) immunity at the level of the palatine tonsils.

SAFETY ISSUES

Colostrum and lactoferrin do not seem to cause any significant side effects. However, comprehensive safety studies have not been performed. Safety in young children or women who are pregnant or nursing has not been established. These guidelines should probably also be followed for pets.

COLTSFOOT (Petasites and Tussilago)

Common Uses
Asthma

The leaves and stems of the mature coltsfoot plant are often recommended by herbalists for the therapy of various respiratory disorders.

THERAPEUTIC USES

Coltsfoot is recommended for pets with respiratory infection, including **kennel cough** (page 120). It acts as an antimicrobial, expectorant, and cough suppressant.

SAFETY ISSUES

The flowers (not the leaves and stems) contain small quantities of alkaloids that can cause liver damage or cancer if taken in large quantities. Use only as directed and for short periods of time (1 to 2 weeks). Do not use in pregnant animals or pets with liver disease.

COMFREY *(Symphytum officinale)*

Common Uses
Skin irritation, wound healing (external only), inflammatory conditions

Comfrey is a plant native to Europe. Generally the roots and leaves are used for herbal healing.

THERAPEUTIC USES

Comfrey can be applied topically for any kind of skin irritation. It contains allantoin which speeds cellular healing. For open wounds, it is suggested to combine comfrey with an antibacterial herb (Oregon grape) to prevent bacteria from being trapped inside of a quick healing wound.

Due to the potential for liver disease (to follow), the FDA has discouraged internal use of comfrey. However, it has been recommended for internal use for pets with gastrointestinal inflammation and for pets with inflammatory respiratory conditions.

DOSAGES

The suggested safe dosage is ½ to 1 teaspoon per pound of food, fed for no more than 1 to 2 weeks at a time to prevent accumulation of alkaloids.

SAFETY ISSUES

Comfrey contains small quantities of alkaloids that can cause liver damage or cancer if taken in large quantities. While the leaves (the most commonly used part of the herb) contain almost negligible amounts of alkaloids (the roots contain the most and should never be used), it is wise to use comfrey only as directed and for short periods of time (1 to 2 weeks). Do not use in pregnant animals or pets with liver disease.

COPTIS AND SCUTE COMBINATION

Common Uses
  Gastroenteritis

In Traditional Chinese Medicine (TCM), herbs are usually used in combination. Coptis and Scute is one of four Chinese herbal combinations discussed in this book.

THERAPEUTIC USES

This formula is used to treat gastroenteritis with vomiting and fever or diarrhea caused by ulcers with bleeding. It should not be used for longer than 2 weeks as prolonged use causes injury to Qi.

CHINESE HERBS

Because of the Chinese diagnosis and classification of diseases, the ingredients in each formula may vary. Individual Chinese pharmacists include herbs in their tented formulas based upon their experiences. However, they can compound formulas to the needs of an individual pet.

For example, a Western diagnosis of allergies allows a selection of treatment based upon this diagnosis. In Traditional Chinese Medicine (TCM), diagnosis and treatment are based upon the need to rebalance the patient so that the individual, not the disease, is treated. As an example, with TCM we might be concerned about selecting herbs to circulate Qi, nurture Yin, or

invigorate Yang. This system has been used for thousands of years, even prior to the advent of Western medicine, and the herbal treatments have been passed down through time.

This doesn't mean that Chinese herbal formulas cannot be used based upon a Western diagnosis, only that if the herbal formula doesn't work, it might indicate the need for another formula or a correct TCM diagnosis so that the correct remedy can be selected. See the Introduction for more information.

DOSAGES

Herbs are usually supplied in powder or capsule form; tinctures can also be found. Many products made for humans can be used in pets. Unfortunately, the "correct" dosage for the pet has not been determined for many herbs and clinical experience, and extrapolation from human data is often used. The lower dosage is usually used and the dosage increased if needed. Compared to traditional drug therapy, herbal treatments usually take longer (several weeks or longer) before an effect is seen. As with Western herbal therapy, quality control in the manufacturing of the product used is important, and only herbs from reliable companies should be used. The following guidelines serve as a starting point for herbal therapy: 1 gm/20 pounds, 2 to 3 times daily of concentrated herbs for dogs and cats; 4 gm of fresh herbs/20 pounds, 2 to 3 times daily for dogs and cats; tinctures 5 to 10 drops/20 pounds, 2 to 3 times daily for dogs and cats.

Alternatively, some herbalists recommend extrapolation based on weight. Since human doses are based on a 150-pound male, a recommended dose of 3 capsules given 3 times daily for this 150-pound male would extrapolate to 1 capsule given 3 times daily for a 50-pound dog. There are some suggestions that dogs and cats require more herb per pound of body weight than humans. This would suggest that a 10-pound cat should receive 20% of the recommended human dosage, whereas a 25-pound dog should receive 25% of the human dosage.

You should consult with a holistic doctor to determine the best starting dose prior to treating your pet with herbs.

SAFETY ISSUES

While many herbs are used safely in pets, remember that many potent drugs (such as digitalis, vincristine, and aspirin) were first described in plants and herbs and have actually been extracted from plants and herbs. This means that working with your holistic veterinarian before using herbal remedies in your pet is essential. For example, a recent report of a Chinese herbal cream used in people for skin disorders showed a high level of the steroid dexamethasone in the product, with the highest levels in the products recommended for children. Other reports of the product ma huang, which contains the potent drug ephedra, revealed varying levels of ephedra in a number of products tested. Stories such as these reinforce the need for proper medical care and advice when using herbs.

CORDYCEPS MUSHROOM (*Cordyceps ophioglossoides,* Caterpillar Fungus, Deer Antler Fungus)

Common Uses
  Anemia, lack of appetite (anorexia), aging pets, antibacterial, cancer, any chronic disease

The cordyceps mushroom comes in the form of a fine powder.

THERAPEUTIC USES

While cordyceps is marketed as a cure-all for many disorders, there is no real evidence that cordyceps is effective for any of these conditions.

SCIENTIFIC EVIDENCE

While there has been a great deal of basic scientific research into the chemical constituents of cordyceps, reliable double-blind studies are lacking.

DOSAGES

The dosage varies with the specific preparation of cordyceps. Most doctors follow package labeling recommendations.

SAFETY ISSUES

In people and pets, cordyceps appears to be extremely safe. Safety in young children, pregnant or nursing women, or those with severe liver or kidney disease has not been established. These guidelines should probably also be followed for pets.

CRANBERRY *(Vaccinium macrocarpon)*

Common Uses
> Bladder stones, bladder infection, kidney disease, FLUTD

The cranberry plant, a relative of the common blueberry plant, has been used as food and as a treatment for bladder and kidney diseases.

THERAPEUTIC USES

Research has shown that drinking cranberry juice makes the urine more acidic. Since common urinary tract infections in pets (especially dogs) are caused by bacteria such as E. coli, which function best in alkaline urine, many holistic doctors promote cranberry juice extracts for treating bladder infections. Additionally, since the most common **bladder stones** (page 40) in dogs and cats, and the sand-like gravel and microscopic crystals that are often encountered in cats with feline lower urinary tract disease (**FLUTD**, formerly called FUS (page 84)) form in alkaline urine, acidifying the urine with supplements such as cranberry extracts may prove helpful.

However, contrary to early research in people, it now appears that acidification of the urine is not so important as cranberry's ability to block bacteria from adhering to the bladder wall. Preventing bacterial adhesion to the bladder wall prevents infection and allows the bacteria to be washed out with the urine.

Cranberry juice is believed to be most effective as a form of prevention. When taken regularly, it appears to reduce the frequency of recurrent bladder infections in women prone to develop them. Cranberry juice may also be helpful during a bladder infection but not as reliably. Similar findings are lacking in pets but may be applicable.

DOSAGES

In people, the recommended dosage of dry cranberry juice extract is 300 to 400 mg twice daily, or 8 to 16 ounces of juice daily. Pure cranberry juice (not sugary cranberry juice cocktail with its low percentage of cranberry) should be used for best effect.

For pets, the recommended dosage varies with the product. One recommended product used in cats recommends a daily dose of 250 mg of cranberry extract. Cranberry juice is not recommended as it is all but impossible to get most pets to drink enough of the juice to be effective.

SAFETY ISSUES

There are no known risks of this food for adults, children, or pregnant or nursing women, nor are there any known risks in pets. However, cranberry juice may allow the kidneys to excrete certain drugs more rapidly, thereby reducing their effectiveness. All weakly alkaline drugs may be affected, including many antidepressants and prescription painkillers.

In dogs and cats, the push to acidify the urine through prescription-type diets has led to a slight increase in oxalate stones, which are more common in acid urine. Pets taking cranberry extract would be more prone to develop crystals and stones, such as oxalate stones, which are more common in acid urine. However, since the crystals and stones that form in alkaline urine are much more commonly diagnosed, pets with chronic stones (and cats with chronic FLUTD) would probably benefit from acidification of the urine even with the slight risk of stones forming in acid urine. Discuss this with your veterinarian.

Cranberry

DANDELION *(Taraxacum officinale)*

Common Uses

Allergies, arthritis, constipation, diabetes, diuretic, fleas, heart conditions, cancer, kidney disease, liver disease, urinary disorders

Dandelion is useful for its ability to stimulate the liver, as a diuretic, and for its anti-inflammatory properties. Dandelion, especially the fresh greens, is also a healthy green food providing a number of vitamins, minerals, and other nutrients to the pet.

THERAPEUTIC USES

The most active constituents in dandelion appear to be eudesmanolide and germacranolide, substances unique to this herb. Other ingredients include taraxol, taraxerol, and taraxasterol, along with stigmasterol, beta-sitosterol, caffeic acid, taraxacin, terpenoides, inulin, and p-hydroxyphenylacetic acid.

In general, the uses and various parts of the plant recommended for dandelion include: fluid retention (leaves), nutritional supplement (leaves), **liver**/gallbladder **disease** (page 127) (root), **constipation** (page 57) (root), and various forms of **arthritis** (page 11) (root).

Dandelion acts as a diuretic (similar to furosemide), but because dandelion contains potassium, it does not deplete the body of necessary potassium like many diuretics (including furosemide).

Dandelion root can stimulate bile production and liver circulation. It is also recommended as a possible therapy for pets with tumors.

Dandelion has demonstrated experimental hypoglycemic effects and may be beneficial in diabetic pets.

Dandelion flowers act as a weak pain killer (analgesic) but do not contain salicylic acid (aspirin) so they can be used safely in cats.

Dandelion is useful for improving digestion and eliminating waste from the body.

The scientific basis for the use of dandelion is scanty. Preliminary studies suggest that dandelion root stimulates the flow of bile. Dandelion leaves have also been found to produce a mild diuretic effect.

SAFETY ISSUES

Dandelion can be used safely in pets; because it may lower blood sugar, it should not be used in pets receiving hypoglycemic therapy without veterinary supervision. There might be some risk when combining it with pharmaceutical diuretics. Do not use in pets with diseases of the gallbladder or bile duct obstruction. Contact dermatitis and allergic reactions have been reported in people. Pets with known allergies to related plants, such as chamomile and yarrow, should use dandelion with caution.

Dandelion is generally regarded as safe. Safety in young children, pregnant or nursing women, or those with severe liver or kidney disease has not been established. Similar precautions probably also apply in pets.

DEVIL'S CLAW *(Harpagophytum procumbrens)*

Common Uses
Arthritis, rheumatoid arthritis, osteoarthritis, heart conditions (possible anti-arrhythmic)

Devil's claw is used as an analgesic and anti-inflammatory and is often recommended for treating arthritis.

THERAPEUTIC USES

Compared with placebo, devil's claw produced a statistically significant reduction in pain experience by people with osteoarthritis. This herb is suggested as an anti-inflammatory for pets with **osteoarthritis** (page 11), but evidence in the form of animal studies is lacking. It may be helpful as an anti-arrhythmic for pets with heart disease.

SCIENTIFIC EVIDENCE

In people, one double-blind study followed 89 individuals with rheumatoid arthritis for a 2-month period. The group given devil's claw showed a significant decrease in pain intensity and improved mobility. Another double-blind study of 50 people with various types of arthritis found that 10 days of treatment with devil's claw provided significant pain relief. A recent double-blind study of 118 participants suggests that devil's claw may also help relieve soft-tissue pain (for example, muscles and tendons). It is un-

known how devil's claw works. Some studies have found an anti-inflammatory effect but others have not. Apparently, the herb doesn't produce the same changes in prostaglandins as standard anti-inflammatory drugs.

SAFETY ISSUES

The herb appears to be safe for short and long-term use; many doctors do not use it in patients with ulcers since it may work similarly to NSAID medications.

Do not use in diabetic pets as devil's claw can cause hypoglycemia. Excessive doses can interfere with treatment for heart disease and high and low blood pressure. Do not administer to pregnant animals.

Do not use concurrently with aspirin, corticosteroids, or other nonsteroidal anti-inflammatory medications.

In people, no side effects other than occasional mild gastrointestinal distress has been seen. Devil's claw is not recommended for people with ulcers. Safety in young children, pregnant or nursing women, or those with severe liver or kidney disease has not been established. Similar precautions are probably warranted in pets.

 DMG (Vitamin B$_{15}$)

Common Uses
Arthritis, stress

DMG stands for dimethylglycine, also called vitamin B$_{15}$. It is found in low levels in foods, including meats, seeds, and grains. Both the human and animal body make DMG from

choline and betaine. It is suggested that increased dietary intake of DMG can be beneficial.

The metabolic role of DMG is to provide carbon to cells. It is also a precursor of SAMe.

DMG appears to enhance oxygen usage, prevent the accumulation of lactic acid, improve muscle metabolism, function as an anti-stress nutrient to improve the cardiovascular system, and reduce recovery time after vigorous physical activity. (See also Glycosaminoglycans.)

THERAPEUTIC USES

It has been recommended for use in pets with a variety of conditions including **osteoarthritis** (page 11) at a dose of 50 to 500 mg per day. Its mechanism in the treatment of osteoarthritis is via an anti-inflammatory effect. Research indicates that DMG reduces the incidence of arthritis and allows for the reversal of the inflammatory condition of some experimental animals with arthritis. Many doctors prescribe it for horses, dogs, and cats to improve performance and enhance recovery from various health problems. DMG is considered an anti-stress nutrient.

DMG has also been recommended by holistic veterinarians as a supplement for pets with seizures and allergies. Research suggests that

DMG may in fact be beneficial for these conditions, although the actual benefit for these conditions is unproven through controlled studies.

Studies have shown that DMG can improve the immune response by potentiating both cell-mediated and humoral (antibody) immunity. Some holistic doctors also recommend DMG for pets with immune disorders such as **cancer** (page 44), **feline leukemia virus infection** (page 82), **feline immunodeficiency virus infection** (page 76), and **diabetes** (page 66) for this reason (at a dosage of 0.5 to 1.0 mg per pound daily).

DMG is included in formulas for pets with heart disease. It is proposed to work by improving oxygen uptake and utilization.

DMG is also recommended as a natural therapy for pets with epilepsy at a dosage of 50–500 mg per pet per day.

SAFETY ISSUES

DMG is extremely safe. The body converts it into its metabolites that are either used or excreted from the body.

ECHINACEA *(Echinacea purpurea, E. angustifolia, E. pallida)*

Common Uses
Allergies, rheumatoid arthritis, cancer, infections, kidney disease, urinary disorders

There are a number of classes of pharmacologically active chemicals in echinacea, including polysaccharides, flavonoids (calculated as quercetin), caffeic acid, essential oils, alkylamides, and polyacetylenes.

Echinacea has strong immune-stimulating properties. This herb increases phagocytosis (the ability of white blood cells to destroy invading organisms), stimulates the lymphatic system (to remove waste materials), and reduces the production of hyaluronidase (an enzyme that breaks down hyaluronic acid; hylauronic acid is needed to bind cells together to prevent infection). The reduction of hyaluronidase is responsible for tissue regeneration and decreased inflammation.

THERAPEUTIC USES

Echinacea is used as an immune stimulant and as an antimicrobial (antiviral and antibacterial) herb. In people, echinacea was the number one cold and flu remedy in the United States until it was displaced by sulfa antibiotics. Ironically, antibiotics are not effective for colds, while echinacea appears to offer some real help.

Echinacea remains the primary remedy for minor respiratory infections in Germany, where over 1.3 million prescriptions are issued each year. The best scientific evidence about echinacea concerns its ability to help people recover from colds and minor flus more quickly. Good evidence tells us that echinacea can actually help people get over colds much faster; it also appears to significantly reduce symptoms while people are sick. In people, studies of echinacea have used all three species of the herb. We don't know which one is better, or whether they are all equivalent.

Echinacea is recommended as an antimicrobial for the urinary system.

Echinacea is also recommended to be used internally and externally as an herbal remedy for snakebite.

SCIENTIFIC EVIDENCE

Both test-tube and animal studies have found that polysaccharides found in echinacea can increase antibody production, raise white blood cell counts, and stimulate the activity of key white blood cells.

However, the meaningfulness of these studies has been questioned. Many other substances induce similar changes, including wheat, bamboo, rice, sugarcane, and chamomile, and none of these have ever been considered immune stimulants. We don't know whether echinacea produces its effects by stimulating the immune system, or in some altogether different way. Its lack of effectiveness in preventing colds when taken over the long-term suggests that echinacea does not actually strengthen the immune system overall.

In an uncontrolled study in people, echinacea decreased inflammation in patients with rheumatoid arthritis.

While controversial, many herbalists recommend using echinacea for 5 to 7 days on, 2 to 3 days off, and then re-administering the herb. This schedule allows the body to rest and hopefully achieve a greater immune boost each time the herb is administered. In people, actual negative results were seen in one study. For a period of 6 months, 200 people were given either echinacea or placebo. Use of the herb was actually associated with a 20% higher incidence of sore throat, runny nose, and sinusitis. The authors suggest that long-term use of echinacea might actually slightly impair immune function.

Since echinacea requires a healthy immune system, it has been proposed that it should not be used in pets with immune disorders without vet-

erinary supervision (feline leukemia or immunodeficiency virus infection, autoimmune diseases). This is based on suggestions made in human medicine, although studies dating back to the 1950s suggest that echinacea is safe in children.

Germany's Commission E warns against using echinacea in cases of autoimmune disorders such as multiple sclerosis, lupus, and rheumatoid arthritis, as well as tuberculosis or leukocytosis. There are also rumors that echinacea should not be used by people with AIDS. These warnings are theoretical, based on fears that echinacea might actually activate immunity in the wrong way. But there is no evidence that echinacea use has actually harmed anyone with these diseases. In fact, it has been used in the therapy of cancer due to its potential immune-stimulating properties.

DOSAGES

Many herbalists feel that liquid forms of echinacea are more effective than tablets or capsules in people, because they feel part of echinacea's benefit is due to activation of the tonsils through direct contact.

Since echinacea works best with a healthy immune system, use of other herbs (such as Oregon grape and goldenseal) and a proper diet with nutritional supplements boosts the effectiveness of echinacea.

It remains controversial which species of echinacea is the "best" to use. Many experts consider the fresh-pressed juice of *Echinacea purpurea* to be the best preparation since this contains the greatest range of active compounds. Many experts recommend a minimum standard of 2.4% beta-1, 2-fructofuranosides, which guarantees the plant was harvested in the blossom stage, was carefully prepared and stabilized. More research is needed to address this area of controversy

Since wild echinacea is becoming endangered, cultivated echinacea or other immune stimulants (such as reishi) may be preferred.

SAFETY ISSUES

For hyper-immune disorders (autoimmune diseases, diabetes) and disorders with diminished immune systems with low white blood cell counts (feline leukemia and immunodeficiency diseases), it may be wise to avoid this herb, as echinacea is used for immune stimulation. It is best used early in the course of the disease at the first signs of infection to properly and fully stimulate the immune system.

Echinacea appears to be safe. Even when taken in very high doses, it has not been found to cause any toxic effects. Reported side effects in people are also uncommon and usually limited to minor gastrointestinal symptoms, increased urination, and mild allergic reactions. The Commission E monograph (an extensive guide to herbal medicine) also recommends against using echinacea for more than 8 weeks. The safety of echinacea in young children, pregnant or nursing women, or those with severe liver or kidney disease has not been established. Similar side effects and warnings might be applied to pets. There are no known drug interactions.

EDTA CHELATION THERAPY

Common Uses
Cancer

Chelation with EDTA (Ethylenediaminetetraacetic acid) or other products is often recommended to treat a variety of cancerous conditions. EDTA can inhibit the metallproteinases that are critical for tumor development and growth. Results are so far inconclusive.

ENZYMES

Common Uses
Nutritional supplement

Enzymes are used for a variety of functions in the pet's body. Cellular processes, digestion, and absorption of dietary nutrients are dependent upon the proper enzymes. Most commonly, owners often think of enzymes as necessary for digestion of food. In fact, enzymes produced by the pancreas are essential for digestion of nutrients in the diet. Once properly digested by pancreatic enzymes, the dietary nutrients can be absorbed by the pet.

The pancreas produces amylase, lipase, and various proteases. Amylase is used for digesting carbohydrates, lipase is used for digesting fats, and proteases are used by the body to digest proteins.

While it is true that the pancreas produces enzymes to aid in food digestion, additional enzymes found in the diet contribute to digestion and absorption as well and may enhance feed efficiency (maximizing the utilization of nutrients in the diet). Natural raw diets contain a number of chemicals including enzymes not found in processed diets. Processing often alters the nutrients found in a pet's food, depleting it of important nutrients and enzymes. Enzymes are broken down in the presence of temperatures in the range of 120 to 160° F and in the presences of freezing temperatures. Supplying additional enzymes through the use of supplementation can replenish enzymes absent in processed foods. Even pets on natural raw diets can often benefit from additional enzymes, which is why they are often recommended as a supplement.

Additionally, various stressors such as illness, stress, allergies, food intolerance, age (older pets may have reduced digestive enzyme capability), and various orally administered medications (antibiotics) can decrease gastrointestinal function. This results in poor digestion and absorption of the nutrients in the diet. Supplying digestive enzymes at these times can improve digestion and absorption.

HOW DO ENZYMES WORK?

How do enzymes actually work? There is nothing magical about the enzymes themselves. They only work by liberating essential nutrients from the pet's diet. While we don't know all the wonderful things that enzymes do, it is known that certain enzyme supplements can increase the absorption of essential vitamins, minerals, and certain fatty acids from the diet. Increased absorption of zinc, selenium, vitamin B6, and linoleic acid have been detected following plant enzyme supplementation (specifically in a small study using a plant enzyme product called Prozyme).

Doctors can prescribe either pancreatic enzymes, microbial enzymes, or plant (vegetable) enzymes. Pancreatic enzymes are adequate for pets with pancreatic disease where enzyme production and function is inadequate.

Proteolytic enzymes are one class of enzymes that help your pet digest the proteins in food. Although the pet's body produces these enzymes in the pancreas, certain foods also contain proteolytic enzymes.

Papaya and pineapple are two of the richest plant sources of digestive enzymes. Papain and bromelain are the respective names for the proteolytic enzymes found in these fruits.

THERAPEUTIC USES

Enzymes have been recommended for treating pets with various disorders, including arthritis, allergies, poor coat condition, bowel disease (especially inflammatory bowel disease), and coprophagia (the condition where the pet ingests its own or another pet's feces). To date, only the plant enzymes seem to be particularly helpful in some pets with medical problems such as arthritis.

(Pancreatic enzymes are only recommended for pets with the rare condition called exocrine pancreatic insufficiency, although due to the cellulase activity seen in plant enzymes, many holistic doctors recommend plant enzymes for pancreatic insufficiency as well as other medical problems.) The plant enzymes are active over a much wider pH range (pH 3–9) than pancreatic enzymes and are the preferred enzymes for most patients. Plants contain the enzyme cellulase. Dogs and cats do not normally have cellulase in their bodies, and that's why they can only digest some of the plant material in their diets. Supplementation with enzyme products that contain cellulase in addition to the normal lipase, amylase, and proteases found in many supplements seems to be more advantageous to pets with medical problems as it liberates chemicals such as zinc, selenium, and linoleic acid that might be bound by fiber.

In one study, supplementing the diet with additional zinc did not confer the same benefits (improved growth rate and efficiency) as supplementing with plant enzymes. Apparently the plant enzymes liberated other nutrients in the diet in addition to zinc, resulting in positive benefits that did not occur simply by increasing the nutrient zinc.

In people (and possibly pets), enzymes have been shown to reduce pain after exercise or soft tissue trauma. Papain, the plant enzyme extracted from papaya, has been shown to be as effective as aspirin in several studies. Bromelain, the plant enzyme extracted from pineapple, was shown in one study to decrease the spread of implanted lung cancer in mice. Bromelain has also shown to be anti-inflammatory and has been suggested for treating inflammatory conditions including skin allergies (atopic dermatitis) and arthritis. It appears to inhibit pro-inflammatory prostaglandins.

Enzymes are recommended for use in cancer and immune diseases in people, including AIDS, although good studies are lacking. Since zinc deficiency impairs immunity, it may be that the increased zinc levels in the blood that occur after plant enzyme supplementation improve the functioning of the immune system in people and pets. Aging decreases immune function and zinc status. Supplementing with plant enzymes may be indicated in older pets to correct this. Supplementing with zinc is not indicated for two reasons: first, other nutrients in addition to zinc are absorbed as a result of enzyme supplementation that are beneficial for pets; second, excessive zinc levels can actually impair the immune system.

Regarding enzyme supplementation for pets with cancer, increased zinc absorption may also play a role in controlling this disease. Zinc can protect against cellular damage caused by the tumor necrosis factor.

Using plant enzymes also increases selenium absorption. Selenium is an antioxidant that works with vitamin E. There is a link between selenium and thyroid hormones. Specifically, selenium appears to be an essential component of the enzyme which converts the inactive form of thyroid hormone (T4) to the active form (T3) in rats and possibly other pets. This link might explain the enhanced hair growth and increased energy levels in pets supplemented with plant enzymes.

Anecdotally, pets taking plant enzyme supplements have been shown to have reduced levels of fleas, improved skin conditions (in pets with dry flaky skin), and improved energy levels (of so-called "poor doers").

Since response is variable regarding the product used, if one supplement does not help, another might.

Since enzymes are inactivated by heat, they cannot be added to warm food or mixed with warm water. Rather, they are simply sprinkled onto the food (at room temperature) at the time of feeding.

Enzyme supplementation is inexpensive, safe, and easy to administer in pill or powder form. Your doctor can help you decide which product is best for your pet's condition.

Bromelain

One popular enzyme is bromelain, a collection of protein-digesting enzymes found in pineapple juice and in the stem of pineapple plants.

Bromelain is actually thought to be useful for a variety of conditions. In Europe, it is widely used to aid in recovery from surgery and athletic injuries, as well as to treat osteoarthritis, rheumatoid arthritis, and gout. Bromelain is also useful as a digestive enzyme. Unlike most digestive enzymes, bromelain is active both in the acid environment of the stomach and the alkaline environment of the small intestine. This may make it particularly effective as an oral digestive aid for those pets who do not digest proteins properly. Since it is primarily the proteins in foods that cause food allergies, bromelain might reduce food-allergy symptoms as well, although this has not been proven.

While most large enzymes are broken down in the digestive tract, those found in bromelain appear to be absorbed whole to a certain extent. This finding makes it reasonable to suppose that bromelain can actually produce systemic (whole body) effects. Once in the blood, bromelain appears to produce mild anti-inflammatory and "blood-thinning" effects. There is at least one experimental report of bromelain inhibiting the spread of implanted lung carcinoma in mice.

Papain

Papain is a popular digestive enzyme that has been shown to be as effective as aspirin as an analgesic and anti-inflammatory agent in a variety of medical conditions.

The primary use of proteolytic enzymes is as a digestive aid (see also betaine hydrochloride). There is some evidence that proteolytic enzymes can be absorbed whole and may produce a variety of effects in the body. As mentioned earlier, many practitioners of complementary medicine believe that proteolytic enzymes can be helpful for a wide variety of other health conditions, especially food allergies (presumably by digesting the food so well that there is less to be allergic to), atopic (allergic) dermatitis, hairballs, arthritis, inflammatory bowel disease, and autoimmune diseases. Theoretically, arthritis and autoimmune diseases (including inflammatory bowel disease) may be made worse by whole proteins from foods leaking into the blood and causing an immune reaction. Digestive enzymes may help foil this so-called "leaky gut" problem. While there are many anecdotal reports of enzymes helping pets with a variety of medical problems, there are few controlled studies to show that they really work for these problems. (In people, two small double-blind studies, involving a total of more than 50 athletes, found that treatment with proteolytic enzymes significantly speeded healing of bruises and other mild athletic injuries, as compared to placebo.)

Pancreatic enzymes are specific extracts of pancreas used to help pets with digestive disturbances, most commonly a very rare condition called exocrine pancreatic insufficiency (EPI). EPI, when it occurs, is seen in dogs (usually German Shepherds). Administering pancreatic enzymes can help increase the digestion and absorption of nutrients in the food (plant enzymes can also be used in place of pancreatic enzymes). Unlike plant enzymes, pancreatic enzymes have no other health benefits as they are not absorbed by the pet.

SAFETY ISSUES

Proteolytic enzymes are believed to be quite safe, although there are some concerns that they might further damage the exposed tissue in an ulcer (by partly digesting it). For this reason, they are often not recommended for people and pets with gastrointestinal ulcerative disease.

Bromelain appears to be essentially nontoxic, and it seldom causes side effects other than occasional mild gastrointestinal distress or allergic reactions. However, because bromelain "thins the blood" to some extent, it shouldn't be combined with drugs such as Coumadin (warfarin) without a doctor's supervision. Safety in young children, pregnant or nursing women, or those with liver or kidney disease has not been established; similar precautions are probably warranted in pets as well.

 # EPHEDRA (Ma Huang, *Ephedra sinica*)

Common Use
Asthma

In Chinese herbal medicine, ephedra is a well-known herbal supplement for people and pets with respiratory conditions including asthma.

THERAPEUTIC USES

Ma huang was traditionally used by Chinese herbalists during the early stages of respiratory infections, and also for the short-term treatment of certain kinds of asthma, eczema, hay fever, narcolepsy, and edema. However, ma huang was not supposed to be taken for an extended period of time, and people with less than robust constitutions were warned to use only low doses or avoid ma huang altogether. Japanese chemists isolated ephedrine from ma huang (only the Asian species of ephedra contains the active compounds ephedrine and pseudoephedrine). It soon became a primary treatment for asthma in the United States and abroad. Ephedra's other major ingredient, pseudoephedrine, became the decongestant Sudafed. Dieters now use ephedrine as a weight-loss supplement.

When used properly, ephedra may be useful as a short-term treatment for sinus congestion and mild asthma.

DOSAGES

In people, it is recommended that ephedrine not be used for more than 1 week. In view of the documented dangers of ephedrine, medical supervision is highly recommended when using ephedra. Some holistic veterinarians recommend not using ephedra in pets due to the potential side effects.

The pet should be prescribed the lowest dosage possible and strict veterinary supervision is essential. For pets with asthma, long-term therapy will probably be necessary. Close monitoring by your veterinarian is essential for pets on long-term ephedra therapy.

SAFETY ISSUES

Ephedra should not be taken by those people or pets with enlargement of the prostate, high blood pressure, heart disease, diabetes, glaucoma, or hyperthyroidism. Furthermore, it should never be combined with monoamine-oxidase inhibitors (MAO inhibitors) or fatal reactions may develop. If symptoms such as a rapid heart rate, rapid breathing, anxiety, or restlessness develops, see your veterinarian.

Cats exhibit idiosyncratic reactions; for this reason, it should probably not be used in cats. Ephedra, most commonly prescribed for pets with asthma or respiratory problems, can cause heart arrhythmias and high blood pressure. Use with great caution in all pets. It should always be combined with other herbs to allow use of the lowest dose of ephedra possible.

Ephedrine mimics the effects of adrenaline and causes symptoms such as rapid heartbeat, high blood pressure, agitation, insomnia, nausea, and loss of appetite. Unscrupulous manufacturers have promoted ma huang as a natural hallucinogen ("herbal ecstasy") and not as a bronchial decongestant. Dosages of ephedrine required to produce psychoactive effects are exceedingly toxic to the heart; the FDA has documented 38 deaths of otherwise healthy young people who reportedly used ephedrine for psychedelic purposes.

Ephedra is not recommended for young children, pregnant or nursing women, or those with severe liver, heart, or kidney disease; similar precautions are probably warranted in pets.

EYEBRIGHT *(Euphrasia officinalis)*

Common Uses
Conjunctivitis

Eyebright is used as an anti-inflammatory and astringent herb for pets with conjunctivitis.

THERAPEUTIC USES

Like many herbs, eyebright contains astringent substances and volatile oils that are probably at least slightly antibacterial. However, there is no evidence that eyebright is particularly effective for treating eye diseases; Germany's Commission E recommends against using it.

Eyebright tea is also sometimes taken internally to treat jaundice, respiratory infections, and memory loss. However, there is no evidence that it is effective for these conditions.

SAFETY ISSUES

Be sure to use sterile products to prevent contamination of the eye. Eyebright can cause tearing of the eyes, itching, redness, and many other symptoms, probably due to direct irritation. However, few pet owners report these side effects. It appears to be safe when taken internally, but not many studies have been performed.

Safety in young children, pregnant or nursing women, or those with severe liver or kidney disease is not established. Similar warnings probably apply in pets.

FEVERFEW *(Tanacetum parthenium)*

Common Uses
Allergies, rheumatoid arthritis, asthma, fleas (topical)

Feverfew contains several chemicals; the major one of interest is the lactone parthenolide. For many years, it was assumed that this was the active ingredient. Numerous articles were published explaining that parthenolide caused platelets to release serotonin and reduce the synthesis of prostaglandins, leukotrienes, and thromboxanes. Based on this premature explanation, authors complained that samples of feverfew on the market varied as much as 10 to 1 in their parthenolide content.

However, a recent study found that an extract of feverfew standardized to a high-parthenolide content is entirely ineffective. Apparently, this high-parthenolide extract lacked some essential substance or group of substances present in the whole leaf. What those substances may be, however, remains mysterious.

As mentioned, feverfew acts similarly to non-steroidals and steroids by inhibiting prostaglandins, leukotrienes, and thromboxane.

THERAPEUTIC USES

Feverfew is often recommended in people with migraines and for its anti-inflammatory effects in the treatment of rheumatoid arthritis. It might be of benefit for pets with rheumatoid arthritis or osteoarthritis (page 11). However, there is no hard evidence that feverfew works for arthritis.

This herb inhibits platelet clumping and inhibits the formation of histamine and serotonin, which might be of benefit in allergic pets.

Feverfew (especially the flowers and upper stems) contain pyrethrins and can be used as a natural flea control rinse.

Feverfew may be useful as a safe "aspirin substitute" in cats as it does not contain salicylic acid.

SAFETY ISSUES

Avoid during pregnancy to prevent abortion. The fresh foliage can cause mouth ulcers, and only the dried herb should be used. Feed a test dose first to check for oral irritation and sensitivity.

The fresh foliage of the plant can cause mouth ulcers; the dried herb is safe. Do not use internally for more than one week at a time. Do not use in pregnant animals.

Feverfew can inhibit platelets and should not be used in animals with platelet problems or bleeding disorders.

Safety in young children, pregnant or nursing women, or those with severe kidney or liver disease has not been established; similar warnings probably apply in pets.

FISH OIL (See Oral Fatty Acids

FLAXSEED OIL (See Oral Fatty Acids)

FLEABANE *(Conyza canadensis)* (See also Canadian Fleabane)

Common Uses
Insecticide

The fleabane plant has been used as an insecticide. It contains limonene, a compound that has shown effectiveness in killing fleas.

THERAPEUTIC USES

Fleabane is used as an insecticide. The active ingredient is limonene, which is a known flea repellant. Little is known regarding other constituents of the plant.

SAFETY ISSUES

Fleabane can elicit allergies in pets.

 # FOLIC ACID (Folate, folacin)

Common Uses
Nutritional supplement

Folic acid is a B vitamin used for proper functioning of the nervous system. It also enhances immunity and is needed for the formation of red blood cells. Because folic acid functions as a coenzyme for DNA and RNA, it is important for normal cell division.

Folic acid plays a critical role in many biological processes. It participates in the crucial biological process known as methylation, and plays an important role in cell division: Without sufficient amounts of folic acid, cells cannot divide properly. In people, adequate amounts of folic acid intake can reduce the risk of heart disease and prevent serious birth defects; it may also lessen the risk of developing certain forms of cancer.

In people, folic acid is best known for preventing neural tube defects in the developing fetus. Folic acid also lowers blood levels of homocysteine, a suspected risk factor in heart disease in people; increased folate supplementation of foods might be able to reduce heart disease deaths.

Studies suggest that a deficiency in folic acid might predispose people to develop cancer of the cervix, colon, lung, and mouth.

SCIENTIFIC EVIDENCE

Although there is no evidence that folic acid supplements can treat cancer, preliminary studies suggest that very high dosages of folic acid may be able to reverse precancerous changes found in the cervix among women taking oral contraceptives.

Based on intriguing but not yet definitive evidence in people, folic acid in various dosages has been suggested as a treatment for depression, bipolar disorder, osteoporosis, osteoarthritis (in combination with vitamin B_{12}), rheumatoid arthritis, vitiligo, migraine headaches, and periodontal disease.

According to a recent study that examined data on 80,000 women, a high intake of folic acid may cut the risk of heart disease in half by reducing blood levels of homocysteine. Individuals with high homocysteine levels appear to have more than twice the risk of developing heart disease than those with low homocysteine levels, and folic acid supplements, alone or in combination with vitamins B_6 and B_{12}, effectively reduce the level of homocysteine in the blood. Pets do not routinely have homocysteine levels measured, nor do they contract the type of heart disease evaluated in this study. Therefore, it is unknown if folic acid supplementation would benefit pets with heart disease.

There is no specific indication for additional folic acid supplementation in pets. Pets with similar conditions to those listed above in people might benefit from additional supplementation with folic acid and B vitamins, although there are no definitive studies to prove this.

SOURCES

Folate is obtained through brewer's yeast, brown rice, milk products, meat, beef liver, mushrooms, poultry, salmon, tuna, dark green leafy vegetables, beans, asparagus, soybeans, soy flour, oranges and other fruits, grains, and wheat.

Folate must be supplied in the diets of dogs and cats. Deficiencies are unlikely but could cause poor weight gain, lack of appetite, low white blood cell counts, decreased immune function, inflammation of tissues of the oral cavity, and megaloblastic anemia.

The AAFCO recommendations for folate are 0.18 mg/kg of food daily for dogs and 0.8 mg/kg of food daily for cats.

SAFETY ISSUES

Too much folic acid can interfere with anticonvulsant medications and may cause seizures!

Extra folic acid may be indicated for pets taking sulfa drugs for extended periods of time due to inhibition of PABA (para-aminobenzoic acid) which is a component of folic acid (easily done by supplementing with a natural B vitamin supplement). Pets taking other medications do not seem to require additional folic acid.

Folic acid is extremely safe; no incidences of toxicity have been reported in pets.

People taking aspirin, other anti-inflammatory medications, antacids, tetracycline antibiotics, sulfa antibiotics, oral contraceptives, estrogen-replacement therapy, triamterene, corticosteroids (prednisone), valproic acid, carbamazepine, isoniazid (INH), nitrous oxide, cholestyramine, colestipol, phenytoin, phenobarbital, or primidone may need to take extra folic acid.

 # GARLIC *(Allium sativum)*

Common Uses

Allergies, asthma, diabetes, fleas (oral), heart conditions, cancer, infections, intestinal parasites, kidney disease

Garlic contains a number of nutrients and a number of sulfur compounds that have been shown to have medical qualities, especially allicin and alliin.

The sulfur compounds present in garlic may increase phase II detoxification enzymes. By increasing phase II detoxification enzymes, the risk of many degenerative conditions may be reduced significantly.

Allicin, one of the active ingredients in garlic, has been shown to have antimicrobial qualities

that may be more effective than tetracycline. While garlic is an effective antibiotic when it contacts the tissue directly, there is no reason to believe that it will work to fight infections systemically if you take it orally. There is no question that raw garlic can kill a wide variety of microorganisms by direct contact, including fungi, bacteria, viruses, and protozoa. This may explain why applying garlic directly to a wound was traditionally done to prevent infection. However, garlic can cause burns when it is applied to the skin.

THERAPEUTIC USES

Garlic has also been proposed as a treatment for asthma and diabetes. Preliminary evidence suggests that regular use of garlic may help prevent cancer. While eating garlic is commonly claimed to raise immunity, there is no real evidence that this is the case. In people, several large studies strongly suggest that a diet high in garlic can prevent cancer. In one study, women whose diets included significant quantities of garlic were approximately 30% less likely to develop colon cancer. The interpretations of studies like this one are always a bit controversial. For example, it's possible that the women who ate a lot of garlic also made other healthful lifestyle choices.

While researchers looked at this possibility very carefully and concluded that garlic was a common factor, it is not clear that they are right. What is really needed to settle the question is an intervention trial, where some people are given garlic and others are given a placebo. However, none have yet been performed.

Moderately good studies have found that garlic (including garlic powder) also appears to slightly improve hypertension in people and pets, protect against free radicals, and slow blood coagulation. Putting all these benefits together, garlic may be a broad-spectrum treatment for arterial disease.

Garlic can be used for **allergic dermatitis** (page 3) as it contains chemicals that can reduce the production of inflammatory prostaglandins.

Garlic is a cardiovascular tonic and can help prevent blood clots. The cholesterol-reducing effects of garlic may also be helpful for pets with **heart disease** (page 91) or high blood cholesterol.

While scientific proof is lacking, garlic (and nutritional yeast) is often used to control **fleas** (page 89) and some owners report positive results.

Garlic is recommended for pets with tapeworms; it has shown effects against roundworms and hookworms in people.

SCIENTIFIC EVIDENCE

Garlic has been shown to stimulate white blood cells (killer cells) in human AIDS patients.

Garlic has been shown to prevent tumor formation in rats (due to its diallyl sulfide component and due to its liver-strengthening chemicals).

Garlic can decrease blood cholesterol and triglyceride levels; certain forms of garlic have been shown to lower total cholesterol levels by about 9 to 12%, as well as possibly improve the ratio of good and bad cholesterol. Virtually all studies in people used garlic standardized to alliin content, whereas garlic oil did not seem to be effective; conflicting results have been shown for garlic powder, although some results are encouraging.

DOSAGES

Allicin is not necessary for all of garlic's purported benefits but is needed to confer the antibiotic properties of garlic. When used for infections, the "allicin potential" of the garlic compound used is important. Since allicin is an unstable compound that is easily destroyed, fresh garlic or products with an identified allicin potential should be used when garlic is chosen for treating infections. (Because it is hard to know if a prepared formula has the guaranteed amount of allicin listed on the label unless the product comes from a reputable manufacturer, many herbalists recommend using fresh garlic cloves when the allicin content is important.) For prepared products, the product should provide a daily dose of at least 10 mg of alliin or a total allicin potential of 4,000 micrograms (4 to 5 mg), which approximates 1 clove (4 grams) of garlic. (In people, a typical dosage of garlic is 900 mg daily of a garlic powder extract standardized to contain 1.3% alliin, providing about 12,000 mcg of alliin daily.) This recommendation needs to be extrapolated for use in pets. Many manufacturers claim an allicin potential "at the time of manufacture." This is not helpful as it does not reveal the allicin potential of the finished product and whether or not the product is stable. Read the label carefully.

However, a great deal of controversy exists over the proper dosage and form of garlic. In people, most everyone agrees that one or two raw garlic cloves a day are adequate for most purposes, but virtual trade wars have taken place over the potency and effectiveness of various dried, aged, or deodorized garlic preparations. The problem has to do with the way garlic is naturally constructed.

A relatively odorless substance, alliin is one of the most important compounds in garlic. When garlic is crushed or cut, an enzyme called allinase is brought in contact with alliin, turning it into allicin. The allicin itself then rapidly breaks down into entirely different compounds. Allicin is most responsible for garlic's strong odor. It can also blister the skin and kill bacteria, viruses, and fungi. Presumably the garlic plant uses allicin as a form of protection from pests and parasites. It also may provide much of the medicinal benefits of garlic.

When powdered garlic is put in a capsule, it acts like cutting the bulb. The chain reaction starts once the garlic is powdered: Alliin contacts allinase, yielding allicin, which then breaks down. Unless something is done to prevent this process, garlic powder won't have any alliin or allicin left by the time you buy it.

Some garlic producers declare that alliin and allicin have nothing to do with garlic's effectiveness and simply sell products without it. This is particularly true of aged powdered garlic and garlic oil. But others feel certain that allicin is absolutely essential. However, in order to make garlic relatively odorless, they must prevent the alliin from turning into allicin until the product is consumed. To accomplish this feat, they engage in marvelously complex manufacturing processes, each unique and proprietary. How well each of these methods work is a matter of finger-pointing controversy.

The best that can be said at this point is that in most of the studies that found cholesterol-lowering powers in garlic, the daily dosage supplied at least 10 mg of alliin. This is sometimes stated in terms of how much allicin will be created from that alliin. The number you should look for is 4 to 5 mg of "allicin potential." Alliin-free aged garlic also appears to be effective when taken at a dose of 1 to 7.2 g daily.

To use garlic for other uses (cancer, antioxidants, nutritional supplement, immune booster), any form will probably work if the garlic has not been subjected to extreme heat (such as roasting). When possible, raw garlic cloves are probably preferred.

SAFETY ISSUES

Too much garlic can be toxic to pets, causing Heinz body anemia. As a rule, I recommend following label directions for commercially prepared products (such as those recommended for flea control). For feeding fresh garlic, I use one clove per 10 to 30 pounds of body weight per day. There do not appear to be any animal toxicity studies on the most commonly used form of powdered garlic standardized to alliin content.

Do not use in pets with anemia. Do not use in pets scheduled for surgery due to the possibility of increased bleeding times. Refrain from use at least 1 week before and 1 week after surgery.

Topical garlic can cause skin irritation, blistering, and even third-degree burns, so be very careful about applying garlic directly to the skin.

Garlic may cause excess intestinal gas (reduce the dosage if this occurs).

Taking garlic at the same time as taking ginkgo or high-dose vitamin E might conceivably cause a risk of bleeding problems.

GERMAN CHAMOMILE (Matricaria recutita, Matricaria chamomilla)

Common Uses

Allergies (topical and herbal rinse), anxiety disorders, arthritis, asthma, diarrhea, infections (topical), intestinal parasites

Two distinct plants are known as chamomile and are used interchangeably: German and Roman *(Chamaemelum nobile)* chamomile. Although botanically far apart, they both look like miniature daisies and appear to possess similar medicinal benefits.

It has been suggested that chamomile's reported effect is due to the constituents of its bright blue oil, including chamazulene, alpha-bisabolol, and bisaboloxides. However, the water-soluble part of chamomile may play a role, too, especially in soothing stomach upset.

THERAPEUTIC USES

Chamomile is useful for digestive disturbances, especially if they occur from nervousness (irritable bowel disorder). Due to the number of chemicals contained in chamomile, this herb can be effective in **inflammatory bowel disease** (page 105) and other gastrointestinal disorders (such as pets with excessive intestinal gas).

It might help protect the stomach against irritation caused by anti-inflammatory drugs.

Concentrated alcohol extracts of chamomile are also sometimes used to treat the pain caused by various forms of arthritis. And, it is common practice in Germany for individuals with asthma or other breathing problems to inhale the steam from boiling chamomile and other herbs.

Chamomile is often recommended as an herbal dewormer for pets with worms, especially roundworms and whipworms, and is safer than other dewormers (wormwood, black walnut).

Chamomile is useful for pets with nervousness and anxiety. Chamomile is an anti-inflammatory herb that is also useful for its antimicrobial properties (for pets with skin infections) and for its ability to heal wounds.

Chamomile can be used as a cooled infusion preparation applied topically to inflamed or infected skin, and applied topically to the eye for pets with allergic conjunctivitis.

SAFETY ISSUES

Avoid using German chamomile in pregnant animals as it may cause abortion. Usually considered a safe herb, the rare pet may be allergic to chamomile, especially those allergic to ragweed, so a small amount should be applied to the skin first to check for inflammation, hives, or other signs of sensitivity. If no reaction occurs, feed a small amount and watch for vomiting, diarrhea, or hives. If no reaction occurs, use as directed by your veterinarian.

Chamomile also contains naturally occurring coumarin compounds that can act as "blood thinners." Excessive use of chamomile is therefore not recommended when taking prescription anticoagulants. Safety in young children, pregnant or nursing women, or those with liver or kidney disease has not been established, although there have not been any credible reports of toxicity caused by this common beverage tea. Similar precautions should probably be observed in pets.

GINGER *(Zingiber officinale)*

Common Uses
Arthritis, heart conditions, infections

Ginger's modern use dates back to the early 1980s, when a scientist named D. Mowrey noticed that ginger-filled capsules reduced his nausea during an episode of flu. Inspired by this, he performed the first double-blind study of ginger. Germany's Commission E subsequently approved ginger as a treatment for indigestion and motion sickness.

One of the most prevalent ingredients in fresh ginger is the pungent substance gingerol, an aromatic ketone. However, when ginger is dried and stored, its gingerol rapidly converts to the substances shogaol and zingerone. Which, if any, of these substances is most important has not been determined.

THERAPEUTIC USES

Ginger dilates blood vessels and may increase blood circulation to the arthritic joints; its anti-inflammatory effects (inhibition of prostaglandins) helps with the treatment of arthritis. It also has pain-relieving effects due to its influence on substance P, a nerve transmitter responsible for relaying the sensation of pain.

Ginger is also well-known for relieving indigestion and nausea in people and can be used for similar problems in pets, including excess intestinal gas; pets taking nonsteroidal or steroidal medications may benefit from ginger use due to the anti-ulcer properties of ginger. It can also be tried for pets who get "car sick" when traveling.

Ginger is known for its antioxidant and antibiotic effects. It can also inhibit platelet clumping, lower blood cholesterol, act as a tonic for the heart, and provide some analgesic effects (possibly by inhibiting the release of substance P).

SCIENTIFIC EVIDENCE

Powdered ginger root and ginger tea have been used in many studies; there is some debate about whether fresh ginger might be preferred.

SAFETY ISSUES

Do not use in pregnant animals or those receiving hypoglycemic therapy or clotting disorders (or in pets on anticoagulant therapies). As ginger may increase body temperature, it should not be used in pets with fever. Do not use in pets scheduled for surgery due to possible effects on blood clotting (refrain from use at least 1 week before and 1 week after surgery).

Like garlic, extracts of ginger inhibit blood coagulation in test-tube experiments. This has led to a theoretical concern that ginger should not be combined with drugs such as Coumadin (warfarin), heparin, or even aspirin. European studies with actual oral ginger taken alone in normal quantities have not found any significant effect on blood coagulation, but it is still possible that combination treatment could cause problems.

GINKGO *(Ginkgo Biloba)*

Common Uses
Allergies, asthma, cognitive disorder, epilepsy, heart conditions, kidney disease, urinary disorders (incontinence)

Ginkgo has a number of important chemical components, including flavonoid glycosides including proanthocyanidins and quercetin (ginkgo extract is standardized to 25% flavonoid glycosides), glucose, rhamnose, and terpenes (ginkgolides and bilobalide).

THERAPEUTIC USES

In traditional Chinese herbology, tea made from ginkgo seeds has been used for numerous problems, most particularly asthma and other respiratory illnesses. The leaf was not used. But in the 1950s, German researchers started to investigate the medical possibilities of ginkgo leaf extracts rather than remedies using the seeds. Thus, modern ginkgo preparations are not the same as the traditional Chinese herb, and the comparisons often drawn are incorrect.

Ginkgo is known for a number of medicinal benefits. By inhibiting platelet activating factor (PAF), ginkgo inhibits platelets from forming clots. Because of this and the ability of ginkgo to strengthen blood vessels, many doctors use it in older pets prone to cognitive dysfunction (as it has been recommended for Alzheimer's patients).

Ginkgo also stabilizes cell membranes and scavenges free radicals, especially in the nervous system. As a result, ginkgo can be tried on pets with any type of nervous system disease, such as seizures, **incontinence** (page 145), deafness, and behavioral disorders.

Ginkgo is also recommended for pets with **kidney disease** (page 121), and is often combined with hawthorn for this condition.

SCIENTIFIC EVIDENCE

The scientific record for ginkgo use in people is extensive and impressive. Numerous studies have found that ginkgo extracts can improve circulation. We don't know exactly how ginkgo does this, but unknown constituents in the herb appear to make the blood more fluid, reduce the tendency toward blood clots, extend the life of a natural blood vessel-relaxing substance, and act as an antioxidant. However, ginkgo's influence on mental function may have nothing to do with its effects on circulation.

In the past, European physicians believed that the cause of mental deterioration with age (senile dementia) was reduced circulation in the brain due to atherosclerosis. Since ginkgo can improve circulation, they assumed that ginkgo was simply getting more blood to brain cells and thereby making them work better. However, the contemporary understanding of age-related memory loss and mental impairment no longer considers chronically restricted circulation the primary issue. Ginkgo (and other drugs used for dementia) may instead function by directly stimulating nerve-cell activity and protecting nerve cells from further injury, although improvement in circulatory capacity may also play a role.

According to a 1992 article published in *Lancet*, more than 40 double-blind controlled trials have evaluated the benefits of ginkgo in treating age-related mental decline. Of these, eight were rated of good quality, involving a total of about 1,000 people and producing positive results in all but one study. The authors of the *Lancet* article felt that the evidence was strong enough to conclude that ginkgo extract is an effective treatment for this condition. Studies since 1992 have verified this conclusion, both in people with Alzheimer's disease and those without the disorder. Interestingly, European physicians are so certain that ginkgo is effective that it's become hard for them to perform scientific studies of the herb. To them, it's unethical to give Alzheimer's patients a placebo when they could take ginkgo instead and have additional months of useful life. This objection doesn't apply in the United States, where physicians generally do not believe that ginkgo is effective. A recent study published in the *Journal of the American Medical Association* reported on the results of a year-long double-blind trial of *Ginkgo biloba* in over 300 individuals with Alzheimer's disease or other forms of severe age-related mental decline.

Participants were given either 40 mg of the ginkgo extract or a placebo 3 times daily. The results showed significant (but not miraculous) improvements in the treated group. Contrary to some reports, the type of ginkgo used in the study is identical to standardized extracts widely available in the United States. This research on people may be applicable to pets and seems quite encouraging.

The bioflavonoids in ginkgo may inhibit histamine release from mast cells and decrease the production of chemicals which promote inflammation including leukotrienes. Ginkgo also contains terpene molecules called ginkgolides. Ginkgolides antagonize PAF (platelet activating factor), which is an important chemical produced by the body that causes inflammation and allergies. In double-blinded studies in asthmatic people, the anti-asthmatic effect of orally administered ginkgolides has been shown to improve respiration. High doses of ginkgo extract were needed to achieve this effect.

DOSAGES

The standard dosage of ginkgo in people is 40 to 80 mg 3 times daily of a 50:1 extract standardized to contain 24% ginkgo-flavone glycosides.

SAFETY ISSUES

Do not use *Ginkgo biloba* in animals with blood-clotting disorders. Do not use in pregnant animals.

Ginkgo

Contact with live ginkgo plants can cause severe allergic reactions, and ingestion of ginkgo seeds can be dangerous. Extremely high doses have been given in animals for long periods of time without serious consequences. Safety in young children, pregnant or nursing women, or those with severe liver or kidney disease, however, has not been established. The same precautions may apply in pets. Ginkgo may cause diarrhea, nausea, or restlessness in excessive doses.

However, because of ginkgo's "blood-thinning" effects, some experts warn that it should not be combined with blood-thinning drugs such as Coumadin (warfarin), heparin, aspirin, and other nonsteroidal medications, and use of such drugs was prohibited in most of the double-blind trials of ginkgo. It is also possible that ginkgo could cause bleeding problems if combined with natural blood thinners, such as garlic and high-dose vitamin E. There have been two case reports in highly regarded journals of subdural hematoma (bleeding in the skull) and hyphema (spontaneous bleeding into the anterior chamber of the eye) in association with ginkgo use in people. As a precaution, do not use in pets with bleeding disorders, pets scheduled for surgery (refrain from use at least 1 week before and 1 week after surgery), and those taking medicines that interfere with blood clotting.

GINSENG *(Panax ginseng, Panax quinquefolius)*

Common Uses
Cognitive disorder (anti-aging effect), diabetes, cancer

There are actually three different herbs commonly called ginseng: Asian or Korean ginseng *(Panax ginseng)*, American ginseng *(Panax quinquefolius)*, and Siberian "ginseng" *(Eleutherococcus senticosus)*. The latter herb is actually not ginseng at all, but the Russian scientists responsible for promoting it believe that it functions identically.

Asian ginseng is a perennial herb with a taproot resembling the human body. It grows in northern China, Korea, and Russia; its close relative, *Panax quinquefolius*, is cultivated in the United States. Because ginseng must be grown for 5 years before it is harvested, it commands a high price, with top-quality roots easily selling for more than $10,000.

Dried, unprocessed ginseng root is called "white ginseng," and steamed, heat-dried root is "red ginseng." Chinese herbalists believe that each form has its own particular benefits.

Ginseng contains many chemicals, the most important of which are triterpenoids called ginsenosides. Different species of ginseng contain different concentrations of the various classes of ginsenosides.

THERAPEUTIC USES

Ginseng can elevate blood pressure. It has also been shown to decrease exhaustion (fatigue) by stimulating the central nervous system and by sparing glycogen use in exercising muscles.

Ginseng is also well-known for its use in the treatment of **diabetes** (page 66). It will decrease blood sugar in diabetic (but not normoglycemic) mice. In non-diabetics, ginseng increases blood cortisol, but it reduces serum cortisol levels in diabetics.

In vitro, ginseng has been shown to increase the lifespan of cells (anti-aging effect).

Ginseng can reduce blood cholesterol and triglyceride levels. Regular intake of ginseng may protect against cancer formation; the extract and powder in people was shown more effective than the tea, juice, or fresh sliced ginseng.

Ginseng also stimulates the immune system by enhancing white blood cell and antibody functions. It should not be used in high doses during acute infections as it may inhibit some immune functions.

DOSAGES

Dosage in people varies based upon ginsenoside content. In general, tonic effects are seen when the product contains at least 10 mg of ginosenoside Rg1, with a ratio of Rg1 to Rb1 of 1:2.

For people, the typical recommended daily dosage of *Panax ginseng* is 1 to 2 g of raw herb, or 200 mg daily of an extract standardized to contain 4 to 7% ginsenosides. *Eleutherococcus senticosus* is taken at a dosage of 2 to 3 g whole herb or 300 to 400 mg of extract daily. Ordinarily, a 2- to 3-week period of using ginseng is recommended, followed by a 1- to 2-week "rest" period. Russian tradition suggests that ginseng should not be used by those under 40. Finally, because *Panax ginseng* is so expensive, some products actually contain very little. Adulteration with other herbs and even caffeine is not unusual.

SCIENTIFIC EVIDENCE

Taken together, the scientific record on ginseng is intriguing but not conclusive. Most studies used injectable ginseng in animals and non-double-blind studies in people. If some of the money spent on animal and non-double-blind human studies had been used to fund more double-blind studies in humans, we might know a lot more. At the present state of knowledge, it is hard to know whether ginseng is as effective as its mystique would make it seem.

SAFETY ISSUES

Ginseng should not be used in pets with hypertension (hyperthyroidism in cats, kidney disease in dogs and cats, cardiomyopathy). Do not use in pets with bleeding or pets with anxiety, hyperactivity, or nervousness. Do not use in pets taking hypoglycemic medications without veterinary su-

pervision. Because patients vary in their response to ginseng, because various species of plants exist with various quantities of ginsenosides, and because of variation in quality control among supplements, long-term ingestion should be avoided and veterinary advice sought when using ginseng.

Ginseng may increase levels of digitalis drugs.

Siberian ginseng (*Eleutherococcus senticosus*) appears to have greater safety due to standardized extracts (typically a 33% ethanol extract, standardized to 5% ginsenosides). It is reported to have antioxidant activity, lowers high blood pressure but raises low blood pressure (an adaptogen effect), dilates coronary arteries, and exhibits a mild diuretic effect. Side effects are rare unless high doses are used. Follow the guidelines for *Panax ginseng*.

In people, unconfirmed reports suggest that highly excessive doses of ginseng can raise blood pressure, increase heart rate, and possibly cause other significant effects. Whether some of these cases were actually caused by caffeine mixed in with ginseng remains unclear. Ginseng allergy can also occur, as can allergy to any other substance. There is some evidence that ginseng can interfere with drug metabolism, specifically drugs processed by an enzyme called "CYP 3A4." There have also been specific reports of ginseng interacting with MAO inhibitor drugs and also digitalis, although again it is not clear whether it was the ginseng or a contaminant that caused the problem. There has also been one report of ginseng reducing the anticoagulant effects of Coumadin.

Safety in young children, pregnant or nursing women, or those with severe liver or kidney disease has not been established. Interestingly, Chinese tradition suggests that ginseng should not be used by pregnant or nursing mothers. Similar precautions are probably warranted in pets.

Ginseng

GLUCOSAMINE

Common Uses
Osteoarthritis, inflammatory bowel disease

Glucosamine is the most commonly used chondroprotective supplement used for the treatment of **osteoarthritis** (page 11) (chondroitin is the second most commonly used supplement for the treatment of osteoarthritis). Glucosamine is produced naturally in the body, where it is a key building block for making cartilage (it serves as a building block for the glycosaminoglycans and proteoglycans). Glucosamine is an aminosugar (made from glutamine and glucose) that is incorporated into articular (joint) cartilage; it is supplied as a supplement in one of three forms: glucosamine sulfate, glucosamine hydrochloride (a salt of D-glucosamine; D-glucosamine is eventually converted by the body into glucosamine sulfate), or N-acetylglucosamine.

THERAPEUTIC USES

N-acetylglucosamine and D-glucosamine (for which glutamine, another supplement recommended for pets with inflammatory bowel disease, is a precursor) may be helpful for pets with inflammatory bowel disease. The cells of the intestinal mucosa have a high rate of cell turnover, and patients with inflammatory bowel disease have a cell turnover rate that is at least three times higher than healthy patients. Patients with inflammatory bowel disease cannot make N-acetylglucosamine. This deficiency of N-acetylglucosamine leads to further intestinal damage including increased permeability (leaky gut syndrome). Supplementing N-acetylglucosamine and D-glucosamine (and giving additional glutamine) can help heal the intestinal mucosa by supporting glycoprotein synthesis. Since glucosamines also are important in producing the glycoproteins that make up the mucous membranes of the urinary and respiratory tracts, supplementing with glucosamine for pets with **bladder disorders** (page 36) and chronic respiratory disease might be helpful.

As we are just beginning to understand how glucosamine products can be helpful in pets, future studies may indicate a variety of disorders for which glucosamine products may be useful.

SOURCES

Glucosamine is not usually obtained directly from food; supplements are derived from chitin, a substance found in the shells of shrimp, lobsters, and crabs.

SCIENTIFIC EVIDENCE

Studies show that while all three forms of glucosamine are effective, glucosamine hydrochloride (which is a salt of D-glucosamine) and glucosamine sulfate were more effective than N-acetylglucosamine. Results take 4 to 8 weeks to develop. Interestingly, these improvements often last for several weeks after glucosamine supplements are discontinued.

Glucosamine is rapidly taken up by cartilage cells and helps stimulate the synthesis of synovial fluid and cartilage and also helps inhibit the destructive enzymes that can destroy cartilage and proteoglycans. The anti-inflammatory aspect of glucosamine may result from the scavenging of harmful free radicals (similar to antioxidants). Glucosamine is used by the cartilage for the synthesis of glycosaminoglycans.

A number of studies in people and pets show that glucosamine is equally effective for treating osteoarthritis when compared to NSAIDs without the side effects. In fact, glucosamine and chondroitin are among the few supplements for which we actually have good studies in people and pets.

In both people and pets, solid evidence indicates that glucosamine supplements effectively relieve pain and other symptoms of osteoarthritis.

In both people and dogs, patients given glucosamine experienced significantly reduced pain and improved movement, to a greater extent than the improvements seen in the placebo groups.

Other studies showed that nonsteroidal medications and glucosamine proved equally effective at reducing symptoms. In people, one group that received combination treatment (the nonsteroidal piroxicam plus glucosamine) didn't show significantly better results than either treatment taken alone.

In this same study, after 90 days into the study, treatment was stopped and the participants were followed for an additional 60 days. The benefits of piroxicam rapidly disappeared, but the benefits of glucosamine lasted for the full 60 days.

While a number of glucosamine products are available from reputable manufacturers, many of the early major studies done in pets have used a proprietary product (Cosequin and Cosequin-DS) containing glucosamine and chondroitin.

Clinical evidence indicates other products from well-known manufacturers are also effective.

DOSAGES

Dosages vary depending upon the product. As a guideline for combination products, a starting dose of 1,000 to 1,500 mg of glucosamine with 800 to 1,200 mg of chondroitin is recommended per day for a 50- to 100-pound dog. This dose is then lowered after 4 to 8 weeks.

While arthritis is rare in cats when compared with dogs, clinical experience suggests that glucosamine and chondroitin products may also be quite helpful for arthritic cats. In general, the doses for smaller dogs are used.

SAFETY ISSUES

Glucosamine appears to be extremely safe with no side effects; mild GI upset is rarely observed. No significant side effects have been reported in any of the studies of glucosamine.

GLUTAMINE

Common Uses
  Bowel disorders, arthritis

Glutamine, or L-glutamine, is an amino acid derived from another amino acid, glutamic acid. It serves as a precursor to D-glucosamine, an amino sugar well-known for its ability to relieve pain and inflammation and regenerate connective tissue in people and pets with osteoarthritis. Severe stresses may result in a temporary glutamine deficiency.

SOURCES

There is no daily requirement for glutamine as the body can make its own glutamine. High-protein foods such as meat, fish, beans, and dairy products are excellent sources of glutamine.

THERAPEUTIC USES

Glutamine plays a role in the health of the immune system, digestive tract, and muscle cells, as well as other bodily functions. It appears to serve as a fuel for the cells that line the intestines (it serves as a primary energy source for the mucosal cells that line the intestinal tract). Because stress on the intestinal cells (such as chronic inflammatory bowel disease) can increase the need for glutamine as the body replaces the cells lining the intestinal tract, glutamine is often recommended for pets with chronic bowel disorders including **inflammatory bowel disease** (page 105). Heavy exercise, infection, surgery, and trauma can deplete the body's glutamine reserves, particularly in muscle cells.

It has also been suggested as a treatment for food allergies, based on the "leaky gut syndrome." This theory holds that in some pets whole proteins leak through the wall of the digestive tract and enter the blood, causing allergic reactions. Preliminary evidence suggests that glutamine supplements might reduce leakage through the intestinal walls. In people and pets, glutamine is also recommended to reduce the loss of muscle mass (as may occur during injury, stress, or high-endurance activities as might be encountered by dogs competing in field trials).

Glutamine is also a precursor to the enzyme glutamine: fructose-6-phosphate amidotransferase, which plays a role in the development of insulin resistance that may eventually manifest itself as diabetes if there is an imbalance or deficiencies in glutamine levels. Supplementing diabetic pets with glutamine may be helpful, although more research is needed in this area.

Glutamine may reduce the gastrointestinal toxicity of some chemotherapy drugs. It can also prevent inflammation of the intestinal tract caused by radiation therapy of this area. Glutamine should be considered as a supplement for dogs undergoing half-body irridation for the treatment of lymphosarcoma.

SCIENTIFIC EVIDENCE

There is little real evidence that glutamine works as a treatment for true food allergies, although it is highly recommended for pets with various bowel disorders.

In people, there is evidence that glutamine supplements might have significant nutritional benefits for those who are seriously ill. In one study, 84 critically ill hospital patients were divided into two groups. All the patients were being fed through a feeding tube. One group received a normal feeding-tube diet, whereas the other group received this diet plus supplemental glutamine. After 6 months, 14 of the 42 patients receiving glutamine had died, compared with 24 of the control group. The glutamine group also left both the intensive care ward and the hospital significantly sooner than the patients who did not receive glutamine. Adding glutamine to the feeding formulas of hospitalized pets might be warranted.

DOSAGES

Recommended dosages in pets are 250 to 3,000 mg daily.

Maximum safe dosages for young children, pregnant or nursing women, or those with severe liver or kidney disease have not been determined; similar precautions are probably warranted in pets.

SAFETY ISSUES

Glutamine, being one of the body's amino acids, is thought to be a safe supplement when taken at recommended dosages. Because many anti-epilepsy drugs work by blocking glutamate stimulation in the brain, high dosages of glutamine may overwhelm these drugs and pose a risk to pets with epilepsy. If your pet is taking anti-seizure medications, glutamine should only be used under veterinary supervision.

GLYCOPROTEINS/GLYCOCONJUGATE SUGARS
(Mannose, Mannans)

Common Uses
Immune diseases, arthritis, asthma, wound healing

Glycoproteins are protein molecules bound to carbohydrate molecules. Glycoprotein molecules coat the surface of every cell with a nucleus in the human body. The body uses the glycoproteins on cell surface glycoconjugates as communication or recognition molecules. These communications may then result in other cellular events, including secretion of bioactive substances (interferon, interleukin-1, complement), ingestion of bacteria and cell debris, inhibition of adherence necessary for bacterial infection, and the spread of cancer cell metastasis.

Scientists have identified eight sugars, glycoforms, found on human cell surfaces that are involved in cellular recognition processes. Of the 200 such sugars occurring naturally in plants, to date only these eight had been identified as components of cellular glycoproteins. These eight sugars that are essential for glycoconjugate synthesis (mannose, galactose, fucose, xylose, glucose, sialic acid, N-acetylglucosamine, N-acetylgalactosamine) can be readily absorbed and directly incorporated into glycoproteins and glycolipids.

Recent research has found specific cell surface glycoforms to be characteristic of many disease conditions. In some people with rheumatoid arthritis, some of these patients' defense cells (IgG antibody) bear malformed glycoproteins. These cells are missing required galactose molecules; the extent to which the galactose molecules are missing correlates with disease severity and reverses in disease remission. In people with cancer, more than 20 different malignancies are known to be associated with characteristic glycoproteins. Many diseases, including some autoimmune diseases, have been found to be associated with altered cell surface glycoproteins.

Glyconutritional supplements are designed to provide substrates for the body to use in building part of the glycoconjugates on cell surfaces. These supplements, most commonly acemannan and mannose, are designed to make the necessary sugars available to the cells quicker and in greater quantity.

Acemannan is a glycoprotein (a long chain of mannan polymers with random o-acetyl groups) derived from the aloe vera plant that has been shown to increase the body's production of immune-modulating chemicals including interleukins-1 and 6, interferon-gamma, and Prostaglandin E_2 and tumor necrosis factor alpha by macrophages. Acemannan also enhances macro-

phage phagocytosis and nonspecific cytotoxicity, which increases the ability of white blood cells (macrophages) to destroy infectious organisms. Glycoproteins such as acemannan also offer antiviral activity as well as bone marrow stimulating activity.

THERAPEUTIC USES

Acemannan has been approved as an adjunct therapy for solid tumors called fibrosarcomas. Intralesional injection into the tumor (2 mg weekly for up to 6 weeks), combined with intraperitoneal injections (1 mg/kg of body weight given weekly for 6 weeks, followed by monthly injections for 1 year), has been shown to be effective in shrinking tumors (via necrosis and inflammation). Acemannan has been proposed as an adjunctive therapy for cats with feline leukemia virus infection and feline immunodeficiency infection.

Acemannan has been anecdotally reported to help pets with atopic dermatitis; however, the immune-modulating chemicals are pro-inflammatory and studies in people have shown them to be involved in the increase in inflammation seen in people with atopic dermatitis. Therefore it does not make sense (from a biochemical point of view) that they would be useful in treating atopic pets despite the anecdotal reports in the literature showing effectiveness in some pets. Since acemannan can increase the ability of the white blood cells to destroy microbes, it may be helpful in pets with skin infections. Also, acemannan probably has other properties that have not yet been defined that might allow it to function to relieve itching and inflammation in atopic pets. Product literature for some of these products hint that the ingredients might support cellular communication through a dietary supplement of monosaccharides needed for glycoconjugate synthesis. Good communication between cells is necessary for proper gland and organ function, proper system function, and optimal health.

Acemannan has also been shown to enhance wound healing when applied topically.

There are a number of potential uses for the various glycosugars in disease conditions of people and pets. For example, one of the glycosugars, mannose, has been shown to activate white blood cells called macrophages. These influence the release of substances that modulate the immune response and tissue inflammation and also remove bacteria and cellular debris. Acemannan, a glycoprotein from the aloe vera plant, is also effective in this manner. Both acemannan and mannose enhance the killing of the yeast *Candida albicans* by macrophages.

Wound healing can be improved with mannose and acemannan by decreasing tissue damage and inflammation.

Galactose stimulates macrophages, activates killing of microorganisms, and enhances wound healing.

SCIENTIFIC EVIDENCE

No definitive studies of large numbers of cats with feline leukemia virus infection have shown the cats to revert to a negative viral status, although the administration of acemannan did appear to prolong the life of the cats. In sick cats with leukemia virus infection, 29 out of 41 cats survived a 12-week study period using intraperitoneal acemannan (2 mg/kg weekly for the first 6 weeks of the study). Two months following the 12-week study, 21 cats were still alive (1 had died, 5 cats could not be followed up as their owners had moved). In a similar study of sick cats who were leukemia positive and not treated with acemannan, 40 out of 46 cats died or were euthanized within 5 days of diagnosis.

In one study of feline immunodeficiency virus (FIV) infections, 75% survival rate was obtained for cats in Stage 3, 4, or 5 (seriously ill cats for which life expectancy is up to 1 year for Stage 4 cats and 1 to 6 months for Stage 5 cats). Cats showed increased body weight, decreased lymph node size, and a reduction in sepsis (infections that are commonly seen in end stage FIV cats). Neutrophil counts improved, as well as lymphocyte counts, indicating an improvement in the immune status of the infected cats. Cats responded regardless of route of administration of acemannan (weekly IV injection or weekly subcutaneous injection, of 2 mg/kg acemannan, or daily oral administration of 100 mg/cat acemannan). No signs of toxicity were noted in any cats, although four cats given the IV injections showed an immediate allergic reaction, which commonly occurs in cats given IV push injections of very large molecular weight compounds such as acemannan.

In these studies, all cats remained virus positive but experienced a noticeable improvement in the quality of life. While acemannan (and other glycoproteins) may be helpful for cats with leukemia or immunodeficiency viral infections, more studies are needed to determine what, if any, true long-term benefit infected cats might experience. At the current time, acemannan and other glycoproteins such as mannose, one of eight glycoproteins found in the oral supplement, ambrotose, probably serve as a useful treatment option for these chronic feline viral diseases for which conventional therapies really do not exist (conventional therapies are of no particular benefit and serve mainly to support the sick cat).

All eight of the glycoconjugate sugars are readily absorbed from the intestines when taken orally. Studies have shown intact mannose molecules are rapidly absorbed from the intestine of rats into the blood, elevating the blood mannose levels by 3- to 10-fold, and mannose is cleared from the blood within hours. The conclusion reached was that mannose was absorbed from the intestinal tract into the blood and from the blood into the cells. These studies suggest that dietary mannose may make a significant contribution to glycoform synthesis in mammals.

Other human and animal ingestion studies show that mannose is readily absorbed, and is cleared from the blood over several hours; some of the mannose was incorporated into glycoproteins. After absorption into the blood, glycoconjugate sugars generally become distributed (usually as glycoproteins and glycolipids) into body fluids, organs, and various body tissues.

In one study, healthy humans were given radiolabeled galactose, mannose, or glucose. This study showed that galactose and mannose were directly incorporated into human glycoproteins without first being broken down into glucose. The conclusion was that specific dietary sugars could represent a new class of nutrients and that the use of these nutrients could have important consequences. Therapy with mannose offers a treatment that is easy to administer and is nontoxic.

The glycoprotein N-acetylglucosamine (discussed in more depth under N-TK) inhibits oxygen radical production by neutrophils and also release of neutrophil-derived elastase, limiting tissue damage and inflammation. This has been shown in studies to substantially reduce pain and increase joint flexion and active mobility in arthritis patients.

The data show that there is scientific basis for potential therapeutic benefits from these sugars in the treatment of common immune system diseases, such as arthritis and asthma, and in wound healing.

Most of the essential glycoconjugate sugars have demonstrated an ability to inhibit cancer growth and the spread of tumor cells both in vitro and in vivo (in experiments in pets and people.) The ability of the glycoproteins to inhibit tumor growth may be related to their ability to alter the activities of the immune system. Glycoconjugate sugars stimulate white blood cells (macrophages), which secrete interferons. The interferons activate natural killer cells that help eliminate cancer cells. The glycoproteins may inhibit the spread of tumor cells by preventing tumor cells from adhering to each other as a result of competitive inhibition of glycoconjugate receptor binding.

Glycoconjugate sugars have been shown to kill bacteria and viruses and prevent infection by them. For example, mannose acts to prevent bacterial infection by binding to the sites on the bacteria and preventing attachment of the bacteria to sites on the cells of the host. Glycoconjugate sugars display antiviral activity as a result of their ability to stimulate macrophages to release interferon. They also interfere with normal virus function.

Glycoconjugate sugars may offer hope for treating disorders such as diabetes, as some glycoconjugate sugars share membrane transporters and metabolism pathways with glucose. For example, galactose might be expected to stimulate insulin secretion by stimulating intestinal release of gastric inhibitory polypeptide (GIP). GIP stimulates the intestinal regulation of insulin secretion (at least in intestinal perfusion techniques in experimental studies in rats). Possible roles for specific glycoconjugate sugars in diabetes are unclear and much more additional research is needed. In vitro and in vivo studies in diabetic rats indicate that mannose may protect the diabetic lens from developing cataracts.

Acarbose (Precose) is an oligosaccharide that inhibits alpha-glucosidase enzymes in the intestinal tract and pancreatic alpha-amylase. This results in delayed digestion of carbohydrates, delayed glucose absorption from the intestines, and decreased post-feeding glucose concentrations. Preliminary studies in dogs with type I diabetes have shown positive response when acarbose is given at the time of feeding at a dose of 25 mg per dog twice daily. Side effects (diarrhea and weight loss) are commonly seen in dogs treated with higher doses (100 to 200 mg per dog).

There are other potential uses for glycoprotein supplementation in pets. A derivative of glucosamine (1-deoxy-glucosamine) suppresses feeding activity in rats, apparently by acting through histamine neurons in the hypothalamus of the brain. This sugar might suppress hunger in people or pets and could possibly be useful as an adjunct to dietary calorie restriction in obese patients.

As with so many of our complementary therapies, a number of anecdotal reports show success in some pets when using glycoprotein therapy. More controlled studies are encouraged to give us a better idea of just how effective glycoproteins might be in the treatment of illness in pets.

SOURCES

Popular glycoprotein supplements used in pets are manufactured by Carrington Laboratories and Mannatech Laboratories.

SAFETY ISSUES

Adverse effects caused by glycoconjugate sugars are rare and usually occur when they are injected or when doses greatly exceed levels that would be expected in normal diets. For pets being treated with the most commonly used glycproteins (acemannan and mannose), side effects would not be expected.

GLYCOSAMINOGLYCANS (GAGs)

Common Use
Arthritis

Glucosamine and chondroitin constitute the major GAGs in the joint cartilage; glycosaminoglycans serve as major components of articular cartilage.

Glycosaminoglycans function by decreasing the presence of harmful pro-inflammatory prostaglandins and other inflammatory enzymes that degrade the cartilage matrix. This results in reduced pain and inflammation, decreased enzymatic destruction of the cartilage, and stimulation of anabolic (cartilage-building) pathways. The GAGs also appear to increase the synthesis of proteoglycans, hyaluronic acid (which acts as a joint lubricant), and collagen.

Glucosamine and chondroitin are commonly prescribed chondroprotective nutraceuticals.

When we talk about chondroprotective nutraceuticals (nutritional products), we're talking about "cartilage-protective" compounds. Unlike corticosteroids and other medications, these products actually help the cartilage rebuild and repair itself. In essence, they are "cartilage-friendly" products. These compounds also help relieve pain and inflammation. Interestingly, these improvements seem to last for several weeks after glucosamine supplements are discontinued. Chondroprotective agents can be given orally or by injection; often both forms will be used in the severely arthritic pet who is in pain.

Optimum functioning of the joints is important for pain-free movements by the pet. While any pet can exhibit lameness or arthritis, it is usually the older pet who is more commonly affected. Articular cartilage, that cartilage which lines the joints, must remain healthy to allow the pet to function to its maximum capability. The articular cartilage acts as a shock absorber for the joint, providing a smooth surface between bones to eliminate bone-on-bone contact. As the cartilage is destroyed, bony surfaces contact and irritate each other, causing pain, inflammation, and reduced activity.

While corticosteroids and certain nonsteroidal medications certainly relieve the pain and inflammation, they further destroy the articular cartilage, making a bad situation even worse.

Cartilage is made of cells called chondrocytes, which make a matrix of molecules that add to the strength of the cartilage. This matrix consists of collagen, a protein that connects tissues, and substances called proteoglycans. These proteoglycans are made of glycosaminoglycans (GAGs) and hyaluronic acid. Surrounding the cartilage, and bathing the joint, is joint (synovial) fluid. Cartilage is a tough material that protects the underlying bones and acts as a shock absorber for the joints during movement. There is a normal amount of wear and tear on the joint cartilage. The various cells and fluids are constantly being broken down and synthesized. It is important that the cartilage receive proper nutrition, especially when it is damaged and inflamed. Chondroprotective agents seek to replenish the raw materials that are essential for the healing and synthesis of cartilage, its matrix, and joint fluid.

THERAPEUTIC USES

Various products, each supplying different nutritional products, are available to assist in relieving inflammation and helping cartilage to heal when it is damaged. The following ingredients may be included in the various nutritional chondroprotective products: **chondroitin, glucosamine** (page 212), cetyl myristoleate, **DMG** (page 194), **MSM** (page 242), **sea cucumber** (page 268), **perna** (page 253), **shark cartilage** (page 271), **bovine cartilage** (page 169), **skullcap** (page 273), **mullein** (page 243), and **SAMe** (page 265). Each doctor has a "favorite" product. If one doesn't help your pet, your doctor may suggest trying a different product. Keep in mind that these are true holistic products; there are no harmful side effects such as those often encountered with long-term use of corticosteroids or nonsteroidal medications.

One novel product called Adequan contains glycosaminoglycans (specifically hyaluronic acid, HA) extracted from bovine cartilage and is available in an injectable form (HA is not well absorbed orally). The recommended regimen is a series of 8 injections, 2 each week for 4 weeks. If the pet has responded favorably during the 4-week trial, the pet is then given an injection as needed (which is usually 1 injection every 1 to 12 months, though this varies from pet to pet). This injectable product can be used with oral chondroprotective supplements as well. The injectable product can be used to get a faster response than the oral supplements. Further injections are given as needed, or pets can be maintained on oral supplements according to the response seen and the convenience for the pet owner.

Note: This product has also shown effectiveness when flushed into joints during joint surgery, allowing faster and smoother recovery.

Chondroprotective Therapy

The following points concerning chondroprotective therapy are important to maximize success when using these supplements:

- *Safety.* They are extremely safe and equally effective when compared to NSAIDs.
- *Cost.* Cost may be an issue for some pet owners. The typical daily cost of using a glucosamine-chondroitin supplement is approximately $1.50/day for a 50-pound dog. This cost can decrease as the dosage of the supplement is lowered to allow the owner to use the least amount of supplement to maintain pain relief. The comparable cost of the most popular NSAIDs (Rimadyl and EctoGesic) is approximately $2 to 3/day for a 50-pound dog, making the supplements less expensive, equally effective, and without potential serious side effects.
- *Early diagnosis and use.* Since these supplements work by acting on living cartilage cells, they are most effective when used early in the course of the disease. This requires adequate and early diagnosis.

- *Response time.* Because they are not drugs but rather nutritional supplements, response may not be seen for 4 to 8 weeks. During the first 4 to 8 weeks, an increased "induction" dose is used and then the dose is lowered as improvement is seen. Additional short-term therapy (with NSAIDs or acupuncture, for example) can be used during the induction phase.
- *Effectiveness.* The supplements can also be used effectively when no clinical signs are present but yet disease exists. In many practices, a number of dogs are diagnosed via screening radiographs with hip dysplasia and started on the supplements pending a decision on the owner's part for surgical correction or until clinical signs occur.
- *Purity of the products.* This is important. There are many generic "knock-off" products that sell for much less than patented products produced by reputable manufacturers. Studies that have been done showing the effectiveness of these compounds have used pure grades of products. Products of lesser purity, while often costing less, may also be less effective. Unlike traditional drugs, these compounds are not regulated and labeling can be inaccurate or misleading. Manufacturers are not required to analyze their products regarding purity, uniformity, or content. You should purchase only quality products from reputable manufacturers as recommended by your veterinarian.
- *Recommended revaluation.* Because the chondroprotective supplements are so effective after 4 to 8 weeks in improving signs seen in arthritic pets, the diagnosis should be reevaluated after this period of time if improvement is not seen.

SAFETY ISSUES

Side effects with GAGs are extremely rare but are reported to include a dose-dependent inhibition of blood clotting. Concerned owners may want to have their pet's doctors regularly monitor blood coagulation parameters and use homeopathic remedies to help increase blood-clotting factors.

GOLDENROD *(Solidago virgaurea)*

Common Uses
Urinary disorders, respiratory disorders

Goldenrod

There are a number of species of goldenrod, and all seem to possess similar medicinal properties. The various species are used interchangeably.

THERAPEUTIC USES

Goldenrod is used as a supportive treatment for **bladder infections** (page 36), irritation of the urinary tract, and **bladder**/kidney **stones** (page 40). Goldenrod increases the flow of urine, helping to wash out bacteria and kidney stones, and may also directly soothe inflamed tissues and calm muscle spasms in the urinary tract. It isn't used as a cure in itself, but rather as a support to other, more definitive treatments such as antibiotics.

We don't really know how well the herb works. While some studies have found that goldenrod increases urine flow, there is no direct evidence that the herb is effective in resolving bladder infections or bladder/kidney stones. Its active ingredients are not known.

In pets, goldenrod has also been suggested for pets with respiratory disorders as it seems to decrease the amount of mucus and inflammation in the bronchial passages.

SAFETY ISSUES

The safety of goldenrod hasn't been fully evaluated. However, no significant reactions or side effects have been reported. Safety in young children, pregnant and nursing women, or those with severe liver or kidney disease has not been established. Similar precautions are probably warranted in pets.

GOLDENSEAL *(Hydrastis canadensis)*

Common Uses
Allergies, heart conditions, cancer, infections, intestinal parasites, urinary disorders

Goldenseal is used as an antimicrobial and anti-inflammatory herb. It can be applied topically to open sores or inflamed skin for its soothing effect on inflamed mucous membranes. Goldenseal functions as a topical (contact) antimicrobial rather than as a general systemic (whole body) antibiotic. It does not seem to be an effective oral antibiotic, probably because the blood levels of the active ingredient, berberine, that can be achieved by taking goldenseal orally, are far too low to matter. However, goldenseal may also be beneficial in treating diseases of the digestive tract because it can contact the affected area directly. Since berberine is concentrated in the bladder, goldenseal may be useful in resolving **bladder infections** (page 36). It may be helpful for treating fungal infections of the skin as well.

Goldenseal is also used for topical contact for sores and ulcers of the mouth, eyes, and upper respiratory tract.

The active ingredient, berberine, is helpful in treating tapeworms (in conjunction with garlic) and for treating giardial and E. coli infections of the intestinal tract.

Goldenseal has also shown potent anticancer activity in vitro against rat and human malignant brain tumors. Its berberine content has shown beneficial effects in the treatment of decreased white blood cell counts in patients suffering this side effects as a result of chemotherapy or radiation treatment.

Pets with allergic conjunctivitis (runny eyes) may benefit from eye drops made from goldenseal.

Due to similar qualities (and the fact that goldenseal is an endangered plant), Oregon grape can be used in place of goldenseal.

SAFETY ISSUES

In people, goldenseal appears to be safe when used as directed. Despite a rumor that goldenseal can disrupt the normal bacteria of the intestines, there is no scientific evidence that this occurs. While there has been a concern that small overdoses of goldenseal are toxic, causing ulcerations of the stomach and other mucous membranes, this is not true.

Safety in young children, nursing women, or those with severe liver or kidney disease is also not established; similar precautions in pets are probably warranted.

Side effects of oral goldenseal are uncommon, although there have been reports of gastrointestinal distress and increased nervousness in people who take very high doses.

Goldenseal should not be used in pregnant animals or in pets with low blood sugar (as goldenseal further lowers blood sugar). Long-term use of goldenseal may cause hypertension and should not be used in pets with kidney failure or in cats with hyperthyroidism.

Do not use in pets with jaundice or liver disease due to the potential for overstimulation of the liver.

It is recommended that goldenseal be used for no more than 7 days in a row, with a break of 5 to 7 days before resuming use, to prevent overstimulation of the liver, bile production, and vomiting (to which cats seem particularly sensitive).

GOTU KOLA *(Centella asiatica)*

Common Uses

Arthritis, cognitive disorder, epilepsy, heart conditions, infections, kidney disease, wound healing

The primary chemicals in gotu kola are triterpenoid compounds; flavonoids including quercetin are also contained in this herb. The triterpenes have remarkable wound-healing properties.

THERAPEUTIC USES

Gotu kola has been recommended in people for many clinical applications, including anal fissures, burns, lupus, mycosis fungoides, periodontal disease, surgical wounds, skin ulcers, and various infections including leprosy (mycobacterial infections) and tuberculosis. Similar applications may occur in pets.

Gotu kola is a mild diuretic and may be useful in pets with **heart disease** (page 91) and other conditions where fluid accumulates abnormally.

Used externally, the herb's antioxidants speed the healing of skin.

It has been recommended to promote hair and nail growth.

Gotu kola can be used in older pets (especially those with **cognitive disorder** (page 56)) to increase mental clarity. It has also been suggested for pets with **epilepsy** (page 73).

Gotu kola can reduce inflammation and can be used for **arthritic** pets (page 11).

DOSAGES

In people, the usual dosage of gotu kola is 20 to 40 mg 3 times daily of an extract standardized to contain 40% asiaticoside, 29 to 30% asiatic acid, 29 to 30% madecassic acid, and 1 to 2% madecassoside. Gotu kola takes at least 4 weeks to work.

SAFETY ISSUES

Orally, gotu kola appears to be nontoxic. It seldom causes any side effects other than the occasional allergic skin rash. However, there are some concerns that gotu kola may be carcinogenic if applied topically to the skin. Although gotu kola has not been proven safe for pregnant or nursing women, studies in rabbits suggest that it does not harm fetal development, and pregnant women were enrolled in one research trial.

Safety in young children and those with severe liver or kidney disease has not been established. Similar precautions are probably warranted in pets.

Do not use in pregnant animals or those receiving hypoglycemic therapy. It may sensitize animals to ultraviolet light (in excessive quantities) and may cause excessive sedation.

GREEN FOODS *(Super Green Foods)*

Common Uses
Nutritional support

Green foods most commonly include barley grass, spirulina, alfalfa, chlorella, and blue-green algae. Green foods contain a variety of nutrients. Ingestion of these nutrients seeks to prevent and treat illnesses that may be induced by an imbalance of minerals, enzymes, and vitamins in processed diets.

Barley grass contains large amounts of vitamins C, A, B$_1$, B$_2$, B$_6$, E; biotin; folic acid; choline; pantothenic acid; nicotinic acid; iron; chlorophyll; potassium; calcium; magnesium; manganese; zinc; proteins; and enzymes.

Spirulina is a high-potency fresh-water, blue-green algae. Spirulina contains an antioxidant called superoxide dismutase (a scavenger of free radicals), B-complex vitamins, gamma-linolenic acid, calcium, iron, magnesium, potassium, boron, molybdenum, manganese, phosphorus, sodium, zinc, copper, amino acids, other phytonutrients with antioxidant effects, and mixed carotenoids. In vitro studies show that the pigment in spirulina, phycocyanin, can inhibit **cancer** (page 44) colony formation and may enhance the formation of neurotransmitters.

Alfalfa is a well-known herb that is rich in many nutrients (protein, vitamins, and minerals) and chlorophyll (which serves as an antioxidant).

It is one of the best adjunctive herbal therapies for **arthritis** (page 11) and possesses **cancer**-preventing properties (page 44) by inactivating chemicals that can cause cancer. Alfalfa is often fed to animals who need to gain weight.

Chlorella is a warm-water algae that has slightly less protein than spirulina, but more chlorophyll and nucleic acid. It has a tough cell wall that is poorly digested, but may work as a toxin binder.

Chlorophyll, contained in super green foods, may assist the body in healing due to an anti-inflammatory effect. The enzymes contained in super green foods grass are not just those that can aid in digestion and absorption of nutrients from the diet, but may also assist in reducing oxidative injury to damaged tissues. Other proposed beneficial effects of super green foods include anti-tumor effects in laboratory rodents, protective effects against toxin-induced kidney failure, enhanced effects on intestinal microflora, lowering of blood sugar, lowering of cholesterol, improved weight loss in obese people, lowering of high blood pressure, and antiviral activity. In pets, supplementation with super green foods may also improve skin and haircoat conditions.

GREEN TEA (See Black and Green Tea)

GYMNEMA (*Gymnema sylvestre*)

Common Uses
  Diabetes

Gymnema is an extract from a plant native to India. The leaves of this plant, given the name "sugar destroyer," have been used for over 200 years in Ayurvedic medicine. The active ingredients are gymnemic acids, saponins, stigmasterol, quercitol, and amino acid derivatives betaine, choline, and trimethylamine.

SCIENTIFIC EVIDENCE

The benefits in people with type I diabetes (insulin-dependent) include a noticeable reduction in all the markers for diabetes including insulin requirements, fasting glucose, glycosylated hemoglobin (HbA1c), and blood lipids. The patients on insulin therapy without supplementation had no reduction in any of these markers. A similar study was performed on type II (non-insulin dependent) diabetics with similar results. These patients showed a significant reduction in blood glucose, glycosylated hemoglobin, and blood lipids. The need for oral medication decreased and some patients were able to maintain their blood sugar with only supplementation.

SAFETY ISSUES

Gymnema appears safe, although safety studies are lacking. Dangerous and potentially fatal low blood sugar (hypoglycemia) can occur if treatment with gymnema is successful. Therefore, gymnema should only be used under veterinary supervision.

DOSAGES

In people, standardized extracts supplying 25% gymnemic acids are recommended.

It is unknown whether supplementation in pets would provide the same benefits.

HAWTHORN (*Crataegus oxyacantha*)

Common Uses
  Heart conditions (caution in hypertrophic cardiomyopathy), cancer, kidney disease

Hawthorn is a well-known heart and vascular tonic, often prescribed for pets with early congestive heart failure. It may be a possible alternative to digitalis. Hawthorn also possesses antioxidant properties. Although not as potent as foxglove, hawthorn is much safer. The active ingredients in foxglove are the drugs digoxin and digitoxin. However, hawthorn does not appear to have any single active ingredient, although the flavonoid and proanthocyanidins have been suggested as the active components. This has prevented it from being turned into a drug.

Like foxglove and the drugs made from it, hawthorn appears to improve the heart's pumping ability. But it offers one very important advantage. Digitalis and some other medications that increase the power of the heart also make it more irritable and liable to dangerous irregularities of rhythm. In contrast, hawthorn has the unique property of both strengthening the heart and stabilizing it against arrhythmias by lengthening what is called the refractory period, the short period following a heartbeat during which the heart cannot beat again. Many irregularities of heart rhythm begin with an early beat. Digitalis shortens the refractory period, making such a premature beat more likely, while hawthorn protects against such potentially dangerous breaks in the heart's even rhythm. Also, with digitalis the difference between the proper dosage and the toxic dosage is very small.

Hawthorn has an enormous range of safe dosing.

SCIENTIFIC EVIDENCE

In people, several double-blind studies strongly suggest that hawthorn is an effective treatment for congestive heart failure. Comparative studies suggest that hawthorn is about as effective as a low dose of the conventional drug captopril (a relative of enalapril, used in pets with heart failure), although whether it produces the same long-term benefits as captopril is unknown.

THERAPEUTIC USES

Due to the flavonoid content, hawthorn is often recommended for pets with **heart disease** (page 91), **heartworm disease** (page 98), and **kidney disease** (page 121). The flavonoids appear to decrease "leakiness" of the capillaries, improve cardiac blood flow by dilating coronary arteries, and improve the contractility of the heart. Hawthorn may also be useful in controlling mild heart arrhythmias. It may act by inhibiting the enzyme phosphodiesterase or as an ACE inhibitor, making it a possible substitute for drugs such as enalapril (Enacard). Doctors may prescribe hawthorn for pets with chemotherapy, especially when the drug chosen for chemotherapy may produce cardiac side effects.

DOSAGES

In people, the standard dosage of hawthorn is 100 to 300 mg 3 times daily of an extract standardized to contain about 2 to 3% flavonoids or 18 to 20% procyanidins. Full effects appear to take several weeks or months to develop.

SAFETY ISSUES

Hawthorn is safe to feed to animals; older animals that may be prone to heart or kidney disease can be given hawthorn on a daily basis. Caution is warranted in pets with low blood pressure and hypertrophic cardiomyopathy. In people, side effects are rare, mostly consisting of mild stomach upset and occasional allergic reactions (skin rash).

Safety in young children, pregnant or nursing women, or those with severe liver, heart or kidney disease has not been established. Similar concerns in pets are probably warranted.

HEALTH FORMULA BLENDS

Common Uses
Nutritional support

A number of products exist that claim to be "health formulas." These products contain a variety of ingredients, including barley grass, wheat, rice, enzymes, fatty acids, vitamins, minerals, seaweed, and/or alfalfa. We don't really know why these compounds often seem effective in the treatment of some pets with various medical problems. Obviously, they supply some "nutrient(s)" missing from the diet, most likely antioxidants, vitamins, and minerals. Like fatty acid supplementation, it may be that they in some way interfere with the production of pro-inflammatory compounds. Because so many different products are available, it would be wise to discuss whatever products you may discover with your pet's veterinarian.

While there are many anecdotal reports showing the effectiveness of many of these supplements in the treatment of a variety of disorders in pets, controlled scientific studies are often lacking. Still, numerous reports show positive response when using these supplements in pets. The most evidence we have is from the first manufactured health formula blend called The Missing Link (Designing Health). Anecdotal reports describing the use of this product are numerous. Pet owners have reported positive response in pets with excessive shedding, dry flaky coats and skin, **epilepsy** (page 73), **arthritis** (page 11), hot spots, and **allergies** (page 3) among other problems.

SAFETY ISSUES

Health formula blends can be used safely and without side effects in dogs and cats, and are often considered a complete nutritional supplement that can be added to every pet's diet, even those not currently suffering from medical disorders. When these health formula blends work in pets with medical disorders, they often allow a reduced dosage of medications that we know have the potential to cause serious side effects.

 # HEMP OIL (See Oral Fatty Acids)

 # HORSETAIL (*Equisetum arvense*)

Common Uses
Arthritis, cognitive disorder, infections (urinary system), urinary disorders

Horsetail contains silicon, which serves as the matrix in connective tissue development.

THERAPEUTIC USES

The silicon in horsetail can be metabolized for tissue repair and development of connective tissues including bone, cartilage, skin, trachea, aorta, and other connective tissues. A decoction of the herb can be used for injuries of the bones and joints, including **osteoarthritis** (page 11), and can be combined with glucosamine and chondroitin supplements. It can be administered after surgery on the bones and joints to assist healing.

Horsetail is often recommended for treating urinary problems, including infections and bleeding of the **urinary tract** (page 145). Horsetail is often combined with soothing herbs such as marshmallow for long-term (greater than 2 weeks) treatment of the urinary tract.

Since silicon levels decrease with age, using horsetail in older pets with **cognitive disorder** (page 56) can be tried (and it can be combined with other herbs that support the immune system, such as ginkgo or hawthorn). Dietary supplementation may be useful to prevent degeneration of bone, skin, the nervous system, and other connective tissues of the older pet.

SAFETY ISSUES

Do not use in pets with cardiac disease, high blood pressure, or bladder stones composed of silica or related minerals.

The raw uncooked herb contains thiaminase, which can decrease thiamine levels in pets.

HOXSEY AND ESSIAC FORMULAS

Common Uses
  Cancer

The Hoxsey and Essiac herbal formulas are commonly recommended for people with cancer. There are two reported Hoxsey formulas. The first contains the herbs burdock, red clover, pokeweed root, prickly ash bark, bloodroot, licorice, stillingia, barberry, and potassium iodide. The second formula contains potassium iodide and an extract of the digestive enzyme pepsin.

The Hoxsey formula was named after Harry Hoxsey, who was a coal miner who made a traditional family remedy for cancer into the largest privately owned cancer treatment center in the world, with branches in 17 states. (It was shut down in the 1950s by the FDA. Harry Hoxsey himself subsequently died of cancer.) Despite the historical enthusiasm, there is no significant evidence that this formula is an effective treatment for cancer or any other illness. However, the antioxidant action may offer some preventive activity. There is probably minimal to no toxicity (unless other herbs have been introduced by the manufacturer).

The Essiac formula was named after a Canadian nurse, Rene Caisse (Essiac is Caisse spelled backwards). The original formula is a well-guarded secret but is believed to have contained burdock, sheep sorrel, turkey rhubarb, and slippery elm bark. As with the Hoxsey formula, there are no conclusive human studies to support the use of the Essiac formula in the treatment of cancer. Additionally, there is controversy over whether any of the commercially available products contain the ingredients in the original formula made by Caisse. However, as with the Hoxsey formula, there is probably minimal to no toxicity (unless other herbs have been introduced by the manufacturer), and the antioxidants might be of benefit for cancer patients (unless the antioxidants would interfere with the chemotherapy treatment recommended by an oncologist).

THERAPEUTIC USES

Recommended for pets with **cancer** (page 44) or where immune support should be boosted.

SAFETY ISSUES

While these formulas may be safe in pets, there are no controlled studies to show if they are effective in dogs and cats. Consult with your veterinarian prior to using either the Essiac or Hoxsey formula.

HYDROXYCITRIC ACID

Common Uses
  Obesity

Hydroxycitric acid, also called HCA, is a product extracted from the rind of the tamarind citrus fruit of the *Garcinia cambogia* tree.

HCA suppresses hunger in people and helps prevent the body from turning carbohydrates into fat by inhibiting the ATP-citrate lysase enzyme. HCA may be useful in pets as part of an obesity treatment program.

DOSAGES

The recommended dosage is 500 mg 3 times daily.

SOURCE

HCA is currently available in one supplement (NutriWeight Management, Rx For Pets).

 # IMMUNOAUGMENTIVE THERAPY

Common Uses
   Cancer

This is an experimental form of therapy involving daily injections of blood products to treat cancer. Early studies in dogs with osteosarcoma show that immunoaugmentive therapy can in fact improve disease-free intervals and survival. The suggested mechanism involves an enhancement of factors that stimulate the immune system. More research is needed before this becomes a recommended therapy.

 # INOSITOL

Common Uses
   Cognitive disorder, hair growth

Inositol is present in all animal tissues, with the highest levels in the heart and brain. It is part of the membranes (outer linings) of all cells, and plays a role in helping the liver process fats as well as contributing to the function of muscles and nerves.

This vitamin, unofficially referred to as "vitamin B_8," promotes the growth of hair, reduces cholesterol levels, contributes to the function of muscles and nerves, and has a calming effect. As with choline, inositol is needed for lecithin formation and in the metabolism of fat and cholesterol. Inositol, a naturally occurring isomer of glucose, is also useful for removing fats from the liver and should be used in pets with **fatty liver disease** (page 127).

THERAPEUTIC USES

While there is no scientific proof for this use, holistic doctors have reported regrowth of hair in pets with skin disorders who take inositol.

IP-6 (inositol hexaphosphate) has been recommended for use in people and pets with cancerous tumors. The proposed action is to control cell division, increase the toxicity of natural killer cells, and as an antioxidant. More research is needed to determine if IP-6 is useful as part of the therapy for carcinomatous tumors.

Inositol is also recommended for the treatment of Alzheimer's disease, obsessive-compulsive disorder, and attention deficit disorder. Inositol appears to have therapeutic effects in various mood disorders similar to those seen with serotonin selective reuptake inhibitors (SSRIs), without the side effects. For these reasons, supplementation with inositol may be indicated for dogs and cats with cognitive disorder (as well as other behavioral problems), although no studies have proven its use for this common problem.

Inositol may also be involved in depression in people. Studies have shown that people who are depressed have much lower-than-normal levels of inositol in their spinal fluid. In addition, inositol participates in the action of serotonin, a neurotransmitter known to be a factor in depression. For this reason, inositol has been proposed as a treatment for depression, and preliminary evidence suggests that it may be helpful.

In people, inositol is also sometimes proposed as a treatment for complications of diabetes (specifically diabetic neuropathy), but there have been no double-blind placebo-controlled studies, and two uncontrolled studies had mixed results.

DOSAGES

There do not seem to be any adverse effects at the recommended human and animal dosage of 25 to 100 mg/kg per day.

SOURCES

Brewer's yeast, lecithin, meats, milk, vegetables, and grains supply inositol. Nuts, seeds, beans, whole grains, cantaloupe, and citrus fruits supply a substance called phytic acid, which releases inositol when acted on by bacteria in the digestive tract.

There are no specific indications for inositol supplementation in dogs and cats.

SAFETY ISSUES

No serious ill effects have been reported for inositol. However, no long-term safety studies have been performed. Safety has not been established in young children, women who are pregnant or nursing, and those with severe liver and kidney disease; similar precautions are probably warranted in pets.

As with all supplements used in multi-gram doses, it is important to purchase a reputable product, because a contaminant present, even in small percentages, could pose real problems for pets.

JUNIPER (*Juniperus communis*)

Common Use
Allergies (topical rinse), bladder infections

Juniper is often recommended for treating bladder infections due to its diurectic effects. It has also been recommended for its antiseptic properties that may relieve itchiness and infections of the skin.

THERAPEUTIC USES

Juniper has been recommended for **bladder infections** (page 36), as a diuretic, to treat edema (fluid accumulation in the body,) to treat **arthri-** tis (page 11), and topically to relieve itchy and irritated skin.

SCIENTIFIC EVIDENCE

Studies in rats have shown that juniper can lower blood glucose, making juniper a possible treatment for diabetes. A derivative of the juniper berry called 14 acetoxycedrol has anticoagulant effects and also appears to relax the smooth muscle in blood vessels. This may make juniper a therapy for cardiovascular disease.

SAFETY ISSUES

The volatile oils in the plant and berries can be irritating to the skin unless properly diluted when preparing the rinse. Juniper should not be used internally in pets with kidney disease, or if pregnant or lactating. Juniper should not be used in diabetic pets or pets with cardiac disease without veterinary supervision.

KAVA KAVA *(Piper methysticum)*

Common Use
Epilepsy

Kava, a member of the pepper family, is well known for its use as a sedating herb due to its kavalactone and other chemicals. One of the most active of these is dihydrokavain, which has been found to produce a sedative, painkilling, and anticonvulsant effect. Other kavalactones include kavain, methysticin, and dihydromethysticin.

THERAPEUTIC USES

Kava can be used in place of chemical tranquilizers and may be helpful for pets with **epilepsy** (page 73). The effects appear to occur by action on the limbic center of the brain or the amygdala, different from the actions of enzodiazepenes (such as diazepam), opioids, and nonsteroidal medications. Suggested actions include modulating of neurotransmitters including GABA, MAO, dopamine, and 5-HT. Unlike other sedatives, kava does not appear to interfere with motor function or cause a depression of mental function.

Kava also exhibits analgesic properties in a manner unlike other traditional pain-relieving medications. Kava, unlike other sedatives, does not lose effectiveness with time (a condition called tolerance that can be seen with some sedating medications). Kava also shows muscle-relaxing properties that are superior to the benzodiazepenes. Finally, kava may prove useful during the recovery period following brain injury (similar to the proposed use in stroke patients).

SAFETY ISSUES

Kava kava can be toxic to the liver in excess. Do not use in pets with liver disease. Do not use in pregnant animals.

Little is know about its safety in pets, although it appears to be safe when used as directed by veterinarians. It is not recommended for long-term use. Typical products are standardized to 29 to 31% kavalactones. Excess use can cause liver disease. Use of kava may potentiate anesthetics and other sedatives. In people, excessive use of high doses of kava beverages causes kava dermatitis. For people, the Commission E monograph recommends using kava for no more than 3 months.

When used appropriately, kava appears to be safe. Animal studies have shown that dosages of up to four times that of normal cause no problems at all, and 13 times the normal dosage causes only mild problems in rats. A study of 4,049 people who took a rather low dose of kava (70 mg of kavalactones daily) for 7 weeks found side effects in 1.5% of cases. These were mostly mild gastrointestinal complaints and allergic rashes. A 4-week study of 3,029 individuals given 240 mg of kavalactones daily showed a 2.3% incidence of basically the same side effects. However, long-term use (months to years) of kava in excess of 400 mg kavalactones per day can create a distinctive generalized dry, scaly rash. It disappears promptly when the kava use stops.

The German Commission E monograph warns against the use of kava during pregnancy and nursing. Kava should not be taken along with prescription tranquilizers or sedatives, or other depressant drugs as there have been reports of coma caused by such combinations. Kava can also cause severe drowsiness when combined with hypnotic drugs. Kava might increase blood-clotting time. Safety in young children and those with severe liver or kidney disease has not been established. Similar precautions in pets are probably warranted.

If your pet is taking drugs in the benzodiazepine family, switching to kava will be very hard. You must seek a doctor's supervision, because in people, withdrawal symptoms can be severe and even life-threatening. It's easier to make the switch from milder anti-anxiety drugs, such as BuSpar and antidepressants. Nonetheless, a doctor's supervision is still strongly advised.

LACTOFERRIN (See Colostrum)

LAPACHO (Pau d'Arco, Taheebo, *Ipe Roxo, Tabebuia impestiginosa*)

Common Uses
Cancer, infections

The bark of the lapacho tree is used in the treatment of a variety of illnesses.

THERAPEUTIC USES

The inner bark of the lapacho tree is used by several South American indigenous peoples to treat cancer as well as a great variety of infectious diseases. The inner bark is believed to be the most effective part of the plant. Unfortunately, inferior products containing only the outer bark and the wood are sometimes misrepresented as "genuine inner-bark lapacho."

SCIENTIFIC EVIDENCE

There is intriguing, but far from conclusive, scientific evidence for some of these traditional uses. One of lapacho's major ingredients, lapachol, definitely possesses anti-tumor properties, and for a time was under active investigation as a possible chemotherapy drug. Unfortunately, when given in high enough dosages to kill cancer cells, lapachol causes numerous serious side effects. At standard dosages, blood levels of lapachol high enough to be deemed effective have not been reported.

Another component of lapacho, b-lapachone, continues to be investigated as an anticancer agent, since it may have a better side-effect profile and act similarly to a new class of prescription anti-tumor drugs.

Herbalists believe that the whole herb can produce equivalent benefits with fewer side effects, but this claim has never been properly investigated.

Various ingredients in lapacho can also kill bacteria and fungi in vitro. However, it is not yet clear how well the herb works for this purpose when taken orally.

While some herbalists recommend lapacho as a treatment for **cancer** (page 44), there is no good evidence that lapacho is an effective cancer treatment. Furthermore, the mechanism by which lapacho possibly works (it has both pro-oxidant and antioxidant properties) may cause it to interfere with the action of prescription anticancer drugs.

Do not add it to a conventional chemotherapy regime without consulting your veterinarian.

Lapacho, by virtue of its antibacterial, antiviral, antiparasitic, and possibly antifungal properties, is also sometimes used in people to treat Candida yeast infections, respiratory infections such as colds and flus, infectious diarrhea, and bladder infections. There may be some use for lapacho in pets with similar conditions.

DOSAGES

Lapacho contains many components that don't dissolve in water, so making tea from the herb is not the best idea; capsulized powdered bark is preferred. In people, a standard dosage is 300 mg 3 times daily.

SAFETY ISSUES

Full safety studies of lapacho have not been performed. When taken in normal dosages, it does not appear to cause any significant side effects. However, because its constituent lapachol is somewhat toxic, the herb is not recommended for pregnant or nursing mothers. Safety in young children or those with severe liver or kidney disease has also not been established; similar precautions are probably warranted in pets.

 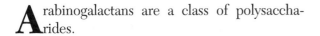

LARCH ARABINOGALACTAN

Common Uses
   Cancer, anti-inflammatory, immune stimulant, diarrhea

Arabinogalactans are a class of polysaccharides.

SOURCE

The primary source of arabinogalactan is the larch tree (mainly the western larch, *Larix occidentalis*).

THERAPEUTIC USES

Studies have shown that these compounds may enhance natural killer cells and cause a release of interferon gamma. For the treatment of **cancer** (page 44), arabinogalactans inhibit the reaction (between the galactose-based glycoconjugate on the cancer cells and a liver-specific, lectin-like receptor) that allows cancer cells to spread to the liver. Arabinogalactan thus has strong immuno-stimulating and anti-inflammatory properties. Its proposed use in people is as an antiviral and for the treatment of allergies, herpes, chronic fatigue, Epstein-Barr virus, pediatric otitis media, as part of HIV therapy, as a anti-radiation nutrient for patients undergoing conventional cancer treatment (chemotherapy), eczema, and general infections.

Arabinagalactan is also an excellent source of dietary fiber and has been shown to increase the production of short-chain fatty acids (SCFA), principally butyrate, a nutrient which has a particularly important role in the colon. Therefore, it may be useful for the treatment of pets with chronic **diarrhea** (page 71).

SAFETY ISSUES

Larch arabinogalactan is extremely safe; rare episodes of bloating and flatulence have been seen.

One brand name supplement exists (Immuno Support, Rx Vitamins for Pets) that contains larch arabinogalactans (and shiitake mushrooms and lutein, a carotenoid) as an immune-enhancing supplement to be used in pets with chronic diseases in which immune stimulation is needed. More clinical studies are needed to determine the effectiveness of larch arabinogalactans in various immune disorders in pets.

LAVENDER

Common Uses

Allergies (herbal rinse), mood elevation, joint irritation, tick repellant

---

Lavender is a plant with purple flowers and a sweet fragrance. The plant itself is not normally used as is true with other herbs. Instead, the oil of the lavender is commonly used to control nervousness and anxiety in pets and is quite popular in aromatherapy applications.

THERAPEUTIC USES

Oil of lavender can be used to calm nervous or aggressive animals. It is also recommended to help "lift the spirits" of depressed animals. Many owners place a small amount of the oil on a cotton ball, and then place this ball in the transport carrier with the pet when taking the pet to the veterinarian's, groomer's, or simply for any travel in the car.

A few drops of oil placed in a vaporizer may help the pet with respiratory congestion.

A tick preventive can be made in the following way (taken from Wulff-Tilford, M, Tilford G. *Herbs for Pets,* BowTie Press, 1999, page 169):

- 100 ml oil of lavender
- 300 ml olive oil
- 500 ml essential oil of terebinth
- 100 ml of St. John's wort-infused oil

A small amount of the oil is rubbed onto the pet to help prevent tick infestation.

SAFETY

Internal use should be avoided due to the potential for toxicity on the liver and kidneys. Topically applied oil should not be licked off by the pet. Do not use the undiluted oil directly on the skin as this may cause irritation. While some sources warn against using the oil around or on cats due to potential liver toxicity, applying a few drops of diluted oil to a cotton ball and placing the ball in the transport cage with the cat has not been shown to be harmful. The oil, even in the diluted form for tick control, should not be used on or in cats.

LECITHIN/CHOLINE (Egg lecithin, soy lecithin, phosphatidylcholine in lecithin)

Common Uses

Cognitive disorder, epilepsy, liver disease

Lecithin contains a substance called phosphatidylcholine (PC) that is presumed to be responsible for its medicinal effects. Phosphatidylcholine is a major part of the membranes surrounding our cells. However, when phosphatidylcholine is consumed, it is broken down into choline rather than being carried directly to cell membranes. Choline acts like folic acid, TMG (trimethylglycine), and SAMe (S-adenosylmethionine) to promote methylation. It

is also used to make acetylcholine, a nerve chemical essential for proper brain function.

SOURCE

For use as a supplement or a food additive, lecithin is often manufactured from soy.

THERAPEUTIC USES

Lecithin has been suggested as a treatment for high cholesterol, although there is surprisingly little evidence that it works. More recently, lecithin has been proposed as a remedy for various psychological and neurological diseases in people, such as Tourette's syndrome, Alzheimer's disease, and bipolar disorder (manic depression).

Choline and phosphatidylcholine are effective for treating human neurological disorders with presumed choline deficiencies, including tardive dyskinesia, Huntington's chorea, and Friedreich's ataxia.

One product containing choline that has been used successfully in pets is Cholodin. Cholodin contains choline, phosphatidylcholine, DL-methionine, and vitamins and minerals. Choline provides methyl groups used by the body in a number of biological reactions and acts as a precursor of acetylcholine. Phosphatidylcholine (lecithin) in part of the plasma membrane of mammalian cells provides additional choline for acetylcholine synthesis. Methinonine and inositol also are involved in neurotransmitter metabolism. Studies have shown effectiveness in improving neurological function in pets with **cognitive disorder** (page 56) (often referred to incorrectly as "senility" in older pets). For those pets who respond favorably, Cholodin can be used in place of the drug Anipryl (selegiline), which has recently been approved for use in canine cognitive disorder.

Cognitive disorder in dogs (and possibly cats) is a disorder of geriatric pets (see Cognitive Disorder under Conditions for a more thorough discussion). It has been erroneously referred to as "senility" in pets. Behavior changes occur as a result of physical and chemical changes in the brains of affected dogs, including accumulation of beta-amyloid protein, decreased neurotransmitter (acetylcholine) activity, or increased activity of the enzyme monoamine oxidase-B, an enzyme that breaks down the neurotransmitter dopamine. Anipryl works by inhibiting monoamine oxidase-B, which allows accumulation of dopamine. (Other pharmacologic effects unrelated to inhibition of monoamine oxidase-B may also be responsible for Anipryl's actions.) While generally safe, side effects that have been seen in dogs treated with Anipryl include diarrhea, vomiting, and loss of appetite. Additionally, Anipryl should not be taken by pets who are also taking other medications such as ephedrine (or the herb ma huang), phenylpropanolamine (commonly prescribed for pets with urinary incontinence), other monoamine oxidase inhibitors (amitraz, commonly used to dip pets with mange), tricyclic antidepressants, tetracycline antidepressants, and selective serotonin reuptake inhibitors. Also, the use of Anipryl may not be cost effective for many dog owners (approximately $100 to $150 per month depending upon the size of the pet). Using lecithin, choline, and related nutritional supplements can be a safe, cost effective, and effective treatment for cognitive disorder in dogs and cats and can serve as a natural substitute for Anipryl. These supplements apparently increase synthesis of the neurotransmitter acetylcholine, which may increase mental function, decrease seizures, and decrease other neurological signs in aging pets (such as decreased hearing, or urinary or fecal incontinence).

Cholodin and similar supplements are also recommended for pets with **fatty liver disease** (page 127) (hepatic lipidosis). In hepatic lipidosis, fat accumulates in the liver. To aid in removing fat from the liver, choline and/or its chemical precursor methionine can be supplemented as part of the therapy (the amino acid arginine, given at 250 mg every 12 hours, is also recommended for cats with hepatic lipidosis). However, choline and methionine should not be used if hepatic encephalopathy and brain depression are present.

Due to its ability to interact with cells of the nervous system, Cholodin is also recommended for pets with **epilepsy** (page 73). Studies have shown decreased seizure frequency in dogs supplemented with products containing increased levels of choline and phosphatidylcholine. Cholodin and other choline-containing products can be tried to determine effectiveness under your veterinarian's supervision.

SAFETY ISSUES

Do not stop anti-epileptic drugs without your veterinarian's permission.

Lecithin is believed to be generally safe. However, some people taking high dosages (several grams daily) experience minor but annoying side effects, such as abdominal discomfort, diarrhea, and nausea. Maximum safe dosages for young children, pregnant or nursing women, or those with severe liver or kidney disease have not been determined; the same precautions are probably warranted in pets.

 # LEMON BALM *(Melissa officinalis)*

Common Use
Hyperthyroidism in cats

Lemon balm may be useful in cats with hyperthyroidism to decrease thyroid output and possibly decrease blood pressure.

THERAPEUTIC USES

Lemon balm is believed to block iodide uptake and inhibit antibody attachment at the thyroid cells. This makes it potentially useful for cats with **hyperthyroidism** (page 101). Secondarily, it may prove helpful for pets with high blood pressure (as lemon balm can lower blood pressure), depression, or indigestion.

SAFETY ISSUES

Do not use in pregnant or lactating pets. Lemon balm should not be used in pets with hypothyroidism due to its ability to decrease thyroid hormone levels. Lemon balm may be useful in cats with hyperthyroidism to decrease thyroid output and possibly decrease blood pressure.

 # LICORICE *(Glycyrrhiza glabra* and *Glycyrrhiza lepidota)*

Common Uses
Adrenal gland, Addison's disease, allergies (topical and herbal rinse), arthritis, asthma, cancer, infections, intestinal parasites, liver disease

Licorice is an herbal anti-inflammatory agent often used to achieve the same effects as corticosteroid medications. Pets with a variety of allergic problems may benefit from therapy using licorice.

THERAPEUTIC USES

Licorice is a fast acting anti-inflammatory agent. Licorice is also known for its antimicrobial and immune-stimulating properties. Many herbalists regard it as "nature's cortisone" due to its glycyrrhizin content, and it is often recommended for pets with **arthritis** (page 11), **allergies** (page 3), **asthma** (page 21), and other inflammatory disorders. Licorice root inhibits inflammatory prostaglandins and leukotrienes (similar in activity to corticosteroids).

Because licorice also exhibits mineralocorticoid as well as glucocorticoid activity, it has been suggested for use in Addison's disease.

The use of licorice may allow pet owners to use decreased doses of more potent corticosteroids.

Licorice is beneficial for the treatment of **liver diseases** (page 127) due to its ability to prevent free radical damage and inhibit formation of free radicals. Licorice also has a protectant effect (due to glycyrrhizin) and enhances interferon and T-cell production (to boost the immune system).

Licorice reduces inflammation in pets with bronchitis and may act as an expectorant.

Licorice has shown antibacterial activity.

In the intestinal tract, licorice helps heal ulcers and may decrease hydrochloric acid in the stomach.

Deglycyrrhizinated licorice (DGL) is a special extract made by removing the glycyrrhizin molecule, leaving the flavonoid components. In people, DGL is used for treating ulcers of the mouth and small intestine and in inflammatory bowel disease. The anti-ulcer effects in people have been shown to be as effective as antacid medications such as Tagamet. DGL is also recommended as an herbal ulcer-preventive (similar to drugs such as misoprostol) for people taking nonsteroidal medications and corticosteroids. However, it is not clear that DGL provides all the same benefits as whole licorice for other problems.

SCIENTIFIC EVIDENCE

Several double-blind studies in people show benefit to patients with HIV infection and AIDS; similar results might occur in cats with leukemia or immunodeficiency infections, although controlled studies are lacking.

DOSAGES

Tinctures appear to be the preferred form in pets.

SAFETY ISSUES

When used in large doses and for extended periods of time, licorice can produce similar cortisone-like effects as steroid medications, including high blood pressure and increased serum potassium. Do not use in pregnant animals.

If used for more than 2 weeks at a time, side effects can include decreased potassium (supplementing with potassium is recommended), fluid retention, high blood pressure, and increased sodium; increased sodium excretion may be needed. These effects can be especially dangerous if you take digitalis, or if you have high blood pressure, heart disease, diabetes, or kidney disease. Licorice may also increase both the positive and negative effects of treatment with corticosteroids, such as prednisone. Dandelion leaf can be added to the regimen to help increased potassium and decrease sodium. In people, side effects occur commonly at levels above 400 mg per day.

DGL is believed to be safe, although extensive safety studies have not been performed. Side effects are rare.

Safety for either form of licorice in young children, pregnant or nursing women, or those with severe liver or kidney disease has not been established. Similar precautions are probably warranted in pets.

If the pet is taking: digitalis, long-term use of licorice can be dangerous; thiazide or loop diuretics, use of licorice might lead to excessive potassium loss; corticosteroid treatment, licorice could increase both its effects and its side effects.

Do not use in animals with cardiovascular disease, high blood pressure, or kidney disease; in pets taking digitalis medications; or in pets with diabetes. Licorice could increase blood-clotting time.

Licorice induces cytochrome P-450 enzymes in the liver; this may alter the metabolism of other drugs, decreasing their serum levels.

If licorice root is used for more than two weeks at a time, the diet should be supplemented with potassium and the sodium should be decreased (adding dandelion can help in this regard). Caution should be used in animals with heart disease or hypertension. In large amounts, steroid overdosage (Cushing's disease) could theoretically occur. It should not be used in pregnant animals and care must be exercised in diabetic pets.

LOBELIA *(Lobelia inflata)*

Common Use
Asthma

Lobelia may be useful in certain respiratory conditions in dogs and cats, including bronchitis and **asthma** (page 21) and as a general respiratory stimulant.

THERAPEUTIC USES

While useful for respiratory problems, lobelia can act as a nervous system depressant. This may make it useful for pets with excess nervous system stimulation, such as those with **epilepsy** (page 73) or hyperactivity.

SAFETY ISSUES

While generally safe, at high doses lobelia can cause vomiting. An active ingredient, lveline, has nicotine-like actions. It should not be used during pregnancy or lactation, and care should be used if combined with other supplements or medications that can depress the nervous system.

LYCOPENE

Common Use
Antioxidant

Lycopene is an antioxidant found in tomatoes, watermelon, guava, and pink grapefruit. Like beta-carotene, lycopene belongs to the family of chemicals known as carotenoids. It is about twice as powerful as beta-carotene as an antioxidant.

SOURCE

Tomatoes are the best source of lycopene, and cooking doesn't destroy lycopene. While not all studies agree, some studies indicate that cooking tomatoes in oil may provide lycopene in a way that the body can use better.

DOSAGES

The optimum dosage for lycopene in people and pets has not been established.

THERAPEUTIC USES

In people, there is some evidence that a diet high in lycopene may reduce the risk of cancer of the prostate as well as other cancers. Lycopene may also help prevent macular degeneration and cataracts; it may be very important for optimal health.

In people, lycopene may help prevent cancer, particularly prostate cancer (since most pets are neutered, this is extremely rare in pets). However, the evidence we have for this idea comes from observational studies in which researchers analyze people's diets, rather than the more definitive intervention trials, in which people are actually given lycopene supplements. In observational trials, it is always possible that other unrecognized factors are at work. Animal studies have also found some cancer-preventative benefits with lycopene.

Weak evidence also suggests that lycopene can reduce the risk of cataracts and macular degeneration in people.

SAFETY ISSUES

Although lycopene is a normal part of the diet for people, there has not been a formal evaluation of lycopene's safety when it is taken as a concentrated supplement. Maximum safe dosages for young children, pregnant or nursing women, or those with severe liver or kidney disease have not been established.

 # MAGNESIUM

Common Uses
Heart disease, diabetes, epilepsy

Magnesium is the third largest mineral constituent of bone (calcium and phosphorus are the first and second largest constituents, respectively). It is found in significant quantities throughout the body and used for numerous purposes, including muscle relaxation, blood clotting, and the manufacture of ATP (adenosine triphosphate, the body's main energy source). Magnesium is involved in the metabolism of carbohydrates and fats; it also acts as a catalyst for a number of enzymes.

Magnesium has been called "nature's calcium-channel blocker," based on its ability to block calcium from entering muscle and heart cells. This may be the basis for magnesium's effects on migraine headaches and high blood pressure.

SOURCES

Magnesium is available in many synthetic forms, including magnesium sulfate, magnesium gluconate, magnesium fumarate, magnesium citrate, magnesium malate, magnesium oxide, and magnesium chloride. Natural sources include kelp, wheat bran, wheat germ, nuts (almonds, cashews), blackstrap molasses, brewer's yeast (not to be confused with nutritional yeast), buckwheat, whole grains, collard greens, dandelion greens, avocado, sweet corn, cheddar cheese, sunflower seeds, shrimp, dried fruit (figs, apricots, and prunes), and many other fruits and vegetables.

THERAPEUTIC USES

In pets, magnesium supplementation is often recommended for pets with **heart disease** (page 91), **diabetes** (page 66), and **epilepsy** (page 73). For pets with epilepsy, it is proposed that magnesium cools the liver down and relaxes the mind and heart electrical complexes.

In people, magnesium has been recommended as a therapy for migraine headaches, noise-related hearing loss, kidney stones, hypertension (high blood pressure), premenstrual syndrome, painful menstruation, diabetes, osteoporosis, low blood sugar, glaucoma, fibromyalgia, fatigue, stroke, autism, various forms of heart disease (such as mitral valve prolapse or congestive heart failure), and asthma.

Low levels of magnesium can cause a variety of clinical signs including lack of appetite, muscle incoordination, slow growth, and seizures. Low levels of magnesium may occur with kidney disease/failure, high levels of blood calcium (hypercalcemia), hyperthyroidism (in cats), and the use of certain medications (diuretics, aminoglycoside antibiotics, cisplatin, cyclosporine, amphotericin, and methotrexate).

When combined with oral diabetes drugs in the sulfonylurea family (Tolinase, Micronase, Orinase, Glucotrol, Diabinese, DiaBeta), magnesium may cause blood sugar levels to fall more than expected.

Excess levels of magnesium may contribute to the increased incidence of calcium oxalate stones.

However, dietary magnesium does not contribute to the more commonly diagnosed struvite stones (high urine pH is more important in the development of these types of bladder stones).

DOSAGES

The recommended starting dosage for pets with heart disease and diabetes is 5 mg/pound daily. Alternatively, magnesium supplementation for epileptic dogs is 100 mg twice daily.

The AAFCO recommendation is 0.08% for growth and reproduction and 0.04% for adult maintenance for cats, and 0.04% for all life stages for dogs.

SAFETY ISSUES

Magnesium may interfere with the absorption of calcium and various other minerals. For this reason it's suggested that pets taking magnesium also take a multimineral supplement.

In general, magnesium appears to be quite safe when taken at recommended dosages. Pets with severe kidney or heart disease should not receive magnesium except under veterinary supervision.

MAITAKE MUSHROOM *(Grifola frondosa, Polyporous umbellatus, Grifola umbellatus, Boletus frondosus)*

Common Uses

Diuretic, edema, immune system stimulant, liver disease, bladder disease (cystitis), cancer support

Maitake is a medicinal mushroom used in Japan as a general promoter of robust health. Like the similarly described reishi fungus, innumerable healing powers have been attributed to maitake, ranging from curing cancer to preventing heart disease.

SCIENTIFIC EVIDENCE

Unfortunately, there hasn't been enough reliable research yet to determine whether any of these ancient beliefs are really true. Maitake contains polysaccharides including beta-D-glucan which may contribute to its ability to stimulate immunity. Contemporary herbalists classify maitake as an adaptogen, a substance said to help the body adapt to stress and resist illness. However, as for other adaptogens, we lack definitive scientific evidence to show us that maitake really functions in this way.

Most investigation has focused on the polysaccharide constituents of maitake. This family of substances is known to affect the human immune system in complex ways, and one in particular, beta-D-glucan, has been studied for its potential benefit in treating cancer and AIDS. In people, highly preliminary studies also suggest that maitake may be useful in treating diabetes, hypertension (high blood pressure), and high cholesterol. However, no real evidence as yet shows that maitake is effective for these or any other illnesses.

SAFETY ISSUES

In people and pets, maitake appears to be extremely safe. Safety in young children, pregnant or nursing women, or those with severe liver or kidney disease has not been established. These guidelines should probably also be followed for pets.

Maitake Mushroom

MANGANESE

Common Uses
Arthritis, nutrition

The trace element manganese is necessary for the synthesis of proteoglycans and serves as an antioxidant. The biochemical reactions that make glycosaminoglycans from glucosamine will not occur efficiently unless manganese is present in the body. In people it has been estimated that approximately 37% of Americans may be marginally deficient in manganese, which limits the rate of glycosaminoglycan (GAG) synthesis.

THERAPEUTIC USES

In pets, manganese is often added to nutritional supplements for pets with **arthritis** (page 11) due to its use in bone and cartilage development. One particular glucosamine-chondroitin supplement includes manganese to help ensure that GAG synthesis occurs at the maximum possible rate. Whether or not animals may exhibit manganese deficiency is not known; therefore, whether or not additional manganese supplementation is necessary is unknown. Still, manganese supplementation as included with this supplement will ensure that the proper amount of manganese is present for the maximum rate of GAG synthesis.

Manganese is available in several synthetic forms, including manganese sulfate, manganese chloride, manganese picolinate, and manganese gluconate.

Manganese is important as a constituent of many key enzymes. It is essential for bone and cartilage development due to the activation of glycosyltransferases, enzymes that are important for the formation of polysaccharides and glycoproteins. Manganese also plays a particularly important role as part of the natural antioxidant enzyme superoxide dismutase (SOD), which helps fight damaging free radicals. It also helps energy metabolism, thyroid function, blood sugar control, and normal skeletal growth.

In people, manganese is often recommended for treating for osteoporosis, although there is no direct evidence that manganese is helpful, except possibly in combination with other minerals. Manganese has also been suggested for dysmenorrhea (painful menstruation), muscle strains and sprains, and rheumatoid arthritis; the evidence that it works in these conditions is very weak.

People with epilepsy and diabetes often have lower-than-normal levels of manganese in their blood. This suggests (but doesn't prove) that manganese supplements might be helpful for these conditions.

SOURCES

The best sources of dietary manganese are fiber sources, menhaden fish meal, dicalcium phosphate, whole grains, legumes, avocados, grape juice, chocolate, seaweed, egg yolks, nuts, seeds, boysenberries, blueberries, pineapples, spinach, collard greens, peas, and green vegetables.

In people, antacids as well as calcium, iron, copper, and zinc supplements can reduce the body's absorption of manganese.

DOSAGES

The AAFCO recommends 5 ppm (parts per million) for dogs and 7.5 ppm for cats.

SAFETY ISSUES

Manganese appears to be safe; signs of deficiency or toxicity are unlikely in pets fed balanced diets.

MARSHMALLOW *(Althaea officinalis)*

Common Uses

Diarrhea, diabetes, cancer, infections, kidney disease, urinary disorders

Marshmallow is an herb recommended primarily for relieving digestive and respiratory problems.

THERAPEUTIC USES

Marshmallow is useful in situations that involve irritation of the skin or mucous membranes. It is often recommended for pets with **urinary tract diseases** (page 84), upper respiratory infections, and irritations of the digestive system. The herb contains very high levels of large sugar molecules called mucilage, which appear to exert a soothing effect on mucous membranes. Marshmallow acts as a soothing, lubricating protective barrier of the membranes of these body systems.

Marshmallow also has antibacterial and immune-stimulating properties.

SCIENTIFIC EVIDENCE

No double-blind studies have been reported at this time.

SAFETY ISSUES

Marshmallow is believed to be entirely safe. However, detailed safety studies have not been performed. One study suggests that marshmallow can slightly lower blood sugar levels. For this reason, it should not be used in animals receiving hypoglycemic therapies. People with diabetes should use caution when taking marshmallow. Safety in young children, pregnant or nursing women, or those with severe liver or kidney disease has not been established. Similar cautions are probably warranted in pets.

Marshmallow may retard the intestinal absorption of drugs when given with medications.

MGN-3

Common Use

Immune stimulant

This product is made by combining the outer shell of rice bran with extracts from the shitake, kawaratake, and suehirotake mushrooms. MGN-3 is theorized to work against cancer by stimulating the immune system by increasing interferon levels, increasing the tumor necrosis factor, increasing the activity of natural killer cells, and increasing the activity of B cells and T cells. Preliminary research in people appears promising, but more research is needed in larger studies before this can be recommended on a large-scale basis.

MILK THISTLE *(Silybum marianum)*

Common Uses
  Cancer, liver disease

Milk thistle, also known as wild artichoke and holy thistle, is well-known for use in the treatment of **liver disease** (page 127).

THERAPEUTIC USES

The silymarin content of milk thistle has been shown effective in treating liver disease. Milk thistle compounds are usually standardized to 70 to 80% silymarin. Milk thistle is one of the few herbs that have no real equivalent in the world of conventional medicine.

The active ingredients in milk thistle appear to be four substances known collectively as silymarin, of which the most potent is named silibinin. When injected intravenously, silibinin is one of the few known antidotes to poisoning by the deathcap mushroom, *Amanita phalloides*. Animal studies suggest that milk thistle extracts can also protect against many other poisonous substances, from toluene to the drug acetaminophen. Silymarin appears to function by displacing toxins trying to bind to the liver as well as by causing the liver to regenerate more quickly. It may also scavenge free radicals and stabilize liver cell membranes. However, milk thistle is not effective in treating advanced liver cirrhosis, and only the intravenous form can counter mushroom poisoning.

Silymarin protects the liver as an antioxidant (it is more potent than vitamin E), by increasing glutathione levels, and by inhibiting the formation of damaging leukotrienes. Silymarin also stimulates the production of new liver cells, replacing the damaged cells.

Due to its liver support, milk thistle is often used anytime the pet becomes ill or toxic. It can also be used anytime drugs are given to the pet that could be toxic to the liver, especially chemotherapy medicines for treating cancer,

heartworm treatment medications, and long-term use of other medications (such as antibiotics and corticosteroids).

In people, treatment produces a modest improvement in symptoms of chronic liver disease, such as nausea, weakness, loss of appetite, fatigue, and pain. Liver enzymes as measured by blood tests frequently improve, and if a liver biopsy is performed, there may be improvements on the cellular level. Some studies have shown a reduction in death rate among those with serious liver disease.

A new form of silymarin, in which the compound is bound to phosphatidylcholine, has been shown to have greater bioavailability than unbound silymarin.

It is best not to use milk thistle as a daily supplement but rather reserve its use for conditions where the liver is under stress.

DOSAGES

The standard dosage of milk thistle is 100 mg per 25 lbs of weight, 2 to 3 times a day. In people, the best results are seen at higher doses (140 to 200 mg 3 times daily of an extract standardized to contain 70% silymarin); the bound form is dosed at 100 to 200 mg twice daily.

SAFETY ISSUES

Do not use in pregnant animals. Long-term use may alter blood liver enzymes and cause depressed liver function unless chronic liver disease is present. High doses may cause diarrhea. Safety in young children, pregnant or nursing women, and individuals with severe renal disease has not been formally established. Similar precautions in pets are probably warranted.

MINERALS (See boron, calcium, chromium, magnesium, manganese, phosphorus, potassium, selenium, sodium, zinc)

 MSM *(Methylsulfonylmethane)*

Common Use
Arthritis

Methylsulfonylmethane, MSM for short, is a natural anti-inflammatory and analgesic. It is a stable metabolite of DMSO (dimethylsulfoxide). MSM supplies sulfur to the body, which can be used for the treatment of a variety of disorders, including **osteoarthritis** (page 11), **allergies** (page 3), and digestive disorders. For example, sulfur is an essential chemical needed for the synthesis of cartilage, which may explain its use in the treatment of arthritis.

SOURCES

MSM is found naturally in a variety of foods, including meat, fish, eggs, poultry, and milk, and to a lesser amount in vegetables, legumes, and fruits. Because of mineral depletion in soil and because MSM is lost during the storage and preparation of food, there is some concern that dietary sources may not provide enough sulfur to our pets. Additionally, the amount of MSM in the body decreases with age, indicating a possible need for this compound in our older pets.

THERAPEUTIC USES

In arthritic cartilage, the concentration of sulfur is about one-third the level found in normal cartilage. MSM may help treat arthritis via an anti-inflammatory benefit and by providing sulfur used by the cartilage in the healing process.

SCIENTIFIC EVIDENCE

Studies in people and animals showed improved joint flexibility, reduced stiffness and swelling, and reduced pain. Animals with rheumatoid arthritis who were given MSM showed no cartilage degeneration.

MSM may be of benefit in pets; more research is needed to determine the optimum dosage, potential benefits, and treatment schedule. In addition to arthritis, some holistic veterinarians recommend it for any type of inflammatory disease (such as gingivitis).

DOSAGES

One recommended starting dose for cats and small dogs is 100 to 200 mg twice daily, mixed in with food (the bitter taste is unpleasant).

SAFETY ISSUES

MSM is considered very safe; the lethal dose of MSM in mice is >20 grams/kg of body weight. No long-term side effects were seen when human volunteers were given MSM for up to 6 months.

MULLEIN *(Verbascum thapsus)*

Common Use
Fleas (topical)

Like marshmallow, mullein contains a high proportion of mucilage that appears to soothe mucous membranes. It also contains saponins that may help loosen mucous. However, there has not been very much scientific investigation into this popular herb. Mullein appears to be most effective when combined with other herbs of similar qualities, such as marshmallow.

Mullein is useful for respiratory inflammation and infection, often being recommended for dogs and cats with common respiratory conditions (such as kennel cough or herpes virus). This herb has been shown to possess antibacterial and antiviral properties.

Mullein can be tried for pets with **urinary incontinence** (page 145).

SAFETY ISSUES

Mullein leaves and flowers are generally regarded as safe. Side effects are rare. Nonetheless, safety in young children, pregnant or nursing women, or those with severe liver or kidney disease has not been established. Similar warnings are probably warranted in pets.

The rotenone content of the herb makes it toxic to fish, amphibians, and birds. The rotenone content also makes it appropriate to try topically for pets with ear mites.

N-ACETYL CYSTEINE (NAC)

Common Uses
Respiratory conditions, degenerative myelopathy

N-acetyl cysteine (NAC) is a modified form of the dietary amino acid cysteine. Technically it is a medication rather than a supplement. It is listed here since it is a derivative of an amino acid and is often used by holistic doctors for the treatment of canine degenerative myelopathy. NAC can help break up mucus, which is the basis for using it in respiratory conditions. It also helps the body make the important antioxidant liver enzyme glutathione, which is necessary to detoxify harmful chemicals.

THERAPEUTIC USES

NAC is used as part of the therapy for treating acetaminophen (Tylenol) poisoning in pets (spe-

cifically cats, who have smaller amounts of liver detoxifying enzymes than dogs). NAC is also included in certain formulations of eye drops to treat pets with corneal ulcers.

Recently, the use of NAC has been promoted as part of the therapy for **degenerative myelopathy** (page 60) as it is a potent antioxidant with neuroprotective effects. Controlled studies are lacking, and there is no treatment for this debilitating disorder, although some pets seem to temporarily stabilize when treated with NAC and other supplements.

DOSAGES

N-acetyl cysteine is given 75mg/kg divided in 3 doses a day for 2 weeks, then every other day. It is made as a 20% solution and can be diluted with chicken broth, using 1 part drug and 3 parts chicken broth. This formula can be compounded by pharmacists, or your veterinarian can order it from Westlab Pharmacy at (352) 373-8111 or toll free at (800) 4WESTLA (or at e-mail info@westlabpharmacy.com).

It is recommended to use low-sodium or no-sodium broth as high sodium levels may cause nausea, diarrhea, or stomach upset. The product should be refrigerated and the lid kept tightly closed as the drug has a tendency to lose its potency and its desired effects.

SOURCES

There is no daily requirement for NAC, and it is not found in food.

SAFETY ISSUES

Because NAC is used as a conventional medication in pets, owners should not use it in their pets without strict veterinary supervision. Safety in young children, women who are pregnant or nursing, and individuals with severe liver or kidney disease has not been established; similar precautions are probably warranted in pets.

 # NEEM (*Azadirachta indica*)

Common Use
Flea control

The neem tree has been called "the village pharmacy" because its bark, leaves, sap, fruit, seeds, and twigs have so many diverse uses in the traditional medicine of India. This member of the mahogany family has been used medicinally for at least 4,000 years.

At least 50 patents have been filed on neem, and neem-based products are licensed in the United States for control of insects in food and ornamental crops, and for flea and insect control on pets.

THERAPEUTIC USES

Currently, neem-based products are recommended for use in pets as natural **flea** (page 89) control products, substituting for shampoos and sprays that contain organophosphates and chemically synthesized pyrethrin analogues. Other veterinary uses include gastroenteritis, wound therapy, genitourinary tract infections, hepatitis, skin problems, and **ringworm** (page 144).

In India, the sap is used for treating fevers, general debilitation, digestive disturbances, and skin diseases; the bark gum for respiratory diseases and other infections; the leaves for digestive problems,

intestinal parasites (page 118), and viral infections; the fruit for debilitation, malaria, skin diseases, and intestinal parasites; and the seed and kernel oil for diabetes, fevers, fungal infections, bacterial infections, inflammatory diseases, fertility prevention, and as an insecticide. Which, if any, of these uses will be verified when proper research is performed remains unclear.

SCIENTIFIC EVIDENCE

At least 100 bioactive substances have been found in neem, including nimbidin, azadiracthins, other triterpenoids and limonoids, beta-sitosterol, and the flavonoids kemferol, quercetin, and myricetin. Although the scientific evidence for all of neem's uses in health care remains preliminary, the intense interest in the plant will eventually lead to proper double-blind clinical trials.

SAFETY ISSUES

Based on its extensive traditional use, neem seems to be quite safe. This is particularly remarkable considering that the oil of neem is a powerful insecticide! However, there has not yet been a full scientific evaluation of the toxicity and side effects of neem and its many constituents.

A recent report suggests that neem might damage chromosomes. Although this information is still highly preliminary, at the present time neem is not recommended for use by young chil-dren, pregnant or nursing women, or those with severe liver or kidney disease; similar precau-tions are probably warranted in pets. Because neem possesses natural contraceptive activity and may cause abortion, it should probably not be used in pregnant animals.

NETTLE *(Urtica dioica)*

Common Uses
Allergies, cancer, liver disease

Some types of nettle are known for causing burning pain when the leaves or stems are touched, but nettle is also used for medicinal purposes.

THERAPEUTIC USES

Nettle contains abundant amounts of vitamins and minerals and protein, and can be used as a vitamin-mineral supplement. Nettle can be used for its antihistamine and other anti-inflammatory properties and to support liver function in pets with chronic skin disorders. In people, one study showed that 58% of patients with allergic rhinitis (runny nose) found relief after taking nettle. Ani-mals with plant allergies can be sensitive to net-tle, so consultation with a veterinarian before using this herb is important.

Nettle drops can be used as an alternative to eyebright.

Nettle root has been recommended for pets with prostate enlargement.

SAFETY ISSUES

Allergic pets may be sensitive to nettle.

Because nettle leaf has a long history of food use, it is believed to be safe, although nettle root does not have as extensive a history.

Although detailed safety studies have not been reported, no significant adverse effects have been noted in Germany where nettle root is widely used. In practice, it is nearly free of side effects. In people, less than 1% reported mild gastrointestinal distress and only 0.19% experi-enced allergic reactions (skin rash).

For theoretical reasons, there are some con-cerns that nettle may interact with diabetes, blood pressure, anti-inflammatory, and sedative medications, although there are no reports of any problems occurring in real life.

The safety of nettle root or leaf for pregnant or nursing mothers has not been established. However nettle leaf tea is a traditional drink for pregnant and nursing women.

If your pet is taking anti-inflammatory, anti-hypertensive, sedative, or blood sugar lowering medications, nettle might conceivably interact with them, although it is unlikely.

NUCLEOTIDES (See Purine and Pyrimidine Nucleotides)

Nucleotides

OLIVE LEAF EXTRACT *(Olea europaea)*

Common Uses
 Infections, inflammation

Extracts from the leaves of olive trees contain large amounts of the chemical oleuropein, as well as bioflavonoids such as quercetin and rutin. The extract apparently works by interfering with several of the amino acid production processes needed for viral growth and/or reproduction, as well as by stimulating phagocytosis (the killing of bacteria and viruses by white blood cells). Olive leaf extract may also interfere with viral infection and spread by preventing virus shedding or budding.

THERAPEUTIC USES

This extracted product exhibits both antiviral and antibacterial effects; it may also be effective against various yeast infections (*Candida*, **ringworm** (page 144)). The anti-inflammatory properties in olive leaf extract may prove useful for the treatment of inflammatory conditions such as **osteoarthritis** (page 11) and dermatitis. Feeding large amounts of olive oil will not achieve the same ef-

fects, as oleuropein is extracted from the leaves before the oil is removed for use. There are anecdotal reports of pets with various **infections** (page 105) (including infections of the skin, urinary tract, and respiratory tract) recovering with its use when traditional therapies did not work.

Little information in the form of controlled studies in pets is available. Anecdotal evidence suggests that olive leaf may be helpful in the numerous conditions mentioned.

DOSAGES

The recommended dose for dogs is 250 to 500 mg per 35 pounds per day of a standardized extract containing 15 to 25% oleuropein for treatment.

SAFETY ISSUE

A rare side effect is transient diarrhea, which usually resolves with a decreased dosage.

 OMEGA-3 FATTY ACIDS (See Oral Fatty Acids)

 ORAL FATTY ACIDS

Common Uses
 Arthritis, allergic dermatitis, heart disease, kidney disease, cancer

Fats in the form of fatty acids have recently become a popular supplement among most veterinarians, not just those interested in holistic care. Fatty acids were first purported to work in some pets with allergic dermatitis, and are in fact

an essential part of every pet's diet. Other practitioners have prescribed them for pets with dry flaky skin and dull haircoats. Recently, they have been advocated in pets with kidney disease, heart disease, elevated cholesterol, and arthritis.

We are just beginning to see that fatty acids may be valuable in a variety of conditions.

When discussing fatty acids, we're not just talking about adding some vegetable oil to the pet's diet to get a nice shiny coat. The fatty acids of most concern to us are the omega-3 and omega-6 fatty acids. Omega-9 fatty acids have no known use in treating our pets. Omega-3 fatty acids—eicosapentaenoic acid (EPA) and docosahexaenoic acid (DHA)—are derived from fish oils of coldwater fish (salmon, trout, or most commonly menhaden fish) and flaxseed, whereas omega-6 fatty acids—linoleic acid (LA) and gamma-linolenic acid (GLA)—are derived from the oils of seeds such as evening primrose, black currant, and borage. Often, fatty acids are added to the diet with other supplements to attain an additive effect.

HOW DO FATTY ACIDS WORK?

Just how do the fatty acids work to help in controlling inflammation in pets? Cell membranes contain phospholipids. When membrane injury occurs, an enzyme acts on the phospholipids in the cell membranes to produce fatty acids including arachidonic acid (an omega-6 fatty acid) and eicosapentaenoic acid (an omega-3 fatty acid). Further metabolism of the arachidonic acid and eicosapentaenoic acid by additional enzymes (the lipooxygenase and cyclooxygenase pathways) yields the production of chemicals called eicosanoids. The eicosanoids produced by metabolism of arachidonic acid are pro-inflammatory and cause inflammation, suppress the immune system, and cause platelets to aggregate and clot; the eicosanoids produced by metabolism of eicosapentaenoic acid are non-inflammatory, not immunosuppressive, and help inhibit platelets from clotting. (This sounds simple, but there is some overlap and the actual biochemical pathway is a bit more complicated than I have suggested here. For example, one of the by-products of omega-6 fatty acid metabolism is Prostaglandin E_1, which is anti-inflammatory. This is one reason why some research has shown that using certain omega-6 fatty acids can also act to limit inflammation.)

Supplementation of the diet with omega-3 fatty acids works in this biochemical reaction. By providing extra amounts of these non-inflammatory compounds, we try to overwhelm the body with the production of non-inflammatory eicosanoids. Therefore, since the same enzymes metabolize both omega-3 and omega-6 fatty acids, and since metabolism of the omega-6 fatty acids tend to cause inflammation (with the exception of Prostaglandin E_1 by metabolism of omega-6 as mentioned previously), by supplying a large amount of omega-3 fatty acids we favor the production of non-inflammatory chemicals.

Many disorders are due to overproduction of the eicosanoids responsible for producing inflammation, including **arthritis** (page 11) and **atopic dermatitis** (page 3). Fatty acid supplementation can be beneficial in inflammatory disorders by regulating the eicosanoid production.

In general, the products of omega-3 (specifically EPA) and one omega-6 fatty acid (DGLA) are less inflammatory than are the products of arachidonic acid (another omega-6 fatty acid). By changing dietary fatty acid consumption, we can change eicosanoid production right at the cellular level and try to modify (decrease) inflammation within the body. By providing the proper (anti-inflammatory) fatty acids, we can use fatty acids as an anti-inflammatory substance. However, since the products of omega-6 fatty acid metabolism (specifically arachidonic acid) are not the sole cause of the inflammation, fatty acid therapy is rarely effective as the sole therapy but is used as an adjunct therapy to achieve an additive effect.

Flaxseed Oil

Flaxseed oil is derived from the seeds of the flax plant and has been proposed as a less smelly alternative to fish oil. Flaxseed oil contains alpha-linolenic acid (ALA), an omega-3 fatty acid that is ultimately converted to EPA and DHA. In fact, flaxseed oil contains higher levels of omega-3 fatty acids (ALA) than fish oil. It also contains omega-6 fatty acids.

As mentioned, many species of pets (probably including dogs and cats) and some people cannot convert ALA to these other more active non-inflammatory omega-3 fatty acids. In one study in people, flaxseed oil was ineffective in reducing

Oral Fatty Acids

symptoms or raising levels of EPA and DHA. While flaxseed oil has been suggested as a substitute for fish oil, there is no evidence that it is effective when used for the same therapeutic purposes as fish oil. Unlike the case for fish oil, there is little evidence that flaxseed oil is effective for any specific therapeutic purpose.

Therefore, supplementation with EPA and DHA is important, and this is the reason flaxseed oil is not recommended as the sole fatty acid supplement for pets. Flaxseed oil can be used to provide ALA and as a coat conditioner.

Flaxseed oil also does contain lignans, which are currently being studied for use in preventing cancer in people.

The essential fatty acids in flax can be damaged by exposure to heat, light, and oxygen (essentially, they become rancid). For this reason, you shouldn't cook with flaxseed oil. A good product should be sold in an opaque container, and the manufacturing process should keep the temperature under 100° F (some products are prepared by cold extraction methods). Some manufacturers combine the product with vitamin E because it helps prevent rancidity.

The best use of flaxseed oil is as a general nutritional supplement to provide essential fatty acids.

Hemp Seed Oil

Hemp seed oil has been referred to as "nature's perfect oil" by several investigators. Its fatty acid ration is 1:4 of omega-3 to omega-6 fatty acids, a ratio suspected to be that which is naturally found in mammals. It contains 1.7% GLA and can be used whenever a combination fatty acid product is needed. However, there are no current studies or recommendations showing any medical benefit of hemp seed oil in pets.

Salvia *(Salvia hispanica)*

The seeds of this plant have been proposed as a more palatable alternative to fish oil and flaxseed oil. The seeds can increase omega-3 fatty acid consumption in the diet.

Little is known about the use of this fatty acid supplement and whether or not it can be of any medical benefit to pets. Studies are needed before this supplement can be recommended as an omega-3 fatty acid supplement.

Fish Oil

Since processed foods have increased omega-6 fatty acids and decreased omega-3 fatty acids, supplementing the diets of all pets with omega-3 fatty acids seems warranted and will not harm your pet. Omega-3 can be derived from fish oils.

Fish oil supplements are usually in the form of a capsule. Since fish oils can easily oxidize and become rancid, some manufacturers add vitamin E to fish oil capsules and liquid products to keep the oil from spoiling (others remove oxygen from the capsule).

SAFETY ISSUES

Flaxseed oil appears to be a safe nutritional supplement when used as recommended.

Note: Flaxseed oil is a popular source of alpha-linoleic acid (ALA), an omega-3 fatty acid that is ultimately converted to EPA and DHA. However, many species of pets (probably including dogs) and some people cannot convert ALA to these other more active non-inflammatory omega-3 fatty acids. In one study in people, flaxseed oil was ineffective in reducing symptoms or raising levels of EPA and DHA. While flaxseed oil has been suggested as a less smelly substitute for fish oil, there is no evidence that it is effective when used for the same therapeutic purposes as fish oil. Therefore, supplementation with EPA and DHA is important, and this is the reason flaxseed oil is not recommended as the sole fatty acid supplement for pets. Flaxseed oil can be used to provide ALA and as a coat conditioner.

Fish oil appears to be safe. The most common side effect seen in people and pets is a fish odor to the breath or the skin.

Because fish oil has a mild "blood-thinning" effect, it should not be combined with powerful blood-thinning medications, such as Coumadin (warfarin) or heparin, except on a veterinarian's advice. Fish oil does not seem to cause bleeding problems when it is taken by itself at commonly recommended dosages. Also, fish oil does not appear to raise blood sugar levels in people or pets with diabetes.

Hemp seed oil appears to be a safe nutritional supplement when used as recommended.

THERAPEUTIC USES

Here are some of the conditions for which fatty acid supplementation may prove beneficial:

Arthritis

There is some evidence in people (which has been extrapolated to pets) that shows that supplementing omega-3 fatty acids in the form of fish oil provided relief from pain associated with rheumatoid arthritis. Twelve double-blind placebo-controlled studies showed a significant reduction of symptoms with minimal side effects in people with rheumatoid arthritis. In another study, reduction of symptoms correlated with dosage of the fatty acid supplement. The group taking the higher dosage of supplement had a greater decrease in signs than the group taking the lower dosage.

However, while osteoarthritis is common in pets, rheumatoid arthritis is very rare in our pets. Still there may be a synergistic effect between the fatty acids and other anti-arthritic supplements, and fatty acid supplementation is often recommended for pets with **osteoarthritis** (page 11).

Allergic (Atopic) Dermatitis

Because of their anti-inflammatory effects, large doses (2 to 4 times the label dose, as the label dose on most products is suspected to be too low to provide anti-inflammatory effects) of omega-3 fatty acids have been shown beneficial in treating allergic dogs and cats. Inhibition of pro-inflammatory prostaglandins, as well as decreased levels of leukotriene B4 production from white blood cells (leukotriene B4 is an important mediator in inflammatory skin disorders) is the explanation for the effectiveness of omega-3 fatty acids in allergic pets. As with the other supplements, they often allow doctors to lower the dosages of drugs such as corticosteroids or nonsteroidal medications.

In allergic dogs, fatty acid supplements were effective in 11 to 27% of dogs treated (over 50% of allergic cats responded to fatty acid supplements). How well fatty acids work in an allergic pet depends upon a number of factors, including product used, dosage used, and the presence of other diseases that may contribute to itching. (Many atopic pets also have flea allergies, bacter-ial skin infections, yeast skin infections with *Malassezia* organisms, and food hypersensitivity. Until these other concurrent problems are identified and treated properly, simply administering fatty acid supplements to a pet suspected of just having **atopic dermatitis** (page 3) is unlikely to be effective.) In general, the literature reports that about 20% of allergic (atopic) dogs and 50% of cats may respond partially or totally to fatty acid supplementation.

Kidney Disease

Ongoing studies seem to support the belief that supplementation with omega-3 fatty acids may benefit pets with **kidney disease** (page 121) or kidney failure. Omega-3 fatty acids can increase beneficial (anti-inflammatory) prostaglandins; these prostaglandins can reduce inflammation in the kidney and improve blood flow to the kidneys (a vasodilatory effect). Since omega-3 fatty acids can also lower blood cholesterol and triglycerides, this effect can also benefit pets with kidney disease as dogs and cats with induced kidney disease have elevated levels of blood cholesterol and triglycerides. (Studies have recommended a starting dose of 0.5 to 1.0 grams of omega-3 fatty acids/100 kcal of food/day.)

Heart Disease

Ongoing research suggests that omega-3 fatty acid supplementation may be beneficial for dogs with **congestive heart failure** (page 91) secondary to dilated cardiomyopathy. Increased levels of tumor necrosis factor (TNF) occurs in dogs (and possibly cats) with congestive heart failure secondary to dilated cardiomyopathy. The increased levels of TNF are responsible for "cardiac cachexia," a chronic wasting of patients with heart failure (and cancer). Omega-3 fatty acids have been shown to reduce TNF levels, improve cachexia, and improve cardiac testing (increased fractional shortening seen on ultrasound studies). More research is needed to determine what other types of heart disease may respond favorably to supplementation with omega-3 fatty acids. Since supplementation is safe, many holistic doctors add omega-3 fatty acids to the diets of many pets with heart disease. While fish oil lowers blood triglyceride

Oral Fatty Acids

levels in people and possibly pets, flaxseed oil does not affect triglyceride levels. Some evidence in people shows that flaxseed oil or whole flaxseed may reduce LDL ("bad") cholesterol and perhaps slightly help hypertension. Finally, increased levels of omega-3 fatty acids can prevent ventricular arrhythmias through their effects on ion channels in excitable heart tissue.

Cancer

In transplanted tumor models, omega-3 fatty acids reduced tumor development while omega-6 fatty acids stimulated tumor development. Omega-3 fatty acids have been shown to inhibit tumor growth as well as the spread of **cancer** (page 44) (metastasis). Reduced radiation damage in the skin was also seen following supplementation with omega-3 fatty acids.

Other proposed uses in people based on preliminary studies include bipolar disease (commonly known as manic-depressive disorder), Raynaud's phenomenon, osteoporosis, inflammatory bowel disease, rheumatoid arthritis, osteoarthritis, cystic fibrosis, and the autoimmune disease lupus. Similar conditions in pets may also show some response to fatty acid supplementation.

While many doctors use fatty acids for a variety of medical problems, there is considerable debate about the use of fatty acids. The debate concerns several areas, including: dosages, capsules vs. liquid, and which fatty acids and in what ratios.

DOSAGES

What is the "best" dose to use in the treatment of pets? Most doctors use anywhere from 2 to 10 times the label dose. Research in the treatment of allergies indicates that the label dose is ineffective; the same theory probably holds true for treating arthritis, but the research is lacking. In people, the dosage that showed effectiveness in many studies were 1.4 to 2.8 gm of GLA per day, or 1.7 gm of EPA and 0.9 gm of DHA per day, which is hard for people to obtain from the supplements currently available. If this were shown to be the correct dosage for pets, a 50-pound dog would need to take 10 or more fatty acid capsules per day to obtain a similar dosage, depend-

ing upon which supplement (and there are many choices on the market) was used. Therefore, while the studies with omega-3 fatty acids show many potential health benefits, it is almost impossible to administer the large number of capsules needed to approximate the same dosage used in these studies. The best that owners can hope for at this time is to work with their veterinarians and try to increase, as best as possible, the amount of omega-3 fatty acids in the diet to try to get to what seems to be the "preferred" ratio of 5:1, omega-6:omega-3 fatty acids.

Which Acids in What Ratio?

What is the "correct" fatty acid to use? Should we use just omega-3 (EPA and DHA) fatty acids, or combine them with omega-6 (GLA) fatty acids? Is there an "ideal" ratio of omega-6 to omega-3 fatty acids? In research on pets with atopic dermatitis, the ideal dietary ratio seems to be 5:1 of omega-6:omega-3 fatty acids, although this is also debated. Whether or not this "ideal" dietary ratio is ideal for the treatment of arthritis and other inflammatory conditions remains to be seen.

Capsule or Liquid?

Is supplementation with fatty acid capsules or liquids the best approach, or is dietary manipulation (adding the "ideal" ratio of omega-6 and omega-3 fatty acids) preferred for the treatment of inflammatory conditions? There are, in fact, diets constructed with this "ideal" ratio. For owners who do not like giving their pets medication, or for those pets who don't take the fatty acid supplements easily, it might be wise to try some of these medically formulated diets (available from your pet's doctor) that contain the fatty acids. However, because these medicated diets may not be as natural as possible due to the inclusion of by-products and chemical preservatives, holistic pet owners may need to try other options. These diets, often prescribed as anti-inflammatory diets for pets with allergies, may be useful as a part of the therapy of arthritic pets.

Since fish oils can easily oxidize and become rancid, some manufacturers add vitamin E to fish oil capsules and liquid products to keep the oil from becoming rancid; others remove oxygen from the capsule.

Since processed foods have increased omega-6 fatty acids and decreased omega-3 fatty acids, supplementing the diets of all pets with omega-3 fatty acids seems warranted and will not harm your pet.

The bottom line is that there are many questions regarding the use of fatty acid therapy.

More research is needed to determine the effectiveness of the fatty acids in the treatment of various medical problems, as well as the proper doses needed to achieve clinical results. Until definitive answers are obtained, you will need to work with your doctors (knowing the limitations of our current research) to determine the use of these supplements for your pet.

 # OREGON GRAPE *(Mahonia aquifolium)*

Common Uses

Allergies (topical and herbal rinse), constipation, heart conditions, infections, intestinal parasites, liver disease, urinary disorders

Oregon grape serves as an alternative to goldenseal. It also shows antimicrobial activity due to its berberine content.

THERAPEUTIC USES

Oregon grape is recommended for treating intestinal giardial infections. Herbal preparations containing Oregon grape have been used for **infections** (page 105) of the ears (including mites) and eyes (conjunctivitis).

This herb is also known for supporting the liver (page 127), and can show good results when treating **constipation** (page 57).

Chronic indigestion and malabsorption can be treated with Oregon grape.

The antibacterial activity of Oregon grape is useful for treating **urinary tract infections** (page 84).

Berberine, contained in this herb, can calm nervous pets and might be tried as an anticonvulsant. Oregon grape can also reduce blood pressure.

SAFETY ISSUES

Do not use in diabetic animals or those with acute liver disease.

Do not use in pregnant animals.

Excessive dosages may deplete vitamin B complex levels.

 # PAPAIN (See Enzymes)

PASSIONFLOWER *(Passiflora incarnata)*

Common Uses
  Anxiety disorders

Passionflower is occasionally recommended as a mild hypnotic and analgesic (pain killer.)

THERAPEUTIC USES

Passionflower may be useful as an herbal alternative to sedatives and analgesics in pets. For pets with mild hyperactive disorders of the nervous system such as mild anxiety, infrequent seizures, and mild pain and discomfort, passionflower can be tried before using conventional medications. Passionflower may be combined in herbal formulas with other sedating herbs.

SAFETY

While there are no reported side effects when used as directed under veterinary supervision, excessive doses may cause sedation. Passionflower may potentiate the side effects from monoamine oxidase inhibitor (MAOI) therapy and should not be used if other medications affecting the nervous system are used. Because passionflower may stimulate the uterus, it should not be used in pregnant animals.

PENNYROYAL OIL *(Mentha pulegium)*

Common Use
  Fleas (topical) (potential toxicity)

Pennyroyal oil, made from the *Mentha pulegium* plant, is often recommended as a topical application for the control of external parasites, particularly fleas.

THERAPEUTIC USES

Pennyroyal oil has been used successfully as a natural **flea** treatment (page 89). However, the oil is quite potent and can cause illness and death. Safer alternative flea control measures are available.

SAFETY ISSUES

While properly diluted pennyroyal oil has been used safely, due to potential toxicity and death if used improperly, it is not generally recommended as a natural form of flea control.

PEPPERMINT *(Mentha piperita)*

Common Uses
Allergies (herbal rinse)

Peppermint, from the *Mentha piperita*, is a popular remedy to relieve gas and indigestion.

THERAPEUTIC USES

Peppermint candies containing the oil of peppermint are popularly ingested by people following a meal. While used to freshen the breath, therapeutically they ease digestion. In pets, the candies should not be used; but the herb fed fresh or as a tea may relieve abdominal discomfort and mild cases of colic.

SAFETY ISSUES

The undiluted oil should not be used. The herb and tea are considered safe. It has been reported that peppermint may interfere with the effectiveness of homeopathic remedies, so it should not be given at the same time as the homeopathic remedy (wait 30 to 60 minutes after administration of the homeopathic remedy before administering peppermint.)

 # PERNA (See Also Glycosaminoglycans)

Common Uses
Arthritis

Perna canaliculus, the green-lipped mussel, is a shellfish that is a natural source of highly concentrated glycosaminoglycans (GAGs) such as chondroitin, as well as a number of other nutrients, including complex proteins, amino acids, nucleic acids, naturally chelated minerals, and an inhibitor of prostaglandin synthesis, which makes it effective as an anti-inflammatory supplement.

THERAPEUTIC USES

Several studies in people have confirmed improvement in patients with osteoarthritis and rheumatoid arthritis. Ongoing studies, as well as many years of anecdotal evidence, show the benefit of perna in dogs with **osteoarthritis** (page 11). As is true with most chondroprotective agents, reports of benefit in cats is scant, as arthritis is quite rare in cats when compared to dogs. However, veterinarians are using many "dog" products safely in cats, and improvement has been noted. If you have an arthritic cat, talk with your veterinarian about using a chondroprotective agent. See **glycosaminoglycans** (page 218) for a general discussion of these agents.

SCIENTIFIC EVIDENCE

Stabilized powder Seatone (MacFarlane Laboratories, Surrey Hills, Victoria, Australia) and the lipid extract Lyprinol (also MacFarlane Laboratories) showed similar results in people with rheumatoid arthritis and osteoarthritis. The lipid extract is a 20-fold concentrate of the original dried mussel. As is true with the powder form, the lipid extract is believed to be a potent but slow-acting anti-inflammatory agent that inhibits cyclooxygenase and 5-lipooxygenase, probably via the omega-3 fatty acid (EPA) content of the mussels. In laboratory experiments in rats, the

Perna

dosage of Lyprinol was 20 mg/kg. In studies in people, a dosage of 300 mg twice daily for the first 30 days followed by a dosage of 150 mg twice daily showed positive results. No dosages for dogs and cats for these specific products have been reported at this time.

DOSAGES

Perna is inexpensive and readily accepted by most dogs; the recommended dosage is 300 mg/15 pounds of body weight. A new product that shows favorable results in many pets called Glyco-Flex Plus combines the benefits of perna with **glucosamine** (page 212) and **methylsulfonylmethane (MSM)** (page 242).

PHOSPHORUS (*Calcium phosphate, sodium phosphate, phosphoric acid*)

Common Uses
Nutritional supplement

Phosphorus is a mineral used in a number of tissues of the body. After calcium, phosphorus is the largest component of bone and teeth. Phosphorus is also a component of DNA and RNA, ATP, and cell membranes. Phosphorus is essential in cell growth and differentiation, energy use and transfer, amino acid and protein formation, and the transport of fatty acids.

Phosphorus availability is generally greater from animal-based dietary ingredients than plant-based ingredients. In animal tissues (meats), phosphorus is mainly in the organic form, whereas in plants it is in an inorganic form (phytic acid).

Regulation of phosphorus in the body is controlled by the intestines and kidneys (under the influence of vitamin D).

SOURCES

Phosphorus is provided through meat tissues, eggs, milk products, and grains.

DOSAGES

The AAFCO recommendation for phosphorus is 0.8% for growth in both puppies and kittens and 0.5% for maintenance of adult dogs and cats.

SAFETY ISSUES

Phosphorus supplements are not needed for any specific disease conditions in dogs and cats. However, pets fed homemade diets should receive supplementation to ensure adequate dietary levels of phosphorus.

PINELLIA COMBINATION

Common Use
Vomiting

Pinellia Combination is a Chinese herbal mix. This formula contains ginseng, ginger, jujube, coptis, and scute, along with pinellia, for treating vomiting in pets.

Because of the Chinese diagnosis and classification of diseases, the ingredients in each formula may vary. Individual Chinese pharmacists include herbs in their tented formulas based upon their experience. However, they can compound formulas to the needs of an individual pet.

For example, a Western diagnosis of allergies allows a selection of treatment based upon this diagnosis. In Traditional Chinese Medicine (TCM), diagnosis and treatment are based upon the need to rebalance the patient so that the individual, not the disease, is treated. As an example, with TCM we might be concerned about selecting herbs to circulate Qi, nurture Yin, or invigorate Yang. This system has been used for thousands of years even prior to the advent of Western medicine, and the herbal treatments have been passed down through time.

This doesn't mean that Chinese herbal formulas cannot be used based upon a Western diagnosis, only that if the herbal formula doesn't work, it might indicate the need for another formula or a correct TCM diagnosis so that the correct remedy can be selected.

Herbs are usually supplied in powder or capsule form; tinctures can also be found. Many products made for humans can be used in pets. Unfortunately, the "correct" dosage for the pet has not been determined for many herbs, and clinical experience and extrapolation from human data is often used. The lower dosage is usually used and the dosage increased if needed. Compared to traditional drug therapy, herbal treatments usually take longer (several weeks or longer) before an effect is seen. As with Western herbal therapy, quality control in the manufacturing of the product used is important, and only herbs from reliable companies should be used. The following guidelines serve as a starting point for herbal therapy.

DOSAGES

Use 1 gram/20 pounds, 2 to 3 times daily of concentrated herbs for dogs and cats; 4 gm of fresh herbs/20 pounds, 2 to 3 times daily for dogs and cats; tinctures 5 to 10 drops per 20 pounds 2 to 3 times daily for dogs and cats.

Alternately, some herbalists recommend extrapolation based on weight. Since human doses are based on a 150-pound male, a recommended dose of 3 capsules given 3 times daily for this 150-pound male would extrapolate to 1 capsule given 3 times daily for a 50-pound dog. There are some suggestions that dogs and cats require more herb per pound of body weight than humans. This would suggest a 10-pound cat should receive 20% of the recommended human dosage, whereas a 25-pound dog should receive 25% of the human dosage.

You should consult with a holistic doctor to determine the best starting dose prior to treating your pet with herbs.

SAFETY ISSUES

While many herbs are used safely in pets, remember that many potent drugs (such as digitalis, vincristine, or aspirin) were first described in plants and herbs and have actually been extracted from plants and herbs. This means that it is essential that you work with your holistic veterinarian before using herbal remedies in your pet. For example, a recent report of a Chinese herbal cream used in people for skin disorders showed a high level of the steroid dexamethasone in the product, with the highest levels in the products recommended for children. Other reports of the product ma huang, which contains the potent drug ephedra, revealed varying levels of ephedra in a number of products tested. Stories such as these reinforce the need for proper medical care and advice when using complementary therapies in pets.

Pinellia Combination

PLANTAIN *(Plantago)*

Common Uses
Urinary disorders

Plantain is an herb used for its ability to lubricate and soothe internal mucous membranes. As such, it is often recommended for pets with disorders of the digestive system and genitourinary tracts.

THERAPEUTIC USES

Plantain is used for pets with urinary tract inflammation and **infection** (page 105). Plantain can be used as a substitute for slippery elm, being useful to reduce inflammation and as an antibacterial. Irritations of the digestive and respiratory tracts can be treated with plantain. Plantain can be used as a mild laxative.

SAFETY ISSUES

Plantain is safe in pets, although some pets may show allergies to it.

POTASSIUM *(Potassium chloride, potassium bicarbonate, chelated potassium* [potassium aspartate, potassium citrate])

Common Uses
Hypokalemia (low potassium), kidney disease

Potassium is one of the major electrolytes in the body, along with sodium and chloride. Potassium and sodium work together to initiate depolarization of cell membranes; depolarization is necessary for cellular functions such as the initiation of nervous impulses or muscle contractions.

Potassium is used for maintaining acid-base balance, maintaining osmotic balance, and serving as a co-factor in several enzyme systems (including energy transfer, carbohydrate metabolism, and protein synthesis).

Like calcium and phosphorus, sodium and potassium are maintained in a ratio to allow proper functioning of a variety of body functions. Sodium and potassium play an intimate chemical role in every function of your body.

THERAPEUTIC USES

In pets, potassium supplementation is often used for pets who develop hypokalemia (low blood potassium) as a side effect of **kidney failure** (page 121). Extra potassium can be added to diets of sick pets who have been anorectic (not eating) as they begin to recover from their illnesses.

The most common use of potassium supplements in people is to make up for potassium depletion caused by diuretic drugs, long-term use of corticosteroid drugs (such as prednisone) or colchicine.

SCIENTIFIC EVIDENCE

There is good evidence that potassium may help prevent kidney stones. In a double-blind study of 57 people with recurring kidney stones, a daily dose of 1.8 to 3.6 g of potassium chloride resulted in a dramatic drop in the average number of kidney stones per year. The treatment group went from an average of 1.2 down to only 0.1 stones per year. The placebo group continued to experience an average of 1.1 stones per year throughout the study. Positive results were seen in another double-blind placebo-controlled study of 64 people. Kidney stones are very rare in dogs and cats, and it is unknown whether potassium supplementation is helpful to prevent or treat kidney stones in pets.

SOURCES

Potassium is provided through bananas, orange juice, potatoes, avocados, lima beans, cantaloupes, peaches, tomatoes, flounder, salmon, cod, chicken, meat, and various other fruits, vegetables, and fish.

Many over-the-counter potassium supplements typically contain 99 mg of potassium per tablet. There is some evidence that, of the different forms of potassium supplements, potassium citrate may be most helpful for those with high blood pressure.

SAFETY ISSUES

Potassium is safe when taken at appropriate dosages. Excess amounts are simply excreted in the urine. Intravenous potassium supplementation, often administered to hospitalized pets, can be dangerous if given too quickly.

If your pet is taking tetracycline antibiotics or antacids, you should administer potassium supplements at a different time of day to avoid absorption problems.

 # PROBIOTICS/PREBIOTICS

Common Use
Bowel health

Probiotics are defined as normal viable bacteria residing in the intestinal tract that promote normal bowel health. Probiotics are given orally and are usually indicated for use in intestinal disorders in which specific factors can disrupt the normal bacterial population, making the pet more susceptible to disease. Specific factors that can disrupt the normal flora of the bowel include surgery, medications (including steroids and non-steroidal anti-inflammatory drugs), antibiotics (especially when used long term), birthing, weaning, illness, and dietary factors (poor quality diet), oxidative damage, and stress. Improving the nutritional status of the intestinal tract may reduce bacterial movement across the bowel mucosa (lining), intestinal permeability, and systemic endotoxemia. Additionally, probiotics may supply nutrients to the pet, help in digestion, and allow for better conversion of food into nutrients.

Prebiotics are food supplements that are not digested and absorbed by the host but improve health by stimulating the growth and activity of selected intestinal bacteria. Currently, there are no well-conducted studies on prebiotics.

Several different probiotic products are available; these can contain any combination of the following organisms: *Lactobacillus* (*L. acidophilus, L. bulgaricus, L. thermophilus, L. reuteri*), *Acidophilus, Bacillus* (specifically a patented strain called *Bacillus CIP 5832* in one patented product), *Streptococcus S. bulgaricus, Enterococcus* (*E. faecium*), *Bifidobacterium, B. bifidus,* and *Saccharomyces* (*S. boulardii,* which is actually a beneficial yeast, not a bacterium).

The intestinal tract, especially the large intestine (colon) is home to millions of bacteria, most of which are harmless and in fact beneficial to the pet. The intestinal bacteria are essential to digestion and the synthesis of vitamin K and many of the B vitamins.

As mentioned, your pet's intestinal tract contains billions of bacteria and yeasts. Some of these internal inhabitants are more helpful than others. *Acidophilus* and related probiotic bacteria not only help the digestive tract function, they also reduce the presence of less healthful organisms by competing with them for the limited space available.

HOW PROBIOTICS WORK

There are several proposed mechanisms by which probiotics can protect your pet from harmful bowel bacteria: Probiotics produce inhibitory chemicals that reduce the numbers of harmful bacteria and possibly toxin production by these harmful bacteria; probiotics may block the adhesion of harmful bacteria to intestinal cells; probiotics may compete for nutrients needed for growth and reproduction by harmful bacteria; probiotics may degrade toxin receptors located on intestinal cells, preventing toxin absorption and damage by toxins produced by harmful intestinal bacteria.

In people, supplementing with probiotics can reduce the risks of rotavirus and can protect against the campylobacter bacterium. Lactobacillus and acidophilus are able to survive hydrochloric acid in the human stomach and inhibited the growth of *Helicobacter pylori*. The numbers of certain bacteria (*E. coli, Klebsiella, Salmonella, Shigella,* and *Proteus*), very common and sometimes deadly pathogens are decreased considerably following *Lactobacillus* and *Bifidus* supplementation. Supplementing with probiotics may also stimulate immune function of the intestinal tract.

Antibiotics can disturb the balance of the intestinal tract by killing friendly bacteria. When this happens, harmful bacteria and yeasts can move in, reproduce, and take over. This is especially true in pets on long-term (several months) antibiotic therapy, and for pets with chronic diarrhea.

Conversely, it appears that the regular use of probiotics can generally improve the health of the gastrointestinal system.

The use of probiotics for treating **diarrhea** (page 71) as well as maintaining health is quite controversial, with no clear scientific evidence (for health maintenance). Although many holistic doctors believe that they are helpful and perhaps even necessary for health, there is no daily requirement for probiotic bacteria. Probiotics are living creatures, not chemicals, so they can sustain themselves in the body unless something comes along to damage them, such as antibiotics.

SOURCES

Cultured dairy products such as yogurt and kefir are good sources of acidophilus and other probiotic bacteria. However, many yogurt products do not contain any living organisms or only contain small numbers of organisms.

Some pets will eat these foods, and others won't. Also, if the pet has any lactose intolerance, he may not tolerate yogurt well and may experience diarrhea (although this is rare). Most doctors recommend supplements to provide the highest doses of probiotics and avoid any lactose intolerance.

Various probiotics, while usually producing the same beneficial effects, may function differently within the intestinal tract. For example, *Lactobacillus acidophilus* produces lactic acid to lower the pH of the intestines and acts as an intestinal bacterial colonizer, *L. casei* lowers oxidation processes, and *L. lactis* acts on hydrogen peroxide as well as amylase and proteases.

DOSAGES

Dosages of acidophilus and other probiotics are expressed not in grams or milligrams, but in billions of organisms. A typical daily dose in people should supply about 3 to 5 billion live organisms. One popular pet supplement provides 500 million viable cells to be given per 50 pounds of body weight. The suggested dosage range of probiotics for pets is approximately 20 to 500 million microorganisms.

Some doctors recommend that when administering antibiotics, the probiotic should be given at least 2 hours later, several times per day, and when the antibiotic treatment has been completed, owners should double or triple the probiotic dose for 7 to 10 days.

Another recommendation is that if taking several species of probiotics, *Acidophilus* is reported to flourish best if taken in the morning, and the *Bifidus* when taken at night. It is suspected that this may follow the diurnal acid/alkaline tide that the body utilizes as part of the detoxification process. However, this is not proven.

Because probiotics are not drugs but living organisms, the precise dosage is not so important. They should be taken regularly to reinforce the beneficial bacterial colonies in the intestinal tract, which may gradually push out harmful bacteria and yeasts growing there.

The downside of using a living organism is that probiotics may die on the shelf. The container label should guarantee living *Acidophilus* (or *Bulgaricus*, and so on) at the time of purchase, not just at the time of manufacture.

THERAPEUTIC USES

Some evidence also suggests that *Acidophilus* and other probiotics may also be helpful for treating irritable bowel syndrome. While rare in pets, probiotics may be preferred over traditional drug therapy for **irritable bowel syndrome** (page 105).

Probiotics are often recommended for treating Crohn's disease (an inflammatory condition in people), and ulcerative colitis, and as a preventative measure against colon cancer; but there is no solid evidence that it is effective.

Finally, probiotics may be helpful in a condition known as yeast hypersensitivity syndrome, also known as chronic candidiasis, chronic candida, systemic candidiasis, or just *"Candida."* Although this syndrome is not recognized by conventional medicine, some practitioners of complementary medicine believe that it is a common problem that leads to numerous symptoms, including fatigue, digestive problems, frequent sinus infections, muscle pain, and mental confusion. In people, yeast hypersensitivity syndrome is said to consist of a population explosion of the normally benign candida yeast that live in the vagina and elsewhere in the body, coupled with a type of allergic sensitivity to it. Probiotic supplements are widely recommended for this condition because they establish large, healthy populations of friendly bacteria that compete with the candida that is trying to take up residence. Pets with chronic disorders may benefit from probiotics for this reason, although evidence is lacking.

If your pet is taking antibiotics, it may be beneficial to supplement with probiotics at the same time, and to continue them for a couple of weeks after the course of drug treatment has stopped. This will help restore the balance of natural bacteria in the digestive tract.

Fructo-oligosaccharides

In people, it is often suggested that in addition to taking probiotics, patients take fructo-oligosaccharides, supplements that can promote thriving colonies of helpful bacteria in the digestive tract. Fructo-oligosaccharides (FOS) are naturally occurring sugars found in many fruits, vegetables, and grains. (Fructo means "fruit," and an oligosaccharide is a type of carbohydrate). These nondigestible complex carbohydrates resist digestion by salivary and intestinal digestive enzymes and enter the colon where they are fermented by bacteria such as *Bifidobacterium* and *Bacteroides spp.*

The most beneficial effect of fructo-oligosaccharides is the selective stimulation of the growth of *Bifidobacterium*, thus significantly enhancing the composition of the colonic microflora and reducing the number of potential pathogenic bacteria. *Lactobacillus*, another beneficial bacteria, was also seen to proliferate with addition of FOS supplements. Because FOS increases the colonization of healthy bacteria in the gut, they are considered to be a prebiotic rather than a probiotic.

Taking FOS supplements are thought to foster a healthy environment for the beneficial bacteria living in the intestinal tract. Studies using FOS at a dosage of 0.75 to 1.0% (dry matter basis) showed decreased E. coli and increased lactobacilli intestinal bacteria in cats and dogs. The typical daily dose of fructo-oligosaccharides for people is between 2 and 8 g. The correct dose for pets has not been determined. One supplement contains 50 mg per dose for a 50-pound dog; research on FOS showed positive benefits when the dosage was 0.75 to 1.0% of the food when fed on a dry matter basis.

Other reports describing the benefits of FOS suggest that they can suppress triglyceride and cholesterol levels, can control glucose metabolism,

Probiotics/Prebiotics

and may inhibit the formation of precancerous lesions in the colon.

SCIENTIFIC EVIDENCE

There is fairly good evidence that many probiotics can help with various types and causes of diarrhea. *Saccharomyces boulardii, Enterococcus faecium*, and *Lactobacillus spp.* have been shown to help prevent antibiotic-induced diarrhea. *Saccharomyces* has demonstrated the most promise for use in diarrhea caused by the intestinal bacterium *Clostridium difficile*, a common cause of bacterial overgrowth in pets and people (*Lactobacillus spp.* are also helpful in bacterial overgrowth). Some evidence suggests that a particular type of probiotic, *L. reuteri*, can help treat diarrhea caused by viral infections in children. According to several studies conducted on the subject, it appears that regular use of acidophilus can help prevent "traveler's diarrhea" (an illness caused by eating contaminated food).

Some preliminary evidence shows that probiotics may protect the bowel from cancer. The proposed mechanisms for this include inhibiting the bacteria in the bowel from converting procarcinogens into carcinogens, inhibiting tumor cell formation directly, and directly binding to or inactivating bowel carcinogens. More research is needed in this area.

SAFETY ISSUES

There are no known safety problems with the use of *Acidophilus* or other probiotics. Occasionally, some people notice a temporary increase in digestive gas (the same could occur in pets).

PURINE AND PYRIMIDINE NUCLEOTIDES
(*Colostrum*)

Common Uses
  Autoimmune conditions

Purine and pyrimidine complexes are involved in virtually all cellular processes and play a major role in structural, metabolic, energetic, and regulatory functions. Like arabinogalactans, they have been shown to stimulate the activity of NK cells.

Purine and pyrimidine complexes are the active fractions found in colostrum, the first milk produced by mammals. Colostrum contains cytokines and other protein compounds that can act as biological response modifiers. Research supports its use in the treatment of rheumatoid arthritis and **osteoarthritis** (page 11), as well as other autoimmune conditions. Nucleotides also may play an important role in essential fatty acid metabolism, and may have a positive effect on the functions of the gastrointestinal tract and the liver.

THERAPEUTIC USES

Nucleotides are used by holistic veterinarians for a variety of disorders, including immune diseases, cancers, any general illness in which the pet's immune system needs support; and arthritis.

SAFETY

Nucleotides appear safe when used as directed.

PYRETHRUM

Common Use
Fleas (topical)

Pyrethrum is a natural insecticide recommended for the control of fleas and ticks. It is found in flowers of several plants of the *Chrysanthemum* genus. Pyrethrin is a chemically synthesized version of natural pyrethrum.

THERAPEUTIC USES

In its natural form, pyrethrum is safe and fairly effective against topical parasites such as **fleas and ticks** (page 89). The flowers of pyrethrum-containing plants can be ground and used in herbal powders, or the fresh flowers can be mixed with warm water to make a dip for the pet. As a rule, pyrethrum-bearing flowers lose their flea-killing potency after drying, so additional insecticidal measures may be needed for total parasite "kill."

SAFETY ISSUES

Natural pyrethrums are safe when used as directed. Toxicity is increased in commercially prepared products with the addition of chemical insecticides (piperonyl butoxide, synthetic pyrethrins and related compounds.)

 # RASPBERRY LEAF

Common Uses
Diarrhea

Raspberry leaf is a safe nutritious food (it is high in vitamin C.) It is most often recommended for mild gastrointestinal inflammation and diarrhea.

THERAPEUTIC USES

Raspberry leaf is recommended for the treatment of mild **diarrhea** (page 71). It has also been used as an eye wash for treating mild conjunctivitis. Raspberry leaf is a well-known uterine tonic that can be used following pregnancy to help evacuate and tone the uterus.

SAFETY ISSUES

Due to its ability to increase uterine tone, raspberry leaf should not be used in pregnant animals, except under veterinary supervision during the labor and delivery process if needed.

RED CLOVER *(Trifolium pratense)*

Common Uses
Allergies, diuretic, fleas (oral), cancer, liver disease

Red clover has been grown for centuries, primarily as feed for animals, but it is also a popular medicine.

THERAPEUTIC USES

Red clover is used as a tonic, diuretic, and blood cleanser. Red clover contains a number of nutrients (including B and C vitamin complexes and protein) that act synergistically to help pets with various disorders. The herb can be used internally and externally as a rinse for pets with skin disorders. The bioflavonoids in red clover (including quercetin) are purported to help pets with **cancer** (page 44) (and red clover is included in the popular herbal anticancer formulas Hoxsey and Essiac). For pets with skin cancer, red clover can be taken internally or a poultice of the flowers can be applied directly to the skin cancers. While definitive studies are lacking, it may be that these bioflavonoids also improve the immune system of pets with **allergic dermatitis** (page 3).

There is no hard evidence that red clover can help cancer. However, its usage in many parts of the world as a traditional cancer remedy has prompted scientists to take a close look at the herb. It turns out that the isoflavones in red clover may possess anti-tumor activity. However, such preliminary research does not prove that red clover can treat cancer.

SAFETY ISSUES

Red clover should not be used in pets with clotting disorders (due to the presence of coumarin), hormonal disorders involving estrogen, pregnant or lactating animals, and in pets sensitive to aspirin (including cats), as red clover contains small amounts of salicylic acid, the active ingredient in aspirin. Only a tiny amount of salicylic acid exists in normal doses of red clover, but you should consult with your holistic veterinarian prior to using it in your cat.

Care should be used in pets taking corticosteroids or nonsteroidal medications.

Safety in young children, or those with severe liver or kidney disease also has not been established; similar precautions are probably warranted in pets.

REHMANNIA SIX/REHMANNIA EIGHT

Common Uses
Kidney disease

The Rehmannia Six and Rehmannia Eight formulas are classic formulas in Traditional Chinese Medicine (TCM). They are useful to strenghten the kidneys and urinary system. The herbal formula uses six or eight herbs in combination to maximize the therapeutic effects and minimize unwanted effects. The herbs in the formula nourish the kidneys and liver and tonify the spleen.

THERAPEUTIC USES

Rehmannia Six/Rehmannia Eight are well-known formulas used as a kidney yin and blood tonic for pets with **kidney disease** (page 121). Ingredients include rehmannia, cornus, dioscorea, moutan, hoelen, alisma (Rehmannia Six and Rehmannia Eight) and cinnamon bark and aconite (Rehmannia Eight).

CHINESE HERBS

A Western diagnosis of allergies allows a selection of treatment based upon this diagnosis. In Traditional Chinese Medicine (TCM), diagnosis and treatment are based upon the need to rebalance the patient so that the individual, not the disease, is treated. As an example, with TCM we might be concerned about selecting herbs to circulate Qi, nurture Yin, or invigorate Yang. This system has been used for thousands of years even prior to the advent of Western medicine, and the herbal treatments have been passed down through time.

This doesn't mean that Chinese herbal formulas cannot be used based upon a Western diagnosis, only that if the herbal formula doesn't work, it might indicate the need for another formula or a correct TCM diagnosis so that the correct remedy can be selected.

DOSAGES

Herbs are usually supplied in powder or capsule form; tinctures can also be found. Many products made for humans can be used in pets. Unfortunately, the "correct" dosage for the pet has not been determined for many herbs; therefore, clinical experience and extrapolation from human data is often used. The lower dosage is usually used and the dosage increased if needed. Compared to traditional drug therapy, herbal treatments usually take longer (several weeks or longer) before an effect is seen. As with Western herbal therapy, quality control in the manufacturing of the product used is important, and only herbs from reliable companies should be used.

The following guidelines serve as a starting point for herbal therapy.

Use 1 gm/20 pounds, 2 to 3 times daily of concentrated herbs for dogs and cats; 4 gm of fresh herbs/20 pounds, 2 to 3 times daily for dogs and cats; tinctures 5 to 10 drops per 20 pounds, 2 to 3 times daily for dogs and cats.

Alternately, some herbalists recommend extrapolation based on weight. Since human doses are based on a 150-pound male, a recommended dose of 3 capsules given 3 times daily for this 150-pound male would extrapolate to 1 capsule given 3 times daily for a 50-pound dog. There are some suggestions that dogs and cats require more herb per pound of body weight than humans. This would suggest a 10-pound cat should receive 20% of the recommended human dosage, whereas a 25-pound dog should receive 25% of the human dosage.

You should consult with a holistic doctor to determine the best starting dose prior to treating your pet with herbs.

SAFETY ISSUES

While many herbs are used safely in pets, remember that many potent drugs (such as digitalis, vincristine, and aspirin) were first described in plants and herbs and have actually been extracted from plants and herbs. This means that it is essential that you work with your holistic veterinarian before using herbal remedies in your pet. For example, a recent report of a Chinese herbal cream used in people for skin disorders showed a high level of the steroid dexamethasone in the product, with the highest levels in the products recommended for children. Other reports of the product ma huang, which contains the potent drug ephedra, revealed varying levels of ephedra in a number of products tested. Stories such as these reinforce the need for proper medical care and advice when using complementary therapies in pets.

Rehmannia Six/Eight

REISHI MUSHROOM *(Ganoderma lucidum)*

Common Uses
Enhance the immune system of sick pets

The tree fungus known as reishi has a long history of use in China and Japan as a semi-magical healing herb. Presently, reishi is artificially cultivated and widely available in stores that sell herb products.

THERAPEUTIC USES

In people, this mushroom has been suggested for treatment in the following ways: improve resistance to stress; strengthen immunity against colds and other infections; improve mental function; and prevent altitude sickness, asthma, bronchitis, viral hepatitis, cardiovascular disease, ulcers, and cancer.

In pets, reishi has been used for the following disorders: **internal parasites** (page 118), demodectic mange, **upper respiratory infections** (page 88) (especially in kittens), **feline leukemia virus infection** (page 82), **feline immunodeficiency virus infection** (page 76), lack of appetite, post-operative recovery, chemotherapy support, various disorders of aging pets, side effects of corticosteroid therapy, and poisonous mushroom toxicity (as an antidote).

While reishi is marketed as a cure-all for many disorders, no real evidence indicates that reishi is effective for any of these conditions. Contemporary herbalists regard it as an adaptogen, a substance believed to be capable of helping the body to resist stress of all kinds. However, while a great deal of basic scientific research has explored the chemical constituents of reishi, reliable double-blind studies on its effectiveness in treating various disorders are lacking.

DOSAGES

The dosage varies with the specific preparation of reishi. Most doctors follow package labeling recommendation.

SAFETY ISSUES

In people and pets, reishi appears to be extremely safe. Occasional side effects include mild digestive upset, dry mouth, and skin rash. Reishi can "thin" the blood slightly, and therefore should not be combined with drugs such as Coumadin (warfarin) or heparin. Safety in young children, pregnant or nursing women, or those with severe liver or kidney disease has not been established. These guidelines should probably also be followed for pets. Dizziness has been seen in people using reishi for several months.

SAGE

Common Uses
Infections

Sage is recommended as an antiseptic and astringent. It is commonly prepared as a tea or tincture. The tea can be made by mixing 1 tablespoon of the dried leaves with 1 cup of boiling water, and dosed at 1 ounce per 20 pounds of body weight for dogs and cats.

THERAPEUTIC USES

Sage is often recommended for infections or sores of the mouth, skin (including **ringworm,** page 144), and digestive tract. Sage contains a volatile oil called thujone, which is believed responsible for its antimicrobial activity. Applied topically, sage may be helpful for pets with gingivitis (gum disease).

SAFETY ISSUES

Sage is considered safe. The undiluted oil can cause skin irritation and should not be used internally. It should not be used in pregnant or lactating animals as it may cause abortion and inhibit lactation. Sage may lower blood sugar and may interfere with hypoglycemic or anticonvulsant therapies.

 SALVIA (See Oral Fatty Acids)

 SAMe

Common Uses
   Arthritis

SAMe stands for S-adenosylmethionine. It is closely related to the ATP molecule which the body uses for energy for the cells. When ATP combines with the amino acid methionine, S-adenosylmethionine is formed.

SAMe was discovered in Italy in 1952. First investigated as a treatment for depression, along the way it was accidentally noted to improve arthritis symptoms, which was a positive "side effect." SAMe is presently classed with glucosamine and chondroitin as a potential "chondroprotective" agent, one that can go beyond treating symptoms to actually slowing the progression of arthritis. However, this exciting possibility has not yet been proven. See the discussion of these agents under **Glycosaminoglycans** (page 218).

The body makes all the SAMe it needs, so there is no dietary requirement. However, deficiencies in methionine, folic acid, or vitamin B_{12} can reduce SAMe levels. Since SAMe is not found in appreciable quantities in foods, it must be taken as a supplement.

THERAPEUTIC USES

Unfortunately, there is scant information about whether SAMe is beneficial in our pet dogs and cats. Some holistic veterinarians have seen good results when SAMe was used to treat canine **cognitive dysfunction** (page 56). Anecdotally, several large breed dogs treated at 200 mg twice daily showed improvement of 50% or more. Owners reported better results than when using Anipryl or *Ginkgo biloba.*

DOSAGES

The recommended human dosages range from 600 to 1,600 mg/day; there are no published veterinary doses as of this writing. Additionally, the cost of SAMe is quite high (several hundred dollars each month for the typical human dose). SAMe remains a possible supplement for use in pets; more research is needed, and the cost is prohibitive for most owners at this time.

SCIENTIFIC EVIDENCE

In people, the result of one double-blind placebo-controlled study showed that SAMe was more effective at relieving pain than the placebo and as effective as the NSAID naproxen. In this study, naproxen worked faster than SAMe (which took 4 weeks to achieve effect). At the end of the study, both treatments produced positive benefit. However, naproxen produced more side effects, namely gastrointestinal distress (a common side effect of potent NSAIDS like naproxen).

Another similar study compared SAMe to the potent NSAID piroxicam, with similar results and positive effects for the SAMe.

It is unknown exactly how SAMe is effective when treating osteoarthritis, but there are some theories. SAMe does show anti-inflammatory and pain-relieving properties. Additionally, laboratory research (in the test tube) suggests that SAMe might work similar to glycosaminoglycans such as glucosamine and chondroitin by stimulating cartilage cells to produce more proteoglycans. This research suggests the possibility that SAMe might help heal the joints as well as relieve pain and inflammation. In one study in rabbits in which surgery was performed on the joint in an attempt to cause arthritis, SAMe-treated rabbits showed protection against the development of arthritis when compared to control animals. The treated rabbits had thicker cartilage, more joint cartilage cells, and higher proteoglycan levels.

While SAMe shows promise as a treatment for osteoarthritis, it does not appear effective for other forms of arthritis such as rheumatoid arthritis.

SAMe also has some positive side effects. It appears effective as an antidepressant (and is used in people for this reason) and protects the lining of the stomach and offers protection of the liver against various toxins.

SAFETY ISSUES

Regarding the safety of SAMe, there is good news here. Current evidence suggests the toxicity is as close to zero as possible, making SAMe much safer than any drug currently used to treat osteoarthritis. However, some people can develop mild stomach distress if they start full dosages of SAMe at once.

Safety in young children, pregnant or nursing women, or those with severe liver or kidney disease has not been established. However, SAMe has been given to pregnant women in scientific studies, with no apparent ill effects. Until more investigation is done in dogs and cats, these same precautions should probably be followed in pets.

 # SAW PALMETTO *(Serenoa repens* or *Sabal serrulata)*

Common Use
  Prostate enlargement

Saw palmetto contains a number of chemicals; the lipid soluble ones are most likely those that are responsible for the action of the herb.

THERAPEUTIC USES

Saw palmetto has recently been recommended for men with prostatic enlargement. Saw palmetto works by inhibiting the conversion of testosterone to dihydrotestosterone (DHT, the more potent form of the hormone) by inhibiting 5-alpha reductase in the prostate; the cellular binding and transport of DHT is also inhibited. An anti-estrogenic activity is also noted. It may

prove useful for dogs with the same condition, although this condition is rare in dogs as most are neutered at a young age.

In men, a dosage of 160 mg twice daily of the fat-soluble extracts standardized to 85 to 95% fatty acids and sterols is used. Similar doses of crude berries, fluid extracts, and tinctures cannot be achieved. Benefits require approximately 4 to 6 weeks of treatment to develop and endure for at least 3 years. It appears that about two-thirds of men respond reasonably well. Furthermore, while the prostate tends to continue to grow when left untreated, saw palmetto causes a small but definite shrinkage. In other words, it isn't just relieving symptoms, but may actually be retarding prostate enlargement.

Saw palmetto may be useful for treating benign prostatic hypertrophy in dogs, although one recent study failed to document significant benefits.

SAFETY ISSUES

Saw palmetto appears to be essentially nontoxic. Safety for those with severe kidney or liver disease has not been established; similar precautions in animals are probably warranted.

🐾 SEA CUCUMBER (*Cucumaria frondosa*)

Common Uses
Osteoarthritis

The sea cucumber, also known by the names "trepang" and "beche de mer" is a marine animal related to urchins. It is believed that these organisms inhibit harmful prostaglandins involved in causing pain and arthritis. They are also rich in nutrients needed by cartilage, including chondroitin and mucopolysaccharides, and several vitamins and minerals. One popular product supplies the sea cucumber in a unique "jerky-type" treat (Sea Jerky-R), which dogs find quite palatable. Other compounds found in this product include sea kelp, natural vitamin E, lecithin, garlic, omega-3 fatty acids, and glucosamine hydrochloride. Each jerky treat provides 1,200 mg of chondroitin.

THERAPEUTIC USES

In research testing by an independent laboratory, the product showed excellent anti-inflammatory activity in rats in which inflammation was induced by injection of adjuvant and no side effects were seen. The anti-inflammatory response was superior to that of Rimadyl and phenylbutazone. This study also showed that the product had higher anti-inflammatory activity than a product made from perna mussels and a glucosamine/chondroitin supplement, indicating that this product might be preferred if a dog fails to respond to another supplement (since the response to various supplements varies among patients, if one fails to provide relief another should be tried). However, to my knowledge, the product has not been evaluated in double-blind placebo-controlled studies in dogs with naturally occurring **arthritis** (page 11). Clinical reports from the veterinary community indicates high acceptance and effectiveness.

DOSAGES

The recommended dosage for this unique product is 1 piece of "jerky" per day for a 60- to 70-pound dog.

While it was assumed that the active ingredient in the product was chondroitin, further research showed that while the sea cucumber contains chondroitin, another substance called InflaStatin (now under research and development) appears to be the active ingredient.

These treats are perfect for the dog who is hard to medicate. While some supplements are flavored pills, there are of course those dogs who will not eat anything in a pill form. There are also those dogs whose owners simply can't medicate. This may be because the dog was never taught to take medications as a puppy and now will not allow the owner to give it a pill. There are also those owners who find it a hassle to give their dogs pills each day. However, offering the dog a jerky treat is an easy way to allow the pet to receive the daily recommended dose of medication.

The jerky treats can also be used in conjunction with other similar pill supplements, as it is unlikely that a pet can overdose on glucosamine or chondroitin. Many owners will give their dogs the recommended amounts of daily pills but will also reward the dog with a jerky treat. For those pets with arthritis, most owners and doctors like the idea of giving them a daily treat that is good for them, as is the case with this jerky product.

SELENIUM (Selenite, sodium selenite, sodium selenate, selenomethionine, selenized yeast, selenium dioxide)

Common Uses
Cancer, shedding

Selenium is a trace mineral that our bodies use to produce glutathione peroxidase, an enzyme that serves as a natural antioxidant. Selenium is also required for normal pancreatic function and lipid absorption. Glutathione peroxidase works with vitamin E to protect cell membranes from damage caused by dangerous, naturally occurring substances known as free radicals. Adequate amounts of selenium can spare vitamin E, and adequate amounts of vitamin E can reduce the selenium requirement. By ensuring that pets receive adequate amounts of both vitamin E and selenium, these important nutritents will not be deficient and will work together to help fight oxidative damage in your pet's body.

Selenium also has an important role in maintaining normal levels of thyroid hormones and in the metabolism of iodine, which is involved in thyroid hormone metabolism. Supplementing the diets of pets with plant enzymes (see **enzymes**, page 197) can increase selenium levels.

THERAPEUTIC USES

Many pets with excessive shedding will show decreased shedding as a result of enzyme supplementation. This may occur as a result of increased selenium levels and the impact selenium has on thyroid hormones.

In pets, selenium is often prescribed (along with other antioxidants) for pets with a variety of disorders, including **epilepsy** (page 73), **inflammatory bowel disease** (page 105), **feline leukemia** (page 82), **feline immunodeficiency virus** (page 76), and **cancer** (page 44) (see Orthomolecular Therapy in Part Four for a greater discussion).

There is some real evidence that selenium supplements can provide some protection against several types of cancer. This "chemopreventive" effect isn't fully understood. It might be due to the protective effects of the antioxidant glutathione peridoxase, but other explanations have also been suggested.

In people, selenium has been recommended for cancer prevention, AIDS, acne, cataracts, heart disease, multiple sclerosis, cervical dysplasia, asthma, rheumatoid arthritis, anxiety, gout, infertility in men, psoriasis, and ulcers.

Treatment with corticosteroids may induce selenium deficiency; supplementation may be recommended in pets receiving long-term corticosteroid therapy.

SCIENTIFIC EVIDENCE

A large body of evidence has found that increased intake of selenium is tied to a reduced risk of cancer. The most important blind study on selenium and cancer in people was a double-blind intervention trial conducted by researchers at the University of Arizona Cancer Center. In this trial, researchers saw dramatic declines in the incidence of several cancers in the group taking selenium. The selenium-treated group developed almost 66% fewer prostate cancers, 50% fewer colorectal cancers, and about 40% fewer lung cancers as compared with the placebo group. Selenium-treated subjects also experienced a statistically significant (17%) decrease in overall mortality, a greater than 50% decrease in lung cancer deaths, and nearly a 50% decrease in total cancer deaths.

Further evidence for the anticancer benefits of selenium comes from large-scale Chinese studies showing that giving selenium supplements to people who live in selenium-deficient areas reduces the incidence of cancer. Also, observational studies have indicated that cancer deaths rise when dietary intake of selenium is low.

The results of animal studies corroborate these results. One recent animal study examined whether two experimental organic forms of selenium would protect laboratory rats against chemically induced cancer of the tongue. Rats were given one of three treatments: 5 parts per million of selenium in their drinking water, 15 parts per million of selenium, or placebo. The study was blinded so that the researchers wouldn't know until later which rats received which treatment. Whereas 47% of rats in the placebo group developed tongue tumors, none of the rats that were given the higher selenium dosage developed tumors.

Another study examined whether selenium supplements could stop the spread (metastasis) of cancer in mice. In this study, a modest dosage of supplemental selenium reduced metastasis by 57%. Even more significant was the decrease in the number of tumors that had spread to the lungs: Mice in the control group had an average of 53 tumors each, whereas mice fed supplemental selenium had an average of one lung tumor.

Putting all this information together, it definitely appears that selenium can help reduce the risk of developing cancer.

SOURCES

Wheat germ, brazil nuts, other nuts, oats, fish, eggs, liver, whole-wheat bread, bran, red Swiss chard, brown rice, turnips, garlic, barley, and orange juice contain selenium. There is some concern with conventional farming practices that mineral levels in the soil are inadequate. This means that the soil used for growing vegetables and fruits may be deficient in minerals such as selenium. According to information from the *Organic View*, 1: 17 (www.purefood.org/organicview.htm), there is great variability in the nutrient contents of foods raised by industrial agricultural practices when compared to organically raised foods. For example, they report that in an analysis of USDA nutrient data from 1975 to 1997, the Kushi Institute of Becket, Massachusetts, found that the average calcium levels in 12 fresh vegetables declined 27%; iron levels dropped 37%; vitamin A levels 21%; and vitamin C levels 30%.

They also report that a similar analysis of British nutrient data from 1930 to 1980 published in the *British Food Journal* found that in 20 vegetables, the average calcium content had declined 19%; iron 22%; and potassium 14%. In addition, a 1999 study out of the University of Wisconsin found that three decades of the overuse of nitrogen in U.S. farming has destroyed much of the soil's fertility, causing it to age the equivalent of 5,000 years. Finally, a new U.S. Geological Survey report indicates that acid rain is depleting soil calcium levels in at least 10 eastern states, interfering with forest growth and weakening trees' resistance to insects. Findings such as those reported here prompt many owners to search for the most wholesome produce available to include in their pets' diets.

Check with stores in your area to see whether they offer organically raised vegetables and animal meats. Also, ask them what they mean by the term "organically raised," as many producers may make this claim but still use conventional agricultural practices. Find out everything you can about the farmers who supply the stores where you shop.

Since most of us have no way of knowing what kind of soil our food was grown in, supplementing pets with selenium and other vitamins and minerals may be a good idea.

The two general types of selenium supplements are organic and inorganic. However, these terms have nothing to do with "natural" but rather refer to the chemical form (the terms have very specific chemical meanings and have nothing to do with "organic" foods).

The inorganic form of selenium, selenite, contains no carbon atoms and is essentially selenium atoms bound to oxygen. Some research suggests that selenite is harder for the body to absorb than organic (carbon-containing) forms of selenium, such as selenomethionine (selenium bound to methionine, an essential amino acid) or high-selenium yeast (which contains selenomethionine). However, other research on both animals and humans suggests that selenite supplements are almost as good as organic forms of selenium, and both forms were equally effective in supporting glutathione peroxidase activity. In pigs, studies have shown that selenium stores in the liver and muscle tissues were greater when organic selenium was fed. Supplying selenium in whole food supplements is the most natural way to supply selenium and is recommended for maintenance.

DOSAGES

The AAFCO recommendation is 0.11 mg/kg of food (dry matter basis) for dogs and 0.1 mg/kg of food for cats. However, recent research in puppies has shown that the level of dietary selenium needed to maximize serum glutathione and selenium levels is 0.21 ppm, which is double current AAFCO recommendations. Therefore, supplementation with a natural vitamin-mineral supplement containing selenium might be indicated for all pets eating commercial diets.

SAFETY ISSUES

Selenium is safe when taken at the recommended dosages. However, very high selenium dosages in people are known to cause selenium toxicity. Signs of selenium toxicity include depression, nervousness, emotional instability, nausea, vomiting, and in some cases, loss of hair and fingernails. Similar precautions are probably warranted in pets taking supplements, although toxicity has not been noted in pets despite concentrations greater than 4 mg of selenium/kg of food in cat foods containing fish or other seafoods. (Cats may be able to tolerate higher selenium levels as their higher dietary protein foods are protective against high selenium levels; the low availability of selenium in pet foods may also contribute to rare reports of toxicity in dogs and cats fed commercial diets.)

 # SENNA *(Cassia angustifolia, Cassia senna)*

Common Uses
 Laxative

Senna is a shrub grown primarily in India and China. Its leaves and pods are used for medicinal purposes.

THERAPEUTIC USES

Cassia is recommended as a laxative due to its anthroquinone glycosides, which increase intestinal fluid secretion and peristalsis. However, it is quite strong and can result in diarrhea or intestinal dysfunction.

SAFETY ISSUES

Prolonged use may cause dependence. Cassia should not be used in cases of obstruction or where a diagnosis has not been reached. Do not use in pets with diarrhea or inflammatory bowel disease. Safer, gentler alternative exist for pets with constipation (a rare disorder in dogs and cats).

Avoid in pregnant animals.

SHARK CARTILAGE (See Also Glycosaminoglycans)

Common Use
Arthritis

There is reported a link between blood vessel growth and the development of osteoarthritis. In the synovial (joint) fluid of arthritic pets, there is an increasing amount of a chemical called endothelial cell-stimulating angiogenic factor. This chemical encourages growth of new blood vessels in the arthritic joint. It is theorized that by inhibiting angiogenesis (new blood vessel growth), further degeneration of cartilage might be prevented.

See **glycosaminoglycans** (page 218) for a discussion of these kinds of agents in general.

THERAPEUTIC USES

In the laboratory, shark cartilage has been shown to contain chemicals that inhibit blood vessel formation. Because **arthritis** (page 11) is an inflammatory condition, and inflammation requires blood vessels, it has been suggested that by inhibiting the formation of new blood vessels, shark cartilage can benefit arthritic pets. And in fact, research has shown this to be the case.

Shark cartilage has also been recommended for the treatment of cancerous tumors in people and pets. In fact, shark cartilage contains chemical compounds that prevent new blood vessel growth in test-tube experiments (a number of test-tube experiments have found that shark cartilage extracts prevent new blood vessels from forming in chick embryos and other test systems). Developing drugs to prevent blood vessels from forming in tumors is an exciting new approach to treating cancer.

SCIENTIFIC EVIDENCE

In studies in both people and in dogs, significant improvement is seen in patients suffering from arthritis. Arthritic pets and people taking shark cartilage supplements often experience increased mobility and decreased pain. In one study, 8 of 10 dogs showed improvement (improvement was defined as no continuing lameness, lack of swelling and pain, and improved movement) when treated at a dosage of 750 mg/5 kg of body weight for 3 weeks. When treatment was temporarily discontinued, pain and lameness returned. Administering additional shark cartilage at 50% of the original dose resulted in improvement. The relief from pain and inflammation was theorized to occur as a result of decreased blood vessel formation. Improvement may also result from a relief from pain due to the large amount of mucopolysaccharides (GAGs) contained in the cartilage, which can help nourish and heal the cartilage. As a result of studies such as this one, many veterinarians feel it is prudent to prescribe shark cartilage as it can be beneficial in some pets with arthritis and can substitute for therapy with medications like nonsteroidal drugs that have potential side effects.

DOSAGES

The main problem with using shark cartilage to treat arthritis is the large dosage required. This suggested dosage would require giving a large number of capsules to the pet each day. And since shark cartilage is among our more expensive supplements, the dosage of shark cartilage needed for medium to large breed arthritic dogs would be unaffordable for most pet owners.

There are several products on the market that supply a much lower dosage of shark cartilage than that listed in the studies reported to date. This lower dosage has proved beneficial in some arthritic dogs. Because shark cartilage is very expensive to use in larger dogs (approximately $40 to $50 for a 2-week supply), some owners are tempted to give less than the recommended dosage to decrease cost. This can be acceptable after a 1- to 2-month stabilization period. Work with your doctor to determine the most effective dose

Shark Cartilage

for your dog. As is often the case with nutritional supplements, we don't know the best or most effective dose for shark cartilage. Therefore we must use the products currently available and adapt the dosage to the individual pet's needs.

Because cancers must create new blood vessels to feed them, shark cartilage has been touted as a cure for cancer. However, there is conflicting evidence as to its effectiveness. In several small but controversial studies, human patients with cancerous tumors did show regression (reduced size of the tumors). Other studies did not show any benefit. Because dogs and cats require a large dose to approximate the dose used in the human studies, this could be costly, especially for owners of larger dogs. Currently, most doctors do not use shark cartilage for the treatment of tumors in people or pets, as convincing research showing positive results is lacking. Additionally, factors such as the cost of the supplements, the potential for interference with proven cancer treatments, and the potentially devastating impacts on marine ecosystems have caused doctors to not routinely recommend this supplement for pets with cancer. While shark cartilage can be helpful for arthritic pets, the concerns mentioned above prompt doctors to recommend glucosamine and chondroitin supplements as their first choices for nutritional supplements.

SAFETY ISSUES

Shark cartilage should not be used in people who have recently suffered a heart attack, in pregnant women, and those who have are recently recovering from deep surgery; similar precautions probably apply towards pets.

Because of conflicting evidence and the potential for impure product (quality control issues are important for all nutritional supplements), owners should consult with their doctors before using shark cartilage for any medical needs.

 # SHIITAKE MUSHROOM (*Lentinula edodes*)

Common Uses
Immune system stimulation (such as cancer and allergies), chemotherapy and radiation support, incontinence, back pain

---

The shiitake mushroom is believed to be a cure-all for many disorders and is used as a cancer preventative in Japan and China.

THERAPEUTIC USES

The more common uses are immune stimulation, cancer therapy support, **incontinence** (page 145), and back pain. In people, shiitake has also been recommended for patients with bronchial inflammation and for cholesterol reduction.

SCIENTIFIC EVIDENCE

While shiitake is marketed as a cure-all for many disorders, there is no real evidence that it is effective for any of these conditions. Contemporary herbalists regard it as an adaptogen, a substance believed to be capable of helping the body to resist stress of all kinds. However, while there has been a great deal of basic scientific research into the chemical constituents of shiitake, reliable double-blind studies are lacking.

DOSAGES

The dosage varies with the specific preparation of shiitake. Most doctors follow package labeling recommendations.

SAFETY ISSUES

In people and pets, shiitake appears to be extremely safe. Occasional side effects include mild digestive upset, dry mouth, and skin rash. Shiitake can "thin" the blood slightly, and therefore should not be combined with drugs such as Coumadin (warfarin) or heparin. Safety in young children, pregnant or nursing women, or those with severe liver or kidney disease has not been established. These guidelines should probably also be followed for pets.

 # SKULLCAP *(Suctellaria laterifolia)*

Common Uses
Anxiety disorders, epilepsy

Skullcap is a variety of "natural" pain reliever and may be included in chondroprotective supplements (see **Glycosaminoglycans** (page 218)).

THERAPEUTIC USES

Skullcap is used for anxiety and to relieve pain from nerve injury. Skullcap contains scutellarian, which is a flavonoid chemical that possesses sedative qualities that allow skullcap to function as an herbal sedative.

Unlike other herbs used for anxiety (valerian), skullcap does not cause drowsiness but rather alleviates restlessness and nervous twitching.

The pain-relieving agents in skullcap may help make the pet more comfortable and may prevent the need for additional conventional analgesics (pain killers).

Skullcap is recommended for pets with seizure disorders. It can also decrease blood cholesterol.

SCIENTIFIC EVIDENCE

Unfortunately, there has been virtually no scientific investigation of how well the herb really works. In practice, skullcap seems to produce a mild calming effect, generally not as strong as that of kava. It appears to take the edge off mild anxiety.

SAFETY ISSUES

There have been reports of liver damage following consumption of products labeled skullcap; however, since skullcap has been known to be adulterated with germander, an herb toxic to the liver, it may not have been the skullcap that was at fault. Safety in young children, pregnant or nursing women, or those with severe liver or kidney disease has not been established; similar precautions are probably warranted in pets.

Skullcap is usually not taken long-term.

 # SLIPPERY ELM *(Ulmus fulva, Ulmus rubra)*

Common Use
Diarrhea

Slippery elm is well-known for its use as a protecting and lubricating herb for pets with **gastrointestinal disease** (page 91).

THERAPEUTIC USES

The tannins in slippery elm reduce inflammation, and the oily mucilage components lubricate the digestive tract and assist in waste elimination.

The lubricating qualities make it desirable to try for pets with constipation. These qualities can also help comfort the respiratory passages for pets with bronchitis and excessive coughing.

SAFETY ISSUES

Slippery elm is safe, although a rare animal may show allergies to it. Do not use the outer bark as it can irritate urinary and digestive systems and cause abortion in pregnant animals.

 # SODIUM (See Part Three, Diet)

 # SODIUM POLYSORBATE (See Part Three, Diet)

 # SOY PROTEIN/ISOFLAVONES

Common Use
  Liver disease

The soybean has been prized for centuries in Asia as a nutritious, high-protein food with many potential uses.

THERAPEUTIC USES

For example, in pets with severe **liver disease** (page 127), diets using soy protein are preferred to decrease formation of chemicals that may be toxic to the pet. Today soy protein is popular for people as a cholesterol-free meat and dairy substitute (soy burgers, soy yogurt, tofu hot dogs, and tofu cheese can be found in a growing number of grocery stores alongside the traditional white blocks of tofu).

Soy has also been suggested as part of the therapy for treatment of cancer. A protease inhibitor called Bowman-Birk Inhibitor (BBI) has been shown in several laboratory experiments in mice and rats to inhibit the formation and spread of cancer. More research is needed to determine if BBI might be of benefit to pets with cancer.

SCIENTIFIC EVIDENCE

Several elements in soybeans, including soy protein, have been studied for possible health benefits. Soy protein appears to reduce blood cholesterol levels, and the U.S. Food and Drug Administration has proposed allowing soy protein foods to carry a "heart-healthy" label. In 1995, a review of all studies performed to date on soy protein and heart disease concluded that soy is definitely effective at reducing total cholesterol, LDL ("bad") cholesterol, and triglycerides. A more recent double-blind study involving 66 older women found improvements in HDL ("good") cholesterol as well. Compared with the placebo group, the soy groups showed significant improvements in both total cholesterol and HDL cholesterol. One added benefit of soy protein is that, unlike most other sources of protein, it contains no fat.

Soy-based diets (using tofu as the protein source) may also be helpful for pets with high blood cholesterol levels, although controlled studies are lacking at this time. Soy protein can reduce blood cholesterol levels and improve the ratio of LDL ("bad") versus HDL ("good") cholesterol in people. It is not known whether this same improvement in cholesterol levels occurs in pets. At an average dosage of 47 gm daily, total cholesterol falls by about 9%, LDL cholesterol by 13%, and triglycerides by 10%. Soy protein's effects on HDL cholesterol itself are less impressive.

In addition to protein, soybeans contain chemicals that are similar to estrogen. These may be the active ingredients in soy protein formulations, although this is not known for sure. Due to the estrogenic effects, soy protein also seems to reduce the common menopausal symptom known as "hot flashes" in women. Unlike estrogen, soy appears to reduce the risk of uterine cancer. While its effect on breast cancer is not as well established, there are reasons to believe that soy can help reduce breast cancer risk as well, due to the isoflavone content.

DOSAGES

In people, the FDA has proposed a daily intake of 25 gm of soy protein to reduce cholesterol; the amount for pets with high cholesterol has not been determined. The recommended intake of 25 gm of soy protein is the amount typically found in approximately ½ pound of tofu. If we consider that this is the dose recommended for the "typical" 150-pound adult male, and scale down for pets, we might see health benefits by feeding ½ to 1 ounce per 10 pounds of body weight.

Soy isoflavones have been proposed as a natural therapy for canine urinary incontinence at a starting dose of 2 mg per pound twice daily. The dosage can be increased if there is not response in 7 to 10 days. However, the pet should be examined regularly and have laboratory tests to check for signs of hyperestrogenism, which is a potential side effect. The correct dosage has not been determined, nor has it been determined whether there is any long-term harm to this therapy. If signs of estrogenism do not occur, the regimen is likely to be safe for pets.

SAFETY ISSUES

As a food that has been eaten for centuries, soy protein is believed to be quite safe. However, the isoflavones in soy could conceivably have some potentially harmful hormonal effects in certain specific situations. In particular, we don't know whether high doses of soy are safe for women who have already had breast cancer (for more information, see the chapter on isoflavones). They may also interact with hormone medications.

If people are taking zinc, iron, or calcium supplements, it has been suggested that it may be best to eat soy at a different time of day to avoid absorption problems. Patients taking the medications estrogen, tamoxifen, or raloxifene might experience interactions if eating large amounts of soy, as it is possible that soy might interfere with their effects. The same precautions may also be warranted in pets.

Isoflavones are water-soluble chemicals found in many plants; soy protein contains a fair amount of isoflavones. One group of isoflavones is known as phytoestrogens (plant estrogens), named because they cause effects in the body somewhat similar to those of estrogen. The most investigated natural isoflavones, genistein and daidzen, are found in soy products and the herb red clover. Another isoflavone, ipriflavone, is an intentionally modified form of daidzen used as a seminatural drug. Ipriflavone is a synthesized type of phytoestrogen that possesses the bone-stimulating effects of estrogen without any estrogen-like activity elsewhere in the body. After 7 successful years of experiments with animals, human research was started in 1981. Today, ipriflavone is available in over 22 countries and in most drugstores in the United States as a nonprescription dietary supplement. It is an accepted treatment for osteoporosis in people in Italy, Turkey, and Japan.

Like estrogen, ipriflavone appears to slow bone breakdown. Since it does not appear to have any estrogenic effects anywhere else in the body, it shouldn't increase the risk of breast or uterine cancer.

Isoflavones appear to work by latching on to the same places (receptor sites) on cells and not allowing actual estrogen to attach. In this way,

St. John's Wort

when there is not enough estrogen in the body, isoflavones can partially make up for it; but when there is plenty of estrogen, they can partially block its influence. In people, the net effect of this interaction may be to reduce some of the risks of excess estrogen (breast and uterine cancer) while still providing some of estrogen's benefits (prevention of osteoporosis).

Roasted soybeans have the highest isoflavone content, about 167 mg for a 3.5-ounce serving. Tempeh is next, with 60 mg; followed by soy flour, with 44 mg. Processed soy products such as soy protein and soy milk contain about 20 mg per serving. Similar isoflavones are also found in the herb red clover. The synthetic isoflavone ipriflavone is not found in foods and must be obtained as a supplement.

The proper dosage of the synthetic isoflavone ipriflavone has been well established through human studies: 200 mg 3 times daily, or 300 mg twice daily.

The optimum dosage of natural isoflavones obtained from food is not known. We know that Japanese women eat up to 200 mg of isoflavones daily, but we don't really know what amount of natural isoflavones is ideal. Most experts recommend 25 to 60 mg daily for people.

In pets, a dosage for soy isoflavones of 2 mg per pound of body weight twice daily has been suggested as an alternative therapy for dogs with urinary incontinence (as mentioned). Long-term side effects are unknown, and pets taking soy isoflavones should be monitored for side effects associated with estrogen, including bone marrow suppression.

Studies on the benefits of isoflavones isolated from red clover are pending at this time.

Natural soy isoflavones have not been subjected to rigorous safety studies. However, because they are consumed in very high quantities among those who eat traditional Asian diets, they are thought to be safe when used at the recommended dosages. However, because isoflavones work somewhat like estrogen, there are at least theoretical concerns that they may not be safe for women who have already had breast cancer.

Nearly 3,000 people have used the seminatural isoflavone ipriflavone in clinical studies, with no more side effects than those taking placebo. However, because ipriflavone is metabolized by the kidneys, individuals with severe kidney disease should have their ipriflavone dosage monitored by a physician. Similar precautions are warranted in pets until we have more information on the usage and safety of soy isoflavones. Feeding pets soy-based diets (tofu) are not likely to be of any harm.

ST. JOHN'S WORT *(Hypericum perforatum)*

Common Uses
Anxiety disorders, cancer, infections

The active components in St. John's wort are found in the buds, flowers, and newest leaves. Extracts are usually standardized to the substance hypericin, which has led to the widespread misconception that hypericin is the active ingredient. However, there is no evidence that hypericin itself is an antidepressant. Recent attention has focused on another ingredient of St. John's wort named hyperforin as the potential active ingredient. It appears that standard St. John's wort extract contains about 1 to 6% hyperforin.

We don't really know how St. John's wort works. Early research suggested that St. John's wort works like the oldest class of antidepressants, the MAO inhibitors.

However, later research essentially discredited this idea. More recent research suggests that St. John's wort may raise levels of serotonin, norepinephrine, and dopamine. This probably increases neurotransmitters to maintain normal mood and emotional stability (the herb may also cause binding of GABA and act as a serotonin reuptake inhibitor). Studies have used the standardized extract containing 0.14% hypericin.

Evidence from animal and human studies suggests that hyperforin is the ingredient in St. John's wort that raises these neurotransmitters. However, there may be other active ingredients in St. John's wort also at work.

THERAPEUTIC USES

The herb has been recommended for depression, separation anxiety, and certain forms of aggression in pets.

In people, St. John's wort is one of the best-documented herbal treatments, with a scientific record approaching that of many prescription drugs. It is a prescription antidepressant in Germany, covered by the national health-care system, and is prescribed more frequently for depression than any synthetic drug.

St. John's wort is also useful for its antiviral and antibacterial properties. It also has tonic effects on nerves.

Interest in St. John's wort is ongoing regarding antiviral activity and the potential to treat diseases including both human and feline AIDS infections. While definitive proof is lacking, it may be worthwhile to try St. John's wort in pets with severe viral infections (canine **distemper** (page 71), **feline leukemia** (page 82), and **immunodeficiency infections** (page 76)).

Applied locally, this herb is useful to heal wounds.

DOSAGES

In people, the current recommendation is 300 mg 3 times daily of the 0.3% hypericin standardized solution as a treatment for depression. A few new products on the market are standardized to hyperforin content (usually 3 to 5%) instead of hypericin. These are taken at the same dosage.

In dogs, a dose of 250 to 300 mg twice daily for large dogs has been recommended, although no scientific studies have been done to verify this dosage.

SCIENTIFIC EVIDENCE

In people, research suggests that St. John's wort is effective in about 55% of cases. As with other antidepressants, the full effect takes approximately 4 to 6 weeks to develop. Although St. John's wort appears to be somewhat less powerful than standard antidepressants, it rarely causes side effects.

SAFETY ISSUES

Use of St. John's wort may potentiate anesthetics and other sedatives; photosensitivity has been reported in people taking high doses. The herb should not be taken with other drugs that can inhibit MAO. In people, it is recommended to take the herb with food to decrease gastrointestinal upset.

In people, the most common are mild stomach discomfort allergic reactions (mainly a rash), lethargy, and restlessness.

Animal studies involving very large doses for 26 weeks have not shown any serious effects.

Do not combine St. John's wort with prescription antidepressants, especially drugs that increase serotonin levels, except on the specific advice of a veterinarian. Since some antidepressants, such as Prozac, linger in the blood for quite some time, caution is advised when switching from a drug to St. John's wort. Since no one knows whether it is absolutely safe to combine the herb with medications, the safest approach is to stop administering similar medications and allow them to wash out of your pet's system before starting St. John's wort. Consult with your veterinarian on how much time is necessary.

There has also recently been an informal report of St. John's wort lowering blood levels of theophylline, an asthma medication, in people. Preliminary investigation suggests that the hypericin in St. John's wort may increase the activity of a liver enzyme called cytochrome P-450. Because this enzyme can break down drugs, St. John's wort may cause the body to speed the breakdown of various drugs (such as theophylline), thereby decreasing their effectiveness.

Finally, preliminary reports from the University of Colorado suggest that St. John's wort may interfere with the action of the anti-tumor drugs etoposide (VePesid), teniposide (Vumon), mitoxantrone (Novantrone), and doxorubicin (Adriamycin).

Safety in young children, pregnant or nursing women, or those with severe liver or kidney disease has not been established; similar precautions in pets is probably also warranted.

 # TAURINE

Common Use
Heart disease

Taurine is a beta amino acid required by cats but not dogs. There are two reasons for this. First, the liver of the cat has a limited ability to make taurine as the rate-limiting enzymes required for converting methionine and cysteine to taurine are only minimally active in the feline liver. Second, cats lose taurine in the secretion of bile acids (whereas other mammals also use glycine in the conjugation and secretion of bile acids, freeing up taurine for other uses). Found in the nervous system (including the retina) and muscles (especially the heart), taurine is one of the most abundant amino acids in the body (and is the most abundant free amino acid in the heart). It is thought to help regulate heartbeat, maintain cell membranes, and affect the release of neurotransmitters in the brain. Taurine also protects the heart from calcium overload and assists in calcium uptake by the heart cells during peroids of hypoxia (reduced oxygen levels).

THERAPEUTIC USES

In people, taurine's best-established use is to treat congestive heart failure. Animal research as well as other, much smaller studies in humans have also found positive effects. One very small study compared taurine with another supplement commonly used for congestive heart failure, Coenzyme Q_{10}. The results suggest that taurine is more effective.

Taurine may also be useful for treating patients with hepatitis.

As mentioned above, dogs do not have a dietary requirement for taurine, since they can make it out of vitamin B_6 and the amino acids methionine and cysteine. Cats cannot do this; as true carnivores, they require dietary taurine.

Deficiencies can occur in dogs and cats fed vegetarian diets, as taurine (or the precursors for taurine) is present in meat but not in vegetables.

In cats, dilated **cardiomyopathy** (page 91) is a condition where the heart enlarges due to the heart muscle becoming thin and flabby. This weakened heart muscle fails to pump blood properly, leading to congestive heart failure. Several years ago, even commercial pet foods with the "correct" levels of taurine caused dilated cardiomyopathy in cats. The cause was unknown but may have been due to a defect in the absorption of dietary taurine. It was also possibly caused by the fact that the "correct" level of taurine was no longer "correct." As a result, manufacturers of commercial pet foods responded by increasing levels of taurine in the diet (so that we now have new "correct" levels in commercial food). Currently, this move seems to have worked, as dilated cardiomyopathy is almost never seen. Interestingly, cats fed homemade meat or fish-based diets did not seem to have this problem with increased incidences of cardiomyopathy.

In cats with taurine deficiency that causes dilated cardiomyopathy, clinical improvement is usually seen within 2 to 3 weeks following supplementation. Improvements in the EKG and radiographs will often take 3 to 6 weeks. The goal of taurine supplementation is to achieve plasma taurine levels of at least 60 nmol/mL (normal cats usually have levels >40 nmol/mL). Not all cats with dilated cardiomyopathy have taurine deficiency as the cause of the cardiomyopathy; those cats with normal taurine levels would not be expected to respond to supplementation with taurine.

In dogs, dilated cardiomyopathy can also occur, leading to congestive heart failure. Preliminary work shows that supplementation with taurine may be beneficial in American Cocker Spaniels and Golden Retrievers with dilated cardiomyopathy. Supplementation with taurine (500 mg twice daily) and L-carnitine (1,000 mg twice daily) in a small number of dogs with low plasma taurine levels resulted in improvement in a few of the patients. While not all doctors agree, many practitioners feel that since American Cocker Spaniels are predisposed to dilated cardiomyopathy with concurrent taurine and (possibly) carnitine deficiencies, supplementation with these two compounds is suggested for Cocker Spaniels with dilated cardiomyopathy.

Dogs with chronic valvular disease, the most common heart disease reported in dogs, usually have normal plasma taurine levels, making routine supplementation unlikely to be of benefit (although supplementation would not be harmful).

Taurine deficiency can be diagnosed based upon testing levels in the blood. Plasma levels are more indicative of recent taurine intake; whole blood levels are more suggestive of chronic taurine intake. However, even with normal blood levels, it is possible that levels of taurine in the heart muscle cells might not be adequate. Even for those pets without low blood taurine levels, supplementation can be tried without side effects.

In people, taurine has additionally been proposed as a treatment for numerous other conditions, including heart attack (to prevent dangerous disturbances in heart rhythm), stroke, hypertension, epilepsy, gallbladder disease, alcoholism, cataracts, multiple sclerosis, psoriasis, and dia-betes. The evidence for using taurine to treat these disorders is weak and, in some cases, contradictory.

People with diabetes have lower-than-average blood levels of taurine, but whether this means they should take extra taurine is unclear.

Taurine has also been recommended for pets with **epilepsy** (page 73). However, the only evidence to date is experimental. Still, since taurine supplementation will not hurt the pet, it can be added to the therapeutic regimen for epileptic pets following your veterinarian's advice.

SOURCES

Meat, poultry, eggs, dairy products, and fish are good sources of taurine.

DOSAGES

For cats, a typical therapeutic dosage of taurine is 250 to 500 mg 2 to 3 times daily.

For dogs, a typical therapeutic dosage is 500 mg 2 to 3 times daily.

SAFETY ISSUES

Taurine is thought to be quite safe. However, maximum safe dosages of taurine supplements for children, pregnant or nursing women, or those with severe liver or kidney disease have not been determined; similar precautions are probably warranted in pets.

As with any supplement taken in multigram doses, it is important to purchase a reputable product, because a contaminant present even in small percentages could cause problems.

 # TEA TREE *(Melaleuca alternifolia)*

Common Uses
  Flea repellant, sarcoptic mange, intestinal parasites, asthma, bronchitis

Tea tree oil has been used for the prevention and treatment of wound infections. However, tea tree oil fell out of favor when antibiotics became widely available.

THERAPEUTIC USES

There is little question that tea tree oil is an effective antiseptic, active against many bacteria and fungi. It also possesses a penetrating quality that may make it particularly useful for treating infected wounds. However, it is probably not effective when taken orally as an antibiotic.

One of the main active ingredients is cineole which is relatively nontoxic. Terpinen-4-ol, another ingredient, has germicidal activity. Other ingredients include various terpene hydrocarbons (pinene, terpinene, cymen) and small amounts of sesquiterpene hydrocarbons and oxytenated sesquiterpenes.

Australian dentists frequently use tea tree oil mouthwash prior to dental procedures and as a daily preventive against periodontal disease.

Tea tree oil also appears to possess deodorant properties, probably through suppressing odor-causing bacteria.

In pets and people, tea tree oil has been used externally for arthritis and muscle pain, and toothaches; in pets, it's used to repel fleas and external parasites, and for treating sarcoptic mange. Internally, the oil has been used for treating **parasites** (page 118), **asthma** (page 21), bronchitis, and sore throat.

SAFETY ISSUES

For people, tea tree preparations contain various percentages of tea tree oil. For treating acne, the typical strength is 5 to 15%; for fungal infections, 70 to 100% is usually used. It is usually applied 2 to 3 times daily, until symptoms resolve. However, tea tree oil can be irritating to the skin, so people are encouraged to start with low concentrations.

The best tea tree products contain oil from the alternifolia species of Melaleuca only, standardized to contain not more than 10% cineole (an irritant) and at least 30% terpinen-4-ol.

SAFETY ISSUES

Like other essential oils, tea tree oil can be toxic if taken orally in excessive doses. Since the maximum safe dosage has not been determined, many doctors recommend using it only topically, where it is believed to be quite safe. Safety in young children, pregnant or nursing women, or those with severe liver or kidney disease has not been established; similar precautions are probably warranted in pets.

Do not use in cats. Small-breed dogs may also be sensitive to undiluted oil. Dilute the oil with vegetable oil (at least 50:50). Test a small patch of skin prior to use as some pets may be sensitive.

TURMERIC *(Curcuma longa)*

Common Uses

 Arthritis, asthma, cancer, infections, liver disease

The volatile oils and curcumin are the active ingredients of this herb, which is well-known as a spice in curry powder and as an herb in Chinese and Ayurvedic medicine.

THERAPEUTIC USES

Whole turmeric possesses anti-inflammatory properties. Much of this observed activity seems to be due to the presence of curcumin, which also acts as a powerful antioxidant.

Turmeric has shown anticancer effects by its antioxidant, free radical scavenging effects, inhibition of nitrosamine formation, and by its ability to increase glutathione levels.

The anti-inflammatory effects, due to lipooxygenase inhibition, have been shown to be comparable to cortisone and phenylbutazone. Topically, it acts similarly to capsaicin by inhibiting substance P to relieve pain and inflammation.

Turmeric lowers blood cholesterol levels and prevents platelet clumping. Similar to glycyrrhizin and silymarin, curcumin shows protective effects on the liver.

Turmeric has beneficial effects on the **gastrointestinal tract** (page 91), including decreased gas formation and spasm.

The herb shows antimicrobial effects.

The antioxidant effects are comparable to BHA, BHT, and vitamins C and E.

Unlike anti-inflammatory drugs, curcumin does not appear to cause stomach ulcers and might even help prevent them. While curcumin has been recommended for people with rheumatoid arthritis and osteoarthritis, more evidence will be necessary before curcumin can be described as an effective treatment for arthritis.

In animal models, the curcurmin was found to have anti-inflammatory effects in arthritic pets comparable to the nonsteroidal medication phenylbutazone.

Turmeric is often used for pets with a number of conditions, including **arthritis** (page 11), **asthma** (page 21), **cancer** (page 44), inflammatory diseases, **infections** (page 105), and can be used as a liver tonic.

In people, the absorption of curcumin is reportedly increased when compounded with bromelain, although there is no evidence to support this. However, since bromelain possesses some anti-inflammatory powers of its own, the combination may be synergistic.

SAFETY ISSUES

Do not use in pets with bile duct obstruction, gallbladder stones, or gastrointestinal upset. Safety in young children, pregnant or nursing women, or those with severe liver or kidney disease has not been established; similar precautions are probably warranted in pets.

UVA URSI *(Arctostaphylos uva-ursi)*

Common Uses

Allergies (herbal rinse), infections (urinary system, alkaline urine), urinary disorders (alkaline urine)

Uva ursi is a berry-producing, evergreen bush. Only its leaves are used for medicinal purposes.

THERAPEUTIC USES

Uva ursi contains tannins and hydroquinones that are astringent and antibacterial. Until the development of sulfa antibiotics, its principal active component, arbutin, was frequently prescribed as a urinary antiseptic. It appears that the arbutin contained in uva ursi leaves is broken down in the intestine to another chemical, hydroquinone. This chemical is altered by the liver and then sent to the kidneys for excretion. In the bladder, it acts as an antiseptic.

Uva ursi is therefore recommended for pets with urinary **infections** (page 105) (but the urine must be alkaline for the antibacterial activity to occur; if the urine is acid, uva won't act as an antibacterial and should be combined with another antibacterial herb using uva ursi for its astringent activity). Since uva ursi is most effective in an alkaline urine, taking vitamin C or cranberry extract with it, which would acidify the urine, is not advised.

Since the tannins in the herb can irritate the kidneys, it should only be used for no more than 5 to 7 days at a time.

SAFETY ISSUES

Hydroquinone is a liver toxin, carcinogen, and irritant. Uva ursi is not recommended for young children, pregnant or nursing women, or those with severe liver or kidney disease. Similar precautions are probably warranted in pets.

Significant problems are rare among individuals using prepared uva ursi products in appropriate doses for a short period of time. Gastrointestinal distress (ranging from mild nausea and diarrhea to vomiting) can occur, especially with prolonged use.

If your pet is taking medications or supplements that acidify the urine, such as cranberry juice or vitamin C, uva ursi may not work very well.

VALERIAN *(Valeriana officinalis)*

Common Uses
Anxiety disorders, epilepsy

Valerian is well-known for its use as an herbal sedative and use as a treatment for anxiety, although there is much more scientific evidence for kava.

THERAPEUTIC USES

Valerian can help restless animals and those pets with trouble sleeping. It can be tried for pets with **epilepsy** (page 73) and those with fear-induced phobias (trips to the doctor or groomer, thunderstorms).

The active components in valerian—valepotriates and valerenic (valeric) acid—appear to work similarly to diazepam, preventing the breakdown of the inhibitory nerve transmitter GABA. (Some researchers question the effectiveness of valepotriates and speculate that the valerenic acid may be the active component.) Valerenic acid also appears to bind to the same brain receptors as diazepam and similar medications. The actual mechanism of action has not been proven.

Unlike diazepam and similar compounds, valerian does not appear to cause side effects such as dependency or impaired mental function.

Valerian can also be used as an antispasmodic for pets with digestive disturbances.

SAFETY ISSUES

Valerian is an extremely safe herb. However, the following precautions are in order. Large amounts can cause nausea and vomiting. Similar to diazepam (Valium), in a few people and pets valerian can act as a stimulant (similar to catnip in cats).

Do not use in pregnant animals. Do not use in large doses, as it can cause gastrointestinal upset. Do not use with other drugs that can cause sedation without veterinary supervision. Since the safety of valepotriates has been questioned, the use of water-soluble extracts has been standardized for valerenic acid content.

Safety in young children, pregnant or nursing women, or those with severe liver or kidney disease has not been established; similar precautions are probably warranted in pets.

VANADIUM (Vanadyl sulfate, vanadate)

Common Use
Diabetes

Vanadium is a mineral, and evidence from animal studies suggests it may be an essential micronutrient.

THERAPEUTIC USES

In people as well as pets, there are no well-documented uses for vanadium, and there are serious safety concerns regarding its use. However, vanadium has been proposed to be of benefit in patients with diabetes as vanadium has insulin-like properties and may inhibit protein tyrosine phosphatase (PTP).

Studies in rats with and without diabetes suggest that vanadium may have an insulin-like effect, reducing blood sugar levels. Based on these findings, preliminary studies involving human subjects have been conducted, with promising results.

Based on promising animal studies, high doses of vanadium, like chromium, have been tested as an aid to controlling blood sugar levels in people with diabetes. However, animal studies suggest that taking high doses of vanadium can be harmful.

In various studies in people, vanadium has been used at doses thousands of times higher than is present in the diet, as high as 125 mg per day. However, there are serious safety concerns about taking vanadium at such high doses. Many doctors do not recommend that people exceed the nutritional dose of 10 to 30 mcg daily (some people with diabetes are prescribed 50 to 100 mcg/day).

To date, most doctors feel that studies using vanadium were all too small to be taken as definitive proof. More research is needed to definitely establish whether vanadium is effective (not to mention safe) for the treatment of diabetes.

New organic forms of vanadium have been synthesized; these include vanadyl acetylacetonate, vanadyl 3-ethylacetylacetonate, bis (malto-lato) oxovanadium. These forms appear to be safer than vanadyl sulfate and are well tolerated in diabetic cats.

In small studies in cats, the use of vanadium did improve clinical signs and reduce blood glucose levels with minimal signs of toxicity.

With insulin-resistant type II diabetics, vanadium may help balance glucose levels by increasing glycogen synthesis (glycogen is a storage form of glucose). Because vanadium mimics many of the effects of insulin, it may improve blood sugar balance. In some studies, vanadium supplements have been shown to lower plasma glucose levels, improve insulin sensitivity, increase glucose uptake and decrease blood fat levels in type I and type II **diabetes** (page 66).

DOSAGES

In pets with diabetes, dosages of 0.2 mg/kg daily for vanadium and 1 mg/kg daily for vanadyl sulfate seem safe. Some holistic veterinarians adapt the recommended human dose of vanadium to pets, using 50 mcg/day for small dogs and cats, 75 mcg per day for medium-sized dogs, and 100 mcg per day for larger dogs. The dosage of one-half of a capsule of Super Vanadyl Fuel (Twin Laboratories, Hauppage, New York) given once daily on the food of diabetic cats appears safe. However, you should not administer vanadium (or chromium) to your pets unless they're under veterinary supervision.

SAFETY ISSUES

Studies of diabetic rats suggest that, at high dosages, vanadium can accumulate in the body until it reaches toxic levels. Based on these results, high dosages of vanadium can't be considered safe for human use; similar concerns are probably reasonably applied to dogs and cats.

Vanadium

Vitamin Requirements for Growing and Adult Cats and Dogs

Vitamin	Growing Cat	Adult Cat	Growing Dog	Adult Dog
A	200 IU	75 IU	202 IU	75 IU
D	20 IU	8 IU	22 IU	8 IU
E	1.2 IU	0.5 IU	1.2 IU	0.5 IU
K	2 μg	2 μg	2 μg	2 μg
Thiamin	200 μg	200 μg	54 μg	20 μg
Riboflavin	160 μg	160 μg	100 μg	50 μg
Pantothenate	200 μg	200 μg	400 μg	200 μg
Niacin	1600 μg	1,600 μg	450 μg	225 μg
Pyridoxine	160 μg	160 μg	60 μg	22 μg
Folic Acid	32 μg	32 μg	8 μg	4 μg
Biotin	2.8 μg	2.8 μg	—	—
B$_{12}$	.8 μg	.8 μg	1 μg	.5 μg
Choline	96 mg	96 mg	50 mg	25 mg

Reprinted from Home-Prepared Dog & Cat Diets, *by Donald R. Strombeck, D.V.M., Ph.D. ©1999 Iowa State University Press. Used with Permission.*

VITAMIN A (Retinol)

Common Uses
Nutritional Supplement

Vitamin A is a fat-soluble antioxidant that protects the cells against damaging free radicals and plays other vital roles in the body. However, it is potentially more dangerous than most other vitamins because it can build up to toxic levels, causing liver damage and birth defects. Because of this risk, pure vitamin A supplements have few therapeutic uses.

Cats cannot convert the vitamin A precursor beta-carotene (often called "pro-vitamin A") into vitamin A. Cats require pre-formed vitamin A, which is available in animal tissue. Dogs can convert beta-carotene in plant tissue into vitamin A.

Vitamin A is an essential nutrient, meaning that the pet must get it in the diet.

Vitamin A is needed for maintaining normal epithelial tissue (skin, mucous membranes). It can prevent various eye problems, enhances immunity, treats several skin disorders, may protect against cancer formation (by scavenging free radicals that occur as a result of cell oxidation), is important in bone formation, aids in fat storage, and helps prevent infections of the **bladder** (page 36), kidneys, and lungs. Vitamin A acts an antioxidant and is used as a nutritional supplement for this reason. Vitamin A is necessary for protein utilization and has been suggested to slow the aging process.

Vitamin A deficiency results in abscesses and secondary bacterial infections, night blindness (in people), frequent infections (especially of the respiratory tract), and various skin disorders.

Vitamin A is often erroneously called beta-carotene. Carotenoids are compounds related to vitamin A and beta-carotene is a precursor to vitamin A. Other carotenoids include alpha-carotene, gamma-carotene, and lycopene. In dogs but not cats, beta-carotene can be converted to vitamin A in the liver; cats require pre-formed vitamin A as they are unable to covert beta-carotene in the diet (cats lack the dioxygenase enzyme necessary to cleave beta-carotene).

Synthetic, but not natural, vitamin A can result in toxicity if large doses are ingested. Clinical signs are related to skin disease (just as a deficiency of vitamin A can also cause skin lesions including dryness, abscesses, and cracking of the skin).

Betatene is the trade name for a carotenoid complex extracted from sea algae that is used in various vitamin products.

SOURCES

Vitamin A sources include liver, dairy products, fish liver oils, green vegetables (broccoli, dandelion greens, kale, mustard greens, spinach, parsley, collard greens, chard, turnip greens, beet greens), yellow vegetables (carrots, red peppers, sweet potatoes, yellow squash), and fruit (apricots, cantaloupe, peaches, papaya). Green foods such as spirulina, alfalfa, kelp and herbs (including cayenne, horsetail, lemongrass, nettle, oat straw, paprika, peppermint, red clover, rose hips, yellow dock) all are sources of vitamin A.

DOSAGES

The usual nutritional daily dose of vitamin A in dogs and cats recommended by the AAFCO is 100 IU to 200 IU/kg/day; the toxic dose in dogs is approximately 20,000 IU/kg/day. Cats seem to tolerate excess vitamin A with minimal or no toxicity. Recent research has shown that adult cats were fed diets with varying vitamin A levels (20,000 to 2,000,000 IU/kg) for 3 to 4 years without toxicity. It is theorized that this resistance to vitamin A toxicity may occur as carnivores like cats have adapted to diets high in vitamin A. Their normal diets are higher in vitamin A than carotenoids like beta-carotene; cats cannot convert beta-carotene to vitamin A and therefore require vitamin A in their diets.

Doses of vitamin A above the basic nutritional requirement are not recommended except for specific therapeutic uses.

THERAPEUTIC USES

As is the case in people, diabetic pets should not receive additional supplementation with high levels of vitamin A without the advice of a veterinarian. It is unknown whether supplementation with vitamin A would help control blood sugar levels in diabetic dogs and cats.

In pets, vitamin A is recommended for treating pets with several disorders that may benefit from high doses of antioxidants. These include **epilepsy** (page 73), allergies (**atopic dermatitis,** page 3), food allergies, **feline leukemia** (page 83), and **immunodeficiency virus infections** (page 76).

For pets with atopic dermatitis, treatment uses vitamin A (10,000 IU for small dogs and cats, and up to 30,000 IU for large dogs), crystalline ascorbic acid (750 mg for small dogs and cats, and up to 3,000 mg for large dogs), and vitamin E (800 IU for small dogs and cats, and up to 2,400 IU for large dogs). The antioxidant mineral selenium (20 mcg for small dogs and cats, and up to 60 mcg for large dogs) is also added to the regimen. Once asymptomatic, a maintenance protocol using lower dosages of vitamins A and E and the mineral selenium is prescribed to reduce the chance for toxicity.

For pets with epilepsy, feline leukemia and feline immunodeficiency virus infections, the same dosing guidelines are used.

Pets with **inflammatory bowel disease** (page 105) are treated similarly, except that the ascorbic acid is not used, as ascorbic acid can worsen diarrhea. (See the section on Orthomolecular Medicine, Part Four, page 415 for a greater discussion of these various disorders.)

Vitamin A is also used in dogs with a specific skin disorder called vitamin A–responsive dermatosis at a dose of 1,000 IU/kg/day. Vitamin A–responsive dermatosis has been seen mainly in Cocker Spaniels but has also been seen in a few Labrador Retrievers and Miniature Schnauzers. A true vitamin A deficiency is usually not the cause of the disorder even though the condition (which occurs for unknown reason) does respond to vitamin A therapy. The condition occurs in adult dogs and is characterized by a seborrheic skin condition not responsive to traditional therapy for seborrhea. The skin exhibits plugging of the hair follicles, plaques, and fronds on the skin. The lesions occur mainly on the sides and underside of the chest and abdomen. The follicular plugging seen by the pathologist on a skin biopsy is highly suggestive of this disease (only a few other conditions cause similar pathological signs, including Cushing's disease, true vitamin A deficiency or toxicity, and atypical generalized demodectic mange).

Vitamin A

Vitamin A, plus omega-3 fatty acids and regular anti-seborrheic shampoo therapy are usually needed for the life of the pet.

Sebaceous adenitis is another condition that can respond to therapy with vitamin A. The condition of unknown cause occurs mainly in dogs, although cats have also been affected.

There is no age predisposition, and in dogs the breeds mainly affected include Vizslas, Akitas, Samoyeds, and Standard Poodles. In general, the lesions are most prominent on the head, face, ears, and trunk, although they will often spread down the body. In short-coated dogs, lesions begin as areas of scaling and hair loss that eventually enlarge and coalesce (come together). Many owners and doctors could easily confuse the lesions with those seen in dogs affected with ringworm fungus.

Long-coated dogs may have some greasiness of the coat and skin, show severe hair loss, and rarely may show systemic signs (fever, lethargy, weight loss).

Itching is not common unless secondary skin infections (usually bacterial) occur.

In cats, lesions are areas of scale, crust, broken hairs, and loss of hair. The lesions are also prominent on the face, head, ears, and neck and then spread down the body.

The diagnosis is made by skin biopsy by ruling out other causes of similar lesions (ringworm, demodectic mange, bacterial follicular infection). Areas of sebaceous adenitis with granulomas or pyogranulomas are seen on microscopic examination of skin biopsies.

Response to treatment in dogs is quite variable; prognosis is poorest when sebaceous glands have been completely destroyed as determined by biopsy. Vitamin A (Isotretinoin at 1 to 2 mg/kg/day or Etretinate at 1 to 2 mg/kg/day) can be used. Isotretinoin seems to work best in Vizslas but not other breeds. Omega-3 fatty acids and anti-seborrheic shampooing are also used, and recently cyclosporine (5 mg/kg twice daily given by mouth) has been reported to be effective in some dogs not responding to synthetic vitamin A therapy. No information on treatment in cats is available.

In place of synthetic vitamin A, whole food sources of vitamin A and skin glandular therapy can be tried, although no controlled studies have been done to assess this natural therapy in dogs or cats with these two very rare skin disorders.

Retinoids refer to any natural or synthetic form of vitamin A. Retinol, retinoic acid, and retinal derivatives are synthetic forms of vitamin A. Only retinol has all the known functions of vitamin A. Over 1,500 synthetic retinoids have been created, each of which may show different effects, side effects, and specific disease indications.

Naturally occurring vitamin A (all-trans retinol) is oxidized in the body to retinal and retinoic acid.

Isotretinoin (13-cis-retinoic acid, Accutane, synthesized as a natural metabolite of retinol) and etretinate (Tegison, a synthetic retinoid) are the synthetic forms of vitamin A most commonly prescribed for various diseases in pets. Isotretinoin is prescribed for Schnauzer comedo syndrome, sebaceous adenitis, feline acne, sebaceous gland adenomas, and epitheliotropic lymphoma (a type of skin cancer). Isotretinoin has not proved effective for treating idiopathic seborrhea of Cocker Spaniels or squamous cell carcinomas of cats.

Etretinate is effective for idiopathic seborrhea of Cocker Spaniels and other breeds (Golden Retrievers, Irish Setters, and several mixed breeds).

Neither drug should be used in pregnant female dogs or cats or those that will be used for breeding, as effects may persist for up to 2 years following the end of treatment.

Dogs and cats that require treatment with these and other synthetic forms of vitamin A must be monitored every 1 to 2 months for side effects with measurements of tear production, blood profiles, and a urinalysis. Lowfat diets are recommended to decrease the chance of causing increased triglyceride levels when using synthetic vitamin A analogues.

SCIENTIFIC EVIDENCE

In people, vitamin A and beta-carotene are often recommended for treating viral infections in children (in developing countries), diabetes, skin disorders (such as acne and psoriasis), menorrhagia (heavy menstruation), Crohn's disease, ulcerative colitis, cancer, impaired night vision, ulcers, ear infections, eating disorders, lupus, AIDS, gout, glaucoma, multiple sclerosis, kidney stones, and Down's syndrome.

In people, there is some evidence that vitamin A supplements reduce deaths from measles and other causes among children in developing countries, presumably because they correct a deficiency in the children's diets. However, this doesn't mean that vitamin A supplements above and beyond the basic nutritional requirement are a useful treatment for measles or any other childhood disease. Vitamin A has been tried as a treatment for various viral infections, including measles, respiratory syncytial virus (RSV, a common childhood viral disease of the respiratory tract), chicken pox, and AIDS. Most of the research on vitamin A has concentrated on children in developing countries. A review article examining 12 studies suggested that vitamin A supplements can protect such children from dying, and should be used more widely. Success with measles led researchers to study its use in another childhood viral disease, respiratory syncytial virus. However, the results were not impressive.

Vitamin A may be helpful for people with diabetes as well, although there are concerns that people with diabetes may be especially vulnerable to liver damage from excessive amounts of vitamin A. According to many but not all studies, people with diabetes tend to be deficient in vitamin A. A recent uncontrolled study suggests that vitamin A supplements may improve blood sugar control in people with diabetes. However, due to safety concerns, they should not supplement with vitamin A except under medical supervision.

High doses of vitamin A have been used in the past for a variety of skin diseases such as acne and psoriasis in people. However, generally vitamin A has to be taken in potentially toxic dosages to produce good effects and should only be taken under a doctor's supervision (and in non-pregnant women, as vitamin A can produce serious birth defects).

In addition, vitamin A has been proposed as a treatment for a wide variety of other conditions in people, including ulcerative colitis, impaired night vision, ulcers, ear infections, eating disor-

ders, lupus, AIDS, gout, glaucoma, multiple sclerosis, kidney stones, and Down's syndrome. There is little to no evidence that it is effective for any of these conditions. According to a double-blind study of 86 people with Crohn's disease, vitamin A did not help prevent flare-ups.

SAFETY ISSUES

In people, dosages of vitamin A above 50,000 IU per day taken for several years can cause liver injury, bone problems, fatigue, hair loss, headaches, and dry skin. People with liver disease should check with their doctors before taking vitamin A supplements because even small doses may be harmful. It is thought that people with diabetes may have trouble releasing vitamin A stored in the liver, which may mean that they are at greater risk for vitamin A toxicity. Women should avoid supplementing with vitamin A during pregnancy, because at toxic levels it may increase the risk of birth defects.

Dogs may show vitamin A toxicity when daily dosages above 20,000 IU/kg are ingested. In foods, the maximum amount of vitamin A recommended for dogs is 250,000 IU/kg of food; for cats, the maximum amount is 750,000 IU/kg of food (although as mentioned earlier, cats eating diets containing up to 2,000,000 IU/kg of vitamin A for 3 to 4 years have not shown vitamin A toxicity). There are rare reports of cats eating fresh beef liver on a daily basis who have been diagnosed with vitamin A toxicity. For owners who choose to feed cats homemade diets, caution is probably warranted and extra vitamin A in the form of synthetic supplements is not needed without veterinary supervision. Vitamin A blood levels can be determined to make sure toxicity does not occur (normal level is 20 to 80 microgram/dl).

Vitamin A toxicity will not occur when using whole food sources rather than synthetic forms of vitamin A.

The older cholesterol-lowering drugs cholestyramine or colestipol may reduce levels of vitamin A. The drug isotretinoin (Accutane) is a vitamin A analogue; additional vitamin A supplementation could be harmful as both products enhance each other's toxicity.

Vitamin A

VITAMIN B

Vitamin B (sidebar)

Common Uses
Nutritional supplement

There is no one "vitamin B," but rather a complex of many B vitamins. All of them help maintain health of the nervous system, skin, eyes, hair, liver, muscle, and brain. They function as coenzymes in energy production and may help reduce anxiety or depression. While we talk about some of the B vitamins individually, keep in mind that in nature these vitamins do not occur as isolated entities but rather as part of the entire B vitamin complex.

Because most foods contain B vitamins, deficiencies of B vitamins are rare in pets. An exception is thiamine deficiency in cats.

Supplementation with the B vitamin choline is indicated in older pets, especially those exhibiting signs of **cognitive disorder** (page 56), often incorrectly referred to as "senility" (see Part One, Conditions). Supplementation with this vitamin may also be helpful for pets with **epilepsy** (page 73) to "calm the brain" and for **liver disease** (page 127).

While they are available from dietary components, the B vitamins are synthesized in the digestive tract by bacteria from nutrients supplied in the diet. Intestinal disease (such as diarrhea) can upset the normal bacterial flora and result in decreased synthesis of these vitamins. Pets with diarrhea and various intestinal diseases should be supplemented with **prebiotics and probiotics** (page 257) to provide healthy bacteria to replace those lost as a result of disease.

B complex vitamins are often recommended for pets with a lack of appetite. In fact, it is theorized that a deficiency of B vitamins (specifically thiamine and niacin) may cause anorexia. Anecdotally, many veterinarians add B vitamins (or force-feeding formulas or intravenous solutions) to the diets of anorectic pets as a "natural" way to stimulate appetite.

The daily B vitamin requirement of cats is estimated to be 6 to 8 times greater than the daily requirement for dogs.

VITAMIN B₁ (Thiamin)

Common Uses
Cognitive disorder, fleas

Vitamin B₁, a water-soluble vitamin, also called thiamin, was the first B vitamin ever discovered. The body uses it to process fats, carbohydrates, and proteins. Every cell in your pet's body needs thiamin to make adenosine triphosphate (ATP), the body's main energy-carrying molecule.

Vitamin B₁ enhances circulation, assists in blood formation, enhances brain activity and cognitive function, acts as an antioxidant, and maintains muscle tone in the intestines, stomach, and heart.

In people, beriberi is the name given to the disease of the nervous system caused by severe vitamin B₁ deficiency. Beriberi, a disease common among sailors through the nineteenth century, is rare today except in developing countries, as well as in alcoholics and people with diseases that significantly impair the body's ability to absorb vitamin B₁.

In people, weak and contradictory evidence suggests that vitamin B₁ may be helpful for Alzheimer's disease. Vitamin B₁ has also been proposed as a treatment for epilepsy, canker sores, and fibromyalgia, but the evidence for these uses is weak.

Alcoholism, Crohn's disease, diabetes, anorexia, kidney dialysis, folic acid deficiency, and multiple sclerosis may all lead to a vitamin B_1 deficiency, and people with these conditions should consider taking B_1 supplements.

THERAPEUTIC USES

Supplementation with B vitamins is often recommended as part of the therapy for pets with **cognitive disorder** (page 56) (similar to Alzheimer's) and **epilepsy** (page 73). Controlled studies are also lacking in pets, but since B vitamins are important for proper functioning of neurological tissues and are safe, it seems reasonable to recommend their use as part of a holistic treatment program for dogs and cats with these disorders.

In pets, pure thiamin deficiency is rare but can occur in cats. Thiamin deficiency occurs as a result of feeding highly processed food (especially canned food, as processing destroys thiamin) or feeding large amounts of raw fish that contain the thiaminase enzyme which destroys thiamin. Thiamin is needed for the conversion of pyruvate to acetyl CoA for use in the Krebs cycle. With deficiency, this reaction cannot occur properly, and blood levels of lactate and pyruvate rise. Since energy metabolism is compromised and acidosis develops, the central nervous system tissue, which has a high metabolic rate, is affected, causing clinical signs. Signs seen with thiamin deficiency include lack of appetite followed by ataxia (a wobbly, drunken gait), recumbency, convulsions, and a downward flexion of the neck. Treatment involves prompt diagnosis (organophosphate poisoning and potassium deficiency cause similar signs) and adminstration of thiamin, along with dietary improvement.

Thiamin, in the form of brewer's yeast, has been advocated as a natural therapy to prevent flea infestation. The theory is that the thiamin is excreted through the eccrine sweat glands and produces a foul odor or taste found unacceptable to fleas. The problem is that eccrine sweat glands, which are responsible for sweating in people, only occur in dogs and cats in certain locations, most notably the footpads and nose. In controlled studies thiamin was not found to help control fleas. Still, the addition of brewer's yeast is not harmful to pets (unless they exhibit an allergy to the yeast). Since many pet owners feel that the addition of yeast to the diet does help with parasite control despite controlled studies to the contrary, it can be used by pet owners as part of a comprehensive **flea control** (page 89) program.

SOURCES

Brown rice, egg yolks, fish, liver, pork, poultry, whole grains, brewer's yeast, nutritional yeast, broccoli, brussels sprouts, and kelp provide vitamin B_1. Peas, beans, nuts, seeds, and whole grains also provide fairly good amounts of vitamin B_1.

Certain foods may impair the body's absorption of B_1 as well, including fish, shrimp, clams, mussels, and the herb horsetail. The green foods alfalfa and spirulina contain vitamin B_1, as do the herbs catnip, cayenne, chamomile, hops, nettle, peppermint, raspberry leaf, red clover, rose hips, and yellow dock.

SAFETY ISSUES

Vitamin B_1 appears to be quite safe even when taken in very high doses.

Additional vitamin B_1 is recommended for people taking certain diuretics (loop diuretics such as furosemide). Similar recommendations are probably prudent for pets as well.

Vitamin B_1

VITAMIN B₂ (Riboflavin, Riboflavin-5-phosphate)

Common Use
Nutritional supplement

Riboflavin, also known as vitamin B₂, is an essential nutrient required for life.

Riboflavin functions as part of a number of coenzymes in most cells. It is an integral part of flavin mononucleotide and flavin adenine dinucleotide. These enzymes are used to transfer hydrogen ions (which are supplied by sugars and fatty acids in the diet) to the cytochrome and hydrogen ion transfer systems to supply energy to the body (via the body's production of adenosine triphosphate, or ATP).

Vitamin B₂ is also used for the production of red blood cells and antibodies that help fight disease. It helps prevent cataracts and aids in energy production by cells of the body. Riboflavin works with vitamin A to maintain mucous membranes and helps the absorption of iron and vitamin B₆ in the intestines. Riboflavin is needed for metabolism of the amino acid tryptophan, which is then converted into niacin. Like other B vitamins, riboflavin assists in the metabolism of nutrients including fats, carbohydrates, and proteins, and helps activate vitamin B₆ and folic acid.

Deficiency resembles signs seen with vitamin A deficiency and includes cracks and sores of the mucous membranes, dermatitis, weight loss, and hair loss.

THERAPEUTIC USES

There are no specific needs for additional supplementation with riboflavin for pets; there are no studies suggesting their use as a cataract preventive.

SCIENTIFIC EVIDENCE

In people, preliminary evidence suggests that riboflavin supplements may offer benefits for two illnesses: migraine headaches and cataracts.

For migraine headaches, the typical recommended dosage of riboflavin—400 mg daily—is much higher than nutritional needs. According to a recent 3-month double-blind study of 55 people with migraines, 400 mg of riboflavin daily can reduce the frequency of migraine headaches by 50%.

For cataract prevention, riboflavin may be taken at the nutritional dosages described.

One very large study suggests that riboflavin at nutritional doses may be helpful for cataracts, but in this study it was combined with another B vitamin, niacin or vitamin B₃, so it's hard to say which vitamin was responsible for the effect. In this large, double-blind placebo-controlled study, 3,249 people were given either placebo or one of four nutrient combinations (vitamin A/zinc, riboflavin/niacin, vitamin C/molybdenum, or selenium/beta-carotene/vitamin E) for a period of 6 years. Those receiving the niacin/riboflavin supplement showed a significant (44%) reduction in the incidence of cataracts. Strangely, there was a small, but statistically significant higher incidence of a special type of cataract (called a subcapsular cataract) in the niacin/riboflavin group. However, it is unclear whether the effects seen in this group were due to niacin, riboflavin, or the combination of the two.

Riboflavin has also been proposed as a treatment for sickle-cell anemia and canker sores, and as a performance enhancer for athletes, but there is no real evidence that it is effective for these uses.

SOURCES

Cheese, fish, egg yolks, milk, beef, pork, poultry, yogurt, spinach, whole grains, broccoli, brussels sprouts, kelp, leafy greens, and mushrooms are sources of riboflavin. The green food alfalfa as well as the herbs catnip, cayenne, chamomile, chickweed, ginseng, hops, mullein, nettle, peppermint, raspberry leaves, red clover, rose hips, sage, and yellow dock also contain vitamin B₂.

Riboflavin is also found in organ meats (such as liver, kidney, and heart) and in many nuts, legumes, and leafy greens. The richest sources are torula (nutritional) yeast, brewer's yeast, and calf liver. Almonds, wheat germ, and wild rice are good sources as well.

For pets, riboflavin must be supplied in the diet, as little is stored in the body (as is true with most water-soluble vitamins).

DOSAGES

The new recommendation for adult dogs is 2.7 mg/kg of food, which is higher than the amount (2.2 mg/kg of food) currently recommended by the AAFCO.

SAFETY ISSUES

Riboflavin seems to be an extremely safe supplement. Toxicity has not been reported in pets.

If your pet is taking tetracycline-family antibiotics, he may need extra riboflavin.

VITAMIN B₃ (Niacin, niacinamide, nicotinamide, inositol hexaniacinate)

Common Uses
Nutritional supplement

Vitamin B₃ is required for the proper function of more than 50 enzymes. Without it, your body would not be able to release energy or make fats from carbohydrates. Vitamin B₃ is also used to make sex hormones and other important chemical signal molecules.

Vitamin B₃, is needed for healthy skin and proper circulation of the blood throughout the body. As with other B vitamins, it also aids in proper functioning of the nervous system and in metabolism of proteins, fats, and carbohydrates. The secretion of bile and stomach acids requires niacin. Niacin lowers cholesterol and helps with the synthesis of hormones, including estrogen and testosterone. It is often used to enhance memory.

Similar to riboflavin, vitamin B₃ is used in energy production by the cell. It is an integral part of nicotinamide adenine dinucleotide phosphate and nicotinamide adenine dinucleotide. These enzymes are also used to transfer hydrogen ions (which are supplied by sugars and fatty acids in the diet) to the cytochrome and hydrogen ion transfer systems to supply energy to the body.

Tryptophan metabolism is intrinsically linked to niacin (niacin may also be synthesized from dietary tryptophan if the diet is low in niacin and adequate tryptophan is available). In cats, however, one of the intermediate compounds formed during tryptophan metabolism to niacin is quickly utilized by another pathway; therefore, cats cannot convert tryptophan to niacin. Thus, cats, unlike dogs, have a strict dietary requirement for niacin.

Vitamin B₃ comes in two principal forms: niacin (nicotinic acid) and niacinamide (nicotinamide). When taken in low doses for nutritional purposes, they are essentially identical. However, each has its own particular effects when taken in high doses. High-dose niacin is principally used for lowering cholesterol. High-dose niacinamide may be helpful in preventing type I (childhood-onset) diabetes and reducing symptoms of osteoarthritis in people. However, there are concerns regarding liver inflammation when any form of niacin is taken at high dosages.

SCIENTIFIC EVIDENCE

There is no question that niacin (but not niacinamide) can significantly lower total cholesterol and LDL cholesterol and raise HDL cholesterol in people. However, unpleasant flushing reactions and the risk of liver inflammation have kept niacin from being widely used. According to numerous studies, niacin can lower total cholesterol and LDL ("bad") cholesterol by 15 to 25%, lower triglycerides by 2 to 50%, and raise HDL ("good") cholesterol by about 15 to 25%. Furthermore, long-term use of niacin has been shown to significantly reduce death rates from cardiovascular disease.

Intriguing evidence suggests that regular use of niacinamide (but not niacin) may help prevent diabetes in children at special risk of developing it. Risk can be determined by measuring the ratio of antibodies to islet cells (ICA antibody test). Niacinamide may improve blood sugar control in both children and adults who already have diabetes.

Exciting evidence from a huge study conducted in New Zealand suggests that niacinamide can prevent high-risk children from developing diabetes. In this study, more than 20,000 children were screened for diabetes risk by measuring ICA antibodies. It turned out that 185 of these children had detectable levels. About 170 of these children were then given niacinamide for 7 years (not all parents agreed to give their children niacinamide or stay in the study for that long). About 10,000 other children were not screened, but they were followed to see whether they developed diabetes.

The results were very impressive. In the group in which children were screened and given niacinamide if they were positive for ICA antibodies, the incidence of diabetes was reduced by as much as 60%. These findings suggest that niacinamide is a very effective treatment for preventing diabetes. (It also shows that tests for ICA antibodies can very accurately identify children at risk for diabetes.)

At present, an enormous-scale, long-term trial called the European Nicotinamide Diabetes Intervention Trial is being conducted to definitively determine whether regular use of niacinamide can prevent diabetes. Preliminary results from the German portion of the study were released at press time, and they were not positive. However, until the entire study is complete, it is not possible to draw reliable conclusions.

If a child has just developed diabetes, niacinamide may prolong what is called the honeymoon period. This is the interval in which the pancreas can still make some insulin, and insulin needs are low. A recent study suggests that niacinamide may also improve blood sugar control in type II (adult-onset) diabetes, but it did not use a double-blind design.

According to several good-size, double-blind studies involving a total of over 500 individuals, a special form of niacin, inositol hexaniacinate, may be able to improve walking distance in intermittent claudication (severe leg cramps caused by hardening of the arteries). For example, in one study, 120 individuals were given either placebo or 2 g of inositol hexaniacinate daily. Over a period of 3 months, walking distance improved significantly in the treated group. (Other treatments that may help intermittent claudication include carnitine and ginkgo.)

Preliminary evidence (one small double-blind study) suggests that inositol hexaniacinate may be able to reduce symptoms of Raynaud's phenomenon as well. This condition includes an extreme response to cold, usually most severely in the hands. The dosage used in the study was 4 g daily, again a dosage high enough for liver inflammation to be a real possibility.

Preliminary evidence suggests that niacinamide may be able to reduce symptoms of osteoarthritis. There is some evidence that niacinamide may provide some benefits for those with osteoarthritis. In a double-blind study, 72 individuals with arthritis were given either 3,000 mg daily of niacinamide (in 5 equal doses) or placebo for 12 weeks. The results showed that treated participants experienced a 29% improvement in symptoms, whereas those given placebo worsened by 10%. However, at this dose, liver inflammation is a concern that must be taken seriously.

Very weak evidence suggests one of the several forms of niacin may be helpful in bursitis, cataracts, and pregnancy.

THERAPEUTIC USES

Niacin was discovered to be the specific chemical that cured black tongue (pellagra) in dogs fed niacin-deficient diets. Niacin deficiency (pellagra) causes dermatitis, diarrhea, dementia, and death.

Niacinamide has been recommended for the treatment of several disorders in pets, including discoid lupus erythematosus and pemphigus erythematosus in dogs. When combined with tetracycline, niacinamide (at a dosage of 500 mg of tetracycline and 500 mg of niacinamide per dog given every 8 hours for dogs weighing more than 10 kg) has been found to show an excellent response in 25 to 65% of cases. While no studies support the use of niacinamide for dogs with atopic dermatitis, since niacinamide works by inhibiting antigen-IgE–induced histamine release, it may be an option for atopic dogs.

SOURCES

Good food sources of niacin are seeds, yeast, bran, peanuts (especially with skins), wild rice, brown rice, whole wheat, barley, almonds, liver, brewer's yeast, broccoli, carrots, cheese, eggs, fish, milk, pork, potatoes, and peas. Tryptophan is found in protein foods (meat, poultry, dairy products, and fish). Turkey and milk are particularly excellent sources of tryptophan. Other sources include the green food alfalfa and the herbs catnip, cayenne, chamomile, chickweed, licorice, mullein, nettle, peppermint, raspberry leaf, red clover, rose hips, slippery elm, and yellow dock.

DOSAGES

The AAFCO recommends 11.4 mg/kg of niacin daily for dogs and 60 mg/kg of niacin for cats each day.

SAFETY ISSUES

In people, when taken at a dosage of more than 100 mg daily, niacin frequently causes annoying skin flushing, especially in the face. This reaction may be accompanied by stomach distress, itching, and headache. In studies, as many as 43% of individuals taking niacin quit because of unpleasant side effects.

A more dangerous effect of niacin is liver inflammation. Although most commonly seen with slow-release niacin, it can occur with any type of niacin when taken at a daily dose of more than 500 mg. Regular blood tests to evaluate liver function are therefore mandatory when using high-dose niacin (or niacinamide or inositol hexaniacinate). This side effect almost always goes away when niacin is stopped. People with liver disease, ulcers (presently or in the past), gout, or diabetes should not take high-dose niacin except on medical advice.

Maximum safe dosages for young children and pregnant or nursing women have not been established. Pets are not routinely treated with niacin. However, similar precautions are probably warranted if your pet is prescribed niacin.

As is the case in human medicine, if your pet is taking cholesterol-lowering drugs in the statin family, he should probably not take additional niacin. Pets taking older cholesterol-lowering drugs such as cholestyramine or colestipol should take niacin at a different time of day to avoid absorption problems based on the recommendation in human medicine.

Pets taking the antituberculosis drug isoniazid may need extra niacin. However, because niacin can interfere with INH, doctor supervision is necessary.

 # VITAMIN B$_5$ (Pantothenic acid, Calcium pantothenate)

Common Use
  Stress

Pantothenic acid, vitamin B$_5$, is known as the anti-stress vitamin since it is involved in the production of adrenal hormones and antibodies produced by the body's white blood cells. Like other B vitamins, it assists in vitamin metabolism and helps in the conversion of fats, proteins, and carbohydrates into energy for the body.

It is an essential part of acetyl coenzyme A, also called coenzyme A (by acetylating acetic acid in the cell). Acetyl coenzyme A is involved in energy production for the cell via the production of ATP.

Vitamin B_5 enhances stamina, and is involved in the production of neurotransmitters. It may help prevent and treat depression and anxiety and is useful for normal function of the intestinal tract.

In people, vitamin B_5 deficiency causes fatigue, nausea, and headache.

There are no specific disease conditions in pets for which vitamin B_5 therapy is indicated.

SOURCES

Vitamin B_5 is obtained in the diet from beef, brewer's yeast, eggs, vegetables, organ meats (especially liver and heart), rice and wheat bran, mushrooms, saltwater fish, and whole wheat.

The AAFCO recommends levels of 10 ppm for dogs and 5 ppm for cats.

SAFETY ISSUES

Vitamin B_5 is considered a safe vitamin.

VITAMIN B_6 (Pyridoxine, Pyridoxine hydrochloride, pyridoxal-5-phosphate)

Common Use
Nutritional supplement

Vitamin B_6 plays a major role in making proteins, hormones, and neurotransmitters (chemicals that carry signals between nerve cells).

Cats have a higher requirement for vitamin B_6 (pyridoxine) due to high transaminase activity from their high protein requirement.

Pyridoxine affects physical and mental health and is needed for most body functions. It maintains sodium and potassium balance and is necessary in water regulation by the body. It is needed for fat and protein absorption. Vitamin B_6 is a coenzyme to over 50 different reactions in the body's cells transamination (where nitrogen is added to a fatty acid to form an amino acid) and decarboxylation (where a carbon is removed to shorten an amino acid chain).

Pyridoxine promotes red blood cell production, is needed for normal brain function, and also is needed for DNA and RNA synthesis. Vitamin B_6 is needed for the absorption of vitamin B_{12} and is also used for antibody formation and immune system functioning.

SCIENTIFIC EVIDENCE

Homocysteine, which in people is involved in heart muscle damage and the formation of atherosclerosis, is inhibited by pyridoxine. There is convincing evidence in people that an adequate nutritional intake of vitamin B_6 (as low as 2 to 4 mg daily) can significantly reduce the risk of heart disease. According to data gathered in the Nurses' Health Study, one of the largest long-term medical studies ever performed, vitamin B_6 supplements can significantly reduce a woman's risk of developing heart disease. A total of 80,000 women with no history of heart disease were studied for possible links between vitamin B_6, folic acid, and the development of heart disease. The results showed that adequate intake of B_6 (3 to 4 mg daily) could significantly reduce the risk of heart disease. Folic acid was also effective.

As mentioned, vitamin B_6 reduces blood levels of homocysteine, a chemical that has been linked to hardening of the arteries and heart disease. At first, it was assumed that the benefits of vitamin B6 were all due to reducing homocysteine. However, a subsequent study found no association between high homocysteine levels and the risk of heart disease. Instead, researchers found a connection between heart disease and low levels of vitamin B6. People with the highest vitamin B6 levels were 28% less likely to develop heart disease than those with the lowest B6 levels. This study has led to the hypothesis that it is vitamin B6 itself that reduces heart disease risk, and the reduction of homocysteine seen at the same time is simply incidental. However, the matter remains controversial.

Vitamin B6 may help the heart in several ways. Preliminary studies suggest that it can reduce the tendency of platelets in the blood to form clots, and also lower blood pressure to some extent.

A large double-blind study suggests that a higher dose (30 mg daily) of vitamin B6 can reduce the nausea of morning sickness (as can the herb ginger).

Other common uses of B6 are not very well established. For example, vitamin B6 is widely recommended by conventional physicians as a treatment for carpal tunnel syndrome. However, there is little to no evidence that it actually works. Similarly, although B6 is frequently suggested as a treatment for PMS (premenstrual syndrome), there is some fairly good evidence that it doesn't work for this purpose.

Some natural medicine authorities state that vitamin B6 is a useful treatment for diabetic neuropathy. This idea is based on the fact that B6 deficiency can cause neuropathy, and people with diabetes may be low in B6. However, there is clinical evidence that B6 supplements do not help diabetic neuropathy.

Very weak evidence suggests that B6 may be helpful for depression, allergy to monosodium glutamate (MSG, a highly allergenic food additive used to enhance flavor), asthma, diabetes caused by pregnancy (gestational diabetes), and kidney stones.

A double-blind study of 76 children with asthma found significant benefit after one month. Children in the vitamin B6 group were able to reduce their doses of asthma medication (bronchodilators and steroids). However, a recent double-blind study of 31 adults who used either inhaled or oral steroids did not show any benefit. The dosages of B6 used in these studies were quite high, in the range of 200 to 300 mg daily. Because of the risk of nerve injury, it is not advisable to take this much B6 without medical supervision.

Finally, an interesting series of studies suggests (but certainly don't prove) that the combination of vitamin B6 and magnesium can be helpful in autism.

THERAPEUTIC USES

Patients with kidney stones made of oxalate can benefit from this vitamin. Like other B vitamins, vitamin B6 may aid in cancer prevention.

In pets, there are no specific indications for additional supplementation with vitamin B6. (Vitamin B6 increases the transamination of glyoxylate, which is a precursor of oxalic acid, to glycine. Experimentally induced B6 deficiency predisposes the precipitation of calcium oxalate in the kidneys of kittens. A naturally occurring form of this syndrome, called oxalate precipitation, has not been identified, although B6 dietary deficiency will increase endogenous production of and urinary excretion of oxalic acid. Additional B6 was associated with decreased oxalic acid excretion in diets of cats consuming diets deficient in vitamin B6. It is unknown whether giving additional vitamin B6 will reduce the urinary excretion of oxalic acid and therefore reduce the incidence of oxalic acid **bladder stones** (page 40).

SOURCES

Good sources of B6 include nutritional (torula) yeast, brewer's yeast, sunflower seeds, wheat germ, soybeans, walnuts, lentils, lima beans, buckwheat flour, bananas, fish, eggs, meat, spinach, carrots, broccoli, brown rice, whole grains, potatoes, and avocados, as well as wheat, green foods, alfalfa, and catnip.

DOSAGES

The AAFCO recommendations for vitamin B6 are 1 mg/kg of food daily for dogs and 4 mg/kg of food daily for cats.

Vitamin B6

SAFETY ISSUES

Vitamin B₆ appears to be completely safe for adults and pets. However, dogs fed more than 200 mg/kg of body weight per day have a very real risk of nerve damage.

In people, dietary deficiency can be worsened by use of estrogen, progesterone, antibiotics in the tetracycline family, corticosteroids (such as prednisone), hydralazine (for high blood pressure), penicillamine (used for rheumatoid arthritis and certain rare diseases), Dilantin (phenytoin for seizures), theophylline (an older drug for asthma), and the antituberculosis drug isoniazid (INH), all of which are thought to interfere with B₆ to some degree. Additional B₆ is recommended for people in these circumstances; similar recommendations may be prudent in pets.

VITAMIN B₈ (See Inositol)

VITAMIN B₁₂ (Cobalamin, methylcobalamin, cyanocobalamin, hydrocobalamin)

Common Use
Nutritional supplement

Vitamin B₁₂, an essential nutrient, is also known as cobalamin. The "cobal" in the name refers to the metal cobalt contained in B₁₂. Vitamin B₁₂ is required for the normal activity of nerve cells (the myelin sheaths covering nerves require B₁₂ for normal growth and development, and vitamin B₁₂ is involved in the production of the neurotransmitter acetylcholine). It works with folic acid and vitamin B₆ to lower blood levels of homocysteine, a chemical in the blood that is thought to contribute to heart disease.

Cyanocobalamin, also called cobalt, is needed to regulate proper red blood cell production. Vitamin B₁₂, like other B vitamins, is needed for the metabolism of proteins, fats, and carbohydrates.

Vitamin B₁₂ also plays a role in the body's manufacture of S-adenosylmethionine, or SAMe.

Anemia is usually the first sign of B₁₂ deficiency. Earlier in this century, doctors coined the name "pernicious anemia" for a stubborn anemia that didn't improve even when the patient was given iron supplements. Today we know that pernicious anemia is usually caused by a condition in which the stomach fails to excrete a special substance called intrinsic factor. The body needs the intrinsic factor for efficient absorption of vitamin B₁₂. In 1948, vitamin B₁₂ was identified as the cure for pernicious anemia.

The vitamin B₁₂ in food comes attached to proteins, and must be released by acid in the stomach in order to be absorbed. When stomach acid levels are low, people and pets don't absorb as much vitamin B₁₂ from food. Fortunately, vitamin B₁₂ supplements don't need acid for absorption. For this reason, people taking medications that greatly reduce stomach acid, such as Prilosec or Zantac, should probably also take B₁₂ supplements (similar recommendations for pets have not been made but may be prudent).

SOURCES

Vitamin B₁₂ is found mainly in animal tissues and few vegetables; owners feeding a mostly vegetarian diet must be sure to use vitamin supplements containing B₁₂. The diets in Part Three, Diet, supply vitamin B₁₂ through the inclusion of sardines.

Good sources are eggs, chicken liver, beef liver, kidney, beef, lamb, dairy products, seafood, fish, brewer's yeast, and soy products. Also green goods, alfalfa, herbs, hops, and bladder wrack supply Vitamin B_{12}.

DOSAGES

The AAFCO recommendation for vitamin B_{12} is 22 micrograms/kg of food per day for dogs and 20 micrograms/kg of food per day for cats.

VITAMIN B₁₅ (See DMG)

VITAMIN C (Ascorbate, ascorbic acid)

Common Uses
Nutritional supplement for arthritis, allergy, epilepsy, cancer prevention, immune support

Vitamin C is a water-soluble vitamin that is required by people and some animals. Humans and certain animals (such as guinea pigs and monkeys) lack the enzyme L-gulonolactone oxidase needed for the formation of vitamin C. Dogs and cats possess this enzyme and can therefore synthesize vitamin C. As such, dogs and cats do not have a specific dietary requirement for this vitamin. Many doctors, however, will supplement with vitamin C during times of stress and illness (as larger amounts of vitamin C may be required during these times).

Ascorbic acid is a term often used interchangeably with vitamin C. While ascorbic acid (as well as ascorbate and other terms) is often used synonymously with vitamin C, this is not technically correct. Ascorbic acid (discovered in 1928, when Albert Szent-Gyorgyi isolated the active ingredient in fruits and called the "anti-scorbutic principle") is the antioxidant fraction of vitamin C. Simply supplementing ascorbic acid is not the same as supplying vitamin C. Holistic veterinarians usually prefer natural vitamin C

SAFETY ISSUES

Vitamin B_{12} appears to be extremely safe.

People taking medications including antacids, phenobarbital, colchicine, corticosteroids, Dilantin (phenytoin), long-term sulfa antibiotics, antipsychotic drugs, isoniazid (INH), methotrexate, methyldopa, metformin, phenformin, oral contraceptives, triamterene, nitrous oxide, cholestyramine, colestipol, or clofibrate may need extra B_{12}; the same recommendations have not been proven in pets but may be indicated.

supplementation when indicated, although studies using the complementary therapy called **orthomolecular medicine** (page 415 in Part Four) have shown benefit to using ascorbate in helping pets with a variety of medical disorders. A novel product called Ester-C has also shown benefit in pets (discussed to follow).

Vitamin C functions as an antioxidant and free radical scavenger, is used for normal repair of tissues, is required for adrenal gland function, is used for collagen synthesis, and is needed for maintaining healthy gums. It is needed for the metabolism of several B vitamins, including folic acid and the amino acids tyrosine and phenylalanine. Vitamin C is needed for norepinephrine (a nerve transmitter) synthesis as well as for cholesterol synthesis.

THERAPEUTIC USES

This vitamin assists in providing some protection against **cancer** (page 44) and **infection** (page 105) and enhances immunity. Hemoglobin synthesis requires vitamin C; deficiency can cause anemia.

Because vitamin C is so vital for the synthesis of the connective tissue collagen, which is an integral part of cartilage, it is often prescribed for pets with **arthritis** (page 11) (and various forms of vitamin C or ascorbate are often included in various nutritional supplements for pets with arthritis).

To have normal collagen metabolism, vitamin C is required for the conversion of proline to hydroxyproline and for the conversion of lysine to hydroxylysine. These reactions take place after proline and lysine are incorporated into the connective tissue.

Vitamin C also protects against unnecessary blood clotting and bruising and aids in healing of wounds; vitamin C deficiency causes slow scar formation.

Ascorbic acid is a precursor of oxalate. It has been suggested that additional ascorbic acid should not be fed to pets prone to oxalate bladder stones. However, at least in people, there is no evidence that high levels of ascorbic acid actually increase oxalate production.

Vitamin C appears to work synergistically as an antioxidant with vitamin E. Vitamin C appears to attack free radicals, those chemicals produced as a by-product of cell metabolism, in cellular fluids, whereas vitamin E attacks the free radicals in the cell membranes.

In people, vitamin C has been recommended for numerous conditions, including colds, cataracts, macular degeneration, cancer prevention and treatment, heart disease prevention, hypertension, asthma, low sperm count, bedsores, Alzheimer's disease, diabetes, hepatitis, herpes, insomnia, osteoarthritis, Parkinson's disease, periodontal disease, preeclampsia, rheumatoid arthritis, ulcers, allergies, general antioxidant, bladder infections, menopausal symptoms, migraine headaches, and nausea.

Ascorbic acid scavenges nitrates, which can reduce nitrosamine-induced cancers.

There is some evidence that supports using vitamin C supplements to help colds, slightly improve asthma, and reduce the risk of macular degeneration and cataracts.

In people, vitamin C deficiency causes scurvy with the clinical signs of swollen, painful joints, abnormal wound healing, bleeding gums, and pinpoint hemorrhages under the skin. Vitamin C deficiency, while common in non-human primates (monkeys) and guinea pigs, does not occur in dogs and cats.

SCIENTIFIC EVIDENCE

Regular use of vitamin C may reduce the risk of cataracts, probably by fighting free radicals that damage the lens of the eye. In an observational study of 50,800 nurses followed for 8 years, it was found that people who used vitamin C supplements for more than 10 years had a 45% lower rate of cataract development. However, unlike the case with other supplements, diets high in vitamin C were not found to be protective; only supplemental vitamin C made a difference. This is the opposite of what has been found with vitamin C in the prevention of other diseases, such as cancer.

It has been suggested that vitamin C may be particularly useful against cataracts in people with diabetes, because of its influence on sorbitol, a sugar-like substance that tends to accumulate in the cells of diabetics. Excess sorbitol is believed to play a role in the development of diabetes-related cataracts, and vitamin C appears to help reduce sorbitol buildup.

Vitamin C levels in the blood have been found to be low in people with diabetes. When vitamin C levels were adequate, the regulation of insulin improved, as vitamin C has been shown to enhance insulin action and improve glucose and lipid metabolism. Therefore, vitamin C supplementation may benefit both insulin-dependent and non-insulin-dependent diabetics. It is unknown if this is the case in diabetic pets, although vitamin C has been recommended for pets with diabetes.

There is also good evidence for using ascorbate for people with gingivitis. Evidence for its effectiveness in treating other conditions is highly preliminary at best.

In people, aspirin, other anti-inflammatory drugs, corticosteroids, and tetracycline-family antibiotics can lower body levels of vitamin C. The same may be true of pets; vitamin C given to pets treated with the medications mentioned above is not harmful and might be helpful.

Pets are often treated with additional vitamin C or ascorbate compounds for various illnesses. Both intravenous and oral supplementation are used, although controlled studies are lacking showing the effectiveness of giving vitamin C or ascorbate compounds for most conditions.

Orthomolecular medicine (page 415) utilizes high doses of antioxidants to help pets with a variety of medical conditions. Ascorbate has shown effectiveness (when combined with other antioxidants) in clinical cases of pets with **epilepsy** (page 73), **atopic dermatitis** (page 3), **feline leukemia virus** (page 82), **periodontal disease** (page 61), and **osteoarthritis** (page 11).

Ester-C Chelated Mineral Blend for Animals is a patented, non-acidic form of calcium ascorbate that contains the essential minerals calcium, magnesium, manganese, and zinc bound in a pH neutral complex along with vitamin C metabolites (naturally occurring dehydroascorbate and threonate) that enhance the absorption of vitamin C. This form of ascorbate is often preferred by some veterinarians as Ester-C permits rapid absorption from the gastrointestinal tract (resulting in less chance of gastrointestinal disturbances such as diarrhea). Also, Ester-C produces higher serum levels, higher WBC levels, less oxalate excretion, and less urinary ascorbate loss than ascorbic acid.

In numerous clinical trials and studies in the U.S. and Norway, Ester-C mineral ascorbates have been shown beneficial in alleviating signs of non-specific lameness in dogs and degenerative joint disease (DJD) in horses and chronic obstructive pulmonary disease (COPD) in horses. Specifically, a study done in arthritic dogs showed that 62% of dogs receiving the Chelated Mineral Blend given at a dosage of 45 mg/kg of body weight twice daily experienced improved locomotion within 5 to 8 days of usage (44% of dogs on plain ascorbic acid at the same dosage showed some improvement, and two dogs experienced mild gastrointestinal disturbances).

SOURCES

Citrus fruits, green vegetables, berries, broccoli, brussels sprouts, collard greens, mustard greens, spinach, chard, turnip greens, red chili peppers, sweet peppers, kale, parsley, watercress, cauliflower, cabbage, and strawberries are good sources of vitamin C, as are green foods, alfalfa, herbs, rose hips, dandelion, fennel, and slippery elm.

DOSAGES

In people, good evidence suggests that there is no reason to take more than 200 mg of vitamin C daily (which is approximately 10 to 100 times less than the amount recommended by vitamin C proponents). The reason is that if people consume more than 200 mg daily (researchers have tested up to 2,500 mg), their kidneys begin to excrete the excess at a steadily increasing rate, matching the increased dose. Additionally, their digestive tracts also stop absorbing it well at higher doses. The net effect is that even with increasing doses, blood levels of vitamin C don't increase. There is no evidence to suggest the maximum dose at which pets stop absorbing vitamin C or begin excreting extra vitamin C (orthomolecular therapy uses higher doses than 200 mg).

As dogs and cats manufacture their own vitamin C, there is no AAFCO recommendation for including vitamin C in the diets or supplements of dogs and cats. Many natural foods will use vitamin C (often supplied as rose hips) or various forms of ascorbate (or ascorbic acid) as a natural preservative. Contacting the manufacturer will allow the owner to determine the level in the food, although pets requiring vitamin C will need more than the amount added to the food as a natural antioxidant.

SAFETY ISSUES

Vitamin C is a safe vitamin. High oral doses (which vary from pet to pet) may cause people and pets to develop diarrhea. This is the "bowel tolerance" dose; in **orthomolecular medicine** (page 415), vitamin C is often dosed to bowel tolerance.

In people, high-dose vitamin C can cause copper deficiency and excessive iron absorption. There have also been warnings that long-term vitamin C treatment can cause kidney stones, but in a large-scale study the people who took the most vitamin C (over 1,500 mg daily) actually

Vitamin C

had a lower risk of kidney stones than those taking the least amounts. Nonetheless, people with a history of kidney stones and those with kidney failure who have a defect in vitamin C or oxalate metabolism should probably restrict vitamin C intake to approximately 100 mg daily. While there is no evidence that stone formation increases in people or pets supplemented with vi-

tamin C, talk with your veterinarian before adding extra vitamin C if your pet is prone to urinary stones.

Vitamin C may also reduce the blood-thinning effects of Coumadin (warfarin) and heparin.

Vitamin C may increase the blood levels of some drugs, such as aspirin and other salicylates.

 VITAMIN D (Cholecalciferol [vitamin D3] Ergocalciferol [vitamin D2])

Common Uses
Nutritional supplement

Vitamin D (a fat-soluble vitamin) is needed for proper absorption of calcium and phosphorus from the intestinal tract. It is needed for normal growth and development of bones and teeth, protects against muscle weakness, and regulates the heart. Vitamin D helps prevent hypocalcemia and osteoporosis, enhances immunity, and is needed for proper thyroid function and blood clotting.

Vitamin D in food or supplements is converted into an active form by ultraviolet light from the sun acting on the vitamin D precursor located in the skin, and then metabolism by the liver and kidney.

Vitamin D is both a vitamin and a hormone. It is a vitamin because your pet's body cannot absorb calcium without it; it's a hormone because your pet's body manufactures it in response to the skin's exposure to sunlight. However, recent research suggests that dogs and cats have low levels of vitamin D activation by UV-B light due to low levels of vitamin D in the skin, indicating that supplementation of vitamin D may be needed. Processed foods contain enough vitamin D and do not need supplementation; homemade diets such as those listed in Part Three contain adequate vitamin D due to the recommendation for supplementation with vitamin supplements.

There are two major forms of vitamin D, and both have the word calciferol in their names (in Latin, calciferol means "calcium carrier"). Vita-

min D_3 (cholecalciferol) is made by the body and is found in some foods. Vitamin D_2 (ergocalciferol) is the form most often added to milk and other foods, and the form most likely to be included in synthetic supplements; it is also the form found in plants.

THERAPEUTIC USES

Vitamin D promotes the intestinal absorption of calcium and subsequent urinary calcium excretion. Reducing dietary phosphorus increases activation of vitamin D, which promotes more intestinal absorption of calcium and urinary calcium excretion. Pets with oxalate urinary (bladder) stones should not be fed diets with restricted levels of dietary phosphorus for this reason.

Vitamin D supplementation is not usually needed as part of a holistic treatment for pets, as vitamin D deficiency is unlikely to occur (unless it occurs as part of calcium deficiency due to the interaction of these compounds).

In people, there is reasonably good evidence that the combination of vitamin D and calcium supplements can be quite helpful for preventing and treating osteoporosis (an extremely unlikely disease in most pets).

Vitamin D deficiency causes a bone disorder called rickets and osteomalacia. Vitamin D toxicity results in calcification of blood vessels and organs.

Vitamin D and the Skin

Vitamin D is the only vitamin that can be produced in the skin. In the epidermis (outer layer of skin), vitamin D_3 (cholecalciferol) is formed from pro-vitamin D_3 (7-dehydrocholesterol) on exposure to sunlight. The cholecalciferol is then transported to the circulation from the skin via the vitamin D-binding protein in plasma. Cholecalciferol is then transported to the liver where it is hydroxylated to 25-hydroxyvitamin D_3, transported to the kidney, and hydroxylated into 12,25-dihydrovitamin D_3, which is used in the regulation in the proliferation and differentiation of the epidermis.

In people, exposure to sunlight provides adequate levels of vitamin D. However, recent research suggests that dogs and cats have low levels of vitamin D activation by UV-B light due to low levels of vitamin D in the skin, indicating that supplementation of vitamin D may be needed.

SOURCES

Fish liver oil (cod liver oil), coldwater fish (such as mackerel, salmon, and herring), butter, egg yolks, dairy products, liver, oatmeal, and sweet potatoes are good sources of vitamin D. Most vegetables provide little vitamin D, but dark-green leafy vegetables do contain some. Also green foods and herbs, including horsetail and nettle, contain vitamin D.

SCIENTIFIC EVIDENCE

Some evidence suggests that vitamin D may help prevent cancer of the breast, colon, pancreas, and prostate, but the research on this question has yielded mixed results.

Vitamin D is sometimes mentioned as a treatment for psoriasis. However, this recommendation is based on Danish studies using calcipotriol, a variation of vitamin D_3 that is used externally (applied to the skin).

Today, severe vitamin D deficiency in people is rare in the developed world. However, it is sometimes seen in elderly people who don't get enough sunlight. Marginal vitamin D deficiency may also occur in people who live in northern latitudes and don't drink vitamin D–enriched milk. Additionally, carbamazepine, phenytoin, primidone and phenobarbital (for seizures), corticosteroids, cimetidine (for ulcers), colestipol and cholestyramine (older drugs used for lowering cholesterol), and the antituberculosis drug isoniazid (INH) may interfere with vitamin D absorption or activity.

It is unlikely for most pets to develop vitamin D deficiency. Reptiles most commonly develop vitamin D and calcium deficiency due to lack of vitamin D and calcium in the diet, as well as lack of exposure to UV light.

DOSAGES

AAFCO recommendations for dietary vitamin D are 500 IU/kg of food for dogs (maintenance, growth, and reproduction) and 500 IU/kg of food (maintenance) to 750 IU/kg of food (reproduction) for cats. Kittens seem to require 250 IU/kg of food, which is less than the current AAFCO recommendations of 750 IU/kg of food.

SAFETY ISSUES

When taken at recommended dosages, vitamin D appears to be safe. However, when taken to excess, vitamin D can build up in the body and cause severe symptoms of toxicity. In people, toxic symptoms (ranging from headaches, weight loss, and kidney stones, to deafness, blindness, and death) are seen when dosages above 1,200 mg daily are taken for long periods of time.

In pets, vitamin D levels should not exceed 10,000 IU/kg of food, although some brands of moist foods exceed this level.

People with sarcoidosis or hyperparathyroidism should never take vitamin D without first consulting a physician. Pets do not get sarcoidosis; however, similar precautions are probably warranted in pets with hyperparathyroidism when taking vitamin D supplements.

Vitamin D toxicity will not occur when using whole food sources rather than synthetic forms of vitamin D.

In people taking antiseizure drugs (carbamazepine, phenobarbital, primidone, valproic acid or phenytoin), corticosteroids, Coumadin (warfarin), H2 blockers (Zantac, for example), heparin, isoniazid (INH), rifampin, verapamil, or the older cholesterol-lowering drugs colestipol and cholestyramine, there may be a need for extra vitamin D. The same need may also apply to pets, although this has not been well researched and most doctors do not give additional vitamin D to pets taking these medications.

Vitamin D toxicity can occur in pets. The D_3 form appears to be more toxic than the D_2 form. In reptiles, vitamin D toxicity commonly occurs due to oversupplementation by owners.

In dogs and cats, vitamin D toxicity most commonly results from poisoning with vitamin D rodenticides (rodent poisons). These poisons cause increased levels of blood calcium that can be fatal.

VITAMIN E

Common Uses
Nutritional supplement

Vitamin E, a fat-soluble vitamin, is an antioxidant that is used in conjunction with vitamin C as a natural antioxidant in some processed foods (replacing the chemicals BHA, BHT, and ethoxyqin for preservation of food). It works in lipids (fats and oils), which makes it complementary to vitamin C, which fights free radicals dissolved in water. Vitamin E works in conjunction with glutathione peroxidase to protect cells from oxidation. Vitamin E in cellular and subcellular membranes acts as a first line of defense against oxidation of vital membrane phospholipids. Selenium works with vitamin E; as a part of the enzyme glutathione peroxidase, selenium acts as a second line of defense against membrane peroxidation.

While alpha-tocopherol is the form of vitamin E most commonly used as a preservative in pet foods, the more natural foods use mixed tocopherols.

Of all the antioxidants so much in the news today, vitamin E has the best evidence for its effectiveness.

THERAPEUTIC USES

Impressive studies in people suggest that it can significantly reduce the risk of heart disease and various forms of cancer. Vitamin E has also shown considerable promise for improving immunity and slowing the progression of Alzheimer's disease.

Vitamin E promotes normal blood clotting, aids in preventing cataracts, maintains healthy nerves and muscles, and promotes healthy skin and hair.

Vitamin E prevents cell damage by inhibiting oxidation of fats (in conjunction with selenium) and inhibiting the formation of free radicals produced by cell damage. It aids in the utilization of vitamin A and protects it and other fat-soluble vitamins from oxidation. Vitamin E requirements increase with increasing dietary levels of fatty acids, oxidizing agents, vitamin A, and trace minerals.

As is the case with vitamin A, vitamin E is recommended for treating pets with several disorders that may benefit from high doses of antioxidants. These include **epilepsy** (page 73), allergies (**atopic dermatitis,** page 3), food allergies, **feline leukemia** (page 82) and **immunodeficiency virus infections** (page 76). (See the section on **orthomolecular medicine** in Part Four for a greater discussion of these various disorders.)

Cognitive disorder is related to Alzheimer's disease in people. While most commonly seen in dogs, cats can also develop cognitive disorder. While there are no controlled studies suggesting that vitamin E is helpful in pets with cognitive disorder, since it does help people with Alzheimer's (a similar condition), it might be helpful to add vitamin E to the treatment regimen of pets with cognitive disorder.

Vitamin E is a mild antagonist to leukotriene formation (leukotrienes are pro-inflammatory chemicals formed from the conversion of arachidonic acid in damaged cell membranes). As such, it is often used in certain immune skin disorders, including discoid lupus erythematosus (DLE), pemphigus erythematosus, epidermolysis bullosa, and acanthosis nigricans with variable results. The dosage in dogs is 100 to 400 mg per pet twice daily, and is usually combined with omega-3 fatty acids.

While some holistic doctors have reported success when using vitamin E (as part of **orthomolecular medicine**, page 415) for pets with atopic dermatitis, using only dl-alpha-tocopherol at doses used for pets with immune skin disorders has not proved effective.

Vitamin E has been recommended for treating dogs with demodectic mange as low serum levels of vitamin E have been reported in some dogs with this disorder. Other studies have failed to support this finding. Vitamin E by itself has not been shown effective in dogs with demodectic mange (although holistic doctors may prescribe it and other antioxidants as part of orthomolecular therapy for any skin disorder to support the immune system).

Vitamin E (and selenium) deficiency results in a neuromuscular disease called white muscle disease. In people, reduced levels of vitamin E have been linked to breast cancer and bowel cancer and heart disease; this link with cancer has not been established in dogs and cats (although the link for white muscle disease of the heart is well-known).

Weak evidence suggests that vitamin E can improve blood sugar control in people with type II diabetes, prevent cataracts, and slow the progression of osteoarthritis.

Vitamin E is frequently recommended for treating asthma in people, but there is no scientific evidence that it works

SYNTHETIC VS. WHOLE VITAMIN

While vitamin E is often erroneously referred to as "tocopherol" or "alpha-tocopherol," the toco-

pherols (alpha, beta, gamma, and delta) and tocotrienols (alpha, beta, gamma, and delta) are just a part of the vitamin E complex. Synthetic vitamins supplying only alpha-tocopherol are only supplying a part (the antioxidant part) of the entire vitamin E complex. For this reason many doctors prefer providing natural vitamins made from raw foods or whole food complexes (often called "mixed tocopherols" on the label) to supply the entire complex of vitamin E to maintain health.

The most common tocopherol used in supplements is a synthetic form called DL-alpha-tocopherol. However, there is some evidence that natural forms of vitamin E (beta-, delta-, and gamma-tocopherols, as well as other compounds in the tocopherol family such as tocotrienols) are more effective. Natural vitamin E also differs from the synthetic form in that natural vitamin E comes in a form called a D-isomer (synthetic vitamin E contains a mixture of D- and L-isomers).

It has been suggested that the best vitamin E supplement would be a natural mixture of tocopherols, including alpha-, delta-, and gamma- ("mixed tocopherols"), all of which should be in the "D" form. Unfortunately, all the scientific evidence we have for the effectiveness of vitamin E supplements comes from studies using synthetic DL-alpha-tocopherol, so at this point we have no direct confirmation that natural vitamin E is better.

Note: If you wish to purchase natural vitamin E, look for a label that says "mixed tocopherols." However, some manufacturers use this term to mean the synthetic DL-alpha-tocopherol, so you need to read the contents closely. Natural tocopherols come as D-alpha-, D-gamma-, D-delta-, and D-beta-tocopherol. Check with your veterinarian for further help.

SOURCES

Dark, leafy green vegetables, whole grains, brown rice, eggs, liver, milk, organ meats, soybeans, kelp, sweet potatoes, wheat, green foods, alfalfa, herbs, nettle, rose hips, and raspberry leaf are all sources of vitamin E.

Vitamin E

Vitamin E

SCIENTIFIC EVIDENCE

Vitamin E is the best-documented antioxidant supplement for the prevention of heart disease in people. It seems to be able to reduce the risk of heart disease and nonfatal heart attacks in people by 40 to 80%, depending on the dose. One large observational study (over 11,000 participants) suggests that intake of both vitamins E and C will give even better results.

Although we don't really know how vitamin E works to prevent heart disease in people, there are several theories. One points out that vitamin E protects fats and cholesterol from being converted by free radicals into an especially damaging form. Another possible explanation hinges on vitamin E's effect on the formation of dangerous blood clots. Platelets stick to the walls of blood vessels damaged by atherosclerosis, forming blood clots that can then break off and cause heart attacks and strokes. Like aspirin, vitamin E interferes with the activity of blood platelets.

Vitamin E appears to offer dramatic benefits for preventing prostate and colon cancer. In an intervention trial that involved 29,133 smokers, those who were given about 50 IU of vitamin E daily for 5 to 8 years showed a 32% lower incidence of prostate cancer, a 41% drop in prostate cancer deaths, and a 16% decrease in the incidence of colon cancer.

Surprisingly, these benefits were seen fairly soon after the start of supplementation, even though prostate cancer is very slow-growing. A cancer that shows up today had its start many years ago. The fact that vitamin E almost immediately lowered the incidence of prostate cancer suggests that it somehow blocks the step at which a hidden prostate cancer makes the leap into becoming detectable.

Vitamin E may be even more effective in people who do not smoke. Researchers at the Fred Hutchinson Cancer Research Center in Seattle found that regular use of supplemental vitamin E (200 IU or more daily) cut colon cancer risk by 57%. Another observational study found a 29 to 59% reduction, based on the length of time of using vitamin E.

A double-blind study suggests that vitamin E may be able to strengthen immunity. In this study, 88 people over the age of 65 were given either placebo or vitamin E at 60 IU, 200 IU, or 800 IU daily. The researchers then gave all participants immunizations against hepatitis B, tetanus, diphtheria, and pneumonia, and looked at subjects' immune response to these vaccinations. The researchers also used a skin test that evaluates the overall strength of the immune response.

The results were impressive. Vitamin E at all dosages significantly increased the strength of the immune response. However, a daily dosage of 200 IU produced the most marked benefits.

Preliminary evidence suggests that high-dose vitamin E may slow the progression of Alzheimer's disease. In a double-blind placebo-controlled study, 341 subjects received either 2,000 IU daily of vitamin E (an extremely high dose), the antioxidant drug selegiline, or placebo. Those given vitamin E took nearly 200 days longer to reach a severe state of the disease than the placebo group. (The drug selegiline was even more effective.)

DOSAGES

The AAFCO recommendation for vitamin E is 50 IU/kg of food for dogs and 30 IU/kg of food for cats. For foods containing fish oil, additional antioxidation is needed and it is recommended that an additional amount of vitamin E be added to the diet (10 IU of vitamin E/gm of fish oil/kg of food).

SAFETY ISSUES

In people, vitamin E is generally regarded as safe when taken at the recommended dosage of 400 to 800 IU daily. However, vitamin E does have a "blood-thinning" effect that could lead to problems in certain situations. In one study, vitamin E supplementation at the low dose of 50 IU per day was associated with an increase in hemorrhagic stroke, the kind of stroke caused by bleeding.

Based on its blood-thinning effects, there are concerns that vitamin E could cause problems if it is combined with medications that also thin the blood, such as Coumadin (warfarin), heparin, and aspirin. Theoretically, the net result could be to thin the blood too much, causing bleeding problems. However, the results of studies in people suggests that vitamin E up to 1,200 IU daily can be used safely with Coumadin; another study showed that vitamin E plus aspirin is safe and may help prevent the type of stroke caused by obstruction.

Likewise, there is also a remote possibility that vitamin E could also interact with herbs that possess a mild blood-thinning effect, such as garlic and *Ginkgo biloba*. Individuals with bleeding disorders such as hemophilia, and those about to undergo surgery or labor and delivery should also approach vitamin E with caution; similar warnings and precautions are probably warranted in pets.

Vitamin E is one of the safest vitamins; doses above the recommended maximum of 1,000 IU/kg of diet for dogs appear safe. However, higher levels of vitamin E may antagonize other vitamins. Pets taking high doses of vitamin E may need extra levels of vitamins A, D, and K. Once again, most pets taking whole food sources of vitamin E will not have this problem as most of these supplements will contain vitamin K as well (be sure to check with your veterinarian).

VITAMIN K

Common Use
Nutritional supplement

Vitamin K, a fat-soluble vitamin, is needed for the proper clotting of blood (it plays a major role in the carboxylation of clotting proteins II, VI, IX, and X and proteins C and S). It may also help prevent osteoporosis, as it is needed for the synthesis of the bone protein (osteocalcin) involved in calcium crystallization (via the incorporation of calcium phosphates in growing bone). Vitamin K exists as vitamin K_1 (phylloquinone) and K_2 (menaquinone), the natural forms found in food, and as vitamin K_3, the synthetic form called menadione. Both vitamins K_1 and K_2 are converted to dihydrovitamin K upon digestion.

Intestinal (colonic) bacteria manufacture a large amount of the vitamin K (K_2) present in tissues throughout the body; therefore, supplementation with dietary vitamin K is usually not necessary in people and pets.

Deficiency of vitamin K causes excess internal or external bleeding due to a failure of the body to properly clot blood. In dogs and cats, this most commonly occurs as a result of rodent poisons containing warfarin or warfarin-type chemicals. Diseases causing maldigestion and malabsorption as well as destruction of bacteria in the colon by antibiotic therapy can also cause vitamin K deficiency. Supplementation with probiotic bacteria can help restore vitamin K production.

Severe liver deficiency may decrease the activation of vitamin K in the liver, resulting in defective carboxylation of vitamin-K dependent coagulation cofactors, resulting in bleeding disorders due to faulty blood clotting.

Vitamin K also aids in converting glucose into glycogen for energy storage in the liver. Healthy liver function is also promoted by vitamin K.

THERAPEUTIC USES

Protection against cancers that involve the inner lining of body organs is attributed to vitamin K; vitamin K may also promote longevity.

While vitamin K has been recommended for use in people with osteoporosis, so far the evidence that it actually works is somewhat slim. There are no well-established therapeutic uses of vitamin K, other than its conventional use as an antidote for blood-thinning medications.

SCIENTIFIC EVIDENCE

A study of people suggests that an intake of vitamin K higher than the RDA, in the range of

110 mcg daily, might be helpful for preventing osteoporosis. Research has found that people with osteoporosis have much lower blood levels of vitamin K than other people. For example, in a study of 71 postmenopausal women, participants with reduced bone mineral density showed lower serum vitamin K_1 levels than those with normal bone density. Similar results have been seen in other studies. A recent report from 12,700 participants in the Nurses' Health Study found that higher dietary intake of vitamin K is associated with a significantly reduced risk of hip fracture. Interestingly, the most common source of vitamin K used by individuals in the study was iceberg lettuce, followed by broccoli, spinach, romaine lettuce, brussels sprouts, and dark greens. Women who ate lettuce each day had only 55% the risk of hip fracture of those who ate it only weekly. However, among women taking estrogen, no benefit was seen, probably because estrogen is so much more powerful. Research also suggests that supplemental vitamin K can reduce the amount of calcium lost in the urine. This is indirect evidence of a beneficial effect on bone. Taken together, these findings suggest that vitamin K supplements might help prevent osteoporosis.

SOURCES

Vitamin K (in the form of K_1) is found in dark green leafy vegetables. Kale, green tea, and turnip greens are the best food sources, providing about 10 times the daily human adult requirement in a single serving. Spinach, broccoli, lettuce, and cabbage are very rich sources as well. Vitamin K is also found in such common foods as oats, green peas, whole wheat, green beans, brussels sprouts, egg yolks, liver, oatmeal, safflower oil, soybeans, wheat, watercress, and asparagus. Green foods, alfalfa, and the herbs green tea, nettle, and shepherd's purse are also sources.

DOSAGES

There is no AAFCO recommended level of vitamin K in dog foods. However, there have been reports of vitamin K deficiency in cats fed several commercial foods containing high levels of salmon or tuna. The AAFCO recommends supplementation for any cat eating a diet containing greater than 25% fish (0.1 ppm vitamin K recommended and is usually included in the processed diets). Supplementation with the multivitamins recommended in the Part Three, Diet (page 344) will provide cats fed homemade diets with vitamin K.

SAFETY ISSUES

Vitamin K is probably quite safe at the recommended therapeutic dosages, since those quantities are easily obtained from food.

Certain drugs can interfere with the action or absorption of vitamin K, including the antituberculosis drug isoniazid (INH), phenytoin (for seizures), cholestyramine (for high cholesterol), and even high doses of vitamin E. Additional vitamin K may be needed in these situations

The blood-thinning drugs Coumadin (warfarin) and dicumarol work by antagonizing the effects of vitamin K. Conversely, vitamin K supplements, or intake of foods containing high levels of vitamin K, blocks the action of these medications, and is used as an antidote.

Excess vitamin K (vitamin K toxicity) is unlikely to be a problem in pets. However, menadione (synthetic vitamin K_3) toxicity can occur and cause fatal anemia and jaundice.

WHITE WILLOW BARK *(Salix alba)*

Common Uses

Arthritis (dogs), pain (dogs), inflammation (dogs)

In 1828, European chemists extracted the substance salicin from white willow, which was soon purified to salicylic acid. Chemists later modified salicylic acid (this time from the herb meadowsweet) to create acetylsalicylic acid, or aspirin. Willow bark contains salicin and can be considered a natural form of aspirin. It is used for pain relief and anti-inflammatory action. In people, the tea seems more effective than the powdered herb. Salicin is converted by the body to salicylic acid, which means that the side effects of chemically produced aspirin (specifically gastrointestinal ulcers) could occur with willow bark. However, a very large amount of the herb is required to get the same dose of active ingredient. Also, white willow is reportedly not particularly hard on the stomach. This may be due to the fact that most of the salicylic acid in white willow is present in chemical forms that are only converted to salicylic acid after absorption into the body.

Salicin is slowly absorbed in the intestines. This means that it takes longer for relief to occur after taking willow bark, but that the effects are longer lasting than salicylic acid.

THERAPEUTIC USES

In dogs, white willow bark can be used for the control of pain and inflammation.

SCIENTIFIC EVIDENCE

One study reported in the poceedings of the *JAHVMA* (1997) compared a combination of Western herbs (devil's claw, yucca, and white willow in a base of alfalfa, watercress, parsley, kelp, and fenugreek), traditional Chinese herbs (white peony root, licorice, epimedium, oyster shell, lucid ganoderma, isatidis, corydalis), aspirin, and a placebo in the treatment of dogs with osteoarthritis. Results of the study showed most improvement in dogs treated with aspirin. Therapy with the Chinese herbs, while not consistent, were better than placebo (the authors suggested that a higher rate of improvement might have occurred if Traditional Chinese Medicine diagnostics, rather than Western diagnostics, were used). The Western herbs were no more effective than placebo. In this study at least, the NSAID was most effective, the Chinese herbs were next most effective, and the Western herbs were ineffective, as was the placebo.

SAFETY ISSUES

Because cats are sensitive to aspirin, white willow bark should only be used in cats with proper veterinary supervision.

Do not use concurrently with aspirin, corticosteroids, or other nonsteroidal, anti-inflammatory medications.

Although white willow doesn't appear to upset the stomach as easily as aspirin, based on its chemical constituents it is almost certain that white willow can cause stomach irritation and even bleeding ulcers if used over the long-term. It should also not be used by pets with aspirin allergies, bleeding disorders, ulcers, kidney disease, liver disease, or diabetes. Safety in pregnant or nursing women, or those with severe liver or kidney disease has not been established; similar precautions are probably warranted in pets.

WORMWOOD (*Artemesia absinthum*)

Common Uses
Intestinal parasites (potential toxicity)

Wormwood is known as an herbal deworming agent. It is not usually recommended as it can be quite harsh on the pet, and can cause damage to the kidneys, liver, and nervous system. Safer deworming herbs (and even many conventional deworming medications) exist.

SAFETY ISSUES

Wormwood is unsafe for internal use in people. Do not use in pets with seizures, kidney disease, liver disease, or in pregnant animals. Safer herbs for deworming exist.

YARROW (*Achillea millefolium*)

Common Uses
Allergies (topical), arthritis, infections, intestinal parasites, urinary disorders

The herb yarrow is used for treating open wounds, where it can stop bleeding and inhibit bacteria.

THERAPEUTIC USES

Yarrow also serves as a vascular tonic, removing small blood clots and improving circulation. It can be tried in cats with **cardiomyopathy** (page 91), especially those who have developed embolic disease.

Anti-inflammatory properties also make yarrow useful for pets with **osteoarthritis** (page 11) and dermatitis.

For pets with **urinary infections** (page 105), yarrow's antibacterial properties may prove useful.

Yarrow is used for pets with respiratory diseases, including pneumonia, because it can dilate respiratory blood vessels.

Yarrow is useful for relieving inflammation of the digestive tract and can act as a mild dewormer.

Yarrow can reduce fever and stimulate appetite.

SAFETY ISSUES

Do not use in pregnant animals. Yarrow may cause allergic reactions. Do not use for extended periods of time as yarrow contains thujone, which can be toxic if consumed in large amounts for extended periods of time.

YELLOW DOCK *(Rumex crispus)*

Common Uses

Allergies (topical), rheumatoid arthritis, constipation, cancer, liver disease

Yellow dock is a cleansing herb that stimulates liver function and evacuation of the bowels to remove wastes from the body. Yellow dock is useful for chronic skin disorders that may be attributed to toxicity within the body. It can also be used as treatment for rheumatoid arthritis, in **cancer** (page 44) patients, and as a remedy for anemia due to its high iron content. Yellow dock is most commonly recommended for short-term use at the beginning of therapy to get a "quick cleansing," as its action is often quick and dramatic.

SAFETY ISSUES

Excess yellow dock can lead to intestinal cramping, vomiting, and diarrhea; it should not be used during pregnancy or in pets with intestinal blockages or bleeding. It should not be used in pets in whom excess iron could be harmful. Large amounts can cause cramping and diarrhea.

YUCCA *(Yucca schidigera)*

Common Uses

Arthritis, diabetes, intestinal parasites, anti-inflammatory

Yucca contains many nutrients and chemicals, including plant glycosides called saponins. Two saponins, smilagenin and sarsasapogenin, optimize nutrient assimilation in the intestinal tract.

The saponins act as precursors to corticosteroids produced by the body.

THERAPEUTIC USES

The saponins allow yucca to be used for pets with inflammatory diseases such as **osteoarthritis** (page 11) or rheumatoid arthritis.

Yucca can inhibit urease, making it ideal to use for pets with excessive urine or fecal odors.

The yucca plant is viewed as an anti-inflammatory that may be included in some nutritional supplements for pets with arthritis (see also Glycosaminoglycans). Response of pets with osteo-

arthritis to supplementation with yucca is usually good. Some doctors have reported that a point of tolerance may be reached in some patients where good results are no longer obtained. In the laboratory, the yucca plant contains chemicals that can be converted into steroids (it is not known if this also occurs in the body).

DOSAGES

Use for only 5 days at a time (5 days on and 2 days off is recommended).

SAFETY ISSUES

In large doses (in excess of 15% yucca root) or for long periods of time, vomiting may occur. Do not use for more than 5 days at a time (5 days on, 2 off is often recommended).

Yucca is generally accepted as safe based on its long history of use as a food. However, it sometimes causes diarrhea if taken to excess. Safety in young children, pregnant or nursing women, or those with severe liver or kidney disease has not been established; similar precautions in pets is probably also warranted.

ZINC (zinc sulfate, zinc acetate, zinc gluconate, zinc citrate, zinc picolinate, chelated zinc)

Common Uses
Zinc deficiency, copper poisoning, diabetes

Zinc is an important mineral found in every cell in the body and required by more than 300 enzymes in the body. In people, mild zinc deficiency seems to be fairly common.

Severe zinc deficiency can cause a major loss of immune function, and mild zinc deficiency might impair immunity slightly.

In people, zinc supplements may have benefits, including directly killing cold viruses in the throat, helping stomach ulcers heal, and relieving symptoms of rheumatoid arthritis. Although the evidence that it works is not yet meaningful, zinc is sometimes recommended in people for the following conditions as well: macular degeneration, benign prostatic hyperplasia, Alzheimer's disease, wound healing, inflammatory bowel disease (ulcerative colitis and Crohn's disease), osteoporosis, diabetes, AIDS, bladder infection, cataracts, and periodontal disease. With the exception of short-term use for people with colds, these other uses involve long-term use of high dosages of zinc, which can cause toxic effects.

Zinc is necessary for normal growth, formation of the epidermis, metabolism of protein, metabolism of carbohydrates, and normal immune function. Zinc-deficient diets fed to puppies produce fewer T lymphocytes (an important constituent of the immune system) in the lymph nodes, spleen, and thymus gland.

There are two specific, rarely seen zinc-responsive skin disorders in dogs. The first is seen in dogs (usually puppies) fed a zinc-deficient diet (diets high in plant material such as vegetable fiber and soybean meal). Plant materials contain calcium phytate, which binds zinc, interfering with intestinal absorption and leading to a zinc deficiency. The diets most likely to cause zinc deficiency are those generic (least expensive) diets that use the less expensive plant ingredients rather than meat ingredients as protein sources.

The second syndrome is a genetic defect that causes a decreased absorption of zinc from the intestines in Siberian Huskies, Malamutes, and Bull Terriers that carry the gene for lethal acrodermatitis.

Clinical signs include a crusting dermatitis, mainly around the eyes, nostrils, and mouth.

THERAPEUTIC ISSUES

Zinc administration (10 to 15 mg/kg IV weekly for 4 to 6 weeks, zinc sulfate at 10 mg/kg daily, or zinc methionine at 4 mg/kg/day) is curative of acrodermatitis. Higher doses may be needed in some pets, and those pets with the genetic form may only respond to the IV administration of zinc (the oral form was found ineffective in some but not all studies). Changing generic diets to better diets (preferably homemade) is also important.

Oral administration of zinc was not found to be effective in treating dogs with atopic dermatitis.

In dogs, oral administration of zinc acetate has been helpful for treating copper hepatotoxicosis. Zinc induces increased concentrations of metallothionein in intestinal cells (preventing copper absorption) and in liver cells (which binds to copper in the damaged liver cells). Zinc acetate is administered at 100 mg per dog twice daily for 3 to 6 months with the goal of achieving plasma zinc concentrations of 200 to 600 micrograms/dl. After 3 to 6 months, the zinc acetate dosage is reduced to 50 mg twice daily. Treatment may need to continue for the life of the pet. Zinc acetate is best administered without food (give at least 1 hour before meals) to decrease zinc binding by constituents (such as phytates) in the food.

Zinc is found in high concentrations in the pancreatic islet cells and performs a distinct role in the synthesis, secretion, and storage of insulin. Zinc deficiency has been shown to increase the risk of diabetes while zinc supplementation seems to have positive effects on glucose balance.

Zinc is also a precursor to the antioxidant enzyme superoxide dismutase (SOD), a powerful antioxidant that destroys the highly reactive form of oxygen known as superoxide. In order to maintain adequate levels of SOD, it is critical to consume adequate amounts of selenium and zinc.

Deficiencies of zinc can lead to decreased SOD production, increasing the risk of lipid peroxidation. Diabetics have been found to have elevated levels of peroxidation end-products. Supplementing with 30 mg of zinc daily has been shown to increase plasma concentrations, which may have a positive effect on SOD activity.

Manganese and high intake of copper and iron may impair zinc absorption. Neither calcium nor folic acid appears to significantly affect zinc absorption. Diuretics can cause excessive loss of zinc in the urine.

SOURCES

Zinc can be taken as a nutritional supplement, in one of many forms. Zinc citrate, zinc acetate, or zinc picolinate may be the best absorbed, although zinc sulfate is less expensive. The most holistic approach is to feed your pet a whole food supplement containing zinc.

SAFETY ISSUES

In people, zinc seldom causes any immediate side effects other than occasional stomach upset, usually when it's taken on an empty stomach. Some forms do have an unpleasant metallic taste. However, long-term use of zinc at dosages of 10 mg or more daily can cause a number of toxic effects, including severe copper deficiency, impaired immunity, heart problems, and anemia.

Use of zinc can interfere with the absorption of manganese, soy, Coumadin (warfarin), verapamil, penicillamine, and antibiotics in the tetracycline or quinolone (Cipro, Floxin, enrofloxcin) family.

Zinc

PART

THREE

Diet

NUTRIENTS

Nutrients

Choosing and feeding the best diet for your pet is such an easy thing to do, yet it is one area of health care often overlooked by both doctors and pet owners. Feeding the best diet is so important for total holistic health for your pet that most holistic doctors stress diet. By getting your pet on the best diet, some mild conditions (such as allergies) may respond without your needing to use other therapies. Even when other conventional or complementary therapies are indicated, feeding the most appropriate diet is the first rung on the ladder of holistic health care, often working synergistically with other supplements and therapies to provide the best health possible for your pet. Here are some important questions to keep in mind as you read this chapter.

- How do you determine which diet is best for your pet?
- Should you simply purchase the least expensive diet for your pet?
- Should you purchase the well-known, heavily advertised, and promoted brands?
- Should you trust your veterinarian to recommend the best diet for your pet?
- Is a processed food best for your pet, or would a homemade diet be more suitable?
- If you prepare a diet at home, should you cook the food, or is feeding it "raw" better for your pet?

In truth, it is up to you, the pet owner, to work with your veterinarian to help determine the most appropriate diet for your pet. This entire diet section is designed to give you the basic information you need to do just that.

Most pet owners, unfortunately, don't really think a lot about what their pets eat. Sure, we all pay attention to ads touting one brand of food over another. Yet most pet owners (and some veterinarians) don't know what's really in the food they feed. Even though the answer is only a glance away, listed on the label required on each bag or can of food (assuming we can understand the label!), most of us never think to look.

Getting the proper diet is extremely important for pets. Because we are finally beginning to realize how important proper diet is for ourselves, many of us are trying to eat a more healthful diet. This may mean cutting back on calories, eating more fiber, or adding multivitamins and minerals to our diets. We know that certain diseases, including liver disease, heart disease, obesity, and cancers can be traced to improper diets, such as those too high in saturated fats or too low in fiber.

As owners make healthful dietary choices for themselves, it's only natural they would do the same for their pets.

All food is not created equal. Turning to the ever-present pet food label we mentioned earlier, stop and take a look at the label on your pet's food right now. Read the top three ingredients. Are they healthful ingredients such as whole dressed chicken (or another protein source), corn, and rice—or are they items such as chicken by-products, corn by-products, animal meal, blood meal, and the like? Exactly what are you feeding your pet? Is it possible that your choice of pet food may actually be hurting your pet? Is it possible that his food might be contributing to some of your pet's health problems?

These questions must be answered so you can have the healthiest pet possible, but first you must understand the nutrients essential for your pet to determine how to feed your pet properly.

Whether you choose to prepare a diet at home or feed a natural, processed food, this part of the book will help you understand how to choose the best diet for your pet. For those of you who choose a processed food, feeding your pet the most natural, healthful diet possible is important. You will also learn how to do that in the *Natural Health Bible for Dogs & Cats.*

For readers who prefer, like many pet owners who seek the help of holistic veterinarians, to prepare a natural, balanced diet at home, the second half of this Diet section will help you do that as well.

Regardless of whether you feed a prepared diet or make one yourself, you'll spend good money feeding your pet each and every day; therefore, it's important that you know how to feed your pet most appropriately.

While it's not common for veterinarians to see many obvious nutritional diseases in dogs and cats, there is no doubt that diet plays an important role in a pet's health. As owners become more holistic in their approach to pet care, including their choice of diet, their pets will enjoy longer and healthier lives. Simply stated, an educated owner is the best pet owner.

Your pet needs many nutrients to not only sustain life but to encourage growth, promote a healthy coat, and allow proper function of his organs and immune system. An improperly nourished pet is unhealthy and prone to illness. Preventing illness with proper nutrition may be the most important part of a pet owner's responsibility.

There are seven dietary classifications of nutrients—water, protein, carbohydrates, fats, vitamins, minerals, and food additives—each of which is important. Additives, though not technically nutrients, are found in many processed foods; therefore, it's important to address them in this discussion. In formulating the best diet for pets, nutritionists take into account the percentage of each nutrient class the pet needs. It is extremely important for owners who choose to prepare homemade diets for their pets to carefully consider each class of nutrients. Dietary nutrient deficiencies are most likely to occur when owners prepare pets' meals without following a tested recipe, or feed the least expensive, least healthful commercially prepared diets.

WATER

While most people don't consider water a nutrient, it is without a doubt the most important one. An animal can survive after losing most of its fat or protein, but a 15% loss of body water results in death! Your pet's body, just like your body, is made up mostly of water. The water content of the pet's body varies with age; on average, water content of the pet's body at birth is approximately 75 to 80%, while the percent of body water in an older pet might be more on the order of about 40%. The water content of plants can be anywhere from just above 0% (very dry plant matter such as aged hay), to about 11 to 16% for cereal grains, to about 99% for seaweed. Most people forget how important water is to a pet's diet, yet water may be the most important nutrient. Too much or too little water can be fatal. For those interested in a holistic approach to feeding pets, you would be wise to consider using distilled water or pure spring water to reduce the possibility of contaminants.

While your pet's food can supply a little or a lot of your pet's daily water needs, water is usually supplied by always having available a fresh bowl of clean water.

There is some debate concerning whether tap water is adequate, or whether bottled or distilled water is preferable. No published studies prove one type of water is better than another, or that any type of water causes disease in pets. Many holistic pet owners prefer bottled or filtered water to tap water. A recent report in a popular periodical tested a number of brands of bottled water and found them no different from plain tap water. City tap water is chlorinated. While this causes concern to some owners, chlorination also kills various bacteria that could cause food poisoning in pets if the bacteria were present in high numbers. Using non-chlorinated water could predispose the pet to poisoning by these bacteria (as well as any protozoal organisms) if they are present in the water source. Cities will usually provide a chemical analysis of the water supply if requested by owners. The decision about which water source to use is a personal one; most clients offer their pets whichever type of water they themselves drink.

Body water serves several useful functions. First, water is used for body heat regulation. Water in the body transfers heat produced during metabolism by the cells to the outside surface of the body. The heat is released through sweating (although our pets can't do this) and through evaporation in the lungs. Second, water is used for transportation of body nutrients, from the food the pet eats into the cells where the nutrients are used for cellular processes such as energy production, cellular metabolism, and making hormones. Third, water allows the body to transport waste material from the cells to the outside of the body (in the form of urine and fecal production). Finally, water assists in lubricating the various body surfaces (joints, intestines, and organs of the abdomen and chest).

Dry food is 6 to 10% water, soft-moist is 23 to 40% water, and canned food is 68 to 78% water. As a rule, the amount of water consumed by mature dogs and cats maintained at a comfortable environmental temperature is about 2.5 times the amount of dry matter consumed in food.

Dry food is the least expensive per pound. Soft-moist food often contains a high sugar or propylene glycol content. Excess sugar may contribute to diabetes in dogs and cats, and propylene glycol can cause anemia in cats. Soft-moist (semi-moist) foods are best avoided by owners desiring a more holistic diet. Canned food contains a lot of water; therefore, a dog or cat consuming a lot of canned food (or homemade diet) will drink less water. For owners choosing to feed a wholesome, natural processed diets, offering dry food (supplemented with canned food as desired) seems a popular option. Dry food is not quite as messy as canned food, costs less, is less likely to spoil quickly, and promotes healthy gums and teeth. Periodontal tartar seems to build up more slowly when pets eat a diet of dry food, although pets who chew a lot (pets fed bones) also build up tartar less quickly. Tartar buildup and periodontal disease occur differently in every pet, usually as a result of diet plus individual susceptibility to this common infectious disease of dogs and cats.

Water should be increased in times of illness, when fever is present, when the environmental temperature increases, if your pet pants excessively, or when your pet is taking certain medications (such as corticosteroids or diuretics) that result in an increased urinary output.

CARBOHYDRATES

Carbohydrates—sugars, starches, and fiber—are excellent sources of energy in pet foods. The body of a pet actually contains only small amounts of unused carbohydrates; carbohydrates in the diet that the pet does not need are stored as glycogen and body fat. Plants, however, contain a large amount of carbohydrates and are included in the diets of pets to provide energy or fiber.

Natural sugars and starches found in plants are useful for supplying energy and are easily digested by the pet (see below). You should avoid feeding your pet excess sugars, especially man-made sugars that often added to increase the flavoring of the food. Sugars compete with essential dietary nutrients for digestion and absorption, can contribute to obesity, and may predispose pets to diabetes.

Also avoid excess quantities of poorly digestible carbohydrates (wheat, oats, soybeans) in your pet's diet as they contribute to excess intestinal gas (flatus). Excess fermentation of poorly digestible carbohydrates may contribute to bloat in dogs.

Once digested and absorbed by the pet, one of three things can happen to the sugars and starches: They are immediately used for energy, they are stored as glycogen in the liver (to be used at a future time for energy), or they can be stored as fat. Fiber, however, is not digested by the pet. Fiber serves as the structural part of the plant; common plant fibers include cellulose and lignin. Including fiber in the diet is important for normal intestinal function. Excess dietary fiber is often used when formulating diets for overweight pets, for pets with certain intestinal problems, and for pets with diabetes to help them control their absorption of sugars and starches from the diet.

Fiber is sometimes added to the diet to prevent both diarrhea and constipation. Fiber also helps the animal feel full so he doesn't overfeed and become obese. Cheaper pet foods often have too much fiber as a filler. As a result, pets can become full before consuming the needed nutrients and can exhibit nutritional deficiencies.

While both dogs and cats can digest and absorb carbohydrates, neither has specific dietary requirements for this nutrient form. Cats especially, being true carnivores, do not need carbohydrates in their diets. Cats are able to easily maintain blood glucose levels when fed high-protein, low-carbohydrate diets. The sugar transporting system of the cat's intestinal system does not adapt to varying levels of dietary carbohydrates as cats have low activities of intestinal disaccharidiase (sucrase and lactase) enzymes. Cats also only produce about 5% of the pancreatic

Nutrients

amylase enzyme (the carbohydrate-digesting enzyme) that dogs produce. Also, unlike dogs, cats do not possess the liver enzyme activity (hepatic glucokinase), which limits their ability to metabolize large amounts of carbohydrates. Many commercial cat foods contain large amounts of carbohydrates (especially corn), which lower the price of the food. (Corn, a grain which supplies carbohydrates and protein, is less expensive than animal meats as a protein source.) These foods should not be fed to cats, who require large amounts of animal protein and minimal amounts of dietary carbohydrates.

PROTEIN

Protein is composed of amino acids, which are the building blocks of the body. Proteins are used for energy and in the production of enzymes, hormones, antibodies, and in making muscle and other structural tissues. While people often mistakenly are concerned about the protein content of food, in reality it's the amino acids that are important. The protein sources used in formulating the diet must contain the proper amounts of the essential amino acids needed, or your pet will suffer from an amino acid deficiency despite an adequate protein intake.

While plants can produce all of the 24 amino acids, they can't really produce enough of each or in the right amounts. With few exceptions, an all-plant (vegetarian) diet would not provide enough of the right amounts and right balance of amino acids required for our pets. Keep in mind that cats are true carnivores requiring meat in their diets; and even though dogs are more omnivorous than cats, they too are carnivores and must have meat in their diet.

Pets cannot make all the amino acids they need; therefore, their diets must provide those they cannot make in their bodies. These required amino acids are called essential amino acids. Nonessential amino acids, on the other hand, can be made by the pet's body from other amino acids that they get through their diet. A high-quality protein diet contains all the essential amino acids required in the right amounts and right ratios. Protein is supplied in a pet's diet through animal (preferably) or plant material; in cheaper diets the animal source might be "animal meal" or "animal by-products" rather than whole, dressed animal. These less wholesome ingredients are not desired in the diets of pets.

AMINO ACIDS

Essential	Nonessential
Arginine	Alanine
Citrulline (conditionally in cats)	Asparagine
Histidine	Aspartate
Isoleucine	Cysteine
Leucine	Glutamate
Lysine	Glutamine
Methionine	Glycine
Phenylalanine	Proline
Taurine (essential in cats)	Serine
Threonine	Tyrosine
Tryptophan	
Valine	

The biological value of protein is based on the protein's unique combination of its building blocks, the amino acids. People and animals use the amino acids obtained by digestion of protein for growth and building tissues and organs. When discussing proteins, the biological value of the protein is important. Eggs are ranked at 100, being considered the best food for providing high-quality protein. Digestibility is also important; the protein must be easily digested and assimilated into the body before it can be of any value to the pet. While it would be most helpful to know the amino acid content of the protein in the commercial pet foods, the label only needs to list the crude protein. It's important to read the label to see the quality of ingredients, as crude protein can include items such as feather meal, hair, hooves, tendons, and ligaments. While these animal by-products certainly provide protein, they are essentially non-digestible and provide no biologic value (amino acids) to the pet. Cheaper, generic foods are more likely to contain these by-products as sources of protein for the diet.

Protein deficiency is not common but can occur during illness, when the animal eats less or refuses to eat. In this situation, the pet still requires amino acids. If he isn't eating, the pet will literally break down his own muscle tissue to supply his body with protein. This happens quite

Nutrients

readily when the pet becomes ill, and is an important reason why sick pets don't recover from illness quickly. Providing food for a sick pet is so essential that hospitalized pets are force-fed to maintain a positive energy and protein balance to help them recover quickly. You can see how important it is to make sure that sick pets continue to eat!

There are some unique requirements for amino acids in our pets. For example, cats, being true carnivores, require high levels of the amino acid **taurine** (page 278). Taurine is only found in meat; cats cannot be fed diets based on soy, dairy, or plant material without added taurine. Taurine deficiency has been associated with blindness and dilated **cardiomyopathy** (page 91) in cats.

Taurine is not made into proteins synthesized by the body but instead remains as a free amino acid. It exists as a free amino acid in many body tissues, including the brain, nervous tissue, heart muscle, skeletal muscle, retina of the eye, liver, red and white blood cells, as well as in milk and as a complex with bile salts excreted by the gallbladder.

Since taurine is a free amino acid found in meat, it is important when preparing diets at home that if the meat is cooked in water, the water be added back to the diet to preserve taurine. That's because the longer the meat is cooked, the more taurine will leach into the water. Owners choosing to feed raw meat to their cats will not have this problem.

Cats also require citrulline as they cannot synthesize it. They can convert arginine to citrulline as long as the diet contains adequate amounts of arginine. Diets deficient in arginine, citrulline, and the amino acid ornithine predispose the cat to developing hyperammonemia (too much ammonia in the blood), which can be fatal. Since most protein sources contain adequate arginine, additional supplementation is usually not needed. Cats with **hepatic lipidosis** (page 128) are often supplemented with arginine to help detoxify ammonia and prevent worsening of clinical signs. Diets designed for pets with cancer contain additional arginine as this amino acid decreases tumor growth and spreading (metastasis). Arginine is also involved in the formation of

nitric acid. Nitric acid is used by the body to help regulate blood flow through blood vessels and regulate blood pressure. Nitrates (isosorbide dinitrate, nitroglycerin) may be used by doctors to help pets with heart disease. It may be possible that additional arginine could be helpful in controlling blood flow and blood pressure in dogs and cats with heart disease, but this has not been investigated.

Excess glutamic acid can be detrimental to cats and cause vomiting and thiamin deficiency. Glutamic acid is found in plant proteins and is relatively low in animal proteins. Diets with high levels of vegetable matter may contain excess glutamic acid.

Glutamine (page 213) is present in high-quality proteins and is not often added to pet foods. Additionally, because L-glutamine is destroyed by heating and cooking, supplementation with L-glutamine is best accomplished by adding the supplement (often in a powdered or capsule form) to the food immediately before feeding. (Capsule glutamine supplements can be given directly to the pet as directed by the veterinarian.) Dogs and cats experiencing stress—illness, cancer chemotherapy, immunosuppressive illnesses (such as feline leukemia virus or feline immunodeficiency virus infection), or surgery—may not be able to maintain glutamine stores in their bodies and might benefit from additional supplementation. Glutamine may also retard the cachexia (wasting) seen in many pets with cancer. Glutamine, being the preferred energy source for cells of the intestinal tract, is useful as a supplement for pets with acute and chronic gastroenteritis (especially when diarrhea occurs) and from gastroenteritis that results from cancer chemotherapy.

Excess dietary protein has been linked to fear-related territorial aggression in some dogs. It is theorized that increased protein interferes with the transport of the amino acid tryptophan across the blood-brain barrier, which can decrease serotonin formation. Serotonin is an important neurotransmitter, and low levels have been linked to various behavioral problems. Often feeding these dogs a reduced-protein diet can cure this behavioral disorder.

Nutrients

FAT

Fats are used for energy and are necessary for the absorption of vitamins A, D, E, and K. Fats also are used in the body's production of hormones, for insulation, for protection of vital organs, for lubrication, for buoyancy, and as precursors to amino acids. Fats also make diets more palatable (diets high in fats taste good!). Excess concentrations of fats can lead to obesity, hepatic lipidosis (fatty liver disease), and pancreatitis. Cholesterol is a common animal fat. While excess cholesterol can cause problems in both people and pets, every person and animal needs some cholesterol. Cholesterol is important because important hormones (testosterone, progesterone, estrogen) are made from cholesterol.

Fats are either saturated or unsaturated, which refers to the chemical structure. Excessive amounts of saturated fats are linked to arteriosclerosis in people and may be unhealthy in pets as well. While both plants and animals contain higher amounts of saturated fats than unsaturated fats, animal tissue contains higher amounts of saturated fats than plant tissue. Hydrogenated oils, made chemically by adding hydrogen to vegetable oils, are also harmful to people and pets and interfere with the production of protective prostaglandins.

Fat deficiency, or rather fatty acid deficiency, is rare in pets; it is most likely to occur in pets fed cheaper generic diets, and in pets with maldigestion and malabsorption intestinal conditions. Certain fatty acids (omega-3 fatty acids) can be supplemented by your doctor to help with various skin problems—specifically atopic dermatitis, a form of allergic dermatitis. Fatty acids are being investigated in both people and pets to help control a variety of ailments, including heart disease, arthritis, and kidney disease.

Owners often attempt to supplement fats in a pet's diets by adding a few spoonfuls of vegetable oil to the diet. While this may not be harmful, it is usually not necessary and will not provide essential fatty acids necessary for improved health or disease treatment. Fatty acid supplementation may be indicated for pets with a variety of medical disorders, and can be beneficial for all pets

by increasing the dietary ratio of omega-3 to omega-6 fatty acids.

Omega-3 fatty acids—eicosapentaenoic acid (EPA) and docosahexaenoic acid (DHA)—are derived from fish oils of coldwater fish (salmon, trout, or most commonly menhaden fish) and flax-seed. Omega-6 fatty acids—linoleic acid (LA) and gamma-linolenic acid (GLA)—are derived from the oils of seeds such as evening primrose, black currant, and borage. Omega-9 fatty acids have no known use in treating our pets.

In general, the products of omega-3 (specifically EPA) and one omega-6 fatty acid (DGLA) are less inflammatory than are the products of arachidonic acid (another omega-6 fatty acid). Supplementation of the diet with omega-3 fatty acids (generally considered anti-inflammatory fatty acids) is useful to decrease inflammation in the body. Since metabolism of the omega-6 fatty acids tend to cause inflammation, supplying a large amount of omega-3 fatty acids favors the production of non-inflammatory chemicals.

Note: Flaxseed oil is a popular source of alpha-linoleic acid (ALA), an omega-3 fatty acid that is ultimately converted to EPA and DHA. However, many species of pets (probably including dogs and cats) and some people cannot convert ALA to these other more active non-inflammatory omega-3 fatty acids. In one study in people, flaxseed oil was ineffective in reducing symptoms or raising levels of EPA and DHA. While flaxseed oil has been suggested as a less smelly substitute for fish oil, no evidence supports it as effective when used for the same therapeutic purposes as fish oil. Therefore, supplementation with EPA and DHA is important, and this is the reason flaxseed oil is not recommended as the sole fatty acid supplement for pets. Flaxseed oil can, however, be used to provide ALA and as a coat conditioner.

MINERALS

Minerals include such substances as calcium, phosphorus, iron, and zinc, among others. As a rule, minerals function as coenzymes that help control numerous biochemical reactions in the body. Minerals also are constituents of bone and

Nutrients

muscle, and are involved in the growth and regeneration of tissues. Mineral deficiencies rarely occur in pets. In dogs fed cheap generic diets, zinc deficiency commonly occurs, causing crusting skin lesions, often prominent around the mouth and nose.

Mineral excess can occur by overzealous administration of minerals by owners, specifically calcium and phosphorus. This may be especially problematic in dogs. Many owners give their growing puppies calcium pills, thinking this will help with skeletal growth. Too much calcium can actually cause problems, including hip dysplasia. Excessive iron given to dogs and cats (which can happen if human vitamin products containing iron are given to the pet) can be fatal.

Note: An excess of minerals can occur easily in pets. Mineral supplementation is not recommended unless directed by your veterinarian.

Minerals commonly found in plants include calcium, phosphorus, and magnesium. (These are also found in bone, and are provided in our pets' diets through the addition of bonemeal or similar supplements.) Minerals commonly found in animals (in muscle tissue) include potassium, sodium, and chlorine. See Part Two for a more thorough discussion of minerals.

VITAMINS

Like minerals, vitamins function as enzymes or coenzymes. Pure vitamin deficiencies or toxicities are rarely encountered in pets fed quality processed diets, as pet food manufacturers overcompensate and make sure the food contains more than enough of these compounds. There are a few rare exceptions: vitamin K deficiency that can occur rarely as a result of chronic diarrhea, acute poisoning by warfarin-type rat poisons, poor-quality diets that contain an insufficient amount of fat, and antibiotic therapies (antibiotics can kill the intestinal bacteria which manufacture vitamin K). Also, large amounts of ingested raw egg whites can result in a biotin deficiency, though this is also rare.

Vitamin toxicities can occur if owners supplement their pets' diets with excessive amounts of human or animal vitamin preparations. See Part Two for a more thorough discussion of vitamins.

ADDITIVES

Additives can include a number of substances, such as chemical preservatives, artificial coloring, and artificial flavors.

Preservatives are essential in preventing spoilage of food. As people learned more about food and as chemicals were developed to prevent spoilage, the incidence of food poisoning drastically decreased. However, chemicals also have a bad side. Long-term ingestion of certain chemicals might be harmful and may be linked to chronic diseases including cancers. Purists try to avoid manmade chemicals in diets fed to pets. However, it is important that owners not totally abandon preservatives or they risk causing illness in pets due to food poisoning. Some manufacturers of pet foods have responded to the preference to move away from chemicals and include more natural preservatives. When choosing commercially prepared diets, antioxidants such as vitamin E and vitamin C have replaced chemicals such as ethoxyquin, BHA, and BHT (to follow). Careful reading of the label will inform owners what chemicals, if any, are added to the pet's food. For pet owners who choose to prepare diets at home, it is almost impossible to formulate diets that are resistant to spoiling. Therefore, owners should refrigerate or freeze small amounts of prepared food when making a homemade diet. The food can be defrosted and fed to the pet as needed.

Artificial colors and flavors are really not necessary in pet foods. Because dogs and cats don't have the color vision of people, they don't care about the color of the food you choose. Colors are added to be more attractive to owners who must make purchase decisions regarding the large number of foods available to them. Artificial flavors should not be needed if the food is palatable. Whenever artificial flavors are added to foods, owners should question whether the pet would eat the food without the flavors. If the pet wouldn't, one has to wonder why the owner would choose to purchase that food!

For a more thorough discussion of the chemicals commonly included in **commercial pet foods,** see page 329.

Energy

While not a nutrient in the true sense of the word, the energy content of a food is important, as food must provide energy not only for survival of the pet, but also for processes including normal metabolism, healing, reproduction, lactation for nursing animals, growth, and everyday activity. For simplicity sake, energy is provided in food by fats, carbohydrates, and proteins. The energy content of food is defined in kilocalories, which is 1,000 calories (in nutri-tion language, the word calorie usually means kilocalorie). If the food is a premium food and correctly balanced, as a rule, feeding the amount needed to meet the pet's energy requirement provides the proper amount of all needed nutrients. The amount to feed can be calculated by dividing the animal's energy requirement by the energy density of the food. In practice, most owners don't wish to do this. Pet food companies have already done this and offer suggested feeding amounts that vary with pet weights on the food package.

DIFFERENCES BETWEEN DOGS AND CATS

Dogs and cats are different, and dogs have different dietary requirements than cats have! Unlike cats, which are true carnivores and require a diet high in protein, dogs are more omnivorous therefore require a diet lower in protein than cats do.

The natural diet of dogs is higher in carbohydrates than is the natural diet of cats, although neither has strict dietary requirements for carbohydrates.

Dogs, unlike cats, can make one of the fatty acids called arachidonic acid from linoleic acid thus don't require this in their diets.

Cats, on the other hand, have a dietary requirement for the amino acids arginine and taurine, whereas dogs do not.

Vitamin A occurs only naturally in animal tissue; vitamin A precursors such as beta-carotene are synthesized by plants. Dogs, unlike cats, can make their own vitamin A from beta-carotene and therefore don't require preformed vitamin A.

It's obvious that the dietary requirements of dogs are different from those of cats, and these requirements go hand in hand with dogs being more omnivorous than cats. These are important reasons why puppies and dogs should only eat diets designed specifically for canines, and kittens and cats should only eat diets designed specifically for felines.

What Kind of Food?

WHAT KIND OF FOOD?

Now that you have an understanding of the nutrients involved in feeding your pet, you must decide just what you are going to feed. Will you feed a prepared processed food? If so, which ones are most healthful and natural?

Or would you prefer, like many clients who approach pet care with a holistic mindset, to feed a homemade diet? If you choose a homemade diet, should the food be fed raw or should it be cooked? Many pet owners and doctors have very firm opinions when asked these questions.

Just what constitutes the best or most appropriate diet is quite a controversial topic, and there are as many opinions as there are doctors. Often the opinions are based more on emotion than on objective medical facts. And when it comes to finding facts to back one view or the other, sometimes they are hard to find.

No matter which type of diet—homemade or processed—is chosen, it must meet at least five requirements:

1. The diet must contain the proper amount and balance of essential nutrients required by the pet.
2. The ingredients must be of high nutritional quality so that the animal can effectively digest, absorb, and utilize the dietary nutrients.
3. The diet should be palatable so that the pet will eat it.
4. The diet should contain minimal to no fillers such as animal or plant by-products (or if by-products are present, as in the case of some prescription-type diets for sick pets, the diet should at contain the least amount of by-products).
5. The diet should contain no artificial colors, flavors, chemical preservatives, or additives, when possible.

No matter which type of diet you choose to feed, it should meet the above requirements.

While many holistic pet owners prefer to cook for their pets, many others must choose a processed diet for a variety of reasons. If you are one of those who must feed a processed food, it is important to learn as much as possible about processed pet foods so you can make the most intelligent choice. The following information will be helpful when you make your choice.

PROCESSED FOODS

Processed foods have been around for about 40 to 50 years. Prior to the introduction of processed foods, our pets ate what people ate (or leftovers of what people ate). Many holistic pet owners feel that pets fared much better as a result of these fresher homemade diets, and that many diseases (such as immune disorders and arthritis) are diseases of processed food. (See the section following about raw diets for a greater discussion of this topic.)

Processed foods were introduced (like vitamin-mineral supplements) for two main reasons:

- Convenience
- Prevention/Treatment of Nutritional Diseases

There is no question that it takes time to properly prepare homemade pet diets and that using processed foods saves pet owners a large amount of time. It is convenient to simply open a can or scoop a cup of food from a bag and feed the pet. Processed foods not only save people time when it comes to food preparation, but they make feeding the pet quick and easy.

Processed foods were also introduced to prevent (and treat) nutritional diseases. It takes a lot more than simply tossing him some scraps to give your pet a complete, balanced, and nutritional diet. Prior to our understanding of nutrition, people and pets alike suffered from diseases resulting from dietary imbalances.

For example, people who didn't receive citrus fruits were diagnosed with scurvy as a result of vitamin C deficiency. Pets fed mainly meat developed nutritional osteodystrophy (nutritional secondary hyperparathyroidism) as a result of calcium deficiency. Cats fed only fish develop thiamin deficiency and steatitis. By learning about the nutritional needs of pets and formulating balanced diets, you can avoid these nutritional problems. While many of the nutritional diseases seen prior to the introduction of processed diets have all but been eliminated, many holistic veterinarians believe without question that processed foods, specifically those of little nutritional quality loaded with by-products and chemicals, may actually contribute to a whole new set of problems such as immune diseases, cancers, allergies, and arthritis.

Many years ago, we had but few choices of processed pet foods. As manufacturers have seen the profit in the pet food industry, we now see more players and many more choices. As well-known manufacturers of pet foods have reaped huge profits, large corporations have purchased the ownership of the foods. As a result, even many conventional veterinarians who promoted certain brands of food in the past have seen a decline in food quality and pet health as the dietary formulations have changed.

For example, let's take a look at Hill's Science Diet, formerly manufactured by the Morris

Company. Science Diets were originally designed as a line of medical, therapeutic diets for pets with medical conditions (the first diet in the line was designed for pets with kidney failure). The company, under the leadership of Dr. Mark Morris, was the first pet food company to look at the potential beneficial role of diet in helping pets with medical disorders—many of which can only be managed by dietary therapy as no drug therapy is available to correct the problem.

Science Diet is now owned by Colgate-Palmolive. In 1986, Hill's prescription diet formulation and production was still under the direct supervision of Mark Morris Associates. Since that time there have been some major changes. Mark Morris Associates was reformed as an independent group and Colgate-Palmolive made some major marketing changes. About this time, meals started showing up in the ingredient list. Formulations underwent major changes, supposedly for "nutritional" reasons, though most changes seemed to use cheaper ingredients. They violated the basic principle that premium diets are more expensive because they adhere to consistent formulation, regardless of commodity cost. Thus they were "better" than popular diets because the animal wouldn't be subjected to unexpected variations in the diet, reducing the risk of diarrhea in sensitive animals. Formulations were changed significantly without warning. Many doctors who still promote the Science Diet line believe that current formulations are not of the higher quality they were 15 years ago.

Note: This discussion is not meant to pick on Science Diet, as many of the better-known processed foods are also questioned as to their use for long-term feeding by many holistic veterinarians. These include: Procter & Gamble (Iams), Colgate-Palmolive (Hills), Nestle (Friskies, Alpo), and Heinz (9 Lives, Nature's Recipe, Kibbles 'n Bits). However, since Science Diet is among the better-known foods, it is used here as our example.

While Hill's (and Iams and a few other well-known brands) used to be the "gold standard" in commercial pet foods, most holistic veterinarians do not recommend their long-term use for most pets.

These companies, as a rule, maintain beautiful, spotless, accredited production facilities. Those facilities aren't where the problem lies; instead, the raw materials coming in the back door (not to mention the facilities from whence these raw materials come: slaughterhouses and rendering plants) are suspect. These suspect raw materials, which concern holistic veterinarians, are discussed further on under Common Pet Food Ingredients, Protein Sources.

Individual pets have specific needs, and some do better on one diet than on another. For example, Science Diet is a line of a number of scientifically formulated diets tested on several breeds of dogs during formulation. Some pets can handle their diets, whereas others develop diarrhea, vomiting, or itching.

This is also true with the homemade diets that are discussed at the end of this part. However, the homemade diets are made with human-grade fresh ingredients without the addition of chemical additives, whereas many commercial foods are not made using the best ingredients and have hormones, pesticides, and a number of additives. Ultimately, since your pet is an individual, you will need to work with your veterinarian to see just which diet is "best" for your pet.

Processed foods purport to be complete and balanced. Consumers feed them because they are convenient. Yet processing removes many nutrients (such as enzymes and probiotic bacteria, as well as many of the as yet undiscovered phytonutrients) that are not added back to the diet after processing. While most pets can live seemingly "normal" lives on many processed foods, we have to admit that we really don't know every nutrient (and every level of nutrient) that every dog or cat needs. Many foods contain ingredients dogs and cats were not designed to eat—for example cereals such as wheat, barley, and oatmeal; meat and bonemeal; soybean meal; ground corn; soy flour and soy grits. Additionally, many processed foods designed for feeding cats contain large amounts of grain, especially corn. This occurs as grains are less expensive sources of protein than meat. However, cats are true carnivores, not omnivores; and even dogs, being more omnivorous than cats, benefit from diets composed of meat. A strict dietary carbohydrate requirement for cats has not even been identified. Many holistic diets point to processed, high-grain cat foods as a cause of diseases such as diabetes, which are much less common in cats fed meat-based (true carnivore) diets.

Feeding the better wholesome processed foods (or better yet, homemade diets) supplemented with natural vitamins and minerals, omega-3 fatty acids, enzymes, probiotics, green foods, and health blend formulas allow us to match as closely as possible diets consumed by wild relatives of our domestic pets.

There are at least three classifications of processed diets: the least expensive generic diets, the more expensive premium diets, and the most expensive natural diets.

Generic diets are the least expensive but also the least healthful for your pet. Manufacturers use the cheapest ingredients possible. These are the foods that contain ingredients such as animal and plant by-products. Generic diets also are more likely to contain numerous preservatives and additives. Once again, read the label. Most generic foods are not fed to pets in feeding trials, but rather meet arbitrary nutritional "standards." Owners should not consider this type of food because health problems, due to nutritional deficiencies, may result.

Premium foods are available at many pet stores and veterinary hospitals. They usually have higher quality ingredients than do generic diets. However, you must read the label on these foods (see information on how to read a label on page 325). While these diets are far better than generic diets, many contain animal and plant products raised with chemicals and hormones. While some of these premium foods can be acceptable choices when properly augmented with natural supplements, they are not usually the first choice of holistic veterinarians and pet owners if the more natural diets are available. For many of these diets, however, the only thing premium about them is the price! Reading the label will help give you some guidelines about which

foods to avoid and which ones are appropriate to feed your pet.

The *natural* diets are the most premium of foods. These diets usually contain nothing artificial—no artificial colors or flavors. They use natural preservatives rather than chemical preservatives. Instead of by-products, they use more expensive ingredients; depending upon the brand, these ingredients are raised organically without chemicals or hormones. However, some of these diets may also rely too much on grains, especially in their diets for cats, making homemade diets the best choice when this option is possible. Because of this insistence on quality and health, natural diets are the best processed foods (and many would argue the only prepared foods) that you should feed to your pet if you choose not to prepare a homemade diet. (Once again, read the label! Many new companies see the potential profit in making "natural diets," often leaving it up to the owner or doctor to read the label and pick which foods are truly better for the pets.) Since these natural diets are the most popular with owners seeking a holistic approach to raising pets and the most healthful for the pets, let's take a closer look at what makes these diets so good for your pet.

The natural diets differ from most other prepared diets in four ways:

- They use only human grade, high-quality ingredients. (Other prepared diets may use by-products of foods processed for but declared "unfit" for use by humans.)
- They use foods, especially grains, in their whole state rather than parts of the foods.
- They use no artificial colors, additives, chemicals, or preservatives.
- They formulate diets for optimum nutrition.

In order to appreciate the difference between these three classes of prepared diets, it's important to learn to read the label and understand the differences behind the ingredients listed in the diets.

READ THE LABEL!

Keep in mind that products with nearly identical labeling may have wide variations in digestibility due to lower-cost (and lower-quality) ingredients. The label, unfortunately, does not state the suitability of the ingredients, or whether the ingredients are of high or low quality. Only the manufacturer can provide this information. For many products, the main difference is cost and packaging rather than quality of ingredients.

Reading and understanding pet food labels is *critical* when choosing a commercially prepared diet. However, the label is useful only as a starting point. It is impossible to tell the *quality* of the ingredients from the label although the following suggestions can help you determine whether at least some of the ingredients are of better quality. As a rule, cheaper diets are not as wholesome, although even some higher priced diets may use less-than-nutritious ingredients. Many pet owners feel that since the label of their brand of food says the food is nutritionally complete, it is therefore a good food. Unfortunately, this type of thinking can be quite harmful for the pets as most pet food manufacturers profess their products to be "nutritionally complete."

Foods available for sale must list on the bag that the food met guidelines established by the AAFCO (Association of American Feed Control Officials). The AAFCO statement will either say that the diet has been "formulated to meet the nutrition levels established by the AAFCO" or that "animal feeding tests using AAFCO procedures substantiate that this food provides complete and balanced nutrition." Unfortunately, food that just meets nutrition levels may not be adequate for your dog or cat. First, it is important for owners to learn how to read the label on their pet's food. Here are a few tips on reading the pet food labels:

Guaranteed Analysis. This states the *minimum* levels of nutrients in the food. A food with a minimum level of 5% protein means that the food has at least 5% protein; it may have a lot more, possibly even too much! Also, there is no guarantee that this protein is a good-quality protein. Chicken feathers have at least 5% protein, but your pet won't get any nutrients from this protein source!

Digestibility. Poultry meal is a common protein source, but the digestibility of protein meal varies from poor to excellent depending upon which ingredients are actually included in the meal. Reputable manufacturers use higher quality ingredients; the quality of the ingredient is reflected in the cost of the food. Stay away from poorly digestible, cheaper generic brands.

Nutritional Adequacy. Many products state that the food has been "formulated to meet the nutrition levels established by the AAFCO." Unfortunately, this just guarantees the food meets a mathematical minimum. Your pet may not be able to digest or absorb anything in it because the food never had to go through feeding trials to assess palatability and digestibility, and to show whether the animals in the trials grew or showed signs of malnutrition. "Animal feeding tests using AAFCO procedures that substantiate that this food provides complete and balanced nutrition" means the food has been fed to at least a few pets for some period of time and that no nutritional problems were detected. The more expensive brands use this designation after conducting costly feeding trials. However, read these labels carefully too. Just because the food passed feeding trials does not mean it does not contain chemical, additives, and fillers.

The AAFCO is the official body representing the pet food industry that determines the nutrient needs of dogs and cats. The AAFCO makes dietary recommendations for pet foods. These recommendations made by the AAFCO are derived from the NRC (National Research Council) guidelines. The NRC recommendations, which were formerly used to formulate pet foods, were based on diets using purified nutrients assuming 100%

Read the Label!

bioavailability. (No commercial diets use purified nutrients with 100% bioavailability!) However, the AAFCO has abandoned NRC guidelines and is establishing its own standards. Today, all pet foods must conform to either AAFCO "nutrient profiles" or undergo AAFCO-approved "feeding trials." Since feeding trials can be expensive and time-consuming, manufacturers have the option of formulating diets according to nutrient profiles (most manufacturers do not do feeding trials). However, the nutrient profiles, while serving as guidelines for the minimum amounts of nutrients needed in the diet to prevent diseases caused by nutrient deficiencies, do not tell anything about the quality of the ingredients in the diet—nor about the digestibility, palatability, or absorbability of the nutrients in the diet. It is possible for a diet to be labeled "complete and balanced" yet be deficient if no formal chemical analysis of the diet or feeding trial is performed.

Since diet formulation is imprecise, the industry employs safety factors and allows an excess of nutrients in an attempt to prevent dietary nutrient deficiencies. This is done because it is impossible to guarantee the bioavailability of the nutrients in the foods chosen to be used in the diet. Also, there is obviously individual variability in the amounts of nutrients each pet needs, as well as a natural variation in nutrient amount in foodstuffs. Keep in mind that an excess of nutrients does not promote any greater health than the exact amount required by each pet (and in the case of some added nutrients such as vitamin A, toxicity can occur if too much is added).

While the AAFCO nutrient guidelines would appear sufficient to allow pet food manufacturers to formulate a "complete and balanced" diet, this is not necessarily the case (this is one reason for manufacturers' use of extra nutrients, as mentioned above). According to Dr. Jean Hofve, Companion Animal Program Coordinator for the Animal Protection Institute (API), the data used for AAFCO nutrient recommendations was collected to a significant degree in other species, such as chicks and rats, and in puppies and kittens. There is actually very little data supporting the adult cat requirements; this same lack of supporting data is also true for adult dogs, although

a bit more has been done with working dogs (sled dogs) and large breeds.

According to an article in the *Journal of Nutrition* titled "Assessment of the Nutritional Adequacy of Pet Foods Through the Life Cycle," (Morris and Rogers, 1994), "there is virtually no information on the bioavailability of nutrients for companion animals in many of the common dietary ingredients used in pet foods. These ingredients are generally by-products of the meat, poultry, and fishing industries, with the potential for wide variation in nutrient composition. Claims of nutritional adequacy of pet foods based on the current Association of American Feed Control Officials (AAFCO) nutrient allowances ('profiles') do not give assurances of nutritional adequacy and will not until ingredients are analyzed and bioavailability values are incorporated."

What about using feeding trials rather than just formulating diets by using nutrient guidelines? While manufacturers can use a larger number of pets in their feeding trials, the AAFCO feeding protocols specify that six dogs (or cats) on a given diet for 6 months is an adequate trial. (The trials have to start with eight animals, but 25% may be dropped for "non-diet related" reasons at any time during the trial.) Basic blood profile values cannot fall below the laboratory minimums by the end of the trial. Any food can also be tested with the "growth/lactation" protocol, which is only 10 weeks, but requires more extensive blood testing and record keeping. Thus, a food labeled "for all life stages" may have been tested on six animals for 10 weeks, and that's it.

Feeding trials only really tell about palatability and to some extent digestibility and absorbability of the diet.

Complicating all this is that a company can test one food, and then put a label statement on a whole "family" of "related" foods that are nutritionally "equivalent" (within specified limits on moisture, metabolizable energy, and a handful of individual nutrients—as long as the "family member" also meets either the chemical analysis of the lead product on all other nutrients *or* the nutrient profiles, whichever is less.

Read the Label!

In numerous instances, a food that passed the feeding protocols still did not support long-term maintenance. In one cattery, queens suddenly started having weak litters with a very high mortality rate 8 months after a diet change. The cause was traced to a mineral deficiency. So the six-month trial had meant nothing, even though a food passing feeding trials would always be recommended over one that met the Nutrient Profiles. In fact, a food passing feeding trials need *not* meet the Nutrient Profiles.

In the 1980s, many cats were dying from dilated **cardiomyopathy** (page 91). It was determined that decreased levels of taurine (taurine deficiency) was the underlying cause despite the fact that cats with dilated cardiomyopathy were eating diets that had passed feeding trials! Obviously the short-term trials in a limited number of cats were not adequate to show that long-term use of the diets in some cats predisposed them to dilated cardiomyopathy as a result of taurine deficiency. Once the link was made, pet food manufacturers increased taurine levels in the diets, and dilated cardiomyopathy is rarely seen today (and when it is seen, it is often unrelated to taurine deficiency, or it occurs in cats fed vegetarian diets that are not supplemented with taurine).

No studies have shown adequacies or inadequacies of these AAFCO profiles. While they might be better than nothing, pet owners should view them more as recommendations (a starting point) for the "normal, generic pet." Keep in mind that pets are individuals with unique needs. These needs may differ based on breed, genetics, state of health, or illness.

Since we've talked extensively here about the importance of reading the label on your pet's food, let's take a closer look at an example of three labels from dry pet food. One label comes from a premium food; the second label comes from a cheaper, store-brand (generic) food; the third label comes from a more natural diet. Keep the following four points in mind when examining these labels.

1. A more holistic or natural diet should contain fresh whole ingredients rather than by-products.

2. Ingredients are usually listed in descending order from highest concentration to lowest. The first ingredient makes up the largest amount (by weight) of the ingredients.
3. A more holistic or natural diet should be free of artificial colors, flavorings, and preservatives.
4. A meat-based source of protein should be among the first two or three listed ingredients in the food.

Premium Food Label

> Ingredients: Chicken, Brewer's Rice, Ground Wheat, Ground Yellow Corn, Animal Fat (preserved with mixed tocopherols, a source of vitamin E, and ascorbic acid), Corn Gluten Meal, Egg, Whey, Vitamin A, D_3, E, B_{12}, Niacin.

Generic Food Label

> Ingredients: Ground Yellow Corn, Corn Gluten Meal, Soybean Meal, Poultry By-Product Meal, Animal Fat (preserved with BHA), Fish Meal, Meat and Bone Meal, Ground Wheat, Animal Digest, Salt, Ethylenediamine Dihydriodide, Artificial Coloring, Artificial Flavors.

Natural Food Label

> Ingredients: Turkey, Chicken, Whole Ground Barley, Whole Ground Brown Rice, Whole Steamed Potatoes, Chicken Fat (preserved with natural Vitamins C and E), Herring Meal, Whole Raw Apples, Whole Steamed Carrots, Whole Garlic, Alfalfa Sprouts, Lactobacillus, Dried Kelp, Dried Barley Grass.

Read the Label!

Notice the differences among these three labels. With the premium and natural pet foods, an animal source of protein (chicken) is among the first three ingredients listed. In the generic brand of food, an animal source of protein is not listed until the fourth ingredient.

The premium and natural foods use natural antioxidants (tocopherols) as a preservative, whereas the generic brand of food uses chemicals (however, see Common Chemical Preservatives for a greater discussion of why this may be misleading). Also, to make the food more palatable for the dog and more visually appealing to the owner, the generic brand relies upon artificial flavors and colors (various dyes). While the generic brand is less expensive than the premium or natural brands, it is not the best choice when trying to purchase a natural or holistic diet. Even with supplementation, this diet would not approach the quality of the other two foods.

What are "by-products"? Even the best quality premium foods (and some of the diets advertised as "natural") may have one or two ingredients with the term "by-product" listed. It's impossible to tell exactly what makes up a "by-product" because no law governs what can or can't be considered a by-product. As a rule, animal by-products can include any animal parts such as liver, kidneys, lungs, hooves, hair, skin, mammary glands, connective tissue, or intestinal tract. These "foodstuffs" don't sound too appealing, and their nutritional value is questionable at best (if not downright harmful). As the price of food decreases, the reliance of the manufacturer on by-products increases. (Even some of the more expensive premium brands rely on by-products, chemicals, and artificial colorings and flavorings, leading some to comment that "the only thing that is 'premium' about some premium foods is the price!") Using by-products allows manufacturers the opportunity to state that their food meets a certain minimum percent concentration of protein. However, the amino acid content of ingredients like hair, hooves, and connective tissue can't possibly meet even the minimum needs of a pet. Yet, many owners who feed foods with large amounts of by-products still feel that their pets are "healthy" since they do not "look sick!"

PET FOOD INGREDIENTS

Let's take a look at some of the ingredients that are included in foods so that you can appreciate the differences in the quality and ultimate benefit or detriment of these ingredients to your pet's health.

Protein in Pet Foods

The biological value of the protein, which describes how efficiently the protein is digested, absorbed, and utilized by the pet, is important in protein selection. Meats, eggs, and dairy products have high biological values, whereas many by-products (other than organ meats) do not. Plant proteins have lower biological value than animal proteins, although some plant proteins (such as soy) have biological value similar to meat proteins.

To decrease the cost of pet foods, manufacturers often rely on proteins (such as plant proteins and various animal by-products such as meat and bonemeals) of low biological value and wholesomeness. Many of the pet foods only contain enough animal protein to provide the minimum of the essential amino acids required by the pet and not provided by the less expensive plant proteins contained in the diet. Cost is further lowered when the animal protein chosen is of quality unfit for human consumption (some meat meals made from animals that died or were decomposing might be chosen by the manufacturer).

Many of the lower-quality animal protein sources (such as meat and bonemeal) show a large amount of variability. There is no standard, for example, for how much meat and how much bone must be included in meat and bonemeal. As a result, it is impossible to know what is in meat and bonemeal and other questionable protein sources, and therefore the protein quality of these products is questionable.

The terms *meat meal, meat* and *bonemeal, by-products* and *by-product meal,* while having certain stated definitions as mentioned earlier in the text, are also quite nebulous and difficult to define. In general, diets containing these items are less likely to provide high-quality protein than diets containing whole meat (such as chicken, turkey, lamb, beef). However, some meat by-products are organ meats such as liver and kidneys. These are acceptable sources of protein when offered occasionally for pets. There is, however, no way to tell from the label just what "by-products" are contained in diets that use meat by-products as the protein source. Only a call to the manufacturer can help explain the exact nature of the ingredients in each individual diet.

Dogs require approximately 13% (young adults) to 19% protein (adults) to maintain tissue reserves. Cats, being true carnivores, require ap-

Read the Label!

proximately 24% protein (or more). However, pet foods often have more protein levels since they often contain protein sources of lower biological value (the lower the biological value, the more protein is needed to meet amino acid needs of the pet).

While cooking foods can improve the digestibility of proteins, excessive heating of foods can reduce amino acid levels and availability.

Carbohydrates in Pet Foods

Various carbohydrates (mainly starches) are included in the commercial diets of dogs and cats to provide energy to the pet. However, as is the case with proteins, some carbohydrates are more wholesome than others.

Rice is an easily digestible starch. Potato or macaroni, while not as easily and thoroughly digestible and assimilated as rice, would be second and third choices, respectively, in the diet of dogs and cats. Potatoes cooked with the skin serve as a good source of fiber for pets. Diets higher in fiber are often used for weight loss in pets, and may be helpful in regulating blood glucose levels, which are important for pets with diabetes.

Sucrose is a sugar often used as a preservative in soft-moist foods (burgers). Pets do not need sugar in their diets, and excess sucrose can cause diarrhea. Feeding diets high in sucrose may predispose pets to diabetes.

Soybeans are not easily digested by dogs and cats; diets high in soybeans may cause excessive intestinal gas (flatus).

Many processed foods contain less expensive (and less thoroughly digestible and assimilated) carbohydrates. These include wheat, beans, and oats.

Cooking starch improves its digestibility and therefore availability.

While white rice can be used, brown rice (rice that has not been bleached) is often preferred for its greater nutrient content than white rice.

Even though most, if not all, processed foods (as well as some of the homemade diets mentioned here) include carbohydrates in feline diets, cats are true carnivores and do not have a defined dietary carbohydrate requirement. Owners who choose to feed cats processed foods should choose diets with minimum carbohydrates as they most closely match the cat's diet in the wild. (Even dogs do not require carbohydrates in their diets after weaning, although they can tolerate them more easily than cats because dogs are omnivorous.)

Fat in Pet Foods

Fats are useful to provide energy, allow absorption of fat-soluble vitamins (vitamins A, D, and E), provide essential fatty acids, and give flavor to pet foods.

The three essential fatty acids required by pets are linoleic acid (the source of omega-6 fatty acids), linolenic acid (the source of omega-3 fatty acids), and arachidonic acid. Plants (but not animals) produce linoleic and linolenic acids, and most animals (except cats) can make arachidonic acid from linoleic acid. Therefore, cats, unlike dogs, require arachidonic acid in their diets (which they get from meat).

Fats are usually at least 5% of the diet. Higher levels are not usually harmful as long as adequate protein is present in the diet. High fat diets may cause diarrhea or obesity.

Chemical Preservatives/Antioxidants

Preservatives and antioxidants are added to food to retard the oxidation of fats (prevent them from becoming rancid) and to increase the shelf life of processed foods. Without antioxidants and preservatives in food, fats become rancid; the rancidity destroys nutrients and results in the production of toxic chemicals. Foods without preservatives would need to be ingested shortly after manufacture and could not remain on shelves. Homemade diets do not require preservatives if they refrigerated (or frozen) and then are ingested within a few days of preparation.

Natural antioxidants can be used in place of chemical antioxidants and preservatives, but they are more expensive. This is why lower-cost foods rely on chemical preservatives.

While natural antioxidants are preferred by pet owners who take a holistic approach to pet care, these natural antioxidants (such as vitamin E) can be consumed by the fats in the diet as they undergo oxidation, resulting in a vitamin deficiency. This is another reason why some diets have chemical preservatives added. It is also a reason why additional vitamins might be added

Read the Label!

🐾 COMMON PET FOOD INGREDIENTS

Pet owners experience a great deal of confusion when they read terms like chicken, chicken meal, and chicken by-product meal. Here is how the AAFCO defines these terms. The following information is adapted from a table originally appearing in the August 2000 issue of *Cat Fancy* and is reprinted with permission from Lisa Kobs.

Protein   Used as an energy source, protein also functions to maintain a pet's body. It is the main component of muscles, organs, and glands and acts as the building block for important body regulators such as enzymes and hormones.

Animal by-product meal: Rendered mammal tissue without added hair, hoof, horn, hide trimmings, manure and stomach contents, except in such amounts as may occur unavoidably in good processing practices. This definition is used to cover tissue products that do not meet other definitions and is not intended to be used to label a mixture of animal tissue products.

Corn gluten meal: The dried residue of corn protein with the starch and fat removed, and the separation of the bran by a process employed in wet milling manufacture of corn starch and syrup. Corn gluten meal is a by-product and low in critical amino acids. Ground corn, which contains the entire corn kernel, is preferred.

Dried egg: The egg white and yolk, which have had the moisture removed.

Dried egg white: Dried eggs, with the yolk removed, containing a higher percentage of protein.

Dried whey: A fraction of milk that contains whey protein and lactose, or milk sugar, and has had its moisture removed.

Meat: Clean flesh from slaughtered animals limited to skeletal muscle or that found in the tongue, diaphragm, heart, or esophagus, with or without accompanying fat, sinew, skin, nerve, and blood vessels. Can be from any animal species such as pigs, goats, rabbits, and so forth. If meat has a descriptive name (such as turkey), it must correspond to that species.

Meat and bone meal: Rendered (fat and water removed) mammal tissue, including bone without added blood, hair, hoof, horn, hide trim-mings, manure and stomach contents, except in such amounts as may occur unavoidably in good processing practices. This is a by-product with variable amounts of meat and bone (differing between batches) and variable protein quality. Like meat meal, it can contain meat from "4D" animals (dead, dying, diseased, or disabled), which come from animals condemned for human consumption.

Meat by-product: Nonrendered (contains fat and water) clean parts other than meat, including lungs, spleen, kidneys, brain, livers, blood, bone, stomachs, and intestines freed of contents. Cannot have hair, horns, teeth, and hoofs. While this protein source may be more wholesome than meat meal or meat and bone-meal (since it comes from nonrendered tissue and from slaughtered animals rather than from carcasses of already dead animals), there is no way to tell by reading the label how much of which "by-products" are included in the food.

Meat meal: (Lamb meal, for example) Rendered (fat and water removed) mammal tissue without added blood, hair, hoof, horn, hide trimmings, manure and stomach contents, except in such amounts as may occur unavoidably in good processing practices. It can contain meat from 4D animals (dead, dying, diseased, or disabled), which come from animals condemned for human consumption. However, meat meal can also come from dehydrated meat and can be of high quality (some manufacturers of higher quality natural dog and cat foods make their own meal). As a rule, it should be avoided unless you contact the manufacturer to find out what exactly is in the "meat meal."

Poultry: Clean combination of flesh and skin, with or without accompanying bone, and does not contain feathers, heads, feet, and guts. The origin is any fowl—turkeys, ducks, geese, and so forth. If it bears a descriptive name, it must correspond to that species.

Poultry by-product meal: Ground, rendered, clean slaughtered poultry carcass parts such as necks, feet, undeveloped eggs, and intestines. Cannot contain any feathers, except in such amounts as may occur unavoidably in good processing practices. The quality is very inconsistent between batches. Because it is a by-product, it is best avoided in dog and cat food.

Poultry by-product: Nonrendered, clean, slaughtered poultry such as heads, feet, and viscera free from fecal content and foreign matter, except in such amounts as may occur unavoidably in good processing practices. The quality is very inconsistent between batches. Because it is a by-product, it is best avoided in dog and cat food.

Poultry meal: Dry, rendered flesh and skin, with our without accompanying bone, that does not contain feathers, heads, feet, and guts, except in such amounts as may occur unavoidably in good processing practices. The quality is very inconsistent between batches. Because it is a by-product, it is best avoided in dog and cat food.

Rice gluten: The dried residue of rice protein without starch or fat. Rice gluten is a by-product and low in critical amino acids. Ground or whole rice is preferred.

Soy protein concentrate and soy isolate: Concentrated sources of soy protein. Concentrate is 80% protein, and isolate is 90% protein.

Whey concentrate and whey isolate: More concentrated forms of whey protein.

Carbohydrates   Dogs are more omnivorous and can use carbohydrates in their diets, although they are not essential. Cats can use a limited amount of carbohydrates as energy, but there is no specific carbohydrate requirement for cats.

Brewers rice: A by-product of milling consisting of the small milled fragments of rice kernels that have been separated from larger kernels of milled rice; not as wholesome as ground brown (or white) rice. This is a by-product and is not as healthy as whole rice.

Ground brown rice: The entire product obtained in grinding rice kernels after the hulls and pericarp have been removed. Brown rice is better than white (bleached) rice, which has fewer nutrients than brown rice.

Ground corn: The entire ground kernel of corn including carbohydrates, protein, and fat. This is preferred to corn fractions (such as gluten meal), which are missing nutrients.

Peanut Hulls: This ingredient consists of the outer hull of the peanut shell. It is a by-product that is often added as a source of fiber in "Lite" or restrictive diets. It has no nutritional value. There is the potential for contamination with aflatoxin mold, which can cause disease in pets.

Rice flour: The finely ground meal obtained from milling rice, containing mostly starch and protein with some fine particles of rice bran. This is a by-product and is not as healthful as whole rice.

Sorghum: The ground grain of the sorghum plant.

Soybean meal: The product obtained by grinding flakes, which remain after most of the oil has been removed from soybeans.

Wheat flour: The finely ground meal obtained from milling wheat, containing mostly starch and protein with some fine particles of wheat bran. This is a by-product and is not as healthful as whole wheat.

Wheat middlings: Also called wheat mill run or wheat mids, wheat middlings is a by-product of milling consisting of the particles of wheat bran and flour from the end of the mill from commercial flour milling. This is a by-product and is not as healthful as whole wheat.

Fat   Fat functions as a concentrated source of energy. It carries fat-soluble vitamins, provides essential fatty acids, and enhances food palatability.

Animal fat: Fat from mammal or poultry tissue in the commercial process of rendering or extracting.

Chicken fat: Fat from chickens in the commercial processing of rendering.

Beef tallow: Fat from cattle.

Oil: Liquid fat extracted from plant sources such as corn, soybeans, sunflowers, and so forth.

Fiber   Fiber is used to maintain gastrointestinal functioning and promote normal stools. Cats do not have a strict dietary requirement for fiber.

Beet pulp: Dried residue from sugar beets used in sugar processing used as fiber.

Rice bran: The outer coating of a rice kernel used as fiber.

Peanut hulls: The outer hull of the peanut shell used as fiber.

Read the Label!

to the diet, as well as one of the reasons why additional supplementation with natural vitamins is recommended, even for the better natural diets.

Common Chemical Preservatives

The labeling on the pet's food lists the chemicals (additives) that are required to be listed if they are included in the diet. However, this can be misleading for two reasons. First, the food might contain chemicals that are not required to be listed on the label. Second, while the manufacturer of the final food product may not add chemicals or additives, the suppliers of the raw ingredients (such as fats or animal meals) might add chemicals to the raw products but not notify the manufacturer of the final product. These additives would not be listed on the diet's label, and there is unfortunately no way to determine whether this occurs.

Butylated hydroxyanisole (BHA) is a chemical preservative and antioxidant used in many foods. It can cause allergic reactions and affects liver and kidney functions. It is listed as GRAS, which means "Generally Regarded As Safe" in certain low concentrations.

Ethylenediamine can be used as a solvent, urinary acidifier, and as a substance to promote color retention. It can be irritating to the skin and mucous membranes and can sensitize individuals leading to asthmatic reactions and allergic skin rashes.

Butylated hydroxytoluene (BHT) is another preservative and antioxidant. Also listed as GRAS, BHT also can cause liver and kidney problems.

MSG (monosodium glutamate) functions as a flavor enhancer. In people experiencing sensitivity to MSG, headaches and a tingling in the fingers is seen (the condition is referred to as "Quick Queasy").

Sodium metabisulphite is another chemical preservative. In people, this chemical has been linked to weakness, loss of consciousness, difficulty swallowing, and brain damage.

Sugar, sorbitol, ethylene glycol, and propylene glycol are used as preservatives and sweeteners. Artificial sweeteners may be related to diabetes, obesity, and are an empty source of calories. Propylene glycol, most commonly used in semi-moist diets, can cause anemia in cats and should also be avoided in diabetic animals. Ethylene glycol, also called antifreeze, can be fatal to pets in high doses.

Ethoxyquin is a preservative also used as a rubber hardener, insecticide, and pesticide. It is permitted in pet foods at a very low concentration of 0.0075% (one-half of the previously allowed 0.0015%). More than 75 years of use have not shown it to be harmful; on the other hand, any pet who receives enough of any chemical could experience toxicity or long-term effects. Additionally, depending upon the dosage, ethoxyquin could prevent cancer (by binding carcinogenic chemicals as well as enzymes that convert inert chemicals into carcinogens) or cause it. While the low use of ethoxyquin in pet foods seems safe, public outcry has caused most pet food manufacturers to instead use natural antioxidant vitamins.

Are any chemicals safe? Certainly, no one would argue that we have received many benefits from a wide variety of chemicals. However, when possible, it would be in the pet's best interest if non-chemical alternatives (natural antioxidants and preservatives) were used, to minimize toxicity to the pet. A number of chronic disorders—such as various cancers, immune diseases, arthritis, and allergies—are blamed on the use of a number of chemicals contained in pet foods. Although direct proof of this is lacking, these chemicals are not inert and can be metabolized in the intestines and absorbed by the pet.

While the use of these chemicals has not been proven to cause specific diseases when fed at the levels found in pet foods, and while most animals eating commercial foods appear "healthful" (although from a holistic standpoint, looks can be deceiving), we have no firm data on whether or not they may be related to many of these chronic immune disorders when ingested long-term. Therefore, whenever possible, the most healthful alternative is to prepare foods at home or use the natural diets that do not contain these chemicals.

Flavorings

Garlic and onion are often added to diets for flavoring, and in the case of natural diets, garlic is often added for its purported medicinal proper-

Read the Label!

ties (antibacterial, anticancer, immune stimulating). At the dosages listed, the concentration of **garlic** (page 204) is unlikely to be toxic and may be helpful to the pet. Onions are potentially more toxic, especially for cats in which severe anemia could result. It is not recommended to add onions to the diets of dogs and cats.

Miscellaneous Processing Ingredients

- **Digest:** Enzymatic liquefaction or hydrolysis of animal tissue used for flavor.
- **Erythorbic acid:** Prevents the heat of canning from destroying food color.
- **Guar gum, carrageenan, locust bean gum, corn starch-modified, xanthan gum:** Thickening ingredients used to hold canned food together.
- **Sodium tripolyphosphate:** Helps to hold food together by binding water. This also keeps the food tender and helps it to come out of the can.
- **Phosphoric acid:** Used to provide the acid flavor cats love.
- **Propylene glycol, glycerin, sorbitol:** Used to control water in semi-moist foods. Propylene glycol can cause anemia in cats, and both propylene glycol and sorbitol may contribute to diabetes in dogs and cats.

Coloring Enhancers

These ingredients are used to modify the appearance of the food.

- **Caramel color:** A brown coloring agent used to enhance and darken food color.
- **Sodium nitrite:** Used as an antimicrobial agent to kill bacteria and to help canned food maintain a pink color after processing.
- **Titanium dioxide:** A white powder used to lighten up food color.
- **Yellow #5, Yellow #6, Red #3:** Food dyes used in chicken-based food to enhance color.

Preservatives

Preservatives are used to extend shelf life and reduce fat spoilage (rancidity), which can lead to "off" flavors.

- **Ascorbic acid:** Natural source of preservative from vitamin C.

- **BHA, BHT, ethoxyquin:** Artificial sources of preservatives.
- **Mixed tocopherols:** Natural source of preservative from vitamin E but does not keep food fresh as long as artificial sources.

While this discussion may seem like an attack on all processed foods, that is not the case. It is true that many of the diets on the market today may not be the best choice for maintaining health and preventing disease, and may even contribute to a lack of health (or outright disease) in our pets. However, some companies are now promoting more natural diets made from higher quality ingredients without chemical additives. Are these any different or better than many of the other foods? For the most part, while not quite as good as natural homemade diets made from wholesome ingredients, with proper supplementation, some of these newer diets are acceptable alternatives for owners who are unable to prepare diets at home for feeding their pets. Ultimately you will still need to read the label and question the manufacturer to separate the good ones from the bad. Working with the information in this book and with your holistic veterinarian will help you select the better diets if you choose to feed those rather than prepare diets at home.

To summarize, when selecting a commercially prepared product, try to choose one with the least number of by-products, fillers, and chemicals. Reading the label is a starting point, but realize that not everything contained in the diet has to be listed on the label. A phone call to the manufacturer should help answer most questions (if the manufacturer is evasive on the phone, the diet probably is not one to select for your pet). Also keep in mind that if the manufacturer of the final product purchases meals from other sources, even the final manufacturer may not know everything in the food. For this reason, many holistic diets recommend owners prepare diets at home whenever this is possible.

COST VERSUS PRICE

Obviously, many sources compete for your pet food dollar. Making the decision about what food to feed is important and should not be done hastily.

Read the Label!

The price of pet foods is determined by many factors. These include marketing and advertising, feeding trials, and quality of ingredients. If you decide to feed processed foods, it is important to understand the difference between cost and price. The *cost* of pet foods, which is different from the *price* of the foods, is exactly how much it costs to feed the pet at each meal.

The cost of the food is really more important than the price. For example, a generic brand of food has a lower price than a more wholesome natural brand, but actually costs more. Why? Let's suppose that due to the high bulk content of the generic food, a 10-pound bag lasts only 2 weeks for your pet because he has to eat so much of it to get his required daily energy. Let's suppose that same 10-pound bag of natural food lasts 8 weeks; due to the high-quality ingredients, the pet doesn't need to eat as much. The price of the natural food may be more for each bag; but because it lasts longer, the cost is lower. With the natural food, there may be less stool volume produced each day (a desirable feature for most owners), and there may be fewer doctor bills since the food is a better diet for the pet. While the cost of the ingredients in natural diets is higher than generic diets, the health benefits and the lower amount of food needed at each feeding compensate for the higher-priced ingredients.

PALATABILITY AND ACCEPTABILITY

While the quality of ingredients, as well as the inclusion or exclusion of chemical additives are important factors to consider when deciding upon the selection of a processed food, you should consider other factors when selecting a food as well.

No matter how good the nutrients are in a particular pet food, the pet must eat it! While that may sound obvious, not every dog or cat likes every food. Palatability is a measure of how palatable or tasty a particular food is. Several factors influence the palatability of a food. These include:

- **Temperature.** Food warmed to body temperature is more palatable than room temperature; warming the food is often advised for puppies and dogs who don't seem interested

in a food or for pets who are ill. Warming only works for canned food; warm water can be added to dry food for a similar effect.
- **Odor.** Cats in particular have a great sense of smell; therefore, the food must smell good for the pet to eat it. Warming increases odor. Pets with blocked nasal passages (from illness) may not be able to smell and therefore won't eat the food.
- **Texture.** Some pets prefer a certain feel or shape of the food in the mouth; canned food is always preferred over dry food and texture has something to do with this.
- **Nutrient content.** Foods with a higher fat content are usually preferred over foods that are high in fiber, so-called "diet" foods.
- **Habit.** Most pets prefer the diet to which they are accustomed; new foods should be introduced slowly.

Just because a food is palatable doesn't mean your pet will accept it. In order for food to be accepted, the dog or cat must obviously be hungry and have a need for the food. Additionally, the pet must not be averse to the food (if the food previously made the pet sick, he may be unlikely to eat it).

HYPOALLERGENIC DIETS

Often, the advertising developed to sell pet food can be misleading. Recently, many pet owners have jumped on the "lamb and rice" bandwagon. By itself, there is nothing inherently good or bad about lamb and rice diets. However, some pet food manufacturers have misled pet owners by claiming that lamb and rice diets are "hypoallergenic." Pet food manufacturers, in their attempts to sell yet another type of food, have pushed lamb and rice diets as the newest, best things for pets.

While nothing is wrong with lamb and rice diets, the PR people at the pet food companies have put one over on the average pet owner. Here are some factors to consider before you spend extra money on this special diet:

Any food can cause allergy. While doctors debate just how common food allergies really are (many practitioners feel feeding commercial diets

Read the Label!

contributes to many illnesses, including food allergies and general ill health, whereas others feel that true "food allergies" are rare), it is important to know that *any* food can cause food allergies. As a cause of skin disease, food allergies are extremely rare in pets; less than 10% of puppies, dogs, kittens, and cats will ever develop a true food allergy.

There is nothing inherently hypoallergenic about lamb or rice. Food allergies are more likely to be caused by a protein source that a pet has eaten for some period of time, often several years. Assuming your pet is never exposed to lamb, he'll never develop an allergy to lamb. However, if you start feeding him a lamb-based diet, he can certainly become allergic to lamb later in life. The homemade diets for pets with food allergies presented later use other protein sources, such as venison and rabbit, as most pets have not been exposed to these rarer and more expensive protein sources.

Pets who are diagnosed with food allergies need a hypoallergenic diet. If your pet is used to eating lamb, you may find it difficult (and expensive) to find a suitable diet (other choices of diets for pets with food allergies include rabbit, fish, turkey, shrimp, lobster, or venison).

Many "lamb and rice diets" also contain egg, wheat, soy, beef, fish, and chicken. Your pet could develop allergies to any or all of these substances despite eating a "lamb and rice" diet. Read the label to see what else is in your pet's "lamb and rice" diet.

Since your pet doesn't derive any extra nutritional benefit from lamb, it would probably be better to feed a diet with a different protein source. If your pet is ever diagnosed with a food allergy, then your veterinarian may recommend a lamb-based diet as a treatment.

 # HOMEMADE NATURAL DIETS

Many holistic pet owners choose to prepare food for their pets at home. The following information will help you prepare the best diet possible for your pet. As is true with the selection of processed diets, you should work with your veterinarian to make sure that any homemade diet you prepare is best for your pet.

The idea behind the homemade diets is that the owner will use fresh, minimally processed ingredients. By offering fresh food, you include more nutrients in the diet that would otherwise be removed as a result of processing. Homemade diets seek to emphasize freshness and wholesomeness of ingredients. These homemade diets seek to mimic the diet the pet would encounter in the wild. The diets avoid the harmful chemical preservatives, additives, and artificial colorings and flavors that may occur in some commercially prepared diets. Homemade diets address common concerns owners may express concerning commercial pet foods, such as these:

- By-products that may lack nutritional value and may be toxic
- Food additives, flavoring, and colors that are added for the benefit of the consumer but which are of no nutritional value to pets (and may be harmful)
- Failure to include fresh, wholesome ingredients which could benefit the pet by providing a readily and easily digestible and absorbable source of vitamins, minerals, and enzymes
- Fillers such as animal and plant by-products that are of questionable nutritional value yet are often added to generic diets so the manufacturer can meet the minimum nutrient values required to be in the food

While owners have often been told "Don't feed your pet people food," this advice is erroneous for two reasons. First, processed dog food and cat food is nothing more than "people food" processed into pellets and put in a bag for pets (although many manufacturers do use ingredients not fit for human consumption). Second, prior to the origin of processed foods in the early 1900s, our dogs and cats ate nothing but people food (unless the dog or cat hunted its own meals). Many holistic veterinarians think that the diseases we now see (such as immune disorders, allergies, and arthritis that were rare in past years) are a direct result of processed foods.

Fresh foods prepared at home with minimal processing provide phytonutrients (nutrients found in plants) such as bioflavonoids and many nutrients not yet discovered. This is why studies showing the use of vitamins and minerals from food sources often show positive results whereas studies using selected chemically synthesized vitamins and minerals do not show the same positive results and often show negative results. Obviously, the whole food sources contain as yet undiscovered nutrients (not found in most vitamin pills) that are helping the pet. This is another good reason to consider preparing food for your dog or cat at home.

If you choose to feed a homemade diet, you will need to make the distinction between feeding a diet containing cooked ingredients (meat) or a diet where the protein source (meat) is fed raw. The following discussion will take a look at a popular and often recommended raw diet, and will present an objective overview of some of the debate both for and against feeding raw diets.

RAW VERSUS COOKED FOOD

As a pet owner, you may have heard a lot of arguments for or against feeding your dog or cat a diet in a raw, fresh, uncooked state. Many owners feel that feeding a raw diet is the only way to offer a truly healthful diet, and that cooking somehow destroys many of the nutrients in the diet.

Because this topic is so controversial and there is so little science to back up many of the arguments on both sides, it is important that we address both the pros and the cons concerning feeding raw foods.

The argument really concerns what has become known as the BARF diet, also called the Billinghurst diet after Dr. Ian Billinghurst, the doctor who came up with this concept. BARF is an acronym which stands for "Bones and Raw Food." In this diet, the pet is fed raw bones, raw

meat, raw vegetables, and a carbohydrate source such as rice. The concept is simple: Since the wild relatives of our pets eat raw meat, and they seemed to be "healthier" than our domesticated dogs and cats, that is what our pets should eat. This diet has been fed to many pets with little harm, produces great-looking animals, and results in very few problems. Let's take an objective look at many of the claims made by proponents of this diet.

1. *Our pets should eat what their wild ancestors eat.* While it is true that the wild ancestors eat raw, freshly killed foods, our pets are not wild animals but rather domestic relatives of wild animals. That doesn't mean we can't feed them a similar diet, only that we keep in mind that we are talking about totally different groups of animals with different lifestyles, exercise patterns, and health concerns.

2. *Raw meat is safe for our pets; wild animals suffer no ill effects from raw meat.* Whether or not raw meat is safe is debatable, although most pet owners and holistic veterinarians report no obvious health problems in pets fed raw meat. Conversely, many owners and doctors report healthier-looking coats and skin, less itching, less arthritis, and general overall health improvement once pets are slowly switched from processed food to raw food in homemade diets. Health concerns with feeding raw meat, including parasites and bacterial contamination, are discussed at length further along in this discussion.

To say that wild animals suffer no ill effects from eating raw meat is ignorant and presupposes we know everything that happens to every wild animal. While most wild animals thrive on their diets (as would be expected), we also know that wild prey (such as rabbits and rodents) carry parasites (which are obviously transmitted to wild animal predator relatives of our pets who eat the infected prey) and that any infected meat could certainly cause illness in a wild animal. Unfortunately we don't have any studies showing the effects of what happens when this infected prey is eaten by wild relatives of our dogs and cats.

3. *Animals are more acidic compared to people. That is why they don't get sick eating raw meat.* It isn't clear what this statement means, or how someone could even measure a pet's "acidity." We can only assume that those who make this statement somehow assume that the "acid" in the pet's body or stomach in some way can detoxify anything bad in the diet. While it is true that wild animals have adapted to their diets, this in no way means that they are immune to problems associated with the diet. For example, if a wild animal were only able to eat the muscle meat on the prey as the sole dietary ingredient, that animal would develop calcium deficiency. If the meat were rancid and infected with bacteria, the animal could certainly develop food poisoning (as often happens with our own pets who get into and eat garbage). Meat infected with parasites can be eaten by animals and will result in the animal becoming infected with the parasites. So this statement about acidity just doesn't hold up.

4. *Raw meat is safe for our pets. Their systems are designed to handle any problems with the meat.* This all depends what is meant by "safe." Certainly raw meat that was raised free of chemicals and hormones, and that isn't infected with bacteria or parasites, is safe. Many strains of resistant bacteria have become more prevalent today; food safety should be a major concern among pet owners. A recent report mentioned a resistant strain of *Camphylobacter jejuni* bacterium that was highly prevalent in chicken, which is the main recommended raw food. While many dogs and cats may be able to handle the bacterial load of the BARF program, some, especially those not already in good health, may not, which can lead to potentially serious consequences. There are reports of supposedly healthy pets doing fine on diets like the BARF diet who then develop illness (such as *Salmonella*-induced diarrhea) when the owner feeds raw chicken from another supplier or from a contaminated source. Switching the pet to a better source (non-contaminated source) of meat then clears up the problem. Most holistic veterinarians believe that some dogs and cats can tolerate exposure to the pathogens in uncooked meat (and in today's world there will probably always be some) and others cannot, depending on their own health status.

One area of disagreement concerns the feeding of raw meat to pets with illness (such as immune problems like cancer). While some people feel that these severely ill pets are most likely the ones who need the additional nutrition found in raw food, others prefer not to feed raw food to these pets as their immune systems are suppressed and are less likely to fight off any infectious organisms that may be found in the food. This issue should be thoroughly discussed with your veterinarian before feeding raw meat diets to any ill pet.

Owners who choose to feed raw meat must do all they can to ensure that this meat is "safe" and free from pesticide, chemical, and hormonal residues as well as parasite ova (eggs). Proper handling of the meat is needed to ensure that it stays "safe" at home. Most food poisoning results from improper handling at home rather than a problem with the actual source of the meat itself.

When pet owners say that animals can handle problems with raw meat, they seem to mean that the digestive tracts and immune systems of our pets (and wild animals) can eliminate any infections or parasites before they cause problems for the animals. While it is true that a healthy pet is less likely to become ill, and is less likely to develop disease when infected with parasites (although this depends upon the parasite and the number of parasites infecting the animal), raw meat can still make an animal sick. When following the guidelines listed to follow, however, this is highly unlikely and may be a risk you are willing to assume.

What seems interesting is that proponents of feeding raw meat state that it is acceptable to feed pets raw meat *except* raw pork or raw wild meat (such as venison or rabbit). The reason for this warning (which, by the way, many veterinarians do agree with) is that these meats are more likely than beef or lamb to harbor parasites. However, this warning seems contradictory: If our pets "can handle" raw meat because of their "acidity" and their immune systems, why couldn't they "handle" the parasites present in any raw meat? To many doctors, this is an obvious discrepancy that discredits the argument about raw meat being "totally safe" for pets.

5. *Feeding bones is safe for pets.* Once again we need to define safe. Most pets eating raw bones do not die, develop impactions of the digestive tract, fracture teeth, or develop any other problems. Still, some do, as most veterinarians will attest. Some proponents state that only cooked bones, which are softer than raw uncooked bones, are likely to splinter and cause problems. Other suggestions include smashing them with a hammer first, so they are in smaller pieces that should pass easily. (Of course, even small pieces can potentially cut intestinal mucosa or become lodged somewhere, unless the pieces are ground into a bone powder.) Another suggestion is to grind up chicken and bones into a homemade meal for the pet. While this loses some of the dental benefits seen in pets who eat whole bones, it gains some safety and adds usefulness for toothless patients.

Once again, the choice about feeding any bones is left up to your discretion after a thorough discussion with your holistic veterinarian.

6. *The BARF diet, since it is the same food wild animals eat, is balanced for a pet's nutritional needs.* While a properly balanced diet is the basis of any health program for pets, some concern has been expressed about using the basic BARF diet for each and every pet. Each pet is different, and each pet has his own nutritional needs in times of health as well as times of illness. Regarding the basic BARF diet, the daily ration has about 6,900 kcals/kg on a dry basis, has higher levels of calcium and phosphorus recommended by most nutritionists for growth and not maintenance, and contains high levels of fat. In addition, some question exists regarding levels and bioavailability of essential vitamins and minerals.

Still, many pets do well on this diet. Working with your veterinarian to properly supplement and formulate the diet for your pet's needs can be a viable alternative to most commercial processed foods.

Here are some additional concerns and problems expressed by holistic veterinarians who have seen some problems with the BARF diet.

Fractured teeth have been seen in dogs eating bones. Commonly, the fourth premolars, the large upper cheek teeth that do a lot of the grinding of food, are the ones most commonly broken. The fractures occur more frequently when pets eat bones that have the shaft chewed or broken longitudinally; this broken piece of bone can act as a wedge and causes a lateral slab fracture of the fourth premolar. In addition, broken bones can lodge into the hard palate between the teeth. Removal of this piece of bone would require anesthesia. One suggestion to minimize fractured teeth and lodged bones is to supervise bone chewing by the pet, discarding the bone after the "knuckle" part (the soft part) is chewed off.

It is suggested that raw bones (rather than cooked bones) be fed to dogs and cats. The raw bones are softer than cooked bones and less likely to break apart. While raw bones are not as hard as dry bones or cow hooves, dogs who were fed a raw diet similar to the BARF diet are reported to have a significantly higher level of tooth fractures than are dogs on a "normal" diet.

Other reported problems seen in dogs eating the BARF diet include eclampsia (low blood calcium following delivery of puppies); pancreatitis (from eating a lot of marrow); intestinal perforations (punctured holes in the intestines from the sharp edges of the bones); iron-deficiency anemia associated with puppy deaths; "rage" syndrome in dogs whose rectum was impacted with small, sharp pieces of bone (the "rage" resolved after the bone pieces were removed and bones were eliminated from the diet); straining to defecate due to obstruction by bones; fever and toxemia; and death in pets with deficient immune systems (possibly due to bacterial contamination and toxemia).

Cautions for a Raw Diet

While some of these concerns are obviously serious health problems, most pet owners report no problems when feeding their pets raw bones and raw diets. It appears that the following cautions are in order to minimize the possibility of any side effects that can occur when feeding bones as part of the BARF diet:

Give bones in moderation. Bones should be a small part of the diet, and veterinary supervision is critical in converting a pet to the BARF diet or any diet that is new to the pet.

Use raw, meaty smaller bones. Bones such as chicken wings and necks are less likely to cause problems than larger, cooked bones. It appears that most problems occur when meaty bones are not used or when mainly beef bones are used.

Balance the diet with fibrous vegetables. This will increase bulk and encourage movement of the bones through the intestinal tract.

While it may seem that the evidence suggests pets should not eat raw meat or bones, that is not necessarily the case. Anecdotal reports (and some "feeling" among pet owners and holistic veterinarians) supports the idea that pets eating raw foods look better and are healthier than pets eating cooked foods. Unfortunately, no good current studies compare the "health" of pets eating raw versus cooked foods, nor do we have any studies comparing the safety of either diet. Based on personal experiences, most doctors would say that many pet owners feed raw meat and bones and have not reported problems in their pets.

The final choice will be left to the owner. Regardless of how you choose to feed your pet, properly supplementing your pet's diet to prevent deficiencies and ensure maximum health is important. For a complete discussion of supplements, see Part Two.

For now, here are some helpful hints (followed by a number of recipes) for those who choose homemade natural diets.

Proceed with caution! While holistic purists often recommend feeding the uncooked diets and have not had problems with food poisoning as a result of this recommendation, owners would be wise to be concerned about the possi-

bility of infection from raw meat. The bacteria of immediate concern are *E. coli* and *Salmonella*. Stories exist in the media about human illness and death from both of these organisms. *E. coli* seems to be of most concern from beef, whereas *Salmonella* seems to occur mostly as a result of ingestion of poultry products (raw chicken, turkey, and eggs). Most homemade diets use beef or poultry as the main protein source. Although lamb, venison, or rabbit can be used, it is preferable to reserve these protein sources for pets who have medically confirmed food allergies. Pork, venison, and rabbit should definitely be cooked (I'd would be inclined to cook *any* meat in a pet's diet). For owners who choose to feed raw meat, it would be wise to choose only animal meat that was raised "naturally" (without antibiotics or hormones), thoroughly wash the meat at home, and maybe even prepare the meat by grinding it at home (to prevent cross-contamination with other foods at the local grocery or butcher shop). Any signs of illness as a result of feeding raw meat diets should be evaluated by a veterinarian at once.

Cook foods to ensure safety. A better alternative would be to feed the meat cooked and the other dietary constituents (vegetables) raw or lightly cooked.

Beware of dietary deficiencies. Dietary deficiencies (mainly vitamins and minerals) are more common with homemade diets. Careful attention to proper preparation is critical to prevent both vitamin and mineral deficiencies and excesses. Multivitamin and mineral preparations designed for kittens or adult cats should be used. Some holistic practitioners also recommend the addition of colloidal minerals, which may be a better vehicle in which to deliver minerals to the pet. Child dosages (for puppies) and adult human dosages (for dogs) of human vitamin C and E preparations can also be added for their antioxidant effects. Calcium can be added in the form of bonemeal or calcium tablets (gluconate, carbonate, or the lactate forms are acceptable).

Read the labels. For owners who choose not to prepare a diet at home but prefer a commercially

Homemade Natural Diets

❧ SAFETY

Endotoxins and Mycotoxins
Cooking food improves digestibility and kills many of the bacteria that might cause illness. Since many commercial pet foods use low-quality protein sources (such as meat and bone-meal that are easily contaminated with bacteria), cooking is essential.

However, cooking cannot kill endotoxins, a bacterial by-product. When certain bacteria (E. coli) are cooked and killed, they can release en-dotoxins. The level of endotoxins in the food reflects the amount of bacterial contamination and the quality of the meat (meal) used in the diet. Nothing can be done to remove endotoxins from the contaminated pet food. Endotoxins can cause illness in pets.

Mycotoxins, toxins from molds, may also contaminate pet foods. This is most commonly a problem when the raw grain (especially peanut and cottonseed meals) used in the food persists during processing. As can endotoxins, mycotoxins can cause illness in pets.

prepared diet that is close to natural, read the label to check for quality of ingredients (fresh meat or animal by-products) and lack of additives (look for natural antioxidants such as vitamin E and vitamin C and a lack of artificial coloring and flavoring). Supplementation with natural products such as brewer's yeast, fatty acids, kelp, barley grass, cooked liver, enzyme products, and sprouted beans or seeds are often helpful to replace ingredients that may be lost during processing.

Be cautious when supplementing. Keep in mind when formulating homemade diets that the AAFCO standards mentioned earlier in the chapter are intended for use in manufacturing, not supplementing at home.

When switching from a lower quality food to a more natural diet (either cooked or, especially, raw), you may need some time to get your pet to accept the new diet. Additionally, it will take some time (usually 4 to 8 weeks) for the new diet to work so you can see any positive effects in your pet (more energy, brighter skin and hair-coat, healthier skin, decreased allergies or arthritis) as the body detoxifies itself. There is a secret to switching your dog or cat to a new, more healthful diet. Switching to the new food overnight may cause vomiting or diarrhea in a few dogs or cats; some pets are finicky and may not eat a new diet that is suddenly introduced.

The best way to offer your pet a new diet is by gradually introducing it to the pet. When you have about a week's worth of the old diet remain-ing, purchase or prepare the new, more healthful diet. Add about 10% of the new diet each day, gradually adding more until you run out of the old food and the pet is eating only the new diet. This trick usually prevents upset tummies and eases the transition to the new food.

NATURAL DIETS FOR DOG AND CATS

While several quality natural prepared foods are on the market, there is no question that the freshest, most wholesome diet, over which you have most control, is a homemade diet. Only by preparing your pet's food at home can you exercise complete control over the quality and the type of ingredients that your pet will eat.

Many owners have heard that "pets shouldn't eat people food." However, even "dog food" and "cat food" is basically "people food" (although many diets use such poor-quality ingredients that most people would not want to eat those foods). All dog food and cat food starts out with similar (although usually poorer quality) ingredients, the same types of foods that you will use in formulating your pet's diet. However, these ingredients, after being mixed together, are usually heated and pressurized to force the basic mix into extruded pellets that then go into a bag called "dog food" or "cat food."

The homemade diet uses higher quality protein and carbohydrate sources and does not require heating to extremely high temperatures. Also, the homemade food is not extruded into pellets under high pressure. This heating and pressurizing of food destroys most of the nutrients—enzymes, healthy bacteria (probiotics) and vitamins and minerals—that your pet requires. This extensive processing forces pet food manufacturers to add extra vitamins and minerals to the food. Most manufacturers, however, do not add back probiotics or enzymes; supplementation with these ingredients is still necessary to achieve levels found in homemade diets. By making your pet's diet at home, you can achieve minimal destruction of enzymes, probiotics, and vitamins and minerals, ensuring your pet a maximum amount of these important nutrients.

An important advantage to preparing diets for your pet yourself at home is that you can choose the best ingredients available. Many clients prefer to use organically raised plant and animal tissues, which are raised without hormones and chemicals, pesticides, and chemical fertilizers. According to information from the *Organic View* 1:17 (www.purefood.org/organicview.htm), the nutrient contents of foods raised by industrial agricultural practices differs greatly from the nutrients of organically raised foods. For example, *Organic View* reported that in an analysis of USDA nutrient data from 1975 to 1997, the Kushi Institute of Becket, Massachusetts, found that the average calcium levels in 12 fresh vegetables declined 27%; iron levels dropped 37%; vitamin A levels 21%; and vitamin C levels 30%.

They also report that a similar analysis of British nutrient data from 1930 to 1980 published in the *British Food Journal* found that in 20 vegetables, the average calcium content had declined 19%; iron 22%; and potassium 14%. In addition, a 1999 study out of the University of Wisconsin found that three decades of the overuse of nitrogen in U.S. farming has destroyed much of the soil's fertility, causing it to age the equivalent of 5,000 years. Finally, a new U.S. Geological Survey report indicates that acid rain is depleting soil calcium levels in at least ten eastern states, interfering with forest growth and weakening trees' resistance to insects. Findings such as those reported here prompt many owners to search for the most wholesome produce available for including in diets fed to their pets.

Check with stores in your area to see whether they offer organically raised vegetables and animal meats. Also, ask them what they mean by the term "organically raised," as many producers may make this claim but still use conventional agricultural practices. Find out everything you can about the farmers who supply the stores where you shop.

Since every pet is an individual, homemade diets are easily supplemented with additional nutritional supplements as recommended by your veterinarian.

The main drawback to preparing diets at home is that unless you follow properly formulated recipes, it is easy to create nutrient deficiencies or excesses that could cause illness in your pet. Many of the diets listed here are adapted from *Home-Prepared Dog & Cat Diets* by leading gastroenterologist Donald Strombeck. Dr. Strombeck has gone to great lengths to ensure that all of the diets are complete and balanced. He has used these diets for many years with his clinical patients at the University of California at Davis with excellent results.

A homemade diet can be used occasionally to supplement one of the better natural prepared diets, or as the sole diet for the pet. For pets with various medical problems such as heart disease or kidney disease, a homemade diet is probably the best way to go, as no "natural" prepared diets at this time serve the needs of pets with medical disorders. There are medical-type "prescription" diets for pets with various diseases, but these do not always contain wholesome ingredients and may contain by-products and chemicals not desired by owners who opt for holistic care for their pets.

Balancing the following diets is quite simple and only requires a few supplements; a balanced diet using fresh, wholesome ingredients ensures optimal proportions of nutrients and may prevent disease as well as help treat pets with diseases. The optimum amount of any specific nutrient is not always well known; the following diets are formulated with nutrient ranges that can be adjusted under veterinary supervision as needed. Pets are individuals with specific individual nutritional needs. There is no one specific requirement for each nutrient for every pet, despite commercial foods claim to include the "correct" level of nutrients. Depending upon an animal's needs, nutrient levels will vary; owners

Homemade Natural Diets

preparing diets at home for their pets can easily adjust nutrient levels as well as the composition of the diet to meet the pet's changing needs.

For owners who desire to feed a more natural, chemical-free diet, preparing diets at home is easy and cost-effective. Select the freshest ingredients; ideally the vegetables and meats should be from plants and animals raised without chemicals, hormones, or pesticides.

While many veterinarians suggest that feeding raw meat is best, there is always the concern about bacterial contamination and infestation with microscopic parasites. For these reasons, owners should take every precaution when preparing the meat part of the diet. Ideally, the meat should be thoroughly cooked. For those owners who prefer to feed raw meat, the following tips can be helpful (but are not foolproof):

Only chicken, turkey, lamb, or beef should be fed raw; it is best to cook rabbit, venison, wild game, and pork.

Ground meats should ideally be cooked unless the owner grinds the meat at home. (This prevents illnesses from cross-contamination that might have occurred at the store.)

Freeze all meats for at least one week prior to feeding.

Thoroughly wash all meat in clean water prior to feeding; only prepare the amount that will be fed at that meal, keeping the remaining meat frozen.

For pets with illness, especially chronic diseases in which the immune system may not be functioning properly, it may be best to cook the meat and thoroughly clean the vegetables before feeding them to your pet.

Thoroughly clean all utensils used at home in the preparation of raw foods. Do not use utensils that have touched raw foods on cooked foods; clean the utensil or get a new utensil to use on the cooked foods.

Wash your hands thoroughly after handling raw foods.

Use only high quality brand-name supplements recommended by your veterinarian. A discussion of common supplements that can be added to the diet of most pets can be found on page 344.

Note: See the section on **Raw Versus Cooked Food** (page 336) including the discussion of the BARF diet.

Here are some additional tips on preparing the following diets:

Follow the recommendations made on the label of the specific products unless noted otherwise in the diet recipe. Most diets call for chicken fat or canola oil. Chicken fat is best obtained by cooking a whole chicken and reserving the fat (which floats on the top of the water). Many doctors like to add additional omega-3 fatty acids to the diets of dogs and cats to take advantage of the health benefits found in fish oil. (For a thorough discussion of the benefits of **fish oil,** see Part Two, page 202).

Use a calcium/phosphorus source, usually bonemeal, as called for in diets. Use either bonemeal or bonemeal tablets. Alternatively, use a natural product from Standard Process called Calcifood Wafers (calcium/phosphorus) or Calcium Lactate (calcium only). Use 1 Calcifood Wafer or 2 Calcium Lactate tablets for each ½ teaspoon of powdered bonemeal or 2 bonemeal tablets recommended in the diet, unless otherwise noted.

Consider supplementing with a multivitamin/mineral supplement as recommended. You can use a natural, raw human supplement (follow your veterinarian's recommendation if you choose to do this), although a better suggestion is to use a natural product made for pets such as Canine Plus for dogs (VetriScience) or Nu-Cat for cats (VetriScience) following the label dose. Another product that can be used synergistically with the Canine Plus and Nu-Cat is called Catalyn (from Standard Process). The Catalyn is dosed as follows: 1 Catalyn tablet per cat per day; for dogs, use 1 pill per 25 pounds. Follow your veterinarian's advice regarding vitamin-mineral supplementation, as other products are coming onto the market regularly.

Include plant enzymes, which can help improve the digestive efficiency of all diets. This is especially true of processed foods that do not contain natural digestive enzymes. Prozyme and Shake-N-Zyme are two recommended plant enzyme supplements that have proven beneficial for dogs and cats (other products are coming onto the market daily). Follow label directions.

Obtain additional phytonutrients and antioxidants by using green food products containing barley grass and spirulina. Use either Granular Greens from Ark Naturals, which contains spirulina and other green foods, or use Barley Dog or Barley Cat, which only contain barley grass. Other products are coming onto the market; check with your veterinarian for his recommendations.

Add a top dressing of raw or steamed shredded vegetables, which many pets will appreciate. Vegetables including kale, brussels sprouts, broccoli, and carrots will provide additional phytonutrients.

Consider feeding a health blend formula. Missing Link, for example, is quite popular with pet owners and provides vitamins, minerals, fatty acids, enzymes, and probiotics. Check with your veterinarian for her recommendations on using health blend formulas.

A BRIEF PRIMER ON SUPPLEMENTS

A number of nutritional supplements (some were mentioned previously) are available for your pet. Is there such a thing as the perfect or best supplement? Probably no one supplement is perfect for every pet or every condition. However, the best supplement should meet the following conditions:

- *It must be cost-effective.* This does not necessarily mean the supplement should be cheap or the least expensive one available. Several factors influence the cost of a supplement. These include the quality of the ingredients, patents on the product, and advertising costs. Regarding ingredient quality, you should expect that, in general, the more expensive supplements should be expected to contain "better" or larger amounts of ingredients than a

lower-priced alternative. Some supplements may be higher priced because a manufacturer holds a patent on a product. A patent only lasts a few years, and manufacturers must try to recoup the cost of the research, development, and advertisement of the product. Usually, the higher-priced supplements are of better quality than the least expensive, generic supplements. While there is not a large amount of research on many products on the market, it may be wise to select supplements that have proven effectiveness in well-designed research trials when possible.

- *It must be easy to administer.* Supplements are available as powders, capsules, tablets, and liquids. Some pets are notorious for being difficult to medicate. Therefore, the easier it is to administer the product, the more likely it will be used. Supplements such as powders or liquids, which can be easily mixed with the pet's diet, are often the most effective. Products that are designed to be mixed with the food must be palatable or the pet won't eat them. Supplements are more easily mixed with natural canned foods or homemade diets than commercially prepared dry foods.

- *It must be effective and work, especially when it is used in the course of treating a specific illness.* No supplement works all the time. Just because your friend's dog or cat recovered from his disease after supplementation with oral fatty acids doesn't mean that your pet would benefit from this choice of supplement. While working with your doctor, it may be necessary to try several different supplements before finding one that is effective (sometimes, no supplement seems to help the pet). While there are "bogus" products that don't work despite their outrageous claims, by working with your doctor, you can choose supplements that have the most chance for success.

- *It must be free of side effects.* Only rarely do any nutritional supplements cause side effects. The most common side effects are vomiting and diarrhea if the pet does not tolerate the supplement, or if too many supplements are given at one time. Some pets may refuse to eat the diet containing the supplement because of taste. Starting with just a pinch of powdered supplement or a few drops of the liquid form and gradually working up to the recommended amount usually solves this problem.

BASIC SUPPLEMENTS FOR YOUR PET

Numerous supplements are available for maintaining health and improving your dog or cat's nutritional status. Using these supplements will benefit pets whether they eat processed diets (especially if they eat processed diets!) or foods prepared at home. Here is a brief overview of supplements most commonly recommended for augmenting the diets of healthy dogs and cats (many more supplements are discussed in Part Two). For supplements that you may be considering using in your dog or cat's diet that are not mentioned in the text, consult with your holistic veterinarian for advice.

Vitamin-Mineral Preparations

Every pet can benefit from a good natural vitamin-mineral supplement. No diet is perfect, and using a natural vitamin-mineral preparation assures us that the pet has at least obtained the essential macro and micronutrients each day.

A number of vitamin-mineral preparations are available. The best preparations are whole food preparations rather than synthetic, chemically processed multivitamins. These whole food products provide proper nutrition for your pet, as they provide vitamins and minerals in their natural raw states, similar to those your dog or cat would acquire by eating a natural, raw diet. By providing nutrients in this form, your pet is assured of receiving vitamins and minerals as well as all the extra nutrients and cofactors not found in processed, synthetic vitamins. These supplements should be the basic supplements for your pet, and then you can build on your pet's individual needs from this point. See the more extensive discussion of vitamins and minerals in Part Two.

Green Foods

Green foods, often referred to as super green foods, contain a variety of nutrients that can supplement your pet's diet. The most popular green foods contain barley grass, spirulina, blue-green algae, or wheat grass. These supplements are basically processed green plants, rich in chloro-phyll, which serves as the lifeblood of the plant and is similar in composition to hemoglobin in the pet's blood.

Green foods contain phytonutrients, which are chemicals derived from plant sources that exhibit powerful antioxidant properties. The method of action for these phytochemicals appears to be their ability to decrease oxidative stress by strengthening the powerful antioxidant glutathione, located in the liver. Carotenoid and indole compounds found in spinach, broccoli, and tomatoes have been shown to modify liver detoxification enzymes and inhibit tumor cell growth. Antioxidant-rich phytonutrients have been well researched and can help forestall cell death and help reduce the aging process due to oxidative damage. A greater discussion of **super green foods** can be found on page 222.

Health Blend Formulas

Health Blend Formulas are products that combine a number of plant and animal tissues in one easy-to-use powdered formula. The powder formulation allows easy administration of the product. Most products are palatable, which makes their acceptance by pets quite high.

The idea behind health blend formulas is that the heat and pressure used when preparing commercially processed foods may alter some of the nutrients contained in the foods. Providing a health blend formula gives back to the pet those nutrients that may be lacking in processed foods, including enzymes, protein and amino acids, fiber, beneficial bacteria (probiotics), phytochemicals (plant chemicals that may prove beneficial in helping your pet maintain good health and assist in fighting disease), and vitamins and minerals.

Fatty Acids

Fatty acids are important parts of your pet's diet. In large amounts, they are useful not just as dietary supplements but as the sole or complementary therapy for several pet diseases, most commonly skin allergies.

The major fatty acids belong to the omega-3 or omega-6 series. Omega-3 and omega-6 simply refer to the chemical structure of the fatty acid. In general, omega-3 fatty acids combat inflammation (are anti-inflammatory), whereas the omega-6 series promotes inflammation (pro-inflammatory). The omega-3 fatty acids, supplied by several plants (such as flax) and some coldwater fish (salmon), are often recommended to add to the diets of pets. However, while flaxseed oil can improve the skin and coat of pets, only the omega-3 fatty acids in fish oil have been shown to act to reduce inflammation and provide other health benefits within the body. A greater discussion of fatty acids can be found in Part Two under **Oral Fatty Acids** (see page 246).

Enzymes

As pet foods are processed, many nutrients including enzymes are altered or destroyed. Therefore, many nutritionists recommend providing a source of enzymes to help dogs and cats liberate the nutrients contained in the food.

Certainly, without supplemental enzymes pets can still process nutrients in their diets. However, providing extra enzymes (that would normally be present in unprocessed food in its natural state) helps pets digest their food even further, resulting in optimum nutrition. Therefore, your dog or cat receives extra nutrition from his or her food rather than the nutrients being passed into the feces.

Keep in mind that enzymes work to free nutrients from the diet as a result of increased digestion. Therefore, feeding a premium natural diet or a homemade diet is essential in order to get the most out of enzyme supplementation.

Studies have shown that supplementation with plant enzymes results in increased absorption of vitamins, minerals, and fatty acids, including zinc, selenium, vitamin B_6, and linoleic acid. Through the absorption of these nutrients, many disease conditions (including excessive shedding, dry and scaly skin, hairballs, digestive disturbances including diarrhea, allergies, arthritis, and reduced energy levels) improve as a result of improved nutrition.

While enzymes are available as animal enzymes (pancreatic enzymes) or plant enzymes, most holistic doctors prefer plant enzymes rather than animal enzymes. Plant enzymes supply the specific enzyme cellulase, which is not found in animal enzymes. Cellulase helps break down the cell walls of plants, which allows even more nutrients to be released and absorbed for utilization by the pet's body. For a greater discussion of **enzymes**, see page 197.

HOMEMADE DIETS FOR DOGS AND CATS

Note: *Before you start to feed your dog or cat a home-prepared diet, it is strongly recommended that you discuss your decision with your veterinarian or a holistic veterinarian in your area. It*

Table 3.1 Daily caloric requirements for adult dogs

lb	kcal	lb	kcal	lb	kcal
1	70	65	1,581	130	2,660
5	231	70	1,672	135	2,736
10	389	75	1,760	140	2,811
15	526	80	1,848	145	2,887
20	653	85	1,934	150	2,961
25	772	90	2,019	155	3,034
30	886	95	2,102	160	3,108
35	994	100	2,184	165	3,180
40	1,099	105	2,266	170	3,252
45	1,200	110	2,346	175	3,324
50	1,299	115	2,426	180	3,395
55	1,395	120	2,504		
60	1,489	125	2,582		

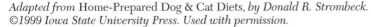

Adapted from Home-Prepared Dog & Cat Diets, *by Donald R. Strombeck.*
©1999 *Iowa State University Press. Used with permission.*

Table 3.2 Daily caloric requirements for cats

Indoor		Outdoor		Growing		Pregnancy		Lactation	
lb	kcal	lb	kcal	lb	kcal	lb	kcal	lb	kcal
4.0	127	4.0	145	1.0	141	4.0	182	4.0	455
4.5	143	4.5	164	1.5	192	4.5	205	4.5	511
5.0	159	5.0	159	2.0	231	5.0	227	5.0	568
5.5	175	5.5	200	2.5	260	5.5	250	5.5	625
6.0	191	6.0	218	3.0	281	6.0	273	6.0	682
6.5	207	6.5	236	3.5	294	6.5	295	6.5	739
7.0	223	7.0	255	4.0	302	7.0	318	7.0	795
7.5	239	7.5	273	4.5	305	7.5	341	7.5	852
8.0	254	8.0	291	5.0	307	8.0	364	8.0	909
8.5	270	8.5	309	5.5	305	8.5	386	8.5	966
9.0	286	9.0	327	6.0	300	9.0	409	9.0	1,023
9.5	302	9.5	345	6.5	298	9.5	432	9.5	1,080
10.0	318	10.0	364	7.0	299	10.0	455	10.0	1,136
10.5	334	10.5	382	7.5	303	10.5	477	10.5	1,193
11.0	350	11.0	400	8.0	312	11.0	500	11.0	1,250
11.5	366	11.5	418	8.5	324	11.5	523	11.5	1,307
12.0	382	12.0	436	9.0	343	12.0	545	12.0	1,364

Reprinted from Home-Prepared Dog & Cat Diets, *by Donald R. Strombeck.*
©1999 Iowa State University Press. Used with permission.

is essential that you follow any diet's recommendations closely, including all ingredients and supplements. Failure to do so may result in serious health consequences for your pet.

The following diets have been adapted with permission from: *Home-Prepared Dog & Cat Diets*, by Donald R. Strombeck, Iowa State University Press, Ames, Iowa, 1999. Remember that these recipes are guidelines only. As a feeding guideline, see tables 3.1 and 3.2 on pages 345–346. The final actual diet, including the amounts to feed and the need for supplementation, should be determined after consultation with your veterinarian.

Basic Diet for Dogs

3 large hard-boiled eggs
2 cups of long grain cooked rice (brown rice is ideal)
2 tablespoons sardines (to provide vitamin B$_{12}$ and flavor), in tomato sauce
2 tablespoons chicken fat or canola oil
¼ teaspoon potassium chloride (salt substitute)

This diet provides 964 kcal, 34.1 gm of protein, and 49.4 gm of fat. The diet supports the daily calorie needs of a 33- to 34-pound dog.

Variations

1. Substitute cottage cheese (1 cup of 2% fat cottage cheese), ⅓ pound chicken, turkey, beef, or other meat (pre-cooking weight) for the eggs. Use lean meat. Occasionally, for variety, also substitute ½ to ⅔ cup of tofu or 1 cup of soybeans for the eggs. Since dogs are not designed to be vegetarians, most doctors prefer to use meat most of the time.

2. Substitute 2 to 3 cups of potato, cooked with the skin, or 2 cups of cooked macaroni for the rice.

3. If desired, supply vitamins and minerals as follows: 4 bonemeal tablets (10-grain or equivalent) or 1 teaspoon of bonemeal powder to supply calcium and phosphorus with a multivitamin/mineral supplement, using the label instructions. Alternatively, use a natural product from Standard Process (1 Calcifood Wafer or 2 Calcium Lactate tablets for each 2 bonemeal tablets). When possible, use natural vitamins made from raw whole

foods, rather than synthetic vitamins (although both can be used in combination), as the natural vitamins also supply plant phytochemicals, enzymes, and other nutrients not found in chemically synthesized vitamins. Use either Catalyn from Standard Process (at a dose of 1 Catalyn per 25 pounds) or Canine Plus from Vetri-Science (following label dosages) for the natural vitamin in this recipe.

4. Fresh, raw or slightly steamed vegetables, such as carrots or broccoli (approximately ½ to 1 cup per recipe) can be used as a top dressing for the diet for extra nutrition and variety. Most vegetables provide approximately 25 kcal per ½ cup.

5. Keep in mind that the nutrient composition of the diet will vary depending upon which ingredients are used. In general, the previous recipe supplies the daily nutritional and calorie needs for a 25- to 35-pound dog. The actual amount to feed will vary based upon the pet's weight (feed less if weight is gained, more if weight is lost).

6. As desired, add supplements that can be beneficial, such as omega-3 fatty acids, plant enzymes, and a super green food or health blend formula.

Basic Diet for Healthy Puppies

Puppies require greater amounts of proteins, calories, and vitamins and minerals than adult dogs. Diets for puppies are suitable for puppies up to 12 months of age for pets whose adult weight is 40 pounds or less, and up to 18 months of age for pets whose adult weight is estimated to be greater than 40 pounds.

Diets for puppies are similar to those for adult dogs, as long as the protein, calories, and vitamins and minerals are increased. The diet for adult dogs can be adapted by using 5 hard-boiled eggs (rather than 3) and slightly less carbohydrates (approximately 1½ cups of cooked long grain brown (prefered) or white rice.

The puppy diet will provide about 765 kcal, 44.5 gm of protein, and 32 gm of fat. As a feeding guideline, follow the guidelines in table 3.1. Confer with your veterinarian to help determine the ideal amount based upon your puppy's growth.

If your puppy does not like eggs, 1½ cup of cottage cheese or ½ pound of meat could be sub-

stituted. Vitamins and minerals can be supplied as follows:

4-6 bonemeal tablets (10 grain or equivalent) or 1–1½ teaspoons of bonemeal powder to supply calcium and phosphorus with a multi-vitamin mineral supplement using the label instructions. Alternatively, a natural product from Standard Process (Calcifood Wafers or Calcium Lactate) can be used (use 1 Calcifood Wafer or 2 Calcium Lactate tablets for each 2 bonemeal tablets.)

When possible, natural vitamins made from raw whole foods, rather than synthetic vitamins (although both can be used in combination) are preferred, as the natural vitamins also supply plant phytochemicals, enzymes, and other nutrients not found in chemically-synthesized vitamins. Catalyn from Standard Process can be used as the natural vitamin in this recipe, at a dose of 1 Catalyn per 25 pounds; Canine Plus (VetriScience) could also be used following label dosages.

Fresh, raw or slightly steamed vegetables (carrots, brocoli, etc.) can be used as a top dressing for the diet for extra nutrition, phytonutrients, and variety (approximately ½ -1 cup per recipe.) Most vegetables provide approximately 25 kcal per ½ cup. Phytonutrients are chemicals derived from plant sources that exhibit powerful antioxidant properties. The method of action for these phytochemicals appears to be their ability to decrease oxidative stress by strenghtening the powerful antioxidant, glutathione, located in the liver. Carotenoid and indole compounds found in vegetables such as spinach, broccoli and tomatoes have been shown to modify liver detoxification enzymes and inhibit tumor cell growth. Antioxidant-rich phytonutrients may help forestall cell death and help reduce the aging process due to oxidative damage.

The nutrient composition of the diet will vary depending upon which ingredients are used. The actual amount to feed will vary based upon the pet's weight (feed less if weight gain, more if weight loss.)

Added supplements which can be beneficial include omega-3 fatty acids, plant enzymes, and a super green food or health blend formula following your doctor's recommendations.

One teaspoon to 1 tablespoon of chicken fat or canola oil should be added to the diet if a protein source (meat) other than eggs are used to provide additional fat.

Adding the chicken fat or canola oil to the diet if eggs are used as the protein source is not harmful but will add extra calories that may not be needed by many puppies.

Basic Diet for Cats

The same diets can be used for both kittens and cats, the difference being the amount fed to meet the greater calorie requirements of the kittens. Adult cats are fed approximately 70 to 80 kcal/kg (1 kg = 2.2 pounds) of body weight each day. Since cats are not born finicky but are made that way, it is strongly recommended that kittens be offered a variety of ingredients and flavors in their diets. Taste preferences in kittens are generally set by 6 months of age. Since cats are true strict carnivores, a totally vegetarian diet will result in nutritional deficiencies.

> ⅓ to ½ pound of ground meat (turkey, chicken, lamb, beef)
> ½ to 1 large hard-boiled egg
> ½ ounce of clams chopped in juice
> 4 teaspoons chicken fat or canola oil
> ⅛ teaspoon potassium chloride (salt substitute)
> 100 mg taurine

If using ½ pound of chicken and ½ egg, the diet will provide 471 kcal, 53.1 gm of protein, and 27.4 gm of fat. An adult, indoor, 10-pound cat requires approximately 300 kcal of energy per day; an adult, outdoor, 10-pound cat requires approximately 360 kcal of energy per day; and a 5-pound kitten requires approximately 300 kcal of energy per day. See table 3.2 for more information and feeding guidelines.

Variations

1. Substitute tuna (4 ounces in water without salt), sardines (4 to 6 ounces in tomato sauce), or other fish (such as 5 ounces of salmon) for the meat protein. If desired, also occasionally substitute ½ to ⅔ cup of tofu for variety. Since cats are true carnivores, most doctors prefer to feed tofu on only an occasional basis.

2. Add ⅓ cup of potato (cooked with the skin), rice, or macaroni, although kittens and cats do not have a defined dietary requirement for carbohydrates.

3. If desired, supply vitamins and minerals as follows: 3 to 4 bonemeal tablets (10-grain or equivalent) or ¾ to 1 teaspoon of bonemeal powder to supply calcium and phosphorus with a multivitamin/mineral supplement, using the label instructions. Alternatively, use a natural product from Standard Process (1 Calcifood Wafer or 2 Calcium Lactate tablets for each 2 bonemeal tablets). When possible, use natural vitamins made from raw whole foods, rather than synthetic vitamins (although both can be used in combination), as the natural vitamins also supply plant phytochemicals, enzymes, and other nutrients not found in chemically synthesized vitamins. Substitute either Catalyn from Standard Process (at a dose of one Catalyn per 10 pounds) or NuCat from VetriScience (following label dosages) for the natural vitamin in this recipe.

4. Use fresh, raw or slightly steamed vegetables, such as carrots or broccoli (approximately ½ to 1 cup per recipe) as a top dressing for the diet for extra nutrition and variety. Many cats, however, will not eat vegetables. Most vegetables provide approximately 25 kcal per ½ cup.

5. Keep in mind that the nutrient composition of the diet will vary depending upon which ingredients are used. See table 3.2 to determine how much to feed your kitten or adult cat. The actual amount to feed will vary based upon the pet's weight (feed less if weight is gained, more if weight is lost).

6. If desired, add supplements that can be beneficial, such as omega-3 fatty acids, plant enzymes, and a super green food or health blend formula.

Homemade Natural Diets

DIETS FOR PETS WITH MEDICAL CONDITIONS

Prior to using any of the following diets, check with your doctor to be sure the selected diet is appropriate for your pet's medical condition. Once your pet's medical condition has stabilized, your doctor may suggest changing back to a maintenance diet for normal pets, such as one of those listed on the previous pages.

ALLERGIC CONDITIONS (SKIN CONDITIONS)

The most common skin disorder seen in many veterinary practices is allergic (atopic) dermatitis. This condition results in itchiness after exposure to environmental (usually airborne) allergens (foreign proteins that induce allergies). True food allergies are quite rare in pets. Food intolerances, in which the pet develops an allergic response to a non-nutrient in the food (such as an additive), occur in pets, but the true incidence is hard to gauge. While dietary therapy is not a mainstay in the treatment of itchy pets, feeding the best, most natural and holistic diet possible is recommended for at least three reasons:

1. All pets, regardless of the presence of disease, benefit from eating the best diet.
2. Supplements work best when fed with a good diet. Supplements form the foundation of the treatment of many pets with allergic dermatitis, so feeding the best diet to these pets is indicated.
3. Some pets experience modest to dramatic improvement in their skin disorders (such as less itching, less flakiness, less redness, or less body odor) when fed a wholesome diet, even when the diagnosis of "food allergy" is not technically the correct diagnosis. This may be the result of contamination of the commercially purchased diet with additives, chemical preservatives, pesticides, or hormones. It may also occur as the result of processing the food, which removes nutrients from the diet and alters the nutrients (for example, heating of the foods to

temperatures over 400° F causes an increased level of trans-fatty acids). Many foods contain increased levels of omega-6 fatty acids relative to omega-3 fatty acids; increased omega-6 fatty acids predispose to inflammation. Because feeding a wholesome diet designed to be hypoallergenic is easily done by most owners, dietary therapy is often recommended for pets with skin disorders.

Diets designed for pets with gastrointestinal disease can be useful for pets with skin disorders with some modification. These modified diets are used to assess and treat food allergies as well as assess any improvement in the pet with any skin disorder, including atopic dermatitis. Keep in mind that even itchy pets without true food allergy may still show improvement when fed the diet used to test and treat food allergies.

Several medicated diets contain the "correct" amount of fatty acids that supposedly help the pet with allergic dermatitis. Other medicated diets contain novel or chemically modified protein sources that supposedly reduce the allergic reaction and may help the itchy pet. While these diets can and do help some allergic pets, there are two important considerations for the holistic pet owner before feeding these diets. First, it appears that the "correct" ratio of omega-6 to omega-3 fatty acids is 5:1, although more research is necessary before this becomes accepted as fact. While this ratio is difficult to achieve simply by adding omega-3 fatty acids to the diet, a large amount of research shows positive benefit in some allergic pets when omega-3 fatty acid supplements are added to the diet, even when the 5:1 ratio is not achieved. Therefore these special supplemented diets are not always needed in pets with allergic dermatitis.

Second, most of these special diets may still use animal by-products and chemical preservatives. (It is difficult to say that a commercial diet is free of pesticides and preservatives.) This practice defeats the purpose of trying to feed

Diets/Medical Conditions

pets a natural wholesome diet. The best diet is a homemade one, ideally with organically grown vegetables and organically raised animal tissues. If your pet will not eat the homemade diet and does require one of these special diets, be sure to work with your veterinarian to pick the one that is most wholesome.

For pets with allergies, hypoallergenic diets can be tried to see whether the level of itching and redness decreases. Hypoallergenic diets are those that contain nutrients to which the pet is unlikely to react with an allergic response. The most common allergic foods are protein sources that the pet has eaten for months or years, rather than a new diet to which the pet has just been introduced. As a result, protein sources that the pet has not eaten before (most often rabbit, lamb, or venison) are used. Gluten-free carbohydrate sources are used to prevent gluten allergies.

To evaluate the response of a pet with a suspected reaction to food, it is necessary to feed the hypoallergenic diet (and nothing else) for at least 8 weeks. Monthly flavored heartworm preventive should be discontinued and replaced with a non-flavored product. Fresh water (or distilled water) can be used. No treats or table scraps can be given to the pet, or the 8-week dietary trial must begin again. The most common reason for failing to improve is one of two causes: The pet's itching is not related to a food allergy/hypersensitivity, or the owner rushes the dietary trial and does not give the pet at least 8 weeks to see whether the hypoallergenic diet will work.

Note: See **Hypoallergenic Diets** on page 334 for a discussion about lamb and rice diets and whether or not they are hypoallergenic.

Vitamins and minerals, which most often contain flavoring, are added after the trial diet and after the pet has been assessed for any reaction to these supplements. Because food allergy trials are difficult, they should be done under veterinary supervision.

Supplements

Glutamine, recommended for pets with inflammatory bowel disease, has also been suggested as a treatment for food allergies, based on the "leaky gut syndrome." This theory holds that in some pets, whole proteins leak through the wall of the digestive tract and enter the blood, causing allergic reactions. Very preliminary evidence suggests that glutamine supplements might reduce leakage through the intestinal walls. It can be tried for pets with allergic skin disease.

Omega-3 fatty acids (and supplements containing both omega-3 and omega-6 fatty acids) are often used in the treatment of skin disease in pets. Omega-3 fatty acids—eicosapentaenoic acid (EPA) and docosahexaenoic acid (DHA)—are derived from fish oils of coldwater fish (salmon and trout) and flaxseed, whereas omega-6 fatty acids—linoleic acid (LA) and gamma-linolenic acid (GLA)—are derived from the oils of seeds such as evening primrose, black currant, and borage.

How do the fatty acids help pets with skin disease and allergies? Cell membranes contain phospholipids. When membrane injury occurs, an enzyme acts on the phospholipids in the cell membranes to produce fatty acids including arachidonic acid (an omega-6 fatty acid) and eicosapentaenoic acid (an omega-3 fatty acid). Further metabolism of the arachidonic acid and eicosapentaenoic acid by additional enzymes (the lipooxygenase and cyclooxygenase pathways) yields the production of chemicals called eicosanoids. The eicosanoids produced by metabolism of arachidonic acid are pro-inflammatory and cause inflammation, suppress the immune system, and cause platelets to aggregate and clot. The eicosanoids produced by metabolism of eicosapentaenoic acid are non-inflammatory, not immunosuppressive, and help inhibit platelets from clotting. (The actual biochemical pathway is a bit more complicated than suggested here. For example, one of the by-products of omega-6 fatty acid metabolism is Prostaglandin E_1, which is anti-inflammatory. This is one reason some research has shown that using certain omega-6 fatty acids can also act to limit inflammation.)

Supplementation of the diet with omega-3 fatty acids works in this biochemical reaction. By providing extra amounts of these non-inflammatory compounds, we try to overwhelm the body with the production of non-inflammatory eicosanoids. Therefore, since the same enzymes metabolize both omega-3 and omega-6 fatty acids, and since metabolism of the omega-6 fatty acids tend to cause inflammation (with the exception of Prostaglandin E_1 by metabolism of DGLA as mentioned above), by supplying a large amount of omega-3 fatty acids, we favor the production of non-inflammatory chemicals.

In general, the products of omega-3 (specifically EPA) and one omega-6 fatty acid (DGLA) are less inflammatory than the products of arachidonic acid (another omega-6 fatty acid). By changing dietary fatty acid consumption, we can change eicosanoid production right at the cellular level and try to modify (decrease) inflammation within the body. By providing the proper (anti-inflammatory) fatty acids, we can use fatty acids as an anti-inflammatory substance. However, since the products of omega-6 fatty acid metabolism (specifically arachidonic acid) are not the sole cause of the inflammation, fatty acid therapy is rarely effective as the sole therapy but is used as an adjunct therapy to achieve an additive effect.

Note: Flaxseed oil is a popular source of alpha-linoleic acid (ALA), an omega-3 fatty acid that is ultimately converted to EPA and DHA. However, many species of pets (probably including dogs) and some people cannot convert ALA to these other more active non-inflammatory omega-3 fatty acids. In one study in people flaxseed oil was ineffective in reducing symptoms or raising levels of EPA and DHA. While flaxseed oil has been suggested as a less smelly substitute for fish oil, there is no evidence that it is effective when used for the same therapeutic purposes as fish oil. Therefore, supplementation with EPA and DHA is important, and this is the reason flaxseed oil is not recommended as the sole fatty acid supplement for pets. Flaxseed oil can, however, be used to provide ALA and as a coat conditioner.

Because of their anti-inflammatory effects, large doses (2 to 4 times the label dose, as the label dose on most products is suspected to be too low to provide anti-inflammatory effects) of omega-3 fatty acids have been shown to be beneficial in treating allergic dogs and cats. Inhibition of pro-inflammatory prostaglandins, as well as decreased levels of leukotriene B4 production from white blood cells (leukotriene B4 is an important mediator in inflammatory skin disorders) is the explanation for the effectiveness of omega-3 fatty acids in allergic pets. As with the

other supplements, they often allow doctors to lower the dosages of drugs such as corticosteroids or non-steroidal medications.

What is the "best" dose to use in the treatment of pets? Most doctors use anywhere from 2 to 4 times the label dose. Research in the treatment of allergies indicates that the label dose is often ineffective. In people, the dosages that showed effectiveness in various studies were 1.4 to 2.8 gm of GLA per day, or 1.7 gm of EPA and 0.9 gm of DHA per day, which is difficult for people to obtain from the supplements currently available. If this were shown to be the correct dosage for pets, a 50-pound dog would need to take 10 or more fatty acids capsules per day to obtain a similar dosage, depending upon which supplement (and there are many choices on the market) was used. Therefore, while the studies with omega-3 fatty acids show many potential health benefits, it is almost impossible to administer the large number of capsules needed to approximate the same dosage used in these human studies. However, this extremely high dosage may not be necessary to provide benefits in pets. In veterinary studies, using anywhere from 2 to 4 times the label dosage was effective in some pets with allergic dermatitis. The best that owners can hope for at this time is to work with their veterinarians and try to increase, as best as possible, the amount of omega-3 fatty acids in their pet's diet to try to get what seems the "preferred" ratio of 5:1, omega-6:omega-3 fatty acids. Whether or not this "ideal" dietary ratio is ideal for the treatment of allergic dermatitis remains to be seen.

Is supplementation with fatty acid capsules or liquids the best approach? Or is dietary manipulation (adding the "ideal" ratio of omega-6 and omega-3 fatty acids) preferable for the treatment of inflammatory conditions like allergic dermatitis? Currently, there are no definitive answers.

Fish oil supplements appear to be safe. The most common problem is a fish odor to the breath or the skin.

Because fish oil has a mild "blood-thinning" effect, it should not be combined with powerful blood-thinning medications, such as Coumadin (warfarin) or heparin, except on a veterinarian's advice. Fish oil does not seem to cause bleeding problems when it is taken by itself at commonly recommended dosages. Also, fish oil does not appear to raise blood sugar levels in people or pets with diabetes.

As mentioned, studies have shown that flaxseed oil is not effective in treating allergic disorders; however, flaxseed oil is safe and can be used to provide ALA and as a coat conditioner.

Hemp seed oil has been referred to as nature's perfect oil by several investigators. Its fatty acid ratio of 1:4 of omega-3 to omega-6 fatty acids is suspected to be the ratio natural in mammals. It contains 1.7% GLA and can be used whenever a combination fatty acid product is needed. As is the case with flaxseed oil, studies have not shown any benefit.

The seeds of the salvia (*Salvia hispanica*) plant have been proposed as a more palatable alternative to fish oil and flaxseed oil. The seeds can increase omega-3 fatty acid consumption in the diet. Little is known about the use of this fatty acid supplement and whether or not it can be of any medical benefit to pets. Studies are needed before this supplement can be recommended as an omega-3 fatty acid supplement.

Diet for Dogs with Allergies

Diets for dogs with allergies must contain protein sources the dog has not previously eaten. Using the **basic dog diet (pg 347)**, we would substitute ½ cup of a meat such as rabbit or venison. Brown rice (2-3 cups) or baked or boiled potato with skin (2-3 cups) serves as the carbohydrate source. Canola oil is added as per the basic diet. The diet provides approximately 650 kcal with 29 grams of protein and 18 grams of fat.

Fresh, raw or slightly steamed vegetables (carrots, broccoli, etc.) can be used as a top dressing for the diet for extra nutrition and variety (approximately ½–1 cup per recipe.) Most vegetables provide approximately 25 kcal per ½ cup.

Since this diet is not totally balanced, vitamins and minerals are added later (4-8 weeks), as the dog improves, to balance the diet. Four bonemeal tablets (10 grain or equivalent) or 1 teaspoon of bonemeal powder to supply calcium and phosphorus with a multi-vitamin mineral supplement using the label instructions.

Alternatively, a natural product from Standard Process (Calcifood Wafers or Calcium Lactate)

can be used (use 1 Calcifood Wafer or 2 Calcium Lactate tablets for each 2 bonemeal tablets.)

When possible, natural vitamins made from raw whole foods, rather than synthetic vitamins (although both can be used in combination) are preferred, as the natural vitamins also supply plant phytochemicals, enzymes, and other nutrients not found in chemically- synthesized vitamins. Catalyn from Standard Process can be used as the natural vitamin in this recipe, at a dose of 1 Catalyn per 25 pounds; Canine Plus (VetriScience) could also be used following label dosages.

Add one new ingredient at a time. If itching does not worsen within 3 to 5 days, add another ingredient if desired.

The nutrient composition of the diet will vary depending upon which ingredients are used. In general, the above recipe supplies the daily nutritional and calorie needs for a 20 pound dog. The actual amount to feed will vary based upon the pet's weight (feed less if weight gain, more if weight loss.)

Added supplements which can be beneficial include omega-3 fatty acids, plant enzymes, and a super green food or health blend formula The health blend formula may contain nutrients that could exacerbate the pet's allergies and should only be added after clinical signs resolve.

Diet for Cats with Allergies

Diets for cats with allergies must contain protein sources the cat has not previously eaten.

Using the **basic cat diet** (page 348) we would substitute ¾ cup of a meat such as rabbit or venison. Canola oil is added as per the basic diet. Taurine (100 mg) is also added. This diet will provide about 350 kcal with 31 grams of protein and 25 grams of fat, which would provide the daily amount of nutrients needed for a 10 pound cat.

Since this diet is not totally balanced, vitamins and minerals are added later (4-8 weeks), as the cat improves, to balance the diet. Two or three bonemeal tablets (10 grain or equivalent) or ¾ teaspoon of bonemeal powder to supply calcium and phosphorus with a multi-vitamin mineral supplement using the label instructions.

Alternatively, a natural product from Standard Process (Calcifood Wafers or Calcium Lactate) can be used (use 1 Calcifood Wafer or 2 Calcium Lactate tablets for each 2 bonemeal tablets.)

When possible, natural vitamins made from raw whole foods, rather than synthetic vitamins (although both can be used in combination) are preferred, as the natural vitamins also supply plant phytochemicals, enzymes, and other nutrients not found in chemically-synthesized vitamins. Catalyn from Standard Process can be used as the natural vitamin in this recipe, at a dose of 1 Catalyn per 10 pounds; NuCat (VetriScience) could also be used following label dosages.

Brown rice (½ cup) or baked or boiled potato with skin (¾ cup) can be added to serve as the carbohydrate source, although cats do not have a true carbohydrate requirement.

Add one new ingredient at a time. If itching does not worsen within 3 to 5 days, add another ingredient if desired.

The nutrient composition of the diet will vary depending upon which ingredients are used. In general, the above recipe supplies the daily nutritional and calorie needs for a 10 pound cat. The actual amount to feed will vary based upon the pet's weight (feed less if weight gain, more if weight loss.)

Added supplements which can be beneficial include omega-3 fatty acids, plant enzymes, and a super green food or health blend formula The health blend formula may contain nutrients that could exacerbate the pet's allergies and should only be added after clinical signs resolve.

For more information on helping the pet with allergies, see *The Allergy Solution for Dogs* in THE NATURAL VET series by Prima Publishing.

ARTHRITIS (SEE OBESITY)

BLADDER STONES

Several different types of stones can occur in the bladder and urinary system of cats and dogs. Generally, struvite stones (composed of the minerals magnesium, ammonium, and phosphate) are most commonly diagnosed. Clinical signs of bladder stones in cats and dogs include frequent urination (pollakiuria), straining to urinate (dysuria) and blood in the urine (hematuria). Radiographs (x rays) of the entire urinary system are taken to determine whether stones are present in the kidneys, ureters, bladder (the most common location for urinary stones), or urethra. Not every type of stone is easily visualized on radiographs (struvite stones are easily visualized though), and often another test such as an abdominal ultrasound is needed to allow a definitive diagnosis.

Dietary therapy is a useful adjunct (and possible preventive measure) for pets with struvite stones. Since the struvite stones most commonly form in alkaline urine (urine with a high pH) when the urine is saturated with magnesium, ammonium, or phosphate, diets should help maintain an acidic urine (low pH) as much as possible. Diets with animal-based protein sources are most important in maintaining an acidic pH (vegetarian or cereal-based diets are more likely to cause an alkaline urine).

In cats, struvite stones most commonly form in the absence of a bladder infection (unlike the situation in dogs, in which a bladder infection is usually the initiating factor in causing the formation of stones). Unless a secondary infection is present, large amounts of urinary bleeding are encountered, or surgery is performed for stone removal, antibiotic therapy is usually not needed in cats with struvite bladder stones.

Crystals, stones, and the condition called feline lower urinary tract disease (FLUTD) most commonly form in cats (which are true carnivores adapted to eating meat-based diets) who are fed dry commercial foods (which are usually high in vegetable materials and grains). Most holistic veterinarians see a lower incidence of these urinary disorders in cats fed meat-based homemade diets.

Diets designed for cats with struvite bladder stones are designed to produce an acid urine (pH of 6.2 to 6.6 lasting 4 to 6 hours after feeding in cats fed free-choice), which allows for crystals and stones to be dissolved. While some commercial foods have decreased levels of magnesium and phosphorus, it has recently been shown that these minerals only contribute to stone formation if the urine is alkaline. If the urine can be maintained with an acidic pH, the dietary concentrations of magnesium and phosphorus do not need to be lowered below recommended daily amounts. In fact, reducing the magnesium levels in cat food can cause increased excretion of calcium from the kidneys, leading to the formation of calcium oxalate stones in the bladder. The increased incidence of calcium oxalate stones in cats and dogs has coincided with an increased use of commercial "stone" diets containing reduced magnesium and phosphorus (often labeled under the term "ash"). Feeding recommended levels of phosphate to normal cats does not promote stone formation. Phosphate is needed to allow the urine to maintain an acid pH, which helps discourage crystal and stone formation. To increase urination (which reduces the amount of time crystals can form and remain in the bladder), extra salt (sodium chloride) can be added to the diet.

In dogs, struvite stones most commonly form as a result of a urinary tract infection. The infection serves as a nidus (place of origin) for stone formation in alkaline urine saturated with magnesium, ammonium, and phosphorus. The infection must be treated (usually with an extended course of antibiotics for at least 2 to 3 weeks) in order for crystals and stones to dissolve. Diets for dogs with struvite stones contain reduced amounts of high-quality proteins (to reduce urea in urine), and reduced levels of phosphorus and magnesium to reduce the concentration of these minerals in alkaline urine. Diets designed for dogs with struvite bladder stones contain near normal levels of minerals such as magnesium; reduced magnesium levels may increase the risk of formation of calcium oxalate stones. To increase urination (which reduces the amount of time crystals can form and remain in the bladder), extra salt (sodium chloride) can be added to the diet.

While urinary acidifiers can be useful, some doctors discourage their use, as the exact dosage which is safe and effective is often not known. If urinary acidifiers are used for short-term acidification, a natural therapy such as cranberry extract might be preferred to conventional medications (such as methionine). See Part Two, **Cranberry** (page 192) for a discussion of when cranberry might be indicated for dogs and cats with bladder infections and bladder stones.

Diet for Dogs with Bladder Stones

⅔ *cup lowfat cottage cheese*
1 large hard-boiled egg

2 *cups long grain, cooked brown rice*
2 *teaspoons chicken fat or canola oil*
½ *ounce brewer's yeast*
¼ *teaspoon potassium chloride (salt substitute)*

This diet provides 780 kcal (enough to fulfill the daily amount required for a 25-pound dog), 42.9 gm protein, 22 gm fat, and 92 mg sodium/100 kcal (a high-sodium diet).

Variations

1. Substitute 4 ounces of tuna (in water without sodium) or ¼ pound of lean ground beef (or ground chicken or lamb) for the cottage cheese.
2. Substitute 2 to 3 cups of potato, cooked with the skin on, or 2 cups of cooked macaroni for the rice.
3. If desired, add vitamins and minerals as follows: bonemeal tablets (10-grain or equivalent) or 1 teaspoon of bonemeal powder to supply calcium and phosphorus with a multivitamin/mineral supplement using the label instructions. Alternatively, use a natural product from Standard Process (1 Calcifood Wafer or 2 Calcium Lactate tablets for each 2 bonemeal tablets). When possible, use natural vitamins made from raw whole foods, rather than synthetic vitamins (although both can be used in combination), as the natural vitamins also supply plant phytochemicals, enzymes, and other nutrients not found in chemically synthesized vitamins. Use either Catalyn from Standard Process (at a dose of 1 Catalyn per 25 pounds) or Canine Plus from VetriScience (following label dosages) as the natural vitamin in this recipe.
4. Use fresh, raw or slightly steamed vegetables (carrots or broccoli, for example) as a top dressing for the diet for extra nutrition and variety (approximately ½ to 1 cup per recipe). Most vegetables provide approximately 25 kcal per ½ cup.
5. If desired, add supplements such as omega-3 fatty acids, plant enzymes, and a super green food or health blend formula.

Safety Note: If you choose to add vegetables or other supplements, monitor urine pH when feeding the diet both with and without the supplements to be sure the pH does not change from

Diets/Medical Conditions

acid to alkaline. Some dogs have a difficult time producing acid urine even when fed the above diet or when administered urinary acidifiers.

Diet for Cats with Bladder Stones

3½ ounces firm raw tofu
2¼ ounces sardines, canned in tomato sauce
½ ounce clams, chopped in juice
½ yolk of large hard-boiled egg
⅓ cup long grain, cooked brown rice
2 teaspoon chicken fat or canola oil
½ ounce brewer's yeast
100 mg taurine

This diet provides 501 kcal (enough to fulfill the daily amount required for a 16-pound cat), 37.4 gm protein, 29.6 gm fat, and 62.2 mg sodium/100 kcal (a high-sodium diet).

Variations

1. Substitute 2 ounces of tuna (in water without sodium), 2 ounces of canned salmon (with bones), 2⅔ ounces of chicken breast, 4 ounces of lean ground beef, or 4 ounces of lean ground lamb for the sardines.
2. Substitute ⅓ cup of potato, cooked with the skin, or ⅓ cup of cooked macaroni for the rice.
3. If desired, supply vitamins and minerals as follows: 1 bonemeal tablet (10-grain or equivalent) or ¼ teaspoon of bonemeal powder to supply calcium and phosphorus with a multivitamin/mineral supplement using the label instructions. Alternatively, use a natural product from Standard Process (1 Calciofood Wafer or 2 Calcium Lactate tablets for each 2 bonemeal tablets). When possible, use natural vitamins made from raw whole foods, rather than synthetic vitamins (although both can be used in combination), as the natural vitamins also supply plant phytochemicals, enzymes, and other nutrients not found in chemically synthesized vitamins. Or use Catalyn from Standard Process (at a dose of 1 Catalyn per 10 pounds) or NuCat from VetriScience (following label dosages) as the natural vitamin in this recipe.
4. Use fresh, raw or slightly steamed vegetables (such as carrots or broccoli) as a top dressing for the diet for extra nutrition and variety (approximately ½ to 1 cup per recipe). Many cats,

however, will not eat vegetables. Most vegetables provide approximately 25 kcal per ½ cup.
5. If desired, add supplements that can be beneficial, such as omega-3 fatty acids, plant enzymes, and a super green food or health blend formula.

Safety Note: If choosing to add vegetables or other supplements, monitor urine pH when feeding the diet both with without the supplements to be sure the pH does not change from acid to alkaline.

Diets for cats with struvite stones should contain 20 to 40 mg/100 kcal of magnesium and 125 to 250 mg/100 kcal of phosphorus. These levels are higher than those recommended by the NRC for adult cats. Eliminating the oil and rice from this diet will further increase the magnesium and phosphorus.

CANCER

Cancer is becoming a more commonly diagnosed condition in both dogs and cats. The rapidly growing specialty of veterinary oncology provides caregivers the choices to battle cancer that are similar to those offered human family members, so until recently, dietary therapy has often been neglected for pets with cancer, yet feeding them the proper diet is very important.

Studies demonstrate that both people and pets with inadequate nutrition cannot metabolize chemotherapy drugs adequately, which predisposes them to toxicity and poor therapeutic response. This makes proper diet and nutritional supplementation an important part of cancer therapy.

Several metabolic derangements are common in the cancer patient. First, cancer patients often have hyperlactatemia (increased lactic acid in the blood). In addition, since metabolism of simple carbohydrates produces lactate, a diet with a minimum of these carbohydrates might be preferred.

Research has shown a pronounced decrease in certain amino acids such as arginine in the plasma of cancer patients. If left uncorrected, these amino acid deficiencies could result in serious health risks to the patient. Supplementation with the deficient amino acids might improve immune function and positively affect treatment and survival rates.

Diets/Medical Conditions

Weight loss often occurs in cancer patients as a result of cachexia (wasting). Most of the weight loss seen in cancer patients experiencing cancer cachexia occurs as a result of depleted body fat stores. Tumor cells, unlike normal healthy cells, have difficulty utilizing lipids for energy. Dogs with lymphoma fed diets high in fat had longer remission periods than dogs fed high carbohydrate diets.

The use of omega-3 fatty acids can promote weight gain and may have anticancer effects and warrants special mention. In people, the use of omega-3 fatty acids, such as those found in fish oils, improve the immune status, metabolic status, and clinical outcomes of cancer patients. These supplements also decrease the duration of hospitalization and complication rates in people with gastrointestinal cancer. In animal models, the omega-3 fatty acids inhibit the formation of tumors and metastasis (spread of the cancer). Finally, in addition to having anticachetic (antiwasting) effects, the omega-3 fatty acids can reduce radiation damage to skin.

While many treatment options are often available for the various malignancies our patients experience, doctors sometimes overlook the simple aspect of nutrition. In the next decade, prevention and treatment will most likely include a focus on nutrition in veterinary medicine, just as our counterparts are now doing in the human medical field. The definitive research is out there, leaving no doubt that cancer patients have deranged nutrient metabolism that can negatively affect the outcome of conventional therapies. Additions of omega-3 fatty acids and antioxidant vitamins and minerals to the diet of cancer patients may help improve survival and possibly decrease the risk of currently cancer-free pets contracting the disease.

Recently, Hill's Pet Food Company introduced the first cancer diet for dogs, called n/d. The diet contains increased protein and fat, decreased carbohydrates, increased omega-3 fatty acids, and increased arginine (the reasons for this formulation are discussed to follow). The composition of the diet is: protein, 37%; fat, 32%; carbohydrates, 21%; arginine, 3.1% (647 mg/100 kcal); and omega-3 fatty acids from fish oil, 7.3% (1518 mg/100 kcal). In controlled studies, dogs with lymphoma (lymphosarcoma) who were being treated with chemotherapy and being fed n/d had increased survival times when compared to dogs being treated with the same chemotherapy medications and eating a controlled diet. Similar findings were found for dogs with nasal and oral cancer who were treated with radiation therapy and eating n/d. The conclusions from this study showed that survival time increased 56%; quality of life improved due to decreased pain from dogs treated with radiation; remission periods were longer; and the metabolic changes seen in pets with cancer reversed.

While these findings are quite impressive, there is no evidence that this diet helps dogs or cats with other forms of cancer. Despite this need for additional research, it is likely that any pet with any type of cancer could benefit from this or similar diets (see below for further discussion).

There are three potential problems with diet n/d: first, it is an expensive diet, especially for owners of large breed dogs. Second, it is only available in a canned variety, most likely due to the high fat content. Finally, the protein source is an animal by-product (beef lung). Owners who desire the most holistic and natural diet possible might object to this protein source.

A homemade diet that approximates n/d can be attempted. However, due to the high level of omega-3 fatty acids in the food, it is difficult (if not impossible) and expensive to prepare a similar diet at home. Nevertheless, I have included a recipe that roughly approximates this "anticancer" diet.

Tofu (soy protein) protects the intestinal tract from damage that could occur with certain chemotherapy drugs and result in diarrhea. While not proven, tofu diets might be preferred for pets with cancer, especially those whose treatment regimen includes chemotherapy.

The homemade anticancer diet for dogs should have the following nutrient levels: protein, 35 to 40%; fat, 30%; carbohydrates, 20%. Cats can have higher protein and fat levels and minimal or no carbohydrates (cats do not have a strict dietary carbohydrate requirement).

Antioxidants can be added to the diet. However, high doses of antioxidants might interfere with any chemotherapy medications, such as doxorubicin (Adriamycin), that work to kill can-

Diets/Medical Conditions

cer cells by oxidation. Several studies indicate that high levels of antioxidants my help cancer cells grow and spread. For example, a recent study showed that cancer cells contain high levels of vitamin C, probably serving as an antioxidant to protect the cancer cell from oxidation. Because of the possibility of high levels of antioxidants interfering with treatment or cure, pet owners should discuss this topic with the pet's oncologist (cancer specialist) prior to using increased levels of antioxidants.

Arginine decreases tumor growth and spread (metastasis), therefore supplemental arginine is useful for pets with cancer. Glutamine may retard the cachexia (wasting) seen in many pets with cancer and may help protect against intestinal injury. However, some experimental studies have shown no benefit and occasionally see increased vomiting or diarrhea in pets supplemented with glutamine. At this time, no clear-cut evidence supports or opposes glutamine supplementation. The need for glutamine will vary from case to case.

Other recommendations include adding 60 to 100 mg of Coenzyme Q_{10} (an antioxidant) and 500 mg of vitamin E/450 kcals of food. The precaution mentioned concerning antioxidants should be heeded.

Finally, many holistic veterinarians will add fresh vegetables (especially those high in indoles and antioxidants) such as broccoli, kale, and cabbage and fresh **garlic** (pages 204). Other supplements (such as herbs or mushrooms) can be used as needed. After consulting with you and thoroughly examining your pet, your veterinarian can decide which additional supplements might be helpful.

Diet for Dogs with Cancer

½ cup tofu, raw, firm
1 cup boiled lentils
2 cups of potatoes boiled with skin
2 teaspoons chicken fat or canola oil
1/10 teaspoon salt
Multivitamin/mineral supplement

Provides 775 kcal and supports the daily needs of a 25-pound dog. Provides 43.9 grams of protein and 22 grams of fat. Adding 2 tablespoons of canned sardines increases the protein content by 6.2 grams and the fat content by 4.6 grams.

Variations

1. Add arginine at 647 mg/100 kcal of food.
2. Add omega-3 fatty acids (fish oil) at 1,518 mg/100 kcal. This is very difficult to do, as the average omega-3 fatty acid capsule contains 180 mg. Work with your doctor to increase the fatty acid content as much as possible—adding fish such as salmon to the diet can help achieve this goal.
3. Occasionally substitute ⅓ pound of cooked chicken, turkey, or lowfat beef for the tofu (in which case the lentils can be eliminated).
4. Occasionally substitute 2 cups of rice or macaroni for the potatoes.
5. Add fresh, raw or steamed vegetables to increase the level of natural vitamins and minerals, as well as add flavor. Most vegetables provide approximately 25 kcal per ½ cup.
6. Add 4 bonemeal tablets (10-grain or equivalent) or 1 teaspoon of bonemeal powder to supply calcium and phosphorus with a multivitamin/mineral supplement using the label instructions. Alternatively, use a natural product from Standard Process (use 1 Calcifood Wafer or 2 Calcium Lactate tablets for each 2 bonemeal tablets).
7. When possible, use natural vitamins made from raw whole foods, rather than synthetic vitamins (although both can be used in combination), as the natural vitamins also supply plant phytochemicals, enzymes, and other nutrients not found in chemically synthesized vitamins. Use either Catalyn from Standard (at a dose of 1 Catalyn per 25 pounds) or Canine Plus from VetriScience (following label dosages) for the natural vitamin in this recipe.

Diet for Cats with Cancer

½ pound chicken
½ large hard-boiled egg
½ ounce clams, chopped in juice
4 teaspoons chicken fat or canola oil
⅛ teaspoon potassium chloride
Multivitamin/mineral supplement
100 mg taurine

This diet provides 471 kcal, 53.1 grams of protein, and 27.4 grams of fat and provides the daily needs for a 15-pound cat.

Variations

1. Add arginine at 647 mg/100 kcal of food. This is a recommendation for dogs and has not been proven in cats.
2. Add omega-3 fatty acids (fish oil at 1,518 mg/100 kcal). This is very difficult to do, as the average omega-3 fatty acid capsule contains 180 mg. Work with your doctor to increase the fatty acid content as much as possible. Adding fish such as salmon to the diet can help achieve this goal for dogs (but has not been proven in cats).
3. Occasionally add ⅓ cup of rice, macaroni, or potatoes. However, cats do not have a proven need for dietary carbohydrates, and adding additional carbohydrates supplies substrate (food) for cancer cells.
4. Add fresh, raw or steamed vegetables to potentially increase the level of natural vitamins and minerals, as well as add flavor. Most vegetables provide approximately 25 kcal per ½ cup. Many cats will not eat vegetables.
5. Add 3 bonemeal tablets (10-grain or equivalent) or ¾ teaspoon of bonemeal powder to supply calcium and phosphorus with a multivitamin/mineral supplement, using the label instructions. Alternatively, use a natural product from Standard Process (1 Calcifood Wafer or 2 Calcium Lactate tablets for each 2 bonemeal tablets).
6. When possible, use natural vitamins made from raw whole foods, rather than synthetic vitamins (although both can be used in combination), as the natural vitamins also supply plant phytochemicals, enzymes, and other nutrients not found in chemically synthesized vitamins. Use either Catalyn from Standard Process (at a dose of 1 Catalyn per 10 pounds) or NuCat from VetriScience (following label dosages) as the natural vitamin in this recipe.

DIABETES

Dietary therapy is useful in both dogs and cats with diabetes, although one author, Dr. Donald Strombeck, disputes the belief that diet is useful for diabetic cats. Most diabetic dogs require insulin as they have type I diabetes (insulin-dependent diabetes). Many cats may not require insulin, as they have type II diabetes (non-insulin-dependent diabetes). These cats are most likely to respond to therapies that may include dietary therapy, nutritional supplementation, and exercise.

While not proven, some holistic veterinarians believe that years of feeding corn-based foods to cats (which amounts to feeding a high carbohydrate food to a true carnivore, which is not natural) may be contributing to the high incidence of diabetes in cats.

The homemade diet recommended for dogs with diabetes is composed of 50 to 55% high-quality complex carbohydrates (oats, vegetables, potato) with no simple sugars (such as sucrose, which may be included in commercial processed diets, especially soft-moist foods). Fat is restricted (no more than 20%), and moderate amounts of protein (15 to 30%) are included.

Diets high in complex carbohydrates (fibers) allow slower digestion and absorption of carbohydrates, which helps prevent wide fluctuations in blood glucose levels by minimizing postprandial glucose concentrations (postprandial refers to the period after a meal is eaten when blood glucose is most likely to spike to a high level, usually within 1 to 4 hours after eating). High complex-carbohydrate diets also appear to increase the sensitivity of the cells of the body to insulin, which can improve blood sugar regulation. Carbohydrates such as vegetables, oats, and potatoes are more slowly digested and absorbed than rice and are preferred sources of carbohydrates for inclusion in the diets of diabetic dogs.

Soluble and insoluble fibers are carbohydrates commonly included in diets for dogs with diabetes. Soluble fiber (such as guar gum, which can be sprinkled on food at 8 gm/400 kcal of food) reduces blood sugar levels by absorbing water and forming gels that slow the movement of food from the stomach, reduces absorption of glucose, and increases the passage of food throughout the intestinal tract (which serves to slow glucose absorption). Insoluble fibers (such as wheat bran added to the diet at 8 gm/400 kcal of food) have similar effects. Pumpkin, squashes, and similar vegetables can be used to add fiber to pet diets. Products such as sugar-free Metamucil can also be added to the pet's diet to provide additional fiber.

Dogs and cats with diabetes who are thin should not be fed high-fiber diets initially, as they may continue to lose weight. These pets should be fed wholesome maintenance diets with small amounts of fiber added slowly once normalization of weight is achieved.

Diet for Dogs with Diabetes

1¼ cups oatmeal or rolled oats, cooked
3½ ounces (¼ cup) kidney beans
1 large hard-boiled egg
1 cup mixed vegetables, cooked and drained

This diet provides 452 kcal, 24.5 gm protein, 8.9 gm fat, and supports the daily caloric needs of a 12- to 13-pound dog. (See table 3.1 on page 345)

Variations

1. Substitute ⅓ pound chicken or turkey breast and 2 cups of potato cooked with the skin for the rolled oats and the kidney beans. If this substitution is made, 30 gm (1 ounce) of wheat bran should also be added to the diet.
2. Add 1½ to 2 bonemeal tablets (10-grain or equivalent) or ½ teaspoon of bonemeal powder to supply calcium and phosphorus with a multivitamin/mineral supplement, using the label instructions. Alternatively, use a natural product from Standard Process (1 Calcifood Wafer or 2 Calcium Lactate tablets for each 2 bonemeal tablets).
3. When possible, use natural vitamins made from raw whole foods, rather than synthetic vitamins (although both can be used in combination), as the natural vitamins also supply plant phytochemicals, enzymes, and other nutrients not found in chemically synthesized vitamins. Use either Catalyn from Standard Process (at a dose of 1 Catalyn per 25 pounds) or Canine Plus from VetriScience (following label dosages) as the natural vitamin in this recipe.

Diet for Cats with Diabetes

Most doctors also recommend similar diets for diabetic cats. However, cats are true carnivores and require meat in their diets. Therefore, the diet that may prove most helpful for diabetic cats uses the maintenance diet with added fiber. Keep in mind, however, that cats will usually not accept diets high in fiber.

⅓ to ½ pound of ground meat (turkey, chicken, lamb, beef)
½ to 1 large hard-boiled egg
½ ounce of clams chopped in juice
4 teaspoons chicken fat or canola oil
⅛ teaspoon potassium chloride (salt substitute)
100 mg taurine

If using ½ pound of chicken and ½ egg, the diet will provide 471 kcal, 53.1 gm of protein, and 27.4 gm of fat. An adult, indoor, 10-pound cat requires approximately 300 kcal of energy per day; an adult, outdoor, 10-pound cat requires approximately 360 kcal of energy per day; and a 5-pound kitten requires approximately 300 kcal of energy per day.

Variations

1. Substitute tuna (4 ounces in water without salt), sardines (4 to 6 ounces in tomato sauce), or other fish (such as 5 ounces of salmon) for the meat protein. Or occasionally substitute ½ to ⅔ cup of tofu for variety. Since cats are true carnivores, most doctors prefer to recommend tofu only on an occasional basis.
2. Add ⅓ cup of potato (cooked with the skin), rice, or macaroni (although cats do not have a defined dietary requirement for carbohydrates).
3. If desired, supply vitamins and minerals as follows: 3 to 4 bonemeal tablets (10-grain or equivalent) or ¾ to 1 teaspoon of bonemeal powder to supply calcium and phosphorus with a multivitamin/mineral supplement using the label instructions. Alternatively, use a natural product from Standard Process (1 Calcifood Wafer or 2 Calcium Lactate tablets for each 2 bonemeal tablets). When possible, use natural

Diets/Medical Conditions

vitamins made from raw whole foods, rather than synthetic vitamins (although both can be used in combination), as the natural vitamins also supply plant phytochemicals, enzymes, and other nutrients not found in chemically synthesized vitamins. Use either Catalyn from Standard Process (at a dose of 1 Catalyn per 10 pounds) or NuCat from VetriScience (following label dosages) as the natural vitamin in this recipe.

4. Use fresh, raw or slightly steamed vegetables (such as carrots or broccoli) as a top dressing for the diet for extra nutrition and variety (approximately ½ to 1 cup per recipe, though many cats will not eat vegetables). Most vegetables provide approximately 25 kcal per ½ cup.

5. The nutrient composition of the diet will vary depending upon which ingredients are used. See table 3.2 on page 346 to determine how much to feed to your kitten or adult cat. The actual amount to feed will vary based upon the pet's weight (feed less if weight is gained, more if weight is lost).

6. Add extra fiber by supplementing with kidney beans (⅛ cup), oatmeal (¼ cup), wheat bran (¼ ounce), pumpkin or squashes, and sugar-free fiber products such as Metamucil.

GASTROINTESTINAL DISEASE

Pets with gastrointestinal disease (the most common of which is inflammatory bowel disease) manifested by vomiting and/or diarrhea can benefit from dietary therapy. After proper veterinary evaluation to rule out serious diseases, pets with vomiting and/or diarrhea are prescribed a period of fasting and dietary therapy.

For pets with mild acute vomiting, food and water should be withheld for 8 to 12 hours to allow the intestinal tract to rest (puppies and kittens are usually fasted for shorter periods of time). After this brief fasting period, water (usually in the form of ice cubes or crushed ice) can be offered in small amounts (alternatively, make ice cubes of an electrolyte solution rather than plain water to offer the pet). If the pet can han-

dle the ice without vomiting, offer a bland diet in small amounts by feeding frequent meals (3 to 6) for 1 to 3 days. Small, frequent feedings are needed to allow maximum digestion and absorption of nutrients. After this period, the regular diet can be added back to the gastrointestinal diet and the pet slowly (over 3 to 5 days) weaned back onto the regular diet.

Treat pets with mild acute diarrhea similarly except do not withhold water from the pet. Offer water or preferably electrolyte solution throughout the healing phase, which typically lasts 5 to 7 days. Withhold food from the pet for 12 to 24 hours (usually 8 to 12 hours for puppies and kittens, 24 hours for adult pets). Feed a gastrointestinal diet then slowly reintroduce the pet to the regular maintenance diet.

Pets with more serious problems such as inflammatory bowel disease may develop chronic vomiting, diarrhea, weight loss, or a combination of these signs. Severe inflammation of the intestinal tract can cause increased absorption of large food particles (molecules) that normally do not cross the intestinal barrier. This can possibly cause the formation of autoantibodies that may lead to autoimmune diseases (and further intestinal damage). Bacteria and yeasts (such as *Candida albicans*) may overgrow in the intestines of pets with chronic gastrointestinal disease who are being treated for extended periods of time with antibiotics. This may contribute, through toxin formation, to leaky-gut syndrome and food allergies or hypersensitivities. Many of these pets may require chronic therapy with medications (such as corticosteroids and antibiotics) and/or natural supplements (such as herbs or glutamine). Dietary therapy is quite helpful in these pets and, when combined with appropriate supplements in pets with mild disease, may be the only therapy needed.

The diet for pets with gastrointestinal disease should contain highly digestible nutrients. The typical diet is low in fat and contains hypoallergenic and easily digestible carbohydrate and protein sources. Diets requiring minimal digestion reduce digestive enzyme production protecting the intestinal tract. Excess fat aggravates diar-

Diets/Medical Conditions

rhea; excess dietary sugars and glutens are not easily digested in pets with gastrointestinal disease. Fiber may be added during the recovery stage if needed to allow continued healing or to prevent diarrhea in pets with chronic gastroenteritis; potatoes and vegetables serve as healthful, natural sources of fiber.

Boiled white rice, which is highly digestible, is the recommended carbohydrate source. Alternatively, tapioca or potatoes can be used if pets cannot tolerate rice (which is very rare) or if they will not eat rice-based diets. Gluten-based grains (wheat, barley, rye, oats) can cause persistent diarrhea due to gluten sensitivity therefore are not recommended.

Proteins that are highly digestible and have a high biological value, such as cottage cheese or tofu, are recommended. Cottage cheese is easily digested, and most pets do not have milk protein allergies. Meat can also be tried, although some pets may lose tolerance to meat (and develop a temporary sensitivity to meat during injury to the intestinal tract caused by vomiting or diarrhea). Additionally, meat stimulates more acid secretion in the stomach than tofu. If meat is fed, try lowfat beef or preferably chicken or turkey.

Supplements that may be useful for pets with chronic gastrointestinal disease include glutamine, glucosamine, various herbs, and omega-3 fatty acids (see Part Two for more on these supplements).

Glutamine (L-glutamine) is an amino acid derived from glutamic acid; it serves as a precursor to D-glucosamine. Severe stresses may result in a temporary glutamine deficiency. Glutamine plays a role in the health of the digestive tract and appears to serve as a fuel for the cells that line the intestines (it serves as a primary energy source for the mucosal cells that line the intestinal tract). Because stress on the intestinal cells (such as chronic inflammatory bowel disease) can increase the need for glutamine as the body replaces the cells lining the intestinal tract, glutamine supplementation is often recommended for pets with chronic bowel disorders including inflammatory bowel disease.

While glutamine supplementation is generally safe, many anti-epilepsy drugs work by blocking glutamate stimulation in the brain. High dosages of glutamine may overwhelm these drugs and pose a risk to pets with epilepsy. If your pet is taking antiseizure medications, glutamine should only be used under veterinary supervision. See Part Two for a greater discussion of glutamine.

N-acetylglucosamine and D-glucosamine (for which glutamine, another supplement recommended for pets with inflammatory bowel disease, is a precursor) may be helpful for pets with inflammatory bowel disease. The cells of the intestinal mucosa have a high rate of cell turnover, and patients with inflammatory bowel disease have a cell turnover rate that is at least three times higher than healthy patients. Patients with inflammatory bowel disease cannot make N-acetylglucosamine. This deficiency of N-acetyl-glucosamine leads to further intestinal damage, including increased permeability (leaky gut syndrome). Supplementing N-acetylglucosamine and D-glucosamine can help heal the intestinal mucosa by supporting glycoprotein synthesis. See Part Two for a greater discussion of glucosamine.

A number of herbs have been recommended for pets with chronic bowel disorders to help relieve inflammation and protect the lining of the intestinal tract. These include German chamomile, slippery elm, aloe vera juice, calendula, raspberry leaf, and marshmallow. See Part One for a greater discussion of herbs that might be helpful for pets with gastrointestinal disease.

Omega-3 fatty acids can reduce inflammation. However, it has been suggested but not proven that high levels of omega-3 fatty acids may reduce the protective prostaglandins in the inner lining (mucosa) of the intestinal tract, worsening diarrhea. More studies are needed to determine if omega-3 fatty acids are helpful or not in pets with chronic gastrointestinal disease. If they are used in pets with gastrointestinal disease, because they add fat to the diet they should not be added until the pet has been stabilized and the diarrhea controlled. They can be slowly added to the diet at that point. See Part Two for a greater discussion of omega-3 fatty acids.

Diet for Dogs with Gastrointestinal Disease

Dogs with gastrointestinal disease need diets with highly digestible proteins that are also low in fat. Low fat cottage cheese (½-⅔ cup) is used to provide protein (tofu with ⅛ teaspoon of added salt can be used if the dog refuses cottage cheese.) Brown or white rice (2 cups) is an easily digestible carbohydrate source (boiled or baked potato can be tried if the dog refuses rice.)

Potassium can be added using supplements such as Tumil-K (available through veterinarians) or by adding ¼-½ teaspoon of salt supplement (potassium chloride.) This diet would provide approximately 500 kcal with 27 grams of protein and 2 grams of fat.

Two to three bonemeal tablets (10 grain or equivalent) or ¾ teaspoon of bonemeal powder to supply calcium and phosphorus with a multi-vitamin mineral supplement using the label instructions is added as the pet improves. Alternatively, a natural product from Standard Process (Calcifood Wafers or Calcium Lactate) can be used (use 1 CalcifoodWafer or 2 Calcium Lactate tablets for each 2 bonemeal tablets.)

When possible, natural vitamins made from raw whole foods, rather than synthetic vitamins (although both can be used in combination) are preferred, as the natural vitamins also supply plant phytochemicals, enzymes, and other nutrients not found in chemically-synthesized vitamins. Catalyn from Standard Process can be used as the natural vitamin in this recipe, at a dose of 1 Catalyn per 25 pounds; Canine Plus (VetriScience) could also be used following label dosages.

Fresh, raw or slightly steamed vegetables (carrots, broccoli, etc.) can be used as a top dressing for the diet for extra nutrition and variety as the pet improves. Most vegetables provide approximately 25 kcal per ½ cup.

In general, the above recipe supplies the daily nutritional and calorie needs for a 12-13 pound dog. The actual amount to feed will vary based

upon the pet's weight (feed less if weight is gained, more if weight is lost.)

Supplements. Omega-3 fatty acids, probiotics, plant enzymes, herbs, glutamine, and glucosamine are often added to the diets of pets with gastrointestinal disease to help nourish the intestinal cells and control clinical signs. Check with your doctor to see whether any of these nutritional "therapies" would be helpful to your pet. Additional fiber can be added under veterinary supervision if diarrhea persists. Rice contains small amounts of fiber, potatoes with the skin have additional fiber, vegetables provide additional fiber; fiber supplements (psyllium) can be added at 1 to 2 teaspoons if needed.

Diet for Cats with Gastrointestinal Disease

Cats with gastrointestinal disease can do well with a slight variation of the **basic cat diet** (page 348) The canola oil and clams should be eliminated. Cats can be fed simply the protein source (such as chicken or turkey, with or without the egg) or a small amount of brown or white rice (¼-½ cup) can be added if desired. Potassium can be added using supplements such as Tumil-K (available through veterinarians) or by adding ¼-½ teaspoon of salt supplement (potassium chloride.) Add 100 mg of taurine.

This diet would provide approximately 275 kcal with 30 grams of protein and 16 grams of fat.

One to two bonemeal tablets (10 grain or equivalent) or ¼-½ teaspoon of bonemeal powder to supply calcium and phosphorus with a multi-vitamin mineral supplement using the label instructions is added as the pet improves. Alternatively, a natural product from Standard Process (Calcifood Wafers or Calcium Lactate) can be used (use 1 Calcifood Wafer or 2 Calcium Lactate tablets for each 2 bonemeal tablets.)

When possible, natural vitamins made from raw whole foods, rather than synthetic vitamins (although both can be used in combination) are preferred, as the natural vitamins also supply plant phytochemicals, enzymes, and other nu-

Diets/Medical Conditions

trients not found in chemically-synthesized vitamins. Catalyn from Standard Process can be used as the natural vitamin in this recipe, at a dose of 1 Catalyn per 10 pounds; NuCat (Vetri-Science) could also be used following label dosages.

In general, the above recipe supplies the daily nutritional and calorie needs for a 9-10 pound cat. The actual amount to feed will vary based upon the pet's weight (feed less if weight is gained, more if weight is lost.)

Supplements.   Omega-3 fatty acids, probiotics, plant enzymes, herbs, glutamine, and glucosamine are often added to the diets of pets with gastrointestinal disease to help nourish the intestinal cells and control clinical signs. Check with your doctor to see whether any of these nutritional "therapies" would be helpful to your pet. Additional fiber can be added under veterinary supervision if diarrhea persists. Rice contains small amounts of fiber, potatoes with the skin have additional fiber, and vegetables provide additional fiber; or fiber supplements (psyllium) can be added at 1 to 2 teaspoons if needed.

HEART DISEASE

Heart disease is a generic term referring to any disorder affecting the heart. Congestive heart failure refers to the syndrome that occurs late in the course of heart disease where fluid backs up into the lungs and other organs of the body as the heart loses its ability to pump blood effectively in a forward direction.

In dogs, the most common form of heart disease is valvular heart disease that can lead to congestive heart failure. In cats, the most common form of heart disease is hypertrophic cardiomyopathy, which can also lead to congestive heart failure. Regardless of the cause of heart disease, with time, some pets may develop heart failure as the diseased heart can no longer compensate. (See Part One for more explanation of heart disease and heart failure.)

Dietary therapy is designed to regulate sodium levels. In heart failure, sodium is re-

tained rather than excreted by the kidneys. Sodium retains fluid in the body, which causes fluid to leak from the blood vessels into the lungs, liver, and other organs causing the signs seen in pets with congestive heart failure such as coughing.

To reduce sodium retention, salt is reduced in diets designed for pets with heart disease. Since commercial pet foods have excessive amounts of sodium to increase palatability and act as a preservative, these diets are not recommended for pets with heart disease. There are several medicated diets prepared for pets with heart disease. However, they may contain by-products and chemical preservatives that are not always consistent with a holistic nutritional program, although they may have a place in the management of heart disease if the owner cannot prepare a homemade diet or if the pet will not eat the homemade diet. Homemade diets can fit the need for holistic, low-sodium diets.

Pets with heart failure may have low potassium levels resulting from decreased food intake (common in pets with heart failure) and the use of diuretics such as furosemide (Lasix). Even with normal blood levels, cellular levels of potassium may be decreased. Extra potassium can be supplied using supplements or potassium chloride (salt substitute). Discuss this with your veterinarian before using potassium supplementation.

Magnesium may also be decreased in pets with heart failure, once again due to reduced food intake and use of diuretics. Magnesium depletion is difficult to prove based on blood levels as, similar to potassium, blood levels do not coincide with cellular levels. Magnesium supplementation under veterinary supervision may be warranted.

Supplementation with Coenzyme Q_{10}, taurine, and carnitine may be helpful in pets with heart disease and heart failure. Taurine deficiency can cause dilated cardiomyopathy in cats. This disease is quite rare today as pet food manufacturers have increased the levels of taurine in commercial pet foods. Cats are true carnivores. Unlike dogs, they cannot make enough taurine to meet their daily needs and must receive taurine from their diets.

Homemade diets for cats containing animal proteins such as meat or fish contain adequate taurine levels. However, processing results in loss of taurine if the meat juices are removed. Pouring the juices over the diet, or feeding raw meats if the owner is comfortable with this (see the earlier discussion on feeding raw diets) can replace this taurine. Eggs and cottage cheese contain little or no taurine and must be supplemented with taurine. Vegetarian diets (including tofu-based diets) do not supply taurine as plants do not make taurine; these diets must also be supplemented with taurine to meet the cat's needs.

In cats with taurine deficiency that results in dilated cardiomyopathy, clinical improvement is usually seen within 2 to 3 weeks following supplementation. Improvements in the EKG and radiographs will often take 3 to 6 weeks. The goal of taurine supplementation is to achieve plasma taurine levels of at least 60 nmol/mL (normal cats usually have levels greater than 40 nmol/mL). Not all cats with dilated cardiomyopathy have taurine deficiency as the cause of the cardiomyopathy; those cats with normal taurine levels would not be expected to respond to supplementation with taurine (although, since taurine supplementation is safe, any cat with heart disease could probably receive a diet containing additional taurine).

In dogs, dilated cardiomyopathy can also occur, leading to congestive heart failure. Preliminary work shows that supplementation with taurine may be beneficial in American Cocker Spaniels and Golden Retrievers with dilated cardiomyopathy. Supplementation with taurine (500 mg twice daily) and L-carnitine (1,000 mg twice daily) in a small number of dogs with low plasma taurine levels resulted in improvement in a few of the patients. Since American Cocker Spaniels are predisposed to dilated cardiomyopathy with concurrent taurine (and possibly) carnitine deficiencies, supplementation with these two compounds is suggested for Cocker Spaniels with dilated cardiomyopathy. Although not all researchers agree on this recommendation, supplementation is safe even in those cases where it is difficult to determine whether it is truly needed.

Dogs with chronic valvular disease (leaky heart valves), the most common heart disease reported in dogs, usually have normal plasma taurine levels, making routine supplementation unlikely to be of benefit.

Taurine deficiency can be diagnosed based upon testing levels in the blood. Plasma levels are more indicative of recent taurine intake; whole blood levels are more suggestive of chronic taurine intake. However, even with normal blood levels it is possible that levels of taurine in the heart muscle cells might not be adequate. Even for those pets without low blood taurine levels, supplementation can be tried without side effects.

Decreased carnitine levels may also be related to dilated cardiomyopathy in dogs, especially in Boxers, Doberman Pinschers, and American Cocker Spaniels. Carnitine deficiency is difficult to diagnose and usually requires heart biopsy for a definitive diagnosis. Carnitine supplementation at 2 grams (2,000 mg) given 3 times daily is often recommended for dogs with cardiomyopathy.

Carnitine can also be used for pets with any type of heart disease (and is included in some heart supplements), but definitive proof for its use in heart diseases other than cardiomyopathy caused due to carnitine deficiency is lacking. However, as with taurine, since carnitine supplementation is safe, supplementation will not hurt, and other nutrients in the supplements (antioxidants and herbs, for example) may be useful.

Carnitine is abundant in red meat (higher in beef than in chicken or turkey) and dairy products, which form the basis of the diets on pages 366 and 367. Diets high in cereal grains and plants (which account for many commercial diets) may not support adequate carnitine levels in the heart.

Supplemental carnitine may improve the ability of certain tissues to produce energy. This effect has led to the use of carnitine in various muscle diseases as well as heart conditions, as carnitine accumulates in both skeletal and cardiac muscle. There is no dietary requirement for carnitine. However, a few individuals have a genetic defect that hinders the body's ability to make carnitine. In dogs, a subset of pets with dilated cardiomyopathy that show variable response to carnitine supplementation has been identified (as was first shown in Boxers).

In addition, diseases of the liver, kidneys, or brain may inhibit carnitine production. Heart muscle tissue, because of its high energy requirements, is particularly vulnerable to carnitine deficiency.

The principal dietary sources of carnitine are meat and dairy products, but to obtain therapeutic dosages, a supplement is necessary.

In people, carnitine is taken in three forms: L-carnitine (for heart and other conditions), L-propionyl-carnitine (for heart conditions), and acetyl-L-carnitine (for Alzheimer's disease). The dosage is the same for all three forms.

Carnitine is primarily used for heart-related conditions. Without adequate carnitine to transport fatty acids into heart muscle cells, reduced levels of energy are available to the heart.

In people, fairly good evidence suggests that it can be used along with conventional treatment for angina or chest pain, to improve symptoms and reduce medication needs. When combined with conventional therapy, it may also reduce mortality after a heart attack. A few studies suggest that carnitine may be useful for cardiomyopathy.

Several small studies have found that carnitine, often in the form of L-propionyl-carnitine, can improve symptoms of congestive heart failure. There is better evidence for Coenzyme Q_{10} for this condition, and in fact, some veterinarians may prescribe both supplements.

In people, carnitine may help reduce death rate after a heart attack. In a 12-month, placebo-controlled study, 160 individuals who had experienced a heart attack received 4 g of L-carnitine daily or placebo, in addition to other conventional medication. The mortality rate in the treated group was significantly lower than in the placebo group, 1.2% versus 12.5% respectively. There were also improvements in heart rate, blood pressure, angina (chest pain), and blood lipids. A larger double-blind study of 472 people found that carnitine may improve the chances of survival if given within 24 hours after a heart attack. As a rule, pets do not experience "heart attacks" as people do. Pets can experience sudden onset of congestive heart failure due to valvular disease or cardiomyopathy. Whether or not administering carnitine following an acute episode improves survival is unknown.

Note: Evidence also suggests that one particular form of carnitine, L-acetyl-carnitine, may be helpful in Alzheimer's disease, although a more recent larger study found no benefit. Dogs and cats do not get true Alzheimer's disease, but instead suffer from cognitive disorder (what many owners mistakenly refer to as "senility"). Whether or not L-acetyl-carnitine may be helpful for pets with cognitive disorder is unknown at this point.

Weak evidence in people suggests that carnitine may be able to improve cholesterol and triglyceride levels. In carnitine deficiency, increased blood trigylceride levels can occur.

In pets, heart levels (myocardial levels) of carnitine have been found to be low in up to 40% of dogs suffering with dilated cardiomyopathy. Diagnosing carnitine deficiency is difficult, as blood levels do not correlate with levels in heart muscle cells (although low plasma carnitine levels appear to be predictive of low myocardial carnitine concentration). Researchers must do heart muscle biopsies in order to determine myocardial carnitine deficiency. If the heart is unable to concentrate carnitine, levels can fall quite low despite normal blood levels. Studies show that only 20% of dogs with dilated cardiomyopathy with myocardial deficiency also had low blood levels of carnitine. Most dogs with myocardial carnitine deficiency and dilated cardiomyopathy suffer from a membrane transport defect that prevents adequate levels of carnitine moving from the blood into the heart muscle cells. (In these pets, blood levels of carnitine are usually normal or higher than normal.)

The dosage of carnitine recommended for dogs with carnitine-deficiency cardiomyopathy is 50 mg/kg 3 times daily, or alternatively 2,000 mg per pet 3 times daily; rare side effects include diarrhea and flatulence (intestinal gas). Improved heart function, appetite, and exercise tolerance are often noted within 2 months following supplementation.

Note: Carnitine supplementation has also been suggested for pets with other heart diseases, including endocardiosis (valvular heart disease), ischemic heart disease, and congestive heart failure. Definitive proof is lacking, although carnitine supplementation is safe and can be tried for pets with these other cardiac disorders under veterinary supervision.

Diets/Medical Conditions

To sum up, current benefits and recommendations regarding carnitine supplementation for dogs with heart disease include:

- Since true carnitine deficiency may exist in a small number of dogs such as Boxers with dilated cardiomyopathy, supplementation with L-carnitine may be of benefit in these pets.
- In some dogs with dilated cardiomyopathy (approximately the 40% who have myocardial carnitine deficiency), supplementation may improve clinical signs and cause some improvement in the echocardiograms of these patients.
- Supplementation with L-carnitine may improve survival in some dogs with dilated cardiomyopathy, especially those that have myocardial carnitine deficiency.

The main disadvantage of carnitine supplementation is the cost, approximately $75 per month. While carnitine deficiency is not the cause of dilated cardiomyopathy in most dogs, supplementation is safe and can be used as an adjunct to other therapies.

L-carnitine in its three forms appears to be safe, even when taken with medications. People are advised not to use forms of carnitine known as "D-carnitine" or "DL-carnitine," as these can cause angina, muscle pain, and loss of muscle function (probably by interfering with L-carnitine). The maximum safe dosages for young children, pregnant or nursing women, or those with severe liver or kidney disease have not been established; similar precautions are probably warranted in pets.

Diet for Dogs with Heart Disease

Diets for dogs with heart disease are usually lower in sodium and higher in potassium.

Extra fat can be added to maintain weight if weight loss due to heart failure occurs. The **basic dog diet** (page 347) can be used, but do not add extra salt. In the place of eggs, ⅓ pound lean ground beef or chicken or other meat can be used. Canola oil is added as per the basic diet. The diet provides approximately 900 kcal with 45 grams of protein and 37 grams of fat.

Fresh, raw or slightly steamed vegetables (carrots, broccoli, etc.) can be used as a top dressing for the diet for extra nutrition and variety (approximately ½–1 cup per recipe.)

Most vegetables provide approximately 25 kcal per ½ cup.

Five bonemeal tablets (10 grain or equivalent) or 1–1¼ teaspoon of bonemeal powder to supply calcium and phosphorus with a multi-vitamin mineral supplement using the label instructions is added. Alternatively, a natural product from Standard Process (Calcifood Wafers or Calcium Lactate) can be used (use 1 Calcifood Wafer or 2 Calcium Lactate tablets for each 2 bonemeal tablets.)

When possible, natural vitamins made from raw whole foods, rather than synthetic vitamins (although both can be used in combination) are preferred, as the natural vitamins also supply plant phytochemicals, enzymes, and other nutrients not found in chemically- synthesized vitamins. Catalyn from Standard Process can be used as the natural vitamin in this recipe, at a dose of 1 Catalyn per 25 pounds; Canine Plus (VetriScience) could also be used following label dosages.

The nutrient composition of the diet will vary depending upon which ingredients are used. In general, the above recipe supplies the daily nutritional and calorie needs for a 30 pound dog. The actual amount to feed will vary based upon the pet's weight (feed less if weight gain, more if weight loss.)

Added supplements which can be beneficial include omega-3 fatty acids, plant enzymes, and a super green food or health blend formula. The health blend formula may contain excess sodium that could be harmful (check with the manufacturer.)

Diet for Cats with Heart Disease

Diets for cats with heart disease are usually lower in sodium and higher in potassium.

Extra fat can be added to maintain weight if weight loss due to heart failure occurs. The **basic cat diet** (page 348) can be used, but do not add extra salt. Low sodium tuna or salmon (5–6 ounces) could be substituted for the meat for variation. Brown or white rice (½ cup) can be added if desired. Taurine (100–500 mg) is also added. The diet provides approximately 550 kcal with 55 grams of protein and 30 grams of fat.

Fresh, raw or slightly steamed vegetables (carrots, broccoli, etc.) can be used as a top dressing for the diet for extra nutrition and variety (approximately ½–1 cup per recipe), but most cats do not like eating vegetables.

Most vegetables provide approximately 25 kcal per ½ cup.

Two bonemeal tablets (10 grain or equivalent) or ¼–½ teaspoon of bonemeal powder to supply calcium and phosphorus with a multi-vitamin mineral supplement using the label instructions is added. Alternatively, a natural product from Standard Process (Calcifood Wafers or Calcium Lactate) can be used (use 1 Calcifood Wafer or 2 Calcium Lactate tablets for each 2 bonemeal tablets.)

When possible, natural vitamins made from raw whole foods, rather than synthetic vitamins (although both can be used in combination) are preferred, as the natural vitamins also supply plant phytochemicals, enzymes, and other nutrients not found in chemically-synthesized vitamins. Catalyn from Standard Process can be used as the natural vitamin in this recipe, at a dose of 1 Catalyn per 10 pounds; NuCat (VetriScience) could also be used following label dosages.

The nutrient composition of the diet will vary depending upon which ingredients are used. In general, the above recipe supplies the daily nutritional and calorie needs for a 10–11 pound cat. The actual amount to feed will vary based upon the pet's weight (feed less if weight gain, more if weight loss.)

Added supplements which can be beneficial include omega-3 fatty acids, plant enzymes, and a super green food or health blend formula The health blend formula may contain excess sodium that could be harmful (check with the manufacturer.)

KIDNEY DISEASE

The most common type of kidney disease/kidney failure that occurs in dogs and cats is chronic kidney disease/failure. This condition usually occurs in older pets, although it may occur in pets of any age. As a matter of fact, kidney failure is one of the most common causes of illness and death in pets 10 years of age and older. (Acute kidney failure, usually caused by toxins such as antifreeze poisoning or acute infections, is much less common in dogs and cats.)

The exact cause of kidney failure in most older pets is unknown except in cases such as tumors of the kidneys in dogs and cats or infection with feline infectious peritonitis virus that can cause kidney failure in cats. One theory relates to the feeding of most commercial processed pet foods. Many pet foods contain excess levels of vitamins and minerals, especially vitamin D, calcium, and phosphorus, which are directly toxic to the kidneys. While definitive proof is lacking, it is interesting to speculate that years of feeding diets containing excess and potentially toxic levels of nutrients could cause chronic damage and ultimately failure of the kidneys. More natural processed diets, and especially properly supplemented homemade diets, would not be expected to have this effect.

Early diagnosis of kidney disease is important, as kidney disease can be irreversible in some pets. Since kidney disease is progressive, early diagnosis and appropriate therapy can prevent further destruction of the nephrons, the microscopic functional units located within the kidneys.

Just when diet should be changed in pets with kidney disease is quite controversial. Certainly altering the diets of pets with kidney failure and uremia, the syndrome that occurs as a result of excessive accumulation of toxins in the blood that are not filtered by the failing kidneys, is accepted by most doctors. In addition, making subtle corrections to the diet for pets with mild and early kidney disease can be helpful in slowing down the progressive quality of the kidney disease seen in many pets.

However, despite recommendations for over 50 years of altering diet in older (middle-aged or geriatric) pets to prevent kidney failure, no definitive proof exists that this works. Currently, unless underlying kidney disease is present, most doctors recommend feeding normal to increased amounts of highly digestible protein to older dogs and cats.

There are several dietary nutrients to consider altering in pets with kidney disease and kidney failure, including protein, phosphorus, sodium, potassium, and fatty acids.

Protein.   Protein restriction is often recommended for pets with kidney disease and kidney failure. Dietary protein is broken down to acid products that are normally excreted by the kidneys. Diseased kidneys cannot excrete these acid products and other toxins as efficiently as normal kidneys; as these products accumulate in the blood, signs of uremia and kidney failure (excess thirst, excess urination, decreased appetite, foul breath, lethargy) occur. Amino acids containing sulfur, as well as extra phosphorus in the diet, contribute to the formation of these acid products and toxins. Excess phosphorus in the body, as occurs in pets with kidney failure, can combine with calcium, forming crystals. These crystals can precipitate into the kidneys and other organs, further contributing to terminal kidney and multi-organ failure. By reducing ingredients in the diet that contain sulfurous amino acids and phosphorus, we can promote kidney health and reduce kidney damage.

Animal sources of protein (meat) are high in sulfur-containing amino acids and phosphorus. Plant protein sources contain less sulfurous amino acids and phosphorus and also contain minerals such as potassium and magnesium that contribute to an alkaline urine, promoting kidney health. Proteins of high biological value that contain little phosphorus are preferred for pets with kidney disease and kidney failure.

Eggs contain the protein of the highest biological value and are often recommended for pets with kidney disease or kidney failure. However, eggs also contain sulfurous amino acids that could contribute to acidosis. Egg protein can be safely fed to most pets with kidney disease without contributing to acidosis except in terminal kidney failure or if blood testing reveals acidosis.

While plant proteins do contain less sulfurous amino acids, the biological value of their proteins is less than egg protein, so more protein would need to be fed if plant proteins were selected as the protein source for the diet. This extra protein

would require that more waste products be excreted by already damaged kidneys, which is why egg protein is usually recommended for kidney diets. Tofu can be used as a compromise if the pet cannot tolerate egg protein.

Phosphorus.   By decreasing meat in the diet, we also reduce phosphorus levels (which are often severely elevated in pets with kidney failure). Phosphorus may be more toxic than protein in pets with kidney failure. Whenever we decrease protein, we also decrease phosphorus. Phosphorus-binding agents given orally can be useful in pets with elevated blood phosphorus levels if the following diet, which is low in phosphorus, cannot maintain acceptable phosphorus levels.

Sodium.   While high blood pressure (hypertension) is rare in pets, it can occur as a result of kidney failure in dogs and cats (and in cats with hyperthyroidism, which can occur concurrently with kidney failure). Most commercial diets have excessive levels of sodium to improve palatability and act as a preservative. Sodium restriction in the diets listed here can be a first line defense against hypertension.

Potassium.   Kidney failure usually results in potassium loss through the failing kidneys, even if the blood potassium level is normal (blood levels of potassium do not reflect cellular levels). Unless increased potassium blood levels are detected (which can occur in some pets with kidney failure), extra potassium supplementation can be of benefit. Potassium chloride, a salt substitute, is recommended in the diet; other sources of potassium supplementation can be obtained through your veterinarian.

Fatty Acids.   Supplementation with omega-3 fatty acids is often recommended for pets with kidney disease or kidney failure, and research continues in this area. Ongoing studies seem to support the contention that supplementation with omega-3 fatty acids may benefit pets with kidney disease or kidney failure. Omega-3 fatty acids can increase beneficial (anti-inflammatory) prostaglandins, which in turn can reduce inflammation in the kidneys and improve blood flow to the kidneys (a vasodilatory effect). Since omega-3 fatty acids can also lower blood cholesterol and triglycerides, this effect can also benefit pets with kidney disease, as dogs and cats with induced kidney disease have elevated levels of blood cholesterol and triglycerides. Studies have recommended a starting dose of 0.5 to 1.0 gram of omega-3 fatty acids/100 kcal of food/day, although this dosage is very difficult to reach with presently available supplements.

The following diets are starting points for feeding pets with kidney disease and kidney failure. Check with your veterinarian to determine the exact needs for your pet.

Diet for Dogs with Kidney Disease

Dogs with kidney disease may do well on the **basic dog diet** (page 347). If kidney failure is present, the diet is adapted to offer lower protein and phosphorus with increased potassium. High quality protein (1–2 hardboiled eggs) is used as the protein source; brown (or white) rice, or baked (or boiled) potato with skin (3 cups of either carbohydrate source) is added to the egg(s.) Canola oil is added as per the basic diet. The diet provides approximately 600 kcal with 15-20 grams of protein and 18 grams of fat.

Fresh, raw or slightly steamed vegetables (carrots, broccoli, etc.) can be used as a top dressing for the diet for extra nutrition and variety and to help bind intestinal phosphorus (approximately ½–1 cup per recipe.) Most vegetables provide approximately 25 kcal per ½ cup.

This diet provides approximately 300% potassium, 50% phosphorus, and 115% of the daily requirements for sodium. Extra potassium (potassium chloride or potassium supplement) can be used if needed; check with your veterinarian.

Calcium carbonate or calcium lactate (which may bind phosphorus) is used rather than bonemeal to decrease the phosphorus levels; 1½–2 pills of either calcium source are added to the diet. If reduced phosphorus is not needed, 3 bonemeal tablets (10 grain or equivalent) or ¾ teaspoon of bonemeal powder to supply calcium and phosphorus with a multi-vitamin mineral supplement using the label instructions is added.

Alternatively, a natural product from Standard Process (Calcifood Wafers or Calcium Lactate) can be used (use 1 Calcifood Wafer or 2 Calcium Lactate tablets for each 2 bonemeal tablets.)

When possible, natural vitamins made from raw whole foods, rather than synthetic vitamins are preferred, as the natural vitamins also supply plant phytochemicals, enzymes, and other nutrients not found in chemically-synthesized vitamins. Catalyn from Standard Process can be used as the natural vitamin in this recipe, at a dose of 1 Catalyn per 25 pounds; Canine Plus (VetriScience) could also be used following label dosages.

The nutrient composition of the diet will vary depending upon which ingredients are used. In general, the above recipe supplies the daily nutritional and calorie needs for a 20 pound dog. The actual amount to feed will vary based upon the pet's weight.

Added supplements which can be beneficial include **omega-3 fatty acids** (page 246), which may be helpful for pets with kidney disease. Check with your veterinarian for guidelines.

Diet for Cats with Kidney Disease

Cats with kidney disease may do well on the **basic cat diet** (page 348). If kidney failure is present, the diet is adapted to offer lower protein and phosphorus with increased potassium. High quality protein (1–2 hardboiled eggs) is used as the protein source (2–3 ounces of salmon or tuna, or 3–4 ounces of poultry or beef can be substituted.) Since cats do not require carbohydrates, none need be added, although adding rice, or cooked potato with skin (½ cup of either carbohydrate source) is acceptable. Taurine (100 mg) is also added. The diet provides approximately 300 kcal with 15 grams of protein and 14 grams of fat. This diet provides approximately 200% potassium, 45% phosphorus, and 160% of the daily requirements for sodium. Extra potassium (potassium chloride or potassium supplement) can be used if needed; check with your veterinarian.

Fresh, raw or slightly steamed vegetables (carrots, broccoli, etc.) can be used as a top dressing for the diet for extra nutrition and variety and to help bind intestinal phosphorus (approximately ½–1 cup per recipe.) Most vegetables provide approximately 25 kcal per ½ cup. Most cats do not like eating vegetables.

Calcium carbonate or calcium lactate (which may bind phosphorus) is used rather than bone-meal to decrease the phosphorus levels; 1½ pills of either calcium source are added to the diet. If reduced phosphorus is not needed, 2–3 bone-meal tablets (10 grain or equivalent) or ¾ tea-spoon of bonemeal powder to supply calcium and phosphorus with a multi-vitamin mineral supplement using the label instructions is added.

When possible, natural vitamins made from raw whole foods, rather than synthetic vitamins (although both can be used in combination) are preferred, as the natural vitamins also supply plant phytochemicals, enzymes, and other nutrients not found in chemically-synthesized vitamins.

In general, the above recipe supplies the daily nutritional and calorie needs for a 10-pound cat. The actual amount to feed will vary based upon the pet's weight.

LIVER DISEASE

Dietary therapy is a mainstay of treating the pet with liver disease, as few conventional medications actually treat liver disease.

High-quality and highly digestible carbohydrates are recommended to supply energy for the pet. Inferior types of carbohydrates that are undigested are fermented by intestinal bacteria, which in turn increases the bacteria in the colon. These bacteria then break down dietary proteins and produce extra ammonia, which is absorbed into the body and contributes to toxicity in pets with liver disease. Frequent feedings of high-quality, simple carbohydrates such as white rice and potatoes are recommended. Vegetables act as a source of complex carbohydrates and provide fiber; the fiber helps bind intestinal toxins and promotes bowel movements to remove these toxins (byproducts of protein digestion and bacterial fermentation of undigested foods) from the body.

Proteins provided by the diet must be of high biological value to reduce the production of ammonia, a by-product of protein digestion. Most commercial foods contain proteins that are not of high biological value. (Many commercial foods may also contain excess vitamin A, copper, and bacterial endotoxins, all of which contribute to the clinical signs in pets with liver disease.) Unless your doctor recommends protein restriction (usually only needed by pets with encephalopathy, a condition producing neurological signs in pets with severe liver disease), normal amounts of protein should be fed as protein is needed by the liver during repair.

Studies show that dogs with liver disease fed diets containing meat-based proteins have shorter survival times and more severe clinical signs than dogs with liver disease fed milk-based or soy-based protein diets. Cats require higher protein diets than dogs. While it may be more beneficial to cats to also feed them diets based on milk-based or soy-based proteins, most cats prefer meat-based diets. Cats fed milk-based or soy-based proteins must have supplemental taurine (100 to 200 mg/day), as milk has minimal taurine and soy (tofu) has no taurine.

In cats, hepatic lipidosis (fatty liver disease) is the most common liver disease and is secondary to starvation (often seen in overweight cats who go without eating for as few as 3 to 5 days). Hepatic lipidosis is a secondary complication of anorexia and obesity rather than a true primary liver disease. Force-feeding cats to help heal the liver and correct the underlying problem is the treatment for hepatic lipidosis. This often requires tube feeding of special diets. When feasible, high-fat (approximately 30%) enteral diets containing milk-based or soy-based proteins are ideal for these cats; taurine supplementation of 150 mg/8 ounces of liquid diet is recommended.

Adding the amino acids arginine or citrulline to the diet may be indicated, as these amino acids accelerate conversion of highly toxic ammonia to urea, reversing the clinical signs of toxicity that may occur in pets with liver disease. Glycine may decrease the toxicity that affects the kidneys when the chemotherapy drug cisplatin is administered.

Fat is used in the diet for energy. Even pets with fatty liver disease (hepatic lipidosis) do well on diets containing 20 to 25% fat. Free fatty acids contribute to increased blood ammonia by interfering with ammonia metabolism. Dietary

Diets/Medical Conditions

fats do not contribute to increased blood levels of free fatty acids; fasting or starvation will contribute to increased levels of free fatty acids. Therefore, pets with liver disease should have diets containing adequate amounts of fats and should receive frequent small feedings. Additionally, small frequent feedings reduce protein breakdown by the body (which can worsen clinical signs), improve glucose metabolism (preventing hypoglycemia), and decrease intestinal ammonia concentrations.

Increasing levels of vitamin A and copper can contribute to liver damage; excess supplementation should be avoided. Zinc supplementation may be of benefit as many pets with liver disease are deficient in zinc, and zinc can reduce copper absorption. Adding vitamins C, E, and K may be warranted for pets with liver disease. Vitamin E protects against metabolism of lipids in cell membranes. Vitamin K is needed for proper blood clotting, which can be a problem in pets with severe liver disease. While dogs and cats, unlike people, can make vitamin C in the liver and do not normally require this vitamin, liver disease may decrease the amount of vitamin C. Supplementation with these vitamins under veterinary supervision may be helpful.

Diet for Dogs with Liver Disease

Dogs with liver disease need different protein sources than those fed to normal pets.

The **basic dog diet** (page 347) is adapted by using cottage cheese (½ cup) and soy protein (typically tofu, ⅔ cup) as the primary protein sources (yogurt can be tried if cottage cheese is refused by the dog.) While not all dogs like cottage cheese or soy protein, try to avoid egg and meat protein whenever possible.

Adding 1½–2 cups of brown or white rice plus the canola oil and potassium chloride as in the basic dog diet completes the diet (adding a few ounces of raw or undercooked potato can increase bowel movements which may decrease bowel toxins.)

This diet would provide approximately 650 kcal with 36 grams of protein and 20 grams of fat.

Fresh, raw or slightly steamed vegetables (carrots, broccoli, etc.) can be used as a top dressing for the diet for extra nutrition and variety and to help bind intestinal phosphorus approximately ½–1 cup per recipe.) Most vegetables provide approximately 25 kcal per ½ cup.

Three to four bonemeal tablets (10 grain or equivalent) or ¾–1 teaspoon of bonemeal powder to supply calcium and phosphorus with a multi-vitamin mineral supplement using the label instructions is added. Alternatively, a natural product from Standard Process (Calcifood Wafers or Calcium Lactate) can be used (use 1 Calcifood Wafer or 2 Calcium Lactate tablets for each 2 bonemeal tablets.)

Supplement if necessary for pets with liver disease, but only after checking with your pet's veterinarian to determine the individual needs of your pet. Here are basic recommendations:

Vitamin C or Ascorbic Acid. Add 25 mg/kg/day. (Ascorbic acid, but not natural vitamin C, can cause release of copper from the liver, which can worsen clinical signs. Add small amounts daily and work up to the recommended dosage if clinical signs do not worsen, or preferably use natural vitamin C.)

Vitamin E. Add 500 mg/day.

Zinc. Add 3 mg/kg/day of zinc gluconate, 2 mg/kg/day of zinc sulfate, or 2 mg/kg/day of zinc acetate. Divide these doses into 3 daily doses; zinc acetate may cause less intestinal irritation.

Supplement with B vitamins. This is important.

Add supplements that can be beneficial, such as omega-3 fatty acids, arginine (250 mg per cat, two times daily), plant enzymes, and a super green food or health blend formula.

When possible, natural vitamins made from raw whole foods, rather than synthetic vitamins (although both can be used in combination) are preferred, as the natural vitamins also supply plant phytochemicals, enzymes, and other nutrients not found in chemically-synthesized vitamins. Catalyn from Standard Process can be used as the natural vitamin in this recipe, at a dose of 1 Catalyn per 25 pounds; Canine Plus (VetriScience) could also be used following label dosages.

The nutrient composition of the diet will vary depending upon which ingredients are used. In general, the above recipe supplies the daily nutritional and calorie needs for a 20-pound dog. The actual amount to feed will vary based upon the pet's weight (feed less if weight is gained, more if weight is lost.)

Diet for Cats with Liver Disease

Cats with liver disease need different protein sources than those to fed to normal pets.

The **basic cat diet** (page 348) is adapted by using cottage cheese (1/2 cup) and soy protein (typically tofu, 2/3 cup) as the primary protein sources (yogurt can be tried if cottage cheese is refused by the dog.) While not all cats like cottage cheese or soy protein, try to avoid egg and meat protein whenever possible. If this is not possible, try using 1/3 pound of turkey instead of the cottage cheese and tofu. Adding 1/3 cup of brown or white rice plus the canola oil and potassium chloride as in the basic cat diet completes the diet (adding a few oucnes of raw or undercooked potato can increase bowel movements which may decrease bowel toxins.) Add 100 mg of taurine. This diet would provide approximately 450 kcal with 40 grams of protein and 22 grams of fat to meet the daily caloric needs of a 15 pound cat.

Two to three bonemeal tablets (10 grain or equivalent) or 3/4-1 teaspoon of bonemeal powder to supply calcium and phosphorus with a multi-vitamin mineral supplement using the label instructions is added. Alternatively, a natural product from Standard Process (Calcifood Wafers or Calcium Lactate) can be used (use 1 Calcifood Wafer or 2 Calcium Lactate tablets for each 2 bonemeal tablets.)

When possible, natural vitamins made from raw whole foods, rather than synthetic vitamins (although both can be used in combination) are preferred, as the natural vitamins also supply plant phytochemicals, enzymes, and other nutrients not found in chemically- synthesized vitamins. Catalyn from Standard Process can be used as the natural vitamin in this recipe, at a dose of 1 Catalyn per 10 pounds; NuCat (VetriScience) could also be used following label dosages.

The nutrient composition of the diet will vary depending upon which ingredients are used. In general, the above recipe supplies the daily nutritional and calorie needs for a 15 pound cat. The actual amount to feed will vary based upon the pet's weight (feed less if weight gain, more if weight loss.)

Supplement if necessary, but only after checking with your pet's veterinarian to determine the individual needs of your pet. Here are basic recommendations:

Vitamin C or Ascorbic Acid. Add 25 mg/kg/day. (Ascorbic acid, but not natural vitamin C, can cause release of copper from the liver, which can worsen clinical signs. Add small amounts daily and work up to the recommended dosage if clinical signs do not worsen, or preferably use natural vitamin C.)

Vitamin E. Add 100 mg/day.

Zinc. Add 3 mg/kg/day of zinc gluconate, 2 mg/kg/day of zinc sulfate, or 2 mg/kg/day of zinc acetate. Divide these doses into 3 daily doses since zinc acetate may cause less intestinal irritation. (These recommendations are extrapolated from recommendations for dogs as the exact requirements are not known for cats.) Additional supplementation with B vitamins is warranted, especially thiamine as cats can easily develop thiamine deficiency with decreased food intake, are important.

Taurine. Add 50 to 100 mg taurine per cat per day, or add ½ to 1 ounce chopped clams to the diet.

Arginine. 250 mg per cat, two times daily.

If desired, supply vitamins and minerals as follows: 2 to 3 bonemeal tablets (10-grain or equivalent) or ¾ to 1 teaspoon of bonemeal powder to supply calcium and phosphorus with a multivitamin/mineral supplement using the label instructions. Alternatively, use a natural product from Standard Process (1 Calcifood Wafer or 2 Calcium Lactate tablets for each 2 bonemeal tablets). When possible, use natural vitamins made from raw whole foods, rather than synthetic vitamins (although both can be used in combination), as the natural vitamins also supply plant phytochemicals, enzymes, and other nutrients not found in chemically synthesized vitamins. Use either Catalyn from Standard Process (at a dose of 1 Catalyn per 10 pounds) or NuCat from VetriScience (following label dosages) as the natural vitamin in this recipe.

OBESITY AND OSTEOARTHRITIS

No diets are specifically designed for the pet with osteoarthritis per se. Many pets with osteoarthritis are overweight. Since increased weight load on the joints significantly contributes to pain and worsening of the inflammation and destruction of the joint cartilage, it is important that overweight pets with osteoarthritis be placed on medically supervised weight-reduction diets. Ideally, pets with osteoarthritis can be kept slightly thin (underweight) to minimize stress on the joints. For more information on helping the pet with osteoarthritis, see *The Arthritis Solution for Dogs*, in THE NATURAL VET series by Prima Publishing.

Understanding Obesity

Obesity is a severe and debilitating condition. It is the most common nutritional disease in pets and people; estimates suggest that up to 45% of dogs and up to 13% of cats are obese. Many doctors think these estimates are low judging by the number of obese pets they see every day in practice. With rare exception (the presence of a disease like thyroid disease), obese pets are made that way, not born that way. In the wild, few, if any, animals are obese. They eat to meet their calorie needs, and are always moving, playing, fighting, mating, and hunting for food (exercising).

Obesity is a disease of domestication. Ideally, you should work with your doctor from the time your pet is a young puppy or kitten so you can prevent obesity as your pet ages.

How can you decide whether your pet fits the definition of "obese?" Current medical opinion states that a pet is obese if it weighs 15% or more over its ideal weight. Pets who weigh 1 to 14% over their ideal weight are considered "overweight" but not yet "obese."

While 15% does not seem like much, consider these figures:

- A dog, such as a Labrador Retriever (one of the most common breeds afflicted with osteoarthritis) who weighs 69 pounds but should weigh 60 pounds, is 15% overweight and is classified as obese.
- An 11½-pound cat who should weigh 10 pounds is 15% over her ideal weight and would be classified as obese.

As you can see, even just a few extra pounds on our pets is cause for concern.

While pet owners often use the pet's actual weight to gauge obesity, it is probably more accurate to use a body composition score. Body composition, measured by looking at the pet from the top and sides and feeling the areas over the ribs and spine, more accurately reflects obesity than does a certain magical number. It also gives us something more concrete to shoot for. For example, while most people who diet strive to achieve a certain numerical weight, a more accurate assessment would be to strive for a certain look. While losing 10 pounds might be an admirable goal, being able to lose a few inches around the waist or fit into a smaller pair of pants is really the ultimate goal. This is not to suggest that you can't have a target weight when designing a weight-control program for your pet, only that this magic number is only a rough guideline of what your pet's "best" weight might be to treat obesity. Many doctors prefer to use the weight as a guideline but ultimately use the look and feel (measured by the body composition score) of the pet to know when we have reached our ultimate goal.

Exactly what causes obesity in our pets? Many theories explaining obesity are put forth by both doctors and pet owners. Here are a few:

Hormones.   Since female pets are more commonly obese than male pets, hormones may play some role in fat retention and deposition. However, doctors really don't know nor do we have good evidence that gender has any primary role in obesity.

Spay or Neuter.   Since most pets are spayed or neutered, and therefore most obese pets are spayed or neutered, it is tempting to blame removal of the sex organs (and therefore sex hormones) as a cause for obesity. No hard-and-fast science supports spaying or neutering as a direct cause for weight problems in pets. Since spayed and neutered pets may be less active than intact pets, that inactivity (caused by removal of the sex hormones) contributes to obesity if the same amount of calories are fed. However, doctors and pet owners have all seen spayed and neutered pets who are quite active. In fact, many pet owners would say that spaying or neutering has not affected their pets' activity level. (Most wish the surgeries *would* calm their pets down, but this rarely, if ever, happens!)

It may be that, despite a normal activity level after spaying and neutering, removal of the sex hormones in some way encourages fat deposition, but this is speculative at this point.

Disease.   Certainly diseases such as hypothyroidism (in dogs) or diabetes (in dogs and cats) are associated with obesity. Metabolic diseases are uncommon causes of obesity in dogs, seen in approximately 5% or fewer pets with weight problems. In hypothyroidism, dogs cannot make enough thyroid hormone. Thyroid hormone is an important hormone that regulates proper metabolism. With too little thyroid hormone, the pet's metabolism is reduced, and obesity can result.

In diabetes, the dog or cat cannot make enough insulin to regulate the blood sugar glucose. As a result, the blood glucose level rises. In people, we know that obesity is related to diabetes as insulin reserves can become exhausted. If inactive pets are fed diets high in simple carbohydrates (sugars), the excess carbohydrate calories are deposited as fat. Years of fluctuating blood glucose (sugar) levels, especially in truly carnivorous animals such as cats (who are not designed to handle high-carbohydrate diets), may exhaust pancreatic insulin supplies and cause diabetes.

In most veterinary hospitals, overweight pets rarely have either of these conditions or any medical problems that are directly related to their weight problem. However, every obese dog should be screened for problems such as hypothyroidism or diabetes; obese cats should be screened for diabetes. If these underlying medical problems are discovered, they will need to be treated in addition to treating the simple obesity.

Age.   Some people speculate that old age contributes to obesity. The theory is that as pets age their metabolic rates slow. While this is true, in the practice experience of many veterinarians, it seems that most overweight pets are young to middle-aged, whereas older pets are often thin as a result of muscle wasting.

Genetics.   Genetics may contribute to obesity, although this link is poorly understood in pets. Rats that were bred to overeat passed this disorder to their offspring, and a lot of circumstantial evidence suggests that this occurs in people. In obese rats (and possibly people and maybe pets), a deficiency of the enzyme that converts tryptophan to 5-HTP and then to serotonin exists. With a low level of serotonin, the rats never feel full and therefore their brains tell them to continue to eat. In people, supplying increased tryptophan, 5-HTP, or medications that raise serotonin levels may help obese subjects feel full and eat less. This may be an area to pursue in pets in the future.

Ultimately, the main cause of obesity in the majority of pets (and pet owners) is overfeeding, either during puppyhood, adulthood, or both. Obesity is a disease of domestication and greed. Wild animals do not become fat. They constantly exercise, often go without food for days, and eat a well-balanced diet of natural foods the way nature intended. Our sedentary pets who are fed anything they want whenever they want have no choice but to become obese (just like many pet owners). The habit of feeding our puppies, kittens, and adult dogs and cats whenever they want to eat (or whenever they beg or whenever we use food in training programs)

❖ SAFETY ISSUE

It is extremely important to differentiate "obesity," which results from fat deposition inside the body as well as under the skin, from "enlargement." Pets can experience abdominal enlargement, for example, from a variety of problems including the adrenal gland disease called Cushing's disease, organ failure (where fluid builds up in the abdominal cavity resulting in a "big belly"), and abdominal tumors. Anytime a pet seems "larger" than normal is a cause for concern that is unlikely to be related to obesity but very probably related to a serious medical disorder.

must stop if pet owners are to control their animals' weights.

Problems associated with obesity in pets and people are numerous and include orthopedic problems (including arthritis), ruptured ligaments, intervertebral disk disease, difficult breathing, reduced capacity for exercise (and in severe cases for any movement at all), heat intolerance, increased chance for complications due to drug therapy (it is more difficult to accurately dose medications in obese pets), cardiac problems, hypertension, and cancer. When you keep in mind that excess body fat occurs in the body cavities of the chest and abdomen (often being deposited there first) as well as under the skin (what we see as "fat"), it is not surprising to discover that many medical problems can be associated with obesity.

Two main kinds of obesity are found in pets (and in pet owners): increased number of fat cells and increased size of fat cells. Increased food intake in adult pets causes more fat to accumulate in existing fat cells. The number of fat cells do not increase but rather simply enlarge.

During growth (puppyhood, which lasts from birth until approximately 12 months in smaller breeds of dogs and 18 to 24 months in large and giant breeds; or kittenhood, which lasts from birth until approximately 12 months of age), overfeeding increases the number of fat cells. Weight reduction is more difficult in pets (and people) with greater numbers of fat cells. To prevent this type of obesity, young, growing animals should not be overfed. Many doctors actually prefer that owners slightly underfeed these pets. While these pet owners are often scorned by apparently well-meaning friends and family members for "starving" their puppies and kittens, they actually are practicing preventive medicine. Slightly underweight, slower-growing puppies and kittens will not develop obesity as a result of increased fat cell numbers (the more difficult type of obesity to treat). Slightly underweight, slower-growing puppies will also experience fewer skeletal disorders so commonly seen in fast-growing, large-breed dogs (hip dysplasia, shoulder dysplasia, elbow dysplasia, osteochondrosis). Since most commercial pet food recommendations result in young animals being overfed, owners should feed their puppies anywhere from 5% (for smaller breeds) up to 15% (for larger breeds) less food than recommended if they choose to feed a premium, natural processed food.

Obesity can often be prevented by not overfeeding puppies and kittens, which will result in fewer numbers of fat cells. Because leaner, more muscular animals have higher metabolic rates than their counterparts with less body musculature, maintaining an exercise program will also contribute to a lean body condition.

The treatment of obesity requires a controlled, low-calorie, lowfat diet with a sensible exercise program. **Nutritional supplements** (page 344) might help reduce weight in selected patients.

So what does all of this have to do with osteoarthritis? Obesity is often present in arthritic pets. It is an important part of the treatment for these pets to get them to lose weight. Extra weight carried by diseased joints adds to the wear and tear on the joints and the pain and discomfort your pain will experience, not to mention other health problems caused by obesity such as heart and lung disease. Weight loss is a desired goal in the treatment of the arthritic pet.

Diet and Arthritis

Realize that obesity does not occur overnight, and neither will it go away overnight. While a very small subset of pets truly cannot lose weight, most pets will reach an acceptable weight within 6 to 12 months of starting an obesity diet coupled with an approved exercise program. This rate of weight loss approximates 2% per week, an acceptable amount that will not cause muscle loss. The actual rate of weight loss recommended by your veterinarian may vary according to your pet's needs.

Prior to starting a weight-reduction diet and exercise regimen, it is important that your pet receive a blood profile to rule out diseases previously discussed, such as diabetes or hypothyroidism that may cause or contribute to obesity. Presence of these diseases would require treatment in addition to dietary therapy.

If your dog or cat needs to lose weight, he should be on a weight reduction diet (ideally a natural, wholesome, homemade diet) recommended by your veterinarian. Store-bought "Lite" foods are not designed for weight loss, but rather weight maintenance once weight loss has been achieved. Therefore, they are not usually recommended for pets requiring weight loss. Additionally, since most of these diets do not contain natural healthful ingredients, it is unlikely they would be recommended as part of a weight-loss program unless other diets could not be used.

Several commercial weight loss or obesity reduction diets are available. While they are effective in reducing weight in many pets, they may also contain artificial ingredients and by-products. If these diets are used, switching to a homemade diet or a more wholesome (natural) processed "Lite" or maintenance diet *once weight reduction has been achieved* would be wise.

Any food (including carbohydrate and proteins) can be converted to and stored as fat if not needed by the body for another metabolic process. Feeding fat is more likely to contribute to fat deposition in fat cells than feeding protein or carbohydrates. Therefore, lower-fat diets are preferred for weight loss in pets.

Foods that increase metabolism, such as vegetables high in fiber, are included in weight-loss diets. Fiber, contained in vegetables, decreases fat and glucose absorption. Fluctuating glucose levels cause greater insulin release. Since insulin is needed for fat storage, decreased or stable levels are preferred. Fiber also binds to fat in the intestinal tract and increases movement of the food in the intestines, which is of benefit to the obese pet.

Weight Control Diet for Adult Dogs

½ pound of cooked chicken
2 cups of cooked long grain rice
¼ teaspoon salt or salt substitute

This diet provides approximately 624 kcal, 49.4 gm of protein, and 4.7 gm of fat. It supplies the daily caloric needs for weight loss in a 45- to 50-pound dog. This diet supplies the calories required for weight reduction in a dog who normally weighs 47 to 48 pounds (non-obese weight). In other words, it should be fed to a dog who weighs more than 47 to 48 pounds but whose ideal weight would be approximately 47 to 48 pounds.

Variations

1. Substitute 4 egg whites (cooked) or ½ cup cottage cheese (1% fat) for the chicken. Usually beef and lamb are too high in fat for canine weight-reduction diets.

2. Substitute 3 cups of cooked potatoes (with skins) for rice.

3. Use fresh, raw or slightly steamed vegetables, such as carrots or broccoli (approximately ½ to 1 cup per recipe; ½ cup of vegetables add about 30 kilocalories to the diet) as a top dressing for the diet for extra nutrition and fiber and variety.

4. If the weight-reduction diet is prescribed for a dog with osteoarthritis, omega-3 fatty acids may be prescribed to help relieve the inflammation and pain seen in pets with osteoarthritis. The inclusion of omega-3 fatty acids adds few calories to the diet, approximately 10 kilocalories depending upon the brand. Because omega-3 fatty acids can be helpful for arthritic pets, and because they also increase metabolic rate, which burns calories, they may be useful in the diets of obese, arthritic pets.

5. Divide this diet into small meals, feeding at least twice daily and preferably 4 to 6 times daily. Frequent small meals will allow the pet to feel full all the time (feeling full reduces appetite and the need to beg, although many dogs who beg have been unintentionally rewarded by their owners for this behavior). Feeding frequent small meals also results in additional weight loss as some of the food consumed is immediately burned into heat (thermogenesis). Frequent feeding results in more burning of calories.

6. If desired, supply vitamins and minerals as follows: 4 bonemeal tablets (10-grain or equivalent) or ¾ to 1 teaspoon of bonemeal powder to supply calcium and phosphorus with a multivitamin/mineral supplement, using the label instructions. Alternatively, use a natural product from Standard Process (1 Calcifood Wafer or 2 Calcium Lactate tablets for each 2 bone-

meal tablets). When possible, use natural vitamins made from raw whole foods, rather than synthetic vitamins (although both can be used in combination), as the natural vitamins also supply plant phytochemicals, enzymes, and other nutrients not found in chemically synthesized vitamins. Use either Catalyn from Standard Process (at a dose of 1 Catalyn per 25 pounds) or Canine Plus from VetriScience (following label dosages) as the natural vitamin in this recipe.

7. As desired, add supplements that can be beneficial, such as plant enzymes and a super green food or health blend formula.

Weight Control Diet for Adult Cats

5 ounces salmon, canned with bone (low-salt)
⅓ cup cooked long grain rice
¼ teaspoon salt or salt substitute
100 mg taurine

This diet provides 284 kcal, 30.2 gm of protein, and 10.4 gm of fat. Feed 75% of this recipe to a cat who would normally weigh 11 pounds, 67% to a cat who would normally weigh 10 pounds, and 60% to a cat who would normally weigh 9 pounds.

Variations

1. Substitute 4 to 8 ounces of tuna or ½ pound of chicken for the salmon. Beef, lamb, and sardines usually have too much fat to be used in feline weight-reduction diets.
2. Rice is optional, as cats do not have a strict dietary carbohydrate requirement.
3. Supplement with additional omega-3 fatty acids if needed. Salmon contains omega-3 fatty acids. Omega-3 fatty acids are often prescribed for pets with osteoarthritis to relieve pain and inflammation. Each extra-strength omega-3 fatty acid capsules contain approximately 10 calories. Omega-3 fatty acids increase metabolic rate so more energy is burned, which can aid weight loss.
4. Use fresh, raw or slightly steamed vegetables, such as carrots or broccoli (approximately ½ to 1 cup per recipe; ½ cup of vegetables add about 30 kilocalories to the diet) as a top dressing for the diet for extra nutrition and fiber and variety. Most cats will not eat vegetables, however.
5. Feed this diet in divided amounts at least twice daily and preferably 4 to 6 times daily. Frequent small meals will allow the pet to feel full all of the time (feeling full reduces appetite and the need to beg, although many dogs who beg have been unintentionally rewarded by their owners for this behavior). Feeding frequent small meals also results in additional weight loss, as some of the food consumed is immediately burned into heat (thermogenesis). Frequent feeding results in more burning of calories.

Supplements for Obesity

Additional supplements for the obese pet may be helpful. Unfortunately, no magic pills exist that will ensure weight loss in pets. Still, some supplements may contribute to weight loss when used as part of a comprehensive plan. *Discuss these supplements with your veterinarian prior to using them in your dog or cat.*

Chromium. Chromium is a trace mineral that can increase the body's sensitivity to insulin. Since decreased sensitivity to insulin can contribute to weight gain (as often happens in diabetic patients), supplying additional chromium (usually at a dose of 200 to 400 mcg/day) is recommended for weight control in people. Research is needed to determine whether chromium would be of benefit to overweight pets.

Carnitine. In people, carnitine is recommended at 500 mg per day to reduce fat deposits. Research is needed to determine whether this recommendation would be of benefit to overweight pets.

Boron. This trace mineral may speed up the burning of calories in people. Your doctor can prescribe a safe dose of this herb if he or she feels it might help your pet.

Herbs. Herbs such as cayenne, mustard, and ginger increase metabolism in people and may also do the same in pets. Your doctor can prescribe a safe dose of these herbs if he or she feels they might help your pet.

Hydroxycitric Acid.   Hydroxycitric acid, also called HCA, is a product extracted from the rind of the tamarind citrus fruit of the *Garcinia cambogia* tee. It suppresses hunger in people and helps prevent the body from turning carbohydrates into fat by inhibiting the ATP-citrate lysase enzyme (the recommended dosage is 500 mg 3 times daily). One particular supplement called NutriWeight Management (from Rx Vitamins for Pets) contains hydroxycitric acid. The recommended dose of this product for dogs is 100 mg of 50% HCA per 25 pounds given twice daily; the recommended dose for cats is 50 to 100 mg of 50% HCA per cat given twice daily. The supplement should be used in conjunction with a weight-reduction diet and exercise program.

Chitosan.   Chitosan is a dietary supplement made from the outer skeletons of shellfish. The product is purported to bind to fat in the intestines, which prevents the absorption of fat. Studies are inconclusive regarding how well the product works in people or pets. One veterinary company is developing a product containing chitosan at this time. Time will tell if it will be of value in any diet programs for pets.

Coenzyme Q$_{10}$.   Coenzyme Q$_{10}$ is used to transport and break down fat into energy. In people, Coenzyme Q$_{10}$ levels were found to be low in approximately 50% of obese individuals. Supplementation with Coenzyme Q$_{10}$ resulted in accelerated weight loss in overweight people.

While Coenzyme Q$_{10}$ is often used in pets with heart disease, periodontal disease, and gastrointestinal disease, reports showing its use as part of a weight-control program are not available. It may be of benefit in overweight pets, and at the recommended dosage, no side effects have been seen. Consult with your doctor about using Coenzyme Q$_{10}$ to help in a weight-reduction program for your pet.

Supplements and medications that are not recommended for weight loss in pets include diuretics and appetite suppressants such as phenylpropanolamine and caffeine. Diuretics, often used for weight loss in people, cause increased urination (followed by increased water consumption) and only temporarily result in weight loss due to water loss. Most pet owners do not cherish the thought of their pets urinating more frequently. Since the result this practice is unaesthetic and can upset the balance of electrolytes, which can be dangerous, giving diuretics is not recommended.

Phenylpropanolamine is a stimulant, appetite suppressant, and decongestant. While it will increase blood pressure and jitteriness, it is not effective over the long term for weight loss in people nor recommended in pets for this purpose.

Caffeine is a mild stimulant that may exhibit a thermogenic (fat-burning) effect. However, since caffeine may contribute to jitteriness and hyperactivity, its use is not recommended for weight control in pets.

Regardless of how helpful supplements may be, they are no substitute for a lifestyle change. Properly feeding and exercising your pet, especially from puppyhood and kittenhood, are the most important factors in weight management.

 # WHY DIET PROGRAMS FAIL

Despite our best efforts, some diet programs just don't seem to work. Reasons for this include:

Underlying disease. While an underlying disorder such as Cushing's disease, thyroid disease, or diabetes is only present in at most 5% of obese dogs, all of our obese patients should be screened for these (and other) diseases prior to starting a comprehensive weight-reduction program. Failure to do so will result in no weight loss and potential serious illness or death in the patient with one of these conditions.

Lack of doctor involvement. Many owners decide to implement a weight-reduction program on their own without proper veterinary supervision. This is unlikely to work for several reasons. First, in those rare cases with underlying medical disorders causing or contributing to the obesity, the true problem will not be diagnosed, and the diet will not work. Second, most owner-implemented diet programs simply consist of the owner feeding a "Lite" diet or just "feeding less." As we have discussed, Lite diets are basically worthless for weight-loss programs. Feeding less rarely results in weight loss for two main reasons:

- Pets who eat less are hungrier, beg more, and ultimately are fed more as the owners become impatient with the constant begging for food.
- As pets (and people) eat less, their metabolism slows down. Pets who are fed less will adapt to this lower metabolism and maintain weight.

Fear of "starving" the pet. Most owners do not want to see their pets starve, and we certainly must question whether or not this procedure is humane. Starvation will reduce fat but also burn muscle. People who starve can develop medical complications due to deranged glucose and fat metabolism. While this may not be as much of a problem in dogs (unlike in cats who can develop serious fatty liver disease within a matter of days), starvation is not recommended, as significant metabolic problems could arise in pets who are starved.

Impatience. Obesity does not happen overnight, and neither does weight loss. Owners must be patient, especially with larger dogs who might require many months of eating a proper diet to slowly lose weight.

To conclude, obesity adds to the stress on damaged joints for our arthritic pets. Therefore, weight control must be an important consideration as part of our overall therapy for the pet with arthritis.

SAFETY

Before feeding a pet with a medical condition one of these natural diets, please check with your doctor first to make sure the diet does not compromise your pet's health care.

Why Diet Programs Fail

Other Complementary Therapies

ACUPUNCTURE

Common Uses

Allergies, arthritis, constipation, diabetes, diarrhea, esophageal disorders, fractures, heart disorders, immune stimulation, inflammation, intervertebral disk disease, kidney disorders, liver disorders, respiratory disorders, sinus disorders, urogenital disorders

Many pet owners think of acupuncture when complementary medicine is mentioned, though many of the other therapies discussed in this book are also valid therapies. Due to the long history of acupuncture, and to the fact that acupuncture may be the best-known complementary therapy, it is no surprise that a large number of pet owners seek out this therapy, especially for conditions, such as osteoarthritis, that are known to improve with acupuncture.

Acupuncture is without a doubt one of the most field-tested techniques available in complementary medicine. While it is hard to pinpoint exactly how long acupuncture has been around, evidence indicates that it is easily more than 4,000 years old, having been used in Asian and Indian cultures for many centuries. For skeptics who question the effectiveness of this popular complementary therapy, a large amount of empirical as well as experimental information and studies show the effectiveness of acupuncture. Certainly a therapy that is a mainstay of Traditional Chinese Medicine (TCM) could not have survived if it were not effective. The theory of Traditional Chinese Medicine has in fact served as the basis of acupuncture instruction for over 4,000 years. While there is certainly no substitute for well-documented research using controlled clinical studies, we cannot ignore thousands of years of clinical experience.

One stumbling block to the Western-trained mind trying to understanding acupuncture is the lack of scientific explanation as to exactly how acupuncture works. The explanations offered by Traditional Chinese Medicine suffice for practitioners of this ancient art, but confuse the traditional Western mind. However, while a number of physiological theories have been proposed to explain how acupuncture works (to follow), we must remain open-minded to the effectiveness of this therapy (and, of course, to all complementary therapies). The wise reader will remember that while we may not know exactly how acupuncture (or other complementary therapies) actually works, we also do not know exactly how certain modern Western medical treatments work. (For example, even Pfizer's own literature states that exactly how their bestselling nonsteroidal drug Rimadyl works is not known.) If we can use traditional drug therapies without formal proof of how they work, we can also use therapies such as acupuncture without formal proof of how they work.

We do know that acupuncture points lie over free nerve endings wrapped in connective tissue or within the walls of blood vessels; this anatomy may help explain why stimulation of acupuncture points elicits therapeutic effects. Additionally, there is a high concentration of tissue-secretory mast cells in and around acupuncture points. The release of histamine (and probably other chemicals) may explain an important part of acupuncture by causing dilation of surrounding blood vessels and stimulating adjacent nerve terminals.

THEORIES OF ACUPUNCTURE

How does acupuncture work? Several proposed theories attempt to explain how acupuncture exerts its effects, though no one theory fully explains how this therapy works. The actual mechanisms are complex and likely to be interrelated.

The theories that explain the workings of acupuncture include the following:

Gate Theory

Inhibitory neurons close a "gate" to ascending pain fibers and thus prevent pain from reaching the higher brain centers that allow conscious recognition of pain. There is a large amount of evidence that acupuncture can induce local pain

Acupuncture

relief; acupuncture points with the highest proportion of type A nerve fibers relative to type C nerve fibers provide the best regional pain relief. However, while probably accounting for some of the action of acupuncture, the gating theory does not explain the delayed onset of some effects seen with acupuncture therapy.

Humoral Theory

Local anesthesia results from some combination of endogenous chemicals, including opioids, serotonin, and cholinergic and adrenergic compounds. These compounds are increased as a result of acupuncture. Additionally, humoral immunity is enhanced during acupuncture treatment.

Autonomic Nervous System

Stimulation of acupuncture points can cause autonomic nervous system dilation of blood vessels (the so-called "somatovisceral reflex"). This helps explain why stimulation of points on the skin can exert strong influences on internal organs. Acupuncture may produce these effects by stimulating cyclic AMP (cAMP) which causes release of catecholamine hormones from the adrenal gland; the catecholamines then affect cellular functions such as dilation of blood vessels.

Local Effects

Acupuncture produces local effects, including increased local tissue immune function, increased blood supply, and muscle and tissue relaxation as well as local pain relief.

Bioelectrical Theory

Acupuncture channels (called "meridians") allow transmission of nervous impulses because of their low electrical impedance (electrical impedances can be measured at acupuncture points). Acupuncture points boost the DC signals carried by the meridian, which short-circuits the current and blocks the pain impulse.

METHODS OF ACUPUNCTURE

What exactly is acupuncture? In its purest sense, acupuncture involves the placement of tiny needles into various parts (acupuncture points) of a pet's body. These needles stimulate the acupuncture points, which can effect a resolution of the clinical signs.

In traditional acupuncture, the acupuncturist places tiny needles at various points on the pet's body. These points are chosen based on diagnostic tests and/or traditional "recipes" or formulas that are known to help pets with specific problems. As mentioned, these acupuncture points correspond to areas of the body that contain nerves and blood vessels. By stimulating these points, acupuncture causes a combination of pain relief, stimulation of the immune system, and alterations in blood vessels, resulting in a decrease in clinical signs.

While traditional acupuncture uses tiny acupuncture needles to stimulate the specific acupuncture points chosen, other forms of acupuncture also exist. These other forms of acupuncture are often chosen to provide the pet more prolonged stimulation of acupuncture points, as they produce higher and more continuous level of stimulation.

They include:

- **Laser therapy.** Acupuncture points may be stimulated by low intensity or cold lasers to promote positive physiologic effects associated with healing and decreased pain and inflammation.
- **Aquapuncture.** Aquapuncture utilizes the injection of tiny amounts of fluid (often vitamins, but also sterile water, antibiotics, herbal extracts, analgesics, local anesthetics, corticosteroids, nonsteroidal medications, or electrolyte solutions) at the acupuncture site for a more prolonged effect.
- **Implantation.** To achieve a more prolonged and intense stimulation of acupuncture points, various objects (usually beads made of gold, silver, or stainless steel) are surgically implanted at acupuncture sites.
- **Electroacupuncture.** This form of acupuncture therapy uses a small amount of non-painful electricity to stimulate the acupuncture site for a more intense effect.
- **Moxibustion.** Moxibustion is the burning of an herb (typically *Artesmisia vulgaris*) on or above acupuncture points. The heat from the burning herb gives additional stimulation to

Acupuncture

the acupuncture points. Care must be taken to avoid burning the patient!

- **Acupressure.** Acupressure involves applying pressure with the fingers to specific acupuncture points. Owners can be taught to apply acupressure on pets at home to the acupuncture points that have been used during veterinary treatments for further relief from pain and inflammation.

Most holistic doctors usually combine acupuncture with other treatments to achieve a truly "holistic" therapy. For example, for pets with osteoarthritis, nutritional supplements that are designed to heal the damaged cartilage are often added to acupuncture treatment, as acupuncture by itself will not heal damaged cartilage. Once the pet has improved, exhibiting decreased pain and inflammation and greater mobility, doctors will use acupuncture on an "as-needed" basis when the pet shows increased stiffness.

As a rule, acupuncture compares quite favorably with traditional therapies (see the discussion below). In some cases, acupuncture may be preferred when conventional therapy is ineffective or potentially harmful (such as long-term therapy for pain relief with medication such as corticosteroids or nonsteroidal anti-inflammatory medications). At other times, acupuncture may be used when an owner cannot afford traditional therapy (such as back surgery for intervertebral disk disease or hip replacement surgery for the pet with severe hip dysplasia). When doctors discuss both acupuncture and conventional therapies, this allows the owner to make the best decision for the pet.

SIDE EFFECTS

Side effects from acupuncture are rare. Accidental puncture of an underlying vital organ can occur; this usually happens if the incorrect needles (the needles come in various sizes, and the correct length of needle must be chosen that corresponds to the size of the pet and the area to be treated) are placed in an area in which there is minimal soft tissue that covers the underlying organs (such as the abdomen). Infection can occur at the site of needle insertion; needles should not be placed in areas in which the skin is infected or inflamed. Occasionally, the needle can break (due to patient movement and incorrect needle placement and removal), and surgery may be needed to remove it. Some pets require sedation in order to allow insertion of the acupuncture needles. In some animals, clinical signs may increase for a few days before they improve. This is not unusual in pets treated with complementary therapies and is explained by the body going through the healing process; additionally, some animals treated with conventional medications also get worse before the medication "kicks in" and the pet begins to show signs of improvement.

Many owners worry that acupuncture is painful and that their pets will suffer. Usually acupuncture is not painful. Occasionally, the animal will experience some sensation as the needle passes through the skin. Once in place, most animals will relax and some may become sleepy. Fractious animals (especially cats and nervous dogs) may require mild sedation for treatment. Alternatively, a complementary therapy, such as an herbal remedy or the flower essence called **Rescue Remedy** (page 391), can be used to calm the pet prior to and during acupuncture treatment.

TREATMENTS

The number of acupuncture treatments that a pet will require varies from pet to pet. Usually, owners are asked to commit to 8 treatments (2 to 3 per week) to assess whether acupuncture will work. On average, treatments last about 15 to 30 minutes for needle acupuncture, and 5 to 10 minutes for aquapuncture or electroacupuncture. If the pet improves, acupuncture is done "as needed" to control the pet's signs. As previously mentioned, other therapies may be used to decrease the number of visits to the doctor's office for acupuncture.

Treating Disk Disease

While acupuncture can be useful for a variety of disorders, most clients seek acupuncture therapy for pets with musculoskeletal or neurological disorders.

Acupuncture

Numerous reports in the human medical literature attest to the benefits of acupuncture. One study showed 65% of people treated for chronic neck and shoulder pain achieved long-term improvement after acupuncture, and another study of 22 patients with chronic low back pain showed a 79.1% success rate. Acupuncture was twice as effective as the nonsteroidal anti-inflammatory medication piroxicam.

In pets, one study found that 70% of dogs with chronic degenerative joint disease (osteoarthritis) showed greater than 50% improvement in mobility after treatment with acupuncture.

In pets with osteoarthritis, acupuncture has been theorized to work by relieving muscle spasms around the affected joint, by producing analgesia (pain relief) by stimulating central endorphin-releasing systems, by improving blood circulation to spastic muscles surrounding affected joints, by direct anti-inflammatory effects, and by releasing local trigger points and relieving stiffness.

Traditional Chinese medical theory holds that acupuncture unblocks *Qi* and blood in the body's meridians and treats the *Bi* syndrome (osteoarthritis is a *Bi* condition in Chinese medicine).

If acupuncture is used to treat osteoarthritis, it is imperative that a proper diagnosis be made prior to starting therapy. Many pets have been prescribed anti-inflammatory medications (corticosteroids or nonsteroidal anti-inflammatory medications) without a proper diagnosis (orthopedic and neurological examinations plus radiographic evaluation of the injured part). Acupuncture cannot be effective for the treatment of osteoarthritis if the pet does not have osteoarthritis!

Many dogs treated incorrectly for osteoarthritis in fact have neurological disease, most commonly **degenerative myelopathy** (page 60). These dogs require different therapy for their problem than do pets with osteoarthritis and will not usually respond to anti-inflammatory therapy for osteoarthritis. Make sure a proper diagnosis is obtained so that the correct treatment can be administered before signs become so severe that no therapy will be successful!

Acupuncture can also be effective for pets with neurological disorders. Most commonly owners whose pets experience **intervertebral disk disease** (page 113) seek acupuncture as an alternative therapy to the conventional treatments of corticosteroids and surgery. While the effectiveness of acupuncture treatment compares favorably with corticosteroids and surgical therapy, for pets in whom surgery is indicated, acupuncture should not replace therapy unless the patient is a poor surgical candidate or the owner is unable to afford surgery. Simply put, *pets who require surgery to treat or cure a problem should have surgery and not a complementary therapy unless there are valid reasons that surgery should not or cannot be performed.*

Intervertebral disk disease commonly affects the middle to lower back (thoracolumbar area) or the neck (cervical area).

Pets with intervertebral disk disease of the thoracolumbar area (thoracolumbar disk disease) are graded based upon clinical signs; the grading allows a more accurate prognosis to be given.

- *Grade I:* Pets have back pain as their only clinical sign.
- *Grade II:* Pets have back pain plus rear leg paresis (partial paralysis) and ataxia (wobbly gait).
- *Grade III:* Pets have back pain and rear leg paralysis (total paralysis), and some dogs and may not have control over bladder and colon function.
- *Grade IV:* Pets have paralysis and no conscious pain perception in the rear legs.

Pets with intervertebral disk disease of the neck area (cervical disk disease) are also graded based upon clinical signs; again, the grading allows a more accurate prognosis to be given.

- *Grade I:* Pets have only neck pain present.
- *Grade II:* Pets have neck pain and show proprioceptive deficits (ataxia, or a wobbly gait) of the front or rear legs.
- *Grade III:* Pets have neck pain and paralysis of the front and rear legs, and some dogs and cats may not have control over bladder and colon function.

Acupuncture

The mechanism of how acupuncture works for pets with intervertebral disk disease of the neck or back is not yet fully understood. Acupuncture may eliminate trigger points (local points of tenderness and muscle spasms and tightness) and abolish muscle pain and stiffness. Acupuncture may also augment endogenous release of corticosteroids to relieve pain and inflammation, but this is disputed by some holistic veterinarians.

How does disk disease respond to treatment with acupuncture? For pets with thoracolumbar intervertebral disk disease, 90% of pets with grade I disease treated with acupuncture recover after 2 to 3 acupuncture treatments over a 1- to 2-week treatment period.

For pets with grade II disk disease, approximately 90% of treated pets receiving 3 to 4 treatments over 3 weeks recovered.

This indicates that for pets with grade I or II thoracolumbar intervertebral disk disease, the results of treatment with acupuncture are comparable to therapy with conventional medications (corticosteroids) or surgical disk decompression. However, while acupuncture can effectively relieve the clinical signs (such as pain and wobbly gait) seen in pets with disk disease, surgery may be preferred for pets with recurring clinical signs. Only surgery can prevent recurrence of the problem, as surgery removes the damaged disks (10 to 25% of patients treated with acupuncture may have recurrences of their clinical signs and require surgery).

For pets with grade III thoracolumbar intervertebral disk disease, 80% recover after 5 to 6 acupuncture treatments over a 6-week treatment period.

For pets with grade IV thoracolumbar intervertebral disk disease, less than 25% of patients recover after 10 or more treatments over 3 to 6 months of treatment.

Acupuncture is only half as effective as immediate decompressive surgery for pets with grade IV intervertebral disk disease. Since few dogs with grade IV thoracolumbar intervertebral disk disease recover from their clinical signs (paralysis, lack of deep pain) regardless of treatment, the prognosis for these dogs is quite grave. How-

ever, even for those pets with this grave prognosis, acupuncture is recommended if the owner chooses not to have surgery even though the prognosis is poor.

For pets with cervical intervertebral disk disease, approximately 80% of dogs with grade I disk disease recover after 3 to 4 treatments over 1 to 2 weeks.

For pets with grade II disk disease, 67% recover after 5 to 6 treatments over 3 to 4 weeks of therapy.

As of this writing, too few grade III cervical intervertebral disk disease patients have been described to evaluate results properly.

Approximately 33% of pets with cervical intervertebral disk disease relapse within 3 years, requiring additional treatment. For pets with chronic disk disease, surgery may be indicated to prevent future recurrences. Surgical removal of damaged disks prevents recurrences of these disks from causing future disease; however, other disks could conceivably develop disease at a future time for which additional treatment would be needed.

To summarize, in general the results of treating pets with intervertebral disk disease with acupuncture approximate those of surgery. However, surgical removal of the damaged disks prevents the possibility of future episodes of disk disease (for those damaged disks) and the chance of relapse is gone. Surgery is recommended for pets with grade IV disk disease (any pet with paralysis and no deep pain) within 24 hours to maximize the chance of cure (although the prognosis for recovery for these pets is poor even with surgery). Acupuncture should only be performed on these pets if presented to the veterinarian after 24 hours or if the owner is unable to afford surgery. This is because the chance for recovery following surgery in these pets is very low once 24 hours has elapsed, due to the high possibility of permanent neurological damage. If the pet is not in severe pain, acupuncture should be attempted on these pets, as there is unlikely to be any harm to the pet from acupuncture therapy and a few pets may recover.

In addition to acupuncture, cage rest is critical to prevent additional stress to the spinal cord, which could increase clinical symptoms. When acupuncture therapy is chosen, the use of corticosteroids should be avoided whenever possible, as corticosteroid administration decreases the effectiveness of acupuncture. However, if corticosteroids are needed to provide immediate relief (decreased pain and inflammation), they should be used. In this case, additional acupuncture treatments may be needed.

AROMATHERAPY

Common Uses

Gastroenteritis, bronchitis, dermatitis, depression, inflammation, pain, insect repellant, sedation, tranquilizer, dental problems, external parasites, skin infections, urinary tract infections, enteritis, skin disorders, diuretic, insecticide, asthma, stimulant, oral infections

Aromatherapy uses volatile oils to achieve a physical or psychological response. Fragrant oils and spices have been used medically for thousands of years in the Middle East. In the 1930s the term *aromatherapy* was coined by Gattefosse, who characterized the chemistry and medical uses of a number of oils. He and other doctors of his time discovered the healing powers and therapeutic uses of the oils.

The volatile oils can be administered by diffusion or nebulization, with massage or topical rubbing, or rarely orally (the oral method of administration is not recommended due to potential toxicity). The nature of the volatile oils allows rapid absorption through the skin (during massage or topical application) or through the mucous membranes of the nose (if nebulization is used to treat the patient).

The oils are generally obtained from various parts of plants, including flowers, buds, fruits, skin, and resins. The oils are obtained from the plant parts by distillation, separation (pressing), or solvent extraction. Volatility is mainly a function of the molecular mass of the oils. As with herbs, most therapists recommend oils only be obtained from organically grown plants to prevent chemical and pesticide contamination.

The oils appear to work by stimulating chemical receptors in the skin and mucous membranes; these receptors relay information to the olfactory cortex of the brain and limbic system, which deals with behaviors.

Topically, certain oils exhibit antibacterial and antifungal effects. This is not surprising when it is remembered that plants produce these oils to protect themselves against infections and parasitic infestations. For example, thyme has been recommended for its antiseptic actions. Thyme has been shown to have the greatest overall inhibition of bacteria in laboratory culture. Tea tree oil has demonstrated antimicrobial action as well. Fungal infections of the nails (onychomycosis) responded similarly to tea tree oil and the antifungal drug clotrimazole in people.

While generally considered safe when used as directed under veterinary supervision, volatile oils can be toxic and even fatal if used incorrectly. Tea tree oil, for example, has shown toxicity when the oil was applied topically in high doses to dogs and cats. Oils taken orally can be quite toxic or fatal, even in small amounts. When applied topically, oils should be applied in areas of the body where the patient as well as other household animals cannot lick off the oils. Cats in particular are very sensitive to toxicity with phenols, and phenols are a major chemical constituent of volatile oils. With proper administration (usually by diffusion through the air) and dilution, most volatile oils can be safely administered to most dogs and cats.

Aromatherapy

While aromatherapy has enjoyed a recent resurgence in popularity for treating people, veterinary medical applications are limited, and current reports of using the volatile oils are quite rare. As a result, indications for using aromatherapy are largely unknown and often extrapolated from human data; more research is needed to determine the best use of volatile oils in pets.

VOLATILE OILS COMMONLY USED

The following list includes the more commonly used volatile oils and their therapeutic uses:

Oil	Therapeutic Use
Aniseed	gastroenteritis, bronchitis
Basil	gastroenteritis
Bergamont	antidepressant
Birch	anti-inflammatory, pain relief
Camphor	bronchitis
Cardamom	gastroenteritis
Cedar	bronchitis, dermatitis, insect repellant
German Chamomile	dermatitis, gastroenteritis, sedative
Cinnamon	dental problems, external parasites
Citronella	insect repellant
Clove	skin infections, gastroenteritis, dental pain
Eucalyptus	bronchitis, urinary tract infections
Fennel	enteritis
Geranium	skin disorders, antidepressant
Hyssop	skin disorders
Juniper	diuretic
Lavender	antidepressant, tranquilizer
Marjoram	sedative
Orange	insecticide
Peppermint	gastroenteritis, bronchitis, asthma
Rosemary	stimulant
Thyme	gastroenteritis, bronchitis, skin infections, oral infections
Turmeric	anti-inflammatory

 # BACH FLOWER ESSENCES

Common Uses

Allergies, excessive licking/grooming, arthritis, chronic illness, pain, nervousness/anxiety/phobias

Flower therapy was developed by Dr. Edward Bach during the 1930s. Dr. Bach was a conventionally trained physician who studied immunology and was involved in the development of a number of vaccines. However, he desired to find a less invasive way of treating patients that would have the same favorable results as he saw with conventional medicine.

During his studies he learned about homeopathy and was attracted to Dr. Samuel Hahnemann's philosophy of treating the individual patient. As a result, Dr. Bach began preparing homeopathic preparations of the vaccines he had created.

During this time, Dr. Bach began to notice that people could be grouped based upon their emotional states. For example, he noticed that some individuals seemed lonely, some were distracted, some were fearful, and some were more outgoing. Dr. Bach further noticed that people that fell into these groupings responded best to the same type of homeopathic vaccine. By matching the homeopathic vaccine with a person's emotional "grouping," Dr. Bach achieved even better results in his patients.

Dr. Bach then began searching for harmless plant-derived materials for his vaccines (rather than relying on the bacterial products used at the time to prepare the vaccines). He desired plants that would have a healing effect on what he thought were the negative emotions that were at the root of many diseases he saw in his patients. This would allow him not just to heal the immediate illness but also heal the root cause of the disorder. By freeing the body from its negative emotional states, the body would be free to heal itself.

The system Dr. Bach discovered during his research led to the creation of the flower essences. The flower essences (flower therapy) are extracts of flowers; each essence addresses a specific trait of mind or personality type.

These flower remedies are used to improve the attitude, personality, and mood of the patient, which Dr. Bach felt was the key to many disorders seen in his patients. According to Dr. Bach, "Health is our heritage . . . and is the complete and full union between the soul, mind, and body. True healing can be obtained by right replacing wrong, good replacing evil, and light replacing dark." Dr. Bach felt that the action of the remedies was to open the patient to healing from within by replacing bad virtue (fear) with good virtue (calm). Since mental and emotional state can determine health or disease, the flower remedies are used to achieve harmony in the patient. According to practitioners of flower essence therapy, harmonious patients are healthier as harmony precludes disease.

There are currently 38 various flower remedies, which correspond to various virtues. Thirty-seven are extracts of flowers, while one remedy is made from natural spring water. They may be given singly or in combination, and are without side effects. Unlike conventional therapies that often rely upon drugs treating the symptoms, the flower remedies attempt a more holistic healing by helping the patient to heal herself.

These 38 remedies are divided among seven personality traits. The traits are fear, uncertainty, insufficient interest in present circumstances, despair, loneliness, oversensitivity, and overconcern for the welfare of others. The remedy or remedies chosen depend upon the most dominant emotion present at the time of the disorder.

While it can be at times challenging to pick the dominant trait in people when attempting to use flower therapy as part of the patient's care, it can be even more difficult to determine a pet's personality type. However, experimentation with the remedies has allowed veterinarians to be able to develop a system for choosing the remedy most likely to work, knowing the "emotions" behind the more common medical disorders that occur in pets. While this cookbook approach can guide the selection of remedies, your knowledge of your pet and how well you convey this to your doctor is of much importance in choosing the best remedy for your pet's particular disorder based upon his nature.

The remedies are not medicines, nor are they meant to replace proper medical therapy. Rather, they can be used with conventional medications (or other complementary therapies). The remedies are best used to treat the emotional state behind the pet's disorder. The process of choosing remedies is not always easy. Because of this, and because of the need to have a proper diagnosis and therapy, pet owners interested in flower essence therapy should work with their holistic veterinarians to determine the proper course of action using a number of therapies based upon the diagnosis.

What is the evidence for the flower essences? While we do not have any controlled studies with the flower essences, we have a wealth of information from doctors and pet owners who have used them for more than 100 years. The positive responses seen in these pets (as well as in people who have used the remedies on themselves) show that the flower remedies do work and the responses are not simply the result of some placebo effect.

BACH'S 38 REMEDIES

Here is a list of the remedies and some of their uses in veterinary medicine:

Agrimony. Often used in stoic animals who do not complain about anything; good for restless animals, and those with skin infestations or irritation.

Aspen. Often used in animals who become anxious, are nervous and jittery, and spook easily; good for impending stresses such as storms and earthquakes.

Beech. Often used in animals who constantly complain or are picky eaters; good for any type of intolerances (for example, grass or insects).

Centaury. Often used in animals who are more submissive and do not stand up for themselves;

Bach Flower Essences

good to increase the desire to fight disease and increase the will to live.

Cerato. Often used for the inattentive animal, the slow learner, and the pet who is easily distracted; good for animals with disorders that are difficult to diagnose and treat.

Cherry Plum. Often used for animals who are destructive, incontinent, hysterical, vicious, or hyperactive.

Chestnut Bud. Often used to break bad habits in animals; good to increase memory and assist in training.

Chicory. Often used in overly possessive animals; good for animals to ease the emotions associated with letting go (going to a new home, separating mother and offspring, for example).

Clematis. Often used to restore consciousness; increases the ability of the pet to focus.

Crab Apple. Often used to cleanse wounds and rashes; helps get rid of odors and poor self-image.

Elm. Often used for high-strung or easily overwhelmed animals; good for pets stressed by traveling, strangers, grooming, boarding, shows, and so on.

Gentian. Often used for animals experiencing any type of setback; good for depression due to chronic illness, separation, abuse, and such.

Gorse. Often used for animals who show signs of hopelessness or giving up; good for cases of abuse, neglect, or separation from the owner (owner death, for example).

Heather. Often used for the animal who always craves attention; good for animals that seem lonely.

Holly. Often used in animals that exhibit negative emotions; good for pets who seem upset, angry, or jealous.

Honeysuckle. Often used for separation anxiety; good for pets with homesickness, separation from loved ones (boarding), and to stimulate vital energies.

Hornbeam. Often used in animals who appear lethargic when training or working but then show energy during play time; good for slow starters.

Impatiens. Often used for nervous animals and those easily agitated; good for pets showing any emotional or physical pain.

Larch. Often used for fearful or cowering animals; good for pets that lack self-confidence.

Mimulus. Often used for fearful animals; good for abused pets and those that have become aggressive or vicious.

Mustard. Often used for animals experiencing profound depression; good for pets with hormone imbalances.

Oak. Often used for animals who are overworked or burdened; good for pets following malnutrition or loss of bodily control.

Olive. Often used for exhausted pets; good for exhaustion of the adrenal glands due to chronic illness, allergies, and such.

Pine. Often used for pets who try hard to over-please owners yet still face rejection; good for the pet who is "co-dependent" and acts guilty when the owner is upset.

Red Chestnut. Often used for pets who worry about the owner or other animals; good when the pet senses impending danger such as storms.

Rock Rose. Often used for terror or panic in pets; good for overly fearful pets and after any terrifying events.

Rock Water. Often used for pets who refuse to accept new training methods; good for pets with stiff joints.

Scleranthus. Often used for neurologic problems such as seizures; good for pets with mood swings or fluctuations in energy levels.

Star of Bethlehem. Often used for comforting the pet; good following emotional or physical trauma.

Sweet Chestnut. Often used to increase energy to deal with competitive events or chronic problems; good for an overall boost to the pet's mental and physical constitution.

Vervain. Often used for hyperactive animals; good for animals who never tire and are restless.

Vine. Often used in pets who are dominant; good for animals in competition to make them more noticeable.

Walnut. Often used to protect against allergens, infectious agents, and other pets; good to aid in transitions, such as moving or changing households.

Water Violet. Often used for pets who are loners or prefer to be alone; good for any form of grief.

Bach Flower Essences

White Chestnut. Often used to quiet an animal's mind; good for pets in training and competition.

Wild Oat. Often used in pets who seem depressed or bored; good for pets who do not do what they are trained to do.

Wild Rose. Often used in apathetic pets; good to use to add some excitement to the pet's life.

Willow. Often used for resentment in pets; good for pets who may have been abused or those who do not receive appropriate attention.

Rescue Remedy. The only combination remedy made by Dr. Bach. It consists of the essences of five flowers (cherry plum, clematis, impatiens, rock rose, and Star of Bethlehem) and is the most popular of the flower remedies. Rescue Remedy has many uses and is recommended for any stressful or traumatic event, such as seizures, separation anxiety, a trip to the doctor's office or grooming salon, and storm phobias.

THERAPEUTIC USES

Here are some commonly suggested flower therapies for the treatment of various disorders in dogs and cats:

Allergies. Agrimony, Cherry Plum, Chestnut Bud, Chicory, Crab Apple (excessive licking, grooming), Olive, Vervain, Walnut

Arthritis. Agrimony, Beech, Gorse, Impatiens, Oak, Willow, Rock Water

Chronic Illness. Centaury, Crab Apple, Gorse, Honeysuckle, Mustard, Willow

Pain. Beech, Impatiens, Star of Bethlehem, Wild Rose

Nervousness/Anxiety/Phobias. Rescue Remedy, Aspen, Chestnut Bud (obsessive-compulsive behavior), Larch, Mimulus, Rock Rose, Sweet Chestnut

Flower essences are administered by either applying a few drops into the pet's mouth as often as needed, or by adding a few drops to the drinking water (or both). Pets can also be bathed in a few drops of the remedy; the remedy can also be misted (sprayed) in the pet's environment. Rescue Remedy also comes in a cream that can be applied to the pet's body (typically an area with minimal hair coverage such as inside the ear or the inner hind leg or abdomen).

There is no wrong remedy, as they are devoid of side effects; there is also no wrong way to take the remedy and no right or wrong number of drops to use. These remedies do not produce side effects, can be used safely in all pets, and can be useful complementary therapies for owners opposed to traditional drug therapies.

CHIROPRACTIC

Common Uses
Spinal/vertebral/neurologic problems, immune response

Chiropractic medicine is the use of spinal manipulation to improve health. Like other complementary therapies, chiropractic medicine is designed to work at the appropriate level of the healing process and to work with the normal inborn homeostasis (the ability of the body to remain "normal and healthy"), rather than simply treating symptoms. Spinal manipulation is an old therapy, almost as old as acupuncture. The Chinese used acupuncture from about 2700 B.C., while Hippocrates used spinal manipulation because he felt that alignment problems with the spine were the cause of many diseases. While chiropractic care has been used in human medicine for many years, only recently has this discipline been applied to animals. While few controlled studies have shown benefits of chiropractic therapy, a number of anecdotal reports have demonstrated positive benefits.

Chiropractic

Chiropractic care focuses on the interactions between neurologic mechanisms (the nervous system) and the biomechanics of the vertebrae. In chiropractic theory, disease arises as a result of spinal misalignment that negatively influences the nervous system. Since all body systems are regulated by the nervous system, anything that interferes with nervous impulses to organs (including spinal misalignment) could impact the proper functioning of those organs and body systems. Chiropractic therapy seeks to realign the spine by a variety of manipulative techniques.

Spinal misalignments are called subluxations by chiropractors (this is not to be confused with the term subluxation, meaning partial dislocation, as used by conventional doctors). A subluxation is technically defined as a "disrelationship of a vertebral segment in association with contiguous (surrounding) vertebrae, resulting in a disturbance of normal biomechanical and neurological function."

CHIROPRACTIC THEORIES

Several hypotheses have been proposed to explain how chiropractic subluxations cause disease. They include:

Facilitation. The subluxation produces a lower threshold for nerve firing in the spinal cord. Realigning the spine stops the nerve firing, relieving signs of disease.

Somatoautonomic Dysfunction. The abnormal responses of the autonomic nervous system result from altered nerve function that occurs as a result of subluxations. The abnormal autonomic nervous system may cause disease in tissues regulated by this branch of the nervous system, including the heart, digestive tract, and urogenital system.

Nerve Compression. The vertebral subluxations cause pressure on spinal nerves, which alters the normal transmission in the nervous system. Chiropractors believe that the nerve compression leads to ischemia (reduced blood supply) and edema (swelling caused by a buildup of fluid) of the compressed nerves, which causes the dysfunction.

Compressive Myelopathy. The vertebral subluxations may compress or irritate the spinal

cord, which can cause ischemia and/or edema, leading to clinical signs.

Fixation. The diseased vertebrae are "fixed" within their normal biomechanical range of motion; the fixation involves local spinal muscles and nerve receptors.

Vertebrobasilar Arterial Insufficiency. The vertebral arteries are constricted due to the subluxations, which leads to ischemia of the spinal cord or structures of the head of the patient.

Axoplasmic Aberration. The intracellular movement of proteins, glycoproteins, or neurotransmitters in the nerve cells is altered as a result of subluxations. The altered axoplasmic transport may result in toxic buildup of proteins, contributing to disease.

Neurodystrophy. Nerve dysfunction is stressful to the body and its organs and this lowered tissue resistance can modify the immune system. This interaction between the nervous system and the immune system (such interaction has been demonstrated in connections between the immune system and the neuroendocrine system of the body) causes disease.

Regardless of which hypotheses may ultimately be proven to be the cause of disease resulting from spinal subluxations, chiropractic medicine seeks to "cure" the disease process by correcting these subluxations. Chiropractors correct subluxations by performing clinical examinations and radiographic (x-ray) examinations to determine which vertebrae are misaligned. Once the location of the subluxation has been determined, the veterinary chiropractor performing the treatment will perform a spinal adjustment. The spinal adjustment, defined as a "specific physical action designed to restore the biomechanics of the vertebral column and indirectly influence neurologic function" is performed as needed to realign the subluxated vertebrae and allow neurologic reprogramming of muscle contractions and healing of damaged ligaments. Usually multiple adjustments are needed, as the body requires time to heal.

SAFETY

Because of the increase in popularity in many complementary treatment techniques such as

Chiropractic

chiropractic, a number of "animal therapists" have advertised chiropractic care (and massage and acupuncture/acupressure) as part of their "specialty." Only veterinarians, or chiropractors using the technique under direct veterinary supervision, should perform chiropractic therapies on pets. Laymen should not be allowed to practice any of these medical techniques on pets.

 # GLANDULAR THERAPY

Common Uses

Thyroid disease, adrenal gland disease, immune diseases, rheumatoid arthritis, degenerative myelopathy, uveitis, diabetes, pancreatic insufficiency, immunodeficiency, neurologic disease, heart disease, liver disease, kidney disease, urinary incontinence

Glandular therapy (cell therapy, tissue therapy) is the use of whole animal tissues or extracts of these tissues for health maintenance and the therapy of mild health problems typically involving the glands of the body. Glandular therapy is "tissue specific." In other words, liver extracts benefit the liver, thyroid extracts benefit the thyroid gland, adrenal extracts benefit the adrenal gland, and so forth. Current research supports this concept that the glandular supplements have specific activity and contain active substances that can exert physiologic effects.

While skeptics question the ability of the digestive tract to absorb the large protein macromolecules found in glandular extracts, evidence exists that this is possible. Therefore, these glandular macromolecules can be absorbed from the digestive tract into the circulatory system and may exert their biologic effects on their target tissues.

Several studies show that radiolabeled cells, when injected into the body, accumulate in their target tissues. The accumulation is more rapid by traumatized body organs or glands than healthy tissues, which may indicate an increased requirement for those ingredients that are contained in the glandular supplements. For example, animals with thyroid cell damage showed rapid uptake of thyroid cells with active regeneration of the damaged thyroids, and liver extracts that were infused into animals caused liver regeneration.

In addition to targeting specific damaged organs and glands, supplementation with glandular supplements may also provide specific nutrients to the pet. For example, glands contain hormones in addition to a number of other chemical constituents. These low doses of crude hormones are suitable for any pet needing hormone replacement, but especially for those pets with mild disease or those that simply need gentle organ support. Pure chemically produced, full-strength hormones, while beneficial in selected pets requiring a quick response to a disease, would not be desired (due to potential side effects) for long-term use in most pets.

Glandular supplements also function as a source of enzymes. Pets with exocrine pancreatic insufficiency need additional pancreatic enzymes to digest food and absorb nutrients from the diet. The use of pancreatic extracts is an accepted "conventional" therapy for this particular disorder. It is possible that all glandular materials provide enzymes that encourage the pet to produce hormones or help the pet maintain health or fight disease.

Finally, glandular supplements are sources of active lipids and steroids that may be of benefit to pets. For example, Coenzyme Q_{10} is a commonly recommended antioxidant for pets with, among other problems, heart disease. The richest sources of this vital enzyme are whole food tissues such as heart, liver, spleen, or kidney. Practitioners who practice glandular therapy would prescribe a glandular supplement (possibly in addition to chemically produced Coenzyme Q_{10}, which might be needed on a short-term basis for

Glandular Therapy

pets with mild heart disease) that would provide the pet with "natural" Coenzyme Q$_{10}$.

SAFETY

An interesting application of cell therapy involves the use of supplements to achieve oral tolerance. Oral tolerization is the "process of turning off patients' rejection of their own tissues by feeding them small amounts of a protein directly or indirectly involved in the attack by the immune system." Oral tolerance involves the use of oral supplements (antigens) that are absorbed from the intestinal tract and then suppress immune responses. In dogs, part of the complementary therapy for **degenerative myelopathy** (page 60) involves administering myelin sheath protein (the protein from the myelin sheath that covers nerves) in an attempt to decrease the autoimmune reaction, which is theorized as the cause of this disorder. While results in people with multiple sclerosis appear encouraging (decreased inci-

dence of major attacks), and anecdotal reports show positive response in some dogs with degenerative myelopathy, more studies would be needed to properly evaluate this therapy.

Therapy with cell or glandular extracts appears safe. However, because these supplements are antigenic and some pets may experience allergic reactions, close observation of the pet may be wise when therapy is first initiated. Also, there is always the need for sterility to prevent viral infection of animal glandular tissues used as supplements. Using only supplements from reputable companies with high-quality manufacturing processes can minimize these potential concerns.

Most pets can benefit from nutritional support with glandular therapy. These supplements may help support the endocrine organs of the body in a more natural way then chemically synthesized conventional medications, and can usually be administered safely on a long-term basis for the majority of pets.

HOMEOPATHY

Common Uses
Gingivitis/periodontitis

Homeopathy is one of several complementary therapies that may be used in the treatment of dogs and cats.

A HOLISTIC VIEW

When discussing homeopathy, it is important to differentiate this therapy from conventional treatments. In conventional medicine, or allopathic medicine, doctors often treat the pet based on signs and symptoms. For example, a common reason many owners seek veterinary care is for the complaint of itchiness in dogs and cats. Usually these pets are treated with various combinations of potentially harmful drugs such as corticosteroids or antibiotics. While these medications can be useful and used safely, many times they

are prescribed without a proper diagnosis and used for extended periods of time without a successful resolution to the case. This is unfortunately all too typical in conventional veterinary medicine. Instead of treating the pet, we treat the problem. It should not be surprising that the pet never recovers with this type of treatment, and that the symptoms return as soon as the symptomatic treatment has worn off. It usually costs more to treat symptomatically for extended periods of time rather than spend a bit more money on the initial visits, collecting data, and treating the pet once a diagnosis has been made.

With complementary therapies such as homeopathy, the goal is to treat "the pet," not just "the problem." Every pet is an individual. Doctors must take time to correctly diagnose the pet's problem before trying to "put out the fire with a bucket of water."

It's not totally the fault of the doctors though. In order for us to treat the pet, we must have cooperative pet owners. Until you give the doctor permission to do what is necessary for your pet, at best all any doctor can do is treat the symptoms. Some owners, who want to do things with the least possible expense, don't give the doctor permission to run various tests to arrive at a diagnosis. Other owners are in a rush, and want a quick fix. Still, some owners request only "minimal care." Owners who fall into these categories are rarely interested in the pet's well-being, and have no interest in holistic care and all that veterinary medicine can offer their pets.

And therein lies the difference between conventional and complementary therapies such as homeopathy. Doctors can't offer a quick fix after a quickie office visit but must spend time carefully collecting a thorough history from the owner and performing a thorough physical examination, uncovering all the pet's medical problems (not just the obvious one that prompted the visit).

How do we know what is best for your pet? Only by slowing down, and taking a holistic view, which puts the needs of your pet first.

Because your pet may be harboring a potentially fatal disease, laboratory testing is needed to maximize his health.

All of this for a simple case of itching? You bet! This is different from the health care most owners receive from the veterinarian; it is holistic care, care that is concerned with the pet's entire well-being.

For homeopathy and other complementary therapies, it is important to realize that each pet possesses on a very deep level the "will" and ability to be healthy, if we will only let the pet try to heal naturally. Homeopathy recognizes this curative power of each person and pet, and attempts to maximize each pet's ability to be healthy and heal itself.

Before discussing veterinary homeopathy, let's take a look at how homeopathy was developed and how it is used for treating people with medical problems.

Homeopathy, developed by Samuel Hahnemann in the nineteenth century, means "similar disease." Conventional medicine, conversely, operates on the system of allopathy, or "different disease." Here's the basic difference. With allopathy, we treat a symptom with a medicine that opposes the symptom (a different treatment). As an example, we might treat a pet who itches with a drug such as cortisone that stops the itching.

With homeopathy, we use the principle of "similars" to treat the pet, not just the symptom of itching. Homeopathic physicians understand that itching is not in itself a disease, but rather a symptom of an underlying disorder. They choose a remedy that in full strength would actually cause itching, so they are treating the patient with a therapy that would normally cause a similar sign.

In human medicine, homeopathic doctors are interested in learning as much as they can about the "entire" or "whole" person. This means that the office visit might take several hours. The patient is questioned about numerous facets of his or her life, including diet, exercise, psychological well-being, sexual health, and numerous emotional factors. Laboratory testing may be performed as needed.

This is in contrast to the scene at many allopathic offices, where the patient is rushed in and out, given a quick diagnosis, and treated symptomatically with conventional drugs. The old saying, "Take two aspirin and call me in the morning if you're not better" would not be consistent with homeopathic therapy!

Why the need for all of this thorough questioning? Simply because the homeopathic physician needs to choose the single (ideally) best remedy to help the patient heal herself. As we shall see, many remedies treat similar constitutional complaints. The "ideal" remedy should always be chosen. The more the doctor can learn from you, the greater the chance that the ideal remedy will be selected. Additionally, the doctor seeks to prevent further disease problems. It is necessary to counsel the patient on various lifestyle choices, such as diet, exercise, relief of stress, proper hygiene, and the like in order to maximize health (when health is maximized, the body can normally defend itself against a number of diseases).

In short, with homeopathy, you are an individual with unique life circumstances. No one treatment can be prescribed for everyone with similar symptoms to the ones you are experiencing. While there is a formulary that lists numerous homeopathic therapies, the final treatment must be individualized to your specific needs. This takes time, and differs from the way many doctors were trained, where they tend to think that "one drug fits all." Instead of treating an itchy patient with cortisone, the homeopath must choose from numerous remedies, and pick one that most closely matches that patient's unique set of circumstances.

Veterinary homeopathic treatment is similar to human homeopathic treatment. However, we veterinarians are at a great disadvantage. From this discussion, you can see the importance of the need for careful questioning of the patient, learning a lot about the patient's emotional and mental state, as well as the physical complaint. We just can't ask a pet how he's feeling, or to share with us any emotional upsets in his life. This puts us at a disadvantage when it comes to trying to choose the "ideal" remedy, and may explain why veterinary homeopathy is more difficult and at times less successful than human homeopathy.

We must rely on a superb history from the owner, in order to maximize our selection of the appropriate remedy.

THEORIES OF HOMEOPATHY

The Remedies

Homeopathic remedies are made from herbs, plants, minerals (elements), and various animal toxins. In their natural, undiluted form, these compounds would be very injurious and possibly even fatal.

Homeopathy uses extremely diluted substances, prepared from a parent compound (mother tincture). There is literally so little of the parent compound left in the diluted final product that none could be detected by chemical means.

How then do homeopathic remedies work? Homeopathy practitioners believe in a "vital force" in each and every organism. When this vital force is altered, disease occurs. By stimulat-

ing the vital force, we can help the body cure itself, which it wants to do (no organism prefers illness over health). Through serial dilution, the vital force of the compound is released.

The more dilute the final product, the more vital force it contains. Extremely diluted substances are very potent homeopathic remedies, and care must be chosen in their selection. The proper dose or dilution is the minimum amount that is required to cure the pet.

Dilutions are made by serially diluting the "mother tincture," which is the full-strength form of the remedy. For example, 1 drop of the mother tincture added to 9 drops of diluent (water or alcohol) gives a 1x potency. One drop of mother tincture diluted in 99 drops of diluent gives a 1c potency. The 1c potency is more dilute than the 1x potency, but it contains more vital force than the 1x potency and is considered a stronger remedy.

This sounds astonishing to many pet owners and doctors who were trained in conventional medicine. It just doesn't make sense that a diluted substance, which contains no measurable trace of chemical, could actually do anything.

Yet many times, homeopathic therapies work. Obviously, something is happening during the dilution to allow the final product to effect a cure. For homeopaths, that something is the release of the "vital force" present in every organism.

The Law of Similars

Homeopaths use similar remedies to effect a cure; they choose a remedy that in full strength would cause similar symptoms, but in diluted strength has the opposite (curative) effect. This important homeopathic doctrine is called the law of similars (like curing like). This concept was not only advanced by Hahnemann but was recorded by other prior physicians, including Hippocrates.

Why is it that therapies should react according to the proposed law of similars? First, Hahnemann observed that many patients of his time were cured with conventional therapies using drugs that produced similar symptoms in the patient as the original illness. He also noticed that many patients with a given disease were cured of this disease when a second, stronger disease in-

Homeopathy

fected the person and caused "displacement" of the primary disorder.

Hahnemann also observed that when a drug is administered to a healthy person, it can produce opposite sets of symptoms, what he called primary and secondary actions of the drug. He concluded that the secondary set of symptoms represented a rebound of the vital force.

Through his investigations, Hahnemann concluded that symptomatic therapy of the patient often did not cure the patient but rather temporarily suppressed symptoms, which would recur because the patient was not living in a true state of health. Remember, too, that during his life many toxic and harmful treatments were administered to people, including bloodletting and toxic doses of compounds. His search for safer, more effective treatments that would improve overall health of the patient resulted in homeopathy.

As an example of using the law of similarities, let's again look at the complaint of itching, a symptom commonly seen in dogs and cats. Numerous reasons for itching abound, but for the sake of our discussion let's just consider the general complaint of itching. One homeopathic remedy that may be useful to control itching is *Rhus tox*, which is prepared from poison ivy. In full concentration, poison ivy causes sores and itching. Yet, the homeopathic preparation of *Rhus tox* is used in the treatment of poison ivy and other itchy disorders. Therefore, we see that a substance which *causes* itching in an undiluted (pure, concentrated) form can be used in a homeopathic, diluted form, to *treat* itching.

As we've already mentioned, some people will question the ability of these diluted, similar remedies to cure a person or pet. Those who do not understand the concept behind homeopathy might bring up the possibility of a placebo effect that may actually be causing the patient to be cured. There are actually two types of placebo effects that can take place. The first, less-discussed effect occurs inherently in any therapy for any disease. No matter what the condition or treatment, some people and pets will simply get better as their bodies heal themselves. Thus, with any type of research study we have to accept that a small percentage of patients being studied will simply get better, and this cure or improvement has nothing to do with the therapy (conventional or complementary) being investigated.

The second and better-known placebo effect deals with the power of suggestion. For example, if your doctor prescribes a medication for you, and tells you that you should feel better within 48 hours after taking the prescription, you may start to feel better based upon the doctor's power of suggestion. This is simply the placebo effect. Maybe the drug is working, maybe not. However, you knew that you were supposed to begin feeling better after taking the drug, and you may convince yourself that you do feel better.

While it is certainly easy to criticize homeopathic medicine as simply a result of the placebo effect, keep in mind that even with conventional drugs, many of us feel better because we know we "should" based upon what our doctors have told us. The placebo effect is very powerful, and it can occur with conventional or homeopathic medicine.

Certainly, in the case of a serious, life-threatening illness, we can't rely on the power of suggestion mediated through a placebo effect to cure the patient. However, most of us rarely have a serious, near fatal illness. We usually have a minor complaint, such as a cold, headache, itching, and the like. These minor complaints may be resolved with successful allopathic or homeopathic treatment, or as a result of the placebo effect.

Even if a patient were to get better by means of the placebo effect, that does not mean homeopathy is bad or ineffective. Remember, earlier discussion mentioned that an important part of homeopathy lies in the belief that the person or pet has the ability to "will" himself healthy. We all know about people who, through prayer or a forceful belief, willed their recovery from an illness. The placebo effect takes advantage of the idea that we can often choose to be healthy or ill, and that we can "will" ourselves to be free of disease. Because of this power of the mind-body connection, some consider the placebo effect the second-best remedy a homeopath could utilize.

Of course, in veterinary medicine, we are free of this particular placebo effect. No matter what we administer to our patients, they don't know if they are taking an allopathic remedy, homeopathic remedy, or placebo. They either respond

Homeopathy

or they don't. They cannot mentally make the decision to recover from illness in 48 hours just because a doctor tells them they should. No dog or cat will stop itching simply because the doctor tells the dog or cat that the itching should be gone in 48 hours! Because homeopathic therapies work in many pets, we know that we can't "blame" the placebo effect when a pet responds. Proponents of veterinary homeopathy believe that pets who get better while on homeopathic therapies do so as a result of the therapy helping the pet heal itself.

There are of course skeptics who may ask, "Wouldn't the pet have gotten better anyway?" That's a very fair question, and of course we could ask the same question of those who prescribe allopathic therapies as well. In some instances, yes, the dog or cat would have improved. In other instances, the pet would not have responded with a self-cure and some form of therapy *was* necessary to assist the pet in healing. This is especially true in chronic medical problems where the pet has failed to respond to numerous conventional medical therapies administered over many months or years. However, even if the pet might have recovered on his own, the remedy administered helped to shorten the pet's illness and speed his recovery. This is another important benefit of homeopathy.

EVIDENCE FOR HOMEOPATHY

Is there proof that homeopathy works in people or pets? Unfortunately, we have few good studies to show the effectiveness of the numerous homeopathic remedies. Most of our information is derived from clinical experiences of doctors practicing homeopathy and the testimony of their patients. This lack of "hard science" is particularly frustrating for pet owners who desire this form of therapy; the lack of scientific studies is often quoted by doctors who do not believe in the effectiveness of homeopathic medicine.

Yet it is important to keep in mind that we have over 200 years of clinical data from doctors and their patients around the world who do believe in the effectiveness of homeopathic therapies. A growing body of evidence does suggest that homeopathic remedies may indeed have bi-

ological actions and clinical usefulness. Since all homeopathic remedies have been tested for toxicosis, we know these remedies are safe when used as prescribed. All remedies have also gone through "provings" or testings in which healthy human volunteers are given repeated doses and observed for physiological effects. These provings show that the microdoses in the remedies do indeed possess biological effects.

In his book, *Dr. Rosenfeld's Guide to Complementary Medicine*, Dr. Isadore Rosenfeld quotes several conflicting studies in people. In one double-blind placebo-controlled study in asthmatic people, there was a 30 to 40% improvement in breathing in patients treated homeopathically compared to 12% improvement in those patients taking placebo. Another study in people failed to show effectiveness of a common homeopathic remedy to control pain following extraction of wisdom teeth. These conflicting studies led Dr. Rosenfeld to conclude that while homeopathy has shown benefit when compared to placebo in some studies, more research would be appropriate before we can fully appreciate the effectiveness (or lack of effectiveness) for the remedies and the number of medical conditions for which they might be indicated.

The exact mechanism for homeopathy has not been determined, although several interesting theories have been proposed. One theory discusses the hypersensitivity that people and animals possess. For example, we know that people can detect the odor of animal musk when it is diluted to portions as small as 0.000000000000032 ounces. We are all familiar with the fact that sharks can detect a single drop of blood in the ocean, and that dogs can detect a person's scent left behind (the concept of using dogs to track missing people utilizes this "homeopathic" principle). It may be that medicine makes use of this hypersensitivity through homeopathy.

It has also been shown that water, which serves as the diluent for the liquid form of the remedies, possesses memory and stores frequencies. Since the remedies can be neutralized if they are subjected to high temperatures or certain magnetic fields, there is no doubt that the water retains some ability to pass on the healing power of the remedies.

Homeopathy

In vitro studies have shown that high dilutions of remedies show a distinct difference in relaxation times (T1 and T2) when compared to placebo-treated water (relaxation times are complex molecular parameters that measure proton interactions and molecular rotation and movement).

Metaanalysis of 107 clinical trials confirmed that in 81 of the trials, homeopathic remedies were effective, 24 showed ineffectiveness of the remedies, and 2 trials were inconclusive.

In their books, homeopathic veterinarians Dr. Christopher Day and Dr. Richard Pitcairn recommend a number of remedies for pets with a variety of medical disorders. Their experiences, as well as the experiences of many holistic veterinarians, serve as the basis for much of the information in this chapter.

While we should encourage further studies in the area of veterinary homeopathy, the lack of acceptable scientific studies should not discourage pet owners from trying homeopathic therapies prescribed by veterinarians for their pets. While certainly not effective in every case (not even prescription medications are effective in every case), homeopathic therapies can have their place in the treatment of a variety of medical disorders in dogs and cats.

A number of remedies are available for use in homeopathic therapy. The doctor must spend time with you and try to arrive at an accurate diagnosis. In people, mental and emotional states are very important when selecting the remedy. In dogs and cats, this is nearly impossible to determine from the patient. Your help in advising the doctor about all aspects of your pet's life will be extremely helpful.

The doctor will often try to prescribe a single homeopathic remedy that most closely matches your pet's problem. Pure homeopathy involves a single remedy to stimulate the patient's vital force. After administration of the remedy, human homeopaths often wait to observe for results. Other remedies are prescribed as needed. This may be a difficult approach for pets. There are several different methods of administering homeopathic remedies. This difficult area of homeopathy is as much an art as a science, and patience is important on the part of the owner and doctor. When treating homeopathically, close

contact with between the owner and doctor and constant reevaluation of the case is essential.

COMMON HOMEOPATHIC REMEDIES

Remedies can be prepared from several sources. Some, such as *sulfur* or *silicea*, are prepared from minerals. Some homeopathic remedies are prepared from plants; examples of homeopathic remedies prepared from plants include remedies such as *belladonna* and *lycopodium*. Animal sources may also be used in the preparation of homeopathic remedies. Examples of animal-derived remedies include venoms of snakes, bees, and spiders. Nosodes, a special type of homeopathic remedy (see the section on **homeopathic vaccination** on page 411), are prepared from infectious organisms such as distemper virus and staphylococcus bacteria. Remember that no matter what the source of the remedy, the actual ingredients are diluted in preparing the remedy. No measurable amount of the original source for the remedy remains, only the vital energy or life force, which imparts healing properties to the remedy. No harm will come to your pet regardless of the toxicity of the original compound used in the preparation of the remedy.

Remember that the original parent compound used in preparing a homeopathic remedy may produce a number of symptoms in the pet. Therefore, it should come as no surprise that a given remedy may be useful in treating a variety of symptoms and illnesses.

Here then, are some of the more commonly used homeopathic remedies, and the indications for which they are often prescribed; specific disease conditions and the remedies most often recommended for them are discussed following this section.

Aconitum Napellus

Aconitum is an herb of the family *Ranunculaceae*. The parent compound is prepared from the entire plant and root, gathered at the start of flowering. The active ingredient in the plant is an alkaloid named aconitine. This toxin initially stimulates and then depresses sensory nerve endings. It also slows heart rate and depresses respiration. Hahnemann prescribed it in people

Homeopathy

for diseases characterized by inflammation and fever, and it was often used as a replacement for bloodletting.

Aconitum is fast acting and its use must be repeated in acute conditions. *Aconitum* is used in people for conditions including violent headache, early stages of the common cold, acute complaints brought on by exposure to cold or heat, restlessness and anxiety, and a number of other inflammatory disturbances.

In dogs, the remedy is useful in the early stages of feverish conditions, and in conditions with disturbances of the mucous membranes and muscular tissues.

In cats, *Aconitum* is used for arthritis of the small joints (the legs and feet), muscle pain, and pain and arthritis of the cervical (neck) vertebrae.

Sulfur, arnica, or belladonna may be useful in cases where aconite is prescribed, often following administration of aconite.

Apis Mellifica

Apis is extracted from honeybees. The remedy is made from the queen and/or worker bees, which contain the poison sac. Rheumatism is treated with *Apis,* and early in medical history, by honeybee venom. Diluted bee antigen is used to desensitize people to the toxin.

Apis is used in people for bee stings and other insect bites and other conditions causing stinging, inflammation, burning, and swelling. Rheumatism is treated with *Apis,* as is congestion of the brain and abdomen.

In dogs, the remedy may be used whenever edematous swellings are noticed. Swollen joints may also benefit. Fluid in the lungs may also improve.

In cats, the remedy is also used whenever edematous swellings are noticed (swollen joints, fluid in the lungs, and such).

Arnica Montana

Arnica is prepared from herbs of the family *Compositae.* The parent compound is prepared from the whole plant including the root.

In people, *Arnica* is useful for promoting wound healing and reducing inflammation of the nasal passages. High blood pressure and heart conditions may also respond. Externally, it was

prescribed for cuts, bruises, and sprains. Currently, it is usually prescribed externally for areas of trauma on unbroken skin. Athletes may use it externally for sore muscles. Internally, it can treat shock and counter the effects of trauma.

In dogs, many wounds and injuries with unbroken skin may benefit. It reduces shock and can be used before and after surgery, and can assist with control of bleeding. If given to pregnant dogs, *Arnica* will promote easy delivery.

Cats often present with similar conditions as dogs for which a homeopathic veterinarian might prescribe *Arnica.* Cats with any type of wound or injury with unbroken skin may benefit. It reduces shock and can be used before and after surgery, and can assist with control of bleeding. If given to pregnant cats, *Arnica* will promote easy delivery.

Arsenicum Album

Arsenicum album is prepared from arsenic, a potent poison, and has been used to poison individuals. In conventional medicine, including veterinary medicines, arsenical compounds may be used to treat parasitic diseases. Until recently, arsenic was the only conventional treatment for heartworm infection.

In people, *Arsenicum album* is useful for many conditions. These include headaches, often with nausea and vomiting, anxiety, burning sensations, putrid body discharges, food poisoning, fever, and heart conditions.

In dogs, *Arsenicum* is a deep-acting remedy, useful in many ailments. Skin conditions manifested by dryness, scaliness, and itching may be treated. It can help in some types of pneumonia, and pets afflicted with intestinal coccidial infections may benefit.

In cats, *Arsenicum* is also a commonly used remedy for many conditions manifested by dryness, scaliness, and itching.

Belladonna

Belladonna is an herb of the family *Solanaceae.* The parent solution is prepared from the whole plant as it is beginning to flower.

In modern medicine, atropine, a potent alkaloid from the plant, is used for a variety of conditions, including the treatment of a slow heartbeat

Homeopathy

and various types of poisonings. Atropine drops are used to dilate the pupils; Italian women used it to dilate the pupils, giving them a "dark-eyed" mysterious appearance (the word *belladonna* means beautiful lady).

In large doses, atropine stimulates then depresses the central nervous system, leading to death. Hahnemann used *Belladonna* to treat scarlet fever.

In people, *Belladonna* is prescribed for convulsions, a feeling of throbbing and heat, vertigo, irritability of nervous centers, hemorrhoids, bladder irritation, menstrual pains, pneumonia, and a number of other complaints.

In dogs and cats, *Belladonna* is used in conditions characterized by dilated pupils and the presence of a bounding pulse with fever.

Bryonia Alba

Bryonia is a perennial vine of the family *Cucurbitaceae*. The parent compound is prepared from the fresh root before flowering.

Bryonia contains a resin called bryoresin. The plant was used as a cathartic, purgative, for rheumatism, and for pleurisy. Hahnemann used it for cholera, typhus, typhoid, and several other conditions.

In people, *Bryonia* is used for fever, chronic conditions, violent headaches, constipation, pleurisy, and painful menstruation.

In dogs and cats, *Bryonia* is useful in many respiratory conditions, especially those in which the mucous membranes are inflamed and produce an exudate consisting of fibrin or serum.

Calcarea Carbonica

Calcarea was first prepared as calcium carbonate from oyster shells. Calcium is a major element in the body.

In people, calcarea is useful for various nutritional impairments. Overweight children, and patients with abscesses, glandular swellings, defective bone formations, withdrawn mental state, recurring headaches brought on by cold, weakened vision, difficulty digesting food, and general weakness or lethargy are often prescribed calcarea.

In dogs, many different calcium salts can be used homeopathically. *Calc. carb.* is useful in the treatment of skeletal problems (especially those

of young pets and older pets with osteomalacia) and in animals which ingest strange objects.

Calendula Officinalis

Calendula is prepared from the leaves and flower of the marigold plant. It is useful for wounds of the eyes and is a good healing agent when applied directly to open wounds. When nerve damage occurs as a result of the open wound, many homeopathic doctors combine *Calendula* with *Hypericum*.

In dogs, *Calendula* may be used locally for open wounds and ulcers and is one of the best homeopathic healing agents available.

In cats, *Calendula* can also be used locally for open wounds and ulcers and is one of the best homeopathic healing agents available. Many doctors also recommend it as a healing agent for rodent ulcers.

Cortisone

Cortisone and other steroids (prednisone, prednisolone, triamcinolone, dexamethasone, and betamethasone) are commonly prescribed for a variety of inflammatory conditions in people and pets. The homeopathic remedy is an extremely diluted form of cortisone.

In dogs, conventional cortisone treatment is useful for numerous inflammatory conditions, such as various allergies and arthritic conditions. The homeopathic remedy is indicated in similar conditions, and when conventional cortisone therapy has been overused and misused.

In cats, homeopathic cortisone can be used for similar conditions, especially when needed to combat the effects of traditional cortisone treatment. The clearing remedies *Nux vomica* or *Thuja* can be given at the same time to help detoxify and heal the body.

Hecla Lava

Hecla is prepared from volcanic ash and contains aluminum, lime, and silica.

In dogs, tumors of the bone (especially of the face) and dental erosions may benefit.

In cats, *Hecla* might be prescribed for any conditions involving the bones, teeth, or lymphoid organs. Bony tumors and conditions affecting the facial bones are indications for this remedy.

Homeopathy

Hepar Sulphuris Calcareum

This homeopathic remedy is made from finely powdered oyster shell and flowers of sulfur.

People who use *Hepar sulph.* are usually very chilly. The patient is overly sensitive and irritable and faints easily. A sharp pain followed by discharge of pus from the affected area may be noticed. Skin and glandular eruptions and discharges may be seen.

In dogs, this remedy may be prescribed in any conditions in which pus is present, especially if the overlying tissue is painful to the touch.

In cats, *Hepar* is also recommended for any process involving pus formation, such as cat bite abscesses.

Hypericum Perforatum

The homeopathic form of *Hypericum* is prepared from the entire St. John's wort plant.

In dogs and cats, this is useful in lacerated wounds and where there are damaged nerve endings. It is good for spinal injuries, in tetanus, and in the treatment of allergies exacerbated by photosensitization. Doctors usually prescribe this remedy in any condition in which nervous tissue injury is seen.

Lycopodium Clavatum

Lycopodium is an evergreen plant. The roots resemble a wolf's foot, which gives this plant its Latin name. The remedy is made from spores located on the scales of the flower.

Historically, *Lycopodium* has been used as a diuretic. The powder is used externally for skin diseases and chafing in infants.

In people, the remedy has been prescribed as a deep-acting remedy producing changes in many internal organs, including the bones, blood vessels, liver, heart, and joints. It is useful for gastrointestinal and liver disorders, and for patients with excess gas. It can be useful in cases where a person develops a headache from missing a meal, or premature signs of aging are seen. Frequency of urination and sexual dysfunction (impotence in the male, painful intercourse in the female) has been seen in people for whom this remedy is prescribed.

In dogs and cats, *Lycopodium* is useful for many conditions involving the digestive, respiratory, and urinary systems. Various conditions causing hair loss may also respond to this treatment.

Nux Vomica

Nux vomica is an evergreen tree; the seeds of the berry are used in preparing the homeopathic remedy.

The seeds contain numerous chemical alkaloids including strychnine and brucine. Strychnine causes severe overstimulation of the nervous system and convulsions that are easily stimulated by sight and sound. Strychnine has been used as a rodent poison. Hahnemann used it as a treatment for paralytic conditions.

In people, *Nux vomica* is used for many conditions. It is an antidote for many products causing nervous system stimulation, including caffeine and alcohol. It is useful for hangovers and gastrointestinal upsets. In general, people who exhibit irritability might be prescribed *Nux vomica.*

Dogs and cats showing digestive disturbances, including excessive gas and indigestion, may benefit. *Nux* is a frequently prescribed homeopathic remedy in veterinary medicine.

Rhus Toxicodendron

Rhus Tox is the poison ivy plant. The fresh leaves of the plant, which can irritate the skin, are used to prepare the remedy.

Originally the remedy was used to treat skin eruptions, scarlet fever, and paralysis.

Presently, *Rhus tox* is used for sprains and strains, numbness and weakness of the limbs, rashes of the face, skin inflammation and blistering, itching, burning eruptions, and hives.

In dogs and cats, *Rhus tox* is a popular remedy for muscle and joint conditions, and some skin disorders.

Ruta Graveolens

Ruta is prepared from the whole plant. In dogs and cats, this remedy is useful in conditions involving bones and cartilage, as well as disorders of the eyes and uterus. It may be helpful in conditions affecting the lower bowel, and is considered helpful in facilitating labor.

Homeopathy

Spongia Tosta

Spongia is prepared from toasted sponge. In dogs and cats, swelling of the lymphatics is an indication for *Spongia tosta*. Following respiratory infections, it has useful action on the heart.

Sulphur (Sulfur)

Sulphur is prepared from the element (mineral). It has historically been used for a variety conditions. It has been prescribed for the plague, as an intestinal antiseptic, for various skin disorders, and as important part of early "sulfa" antibiotics.

Sulphur is often used in people with vague or minimal symptoms, or to complete the action of other remedies. Fetid discharges (sulphur-smelling) may be present; itching and burning may be seen. People with gas and digestive disturbances, diarrhea or constipation, or genital lesions with offensive odors may benefit.

In dogs, the element sulphur is helpful in many skin conditions, including mange.

Cats with skin conditions such as mange, flea allergy, and miliary dermatitis also may benefit from homeopathic sulfur.

SAFETY ISSUES

A word of caution to owners is in order before beginning this discussion of treatments. Numerous homeopathic remedies are available from various sources, including health food stores, pet stores, some grocery stores, and mail-order catalogues. There is certainly nothing inherently wrong with an owner purchasing a "remedy" from one of these sources. Here are some guidelines to follow if you choose to purchase a remedy from these sources rather than seeking veterinary advice first.

- Limit your purchase of any homeopathic remedy from a source other than your veterinarian to remedies for minor disorders. For example, a dog or cat with mild itching, sneezing, mild lameness or an occasional bout of vomiting or diarrhea is probably not in serious danger of succumbing to his illness. If you wish to purchase a homeopathic remedy and try it for no more than 2 to 3 days, then do so. If the pet does not respond within 48 to 72 hours, then you should seek prompt veterinary care.

- *For pets with any serious disorder, seek veterinary care immediately.* Far too many pets get sicker and even die due to an owner waiting too long to seek veterinary care. This is true whether the owner tried home therapy with conventional or homeopathic remedies. If your pet has any serious signs of illness, or does not respond to your choice of homeopathic therapy soon, seek veterinary care.

- *Realize that with pure homeopathy, usually only one, or possibly two, remedies are chosen.* The remedy is chosen only after careful questioning of the owner, thorough evaluation of the patient, and possibly through the use of laboratory testing. There is no way even the most educated owner has the training in medicine to be able to select the best remedy for the specific disorder; often the doctor must try several remedies before finding the best choice for the patient. The homeopathic remedies available for purchase by the consumer are not pure remedies, but rather a mixture of six or more homeopathic therapies that could be indicated for the specific condition. Therefore, while a remedy purchased by the owner might be helpful to a dog or cat with itching, for example, they may also not work as well as if a single "pure" remedy was chosen.

THERAPEUTIC USES: DOGS

Homeopathy has been used to treat most diseases of dogs. This discussion will concentrate on the most common conditions for which an owner might seek treatment for his dog.

Gingivitis/Periodontitis

Oral disease, manifested by excessive amounts of tartar buildup on the teeth, is the most common infectious disease of dogs and cats. It is easily prevented and treated by routine dental care. At least annually, dogs require a thorough dental scaling performed under anesthesia. Often antibiotics are administered to decrease the bacterial count in the mouth.

Inflammation of the teeth and gums can be the result of systemic diseases such as kidney failure, in addition to periodontal disease. Pets with recurrent, severe infections should be thoroughly evaluated for concurrent systemic disease.

Homeopathic remedies may be useful for dogs with periodontal disease. For owners who feed homemade diets, adequate amounts of meat without excessive use of carbohydrates may decrease the incidence of periodontal infections.

Acid. nit. This is indicated when ulceration of the parts of the mouth nearest the lips is present. Ulcers may join together, and salivation is present. Gums bleed easily when this remedy is needed.

Borax. Excessive salivation is present and frothy and is seen as long drooling strands of saliva. Ulcers are present.

Acid. fluor. Fistulae, or holes in the gums and palate that may extend to the jaw, are the indication for this therapy. The saliva may be stained with blood. Damage to the teeth may be seen; the dog prefers cold water as the throat may be ulcerated and irritated.

Merc. corr. Many older dogs with severe periodontal disease may benefit from *Merc. corr.* These dogs have slimy saliva that is stained with blood. The entire mouth is dirty, offensive, and malodorous. Many of these dogs have systemic involvement (the entire body is infected and stressed) and act sick, and may have diarrhea and green discharge from the nose. Many of the older dogs with periodontal disease who have never had their teeth cleaned fall into this category.

Silicea. This can be used when pus in the tooth socket is seen, especially if infection of the underlying jawbone occurs.

Fragaria. This remedy may be useful as a preventive therapy; it may decrease tartar deposition in dogs.

Specific bacterial nosodes, such as *Streptococcus* or *Staphylococcus*, may be useful in place of antibiotics. While many holistic doctors try to avoid the overuse of antibiotics, many dogs, especially older ones who have severe periodontal infection and underlying disorders (including heart, kidney, or liver disease) benefit greatly

from a short dose (3 to 6 days) of antibacterial therapy prior to and immediately after the dental cleaning.

Diarrhea

Diarrhea is a symptom of a disease and not a disease itself. Other than the symptomatic treatment of a mild case of diarrhea, it is important to arrive at a diagnosis so that the proper remedy can be selected. Common causes of diarrhea include parasites, dietary change, various stressors, bacterial overgrowth, viruses, and inflammatory bowel disease.

Proper nutrition and dietary therapy are important for pets with diarrhea.

There are numerous homeopathic remedies for the dog with diarrhea. Dogs with a definable disease such as gastrointestinal parasites can be treated with remedies specific for these conditions. Some of the more common include:

Arsen. alb. This is useful for dogs showing signs of dehydration and restlessness. The feces are watery and foul-smelling, and often worse in the later evening hours.

Podophyllum. Conditions affecting the large and small intestine that result in a gushy feces containing mucus are an indication for this remedy.

Merc. corr. This is used in dogs with slimy, mucoid feces. Symptoms are worse in the evening, and straining may occur.

Carbo. veg. This is useful for many seriously ill animals who have suffered severe fluid loss. The feces are foul-smelling and a large amount of intestinal gas may be present.

China. This is useful with other remedies to restore strength after loss of body fluid.

Nux vomica. Many dogs have diarrhea exhibited by frequent straining with passage of small amounts of feces, and this remedy is particularly helpful. Dietary upsets are usually the cause of the gastroenteritis.

Respiratory Disease

A number of respiratory conditions occur in dogs. Kennel cough and chronic bronchitis are among the most common respiratory disorders often encountered in private practice. Kennel cough is an infectious disease that can be prevented by conventional or homeopathic vaccination. Signs of respiratory disease include coughing (usually a very loud, choking cough) and/or nasal or eye discharge.

Kennel Cough

Spongia tosta. Useful in dogs with a harsh, dry cough; a weak heart may occur.

Phosphorus. Rapid breathing with pneumonia may be seen, and dry cough with flecks of blood in the nasal passages.

Aconitum. Aconitum is always useful early in the course of a disease, and may be useful to calm the dog.

Nosode. The nosode can be useful as a vaccine or in conjunction with other treatments.

Coccus cacti. Coughing is worse at night and difficulty breathing may be seen.

Chronic Bronchitis

Bryonia. This is useful when the dog appears better by resting.

Apis mel. This should help when there is excess congestion in the lungs.

Spongia tosta. This is especially useful in the older dog with a weak heart and bronchitis.

Pneumonia

Aconitum. Usually indicated early in the course of most disease processes.

Ferrum phos. This remedy is particularly useful when pain and anxiety are seen with inhalation. Loose mucus may occur in the throat, and coughing may produce blood.

Phosphorus. This remedy is prescribed when rust-colored sputum is seen; the cough may be dry and unproductive.

Epilepsy

True epilepsy, seen as seizures of unknown cause, occurs quite commonly in dogs. Before a diagnosis of epilepsy is made, numerous tests must rule out other causes of seizures, including poisoning, organ dysfunction, brain infection, meningitis, tumors, abscesses, and hydrocephalus. Standard therapy for epilepsy involves anticonvulsant medication, most often phenobarbital.

Belladonna. A useful remedy for neurological disorders, especially when the pupils are dilated and the dog feels hot.

Hyoscamus. Used when attacks are preceded by shaking of the head and general unsteadiness. Foaming of the mouth may be seen.

Absinthum. Prescribed when attacks are preceded by excitement and twitching.

Intervertebral Disk Disease

A common cause of unsteadiness and paralysis, especially of the rear limbs, is intervertebral disk disease. The intervertebral disks act as shock absorbers between the vertebrae of the bony spine. Occasionally, part of the disk protrudes into the spinal canal, putting pressure on the spinal cord. Depending upon the signs, conventional therapy involves surgery or high doses of corticosteroids; acupuncture is often recommended for pets with intervertebral disk disease as well.

Ruta. This is useful when bony involvement occurs.

Hypericum. Hypericum is used in conjunction with *Ruta.* It is very useful for nerve injuries, especially of the lower back.

Hecla lava. If disk calcification is seen radiographically, this therapy is indicated.

Angustura vera. This can limit nerve damage resulting from disk protrusion.

Urinary Disorders

Kidney failure and bladder stones may occur in dogs. Bladder stones are often removed surgically, and dietary improvement is suggested to try and prevent recurrence. Kidney failure is usually considered irreversible; conventional therapy prolongs life without curing the degenerative processes.

Kidney Disease

Phosphorus. This may be prescribed for dogs with kidney failure, especially if vomiting and hemorrhages are noticed.

Silicea. This remedy may help limit scarring of the kidney.

Thuja. Prescribed as a good general remedy for kidney disease.

Homeopathy

Bladder Stones

Often, the specific remedy is best chosen after microscopic analysis of the stones or gravel. If the composition of the stone is known, the appropriate remedy is matched to the mineral content of the stone.

Lycopodium. This may limit the formation of bladder gravel.

Hydrangea. This remedy may prevent as well as eliminate existing stones.

Urtica urens. This remedy thickens the urine and helps remove gravel.

Congestive Heart Failure

Cardiovascular disease occurs quite commonly in dogs. Small breeds of dogs are most often diagnosed with chronic valvular disease. In this condition, the heart valves become weakened and retract from the heart chambers. As a result, blood not only flows in a forward direction but also flows backwards through the leaky heart valves. With time, the fluid may accumulate in the lungs or other body organs, causing the syndrome called congestive heart failure.

In larger breeds of dogs, valvular heart disease is not commonly detected. Instead, true heart disease called cardiomyopathy most commonly occurs. In this condition, the heart muscle degenerates and becomes thin and flabby. As a result, the heart can no longer effectively pump blood, and congestive heart failure results.

Traditionally, doctors have relied on drug therapy to control signs of congestive heart failure. Diuretics are useful to cause increased urination, which can reduce the excess fluid that builds up in the body. Cardiac glycoside drugs such as digitalis may be helpful to stimulate more forceful heart contractions. Thankfully, conventional doctors are now also prescribing special diets low in dietary sodium that may slow down fluid buildup and help control hypertension.

Homeopathy may be useful to decrease dependence on the cardiac drugs, which may have numerous short- and long-term side effects, and can be toxic on their own.

Lycopus virginicus. This is used when shortness of breath is apparent.

Adonis ver. This is a good remedy for valvular disease; excess fluid accumulates in the body and lungs.

Crataegus. This remedy can regulate cardiac activity.

Laurocerasus. The gums and tongue may turn blue, and exercise may cause shortness of breath.

Strophanthus. This is useful when the heart rate is excessively fast. It may also increase urine output reducing edema.

Arthritis

Arthritis means "inflammation of the joint." Arthritis is a common cause of lameness in older dogs, and may result from secondary joint instability, as is seen with hip dysplasia. Regardless of the cause, arthritis is painful and debilitating; many older pets are euthanized because of severe arthritis or due to the undesirable side effects seen as a result of the drugs used to treat dogs with arthritis.

The main conventional treatment for arthritis relies on drug therapy to relieve pain and inflammation. While these drugs can be effective, they may cause serious side effects (including gastrointestinal ulcers, kidney disease, and suppressed immune systems), damage the joint cartilage (worsening the arthritis), and fail to work after a period of time (necessitating higher dosages to control pain). The main drugs that have been used include corticosteroids and nonsteroidal anti-inflammatory drugs: aspirin, phenylbutazone, ketoprofen, naprosyn, ibuprofen, and acetominophen. (For a more thorough discussion on other complementary therapies for dogs with arthritis, see *The Arthritis Solution for Dogs*, published by Prima Publishing, in THE NATURAL VET series.)

Rhus tox. This remedy is useful if the dog seems to improve after a bit of movement and if the condition appears to worsen in cold, damp weather.

Bryonia. Bryonia is used in the opposite situation, when the dog appears better at rest and worse after movement.

Homeopathy

Calcarea fluorica. Bony deposits may be seen radiographically, and sometimes cracking noises in the joints may occur.

Actaea racemosa. Many older dogs have arthritis of the hips and lower vertebrae; *Actaea racemosa* may be indicated for these patients.

Lithium carbonicum. Once again, this remedy may be helpful for hip arthritis, and when the dog may have difficulty climbing stairs.

Allergic Skin Disease

Allergic skin disease, or atopic dermatitis, is one of the most common causes of skin disease in dogs. There are numerous causes of itching in dogs, including allergies to fleas, various pollens and molds, and occasionally food. Traditional treatment uses corticosteroids and antihistamines to control the signs associated with allergies. Using homeopathy avoids the short- and long-term side effects associated with these other drugs. (See *The Allergy Solution for Dogs*, published by Prima Publishing, in THE NATURAL VET series, for a more thorough discussion on complementary therapies for allergic skin disorders.)

Sulphur (Sulfur). This is a useful remedy for a variety of skin disorders. The skin may be red and itchy, and the problem may be worse in warmer weather.

Rhus tox. Rhus tox can be used when the itching is less severe with warm weather. Once again, the skin is itchy and red when this remedy is indicated.

Arsenicum album. For dry, scaly skin and a dull coat, this remedy may be useful.

Antimonium crudum. Dogs who acquire this condition may show skin lesions that develop scabs after forming pus.

Bacterial Skin Disease

Many dogs develop staphylococcal bacterial dermatitis; the condition is often secondary to allergic skin disease. Antibiotics can be used safely and effectively to treat the condition. Some doctors choose the wrong antibiotic, whereas others stop treatment too soon (the minimum treatment for most bacterial skin disorders is 3 weeks with regular antibacterial shampoo therapy).

Short-term use of antibiotics is not harmful for most dogs. Dogs with chronic skin infections may require almost daily use of antibiotics indefinitely. Treatment of these pets with homeopathy should be attempted.

The same remedies that are prescribed for dogs with itchy skin can also be useful for dogs with bacterial dermatitis. Many dogs with chronic infections have an underlying immune system disorder, including allergic dermatitis.

Additionally, dogs with bacterial skin infections may benefit from a homeopathic bacterial nosode of sorts, called staphylococcinum. In conventional therapy, the use of Staphage Lysate, which is essentially a "vaccine" against staphylococcal bacteria, is used and works in many situations. The staphylococcinum can be viewed as the homeopathic version of this product. It can be used by itself or in conjunction with antibiotics.

Nosodes. Nosodes are homeopathic remedies made from various infectious organisms. I have used the staphylococcal nosode for the treatment of staphylococcal dermatitis.

Homeopathy is an excellent and safe complementary therapy for dogs. There are never any guarantees, and some pets may not respond to homeopathy for a variety of reasons. Still, homeopathy is safe and often effective, even when conventional therapy has failed. Owners should discuss all the treatment possibilities with their doctors and then select that which is most appropriate for their dog's problem. When used properly, homeopathy can be an important therapy for your dog.

THERAPEUTIC USES: CATS

Immune System Disorders

Without question, viral diseases involving the immune system are a big concern among cat owners. These "Big Three" diseases are feline leukemia virus (FeLV), feline immunodeficiency virus (feline AIDS), and feline infectious peritonitis virus (FIP).

Homeopathy

Each of these viral diseases causes havoc with the cat's immune system. In the case of FIP, death usually results from an overactive immune system attacking blood vessels and other organs. In leukemia and immunodeficiency virus infections, the immune system is suppressed, and secondary infections or cancers are the cause of death.

Conventional therapy does not really offer any hope. We can support the cat while he's sick, and treat infections with antibiotics while the pet attempts to heal himself. Ultimately, we must turn to complementary medicine to really offer these patients any semblance of hope.

Realize that homeopathy is not a cure-all, and most, if not all, pets will still be infected with the virus. Our goal is to strengthen the cat's immune system to help it live a longer, fuller life; if we're lucky, the cat might rid himself of the virus.

The actual remedy chosen may depend upon which stage of the infection the cat is in at the time of the visit. Here are some general guidelines for treating these pets with homeopathy.

Sulphur. These cats may have chronic infections, including infections of the bladder, skin, and respiratory tract. The hair coat may appear rough and dry or oily. Anemia may be present, as is gingivitis; swelling of the lower lip at the midline may occur.

Natrum muriaticum. *Natrum* is a deep-acting remedy in cats with immunosuppressive viral infections. These cats are thirsty and may crave fish or salty foods, and don't like to be handled too much. Excess salivation (with thick saliva that dries on the hair after the cat grooms) and facial swelling may be seen. The coat may fade in color and the cat may excessively groom.

Nux vomica. Those cats who seem chilly may benefit, as will those with a history of conventional drug therapy for treatment of the condition. Cats who are somewhat fearful and have vomiting or diarrhea and jaundice may be prescribed *nux.* Bladder disease may also be seen in these cats.

Phosphorus. The cat who may be treated with phosphorus does not like to be picked up and may prefer to hide. These cats may be very thirsty (and may drink from the faucet). Blood may be seen in the vomitus, feces, or urine; ane-

mia may occur, as may liver disease. Cats who regurgitate their food may benefit from this treatment.

In addition to these and other remedies, cats with immunosuppressive viral infections *must* be on a high-quality natural diet with adequate supplementation. Antioxidants may be beneficial and may encourage return of appetite.

Gingivitis/Stomatitis

Oral disease, manifested by excessive amounts of tartar buildup on the teeth, is the most common infectious disease of dogs and cats. It is easily prevented and treated by routine dental care. At least once each year, most cats require a thorough dental scaling performed under anesthesia. Antibiotics may be prescribed to decrease the bacterial count in the mouth.

Inflammation of the teeth and gums can be the result of systemic diseases such as kidney failure, in addition to periodontal disease. Pets with recurrent, severe infections should be thoroughly evaluated for concurrent systemic disease.

Homeopathic remedies may be useful for cats with periodontal disease. For owners who feed homemade diets, adequate amounts of meat without excessive use of carbohydrates may decrease the incidence of periodontal infections.

Mercurius solubilis. This is indicated in cats with inflamed gums with excessive saliva and a "dirty" look to the mouth, which may worsen at night.

Acid. nit. This is indicated when ulceration of the parts of the mouth nearest the lips is present. Ulcers may join together, and salivation is present. Gums bleed easily when this remedy is needed.

Borax. Excessive salivation is present and frothy and is seen as long drooling strands of saliva. Ulcers with a raw red surface are present. The cat tends to not want to jump down from high places.

Acid. fluor. Fistulae, or holes in the gums and palate which may extend to the jaw, are the indication for this therapy. The saliva may be stained with blood. Damage to the teeth may be seen; the cat prefers cold water as the throat may be ulcerated and irritate.

Homeopathy

Mercurius corrosivus. Similar indications to *Mercurius sol.* but the symptoms are more severe. Many older cats with severe periodontal disease that have slimy saliva (that may be blood-tinged) may benefit from *Merc. corr.* These cats may be systemically ill and act sick, showing a slimy bowel movement, especially at night.

Specific bacterial nosodes, such as Streptococcus or Staphylococcus, may be useful in place of antibiotics.

Diarrhea

Diarrhea is frequently seen in cats, but keep in mind that it is only a symptom of a disease and not a disease itself. Other than the symptomatic treatment of a mild case of diarrhea, it is important to arrive at a diagnosis so that the proper remedy can be selected. Common causes of diarrhea include parasites, dietary change, various stressors, bacterial overgrowth, viruses, and inflammatory bowel disease. And for middle-aged to older cats, thyroid disease should be kept in mind as a possible cause of diarrhea. Proper nutrition and dietary therapy are important in the treatment of cats with diarrhea.

There are numerous homeopathic remedies for the cat with diarrhea. Some of the more common remedies include:

Bowel nosode. A bowel nosode may be quite beneficial in cats and kittens with diarrhea. One that is often recommended is the Gaertner-Bach nosode; the *E. coli* nosode may also be useful.

Baryta carb. This remedy is useful in young cats and kittens, and may be used in conjunction with other remedies.

Podophyllum. Conditions affecting the large and small intestine that result in a gushy feces containing mucus are an indication for this remedy. This may also be prescribed in chronic conditions that have failed to respond to other homeopathic or conventional treatment.

China. This is useful with other remedies to restore strength after loss of body fluid.

Veratrum album. Veratrum is often used in severe conditions that cause weakness and collapse, and if the feces are very watery.

Respiratory Disease

Respiratory diseases are among the most common problems in pet cats. In young kittens, they are often caused by viral, bacterial, or chlamydial infections. They often occur before the initial vaccinations have been completed as a result of incomplete immunity. Allergic rhinitis may cause similar signs initially.

In older cats, respiratory problems may occur as a result of immunosuppressive viral infections, heartworm disease, asthma, cancers, and as a sequel to permanent damage to the nasal area from infections occurring in kittenhood.

Arsenicum album. This useful remedy is indicated when signs are first noticed; nasal and ocular discharge is thin and watery.

Mercurius solubilis. This remedy is prescribed for pets with swollen nasal bones and a greenish and thick discharge. Symptoms may be worse at night.

Allium cepa. For cats with thin and watery nasal discharges that may also exhibit sneezing, *Allium* may be helpful.

Kali bichromicum. Cats needing this remedy often have yellow discharges that may form small plugs of pus; streaking of blood may be seen.

For cats with chronic sinus problems, doctors may prescribe *Hepar sulphur, Silicea,* and the Hippozaeninum nosode.

Urinary Disorders

Kidney failure, bladder stones, and the so-called feline lower urinary tract disease (FLUTD, formerly called FUS) are seen frequently in cats. Bladder stones are often removed surgically, and dietary improvement is suggested to try and prevent recurrence. Kidney failure is usually considered irreversible; conventional therapy prolongs life without curing the degenerative processes. Lower urinary tract disorders, where bladder sand forms and obstructive plugs (especially in male cats) occur, are treated with diet and sometimes antibiotics. Obstructive disorders are true emergencies and require urinary catheterization and fluid therapy.

Homeopathy

Kidney Disease

Phosphorus. This may be prescribed for dogs with kidney failure, especially if vomiting and hemorrhages are noticed.

Silicea. This remedy may help limit scarring of the kidney.

Thuja. Prescribed as a good general remedy for kidney disease.

Bladder Stones

Often, the specific remedy is best chosen after microscopic analysis of the stones or gravel. If the composition of the stone is known, the appropriate remedy is matched to the mineral content of the stone.

Lycopodium. This may limit the formation of bladder gravel.

Hydrangea. This remedy may prevent as well as eliminate existing stones.

Urtica urens. This remedy thickens the urine and helps remove gravel.

Congestive Heart Failure

Not as commonly seen in cats as in dogs, congestive heart failure most commonly occurs secondary to hypertrophic or dilative cardiomyopathy. Cats in heart failure may require oxygen, medical therapy to relieve fluid accumulation (diuretics) and strengthen the heart beat (digitalis, calcium channel blockers, ACE inhibitors), nutritional supplements (Coenzyme Q_{10}), or herbal therapy. The following homeopathic remedies may also be indicated.

Lycopus. This remedy is used for cats who appear out of breath and manifest with a quick and irregular pulse.

Adonis. *Adonis* can be used for cats who have diseased heart valves. Secondary kidney problems (decreased urine output) can be secondary to heart disease and may benefit from this remedy.

Lilium. *Lilium* is used for pets with rapid and weak pulses.

Crotalus. For cats with blood clots (arterial thrombosis) secondary to heart disease, homeopathic doctors might recommend this remedy.

Secale. This remedy is also indicated for cats with blood clots, particularly those affecting the rear legs.

Arthritis

Arthritis ("inflammation of the joint") is much less commonly diagnosed in cats as compared with dogs. Regardless of the cause, arthritis can be painful and debilitating; some cats are so severely affected that euthanasia may be recommended.

The main conventional treatment for arthritis relies on drug therapy to relieve pain and inflammation. While these drugs can be effective, they may cause serious side effects (including gastrointestinal ulcers, kidney disease, and suppressed immune systems), damage to the joint cartilage (worsening the arthritis), and they may fail to work after a period of time (necessitating higher dosages to control pain). The main drugs that have been used include corticosteroids and nonsteroidal anti-inflammatory drugs, most commonly aspirin as there are no approved and safe nonsteroidal medications available as of this writing to treat cats with arthritis. As with dogs, the following remedies may be helpful.

Rhus tox. This remedy is useful if the cat seems to improve after a bit of movement and if the condition appears to worsen in cold, damp weather.

Bryonia. *Bryonia* is used in the opposite scenario, when the cat appears better at rest and worse after movement.

Actaea racemosa. Many older cats have arthritis of the hips and lower vertebrae; actaea racemosa may be indicated for these patients.

Allergic Skin Disease

While not as common in cats as in dogs, skin allergies occur most commonly secondary to flea infestation, atopic dermatitis, or mange. While corticosteroids or antihistamines can be used to temporarily relieve itching, owners who prefer homeopathic remedies might use any of the following well-known skin remedies.

Sulphur (Sulfur). This is a useful remedy for a variety of skin disorders. The skin may be red and itchy, and the problem may be worse in warmer weather.

Arsen alb. This is a useful remedy for a variety of skin disorders, especially in cats showing systemic involvement (vomiting, diarrhea).

Lycopodium. This may be used when hair loss occurs secondary to skin disease.

Thallium acetas. This is another useful remedy for cats with hair loss that often occurs during skin disorders and has been reported to help hair regrow.

Special Immunologic Diseases of Cats

The most common devastating feline viral disorders that drastically alter the cat's immune system include feline leukemia virus infection (FeLV), feline immunodeficiency virus infection (FIV, also called feline AIDS), and feline infectious peritonitis virus infection (FIP). These viruses cause a number of chronic problems, and persistently infected cats will usually die as a result of a suppressed immune system or various tumors caused by the viruses.

Conventional treatment is generally unrewarding, and cats are treated symptomatically to improve the quality of life. Natural therapies, including homeopathy, may offer hope to the owner. While homeopathic veterinarians do not like to be overly optimistic, owners should consider complementary therapies as some pets do quite well. It is important to keep in mind that recently infected cats may normally seroconvert and fight off the virus; thus, whether using conventional or complementary therapies, one should not proclaim a miracle cure as the cat may have cured itself. Still, no one can argue that, in persistently viremic cats (those who repeatedly test positive for the virus in question) who live a longer, healthier life than expected, the complementary therapies must be of some value.

In general, homeopathic therapies for cats with these immunosuppressive viral disorders are prescribed nosodes (diluted concentrations of the virus) and other supportive remedies, depending upon the system affected. Other therapies (such as nutritional and herbal) are often used concurrently with the nosodes and other remedies.

VACCINATIONS AND NOSODES

Homeopathic physicians may recommend nosodes instead of conventional vaccinations. Nosodes are simply homeopathic "vaccines" that are prepared from various infectious organisms. As an example, a nosode for panleukopenia (cat distemper) would be prepared from infectious panleukopenia virus, possibly from respiratory secretions from an infected cat. A variety of nosodes are available, both for the treatment of infectious diseases (for example, the staphylococcal nosode is used as part of the treatment of staphylococcal dermatitis).

Veterinarians who practice homeopathy often recommend nosodes in place of conventional vaccines as part of the annual immunization regimen. In some sense, conventional vaccinations are somewhat "homeopathic." Conventional vaccines are made from altered infectious organisms, and they are administered in a diluted form. By administering these infectious organisms, doctors attempt to stimulate the pet's immune system to prevent against infectious diseases.

Recently, several concerns with conventional vaccines have surfaced. First, it appears that many pets may not need vaccinations each year against every infectious organism. Some may have immunity that lasts longer than one year after vaccination with some of our current vaccines. These particular pets would probably not benefit from additional immunizations.

Second, doctors do know that conventional vaccinations can cause both short-term and long-term side effects. Some side effects are not serious, such as mild swelling or pain after the vaccination. Other reactions can be more severe or even fatal, including inducing immune-mediated diseases such as anemia and low platelet counts. In cats, we are now seeing vaccine-induced cancers. While not common, certain studies suggest that vaccine-induced tumors may be seen in anywhere from 1 in 10,000 cats up to 1 in 1,000 cats. (A more thorough discussion concerning **vaccinations** in pets is found on page 147 discussing vaccinosis.)

Homeopathic doctors therefore may recommend the administration of homeopathic nosodes in place of conventional vaccines. Since the

Homeopathy

nosodes do not contain measurable amounts of infectious product, they may be administered without any side effects.

While nosodes are very safe, are they effective? Some doctors seem to prefer nosodes manufactured by specific homeopathic pharmacies, as they feel there is a definite difference in the ability of nosodes to stimulate the immune system. In their opinions, the manufacturer of the nosode is important and some vaccination nosodes work better than others.

Nosodes are supposed to work in the same manner as conventional vaccines, namely by stimulating antibodies to fight off infections. However, while nosodes may be a safe alternative to conventional vaccinations, many doctors question how effective they might be when compared to conventional vaccination protocols.

One way to see whether they work is to subject them to the same testing vaccine companies use. After vaccinating a number of pets with nosodes, we would then expose these dogs and cats to the infectious organisms to see whether they become infected or remain protected. While this technique may be acceptable in the laboratory, most owners do not want to subject their pets to potentially fatal doses of infectious organisms just to see whether nosodes work!

Currently, there are no controlled studies showing the effectiveness of nosodes as an alternative to conventional vaccines despite their use by homeopathic physicians. The use of nosodes in place of vaccines is a personal one to be made after consultation with your veterinarian.

While some veterinarians recommend nosodes as a substitute for vaccinations, other homeopathic veterinarians do not believe nosodes are designed for this purpose. Rather, they use nosodes in two other ways.

First, in the face of an outbreak of disease, they use the nosode to strengthen the pet's immune system with the idea that this will make the pet less susceptible to infection.

Second, some doctors use the nosodes to minimize vaccine reactions (vaccinosis) that may occur in some vaccinated pets (see page 147 to read more about vaccinosis).

Nosodes, and particularly the homeopathic remedies *Thuja* and *Lyssin,* can be used along with conventional vaccinations in an attempt to minimize any reactions or side effects from the vaccinations. Once again, controlled studies are lacking despite this widespread practice.

SAFETY

Many owners, and sadly many veterinarians, are afraid to anesthetize these older pets for periodontal cleaning. This attitude means that many older dogs suffer for years from the pain of periodontal disease, not to mention the systemic infection and illness that occurs secondary to the infected oral cavity. There is absolutely no reason not to anesthetize an older dog. As long as the dog is normal on physical examination and preanesthetic laboratory tests, there is no increased risk with anesthesia (assuming a safe anesthetic is used and proper monitoring takes place) with age. There is a much greater risk of illness and death from the periodontal infection than from a short anesthetic procedure.

MAGNETIC THERAPY

Common Uses

Chronic wound repair; healing of delayed and non-union fractures; sprains and strains; intervertebral disk disease; avascular necrosis; musculoskeletal pain; postsurgical pain and edema (swelling); hip, elbow, and shoulder dysplasia

In recent years, therapy using magnets has gained a following among some pets owners.

It is seen as a safe and simple method of treating various disorders, often producing positive results without side effects or much expense. While magnets are advertised to offer a number of benefits, many owners wonder whether they really work. And if they do, can your dog or cat benefit from magnetic field therapy?

Magnetic therapy is by no means "quackish." The Earth has a normal magnetic field. The cells in our bodies and our pets' bodies also have a normal magnetic field that allow for proper functioning. NASA determined that rats in space that are not provided with a suitable magnetic field perished due to disrupted energy flow (altered calcium metabolism). While direct proof is hard to find, some holistic doctors attribute many of the illnesses we see in pets to the decline over the centuries in the Earth's normal magnetic field.

HOW DOES MAGNETIC THERAPY WORK?

Magnets are believed to work by means of magnetic lines of force; units called gauss measure the strength of the magnetic field. The higher the gauss number, the stronger the magnet (a 1,000-gauss magnet is stronger than a 100-gauss magnet). Magnets are used either as permanent magnets, also called static magnets or as pulsed electromagnetic field magnets (PEMF). Static magnets come in bars, beads, or strips; therapeutic permanent (static) magnets usually range from 200 to 3,000 gauss. PEMF uses a low-frequency (at or below 5 kHz) pulsing current flow through a wire coil to create a magnetic field around the wire. The greater the amount of current flow, and the greater the number of turns of the wire, the greater the magnetic field that forms. In people, PEMF is approved by the FDA for treating non-union fractures (fractures that have failed to heal). Non- or low-thermal pulsed radiofrequency (PRF) signals may also be used, and were originally used for the treatment of infections in people prior to the advent of antibiotics. Since the signals from PRF (13–40 MHz) have frequency components with sufficient amplitude to elicit a possible bioeffect over a broader band than PEMF signals, they may be preferred. This difference also allows PRF to be used for shorter periods of treatment time (30 minutes) than PEMF (1 to 4 hours). Other uses include treatment of avascular necrosis of the hip, osteoarthritis, and rotator cuff injuries. While there have been conflicting findings in studies examining chronic exposure to the magnetic frequencies of people exposed to power lines (50 to 60 Hertz), no toxic effects have been reported using magnetic therapy.

Magnets appear to heal the body by removing inflammation (mainly fluid or edema) and restoring circulation. By increasing blood flow to a diseased site, increased nutrients are available for healing. In fracture healing, for example, the use of magnetic fields increases the adherence of calcium ions to the blood clot formed at the site of the break. This allows proper formation of the callus that is necessary for fractures to heal properly.

In the Eastern view of healing, magnets help restore the energy flow of the body to allow healing and proper metabolism. This is similar to one of the theories used to explain the positive effects of acupuncture as well.

While magnets can be used in both dog and cat therapies, most commonly, dogs are treated with magnets due to their greater incidence of musculoskeletal injuries. In canine medicine, magnets are often used to aid in fracture healing and in the treatment of arthritis, hip dysplasia, osteochondritis, epilepsy, pain relief, chronic organ disorders, and vertebral disorders. Sprains and strains and other traumatic disorders may also benefit. They should not be used in acute infectious conditions, on cancerous growths (although some doctors do find them useful in treating cancerous tumors, see below), in acute injuries, pregnant animals, or in dogs with cardiac pacemakers.

The use of magnetic fields in animals with cancer is controversial. Due to the increased blood flow in areas treated with magnets, the use of magnets in areas with cancerous tumors is problematic, as increased blood flow is needed for tumor growth and spread. Alternatively, increased blood flow to the tumor results in increased oxygen delivery to the cancerous cells, which could result in increased hydrogen peroxide levels and cell death within the tumors. Also, this increased blood flow may be used to the benefit of the patient when magnetic therapy is combined with cancer chemotherapy. For example, in studies in the laboratory involving a human breast cancer cell line (MCF-7) and melatonin and tamoxifen, it was shown that electromagnetic fields interacted with calmodulin, a protein important in cell proliferation pathways. This finding indicated that the magnetic fields may help control cellular activity and influence cellular responses to various medications. More research is needed to determine possible clinical applications.

WHAT IS THE EVIDENCE FOR MAGNETIC THERAPY?

In both people and canine medicine, a number of studies show the beneficial use of magnets for the treatment of a variety of disorders.

In people, a number of double-blind clinical studies have shown positive results for patients with a number of injuries, including chronic wound repair, delayed and non-union fractures, rotator cuff tendinitis, spinal fusions, avascular necrosis, acute ankle sprains, acute whiplash injuries, sleep disorders, fibromyalgia pain, post-liposuction pain and edema, and pain in the feet of patients with diabetic peripheral neuropathy, treated with static magnets, pulsed electromagnetic fields, or non-thermal pulsed radio frequency. Additionally, benefit has been seen in patients with depression and alleviation of some symptoms in people with multiple sclerosis.

In one study of 18 dogs with osteoarthritis treated for 12 weeks with permanent magnetic beds, dogs treated with the magnetic beds showed an overall improvement in the appearance of cartilage when compared with dogs in the control groups. There was a significant protective effect on articular cartilage degeneration. In this study, the magnetic beds had domino-sized ceramic magnets with 1,100 G surface field strength positioned between two layers of foam with a magnetic field on the mattress surface of 400 to 500 G. This suggested that dogs treated with magnetic beds had decreased synovial inflammation (the lining of the joint), decreased cartilage damage, and decreased levels of destructive enzymes in the synovial (joint) fluid. The proposed mechanism of cartilage healing involves increased triated thymidine and sulphate incorporation and calcium influx into the carti-lage cells (which allows production of more cartilage matrix, decreased inflammation, and inhibition of destructive enzymes).

Another study in dogs showed that with regard to fracture healing, there was a reduction of 40 to 50% in the healing time of simple fractures by incorporating magnets into the bandage. This meant that dogs would resume weight-bearing activities sooner when magnets were used along with conventional fracture repair.

A problem often seen in fracture healing is non-union of the fracture. In a non-union, the ends of the fracture fail to heal and the fractured ends of the bones remain. With treatment of more than 50 fracture cases in one report, no cases of non-union developed. Additionally, in two cases of severe non-union referred for evaluation where the fracture had failed to heal, magnetic therapy allowed healing of the fracture site.

This same clinical report also showed good success in treating various types of arthritis with magnets. Included in these clinical cases are dogs with spinal arthritis and paralysis, chronic disk disease, hip dysplasia and arthritis, older dogs who move stiffly or slowly, and stiffness that develops after a morning exercise routine. By using a combination of a magnetic mat for sleeping along with a spinning magnetic field, the report showed a positive response in 60 to 70% of cases.

A double-blind pilot study of people with post-polio syndrome and muscular or arthritic pain showed that the application of a static magnet delivering magnetic fields of 300 to 500 G resulted in significant and prompt relief of pain.

Exposure of mice to magnetic fields produced by either four permanent magnets or electromagnets with alternating polarity suppressed the same stages of excitatory amino acid-induced seizures that were also suppressed by anticonvulsant medications.

Magnets are certainly not a cure-all for every medical problem. Still, they are a safe and relatively inexpensive alternative for pets with chronic problems, and can be of benefit in fracture healing. Magnetic field therapy helps the body to heal by creating a favorable environment for repair. Magnets increase blood flow to the area, bring in essential nutrients, and help relieve pain and inflammation. As with so many

Magnetic Therapy

facets of the complementary health-care market, pet owners should consult with a veterinarian before trying magnetic field therapy. First, the correct diagnosis is essential in order to select the best treatment. Also, your doctor, if he has interest in the field, can recommend a safe and effective magnet. This is preferable to an owner selecting whatever happens to be advertised at the local store or in the recent pet catalogue. For owners researching magnets on their own, it is important to ask the manufacturers for any evidence (clinical studies) that show that their products provide the results that are advertised.

THERAPEUTIC USES

The various therapeutic uses include; chronic wound repair, healing of delayed and non-union fractures, sprains and strains, intervertebral disk disease, avascular necrosis, musculoskeletal pain, postsurgical pain and edema (swelling), and hip, elbow, shoulder dysplasia.

ORTHOMOLECULAR MEDICINE

Common Uses
   Feline leukemia, allergic dermatitis, epilepsy, inflammatory bowel disease, canine hip dysplasia, feline gingivitis/stomatitis

Orthomolecular medicine (often called "megavitamin therapy") seeks to use increased levels of vitamins and minerals (mainly antioxidants) to help treat a variety of medical disorders. While daily amounts of vitamins and minerals have been recommended as an attempt to prevent nutritional deficiencies, orthomolecular medicine uses higher doses as part of the therapy for disease.

The pet food industry relies on recommendations by the National Research Council (NRC) to prevent diseases caused by nutrient deficiencies in the "average" pet; yet, the NRC has not attempted to determine the *optimum* amount of nutrients or their effects in treating medical disorders. While a minimum amount of nutrients may be satisfactory in preventing diseases caused by nutrient deficiencies, it is important to realize that there is no "average" pet, and every pet has unique nutritional needs.

It is unlikely that our current recommendations are adequate to maintain health in every pet. Each pet has unique requirements for nutrients. Additionally, these needs will vary depending upon the pet's health. For example, in times of stress or disease additional nutrients above and beyond those needed for health will be required. Orthomolecular medicine evaluates the needs of the pet and uses increased nutrients to fight disease.

THEORY

The principles of orthomolecular medicine, summarized below, are adapted from "Orthomolecular Medicine: A Practitioner's Perspective," in *Complementary and Alternative Veterinary Medicine: Principles and Practice,* Mosby, 1998.

- Nutrition forms the basis of medical diagnosis and treatment.
- Universal recommended daily amounts of vitamins and minerals are inadequate due to individual needs among pets.
- Drug therapy is used when needed and always with consideration of potential side effects.
- Most foods (even those organically raised, although usually less so) are polluted due to environmental contamination that is unavoidable in our society. We use nutrition to replace those nutrients lacking in the pet's diet due to pollution and leeching of nutrients from the soil.

THERAPEUTIC USES

Orthomolecular medicine has shown promise in treating a variety of medical disorders. These disorders and the recommended therapies are described below.

Feline Leukemia is caused by a retrovirus transmitted by the saliva. There is no cure; conventional therapy seeks to reduce secondary infections and offer support with fluid therapy or force feeding as needed.

Orthomolecular therapy of feline leukemia utilizes 750 mg of sodium ascorbate, 750 IU of vitamin A, and 75 IU of vitamin E. A number of cats on this protocol tested negative for leukemia virus within 2 years of initial diagnosis on both ELISA and IFA tests. Also, many cats displaying signs of chronic illness became devoid of symptoms. Since false negative test results are possible, all cats who tested negative on blood ELISA testing treated with orthomolecular therapy should have follow-up IFA testing done.

Allergic (Atopic) Dermatitis is a common cause of itching in dogs and cats. This genetic disease is most commonly treated conventionally with corticosteroids and antihistamines.

The orthomolecular approach uses a hypoallergenic, healthful diet as the starting point. This diet should be free of chemicals, impurities, and by-products. A blood profile is done to rule out endocrine diseases such as Cushing's disease and hypothyroidism, as antioxidants may create changes in blood values that are normally used to screen for these common disorders. Treatment uses vitamin A (10,000 IU for small dogs and cats, and up to 30,000 IU for large dogs), crystalline ascorbic acid (750 mg for small dogs and cats, and up to 3,000 mg for large dogs), and vitamin E (800 IU for small dogs and cats, and up to 2,400 IU for large dogs). The antioxidant mineral selenium (20 mcg for small dogs and cats, and up to 60 mcg for large dogs) is also added to the regimen. Once the animal is asymptomatic, a maintenance protocol using lower dosages of vitamins A and E and the mineral selenium are prescribed to reduce the chance for toxicity.

Epilepsy is the most common cause of seizures in pets. Anticonvulsant medications such as phenobarbital, diazepam, or potassium bromide are commonly prescribed conventional medications.

Correcting the diet is important as there is anecdotal evidence that food hypersensitivity may be the cause of seizures in some pets. A small number of cases treated concurrently with anticonvulsant medicines plus antioxidants (at the dosages used for treating allergic dermatitis) have shown promise and allowed a reduction or elimination of seizures. While more cases must be treated before any conclusions can be reached, using antioxidant vitamins and minerals may be helpful in selected patients with epilepsy.

Inflammatory Bowel Disease is a common cause of vomiting, diarrhea, and weight loss in dogs and cats. The cause is unknown but is speculated to be an immune reaction to a local hypersensitivity in the digestive tract. Conventional treatment of inflammatory bowel disease usually involves corticosteroids and antibiotics such as metronidazole or tylosin; occasionally, other chemotherapeutic agents are needed for those cases that fail to respond to the initial therapies.

As with other conditions, the initial approach to orthomolecular therapies involves a hypoallergenic diet free of by-products, chemicals, preservatives, fillers, and artificial colorings and flavorings to decrease potential hypersensitivity within the gastrointestinal tract. Antioxidant therapy using the same protocol as for allergic dermatitis and epilepsy is the mainstay of treatment. Ascorbic acid is not used due to its cholinergic effect on the intestinal tract, which can worsen diarrhea.

Canine Hip Dysplasia is most common in large breed dogs (although hip dyplasia can occur in any breed of dog or cat). The exact cause is not known, but a combination of genetics and environmental influences (such as high-calorie diets in rapidly growing puppies) contribute to dislocation of the hip joints. Conventional therapy may involve medical or surgical therapy, or both. For young puppies with moderate to severe dysplasia showing clinical signs, surgical correction (such as total hip replacement) may be recommended to eliminate clinical signs, remove the source of inflammation and pain, and prevent secondary osteoarthritis. Puppies with mild dysplasia, as well as very old dogs who may not be candidates for surgery for a variety of reasons, are treated

Orthomolecular Medicine

medically with corticosteroids or nonsteroidal anti-inflammatory medications such as Rimadyl or EctoGesic.

Complementary therapies utilizing acupuncture, glucosamine, and/or chondroitin are quite popular and successful alternatives to conventional medical therapy. Unlike conventional medications, glucosamine and chondroitin may actually help rebuild damaged cartilage.

Orthomolecular medicine suggests using ascorbic acid as part of the therapy. Ascorbic acid is utilized for collagen synthesis; collagen is the connective tissue necessary for proper muscle, cartilage, bone, and ligament formation. Usually, ascorbic acid or vitamin C makes up part of, rather than the total, complementary approach to treating hip dysplasia.

A controversial report in 1976 described using ascorbic acid in pregnant female dogs to prevent hip dysplasia in puppies. The study looked at eight litters of puppies from German Shepherds who either had dysplasia or produced litters with puppies afflicted with hip dysplasia. No signs of dysplasia were seen in puppies when the pregnant bitches were administered megadoses of sodium ascorbate (doses administered to bowel tolerance) and the puppies were kept on a similar regimen. This study has been criticized by conventional veterinarians for two reasons: first, only a small sample size (eight litters) were utilized, with a small number of parent dogs. Second, long-term follow-up studies (radiographs, orthopedic manipulation of the hip joints, and so forth) were not done. Still, while more studies would be necessary to confirm these initial results, this study suggests that providing sodium ascorbate to pregnant dogs and their puppies may allow sufficient amounts of collagen to be developed to prevent the joint instability that is seen in dogs with hip dysplasia. If the results of this study were repeatable and proved valid, environmental factors that can contribute to hip dysplasia (rapid growth, high calorie diets, excessive exercise) would also need to be avoided to prevent environmental influences.

Feline Gingivitis-Stomatitis is a condition in which cats, and rarely dogs, develop severe inflammation and/or infection of the gums and surrounding oral tissues. The cause of this painful condition is unknown but appears to be a severe immune response to oral antigens. Because cats with feline leukemia virus or feline immunodeficiency virus infection may present with chronic dental disease or gingivitis, cats with recurring gingivitis, stomatitis, or dental disease should be tested for these immunosuppressive viral infections.

Traditionally, many cats can be treated conventionally with frequent dental cleanings, oral antibiotics, and corticosteroids. In severe cases, cats need all teeth extracted to cure the condition.

Orthomolecular therapy involves administration of high doses of vitamins A, C, and E, and selenium to improve cell-mediated immunity and decrease local oxidation that may contribute to destruction of the oral tissues. The antioxidants are administered locally and may also be rubbed onto the gums. Dental cleanings (as needed) and administration of antibiotics and/or corticosteroids are administered as needed at the start of therapy and during any flare-ups. A small number of cases have shown significant improvement when other (conventional) therapies have failed.

SAFETY

Owners should not diagnose and treat their pets without veterinary supervision. Many medical disorders present similar symptoms. Also, megavitamin therapy can be toxic if not used properly.

Orthomolecular Medicine

TTOUCH (TTEAM)

Common Uses

Nervousness, biting, fear, pain, shock, post-operative, trauma

In 1978, Linda Tellington-Jones created TTeam as a gentle approach to help horses with behavioral problems. Later, she refined the technique and created a series of touches using small, circular hand movements on the body. The technique has shown effectiveness when used on people and a variety of animals.

TTouch helps bring about awareness to various parts of the body. Unlike massage, which activates deeper body tissues, TTouch only manipulates the skin and stimulates the nervous system rather than the deeper muscular system. Also, TTouch can be used on small areas of the body, whereas massage usually focuses on larger areas of the body (or in some cases the entire body).

Biofeedback machines have been used to measure brain waves on patients treated with TTouch, and showed that brain waves (especially alpha and beta waves) were activated.

THERAPEUTIC USES

TTouch has been used on dogs and cats for its calming effects. For example, many frightened dogs who may bite (fear biters) and cats that are too nervous to be handled (fear biters) have shown positive response to TTouch exercises, either with direct touching by the hands or a wand or feather (to prevent initial fearful bites to the person doing the exercises). The TTouch approach helps perfect communication between pet owners and pets: People learn new non-threatening methods of handling pets and the animals can relax and learn a new understanding of their owner's expectations.

In dogs and cats, in addition to calming fearful animals, TTouch may be used post-operatively to relieve discomfort or pain. TTouch may be used to help calm animals who resist having their nails trimmed. Animals in shock or with serious injuries may also benefit from TTouch applied to the ears.

The TTouch technique can be used by owners or veterinary staff to calm animals and allow for improved relationships between people and animals. People learn positive interaction technique with pets, and the animals learn how to relax and not fear people but rather work with them in this approach, which can serve as an adjunctive therapy. People interested in learning the TTouch technique can take classes that show the proper techniques and their applications.

Ttouch (TTeam)

APPENDIX I: COMMONLY USED MEDICATIONS

In this appendix you will learn about the most commonly used (and, some would argue, misused or abused) conventional medications. The goal is not to discourage you from using them on your pet if your veterinarian prescribes them. You can use them safely and intelligently as part of a holistic pet program. However, because they are often indiscriminately prescribed, especially when other safer, more natural options exist, it is important that you take an objective look at them so you can use them safely when needed.

CORTICOSTEROIDS

Corticosteroids, or steroids for short, are among the most commonly prescribed medications. Without question, they are also one of the most frequently abused drugs in veterinary and probably human medicine. It's too easy for doctors to reach for the magic "steroid shot" to treat symptoms without really diagnosing and treating the disease. As a result, pets are often incorrectly treated for months or years before someone says "Enough. There must be a better way!"

Because of their frequent improper usage, corticosteroids are viewed by many holistic pet owners as horrible drugs to be avoided at all costs. However, that is far from accurate. Corticosteroids are actually wonderful drugs that can be life-saving *when* used correctly—at the correct dose, for the proper length of time, and in the patient whose diagnosis suggests a disease that is most correctly treated with corticosteroids. The problem is that they are often *not* used at the right dose, for the proper length of time, and in the appropriate patient. With rare exception (for example, some types of cancers and immune disorders), there is seldom if ever a need for their long-term use in the treatment of patients with diseases such as arthritis or allergies, since so many other natural options work just as well.

What Are Corticosteroids?

Corticosteroids, or more correctly glucocorticoids, are hormones produced by the adrenal glands. They are produced under the control of the pituitary gland. When the body needs to produce more of its own glucocorticoids, the pituitary gland produces a hormone called adrenocorticotrophic hormone (ACTH), which stimulates the adrenal gland to produce more glucocorticoids. When the level of glucocorticoids rises, the pituitary gland shuts off its signal (ACTH) to the adrenal gland; when the level of glucocorticoids falls, the pituitary gland puts out more ACTH. This loop keeps the body's production of glucocorticoids in sync with the body's demand. However, if we give the pet corticosteroids as a treatment, the pituitary gland senses this and stops production of ACTH so the adrenal glands won't make steroids. This effectively shuts down the body's normal production of a vitally important hormone. This won't hurt the pet if we use a low dose of steroid for a short period of time (7 to 10 days). However, if we use more potent steroids to treat a pet for longer periods of time, then suddenly stop giving them, the pet's body can't quickly adapt to the need for steroid and we can cause serious problems. This potentially serious side effects that occurs when we treat pets with glucocorticoids is not limited to injectable or oral corticosteroids, but has even resulted from various steroid-based creams and ointments that are applied topically to the pet.

What Effect Do Corticosteroids Have?

Corticosteroids have many benefits and do a number of wonderful things. First, they are anti-inflammatory and analgesic (pain-relieving) medications. They decrease inflammation, swelling, pain (caused by inflammation), and itching. This ability to relieve itching leads many doctors to overprescribe them for pets with allergic dermatitis. They are also very helpful in the initial treatment of patients with severe shock and neurological disease (spinal cord and brain injuries) as they relieve inflammation. They can modulate the pet's immune system, preventing the body from destroying itself in various autoimmune diseases such as lupus, immune anemias and platelet disorders, and rheumatoid arthritis. For pets with various cancers, corticosteroids can actually kill cancer cells.

The negative side to these wonderful effects is that corticosteroids can decrease the ability of wounds to heal and they increase the chance of infection if used for too long or at high doses. (Pets who truly need long-term steroid therapy require careful, frequent monitoring to allow for early detection of infections.) Corticosteroids may also contribute to further destruction of arthritic joints by decreasing collagen and proteoglycan synthesis, making them a poor long-

term therapy choice for most pets with arthritis. Corticosteroids are also immunosuppressive. At a high enough dose, steroids suppress the body's immune system. While this can be useful in immune diseases where the body is attacking itself, as stated before, an animal with a suppressed immune system is more prone to infections.

Corticosteroids exhibit both short-term and long-term side effects. Let's talk about the short-term side effects first, since these are most commonly observed and are the ones pet owners seem most concerned about.

Corticosteroids cause an increase in appetite, an increase in water intake, and an increase in urine output. These side effects are commonly observed in most if not all dogs on corticosteroid therapy; cats are considered somewhat steroid resistant and rarely show these side effects. (This does not mean that we can administer the therapy to cats without regard for the animal's well-being, only that if corticosteroids are necessary, their use

Long-Term Side Effects of Corticosteroid Therapy

Use	Side Effects
Heart (cardiovascular system):	Hypertension (high blood pressure), sodium/water retention
Skin:	Acne, infections, excessive bruising, atrophy (degeneration or thinning) of the skin, hair loss
Hormonal/ Reproductive:	Infertility, growth failure, adrenal gland diseases, birth defects, abortion
Gastrointestinal:	Ulcers, pancreatitis, perforation
Immune System:	Suppression and decreased ability to resist infections
Metabolic:	Increased blood fat, fatty liver disease, obesity
Musculoskeletal:	Osteoporosis (thin bones), muscle weakness, possible further cartilage destruction*
Nervous System:	Hyperactivity, lethargy
Eye:	Glaucoma, cataracts
Respiratory:	Thromboembolism (blood clots in the lungs)
Laboratory Tests:	Artificial changes in liver enzymes, white blood cell values, and thyroid tests

*There are conflicting reports about whether corticosteroids actually destroy cartilage, worsening arthritis. Since they decrease the abnormal formation of new bone and also decrease the destructive enzymes that occur with arthritis, some studies mention a positive benefit from their use. Other studies, especially where the corticosteroid was administered directly into the joint (an intraarticular injection commonly used in people with arthritis), showed microscopic evidence of cartilage damage, even after a single intraarticular injection. Regardless of the amount of potential damage to the joint, and due to the number of other potential side effects, more natural therapies should be used in most pets for the long-term treatment of osteoarthritis. Additionally, since corticosteroids are potent anti-inflammatory and anti-pain medications, the decreased pain from the arthritis may encourage increased patient activity. While this is not in itself bad, activity should be restricted and monitored. Additionally, the increased activity coupled with the cartilage destruction that may occur with corticosteroids adds to the joint damage.

is usually safer than in dogs.) Even those dogs taking corticosteroids for a short time and at a very low dose can show these side effects. The higher the dose and the longer the therapy, the worse the problem. While these side effects are not harmful, they are upsetting to many owners. Therefore, when used as a part of recommended therapy, it is important to use the lowest doses possible for the shortest amount of time.

While the short-term side effects of corticosteroid therapy are not harmful per se, a number of long-term side effects can pose risks to the patient. For that reason, holistic doctors prefer not using steroids for long periods of time unless absolutely necessary. Pets on long-term corticosteroid therapy (especially dogs, who are more likely than cats to develop side effects) must be monitored closely and frequently for side effects (by physical examination and blood and urine tests), usually every 2 to 3 months.

As a rule, pets on long-term corticosteroid therapy are not expected to live as long as they would if not on these medications due to these side effects. It is distressing to see pets sentenced to a (shortened) life of corticosteroid therapy when other therapies have not been tried. Sure, some pets who do not respond to any conventional or alternative therapy must take corticosteroids for life, but these instances are rare. And with appropriate dosing and monitoring, even these pets could live a decent quality of life *if* doctors handle their cases carefully. Sadly, it's too easy for doctors and owners to reach for the steroids any time a pet shows lameness. I would choose chronic therapy with corticosteroids for pets with disorders such as arthritis or allergies (conditions for which complementary therapies are usually quite successful) *only* if all other treatments had failed (it will take over a year of trying various safer therapies to determine this) and *only* if my other choice was euthanasia. For side effects associated with various uses, see table, Long-Term Side Effects of Corticosteroid Therapy.

Once again, my intention in relating all these facts is not to scare you into avoiding corticosteroids, but rather to educate you. For owners who don't mind steroid therapy, or in the few disease for which they may be the best therapy, corticosteroids can be used safely and effectively. All too often, though, doctors reach for the steroids without arriving at a correct diagnosis, or without pursuing other safer alternative therapies.

For those pets who may require corticosteroids (or for those owners who want to use them short-term), a lower dose of corticosteroids can often be used when owners agree to try more natural therapies.

Here are some of the complementary therapies that can be used for pets who require corticosteroid therapy.

Complementary Therapies

For pets with allergies, antioxidants, fatty acids, topical decontamination with hypoallergenic shampoos and conditioners, and herbal remedies can decrease itching and inflammation.

For pets with arthritis, therapies to reduce pain and inflammation including omega-3 fatty acids, antioxidants, magnetic beds, herbs, and acupuncture can be tried. Glucosamine and chondroitin sulfate supplements can also nourish and repair the cartilage.

For pets with immune disorders, herbs and antioxidants are often recommended.

For pets with inflammatory bowel disease, herbs, probiotics, enzymes, glucosamine, and glutamine are usually recommended.

Acupuncture, proper natural diet, and supplementation with raw foods and glandular products can be tried as treatment for any condition that responds to corticosteroid therapy.

NONSTEROIDAL ANTI-INFLAMMATORY MEDICATIONS (NSAIDS)

Nonsteroidal medications are the second group of medications commonly prescribed for dogs (and rarely cats). They are commonly prescribed for people and pets with various painful and inflammatory conditions, including arthritis and post-surgical pain relief. There are a number of these products, including aspirin, ibuprofen, naproxen, phenylbutazone, piroxicam, carprofen (Rimadyl), Etodolac (EctoGesic), and acetominophen (Tylenol).

Duration of Commonly Used Corticosteroids

Short Acting (Duration Lasts 8 to 12 Hours)
Hydrocortisone

Intermediate Acting (Duration Lasts 12 to 36 Hours)*
Prednisone
Prednisolone
Methylprednislone
Triamcinolone

Long Acting (Duration Lasts Longer Than 36 Hours)
Betamethasone
Dexamethasone

---

*The actual duration depends upon a number of factors, including the specific formulation. For example, the acetate and ace-tonid formulations are reposítol (very long-acting) preparations that can act for weeks and last in the body for several months. These preparations are overused in veterinary medicine and are the most harmful if used repeatedly.

Note: Acetominophen is not technically a non-steroidal medication even though it is often and incorrectly prescribed for this purpose; ace-tominophen has no anti-inflammatory properties.

Since dogs have shown greater toxicity (usually increased GI side effects) with most of the human NSAID medications, it is questionable whether NSAIDs should be used in dogs for any reason. As a result of this increased sensitivity toward NSAID side effects, the pharmaceutical companies are developing products that are safer for our canine patients. There are currently no approved NSAID products for cats in the United States; any NSAID use in cats must be done carefully under a doctor's supervision.

Like corticosteroids, NSAIDs work by inhibiting the chemicals (prostaglandins) that cause pain and inflammation. While they can be very useful in controlling pain and inflammation, like corticosteroids they too have side effects, some more serious and dangerous than others. We'll get to these side effects in just a minute. First, understanding how these side effects can occur is important.

Nonsteroidal medications are involved in something called the COX pathway. COX stands for cyclooxygenase, which is another enzyme in the pathway that breaks down the arachidonic acid in the cell membranes of the joint into chemicals such as free radicals and various prostaglandins that damage the articular cartilage.

Two COX enzymes, called COX-1 and COX-2, have been discovered to date. COX-1 is found in various tissues such as the stomach, intestines, and kidneys, and serves an important role in maintaining health. When arachidonic acid is broken down by COX-1, good anti-inflammatory prostaglandins are produced. These prostaglandins keep the kidneys functioning normally and help protect the stomach and intestinal tract against ulcers.

When arachidonic acid is broken down by COX-2, bad pro-inflammatory prostaglandins are produced. These prostaglandins (and other chemicals) are harmful and contribute to the side effects, such as GI ulcers and kidney disease, seen in some patients taking NSAID medications. Drugs that selectively inhibit COX-2 but not COX-1 are most likely to result in fewer side effects and be safer for our patients (although current research shows that while the incidence of side effects is much lower in COX-2 inhibiting NSAIDs than in COX-1 NSAIDs, there is still a concern about side effects as they are not totally safe drugs). Right now the move

Common Nonsteroidal Medications

(Adapted from Hobbs R, Bucco G. *The Natural Pharmacist: Everything You Need to Know About Arthritis,* Prima Publishing, 1999:36–37.)

Active Ingredient	Brand Names
aspirin	Ascriptin, Bayer
carprofen	Rimadyl*
celecoxib	Celebrex
diclofenac sodium	Arthrotec, Cataflam, Voltaren
diflunisal	Dolobid
etodolac	EctoGesic*
fenoprofen	Nalfon
flunixin meglumine	Banamine
flurbiprofen	Ansaid
ibuprofen	Advil, Motrin, Nuprin
indomethacin	Indocin
ketoprofen	
naproxen	Aleve, Anaprox, Naprosyn, Naprelan
piroxicam	Feldene**
phenylbutazone	Butazolidin
salsalate	Salflex
sulindac	Clinoril
tolmetin	Tolectin

*Approved for use in dogs

**Often prescribed for use in dogs with cancer for pain control. The use of piroxicam has rarely been associated with resolution of cancerous tumors.

Note: Most of these medications are unsafe to use in dogs and cats at any dosages.

is on in human medicine to find NSAIDs that inhibit COX-2 but not COX-1; hopefully our veterinary patients will benefit from this research as well.

Current NSAID medications available for veterinary patients inhibit both COX-1 and COX-2 to various degrees. Indomethacin and piroxicam have high COX-2/COX-1 ratios, and result in high incidences of GI problems (bleeding, ulcers). Naproxen, ibuprofen, carprofen (Rimadyl) and etodolac (EctoGesic) have lower COX-2/COX-1 ratios, and as a result have fewer incidences of GI problems. Aspirin has a higher ratio but an intermediate incidence of GI problems, indicating that other mechanisms are involved in causing some of the side effects we may see in patients taking NSAIDs.

The NSAIDs have the potential, like the corticosteroids, to produce a number of undesirable and potentially fatal side effects. One side effect is gastrointestinal bleeding. This bleeding can lead to ulcers of the stomach and intestine, and possibly perforation of the stomach or intestines. This occurs because of prostaglandin inhibition. While a good effect of nonsteroidal medications is inhibition of the prostaglandins that cause joint inflammation and pain (via COX-2 inhibition), the protective prostaglandins that are necessary to help prevent ulcers of the gastrointestinal tract are also inhibited (via COX-1 inhibition).

These protective prostaglandins are needed to maintain the alkaline mucus barrier of the stomach that protects stomach acids from destroying the stomach lining. Inhibition of these protective prostaglandins decreases the protective mucus layer, making bleeding and ulceration more likely to occur.

Therefore, while the nonsteroidal drugs are useful in the treatment of arthritis or for pain relief, the same mechanism which relieves the inflammation and pain also can cause serious side effects of the stomach and intestines.

Since control of pain and inflammation in pets with osteoarthritis is likely to require some type of chronic therapy, it is important to question the incidence of side effects in arthritic pets treated chronically (greater than one year) with nonsteroidal medications. Currently we really don't know the answer to this question; more studies are needed as some of these medications (Rimadyl and EctoGesic) have only recently become available, but here are some interesting statistics.

In one study, four of six dogs developed stomach ulcers after taking double the recommended dose of aspirin for 30 days (little information is available on long-term side effects when dogs are given the recommended dose of aspirin).

Looking to human medicine for clues, here is some information from the package insert from Celebrex, a new nonsteroidal medication made by Pfizer and Searle for people. (Keep in mind that Celebrex is supposed to be a safer NSAID, targeting mainly the COX-2 enzyme.) Reading from the package insert:

> *Serious GI toxicity such as bleeding, ulceration, and perforation of the stomach, small intestine or large intestine, can occur at any time, with or without warning symptoms, in patients treated with NSAIDs. Only ⅕ (20%) of patients who develop a serious upper GI adverse event on NSAID therapy is symptomatic. Upper GI ulcers . . . appear to occur in approximately 1% of patients treated for 3–6 months, and in about 2–4% of patients treated for one year.*

The insert did go on to state that in short-term studies on patients taking Celebrex, only 0.04%

experienced significant upper GI bleeding treated for 3 to 6 months, although the significance of this finding is unknown. While it appears that this product (only used in humans for now) is possibly safer that other NSAIDs (which inhibit both COX-1 and COX-2), I want to call your attention to the general warning signs listed in the insert regarding NSAID administration in general.

Only 20% of people *showed signs* of a serious GI side effect; the other 80% had serious side effects but *did not show signs!* Unfortunately, we don't have good studies in our pets to compare to this study, but I would assume the incidence of asymptomatic patients is similar.

Let's look at some of the information put out by Pfizer, manufacturer of not only Celebrex but the popular NSAID drug Rimadyl. This information is excerpted from the Pfizer Animal Health Technical Bulletin, "First-Year Clinical Experience with Rimadyl (carprofen): Assessment of Product Safety, May 1998" and "Update: Two Years (1997–1998) Clinical Experience with Rimadyl (carprofen), August 1999."

Key Points

1. More than 2.5 million dogs were treated with Rimadyl.
2. The reported rate of adverse reactions is low, approximately 0.2%, in 1997, and 0.18% in the 2-year study.
3. Approximately 70% of possible adverse drug events have been in older dogs.
4. Patient evaluation including physical examination and appropriate diagnostics is prudent before prescribing any medications.
5. When any medication is prescribed, owners should be informed of potential drug-related side effects and signs of drug tolerance.

Let's look at the last three key points, as I believe they are most important.

Key point #3 deals with the fact that most reactions to Rimadyl occur in older dogs. This is not surprising for several reasons (some of which I will discuss as I go into the possible side effects of Rimadyl). First, most dogs with arthritis are older dogs. Second, older pets are more likely to have drug reactions for two reasons: They have decreased ability to metabolize and excrete drugs from their bodies, and many older patients are taking multiple medications, which can interact with each other increasing the chances of a drug reaction. Third, many older pets have additional medical problems (such as kidney or liver disease) that may be undiagnosed at the time a medicine is prescribed; these added problems increase the chance of a drug reaction.

Key point #4 makes sense: Every patient receiving any medication should have a proper physical examination and diagnostic testing. (Blood and urine tests for nonsteroidal medications such as Rimadyl will usually suffice.) Unfortunately, it is the rare pet who receives the necessary diagnostics before chronic administration of Rimadyl is prescribed. It is imperative that your pet receive diagnostic testing to uncover anything that may increase chances for adverse drug reactions if Rimadyl is to be used for more than a short-term (3- to 7-day) treatment.

Key point #5 also makes sense: Owners must know about possible side effects so that at the earliest signs of any side effects, the medication can be stopped and the doctor notified. Yet when it comes to Rimadyl, this is rarely the case. I have yet to have an owner tell me that her previous doctor discussed testing or side effects with her. Most owners are astonished to hear there are any side effects at all! This is no doubt due to the multi-million dollar advertising campaign put on by Pfizer to promote Rimadyl, suggesting that long-term treatment is now available to help restore your old pet back to his younger, more mobile self. (In fairness to Pfizer, the ad briefly mentions that side effects can occur in pets taking NSAID medications. My experience shows that owners overlook this caution and doctors neglect to point it out.)

I would add a key point #6 to this list: Any pet that must receive Rimadyl for long-term therapy should have ongoing examinations and diagnostics to allow for early detection of any possible side effects. In my practice, regular testing for patients receiving any medication on a long-term basis is required or the prescription cannot be refilled! To do anything else is bad medicine and malpractice.

Here is Pfizer's recommendation for the use of Rimadyl in geriatric (6 years of age and older) dogs, as excerpted from the Pfizer Animal Health Technical Bulletin, "First-Year Clinical Experience with Rimadyl (carprofen): Assessment of Product Safety, May 1998."

- Complete history and physical examination are necessary before prescribing Rimadyl.
- Definitive diagnosis should be determined so therapeutic response can be monitored.
- Baseline and repeat laboratory testing should be considered and are valuable in the geriatric dog.
- Follow-up communication between doctor and pet owner is important.
- Owners should be informed of clinical signs of drug intolerance (lack of appetite, vomiting, jaundice, and behavioral changes).
- Repeat laboratory values should be considered before refilling prescriptions.
- Recheck evaluations should be done after 2 to 4 weeks of treatment and then 3 to 6 months later if chronic treatment is needed.

The latest information to come out concerning adverse drug reactions (ADR) to Rimadyl include:

In 1998 (the last year figures were available), Rimadyl led the list of drugs reported to cause adverse reactions in dogs (43.4% of all ADR were due to Rimadyl).

As mentioned, this is due to any of a number of causes: older pets who are often subclinically dehydrated, pets taking multiple medications such as heart medications that could increase toxicity of NSAIDs like Rimadyl, have organ disease or failure, and are not regularly screened for underlying problems and side effects. While NSAIDs can be safely used for short-term pain relief in most pets, other, safer options are preferred for long-term relief in arthritic pets, for whom Rimadyl is most often prescribed.

Now I'd like to share with you some of the side effects that may be seen with Rimadyl, EctoGesic, or any nonsteroidal medication that may be prescribed for your dog.

We've already mentioned gastrointestinal problems like GI bleeding and ulceration. Other side effects include kidney disease (also due to prostaglandin inhibition), liver disease (mild cases display elevated liver enzymes whereas more serious cases can show liver failure), immune diseases (anemia, low platelet count, skin diseases), neurologic signs (seizures, paralysis, unsteadiness), behavioral problems (hyperactivity, aggression, depression, or sedation), and even death.

Kidney Disease

Kidney dysfunction may occur as a result of NSAID administration. Dogs with underlying kidney disease (usually older pets) are at greater risk. Any time dehydration is present, the risk of kidney disease increases. Pre-treatment blood and urine testing can detect some but not all kidney pathology.

Liver Disease

The most serious side effect seen in dogs taking Rimadyl was liver disease. Two subsets of "liver disease" were seen. In the first subset are dogs with elevated liver enzymes detected on a blood test. Most of these dogs were normal, and elevated enzymes were only detected during routine monitoring.

The second and more serious subset included dogs with signs of liver disease or liver failure; these dogs require intensive hospitalization, and death may result. One-third of all dogs in this class were Labrador Retrievers. This may represent a true breed predisposition or may simply reflect the fact that Labrador Retrievers are popular dogs and many of them have osteoarthritis.

Immune Diseases

Anemia, low platelet counts, and skin reactions have been seen.

Neurologic Disease

Seizures, paralysis, and unsteadiness have been seen in a small number of dogs.

Behavioral Problems

Aggression, depression, or hyperactivity can occur in pets taking Rimadyl.

Drug Interaction

NSAIDs like Rimadyl and EctoGesic can interact with other medications. These interactions can result in increased or decreased concentrations of the medications in the pet's blood, which may result in clinical disease. Drug interaction most likely occurs in pets taking medication for epilepsy, such as phenobarbital, or for heart failure, such as Lasix (furosemide), digoxin, and Enacard (enalapril and other ACE inhibitors).

Cartilage Damage

Finally, and perhaps most importantly, as with steroids, many of the nonsteroidal medications destroy cartilage. They do this by inhibiting the enzymes necessary for the multiplication of the chondrocytes and the synthesis of proteoglycans. Both Rimadyl and EctoGesic appear to cause less cartilage destruction than other NSAIDs. Some studies reveal no cartilage damage *in vitro* (in the test tube) depending upon the dose administered (some studies suggested that a low dosage actually increased the glycosaminoglycans, indicating cartilage healing). What significance the *in vitro* tests have has yet to be determined.

I've used Rimadyl as our NSAID example for dogs since it was the first one (and the one most commonly prescribed) for dogs. However, even though EctoGesic favors inhibition of the COX-2 enzyme, it can also cause any of these same side effects. The good news (so far) about EctoGesic is that it is prescribed for once-a-day use (Rimadyl is used twice daily).

Note: I've talked with some doctors who have seen more GI side effects (rectal bleeding) in pets taking EctoGesic than in Rimadyl (although diarrhea and bleeding have also been reported by doctors prescribing Rimadyl). These doctors surmised that the increased incidence of side effects may be due to the higher blood levels of EctoGesic that allow it to be given only once daily. At this point, probably either medication can be used safely short term as long as the pet is monitored for diarrhea, blood in the feces, and any other side effects.

Also, to date I have not seen or heard of any specific liver problems (most common in Lab-

Possible Side Effects in Dogs Treated with Corticosteroids or Nonsteroidal Medications

System	Side Effects
Gastrointestinal System:	GI bleeding, ulceration, perforation, pancreatitis
Kidney:	Kidney failure
Liver:	Elevated liver enzymes, liver failure
Immune System:	Anemia, low platelet counts, and skin reactions
Neurologic System:	Seizures, paralysis, unsteadiness
Miscellaneous:	Aggression, depression, hyperactivity
Drug Interactions:	Phenobarbital, Lasix (furosemide), digoxin, and Enacard (enalapril and other ACE inhibitors)
Musculoskeletal System:	Cartilage damage

rador Retrievers taking Rimadyl) in pets taking EctoGesic. This may indicate that EctoGesic is a better choice for members of this breed with arthritis, or it may simply be that EctoGesic has been available for a shorter period of time than Rimadyl.

The safety of these products has been reported up to 12 months of continuous use, yet a number of dogs take these medications for many years. Time will tell if more side effects appear in pets taking these NSAIDs for longer than the 12 months tested. Also consider that the safety margin in these products is narrow. For example, quoting from the EctoGesic® package insert:

Elevated dose levels of EctoGesic at 2.7 times the maximum daily dose causes gastrointestinal ulceration, vomiting, and fecal blood and weight loss.

Yet, EctoGesic is supposed to be a "safe" NSAID. Ideally the first prescribed dose should start at the low end of the dosage range to minimize side effects. It is important to carefully follow the prescribed dosages if your pet must take these NSAIDs even for short-term use.

Here are some of the complementary therapies that can be used for pets that require nonsteroidal anti-inflammatory therapy.

Complementary Therapies

For pets with arthritis, owners can try therapies to reduce pain and inflammation including omega-3 fatty acids, acupuncture, antioxidants, magnetic beds, herbs, and acupuncture. Glucosamine and chondroitin sulfate supplements can also nourish and repair the cartilage.

Postoperatively, NSAIDs can be used safely in most pets for a short period of time (3 to 5 days). Alternatively, opiod medications are also quite effective (although some studies showed NSAIDs more effective than opiods for pain associated with procedures such as spaying or neutering). Acupuncture and herbal therapies may also be tried to relieve pain.

ANTIBIOTICS

Antibiotics are frequently used in the treatment of diseases of dogs and cats. While they can be life-saving, too often pets are treated indiscriminately with these medications. In many cases, as is true with corticosteroids and nonsteroidal medications, pets are treated with antibiotics for months to years without having even received a proper diagnosis!

Antibiotics are medications made from other living products such as molds. Penicillin is actually produced by the penicillium mold, as a way to prevent bacteria from killing the mold. In the laboratory, these raw antibiotics are chemically altered to reduce toxicity and reduce the chance of bacteria becoming resistant to them. Commonly used classes of antibiotics include amoxicillin, amoxicillin-clavulanic acid, ampicillin,

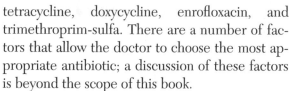
tetracycline, doxycycline, enrofloxacin, and trimethroprim-sulfa. There are a number of factors that allow the doctor to choose the most appropriate antibiotic; a discussion of these factors is beyond the scope of this book.

Antibiotic therapy, while usually safe when used on a short-term basis, is not totally benign. Side effects, most commonly vomiting or diarrhea, can be seen. While not as common as in people, allergic reactions can rarely occur in pets taking antibiotics. In practice, the most common side effects include a failure of the pet to improve and be "cured," as well as an increased incidence of secondary yeast infections, which are common with long-term use of antibiotics (especially tetracycline-type medications and the use of antibiotic therapy in pediatric patients).

There are several reasons pets may not get better while taking antibiotics. Paying attention to these reasons will allow doctors to prevent problems and minimize the length of time pets should take antibiotics for their infections.

- *Incorrect diagnosis.* Since only bacterial infections respond to antibiotics, it is important that the disease process is actually caused by bacteria. Diseases caused by viruses, fungi, and cancer will not respond to antibiotic therapy.
- *Underlying problems.* Pets with allergies and thyroid disease often have chronic bacterial skin infections. Until the underlying problem is diagnosed and treated, the skin will continue to become infected and the pet will continue to require ever longer doses of antibiotics.
- *Wrong antibiotic.* No antibiotic works all the time. If the prescribed antibiotic does not work, the diagnosis should be reassessed. If antibiotics are required, a different antibiotic might be used. The use of culture and sensitivity testing will help guide the clinician in the correct choice of antibiotic.
- *Wrong dose.* Even the right antibiotic won't work if it is under-dosed.
- *Wrong treatment time.* Antibiotic therapy can't be stopped by the owner or doctor just because the pet looks or feels better. Doing so will often cause the disease to relapse by bacteria that not have been killed but just re-

mained dormant. Many doctors, in an attempt to minimize cost, minimize treatment time. This is usually the case when treating larger dogs with skin infections. Skin infections require a *minimum* treatment time of 3 to 4 weeks. Antibiotics for skin infections are expensive; the dose for a large dog could easily cost $50 to $100 or more for 3 to 4 weeks of treatment. To help owners out, some doctors only prescribe a 2-week course. Of course, the pet relapses after temporarily improving and requires more treatment, which ultimately costs more than if the pet had been treated properly in the first place.

- Not only doctors are guilty of treating the pet for less than the appropriate amount of time required to eliminate the infection. Many owners commonly stop antibiotic therapy when the pet begins to "look and feel" better. Doing so will not cure the pet and may allow a relapse that will take longer to treat than the original infection.

Here are some of the complementary therapies that can be used for pets that require antibiotic therapy.

Complementary Therapies

Topical Decontamination

Skin infections are among the most common reasons for chronic antibiotic therapy. One treatment that is extremely helpful for both dogs and cats with skin infections is topical therapy. By using antibacterial shampoos, we treat the pet on the outside of the body as well as the inside.

Antibacterial shampoo therapy does several things:

- Moisturizes and rehydrates the skin
- Removes bacteria
- Removes odor
- Removes crusts and scales
- Flushes out hair follicles

And most importantly, frequent antibacterial shampoo therapy *reduces* the amount of time pets require more potent oral antibiotic therapy.

By bathing your pet every 1 to 2 days with the appropriate product, you minimize the number of days your pet must take oral antibiotics in most cases. In my practice, pets whose owners frequently bathe them only need oral antibiotics for 3 to 4 weeks (the minimum time needed to treat a skin infection) rather than 4 to 8 weeks (which is often required for pets with chronic therapies who are not frequently bathed). Products containing chlorhexidine, povidone iodine, ethyl lactate, and benzoyl peroxide are often useful.

Vaccines

For treating skin infections, some products are designed to boost the immune system that are basically "vaccines" against the staphylococcal bacteria that cause most skin infections. By immunizing the pet, we can often eliminate the need for antibiotics. This might be a consideration if other, more natural remedies fail to produce the desired result.

Homeopathy

Homeopathy uses dilute substances to treat the pet. Homeopathic "antibiotics" (called nosodes) are dilute remedies containing the bacteria for which they are indicated. For example, if the pet has a staphylococcal infection, the homeopathic doctor might prescribe the staphylococcal nosode, which is, in effect, a homeopathic "vaccine" against the staphylococcal bacteria. The goal is to use the nosode to stimulate the pet's body to attack the bacteria.

Other homeopathic remedies may be indicated, depending upon which part of the body is infected. For example, pets with skin infections might be treated with the staphylococcal nosode (since staphylococcal bacteria are the primary cause of skin infections) and the homeopathic sulfur remedy, a good remedy for many skin cases.

Acupuncture

Acupuncture is not really used as an antibiotic, but rather as a way to stimulate the pet's immune system. Pets with conditions that require long-term antibiotic therapy often have less than ideal immune systems. Acupuncture is an excellent way to boost an improperly functioning immune system. Additionally, depending upon where the infection is located, acupuncture points can be chosen to stimulate the desired organ as well. By stimulating the immune system, we can often allow the body to heal itself, reducing the need for antibiotics.

Herbs

Herbal therapies are used for a number of medical conditions. Many herbs are considered "antibacterial" and can be tried in place of antibiotics (under a doctor's supervision, of course!).

Here are some herbs that may be helpful as your pet's doctor attempts to wean her off antibiotic therapy.

"Anti-bacterial" Herbs

- Alfalfa
- Aloe (vera)
- Astragalus
- Blessed thistle
- Coriander
- Cranberry
- Echinacea
- Garlic
- Goldenrod
- Goldenseal
- Sarsaparilla
- Tea tree

Whole Food Supplements

Whole food and glandular supplements are designed to improve a pet's nutritional status. Many doctors believe that a number of diseases, including diseases of the immune system, such as chronic infections, occur due to an inadequate diet. Many doctors believe that pets eating natural diets and receiving nutritional supplementation are healthier, and are less likely to become ill.

While simply giving your pet a multivitamin and mineral tablet will provide some nutrition, using raw foods (like vegetables) as supplements provides vitamins and minerals in their natural forms. These natural foods also provide many other nutrients (enzymes, digestive bacteria) that can help keep pets healthy. Supplementing with these products can maximize the pet's nutrition; the choice of supplements that can be effective will vary with the pet and which body system has suffered from chronic infections. Standard Process makes high-quality whole food supplements. Several of their products are useful as supplements for pets requiring chronic antibiotic therapy, including Catalyn, Lact-enz, Immuplex, and Congaplex.

Olive Leaf Extract

Extracts from olive leaves contain large amounts of the chemical oleuropein. This extracted product exhibits both antiviral and antibacterial effects. Feeding large amounts of olive oil will not achieve the same effects, as oleuropein is extracted from the leaves before the oil is removed for use. There are anecdotal reports of pets with various infections (particularly ear infections) recovering when traditional therapies did not work. Because this is a relatively new product, more research is needed before it can be broadly recommended. However, it may offer pet owners another therapy for pets who have required chronic antibiotic treatment. Pet owners should ask their doctors for any information on this new and possibly helpful treatment.

ANTIHISTAMINES

Antihistamines represent the second class of medications that is often recommended to decrease itching in the allergic pet. Histamine is a chemical that is released by mast cells and basophils (cells in the pet's body) in response to contact with the allergen (foreign substance, such as mold, ragweed, grass protein, and so forth). Histamine "locks onto" histamine receptors (H_1 receptors) located on various cells throughout the body. (Think of histamine as a "key" that fits into its receptor, which acts as the "lock.") When histamine locks onto the receptor, the cell undergoes biochemical changes and produces the clinical signs associated with allergies (itching usually, but also runny eyes and nose). The histamine receptors also cause increased permeability of blood vessels (resulting in edema or fluid formation), release of other chemicals that increase inflammation, and accumulation of inflammatory cells. Antihistamines work by blocking these histamine receptors. By doing so, the antihistamines physically prevent histamine from connecting with its receptor, preventing the clinical signs mentioned above.

A number of studies have shown the effectiveness of various antihistamines in treating allergies in pets. Response has been variable, with anywhere from 10 to 30% of dogs showing clinical improvement. The response in cats is similar.

Antihistamines are not nearly as effective in controlling signs seen in allergic pets as are corticosteroids. This is because antihistamines function to block the histamine receptors on cells in the body, whereas corticosteroids function to prevent the formation of prostaglandins and other chemicals that cause itching as well as stabilize allergy cells to prevent them from "breaking apart" and releasing their chemical mediators of inflammation. Also keep in mind that histamine is only one of many chemicals released by allergy cells. This means that all of the other chemicals released by allergy cells upon contacting the allergen (foreign protein that causes allergies) are free to cause itching even though histamine may be prevented from doing so after the administration of an antihistamine. Additionally, antihistamines work best to prevent itching before allergy signs are seen; they are not as effective in decreasing itching once the pet is severely itchy.

The response to antihistamines is variable in pets. In some pets, none of the available antihistamines produces any effect. In other patients, the first antihistamine tried works great! There is no way to predict which antihistamine might work on which pet. Only through patient trial and error can we determine whether an antihistamine might be of use in allowing us to reduce the pet's need for corticosteroids.

When effective, antihistamines are felt to be a safer alternative to corticosteroids for long-term use in allergic pets. The major side effect that can be seen in pets taking antihistamines is sedation, which is much less of a problem in pets than in people. Sedation will, of course, decrease the pet's itching just because the pet is too sedate to itch. However, long-term sedation is not desirable. In some cases the sedation will wear off in a few days. If this does not occur, you can lower the dosage, increase the dosing interval, or try another antihistamine.

The side effect of sedation in both people and pets is related to individual susceptibility, as some

Chemical Mediators of Itching

Histamine	Prostaglandins	Leukotrienes
Serotonin	Trypsin	Plasmin
Bradykinin	Substance P	Opiods

Common Antihistamines

Brand Name	Active Ingredient
Benadryl	diphenhydramine
Chlortrimeton	chlorpheniramine
Atarax/Vistaryl	hydroxyzine
Tavist	clemastine
Seldane	terfenadine
Periactin	cyproheptadine
Temaril	trimeprazine
Hismanal	astemizole
Claritin	

patients are more likely to experience this side effect than others. The other factor has to do with the individual antihistamine. First-generation antihistamines (including hydroxyzine, diphenhydramine, and chlorpheniramine) can enter the central nervous system (brain) quite easily, and cause sedation. Second-generation antihistamines (such as terfenadine) do not enter the central nervous system as easily and are less likely to cause sedation. However, terfenadine has been reported in people to cause serious heart arrhythmias. This is most likely to occur in people with liver disease; those with low blood magnesium or potassium; and when terfenadine is used with drugs such as ketoconazole, itraconazole, and erythromycin. The same precautions probably apply to pets, although use of terfenadine in pets is not common and it is unlikely (although possible) that the other drugs mentioned above would be used in most pets.

Because antihistamines are metabolized by the liver, they should be used cautiously in pets with liver disease. They should not be used unless absolutely necessary in pets with glaucoma, urinary retention disorders, or intestinal atony (a disorder characterized by lack of intestinal tone). They can cause birth defects and should not be used in pregnant animals.

There is no data on long-term safety, but clinical experience seems to indicate they are relatively safe (much more so than corticosteroids if chronic drug therapy is indicated).

Commonly prescribed antihistamines include chlorpheniramine, amitriptyline, diphenhydramine, hydroxyzine, clemastine, and trimeprazine. Astemizole and terfenadine were ineffective in several studies but can be tried at various dosages if the more common antihistamines do not offer the pet relief.

Here are some of the complementary therapies that can be used for pets who require antihistamine therapy.

Complementary Therapies

Antihistamines are most commonly prescribed for allergic pets in an attempt to decrease the need for corticosteroids, which have more side effects than antihistamines. These pets may benefit from the following therapies:

Antioxidants, fatty acids, topical decontamination with hypoallergenic shampoos and conditioners, and herbal remedies can be used to decrease itching and inflammation.

APPENDIX II: WHAT'S REALLY IN PET FOOD: AN API REPORT

Plump whole chickens, choice cuts of beef, fresh grains, and all the wholesome nutrition your dog or cat will ever need.

These are the images pet food manufacturers promulgate through the media and advertising. This is what the $11 billion per year U.S. pet food industry wants consumers to believe they are buying when they purchase their products.

This report explores the differences between what consumers think they are buying and what they are actually getting. It focuses in very general terms on the most visible name brands—the pet food labels that are mass-distributed to supermarkets and discount stores—but there are many highly respected brands that may be guilty of the same offenses.

What most consumers don't know is that the pet food industry is an extension of the human food and agriculture industries. Pet food provides a market for slaughterhouse offal, grains considered "unfit for human consumption," and similar waste products to be turned into profit. This waste includes intestines, udders, esophagi, and possibly diseased and cancerous animal parts.

Three of the five major pet food companies in the United States are subsidiaries of major multinational companies: Nestlé (Alpo, Fancy Feast, Friskies, Mighty Dog), Heinz (9 Lives, Amore, Gravy Train, Kibbles 'n Bits, Recipe, Vets), Colgate-Palmolive (Hill's Science Diet Pet Food). Other leading companies are Procter & Gamble (Eukanuba and Iams), Mars (Kal Kan, Mealtime, Pedigree, Sheba), and Nutro. From a business standpoint, multinational companies owning pet food manufacturing companies is an ideal relationship. The multinationals have a captive market in which to capitalize on their waste products, and the pet food manufacturers have a reliable source from which to purchase their bulk materials.

There are hundreds of different pet foods available in this country. And while many of the foods on the market are virtually the same, not all of the pet food manufacturing companies use poor-quality and potentially dangerous ingredients.

INGREDIENTS

Although the purchase price of pet food does not always determine whether a pet food is good or bad, the price is often a good indicator of quality. It would be impossible for a company that sells a generic brand of dog food at $9.95 for a 40-lb. bag to use quality protein and grain in its food. The cost of purchasing quality ingredients would be much higher than the selling price.

The protein used in pet food comes from a variety of sources. When cattle, swine, chickens, lambs, or any number of other animals are slaughtered, the choice cuts such as lean muscle tissue are trimmed away from the carcass for human consumption. However, about 50% of every food-producing animal does not get used in human foods. Whatever remains of the carcass—bones, blood, intestines, lungs, ligaments, and almost all the other parts not generally consumed by humans—is used in pet food, animal feed, and other products. These "other parts" are known as "by-products" or other names on pet food labels. The ambiguous labels list the ingredients, but do not provide a definition for the products listed.

The Pet Food Institute—the trade association of pet food manufacturers—acknowledges the use of by-products in pet foods as additional income for processors and farmers: "The growth of the pet food industry not only provided pet owners with better foods for their pets, but also created profitable additional markets for American farm products and for the by-products of the meat packing, poultry, and other food industries which prepare food for human consumption."

Many of these remnants provide a questionable source of nourishment for our animals. The

433

nutritional quality of meat and poultry by-products, meals, and digests can vary from batch to batch. James Morris and Quinton Rogers, two professors with the Department of Molecular Biosciences, University of California at Davis, Veterinary School of Medicine, assert that, "There is virtually no information on the bioavailability of nutrients for companion animals in many of the common dietary ingredients used in pet foods. These ingredients are generally by-products of the meat, poultry and fishing industries, with the potential for a wide variation in nutrient composition. Claims of nutritional adequacy of pet foods based on the current Association of American Feed Control Officials (AAFCO) nutrient allowances (profiles) do not give assurances of nutritional adequacy and will not until ingredients are analyzed and bioavailability values are incorporated."

Meat and poultry meals, by-product meals, and meat-and-bone meal are common ingredients in pet foods. The term "meal" means that these materials are not used fresh, but have been rendered. What is rendering? Rendering, as defined by *Webster's Dictionary,* is "to process as for industrial use: to render livestock carcasses and to extract oil from fat, blubber, etc., by melting." Homemade chicken soup, with its thick layer of fat that forms over the top when the soup is cooled, is a sort of mini-rendering process. Rendering separates fat-soluble from water-soluble and solid materials, and kills bacterial contaminants, but may alter or destroy some of the natural enzymes and proteins found in the raw ingredients.

What can the feeding of such products do to your companion animal? Some veterinarians claim that feeding slaughterhouse wastes to animals increases their risk of getting cancer and other degenerative diseases. The cooking methods used by pet food manufacturers—such as rendering and extruding (a heat-and-pressure system used to "puff" dry foods into nuggets or kibbles)—do not necessarily destroy the hormones used to fatten livestock or increase milk production or the drugs such as antibiotics or the barbiturates used to euthanize animals.

Animal and Poultry Fat

You may have noticed a unique, pungent odor when you open a new bag of pet food—what is the source of that delightful smell? It is most often rendered animal fat, restaurant grease, or other oils too rancid or deemed inedible for humans.

Restaurant grease has become a major component of feed-grade animal fat over the last fifteen years. This grease, often held in fifty-gallon drums, is usually kept outside for weeks, exposed to extreme temperatures with no regard for its future use. "Fat blenders" or rendering companies then pick up this used grease and mix the different types of fat together, stabilize them with powerful antioxidants to retard further spoilage, and then sell the blended products to pet food companies and other end users.

These fats are sprayed directly onto dried kibbles or extruded pellets to make an otherwise bland or distasteful product palatable. The fat also acts as a binding agent to which manufacturers add other flavor enhancers such as digests. Pet food scientists have discovered that animals love the taste of these sprayed fats. Manufacturers are masters at getting a dog or a cat to eat something she would normally turn up her nose at.

Wheat, Soy, Corn, Peanut Hulls, and Other Vegetable Proteins

The amount of grain products used in pet food has risen over the last decade. Once considered filler by the pet food industry, cereal and grain products now replace a considerable proportion of the meat that was used in the first commercial pet foods. The availability of nutrients in these products is dependent upon the digestibility of the grain. The amount and type of carbohydrate in pet food determines the amount of nutrient value the animal actually gets. Dogs and cats can almost completely absorb carbohydrates from some grains, such as white rice. Up to 20% of the nutritional value of other grains can escape digestion. The availability of nutrients for wheat, beans, and oats is poor. The nutrients in potatoes and corn are far less available than those in rice. Some ingredients, such as peanut hulls, are used for filler or fiber, and have no significant nutritional value.

Two of the top three ingredients in pet foods, particularly dry foods, are almost always some form of grain products. Since cats are true carnivores—they must eat meat to fulfill certain physiological needs—one may wonder why we are feeding a corn-based product to them. The answer is that corn is much cheaper than meat.

In 1995, Nature's Recipe pulled thousands of tons of dog food off the shelf after consumers complained that their dogs were vomiting and losing their appetite. Nature's Recipe's loss amounted to $20 million. The problem was a fungus that produced vomitoxin (an aflatoxin or "mycotoxin," a toxic substance produced by mold) contaminating the wheat. In 1999, another fungal toxin triggered the recall of dry dog food made by Doane Pet Care at one of its plants, including Ol' Roy (Wal-Mart's brand) and 53 other brands. This time, the toxin killed 25 dogs.

Although it caused many dogs to vomit, stop eating, and have diarrhea, vomitoxin is a milder toxin than most. The more dangerous mycotoxins can cause weight loss, liver damage, lameness, and even death as in the Doane case. The Nature's Recipe incident prompted the Food and Drug Administration (FDA) to intervene. Dina Butcher, Agriculture Policy Advisor to North Dakota Governor Ed Schafer, concluded that the discovery of vomitoxin in Nature's Recipe wasn't much of a threat to the human population because "the grain that would go into pet food is not a high quality grain."

Soy is another common ingredient that is sometimes used as a protein and energy source in pet food. Manufacturers also use it to add bulk so that when an animal eats a product containing soy, he will feel more sated. While soy has been linked to gas in some dogs, other dogs do quite well with it. Vegetarian dog foods use soy as a protein source.

Additives and Preservatives

Many chemicals are added to commercial pet foods to improve the taste, stability, characteristics, or appearance of the food. Additives provide no nutritional value. Additives include emulsifiers to prevent water and fat from separating, antioxidants to prevent fat from turning rancid, and artificial colors and flavors to make the product more attractive to consumers and more palatable to their companion animals.

Adding chemicals to food originated thousands of years ago with spices, natural preservatives, and ripening agents. In the last 40 years, however, the number of food additives has greatly increased.

All commercial pet foods contain preservatives. Some of these are added to ingredients or raw materials by the suppliers, and others may be added by the manufacturer. Because manufacturers need to ensure that dry foods have a long shelf life to remain edible after shipping and prolonged storage, fats included in pet foods are preserved with either synthetic or "natural" preservatives. Synthetic preservatives include butylated hydroxyanisole (BHA) and butylated hydroxytoluene (BHT), propyl gallate, propylene glycol (also used as a less-toxic version of automotive antifreeze), and ethoxyquin. For these antioxidants, there is little information documenting their toxicity, safety, or chronic use in pet foods that may be eaten every day for the life of the animal.

Potentially cancer-causing agents such as BHA, BHT, and ethoxyquin are permitted at relatively low levels. The use of these chemicals in pet foods has not been thoroughly studied, and long-term build-up of these agents may ultimately be harmful. Due to questionable data in the original study on its safety, ethoxyquin's manufacturer, Monsanto, was required to perform a new, more rigorous study. This was completed in 1996. Even though Monsanto found no significant toxicity associated with its own product, in July 1997, the FDA's Center for Veterinary Medicine requested that manufacturers voluntarily reduce the maximum level for ethoxyquin by half, to 75 parts per million. While some pet food critics and veterinarians believe that ethoxyquin is a major cause of disease, skin problems, and infertility in dogs, others claim it is the safest, strongest, most stable preservative available for pet food. Ethoxyquin is only approved for use in human food for preserving spices, such as cayenne and chili powder, at a level of 100 ppm—but it would be very difficult to consume as much chili powder every day as a dog would eat dry food. Ethoxyquin has never been tested for safety in cats.

Some manufacturers have responded to consumer concern, and are now using "natural" preservatives such as Vitamin C (ascorbate), Vitamin E (mixed tocopherols), and oils of rosemary, clove, or other spices, to preserve the fats in their products. Other ingredients, however, may be individually preserved. Fish meal, and some prepared vitamin mixtures used to supplement pet food, contain chemical preservatives. This means that your companion animal may be eating food containing several types of preservatives. Not all of these are required to be disclosed on the label. However, due to consumer pressure, preservatives used in fat are now required to be listed on the label.

Additives in Processed Pet Foods

Anticaking agents	Lubricants
Antimicrobial agents	Nonnutritive sweeteners
Antioxidants	Nutritive sweeteners
Coloring agents	Oxidizing and reducing
Leavening agent	agents
Curing agents	pH control agents
Drying agents	Processing aids
Emulsifiers	Sequestrants
Firming agents	Solvents, vehicles
Flavor enhancers	Stabilizers, thickeners
Flavoring agents	Surface active agents
Flour-treating agents	Surface-finishing agents
Formulation aids	Synergists
Humectants	Texturizers

While the law requires studies of direct toxicity of these additives and preservatives, they have not been tested for their potential synergistic effects on each other once ingested. Some authors have suggested that dangerous interactions occur among some of the common synthetic preservatives. Natural preservatives do not provide as long a shelf life as chemical preservatives, but

they do not carry the unanswered questions about their safety.

THE MANUFACTURING PROCESS

Although feeding trials are no longer required for a food to meet the requirements for labeling a food "complete and balanced," most manufacturers perform palatability studies when developing a new pet food. One set of animals is fed a new food while a control group is fed a current formula. The total volume eaten is used as a gauge for the palatability of the food. The larger and more reputable companies do use feeding trials, which are considered to be a much more accurate assessment of the actual nutritional value of the food. They keep large colonies of dogs and cats for this purpose.

Dry food is made with a machine called an expander or extruder. First, raw materials are blended, sometimes by hand, other times by computer, in accordance with a recipe developed by animal nutritionists. This mixture is fed into an expander and steam or hot water is added. The mixture is subjected to steam, pressure, and high heat as it is extruded through dies that determine the shape of the final product and puffed like popcorn. The food is allowed to dry, and then is usually sprayed with fat, digests, or other compounds to make it more palatable. Although the cooking process may kill bacteria in pet food, the final product can lose its sterility during the subsequent drying, fat-coating, and packaging process.

Ingredients are similar for wet, dry, and semimoist foods, although the ratios of protein, fat, and fiber may change. A typical can of ordinary cat food reportedly contains about 45 to 50% meat or poultry by-products. The main difference between the types of food is the water content. It is impossible to directly compare labels from different kinds of food without a mathematical conversion to "dry matter basis." Wet or canned food begins with ground ingredients mixed with additives. If chunks are required, a special extruder forms them. Then the mixture is cooked and canned. The sealed cans are then put into containers resembling pressure cookers and commercial sterilization takes place. Some manufacturers cook the food right in the can.

There are special labeling requirements for pet food. The "all-meat" product is covered by AAFCO's 95% Rule: "When an ingredient or a combination of ingredients derived from animals, poultry, or fish constitute 95% or more of the total weight of all ingredients of a pet food, the name or names of such ingredient(s) may form part of the product name of the pet food; provided that where more than one ingredient is part of such product name, then all such ingredient names shall be in the same size, style, and color print. For the purpose of this provision, water sufficient for processing shall be excluded when calculating the percentage of the named ingredient(s). However, such named ingredient(s) shall constitute at least 70% of the total product." Because all-meat diets are not nutritionally balanced, they are uncommon today.

The "dinner" product is defined by the 25% Rule: "When an ingredient or a combination of ingredients constitutes at least 25% but less than 95% of the total weight of all ingredients of a dog or cat food mixture, the name or names of such ingredient or ingredients may form a part of the product name of the pet food if each of the ingredients constitute at least 3% of the product weight excluding water used for processing and only if the product name also includes a primary descriptive term such as 'dinner,' 'platter,' or similar designation so that the product name describes the contents of the product in accordance with an established law, custom, or usage or so that the product name is not misleading. If the names of more than one ingredient are shown, they shall appear in the order of their respective predominance by weight in the product. All such ingredient names and the primary descriptive term shall be in the same size, style and color print. For the purpose of this provision, water sufficient for processing shall be excluded when calculating the percentage of the named ingredient(s). However, such named ingredient(s) shall constitute at least 10% of the total product."

The "flavor" product is formulated to have a specific flavor: "No flavor designation shall be used on a pet food label unless the flavor is detected by a recognized test method, or is one the presence of which provides a characteristic distinguishable by the pet. Any flavor designation on a pet food label must either conform to the name of its source as shown in the ingredient statement or the ingredient statement shall show the source of the flavor. The word flavor shall be printed in the same size type and with an equal degree of conspicuousness as the ingredient term(s) from which the flavor designation is derived. Distributors of pet food employing such flavor designation or claims on the labels of the product distributed by them shall, upon request, supply verification of the designated or claimed flavor to the appropriate control official." In essence, the "flavor rule" allows a food to be labeled as "beef flavor" without actually containing any beef meat at all.

What Happened to the Nutrients?

Dr. Randy L. Wysong is a veterinarian and produces his own line of pet foods. A long-time critic of pet food industry practices, he said, "Processing is the wild card in nutritional value that is, by and large, simply ignored. Heating, cooking, rendering, freezing, dehydrating, canning, extruding, pelleting, baking, and so forth, are so commonplace that they are simply thought of as synonymous with food itself." Processing meat and by-products used in pet food can greatly diminish their nutritional value, but cooking increases the digestibility of cereal grains.

To make pet food nutritious, pet food manufacturers must "fortify" it with vitamins and minerals. Why? Because the ingredients they are using are not wholesome, their quality may be extremely variable, and the harsh manufacturing practices destroy many of the nutrients the food had to begin with.

Contaminants

Commercially manufactured or rendered meat meals and by-product meals are frequently highly

What's Really in Pet Food

contaminated with bacteria because their source is not always slaughtered animals. Animals that have died because of disease, injury, or natural causes are a source of meat for meat meal. The dead animal might not be rendered until days after its death. Therefore the carcass is often contaminated with bacteria such as *Salmonella* and *Escherichia coli.* Dangerous *E. coli* bacteria are estimated to contaminate more than 50% of meat meals. While the cooking process may kill bacteria, it does not eliminate the endotoxins some bacteria produce during their growth which are released when they die. These toxins can cause sickness and disease. Pet food manufacturers do not test their products for endotoxins.

Mycotoxins come from mold or fungi, such as vomitoxin in the Nature's Recipe case, and aflatoxin in Doane's food. Poor farming practices and improper drying and storage of crops can cause mold growth. Ingredients that are most likely to be contaminated with mycotoxins are grains such as wheat and corn, cottonseed meal, peanut meal, and fish meal.

Labeling

The National Research Council (NRC) of the Academy of Sciences set the nutritional standards for pet food until 1974, when the pet food industry created a group called the Association of American Feed Control Officials (AAFCO). At that time the AAFCO chose to adopt the NRC standards rather than develop its own. The NRC standards required feeding trials for pet foods that claimed to be "complete" and "balanced." The pet food industry found the feeding trials too restrictive and expensive, so the AAFCO designed an alternate procedure for claiming the nutritional adequacy of pet food. the AAFCO also formed "expert committees" for canine and feline nutrition and developed its own standards in the early 1990s. Instead of feeding trials, chemical analysis will determine if a food meets the standards.

The problem with chemical analysis is that it does not address the palatability, digestibility, and biological availability of nutrients in pet food. Thus it is unreliable for determining whether a food will provide an animal with sufficient nutrients.

To compensate for the limitations of chemical analysis, the AAFCO added a "safety factor," which was to exceed the minimum amount of nutrients required to meet the complete and balanced requirements.

The digestibility and availability of nutrients is not listed on pet food labels.

The 100% Myth—Problems Caused by Inadequate Nutrition

The idea of one pet food providing all the nutrition a companion animal will ever need for its entire life is a myth.

Cereal grains are the primary ingredients in most commercial pet foods. Many people select one pet food and feed it to their dogs and cats for a prolonged period of time. Therefore companion dogs and cats eat a primarily carbohydrate diet with little variety. Today, the diets of cats and dogs are a far cry from the primarily protein diets with a lot of variety that their ancestors ate. The problems associated with a commercial diet are seen every day at veterinary establishments. Chronic digestive problems, such as chronic vomiting, diarrhea, and inflammatory bowel disease are among the most frequent illnesses treated.

Allergy or hypersensitivity to foods is a common problem usually seen as diarrhea or vomiting. Food allergies have become an everyday ailment. The market for "limited antigen and novel protein" diets is now a multi-million dollar business. These diets were formulated to address the increasing intolerance to commercial foods that animals have developed.

Dry commercial pet food is often contaminated with bacteria, which may or may not cause problems. Improper food storage and some feeding practices may result in the multiplication of this bacteria. For example, adding water or milk to moisten pet food and then leaving it at room temperature causes bacteria to multiply. Yet this practice is suggested on the back of packages of some kitten and puppy foods.

Pet food formulas and the practice of feeding that manufacturers recommend have increased other digestive problems. Feeding only one meal per day can cause the irritation of the esophagus by stomach acid. Feeding two smaller meals is better.

Urinary tract disease is directly related to diet in both cats and dogs. Plugs, crystals, and stones in cat bladders are often triggered or aggravated by commercial pet food formulas. One type of stone found in cats is less common now, but another more dangerous type has become more common. Manipulation of manufactured cat food formulas to affect acidity in urine and the amount of some minerals has directly affected these diseases. Dogs also form stones as a result of their diet.

History has shown that commercial pet food products can cause disease. An often-fatal heart disease in cats and some dogs was shown to be caused by a deficiency of an amino acid called taurine. Blindness is another symptom of taurine deficiency. This deficiency occurred because of inadequate amounts of taurine in cat food formulas. Cat foods are now supplemented with taurine. New research suggests that supplementing taurine may also be helpful for dogs, but as yet no manufacturer is adding extra taurine to dog food.

Rapid growth in large-breed puppies has been shown to contribute to bone and joint disease. Excess calories in manufactured puppy food formulas promote rapid growth. There are now spe-cial puppy foods for large-breed dogs. But this recent change will not help the countless dogs who lived and died with hip and elbow disease.

There is also evidence that hyperthyroidism in cats results from commercial pet food diets. This is a new disease that first surfaced in the 1970s, when canned food products appeared on the market. The exact cause and effect are not yet known. This is a serious and sometimes terminal disease, and treatment is expensive.

Many nutritional problems appeared with the popularity of cereal-based commercial pet foods. Some have occurred because the diet was in-complete. Although several ingredients are now supplemented, we do not know what ingredients future researchers may discover that should have been supplemented in pet foods all along. Other problems may result from reactions to additives. Others are a result of contamination with bacteria, mold, drugs, or other toxins. In some diseases the role of commercial pet food is under-stood; in others, it is not. The bottom line is that diets composed primarily of low-quality cereals and rendered meat meals are not as nutritious or safe as you should expect for your cat or dog.

Adapted with the generous permission of the API (www.api4animals.org) and Jean Hofve, D.V.M., Companion Animal Program Coordinator, Animal Protection Institute.

What's Really in Pet Food

NOTES

NOTES ON CONDITIONS

Arthritis (Osteoarthritis)

1. Tibbitts, D. "Use of Cetyl Myristoleate for Arthritis and Tendinitis in Holistic Veterinary Medical Practice." *Journ AHVMA* 18(2) (1999): 27–31.

2. Hoskins, J., and D. McCurnin. "Implementing a Successful Geriatric Medicine Program." *Supplement to Veterinary Medicine* (1997): 3–11.

3. Whitehouse, M.W., M.S. Roberts, and P.M. Brooks. "Over the Counter (OTC) Oral Remedies for Arthritis and Rheumatism: How Effective Are They?" *Inflammopharmacology* 7(2) (1999): 89–105.

4. Messonnier, S.P. *The Arthritis Solution for Dogs.* Roseville: Prima, 2000.

Allergies

1. Messonnier, S.P. *The Allergy Solution for Dogs.* Roseville: Prima, 2000.

2. Scott, D., W. Miller, and C. Griffin. *Muller and Kirk's Small Animal Dermatology*, 5th ed. Ithaca: WB Saunders, 1995: 236.

Asthma

1. Johnson, L. "Diseases of the Bronchus." In Ettinger, S., and E. Feldman**.** *Textbook of Veterinary Internal Medicine*. 5th ed. WB Saunders, 2000: 1055–1061.

Cancer

1. Powers, B. "The Pathology of Neoplasia." In Withrow, S., and E.G. MacEwen. *Small Animal Clinical Oncology.* 2nd ed. WB Saunders, 1996: 4–15.

2. London, C., and D. Vail. "Tumor Biology." In Withrow, S., and E.G. MacEwen. *Small Animal Clinical Oncology*, 2nd ed. WB Saunders, 1996: 16–31.

3. Ogilvie, G., M. Fettman, and C. Mallinckrodt, et al. "Effect of Fish Oil and Arginine on Remissions and Survival Time in Dogs With Lymphoma: A Double-blind, Randomized, Placebo-controlled Study." *VCS Meeting* (1997): 39–42.

4. Ogilvie, G. "Nutritional Approaches to Cancer Therapy." In Schoen, A., and S. Wynn. *Complementary and Alternative Veterinary Medicine: Principles and Practice.* Mosby, 1998: 93–112.

5. King, G., K. Yates, P. Greenlee, K. Pierce, et al. "The Effect of Acemannan Immunostimulant in Combination With Surgery and Radiation Therapy on Spontaneous Canine and Feline Fibrosarcomas." *JAAHA* 31 (1995): 439–447.

Cognitive Disorder

1. "Senior Care Part 1: Pharmacology and Neurology." In "The Summit on Internal Medicine." *Vet Forum* (November 1999): 50–57.

2. Editor's Comments. *Journ AHVMA,* 16(4) (1997–1998): 4.

Diabetes

1. Nelson, R. "Diabetes Mellitus." In Ettinger, S., and E. Feldman. *Textbook of Veterinary Internal Medicine.* 5th ed. WB Saunders, 2000: 1438–1460.

2. Dowling, P. "Two Transition Metals Show Promise in Treating Diabetic Cats." *Vet Med* (March 2000): 190–193.

Epilepsy

1. Quesnel, A. "Seizures." In Ettinger, S., and E. Feldman. *Textbook of Veterinary Internal Medicine.* 5th ed. WB Saunders, 2000: 148–152.2.

2. Carr, A. "Taurine and Canine Seizure." *Vet Forum* (Forum Letters), December 1999.

Feline Immunodeficiency Virus (FIV)

1. Levy, J. "FeLV and Non-neoplastic FeLV-related Disease." In Ettinger S., and E. Feldman. *Textbook of Veterinary Internal Medicine.* 5th ed. WB Saunders, 2000: 425–432.

2. Sheet, M, B. Unger, G. Giggleman, and I. Tizard. "Studies of the Effect of Acemannan on Retrovirus Infections: Clinical Stabilization of Feline Leukemia Virus-infected Cats." *Mol Biother,* 3 (1991): 41–48.

3. Uates, K.M., L.J. Rosenberg, C.K. Harris, D.J. Bronstad, et al. "Pilot Study of the Effect of Acemannan in Cats Infected With Feline Immunodeficiency Virus." *Vet Immun and Immunopath,* 35 (1992): 177–189.

Feline Leukemia Virus (FeLV)

1. Levy, J. "FeLV and Non-neoplastic FeLV-related Disease." In Ettinger, S., and E. Feldman. "Textbook of Vet-

erinary Internal Medicine." 5th ed. WB Saunders, 2000: 425–432.

2. Sheet, M., B. Unger, G. Giggleman, and I. Tizard. "Studies of the Effect of Acemannan on Retrovirus Infections: Clinical Stabilization of Feline Leukemia Virus-infected Cats." *Mol Biother*, 3 (1991): 41–48.

3. Uates, K.M., L.J. Rosenberg, C.K. Harris, D.J. Bronstad, et al. "Pilot Study of the Effect of Acemannan in Cats Infected With Feline Immunodeficiency Virus." *Vet Immun and Immunopath*, 35 (1992): 177–189.

Feline Lower Tract Urinary Disease [FLUTD]

1. Grauer, G. "Urinary Disorders: Feline Lower Urinary Tract Inflammation." In Nelson, R. and C.G. Cuoto. *Manual of Small Animal Internal Medicine*. Mosby, 1999: 394–399.

2. Conference Review. *Journ AHVMA* 17(4) (1999): 14–15.

Heart Disease

1. Freeman, L.M., H.E. Rush, J.J Kehayias, H.N. Ross, S.N. Meydani, D.J. Brown, G.G Dolnikowski, B.N. Marmor, M.E. White, C.A. Dinarello, and R. Roubenoff. "Nutritional Alterations and the Effect of Fish Oil Supplementation in Dogs With Heart Failure." *Journ Vet Intern Med*, 12 (1998): 440–448.

Hyperthyroidism

1. Peterson M. "Hyperthyroidism." In Ettinger, S., and E. Feldman. *Textbook of Veterinary Internal Medicine*. 5th ed. WB Saunders, 2000: 1400–1419.

2. Taboada J. "Recent Research Explores New Treatment for Feline Hyperthyroidism." *DVM Newsmagazine* (March 2000): 5S.

Intestinal Parasites

1. Wynn, S. "Anthelmintic Therapy in Holistic Veterinary Practice." *Journ AHVMA* 15(1) (1996): 15–19.

Kidney Disease

1. Brown, S., C. Brown, W. Crowell, J. Barsanti, and D. Finco. "Does Modifying Dietary Lipids Influence the Progression of Renal Failure?" *Vet Clinics of North America*, 26(6) (1996): 1277.

2. Hoskins, J., and D. McCurnin. "Implementing a Successful Geriatric Medicine Program." *Supplement to Veterinary Medicine* (1997): 3–11.

Vaccinosis

1. Rivera, P. "Vaccinations and Vaccinosis." *Journal AHVMA* 16(1) (1997): 19–24.

2. Tobin, S. "A Holistic Viewpoint on Vaccinations." *Journal AHVMA*, 16(4) (1997–1998): 31–33.

3. Rivera, P. "Vaccinations and Vaccinosis." *Journal AHVMA*, 16(1) (1997): 19–24.

4. Hershey, A.E., K. Sorenmo, M. Hendrick, F. Shofer, and D. Vail. "Prognosis for Presumed Feline Vaccine–associated Sarcoma After Excision: 61 Cases (1986–1996)." *JAVMA*, 216(1) (2000): 58–61.

5. Scott, F.W., and C. Geissinger. "Do Cats Really Need Annual Boosters?" *Am J Vet Res*, 60 (1999): 652–658.

6. Macy, D., and J. Chretin. "Local Postvaccinal Reactions of a Recombinant Rabies Vaccine," *Vet Forum* (August 1999): 44–49.

7. Ford, R. "Vaccines and Vaccinations: Issues for the 21st Century." In *Vaccine Technology in the 21st Century, Supplement to Compend on Contin Educ for the Pract Vet*, 20(8)(C) (1998): 19–24.

8. Schultz, R., and S. Conklin "The Immune System and Vaccines: Challenges for the 21st Century." In *Vaccine Technology in the 21st Century, Supplement to Compend on Contin Educ for the Pract Vet*, 20(8)(C) (1998): 5–18.

9. Roundtable Discussion. "Vaccines and Recombinant Technology." In *Vaccine Technology in the 21st Century, Supplement to Compend on Contin Educ for the Pract Vet*, 20(8)(C) (1998): 33–39.

10. Hustead, D., T. Carpenter, D. Sawyer, et al. "Vaccination Issues of Concern to Practitioners." *JAVMA*, 214(7) (1999): 1000–1002.

11. McCaw, D., M. Thompson, D. Tate, and A. Bonderer. "Serum Distemper Virus and Parvovirus Antibody Titers Among Dogs Brought to a Veterinary Hospital for Revaccination." *JAVMA*, 213(1) (1998): 72–75.

12. "Feline sarcoma and vaccination: roundtable on the injection-site problem in cats," *Vet Forum* (March 1999): 40–47.

13. Dodds, W.J. "Vaccine-related Issues." In Schoen, A., and S. Wynn. *Complementary and Alternative Veterinary Medicine: Principles and Practice*. Mosby, 1998: 701–712.

14. Oehen, S., H. Hengartner, and R.M. Zinkernagel. "Vaccination for Disease." *Science*, 251 (1991): 195.

15. Personal Communication. Dr. James Richard, Cornell Feline Health Center, Oct 2000.

NOTES ON HERBS AND SUPPLEMENTS AND DIET

General Reference for Remedies:

1. Bratman, S., and D. Kroll, ed. *Natural Health Bible*. Roseville: Prima Publishing, 1999.

2. Kidd, R. "Herbology 101." *Journal AHVMA*, 16(4) (1997–1998): 27–28.

3. Keane, F.M., Se Munn, A.W.P. du Vivier, et al. "Chinese Herbal Creams May Be Laced With Steroids." *British Medical*, 1000(7): 111–113.

4. Wynn, S. *Emerging Therapies: Using Herbs and Nutraceutical Supplements for Small Animals.* AAHA Press, 1999.

5. Wulff-Tilford, M., and G. Tilford. *All You Ever Wanted to Know About Herbs for Pets.* Bowtie Press, 1999.

Anipryl

1. Campbell, S. "Comprehensive Study Confirms Medication's Benefits." *Anipryl Monograph.* Pfizer Animal Health, 1999.

Antioxidants

1. Labriola, D. *Complementary Cancer Therapies.* Roseville: Prima, 2000: 93–105.

2. Blake, S. "Bovine Colostrum: the Forgotten Miracle." *Journ AHVMA*, 18(2) (1999): 39–40.

3. Kendall, R. "Basic and Preventive Nutrition for the Cat, Dog, and Horse." In Schoen, A., and S. Wynn. *Complementary and Alternative Veterinary Medicine: Principles and Practice.* Mosby, 1998: 23–52.

Arginine

1. Ogilvie, G., and N. Robinson. "Controversies in Veterinary Oncology: Complementary Holistic Cancer Therapy—Fact or Fiction?" *Proc 15th ACVIM Forum*, 197: 567–571.

2. Ogilvie, G., M. Fettman, C. Mallinckrodt, et al. "Effect of Fish Oil and Arginine on Remissions and Survival Time in Dogs With Lymphoma: A Double-blind, Randomized, Placebo-controlled Study." *VCS Meeting* (1997): 39–42.

3. Ogilvie, G. "Nutritional Approaches to Cancer Therapy." In Schoen, A. and S. Wynn. *Complementary and Alternative Veterinary Medicine: Principles and Practice.* Mosby, 1998: 93–112.

Burdock Root

1. Messonnier, S. "Getting the Jump on Fleas," *Vet Forum* (July 1996): 42.

Calcium

1. Kurosky, L. "Abnormalities of Magnesium, Calcium and Chloride." In Ettinger, S., and E. Feldman. *Textbook of Veterinary Internal Medicine.* 5th ed. Vol 1. WB Saunders, 2000: 232–235.

Canadian Fleabane

1. Messonnier, S. "Getting the Jump on Fleas." *Vet Forum* (July 1996): 42.

Carnitine

1. Goodwin, J.K. "The Nondrug Therapy of Heart Disease in the Dog and Cat." *Emerging Science and Technology* (Summer 1996): 24–29.

2. Rush, J. "Alternative Therapies for Heart Failure Patients." *Proc 14th ACVIM Forum* (1996): 151–153.

Cetyl Myristoleate

1. Tibbitts, D. "Use of Cetyl Myristoleate for Arthritis and Tendinitis in Holistic Veterinary Medical Practice." *Journ AHVMA*, 18(2) (1999): 27–31.

Chloride

1. Kurosky, L. "Abnormalities of Magnesium, Calcium and Chloride." In Ettinger, S., and E. Feldman. *Textbook of Veterinary Internal Medicine.* 5th ed. Vol 1. WB Saunders, 2000: 232–235.

Chondroitin

1. Kendall, R. "Therapeutic Nutrition for the Cat, Dog, and Horse." In Schoen, A. and S. Wynn. *Complementary and Alternative Veterinary Medicine: Principles and Practice*, Mosby, 1998: 53–72.

2. Whitehouse, M.W., M.S. Roberts, and P.M. Brooks. "Over the Counter (OTC) Oral Remedies for Arthritis and Rheumatism: How Effective Are They?" *Inflammopharmacology* 7(2) (1999): 89–105.

Chromium

1. Dowling P. "Two transition metals show promise in treating diabetic cats," *Vet Med* March 2000: 190–193.

Citronella

1. Messonnier. S. "Getting the Jump on Fleas." *Vet Forum* (July 1996): 42.

Coenzyme Q-10

1. Labriola, D. *Complementary Cancer Therapies.* Roseville: Prima, 2000: 93–105.

2. Blake, S. "Bovine Colostrum: the Forgotten Miracle." *Journ AHVMA* 18(2) (1999): 39–40.

3. Goodwin, J.K. "The Nondrug Therapy of Heart Disease in the Dog and Cat." *Emerging Science and Technology* (Summer 1996): 24–29.

4. Rush, J. "Alternative Therapies for Heart Failure Patients." *Proc 14th ACVIM Forum* (1996): 151–153.

Notes

Colostrum

1. Blake, S. "Bovine Colostrum: the Forgotten Miracle." *Journ AHVMA*, Vol 18, No 2 (July 1999): 39–40.

2. Moriishi, K., S. Inoue, M. Koura, and F. Amano, Department of Veterinary Science, National Institute of Infectious Diseases, Tokyo, Japan. "Inhibition of Listeriolysin O–induced Hemolysis by Bovine Lactoferrin." *Biol Pharm Bull*, 22 (11) (1999): 1167–72.

Cordycheps Mushrooms

1. Basko, I. "The Healing Fungi: Applications for Veterinary Medicine." *Proc AHVMA* (1996): 101–118.

Dandelion

1. Messonnier, S. "Getting the Jump on Fleas." *Vet Forum* (July 1996): 42.

Diatomaceous Earth

1. Messonnier, S. "Getting the Jump on Fleas." *Vet Forum* (July 1996): 42.

Diet

1. Strombeck, D. *Home-Prepared Dog and Cat Diets: The Healthful Alternative.* Iowa State University Press, 1999.

2. Gross, K., K. Wedekind, C. Cowell, W. Schoenherr, et al. "Nutrients." In Hand, M., C. Thatcher, R. Remillard, and P. Roudebush. *Small Animal Clinical Nutrition.* 4th ed. Mark Morris Institute, 2000: 21–110.

3. Cowell, C., N. Stout, M. Brinkmann, E. Moser, and S. Crane. "Making Commercial Pet Foods." In Hand, M., C. Thatcher, R. Remillard, P. Roudebush. *Small Animal Clinical Nutrition.* 4th ed. Mark Morris Institute, 2000: 127–146.

4. Dodds, WJ. "Pet food preservatives and other additives," in Schoen A, Wynn S. *Complementary and Alternative Veterinary Medicine: Principles and Practice*, Mosby, 1998: 73–80.

5. Gross K, Wedekind K, Cowell C, Schoenherr W, et al., "Introduction to commercial pet foods," in Hand M, Thatcher C, Remillard R, Roudebush P. *Small Animal Clinical Nutrition*, 4th ed, Mark Morris Institute, 2000: 21–110.

6. Hofve J. "Building a strong foundation," *Whole Cat Journal* Dec 1999: 8–11.

7. Strombeck D. *Home-Prepared Dogs & Cats Diets*, Iowa State University Press, 1999.

8. Hofve, J. Animal Protection Institute Web site, www.api4animals.org.

9. Kendall R. "Basic and preventive nutrition for the cat, dog, and horse," in Schoen A, Wynn S. *Complementary and Alternative Veterinary Medicine: Principles and Practice*, Mosby, 1998: 23–54.

10. Kendall R. "Therapeutic nutrition for the cat, dog, and horse", in Schoen A, Wynn S. *Complementary and Alternative Veterinary Medicine: Principles and Practice*, Mosby, 1998: 54–72.

11. Kobs, L. "Best bites: the truth about your cat's diet," *Cat Fancy* Aug 2000: 20–25.

12. Miller EP, Cullor J. "Food safety", in Hand M, Thatcher C, Remillard R, Roudebush P. *Small Animal Clinical Nutrition*, 4th ed, Mark Morris Institute, 2000:83–200.

13. Ogilvie G. "Nutritional approaches to cancer," in Schoen A, Wynn S. *Complementary and Alternative Veterinary Medicine: Principles and Practice*, Mosby, 1998:93–112.

14. Ogilvie G, Robinson N. "Controversies in veterinary oncology: complementary holistic cancer therapy—fact or fiction?" *Proc 15th ACVIM Forum* 197: 567–571.

15. Rogers S. "Environmental medicine for veterinary practitioners," in Schoen A, Wynn S. *Complementary and Alternative Veterinary Medicine: Principles and Practice*, Mosby, 1998: 93–112.

16. Roudebush P, Dzanis D, Debraekeleer J, Brown RG. "Pet food labels," in Hand M, Thatcher C, Remillard R, Roudebush P. *Small Animal Clinical Nutrition*, 4th ed, Mark Morris Institute, 2000: 147–162.

17. Wynn S. "Emerging therapies: using herbs and nutraceutical supplements for small animals," AAHA Press, 1999.

Enzymes

1. Silver R. "Enzymes: the catalysts of life," *Journ AHVMA* 16(4): 25–26, 1997–1998.

2. Ackerman L. "Effect of an enzyme supplement (Prozyme) on selected nutrient levels in dogs," *J Vet Allerg Clin Immunol*, March 1994: 25–29.

3. Messonnier S. "Fighting flatulence," *Vet Forum* July 1996: 33.

Feverfew

1. Messonnier S. "Getting the jump on fleas," *Vet Forum* July 1996: 42.

Garlic

1. Messonnier S. "Getting the jump on fleas," *Vet Forum* July 1996: 42.

Glucosamine

1. Kendall R. "Therapeutic nutrition for the cat, dog, and horse," in Schoen A, Wynn S. *Complementary and Alter-*

native Veterinary Medicine: Principles and Practice, Mosby, 1998: 53–72.

2. Whitehouse MW, Roberts MS, Brooks PM. "Over the counter (OTC) oral remedies for arthritis and rheumatism: how effective are they?" *Inflammopharmacology* 7(2): 89–105, 1999.

Glutamine

1. Kendall R. "Therapeutic nutrition for the cat, dog, and horse," in Schoen A, Wynn S. *Complementary and Alternative Veterinary Medicine: Principles and Practice,* Mosby, 1998: 53–72.

Glycoproteins

1. Tizard I, Busbee D, Maxwell B, Kemp MC. "Effects of acemannan, a complex carbohydrate, on wound healing in young and aged rats," *Wounds* 6(6): 201–209, 1994.

2. Swaim S, Riddell K, McGuire J. "Effects of topical medications on the healing of open pad wounds in dogs," *JAAHA* 28: 499–502, 1992.

3. Sheet M, Unger B. Giggleman G, Tizard I. "Studies of the effect of acemannan on retrovirus infections: clinical stabilization of feline leukemia virus–infected cats," *Mol Biother* 3: 41–48, 1991.

4. Uates KM, Rosenberg LJ, Harris CK, Bronstad DJ, et al. "Pilot study of the effect of acemannan in cats infected with feline immunodeficiency virus," *Vet Immun and Immunopath* 35: 177–189, 1992.

5. King G, Yates K, Greenlee P, Pierce K, et al. "The effect of acemannan immunostimulant in combination with surgery and radiation therapy on spontaneous canine and feline fibrosarcomas," *JAAHA* 31: 439–447, 1995.

6. McAnalley B, Vennum E. "Introduction to glyconutritionals," Glycoscience.com: The Nutrition Science Site, Copyright 2000 Mannatech, Inc. Coppell, Texas, U.S.A., all rights.

7. Gardiner T. "Absorption, distribution, metabolism, and excretion (ADME) of eight known dietary monosaccharides required for glycoprotein synthesis and cellular recognition processes: summary," Glycoscience.com: The Nutrition Science Site, Copyright 2000 Mannatech, Inc. Coppell, Texas, U.S.A., all rights.

8. Gardiner T. "Biological activity of eight known dietary monosaccharides required for glycoprotein synthesis and cellular recognition processes: summary," Glycoscience.com: The Nutrition Science Site, Copyright 2000 Mannatech, Inc. Coppell, Texas, U.S.A., all rights.

9. Lefkowitz S. "Glyconutritionals: Implications for cancer," Glycoscience.com: The Nutrition Science Site, Copyright 2000 Mannatech, Inc. Coppell, Texas, U.S.A., all rights.

10. Lefkowitz D. "Glyconutritionals: Implications for rheumatoid arthritis," Glycoscience.com: The Nutrition Science Site, Copyright 2000 Mannatech, Inc. Coppell, Texas, U.S.A., all rights.

11. Lefkowitz D. "Glyconutritionals: Implications for asthma," Glycoscience.com: The Nutrition Science Site Copyright 2000 Mannatech, Inc. Coppell, Texas, U.S.A., all rights.

12. Lefkowitz D. "Glyconutritionals: Implications for inflammation," Glycoscience.com: The Nutrition Science Site, Copyright 2000 Mannatech, Inc. Coppell, Texas, U.S.A., all rights.

13. Levy J. "FeLV and non-neoplastic FeLV-related disease," in Ettinger S, Feldman E. *Textbook of Veterinary Internal Medicine, 5th ed*, WB Saunders, 2000: 425–432.

Green Foods

Messonnier S. "Fighting flatulence," *Vet Forum* July 1996: 33.

Green Tea

McKenna D, Hughes K, Jones K. "Green tea monograph," *Alternative Therapies* 6(3): 61–84, 2000.

Inositol

Nick G. "Inositol: a scientific evaluation of its clinical effectiveness," 2000: 1–8 (available through Standard Process Nutritional Supplements).

Lactoferrin

1. "Inhibition of listeriolysin O–induced hemolysis by bovine lactoferrin." *Biol Pharm Bull* 22(11): 1167–72, 1999. (ISSN: 0918-6158) Moriishi K, Inoue S, Koura M, Amano F. Department of Veterinary Science, National Institute of Infectious Diseases, Tokyo, Japan.

2. "Synergistic fungistatic effects of lactoferrin in combination with antifungal drugs against clinical Candida isolates: antimicrob agents," *Chemother* 43(11): 2635–2641, 1999. (ISSN: 0066-4804) Kuipers ME, de Vries HG, Eikelboom MC, Meijer DK, Swart PJ. Section of Pharmacokinetics and Drug Delivery, Groningen University Institute for Drug Studies, University Centre for Pharmacy, 9713 AV Groningen, The Netherlands.

3. "Effects of topical application of free and liposome-encapsulated lactoferrin and lactoperoxidase on oral microbiota and dental caries in rats."*Arch Oral Biol* 44(11): 901–906, 1999. (ISSN: 0003-9969) Martinez-Gomis J, Fernandez-Solanas A, Vinas M, Gonzalez P, Planas ME, Sanchez S. Department of Pharmacology, School of

Dentistry, University of Barcelona, L'Hospitalet de Llobregat, Spain.

4. "Identification of pneumococcal surface protein A as a lactoferrin-binding protein of Streptococcus pneumoniae." *Infect Immun* 67(4): 1683–1687, 1999. (ISSN: 0019-9567) Hammerschmidt S, Bethe G, HRemane P, Chhatwal GS. Department of Microbial Pathogenesis, GBF—National Research Centre for Biotechnology, 38106 Braunschweig, Germany.

5. "Lactoferrin: a multifunctional glycoprotein involved in the modulation of the inflammatory process." *Clin Chem Lab Med* 1999, 37(3): 281–286, 1999. (ISSN: 1434-6621) Baveye S, Elass E, Mazurier J, Spik G, Legrand D. Unite Mixte de Recherche du Centre National de la Recherche Scientifique n 111 et Laboratoire de Chimie Biologique, Universite des Sciences et Technologies de Lille, Villeneuve d'Ascq, France.

6. "Measurement of urinary lactoferrin as a marker of urinary tract infection." *J Clin Microbiol* 37(3): 553–557, 1999. (ISSN: 0095-1137) Arao S, Matsuura S, Nonomura M, Miki K, Kabasawa K, Nakanishi H. Planning and Development Division, Iatron Laboratories, Inc., 1-11-4, Higashikanda, Chiyoda-ku, Tokyo 101-0031, Japan.

7. "Direct evidence of the generation in human stomach of an antimicrobial peptide domain (lactoferricin) from ingested lactoferrin." *Biochim Biophys Acta* 1429(1): 129– 141, 1998. (ISSN: 0006-3002) Kuwata H, Yip TT, Tomita M, Hutchens TW. Department of Food Science and Technology, University of California, Davis 95616, USA.

8. "Calprotectin and lactoferrin levels in the gingival crevicular fluid of children." *J Periodontol* 69(8): 879–883 (ISSN: 0022-3492), 1998. Miyasaki KT, Voganatsi A, Huynh T, Marcus M, Underwood S. Section of Oral Biology and the Dental Research Institute, UCLA School of Dentistry, Los Angeles, CA 90095-1668, USA.

Larch

Kelly G. Larch "Arabinogalactan: clinical relevance of a novel immune-enhancing polysaccharide," *Alternative Medicine Review* 4(2) 96–103, 1999.

Lavender

1. Wulff-Tilford M., et al. *Herbs for Pets*, Bowtie Press, 1999.

Maitake Mushrooms

1. Basko I. "The healing fungi: applications for veterinary medicine," *Proc AHVMA* 1996: 101–118.

Marshmallow

1. Bratman S. *Natural Health Bible, 2nd ed.* Prima Publishing, 2000.

2. Wulff-Tilford M, Tilford G. *Herbs for Pets*, Bowtie Press, 1999.

MGN-3

1. Williams D. "MGN-3, alternatives for the health conscious individual," *Alternatives* 7(15) Sept 1998.

Milk Thistle

1. Labriola D. *Complementary Cancer Therapies*, Prima Publishing, 2000: 93–105.

2. Blake S. "Bovine colostrum: the forgotten miracle," *Journal of AHVMA* 18(2): 39–40, 1999.

Minerals

1. Peres Y. "Hyponatremia and hypokalemia," in Ettinger S, Feldman E. *Textbook of Veterinary Internal Medicine, 5th ed, Vol 1*, WB Saunders, 2000: 222–226.

2. Schaer M. "Hyperkalemia and hypernatremia," in Ettinger S, Feldman E. *Textbook of Veterinary Internal Medicine, 5th ed, Vol 1*, WB Saunders, 2000: 227–231.

3. Kurosky L. "Abnormalities of magnesium, calcium and chloride," in Ettinger S, Feldman E. *Textbook of Veterinary Internal Medicine, 5th ed, Vol 1*, WB Saunders, 2000: 232–235.

Mullein Rotenone

1. Messonnier S. "Getting the jump on fleas," *Vet Forum* July 1996: 42.

Neem

1. Messonnier S. "Getting the jump on fleas," *Vet Forum* July 1996: 42.

Nematodes

1. Messonnier S. "Getting the jump on fleas," *Vet Forum* July 1996: 42.

Olive Leaf Extract

Baldinger K. "Olive leaf extract: ancient solution to modern ailments", *Nature's Impact* Dec–Jan 1998/1999: 3840.

2. Walker M. "Olive leaf extract," Kensington Books, 1997.

Omega-3 Fatty Acids

1. Labriola D. *Complementary Cancer Therapies*, Prima Publishing, 2000: 93–105.

2. Blake S. "Bovine colostrum: the forgotten miracle," *Journal of AHVMA* 18(2): 39–40, 1999.

3. Ogilvie G, Robinson N. "Controversies in veterinary oncology: complementary holistic cancer therapy—fact or fiction?" *Proc 15th ACVIM Forum* 1997: 567–571.

4. Goodwin JK. "The nondrug therapy of heart disease in the dog and cat," *Emerging Science and Technology*, Summer 1996: 24–29.

5. Rush J. "Alternative therapies for heart failure patients," *Proc 14th ACVIM Forum* 1996: 151–153.

6. Byrne KP, Davis CA, Campbell KL. "The effects of dietary N-3 VS. N-6 fatty acids on ex-Vivo LTB4 generation by canine neutrophils," *14th Proc of AAVD/ACVD* 1998: 109–110.

7. Ogilvie G, Fettman M, Mallinckrodt C, et al. "Effect of fish oil and arginine on remissions and survival time in dogs with lymphoma: a double-blind, randomized, placebo-controlled study," *VCS Meeting* 1997: 39–42.

8. Ogilvie G. "Nutritional approaches to cancer therapy," in Schoen A, Wynn S. *Complementary and Alternative Veterinary Medicine: Principles and Practice*, Mosby, 1998: 93–112.

9. Scott D, Miller W, Griffin C. Muller and Kirk's *Small Animal Dermatology, 5th ed*, WB Saunders, 1995: 236.

Pennyroyal Oil

1. Messonnier S. "Getting the jump on fleas," *Vet Forum* July 1996: 42.

Perna

1. Kendall R. "Therapeutic nutrition for the cat, dog, and horse," in Schoen A, Wynn S. *Complementary and Alternative Veterinary Medicine: Principles and Practice,* Mosby, 1998: 53–72.

2. Gibson SLM, Gibson RG. "The treatment of arthritis with a lipid extract of *Perna canaliculus:* a randomized trial,"*Complementary Therapies in Medicine* 6: 122–126, 1998.

3. Whitehouse MW, Macrides TA, Kalafatis N, Betts WH, Haynes DR, Broadbent J. "Anti-inflammatory activity of a lipid fraction (Lyprinol) from the NZ green-lipped mussel," *Inflammopharmacology* 5: 237–246, 1997.

Potassium

1. Peres Y. "Hyponatremia and hypokalemia," in Ettinger S, Feldman E. *Textbook of Veterinary Internal Medicine, 5th ed, Vol 1*, WB Saunders, 2000: 222–226.

Pyrethrum

1. Messonnier S. "Getting the jump on fleas," *Vet Forum* July 1996: 42.

Red Clover

1. Messonnier S. "Getting the jump on fleas," *Vet Forum* July 1996: 42.

Shark/Bovine Cartilage

1. Kendall R. "Therapeutic nutrition for the cat, dog, and horse," in Schoen A, Wynn S. *Complementary and Alternative Veterinary Medicine: Principles and Practice,* Mosby, 1998: 53–72.

Shiitake Mushrooms

1. Basko I. "The healing fungi: applications for veterinary medicine," *Proc AHVMA* 1996: 101–118.

Sodium Polysorbate

1. Messonnier S. "Getting the jump on fleas," *Vet Forum* July 1996: 42.

Taurine

1. Carr A. "Taurine and canine seizure," *Vet Forum* (Forum Letters) December 1999.

Goodwin JK. "The nondrug therapy of heart disease in the dog and cat," *Emerging Science and Technology*, Summer 1996: 24–29.

Schaer M. "Hyperkalemia and hypernatremia," in Ettinger S, Feldman E. *Textbook of Veterinary Internal Medicine, 5th ed*, Vol 1, WB Saunders, 2000: 227–231.

Vanadium

1. Dowling P. "Two transition metals show promise in treating diabetic cats," *Vet Med* March 2000: 190–193.

Vitamin A

1. Kendall R. "Basic and preventive nutrition for the cat, dog, and horse," in Schoen A, Wynn S. *Complementary and Alternative Veterinary Medicine: Principles and Practice,* Mosby, 1998: 23–52.

2. Freytag TL, Rogers QR, Morris JG. "Adult cats tolerate excess vitamin A with minimal toxicity," in *1998 Purina Nutrition Forum Proceedings* June4–6 1998: 59.

Vitamin C

1. Kendall R. "Basic and preventive nutrition for the cat, dog, and horse," in Schoen A, Wynn S. *Complementary and Alternative Veterinary Medicine: Principles and Practice,* Mosby, 1998: 23–52.

2. "Vitamin A supplements and birth defects," *New England Journal of Medicine* Nov 23, 1995, in Patient's Nutritional Supplement Education Portfolio, Standard Process.

Vitamin E

1. Kendall R. "Basic and preventive nutrition for the cat, dog, and horse," in Schoen A, Wynn S. *Complementary and Alternative Veterinary Medicine: Principles and Practice,* Mosby, 1998: 23–52.

2. "Vitamin E supplements may cause harm," March 26, 1999, Reuters, in Patient's Nutritional Supplement Education Portfolio, Standard Process.

NOTES ON OTHER COMPLEMENTARY THERAPIES

Acupuncture

1. Altman S. "Techniques and instrumentation," in Schoen A. *Veterinary Acupuncture: Ancient Art to Modern Medicine,* Mosby, 2001: 75–105.

2. Hwang Y-C, Egerbacher M. "Anatomy and classification of acupoints," in Schoen A. *Veterinary Acupuncture: Ancient Art to Modern Medicine,* Mosby, 2001: 19–32.

3. Smith FWK. "The neurophysiologic basis of acupuncture," in Schoen A. *Veterinary Acupuncture: Ancient Art to Modern Medicine,* Mosby, 2001: 33–54.

4. Schoen A. "Acupuncture for musculoskeletal disorders," in Schoen A. *Veterinary Acupuncture: Ancient Art to Modern Medicine,* Mosby, 2001: 159–170.

5. Joseph R. "Acupuncture for neurologic disorders," in Schoen A. *Veterinary Acupuncture: Ancient Art to Modern Medicine,* Mosby, 2001: 171–189.

6. Stefanatos J. "Introduction to bioenergetic medicine," in Schoen A, Wynn S. *Complementary and Alternative Veterinary Medicine: Principles and Practice,* Mosby, 1998:227–246.

Aromatherapy

1. Wynn S, Kirk-Smith M. "Aromatherapy," in Schoen A, Wynn S. *Complementary and Alternative Veterinary Medicine: Principles and Practice,* Mosby, 1998: 561–578.

Bach Flower Essences

1. "Bach flower essences for the family," Wigmore Publications, Nelson Bach Company Material (Flower Essence Booklet), 1993:3–55.

2. Blake S. "Bach flower therapy: a practitioner's perspective," in Schoen A, Wynn S. *Complementary and Alternative Veterinary Medicine: Principles and Practice,* Mosby, 1998: 579–588.

3. Moore AK. "Healing with the Bach flower remedies," *Proc of the AHVMA,* 1998 Conference: 47–53.

4. Ball S, Howard J. "Bach flower remedies for animals," CW Daniel Co., 1999.

Chiropractic

1. Willoughby S. "Chiropractic care," in Schoen A, Wynn S. *Complementary and Alternative Veterinary Medicine: Principles and Practice,* Mosby, 1998: 185–200.

2. Homewood AE."The neurodynamics of the vertebral subluxation," 1962, Parker Research Foundation.

Glandular Therapy

1. Lewis A, Schoen A. "Glandular therapy, cell therapy, and oral tolerance," in Schoen A, Wynn S. *Complementary and Alternative Veterinary Medicine: Principles and Practice,* Mosby, 1998: 81–92.

Homeopathy

1. Weiner M. *The Complete Book of Homeopathy: A Comprehensive Manual of Natural Healing,* MJF Books, NY, 1997.

2. Macleod G. *Dogs: Homeopathic Remedies,* CW Daniel Co, Essex England, 1989.

3. Macleod G. *Cats: Homeopathic Remedies,* CW Daniel Co, Essex England, 1990.

4. Day C. *The Homeopathic Treatment of Small Animals: Principles and Practice,* CW Daniel Co, Essex England, 1990.

5. Ullman D. "Homeopathic medicine: principles and research," in Schoen A, Wynn S. *Complementary and Alternative Veterinary Medicine: Principles and Practice.* Mosby, St. Louis Mo, 1998: 469–484.

6. Day C, Saxton JGG. "Veterinary homeopathy: principles and practice," in Schoen A, Wynn S. *Complementary and Alternative Veterinary Medicine: Principles and Practice.* Mosby, St. Louis Mo, 1998: 485–514.

7. Willoughby S. "Chiropractic care," in Schoen A, Wynn S. *Complementary and Alternative Veterinary Medicine: Principles and Practice,* Mosby, 1998: 185–200.

Magnetic Therapy

1. Hudson D, Hudson D. "Magnetic field therapy," in Schoen A, Wynn S. *Complementary and Alternative Veterinary Medicine: Principles and Practice,* Mosby, 1998: 275–298.

2. Rogachefsky R, Markov M. "Treatment of canine osteoarthritis with a permanent magnetic mattress," *XXI Annual Meeting of BEMS,* June 20–24, 1999.

3. Strazza M. "Magnetic field exposure as an adjunct therapeutic modality in the dog, cat, and horse," *Journal of the American Holistic Veterinary Medical Assoc* 15(2): 27–31, 1996.

4. Hudson D, Hudson D. "Magnetic field therapy," in Schoen A, Wynn S. *Complementary and Alternative Vet-*

erinary Medicine: Principles and Practice, Mosby, 1998: 275–296.

5. Benson K. "The magnetism of magnetic therapies," *Pet Product News* Dec 1999: 1.

6. Pilla A. "Pre-clinical evaluations of tectonic permanent magnets: dosimetry and physical and biological mechanisms," Aug 1999, Magnatherapy Literature.

7. Pilla A. "State of the art in electromagnetic therapeutics: soft tissue applications," *Proceedings, 2nd World Congress on Electricity and Magnetism in Biology and Medicine*, New York: Plenum Press, 1999.

8. Vallbona C, Haxlewood C, Jurida G. "Response of pain to static magnetic fields in postpolio patients: a double-blind pilot study," *Arch Phys Med Rehabil* 78: 1200–1203, 1997.

9. Liburdy R. "Electromagnetic fields and control of cell growth: drugs, hormones, and human tumor cells," *Po-*

tential Therapeutic Applications of Magnetic Fields 1st International Symposium, Vanderbilt Univ Med Center, Nov 15–16, 1999.

10. Pilla A. "Time-varying electromagnetic fields: review of basic and clinical studies," *Potential Therapeutic Applications of Magnetic Fields 1st International Symposium*, Vanderbilt Univ Med Center, Nov 15–16, 1999.

Orthomolecular Medicine

1. Belfield W. "Orthomolecular medicine: a practitioner's perspective," in Schoen A, Wynn S. *Complementary and Alternative Veterinary Medicine: Principles and Practice*, Mosby, 1998: 113–132.

TTouch (TTeam)

1. Harman J. "TTeam approach," in Schoen A, Wynn S. *Complementary and Alternative Veterinary Medicine: Principles and Practice*, Mosby, 1998: 217–226.

INDEX

Index

Index

Index

Index

Index

The YOUR PET'S LIFE® Series

KIM CAMPBELL THORNTON
Joanne Howl, D.V.M., Series Editor

Your
BEAGLE'S
Life

Your Complete Guide
to Raising Your Pet from
Puppy to Companion

ISBN 0-7615-2050-3

KIM D.R. DEARTH
Joanne Howl, D.V.M., Series Editor

Your
BORDER COLLIE'S
Life

Your Complete Guide
to Raising Your Pet from
Puppy to Companion

ISBN 0-7615-2536-X

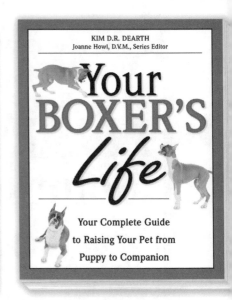

KIM D.R. DEARTH
Joanne Howl, D.V.M., Series Editor

Your
BOXER'S
Life

Your Complete Guide
to Raising Your Pet from
Puppy to Companion

ISBN 0-7615-2048-1

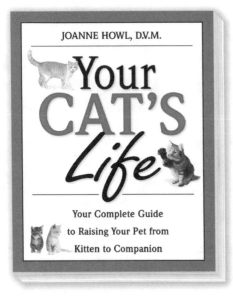

JOANNE HOWL, D.V.M.

Your
CAT'S
Life

Your Complete Guide
to Raising Your Pet from
Kitten to Companion

ISBN 0-7615-1361-2

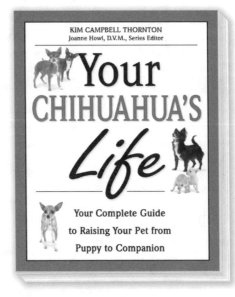

KIM CAMPBELL THORNTON
Joanne Howl, D.V.M., Series Editor

Your
CHIHUAHUA'S
Life

Your Complete Guide
to Raising Your Pet from
Puppy to Companion

ISBN 0-7615-2051-1

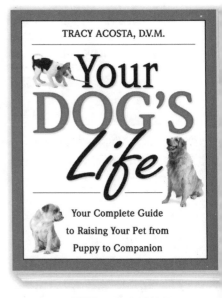

TRACY ACOSTA, D.V.M.

Your
DOG'S
Life

Your Complete Guide
to Raising Your Pet from
Puppy to Companion

ISBN 0-7615-1543-7

THREE
RIVERS
PRESS

Available everywhere books are sold.
Visit us online at www.crownpublishing.com.

Paperback
U.S. $14.99
Can. $22.95